Digital SAT® Workbook

5001 Cordell Avenue
Bethesda, MD
20814

6731 Curran Street
McLean, VA
22101

4646 40th St. NW
Washington, DC
20016

www.prepmatters.com • 301-951-0350
© PrepMatters, Inc., 2023

ACKNOWLEDGMENTS

Author: Rachel Jones

With special thanks to Ned Johnson for his leadership and vision

With additional special thanks to Ana Laura Carignani, Michael DePalatis, Susan Dykeman, Aaron Golumbfskie, John Jones, Daniela Manopla, Laura Moore, and many other past and present PrepMatters employees who made this project possible

TM and © 2023 by PrepMatters, Inc. PREPMATTERS is a registered trademark of Prepmatters, Inc. All rights reserved.

College Board, SAT, and the acorn logo are registered trademarks of the College Board, which is not affiliated with, and does not endorse, this product.

Table of Contents

Introduction to the SAT

Test Overview	5
Scoring	6
Percentiles	7
Computer-Based Testing	8
SAT vs. ACT	10
General SAT Strategies	12
How to Use this Book	13

Reading and Writing

Section Overview — 15

Reading: Information, Ideas, and Structure

Words in Context	18
Central Ideas and Details	27
Structure and Purpose	40
Compare and Contrast	52

Reading: Evidence and Logical Reasoning

Command of Evidence – Illustrate the Claim	65
Command of Evidence – Strengthen/Weaken	75
Command of Evidence – Quantitative	87
Logical Inferences	100

Writing: Standard English Conventions

Sentence Structure	110
Commas	120
Semicolons, Colons, Dashes, and Apostrophes	135
Verbs	153
Pronouns	164
Misplaced Modifiers	172

Writing: Expression of Ideas

Transitions	176
Rhetorical Synthesis	189

TM and © 2023 PrepMatters, Inc. All rights reserved.

Math

Section Overview	201
Strategy in Brief	
Back-Solving and Substitution	203
Mastering the Calculator	214
Approximating and Measuring	226
Algebra	
Algebra Essentials	229
Word Problems	240
Coordinate Geometry	249
Systems of Equations	258
Inequalities and Absolute Value	267
Advanced Math	
Exponents and Roots	274
Factoring, FOILing, and Fractions	282
Function Essentials	296
Linear Functions	307
Quadratic Functions	315
Polynomial, Exponential, Radical, and Rational Functions	324
Problem Solving and Data Analysis	
Data Interpretation	339
Ratios, Proportions, and Unit Conversions	351
Percentages	361
Mean, Median, and Mode	368
Probability	377
Statistics	384
Geometry and Trigonometry	
Area and Volume	390
Angles, Lines, and Triangles	402
Right Triangles and Trigonometry	416
Circles	426

Answers and Explanations   433

Introduction to the SAT
Test Overview

Here's what to expect when you arrive at the testing center to take the SAT.

Check-in and test instructions
at least 30-60 minutes

After presenting your ID, you'll be directed to a testing room where you can set up your laptop or tablet (you can bring your own or use one provided by College Board). Expect to spend some time listening to instructions and filling in your basic information before the test begins.

Reading and Writing, Module 1
27 questions, 32 minutes

Each question in this module will present you with a brief standalone passage, which may or may not be accompanied by a chart, graph, or other figure. You'll be asked to analyze the passage, pick the best version of a sentence, or make logical deductions based on what you've read.

Reading and Writing, Module 2
27 questions, 32 minutes

This module includes the same types of questions as those found in the first module, but you may notice a change in the difficulty level. Depending on how well your first module went, the test will adjust your second module to be either somewhat easier or somewhat harder than the first.

Break
10 minutes

During this break in testing, you'll be allowed to leave the room, stretch your legs, get a snack, and so on. You may not use your cell phone or any other electronic device.

Math, Module 1
22 questions, 35 minutes

The content you'll see tested will include algebra, data interpretation, ratios, percentages, geometry/trig, and some "advanced" math such as quadratic and exponential functions. Both multiple-choice questions and "student-produced response" questions (fill-ins) are included.

Math, Module 2
22 questions, 35 minutes

Just as with the verbal section, the difficulty level of the second math module will be determined based on your performance on the first math module. The content and question types remain the same.

Total testing time: **about 2½ – 3 hours.**

Scoring

When you sit for the SAT, you'll see four "modules" of questions, as discussed on the previous page. The test will calculate your two section scores (one Reading and Writing score and one Math score) based on the number of questions you got right on the corresponding modules. Each of the two sections is scored on a scale of 200 to 800. The two section scores are then added together, so your final SAT score is on a scale of 400-1600.

However, not all questions are treated equally. The reason that the sections are separated into two modules each is that the SAT is now an **adaptive** test, meaning its difficulty level is set based on your performance. That is, if you do well on the first math module, you'll see a harder set of questions in the second math module—and the opportunity for a higher score. The same is true on the Reading & Writing side: the difficulty level of the second module is based on the number of questions you answered correctly on the first one. This means if you score poorly on the first module, there is a limit to how high your section score will be—even if you get every question in the second module right.

On the other hand, this means if you're seeing a lot of tough questions in your second module, that's good news! It means you aced the first module, and you've put yourself in the best position for a high overall score.

> **TIP:** There is no "guessing penalty" on the SAT—you do not lose points for incorrect answers. So there's no reason to ever leave anything blank.

Percentiles

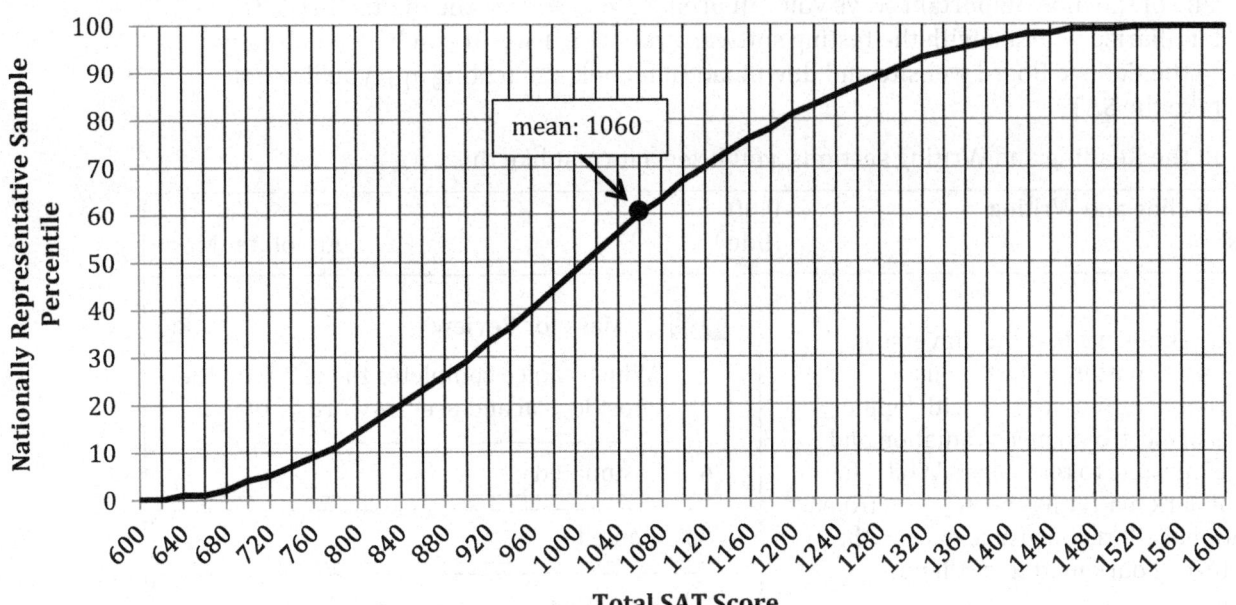

Curious how your score stacks up to those of other students? The graph above shows the 2021-2022 SAT percentiles based on a nationally representative sample of US students in the 11th and 12th grades.

Percentile ranks represent the percentage of students who score equal to or below that score. For example, according to this graph, a total score of 1120 was at about the 70th percentile for this time period: this means that if you scored an 1120, your score was greater than or equal to the scores of approximately 70% of students.

Although these percentiles are based on the previous (written) version of the SAT rather than the current (digital) version, approximately the same curve should apply. The College Board, the company that makes the SAT, asserts that the scoring on the digital test has been carefully formulated so that an 1120 on the new test is equivalent to an 1120 on the old: roughly the same proportion of students should earn that score either way.

Computer-Based Testing

One of the most important ways you can prepare yourself for the digital SAT is to familiarize yourself with the testing software you'll be using. If you haven't already, go to the College Board website and download Bluebook, the testing app you'll use to take the SAT.

In the Reading and Writing sections, you'll see a format like this:

Section 1: Reading and Writing   0:00   Annotate   More
Directions v   (Hide)

Many scientists believe that the universe is made up of dark matter, a mysterious substance that does not interact with light or other forms of electromagnetic radiation and is therefore invisible to telescopes. While the existence of dark matter has been _____ from its gravitational effects on visible matter, the precise nature of dark matter is still not understood.

1 ☐ Mark for Review   ABC

Which choice completes the text with the most logical and precise word or phrase?

(A.) insinuated

(B.) denied

(C.) construed

(D.) inferred

1 of 27   Next

The left side of the screen contains a brief passage, usually no more than one paragraph long. The right side of the screen contains the question and answer choices. Click on an answer to choose it; click the Next button on the bottom right to move to the next question. Immediately above the question, there's a little ☐ symbol with "Mark for Review" written next to it: click that to flag a question to remind yourself to return to it later. Click on the ABC button to the right of that if you want to eliminate answer choices.

Now look at the top row, above the question. Up in the middle is a timer which will count down the number of minutes you have remaining in the section; click the Hide button below it if you don't want this staring at you. In the top right, note the important Annotate button! This is what allows you to mark up the text on the screen as you go. To use it, select some text, then click that button. A pop-up menu will allow you to highlight the text, underline it, or even type a quick note to yourself.

The More button in the top right corner is for assistive technology, IT help, and emergency tools to exit the exam early or take an unscheduled break. Most students won't use this button at all.

The format of the Math questions is very similar.

Section 2: Math
Directions v

0:00 (Hide)

Calculator Reference More

1 ☐ Mark for Review   ABC

If $0 < c < d < 1$, then which of the following has the greatest value?

A. d^2

B. cd

C. c

D. d

1 of 22   Next

This time, the question and answer choices are presented right in the middle of the screen. You no longer have the ability to highlight or underline text, but you now have two other important tools. Click on the [Reference x^2] button to see a list of geometry formulas that you can access at any time. Click on the [Calculator] button to access the built-in graphing calculator, which you definitely should use. All the other buttons are the same as in the Reading and Writing modules.

> ***TIP:***
> Take some time to get comfortable with the built-in calculator. It can be an incredibly powerful tool for your math score.

SAT vs. ACT

Both the SAT and the ACT are well-established standardized tests accepted by all colleges and universities in the US. How can you decide which test is right for you? Here's a breakdown of how they differ.

Digital format — As of 2024, the SAT can only be taken in digital format (on a computer or tablet). Depending on when and where you're testing, the ACT may still be a traditional paper test, or you may have a choice between paper and digital versions. Unlike the SAT, however, the ACT will not be an *adaptive* digital test: the difficulty level of a section will not depend on your previous performance.

Reasoning — Questions on the ACT tend to be more straightforward, with a focus on assessing your knowledge of actual content. SAT questions are often more focused on testing your reasoning ability. The test rewards creative thinking more than subject matter mastery, and a tough problem often presents more like a logic puzzle than a familiar math question out of your textbook.

Reading pace and difficulty — The ACT reading passages are longer, and you have much less time to get through them. On the other hand, the passages are also easier than SAT passages, and the questions are more straightforward.

Science — The ACT includes a Science section, which the SAT does not. However, neither test is actually testing your science expertise. The ACT Science section is really just a test of quickly reading and interpreting charts and graphs in a science context. That task is also included on the SAT, just spread throughout the sections instead of concentrated in one place.

FROM THE BLOG

There's no reason to take *both* the SAT and the ACT. One, I don't know what you do with your Saturday mornings, but you must have more creative/worthwhile/fulfilling ways to spend those hours than in taking every test available to you. Two, grades remain the most important criterion of college admissions. Less time on test prep means more time for school (or friends, sports, sleep, you name it). Three, because the tests are different, the preparation for one is similar to but also meaningfully different than that for the other. It should be. They are different tests. Trying to study for or take both tests at once is akin to trying to switch between shortstop and left field and back, or the roles of Romeo to Juliet on subsequent nights (talk about heartbreak!). Lastly, no college asks for both. They ask for one or the other. Never both. Please choose. Trust me, you will be happy you did.

SAT to ACT Concordance Tables

SAT to ACT:					
SAT Total	ACT Composite	SAT Total	ACT Composite	SAT Total	ACT Composite
1600	36	1260	27	920	17
1590	36	1250	26	910	16
1580	36	1240	26	900	16
1570	36	1230	26	890	16
1560	35	1220	25	880	16
1550	35	1210	25	870	15
1540	35	1200	25	860	15
1530	35	1190	24	850	15
1520	34	1180	24	840	15
1510	34	1170	24	830	15
1500	34	1160	24	820	14
1490	34	1150	23	810	14
1480	33	1140	23	800	14
1470	33	1130	23	790	14
1460	33	1120	22	780	14
1450	33	1110	22	770	13
1440	32	1100	22	760	13
1430	32	1090	21	750	13
1420	32	1080	21	740	13
1410	31	1070	21	730	13
1400	31	1060	21	720	12
1390	31	1050	20	710	12
1380	30	1040	20	700	12
1370	30	1030	20	690	12
1360	30	1020	19	680	11
1350	29	1010	19	670	11
1340	29	1000	19	660	11
1330	29	990	19	650	11
1320	28	980	18	640	10
1310	28	970	18	630	10
1300	28	960	18	620	10
1290	27	950	17	610	9
1280	27	940	17	600	9
1270	27	930	17	590	9

ACT to SAT:	
ACT Composite	SAT Total
36	1590
35	1540
34	1500
33	1460
32	1430
31	1400
30	1370
29	1340
28	1310
27	1280
26	1240
25	1210
24	1180
23	1140
22	1110
21	1080
20	1040
19	1010
18	970
17	930
16	890
15	850
14	800
13	760
12	710
11	670
10	630
9	590

Adapted from "2018 ACT/SAT Concordance Tables," a joint publication of The College Board and ACT, Inc.

TIP:
The best way to tell which test is best suited for you is to take a practice test in each. Use these tables to compare your results.

TM and © 2023 PrepMatters, Inc. All rights reserved.

General SAT Strategies

The SAT is an intellectual marathon in which stamina is a key determinant of success. In order to succeed, you must prepare yourself physically, emotionally, and mentally. Although many students abandon the physical and emotional elements of preparation and focus solely on the mental aspect, they may find it difficult to do their best without the energy, alertness, and focus that physical and emotional preparation supply.

Physical preparation
Be sure to get enough sleep. When you are well rested, you will be more alert, less likely to make careless errors, and better able to devote your attention to the test. Similarly, regular exercise will help you feel more alert for the test and train your body to better handle stress. Nutrition also plays an important role in reaching optimal performance: healthy foods give you energy without leading to a crash later.

Emotional preparation
The best way to be emotionally prepared for the test is to feel in control of it, which comes from the knowledge that you have all the tools and information that you need to succeed. Also, practice a strategy for calming yourself down should you find yourself panicking during the test. Deep breathing is surprisingly effective; talk to a tutor or trusted teacher about other methods that may work for you.

Mental preparation
The best way to prepare for this test—and to lower your stress surrounding it at the same time—is to PRACTICE, PRACTICE, PRACTICE. Continue reviewing topics and doing practice problems until you thoroughly understand each section and have made each topic and strategy your own. Practice will also help you to know the pace at which you need to work.

How to Use This Book

While you're certainly welcome to start this book at page one and make your way in order through all the sections, many students will be better served by a more tailored approach. A good place to begin is the Table of Contents. Which math topics are areas of strength for you, and which ones are you less confident about? Are there any Reading question types that seem completely mysterious? How about topics of Writing mechanics on which you know you could use a refresher?

Each chapter begins with a Preview Quiz that gives you a glimpse of what topics the chapter will cover. Use these to help triage the sections for you. If you can breeze through a quiz with no effort, that's a chapter that's probably not a top priority for your studying time. If the quiz stumps you, focus on that chapter earlier rather than later.

Following the Preview Quiz, you'll see several pages of instruction that walk you through the topic and discuss both content and strategy, starting with the basics and building toward the more difficult content. The answers to all the Preview Quiz questions will be explained along the way. Most chapters also include "Try It" questions so you can test your understanding. You'll also see some "From the Blog" boxes every once in a while: these include excerpts from the PrepMatters blog about important elements of non-academic preparation, such as stress management and the importance of sleep.

After you finish reading the chapter and answering the Try It questions, you're ready to move on to the Practice Sets. Each chapter has two: one with easy to medium level problems, and the other with medium to difficult problems. Depending on your confidence, skill level, and goals, you may want to attack only the first set, only the second, or both. Full answer explanations for both the practice sets and the Try It problems can be found at the back of the book.

You're ready for this! It's time to turn to the Table of Contents, pick a topic, and dive in.

FROM THE BLOG

Some years ago, before we all carried GPS-equipped cell phones in our pockets, a friend of mine called to tell me he was lost. In the panicked, disoriented voice of a person who has lost all perspective, he gasped, "I thought I knew how to get there, because I went once with Derek, and I only have 65 cents and I remember being on a road with a roundish-even-numbered-route like 8 or 80 or 36 or maybe 22 and I'm at a pay phone and I don't know how much gas is left and please help me."

"Take a deep breath," I said. "What do you see?"

Knowing the area well, or having a map handy, is a nice way to keep from getting lost. But telling my friend facts about the area or the map would have been completely useless. What was helpful was being able to imagine how the world looked to him: following his wrong turns or embracing his errant logic. Only after empathizing with how he saw the world could I be helpful in getting him to take inventory of what he knew and helping him to reorient himself.

That panicked, disoriented tone of voice is exactly the same one I hear from my students. They don't know how SAT questions connect to their Algebra II class, or how comma rules relate to semicolons. Their minds race, but they only get more confused, more lost. They worry they don't have enough time. They worry they won't live up to expectations, or that they're inferior to their friends. They resent the test for measuring such inane, uninteresting skills.

Knowing how to test well, and the rules of grammar, and tricky facts of quadratic equations are necessary to help my students. But if they're lost enough, they don't even know how far they are from where they want to be. Telling them the best route is useless unless I know where they are and how they view things. Only then can we gain some perspective and reorient. Take a deep breath, I say. What do you see?

Most of the time, my students find their way, relieved to have the confusion behind them. More exciting, though, is when they learn to orient themselves. When they can retrace their steps and be aware of how their mental routes lead them away from where they want to go. Then, getting a little lost isn't as scary as they feared. Then, getting lost is an interesting side effect of going somewhere new.

Reading & Writing Section Overview

The two modules that make up the SAT's Reading and Writing section will test your proficiency with the written word. In each module, you'll have 32 minutes to answer 27 standalone questions. Unlike on other standardized tests, you will not need to answer multiple questions based on the same lengthy passage. Here, each question is self-contained, based on a passage no more than about one paragraph long.

The topics of the passages will vary. Some will cover history, social studies, the humanities, or science. Others will be fiction passages, often excerpts from a novel or short story. Occasionally, you may be asked to analyze poetry as well.

Roughly half of the questions focus on your skills in **reading** comprehension and analysis. Many of these are familiar types that you've seen before: find the meaning of a word in context, identify the most likely purpose of a particular sentence, state the main idea of a passage, and so on. Other questions will emphasize your logical reasoning skills. For example, for some questions, you'll be asked to demonstrate that you can choose the relevant information from a chart or graph in order to strengthen an author's argument. This requires a fairly advanced understanding of both the chart/graph and the argument, as well as the ways that the two relate to each other.

The other half of the questions are designed to test your **writing** skills. You'll be asked to choose the best version of a sentence, weighing considerations of English mechanics (punctuation, verb agreement, etc.) as well as style (for example, choosing a clean, concise sentence rather than a wordy, awkward one). For a few questions, you'll be given a set of facts and asked to choose the sentence that most effectively incorporates the relevant information to accomplish some specific goal.

These question types may seem unfamiliar, but they all get easier with practice. Helpfully, the SAT Reading & Writing section is very, very predictable. The more you practice it, the more you'll know exactly what to expect on test day.

Section Breakdown

Reading: Information, Ideas, and Structure
17-20 per section
≈ 33%

Reading: Evidence and Logical Reasoning
10-13 per section
≈ 21%

Writing: Standard English Conventions
11-15 per section
≈ 25%

Writing: Expression of Ideas
8-12 per section
≈ 21%

Reading: Information, Ideas, and Structure

These questions test your ability to read and analyze various kinds of texts. After reading a brief passage, you'll answer a single question designed to test your understanding. Some questions are about the details: you may be asked how a particular sentence fits into the passage as a whole, or what specific word best fits into a sentence. Other questions are about the bigger picture, asking you to summarize the main idea or compare one author's viewpoint to another's. For all of these questions, what matters most is the *context* of the passage. Be sure to limit your answers to what the passage explicitly tells you—never rely on your own outside knowledge of the topic, and try to avoid making any big assumptions about what the author is trying to say.

> **TIP:**
>
> In an average SAT Reading and Writing section, about a third of the questions will come from this category. More than half of those will be Words in Context questions.

Strategy in Brief

Unlike in the math portion of the SAT, for which we all agree on the criteria for correct answers, the distinction between two answer choices in the Reading and Writing section can sometimes appear quite subtle. As a result, students sometimes believe this section to be "subjective" or impossible to prepare for. **This is not the case.** Every question has one right answer and three wrong ones. The right answer is right because it has the most evidence *in the text*. Here are a few general principles to keep in mind to help you identify it.

Prediction is key.	We can spend a lot of energy thinking hard about why the answers "might…" "sort of…" "in a way…" "kind of…" work. Comparing answers only to each other is a great way to frustrate ourselves. Instead, the most crucial strategy is—whenever possible—to have an answer to the question *before* looking at the answer choices presented. It's a lot easier to find something if you know exactly what you're looking for.
Put it in your own words.	Have you ever gotten to the end of a passage and realized that you have no idea what you just read? It's easy to do. To keep that from happening, keep your reading **active**. As you go, summarize complex ideas into simple statements. What did the author just tell me? How does it relate to what they told me before? What are they probably going to tell me next?
Weaker is better.	If you're torn between two answer choices, the one using weaker language (e.g., words like "sometimes" or "at least a few") is more likely to be right than one that uses stronger language (such as "always" or "never"). Although some wrong answer choices overtly contradict or distort information in the passage, many are wrong simply because they are too extreme. Be wary, and make sure that the ENTIRE answer is correct.
Make intentional choices.	Depending on your goals, it may make sense to answer the questions out of order. In general, you may want to do fast, easy tasks before difficult, irritating ones. Or you may want to save the fun questions as an incentive to stay on task halfway through the section—managing your energy is another factor, after all. The passage's content and topic are considerations, as is the question type. As with many things on the test, just remember your options and that *you're in charge of your approach.* Take charge of the section and handle it the way that works best for you.

Words in Context

Preview Quiz

What do the following signify?

	contrast	continuation of thought
1) the word *however*	_____	_____
2) the word *moreover*	_____	_____
3) a colon	_____	_____

In each of the following, which choice completes the text with the most logical and precise word or phrase?

4) Janice is an optimistic person with a positive outlook on life. Although she is usually happy, today she seems quite _____

   A) fortunate.
   B) surprising.
   C) sad.
   D) unusual.

5) Bugs Bunny is a _____ character; people around the world recognize his face and his line, "What's up, Doc?"

   A) striking
   B) legitimate
   C) humorous
   D) well-known

6) Insider trading scams would not have flourished in the 1980s, as they clearly did, had regulators not been _____ to crack down on white-collar crime.

   A) motivated
   B) swift
   C) disinclined
   D) predisposed

These questions focus on our understanding of the subtle meanings of individual words, and how those meanings can change with context. In most cases, you'll be presented with a brief passage that has a word missing from one of its sentences, and you'll be asked to choose the word that fits the blank best. Occasionally, you'll see a variation where there is no blank—instead, you'll be asked to analyze an underlined word in the passage and choose the synonym that could best take its place.

The key to getting the correct answer is to understand the natural rhythm and context of the given sentence. Once you understand how the sentence "feels," you ought to be able to fill in the blank with a word of your choosing. Your first instinct will usually be "in the ballpark," if not exactly correct. Understanding, practicing, and adhering to the process described below will ensure that you master the idea of each sentence and that you do not get fooled by incorrect answer choices.

Read.	Cover the answer choices with your hand and read through the text, just saying the word "blank" to yourself when you hit the blank. It is important *not* to look at those answer choices yet so that they don't lead you astray.
Predict.	If no answer choices had been provided, what word would *you* choose to fill this blank? Use all the clues that the text has supplied, and feel free to **reuse the words already in the sentence**.
Evaluate the choices.	Remove your hand and compare the answer choices to the word you predicted. Which one is the best match?
Re-read.	This is a crucial final step! Re-read the text with your choice plugged into the blank to make sure it works.

The right answers to these questions do *not* necessarily involve difficult vocabulary words. In fact, for most of these questions, you will already know the definitions of the words in all four answer choices. The trick is to understand the **context** and make smart use of the **evidence** provided in the text.

TIP:

Avoid the temptation to automatically pick the "fanciest" word as the answer. The only factors that matter are the meanings of the words and the context of the sentence.

The text will always supply **clue words** that help you understand the relationship between the ideas expressed and help you find the correct answer.

Words that indicate a **CONTINUATION** of thought:

and	as well	similarly	furthermore
also	too	moreover	additionally

Words that indicate a **CONTRASTING** ideas:

yet	although	but	rather than
however	even so	in spite of	nevertheless
instead	despite	alternatively	on the other hand

Words that indicate a **CONCLUSION**:

in short	therefore	accordingly	as a result
thus	consequently	hence	in other words

Words that indicate a **CAUSE** or **MOTIVATION**:

because	since	for	to these ends

TIP:

For much more detail about these connecting words and phrases, see the Transitions section on p. 176.

Use these clue words to **predict** a word or phrase that logically would fill the blank. Remember, you can **reuse the words already in the text** to make this step simpler and more accurate.

Example: *Janice is an optimistic person with a positive outlook on life. Although she is usually happy, today she seems quite _____*

Focus on the clue word "although." What does it tell you about the word we're looking for? It indicates a contrast, meaning we're looking for a word that's the opposite of "happy." A simple word like "unhappy" would be a good prediction here. Now look at the choices:

A. fortunate.
B. surprising.
C. sad.
D. unusual.

The answer is **C**.

Words In Context

Try It Which choice completes the text with the most logical and precise word or phrase? First cover the answer choices with your hand and write in your prediction. Then pick the best match from the choices.

1) Many New Yorkers like to escape their crowded cities by visiting the Adirondack Mountains so that they may experience rare moments of _____ when they are truly alone and undisturbed.

   Prediction: _____

   A. solitude
   B. companionship
   C. loneliness
   D. cosmopolitanism

2) Thomas Kuhn's theories on the method of structural change within science were _____ when Kuhn first proposed them, but now they are universally respected and accepted.

   Prediction: _____

   A. well-established
   B. ridiculed
   C. praised
   D. endorsed

Another good source of clues is the **punctuation** of the original text. In general, semicolons and colons link two independent clauses that express similar ideas. On the SAT, semicolons and colons will be used to restate an idea. Similarly, three phrases or words strung together with commas will also express the same idea.

Example: Bugs Bunny is a _____ character; people around the world recognize his face and his line, "What's up, Doc?"

The clue here is the semicolon, which tells us that the second clause is intended to express the same idea as the first. So, according to the second clause, what kind of character is Bugs Bunny? Make it simple and reuse a word from the text: *recognizable* is a great prediction for this one.

A. striking
B. legitimate
C. humorous
D. well-known

The answer is **D**.

TIP:
Notice that some of the incorrect choices may create sentences that are *true*. Many of us do find Bugs Bunny to be a humorous character, after all. But only one choice gives us a sentence that is backed up by the **evidence** in the rest of the text.

Reading: Information, Ideas, and Structure

Try It Which choice completes the text with the most logical and precise word or phrase?

3) Most people think of diamonds as rare gems, but they are actually quite _____; the diamond supply has to be tightly restricted or the value of the gems would drop dramatically.

   Prediction: _____

   A. uncommon
   B. exquisite
   C. common
   D. expensive

4) The photographer was best known for his revealing _____ photographs: he never posed his subjects for fear that the artificiality would ruin the end result.

   Prediction: _____

   A. candid
   B. unnatural
   C. theatrical
   D. brilliant

CHALLENGE:

When these questions get difficult, it is usually due to the twisty structure of the sentence rather than the difficulty of the vocabulary. Be sure to read all the way to the end of the text before making your prediction (or choosing an answer) so that you know exactly where the writer is headed.

Example: Insider trading scams would not have flourished in the 1980s, as they clearly did, had regulators not been _____ to crack down on white-collar crime.

   A. motivated
   B. swift
   C. disinclined
   D. predisposed

Don't move too fast. What's the author's overall point? Scams flourished in the 1980s, and this wouldn't have happened if regulators had cracked down. But there's a "not" in front of the blank, so we need a word that expresses what the regulators did *not* do. Like this: if the regulators had not been so useless, the scams wouldn't have flourished. We need a word that expresses the regulators *not* acting. Choices A, B, and D all go the wrong way. Choice **C** is the only one that works.

Practice Set 1: Easy-Medium

Recycled plastics go through a process called reclamation, where they are collected, sorted, cleaned, melted, and then _____ into new plastic products. During this process, the properties of the plastic can be affected, which can result in some changes in the material's characteristics.

1

Which choice completes the text with the most logical and precise word or phrase?

A. completed
B. embodied
C. formed
D. originated

Mary Oliver was an acclaimed American poet known for her contemplative, lyrical style. Oliver's work often explores themes of the _____ between humans and nature, urging us to deepen our relationship with the world around us.

2

Which choice completes the text with the most logical and precise word or phrase?

A. interconnections
B. articulations
C. fusions
D. illuminations

Many scientists believe that the universe is made up of dark matter, a mysterious substance that does not interact with light or other forms of electromagnetic radiation and is therefore invisible to telescopes. While the existence of dark matter has been _____ from its gravitational effects on visible matter, the precise nature of this fascinating substance is still not well understood.

3

Which choice completes the text with the most logical and precise word or phrase?

A. insinuated
B. denied
C. construed
D. inferred

The simple insight behind graphology is that handwriting is connected in a very deep and very real way to our true selves. Kathi McKnight's <u>take</u> on this idea is that "hand writing is brain writing," and she's so clearly right.

4

As used in the text, what does the word "take" most nearly mean?

A. steal
B. end
C. perspective
D. agenda

The idea of "terraforming" Mars—modifying the planet's environment to make it habitable for humans—has tantalized scientists for years. Some proposed methods include _____ greenhouse gases to warm the planet, melting the polar ice caps to provide water, and introducing genetically engineered plants to produce oxygen.

5

Which choice completes the text with the most logical and precise word or phrase?

A. inflicting
B. asserting
C. suggesting
D. releasing

The practice of traveling over long distances on a seasonal basis is thought to be an important element of the success of a wide variety of species, though scientists still debate the exact mechanism behind this behavior. It is not _____ that the evolution of migratory behavior remains a topic of active research and investigation, as it is a complex and multifaceted phenomenon that is likely influenced by a range of factors.

6

Which choice completes the text with the most logical and precise word or phrase?

A. outstanding
B. surprising
C. unremarkable
D. conspicuous

Recent research has uncovered several magma storage regions under Hawaii's volcanoes. The magma there is located in pockets of partially molten rock at various depths, which allows the magma to move easily and quickly to the surface, leading to more explosive and effusive eruptions. These magma reservoirs are connected through a system of dikes and sills that act as "plumbing systems," _____ magma to move from the deep reservoirs to the surface.

7

Which choice completes the text with the most logical and precise word or phrase?

A. transporting
B. rendering
C. allowing
D. bestowing

Witchweed (*Striga*) is a parasitic plant that reduces the yield of maize grown in infected fields. The impact of witchweed on maize is particularly severe in sub-Saharan Africa, where it is considered one of the major biotic constraints to maize production. Research by C. Li et. al. found that reduction of a single enzyme, ZmCYP706C37, could significantly reduce *Striga* germination and infection, suggesting that it may be possible to breed a strain of maize that is _____ to witchweed.

8

Which choice completes the text with the most logical and precise word or phrase?

A. resistant
B. adverse
C. insubordinate
D. tenacious

For certain types of crystalline materials, a history of exposure to high-energy radiation can instill a hidden superpower known as thermoluminescence. As a result of the electronic excited states trapped in the crystal lattice, these materials emit light when heated. The older an object is, the more light is produced, and in fact the proportion is so well understood that this phenomenon is routinely used to _____ ancient artifacts dug out of the earth after tens of thousands of years.

9

Which choice completes the text with the most logical and precise word or phrase?

A. predict
B. date
C. accompany
D. disinter

Practice Set 2: Medium-Hard

Wildlife biologist Jonathan Slaght has devoted much of his career to the study of the Blakiston's fish owl (*Bubo blakistoni*), an endangered species found in the Russian Far East and in northeastern China. The bird is remarkable not only for its size—with a wingspan of over six feet, it is the largest living owl species—but also for the unusual physiology of its head: it _____ the disk-shaped face characteristic of other owls.

1

Which choice completes the text with the most logical and precise word or phrase?

A. requires
B. lacks
C. maintains
D. distinguishes

It is commonly believed that character motivation in ancient Greek dramas had little to do with individual autonomy. Professor Mellich, for example, argues that even when characters are explicitly faced with a "choice," the situation is crafted by deistic forces who also heavily influence, or in some cases completely control, the outcome. The character _____ the dilemma and his decided course of action as a compulsion, such that any amount of "debating" over the resolution of his problem is nothing more than an agonizing awareness of the tragic situation he finds himself in and the acts he'll have to take as a result. The choice is therefore almost entirely external to the character, lying instead in the hands of the supernatural beings who dominate the story.

2

Which choice completes the text with the most logical and precise word or phrase?

A. sustains
B. develops
C. experiences
D. resolves

If Hollywood is to be believed, Anne Sullivan gave Helen Keller the gift of communication with the outside world. In the famous movie account of the relationship between Keller and her teacher (_____ titled *The Miracle Worker*), Sullivan is hailed as something approaching a saint. By contrast, the film portrays young Keller as a wild, violent child given to fits of uncontrollable rage as she vents her frustration. Sullivan is idealized as the kind soul who refuses to back down, who battles her way past Keller's defenses through stubborn, persistent love.

3

Which choice completes the text with the most logical and precise word or phrase?

A. tellingly
B. artfully
C. proficiently
D. durably

The assumption underlying our reluctance to move proactively into international conflicts that seem poised to escalate to full-scale war is that the risks entailed by all bold actions are not outweighed by the potential dangers inherent to _____.

4

Which choice completes the text with the most logical and precise word or phrase?

A. aggression
B. imperialism
C. hostility
D. inaction

The primary driver behind many dystopian scenarios is the notion that science *must* do all that it *can* do. Those who advocate subsuming scientific inquiry to public discourse and ethical inquiry are often dismissed as reactionary moralists bent on holding back human progress with <u>set</u> worldviews.

5

As used in the text, what does the word "set" most nearly mean?

A. fixed
B. group
C. win
D. collection

In the 1940s, Elizabeth Stern was working at the Los Angeles County Hospital when she noticed a high incidence of cervical cancer in Mexican-American women. She began investigating the cause and discovered a strong association between the human papillomavirus (HPV) and cervical cancer. It is difficult to _____ the importance of this discovery: it was the first time that a virus had been identified as the cause of a human cancer, and it paved the way for the development of HPV vaccines that have saved countless lives.

6

Which choice completes the text with the most logical and precise word or phrase?

A. downplay
B. overstate
C. ascertain
D. evaluate

A recent study investigated the chemical composition and genetic variation of cumin, a spice widely used in food and traditional medicine. The researchers found that cumin contains various bioactive compounds such as essential oils, phenolic compounds, and flavonoids, which contribute to its medicinal properties. Additionally, the study examined the use of somatic embryogenesis, a technique used to produce clones of plants, to _____ cumin. The researchers observed that the somatic embryogenesis technique was effective in producing healthy cumin plantlets, but also noted the occurrence of somaclonal variation, which can result in genetic changes in the plants.

7

Which choice completes the text with the most logical and precise word or phrase?

A. circulate
B. diffuse
C. propagate
D. publicize

Central Ideas and Details

Preview Quiz

Fill in your answer:

1) What should you read first, the passage or the question?

2) As a general rule, an answer choice that uses weak language is (more / less) likely to be right than an answer choice that uses strong language.

3) To help decide on the right answer, it is a (good / bad) idea to rely on your own knowledge of the subject from outside the passage.

Choose the best answer:

4) Elephants are taught to reproduce specific brushstrokes, explains Desmond Morris, a noted naturalist who spent time at Nong Nooch elephant center in Thailand observing the phenomenon. Morris confirmed that the brush strokes are well executed and the result of meticulous training. His research led him to conclude, however, that the paintings are more a product of muscle control than artistic talent.

Based on the text, which of the following is a belief held by Desmond Morris about artistic talent?

A) It is an innate skill.
B) It is less useful than other pursuits.
C) It consists of more than muscle control.
D) It is the only thing that separates humans from other animals.

Reading: Information, Ideas, and Structure

Some of these questions will ask about a specific detail from one part of the passage, while others will ask you to state the main idea of the text as a whole. You do *not* have to "read between the lines" for these questions. The correct answer is typically just a restatement of what the author literally said.

Read the question. It's best to start with the question so that you know exactly what you'll be looking for. Is there a detail to find? A general idea to summarize?

Read the text. Read the *entire* passage. Do not skim. Helpfully, these passages are quite short, so you have time to read it all.

Predict. Come up with your own answer to the question before looking at the answer choices. Stay as literal as possible, basing your answer only on what is contained in the text. Do *not* base your answer on your own outside knowledge of the subject.

Evaluate the choices. Analyze the answers carefully to find the best match for your prediction. Be wary of any choices that use strong, extreme language or take a step beyond what the text literally says. Generally, a correct answer is a bland, wishy-washy reworking of the information in the passage.

Watch out for **tempting wrong answers** that

- rely on outside knowledge
- are *probably* true but don't have specific support in the text
- slightly mischaracterize something from the passage
- are only half-right, half-wrong
- simply go too far (are too extreme)

> **TIP:**
>
> Keep in mind the author's *tone*. Was the passage making an argument? Or was it more a neutral description that didn't take sides? Does it read like a persuasive speech or like a textbook?

A key step in the process is to **predict** your answer *before* you look at the answer choices. This makes spotting the right answer much easier, and it makes the wrong answers much less tempting. Plus, in general, it's just easier to find something if you have a clear idea of what you're looking for.

Try It Write in your own answer.

1) In Europe during the Middle Ages and Renaissance, paper production relied heavily on discarded textiles, such as linen and cotton rags. Rags were collected, sorted, and washed to remove impurities. The fibers were then beaten, mixed with water, and formed into sheets. This method, known as rag papermaking, remained common until the introduction of wood pulp in the 19th century. By then, the limited supply of rags was struggling to meet the increased demand for paper arising from the Industrial Revolution, and the process of collecting and processing them required significant resources. Meanwhile, technological advances had made the processing of wood pulp much more efficient and cost-effective.

   Based on the text, what was a primary reason that European papermakers switched from rag papermaking to the use of wood pulp?

2) The ghazal is a poetic form originating in Arabic literature and subsequently embraced by Persian, Urdu, and other languages. It consists of independent couplets called *bayts*, with each *bayt* functioning as a complete poem. The ghazal follows a specific structure, with a repeating word or phrase (*radif*) appearing at the end of the second line in each couplet, creating a distinctive rhyme scheme. The first line of each couplet often ends with a similar or identical word or phrase (*qafia*) to further contribute to the rhyme pattern. The final *bayt* is typically more personal than the other couplets and often contains the poet's *takhallus*, or pen-name.

   Based on the text, which two elements of a ghazal contribute most directly to the rhyme scheme?

Next, find the answer choice that is the best match for your prediction. If you can't decide between two tempting choices, there are a few reliable tiebreakers to keep in mind.

Weaker is better than stronger. The general rule is that the language of the correct answer choice can be no stronger than the language of the passage. So, all else being equal, a less extreme answer choice (for example, one using words like "sometimes" or "at least a few") is more likely to be right than a more extreme one (for example, one using words like "always" or "never"). It's just easier to support.

General is better than specific. Similarly, it's easier to support a general answer choice than a more specific one. This is true by logical necessity—if you're guessing what object an opaque box contains, you're better off guessing that the object is "red" than that the object is "red and round." An even likelier answer would be that the box contains "something." Answers need not be fulfilling to be correct.

Consider the main idea. Choose the answer that's more in line with the main idea of the passage. For example, if the passage as a whole is about Native American language acquisition projects, an answer that focuses on "Cherokee linguistic techniques" is more likely to be correct than an answer that discusses funding for schools in a state that was only briefly mentioned.

Be a prosecutor, not an advocate. If you find yourself arguing on behalf of your answer choice—trying to build the best case for why it's a good interpretation of what the author said—then you're probably going down the wrong path. Instead, attack each tempting answer choice with a critical eye, doing your best to build the strongest case *against* it. Then choose the answer that best holds up to scrutiny.

> **TIP:**
>
> If a choice is 50% right and 50% wrong—or even 90% right, 10% wrong—it is WRONG.

Of all of these factors, language strength is the most important tiebreaker.

> **Try It**   Practice evaluating choices without a passage. For each of the below, first **underline** any words or phrases in the answers that affect the overall language strength of the choice. Then **select** the choice that's most likely to be the right answer.
>
> 3) Which choice best states the main idea of the (absent) text?
>
>   A) Researchers have developed a revolutionary new method for refining zirconium.
>   B) Chlorination is the most important step in the zirconium refining process.
>   C) A recent experiment has proven the criticisms of the new zirconium refining method to be completely unfounded.
>   D) A new method of refining zirconium appears to be a promising alternative to the traditional approach.
>
>   What is the most likely answer? _____
>
> 4) According to the (absent) text, what does Alfred do on Friday?
>
>   A) He reads at least part of the reference book.
>   B) He starts on his homework to avoid an inevitable confrontation.
>   C) He uses the reference book to complete his entire assignment three days early.
>   D) He asks for help in using the reference book after trying and failing to understand it.
>
>   What is the most likely answer? _____
>
> 5) [a text consisting only of dialogue between two characters]
>
>   Based on the text, what is true about Susan?
>
>   A) She regrets her life choices.
>   B) She thinks her children ought to visit her more.
>   C) She sometimes argues with her family members.
>   D) She privately believes that the picnic is sure to be a disaster.
>
>   What is the most likely answer? _____

Reading: Information, Ideas, and Structure

Let's put it all together by walking through an example question.

Example: *Elephants are taught to reproduce specific brushstrokes, explains Desmond Morris, a noted naturalist who spent time at Nong Nooch elephant center in Thailand observing the phenomenon. Morris confirmed that the brush strokes are well executed and the result of meticulous training. His research led him to conclude, however, that the paintings are more a product of muscle control than artistic talent.*

Based on the text, which of the following is a belief held by Desmond Morris about artistic talent?

A) *It is an innate skill.*
B) *It is less useful than other pursuits.*
C) *It consists of more than muscle control.*
D) *It is the only thing that separates humans from other animals.*

Don't be distracted by all the extraneous detail in this passage. Focus on the question: what do we actually know about *artistic talent* specifically? That was only mentioned in the last sentence. We don't know whether this guy thinks artistic talent is an innate skill, or how useful it might or might not be. We certainly don't know anything as extreme as the idea expressed in choice D. But we do know that Morris distinguishes artistic talent from muscle control: if paintings are more about muscle control than artistic talent, then those two things can't just be the same. Choice C is the only one of these choices that *has* to be true. The answer is **C**.

FROM THE BLOG

Under stress, most people speed up. This is especially true on tests, because students have been conditioned by school to fear not finishing. But on the SAT, answering fewer than all the questions does not spell doom, so panicking over unanswered questions is not called for. And it's a lot easier to accurately answer what you *do* know how to do if you don't rush to answer everything.

Try It   Now let's return to the passages you read earlier. Use the predictions you made and consider the strength of language of the answer choices to help you pick the best answer.

6) In Europe during the Middle Ages and Renaissance, paper production relied heavily on discarded textiles, such as linen and cotton rags. Rags were collected, sorted, and washed to remove impurities. The fibers were then beaten, mixed with water, and formed into sheets. This method, known as rag papermaking, remained common until the introduction of wood pulp in the 19th century. By then, the limited supply of rags was struggling to meet the increased demand for paper arising from the Industrial Revolution, and the process of collecting and processing them required significant resources. Meanwhile, technological advances had made the processing of wood pulp much more efficient and cost-effective.

Based on the text, what was a primary reason that European papermakers switched from rag papermaking to the use of wood pulp?

A) People were concerned about the potential hygiene risks posed by using discarded textiles.
B) The papermaking technology that became available during the Industrial Revolution could only be used with natural materials.
C) Fewer rags were available due to a change in popular fashion tastes.
D) Using wood pulp had become less expensive than using rags.

7) The ghazal is a poetic form originating in Arabic literature and subsequently embraced by Persian, Urdu, and other languages. It consists of independent couplets called *bayts*, with each *bayt* functioning as a complete poem. The ghazal follows a specific structure, with a repeating word or phrase (*radif*) appearing at the end of the second line in each couplet, creating a distinctive rhyme scheme. The first line of each couplet often ends with a similar or identical word or phrase (*qafia*) to further contribute to the rhyme pattern. The final *bayt* is typically more personal than the other couplets and often contains the poet's *takhallus*, or pen-name.

Based on the text, which two elements of a ghazal contribute most directly to the rhyme scheme?

A) The bayt and the qafia.
B) The radif and the takhallus.
C) The radif and the qafia.
D) The bayt and the takhallus.

Practice Set 1: Easy-Medium

Tryptophan is an essential amino acid, meaning it is necessary for the body's functioning but cannot be produced by the body and must come from the diet. When tryptophan is transported across the blood-brain barrier into the brain, it is converted into 5-hydroxytryptophan (5-HTP) and then into the neurotransmitter serotonin.

1

Based on the text, what is true about serotonin?

A. It is synthesized outside the brain.
B. The body cannot function without it.
C. It is a derivative of a substance obtained from food.
D. It is an amino acid transported across the blood-brain barrier.

The following text is adapted from John Burroughs' 1881 essay "An Idyl of the Honeybee."

A colony of honey bees, with its neatness and love of order, its division of labor, its public-spiritedness, its thrift, its complex economies, and its inordinate love of gain, seems as far removed from a condition of rude nature as does a walled city or a cathedral town. Our native bee, on the other hand, the "burly, dozing humblebee," affects one more like the rude, untutored savage. He has learned nothing from experience. He lives from hand to mouth. He luxuriates in time of plenty, and he starves in times of scarcity.

2

Based on the text, what is the primary difference between the honey bee and the native bee?

A. The native bee is less common.
B. The honey bee is more industrious.
C. The native bee is smaller in size.
D. The honey bee is more apt to be imported.

As Heike Kamerlingh Onnes first discovered in 1911, certain materials have the ability to conduct electricity with zero resistance and zero energy loss. This "superconductivity" was at first of only theoretical interest, because the property appeared to exist only in conditions of extreme cold—more specifically, at approximately 4.2 K, a temperature that was highly impractical to maintain. However, in 1986, scientists at IBM's Zurich Research Laboratory dramatically changed that picture. Their experiments showed that some ceramic materials made from copper and oxygen exhibited superconductivity at a much higher temperature point, a breakthrough that paved the way for real-world applications in such varied fields as medical imaging, electronics, and power transmission.

3

Based on the text, which of the following best describes the significance of the 1986 experiments at the Zurich Research Laboratory?

A. They demonstrated that superconductivity was possible at temperatures that were more practical to maintain than was previously believed.
B. They proved that ceramic materials were better superconductors than non-ceramic materials.
C. They suggested that colder temperatures might improve the efficiency of superconductivity.
D. They indicated that Heike Kamerlingh Onnes's discoveries were limited by the inferior materials available to him in 1911.

The following text is from Claude McKay's 1922 poem "When I Have Passed Away."

When I have passed away and am forgotten,
And no one living can recall my face,
When under alien sod my bones lie rotten
With not a tree or stone to mark the place;

Perchance a pensive youth, with passion burning,
For olden verse that smacks of love and wine,
The musty pages of old volumes turning,
May light upon a little song of mine,

And he may softly hum the tune and wonder
Who wrote the verses in the long ago;
Or he may sit him down awhile to ponder
Upon the simple words that touch him so.

Ribbon microphones utilize a thin aluminum ribbon as the primary element for capturing sound. The ribbon is suspended within a magnetic field and acts as a diaphragm that vibrates in response to sound waves. As the ribbon moves, it generates an electrical signal proportional to the sound pressure. Ribbon microphones capture audio with warmth and accuracy, producing detailed and nuanced recordings especially valued for capturing vocals and instruments in studio recordings. As a result, ribbon microphones dominated the recording industry from the 1930s to the 1950s. With advancements of technology and the introduction of new, less delicate microphone types, ribbon microphones declined in popularity during the second half of the twentieth century. However, in recent years, there has been a resurgence of interest in ribbon microphones, driven by their distinct sound qualities and vintage appeal.

4

The "pensive youth" described in the second and third stanzas is best characterized as which of the following?

A. a distant relative of the poet who barely remembers him
B. a hypothetical future student who might ask the poet for advice
C. a stranger who the poet imagines discovering his work after the poet's death
D. a lover of poetry who is a great fan of the poet

5

What is the main idea of the text?

A. Ribbon microphones are ideally suited for the recording of human voices because they capture audio with warmth and accuracy.
B. Some microphones use the vibrations of a metal ribbon to capture sound.
C. Ribbon microphones, which use a thin ribbon to capture sound, were widely used in studio recordings from the 1930s to 1950s and are becoming popular again today.
D. Although ribbon microphones were extremely popular during the mid-twentieth century, they fell out of favor because they were too delicate.

Reading: Information, Ideas, and Structure

The following text is from Sinclair Lewis's 1920 novel *Main Street*. Carol is a senior in college considering her future.

> Carol was determined to earn her living. But how she was to earn it, how she was to conquer the world—almost entirely for the world's own good—she did not see. Most of the girls who were not betrothed meant to be teachers. Of these there were two sorts: careless young women who admitted that they intended to leave the "beastly classroom and grubby children" the minute they had a chance to marry; and studious, sometimes bulbous-browed and pop-eyed maidens who at class prayer-meetings requested God to "guide their feet along the paths of greatest usefulness." Neither sort tempted Carol.

6

Which of the following best characterizes Carol's position toward the two types of students who were preparing to be teachers?

A. She found them unattractive.
B. She was intimidated by their religious convictions.
C. She admired the honesty they displayed about their intentions.
D. She did not wish to join either of the two types.

Penicillin is a widely-used antibiotic obtained from *Penicillium* molds. In the early stages of penicillin's development, researchers found that oxygen posed a major problem. When exposed to oxygen, the *Penicillium* mold would divert its metabolic resources away from penicillin production and instead focus on other metabolic pathways. This resulted in lower penicillin yields and made it difficult to efficiently produce the antibiotic on a large scale. Howard Florey and Norman Heatley overcame this obstacle by developing a method to cultivate the *Penicillium* mold in deep fermentation tanks where oxygen levels could be controlled.

7

Based on the text, which of the following was a major effect of the method developed by Florey and Heatley?

A. It allowed for penicillin to be obtained from substances other than *Penicillium* molds.
B. It made penicillin a more powerful antibiotic.
C. It protected the *Penicillium* culture from potential contaminants.
D. It helped make large-scale production of penicillin more efficient.

Certain animals have evolved specialized visual systems that are particularly adept at perceiving and tracking moving objects. This adaptation is especially useful for animals that rely on hunting or evading predators. For example, the dragonfly is known for its remarkable ability to track and catch flying prey in mid-air. Dragonflies possess large compound eyes that consist of thousands of independent visual units called ommatidia, each containing its own photoreceptor cells. Their specialized neural circuitry quickly processes and combines inputs from various ommatidia, allowing dragonflies to accurately track the movement of prey and swiftly maneuver towards it.

8

According to the text, what is true about dragonflies?

A. Their visual processing capabilities are specialized for detecting and following fast-moving objects such as other flying insects.
B. They are the only type of insect to possess compound eyes consisting of thousands of ommatidia.
C. They are unable to see objects that do not move.
D. They have no need to avoid predators.

Practice Set 2: Medium-Hard

The following text is from Jane Austen's 1817 novel *Persuasion*.

Frederick was, at that time, a remarkably fine young man, with a great deal of intelligence, spirit, and brilliancy; and Anne an extremely pretty girl, with gentleness, modesty, taste, and feeling. Half the sum of attraction, on either side, might have been enough, for he had nothing to do, and she had hardly anybody to love. They were gradually acquainted, and when acquainted, rapidly and deeply in love.

1

Based on the text, which choice best characterizes the motivations for the relationship between Anne and Frederick?

A. mutual convenience
B. mitigated boredom
C. fearful obedience
D. carefree relief

Influential Austrian architect Otto Wagner was a proponent of functionalism, a design philosophy that highlights the practical aspects of a building's design. Wagner believed that architecture should serve the needs of its users and adapt to the demands of modern life. He emphasized the integration of form and function, eliminating unnecessary ornamentation and focusing instead on user experience. His designs aimed to optimize the functionality of buildings, enhance usability, and promote a harmonious relationship between architecture, technology, and society.

2

What is the main idea of the text?

A. Functionalist architecture integrates form and function to optimize the user experience.
B. Otto Wagner's architecture prioritized practicality, usability, and adaptability.
C. Many architects have followed in the footsteps of functionalist Otto Wagner.
D. Otto Wagner, an architect from Austria, aimed to promote harmony between individuals and the buildings they live in.

The following text is from "When You Are Old," an 1893 poem by William Butler Yeats.

When you are old and grey and full of sleep,
And nodding by the fire, take down this
    book,
And slowly read, and dream of the soft look
Your eyes had once, and of their shadows
    deep;

How many loved your moments of glad
    grace,
And loved your beauty with love false or
    true,
But one man loved the pilgrim soul in you,
And loved the sorrows of your changing face;

And bending down beside the glowing bars,
Murmur, a little sadly, how Love fled
And paced upon the mountains overhead
And hid his face amid a crowd of stars.

3

In the first stanza, the phrase "full of sleep" most directly indicates which of the following about the subject?

A. She is drowsy due to illness.
B. She has lost her youthful beauty.
C. She lacks energy due to her advanced age.
D. She was once loved by the speaker.

In 1997, Bilbao, Spain became the new Mecca of art and architecture thanks to Frank Gehry's outstanding new Guggenheim museum. The entire north of Spain, from Santander in the west to the rugged Pyrenees in the east, soon flourished with an incredible influx of tourists. Although urban planners derided early estimates of 500,000 visitors per year, after the first eight months, nearly 700,000 *turistas* had gaped in awe at Mr. Gehry's work. Aside from bringing immediate and significant revenues into Bilbao, the museum catalyzed the city's urban renewal program. The acrobatic Guggenheim and the graceful infrastructure that arose in its wake teamed up to help Bilbao capture a significant role in the expanding European economy.

4

Based on the text, which of the following is true about Bilbao's urban planners around the time the Guggenheim museum opened?

A. They were surprised by the flood of tourists the museum brought in.
B. They understood what new art museums can do to a city's economy.
C. They initiated a program to make Bilbao the dominant economic power in Europe.
D. They reacted to the Guggenheim's success with outpourings of nationalistic pride.

The field of philosophy can be divided into four main branches: logic, ethics, epistemology (the study of knowledge) and metaphysics (the study of reality and existence). By far the most abstract and theoretical of the four, metaphysics seeks to understand the nature of the world, the universe, and the relationship between mind and matter. What is the ultimate reality of time and space? What is the nature of causation and change? What do we mean by terms like "consciousness" or "identity"? These are some of the central questions of metaphysics, and they have no easy answers.

5

According to the text, what is true about metaphysics?

A. It is the most difficult of the four branches of philosophy.
B. Its practitioners have found answers to theoretical questions concerning reality and existence.
C. It serves as the foundation for all philosophical studies.
D. It is more abstract than epistemology.

During the 2016 US presidential election, three Washington state electors, despite having pledged to vote for the candidate who won the statewide popular vote, instead cast their votes for another candidate. Under state law, these "faithless electors" were subject to penalty or replacement due to their actions. But were such laws enforceable? In the resulting case *Chiafolo v. Washington*, the US Supreme Court unanimously held that they were. As a result of this historic holding, the power of states in the Electoral College system was preserved, and the stability of the presidential election process was maintained.

6

Which choice best states the main idea of the text?

A. A group of electors in the 2016 US presidential election inappropriately violated their pledge.
B. The unanimity of the holding in *Chiafolo v. Washington* was a victory for election stability.
C. The central question before the US Supreme Court in *Chiafolo v. Washington* was whether states can enforce "faithless elector" laws.
D. The landmark US Supreme Court case *Chiafolo v. Washington* held that states may penalize or replace faithless electors.

The public health services in Canada and the United Kingdom (UK) differ in several ways. Canada has a decentralized system where healthcare is managed by each province and territory, with federal funding and standards. The UK has a centralized system known as the National Health Service (NHS), which provides healthcare services across the country. Funding in Canada comes from general tax revenues and provincial/territorial insurance plans, while the UK funds the NHS through taxation and national insurance contributions. Coverage and access vary, with both countries aiming for universal access to necessary services. Service delivery involves a mix of public and private providers in Canada, while the UK relies primarily on NHS-employed healthcare professionals.

7

According to the text, what is one key difference between the public health services in Canada and the UK?

A. The funding for Canada's system is decentralized, while the UK's is federally funded.
B. In the UK, most healthcare professionals are employed directly by the government, while in Canada, all healthcare professionals are privately employed.
C. In Canada, unlike in the UK, the goal of the system is to provide universal access to medically necessary services.
D. Delivery of healthcare services falls under the jurisdiction of local authorities in Canada, while in the UK, the system is managed at the national level.

In the 16th century, the invention of the printing press significantly increased the speed and efficiency of book production compared to the previous method of hand-copying texts. The process began with the creation of individual metal letters, called type, which were used to compose the text. The typesetter arranged the individual metal types in a composing stick (a handheld tray with an adjustable frame) to form words, sentences, and paragraphs. Once the text was set, the typesetter transferred the arranged type from the composing stick to a larger frame called a "chase" to hold the type in place. An oil-based ink was applied to the raised surfaces of the type. Next, the press operator would activate the press, bringing a heavy flat plate down onto the inked type and paper. Because each page had to be printed individually, it could take anywhere from two weeks to several months to produce a book from start to finish.

8

Based on the text, what can be inferred about book production in the 16th century?

A. Using the method of hand-copying texts would require more than two weeks to produce a book from start to finish.
B. Producing a book using a printing press required exactly two individuals: a typesetter and a press operator.
C. Errors were more common when texts were hand-copied than when they were produced on a printing press.
D. Oil-based inks were only used in books produced on a printing press, not in books that were produced by other means.

Structure and Purpose

Preview Quiz

Fill in your answer:

1) How are these questions different from the Central Ideas and Details questions?

2) Will you be asked for the purpose of the entire text or for the purpose of a specific piece of it?

Choose the best answer:

3) During photosynthesis, carbon dioxide undergoes a series of reactions to form a nongas molecule, usually one with three carbon atoms. In some of the most important food crops on earth, however, a four-carbon molecule is formed. This "C4" photosynthesis minimizes water loss and maximizes carbon dioxide uptake, which is particularly beneficial in hot and arid environments. Because C4 plants can produce higher yields in regions where water is limited, C4 plants such as cassava and sweet potato are staple foods for millions of people in those regions.

Which choice best describes the function of the first sentence in the text as a whole?

A) It introduces a feature of photosynthesis that is explored in greater detail in the next sentence.
B) It explains how ordinary (non-C4) photosynthesis fails to minimize water loss.
C) It suggests that the nongas molecule formed during photosynthesis can only contain either 3 or 4 carbon atoms.
D) It provides background information that sets up the distinction made later in the text.

Structure and Purpose

These questions ask you about an author's **reason** for including a specific detail or for using a certain word or phrase, or about how the author has **organized** the passage to accomplish a particular goal. The context of the surrounding sentences will point you toward the author's intent.

Watch out for **wrong answer choices** that

- are true statements but don't express the author's intent
- are overly broad or too extreme
- mischaracterize one part of the passage or present the ideas out of sequence

Some of these questions will ask for the purpose of the entire passage as a whole, a variation on the "what is the main idea" questions we've already seen. But most of the time, a purpose question will ask for the function of a particular section of the text, usually a sentence or part of a sentence.

To attack these, first read the text as a whole and summarize the main idea for yourself. Then, re-read the part they're asking about and consider how that section fits into the big picture. Can you predict a description of its role?

As usual, we'll walk through the process with an example.

Example: *During photosynthesis, carbon dioxide undergoes a series of reactions to form a nongas molecule, usually one with three carbon atoms. In some of the most important food crops on earth, however, a four-carbon molecule is formed. This "C4" photosynthesis minimizes water loss and maximizes carbon dioxide uptake, which is particularly beneficial in hot and arid environments. Because C4 plants can produce higher yields in regions where water is limited, C4 plants such as cassava and sweet potato are staple foods for millions of people in those regions.*

Which choice best describes the function of the first sentence in the text as a whole?

TIP: As with the other Reading & Writing questions, the best strategy is to read the **question** before you read the **passage**.

Let's see if we can come up with a prediction before we look at any answer choices. First, read the whole text from start to finish, and try to briefly summarize it in your head. For this one, our summary might be something like this: "C4 plants use a special kind of photosynthesis, which is really important in dry places." Now re-read the first sentence, since that's what the question asked us about. What is it doing there? A good prediction might be "setting the scene" or "explaining the context," or something along those lines.

Now we're ready to read the answer choices.

A) It introduces a feature of photosynthesis that is explored in greater detail in the next sentence.
B) It explains how ordinary (non-C4) photosynthesis fails to minimize water loss.
C) It suggests that the nongas molecule formed during photosynthesis can only contain either 3 or 4 carbon atoms.
D) It provides background information that sets up the distinction made later in the text.

Choice A is half right, half wrong. While this sentence does introduce a feature of photosynthesis (the creation of a nongas molecule), the next sentence does not explore that feature in detail. If it did, the second sentence here would be providing specific information about how the nongas molecule is created. Instead, the second sentence of this text is merely pointing out that some plants do this differently. That's a related point, but it's not exploring the first point in detail. Choice A is out.

Choice B is misusing other parts of the text. The passage does tell us that C4 photosynthesis minimizes water loss, so it's not a crazy step for us to infer that non-C4 photosynthesis *doesn't* minimize water loss. But that's not the purpose of this first sentence! The first sentence doesn't tell us anything about water loss, so this is much too big a leap. (It's also relevant to note that when we predicted an answer, we didn't mention water loss at all.)

Choice C is too extreme. This sentence tells us that the nongas molecule can contain 3 carbon atoms, and a later sentence tells us that it can also contain 4. But nothing in the text establishes that these are the *only* two possibilities. And again, this doesn't match our prediction.

Choice D is the best match. This sentence gives us the background (how photosynthesis generally works) to help us understand the distinction the author is about to make (that in some plants, the nongas molecule contains 4 rather than 3 carbon atoms). Choice **D** is the winner.

Try It

1) Composting is a natural process that converts organic waste into nutrient-rich compost. Organic waste materials, such as kitchen scraps and yard trimmings, are collected and layered in a compost bin or pile. The carbon-to-nitrogen ratio is balanced by alternating between carbon-rich "browns" and nitrogen-rich "greens." Microorganisms break down the organic materials through decomposition, generating heat and transforming the pile into compost. Adequate moisture, aeration, and periodic turning of the pile are essential. After maturation and curing, the resulting compost can be used to enrich soil, providing nutrients and improving its overall health.

Which choice best describes the function of the reference to "kitchen scraps and yard trimmings" in the overall structure of the text?

Predict: _____

A) to introduce a feature of the composting process that is explained in greater detail later in the text
B) to suggest a weakness of the practice of composting
C) to explain how organic waste can be converted into nutrient-rich compost
D) to provide some examples of organic waste materials

TIP:
Some "purpose" questions will ask for the function of a particular section of the text, while others will ask for the overall purpose of the text as a whole. Be sure to read the question carefully so you fully understand your task.

A few questions may ask about the overall **organization** of the passage; for these, you'll need to understand the purpose of multiple parts of the text instead of just one part. Prediction is less important for these questions. Instead, use a process of elimination approach, looking to tie each abstract term in an answer choice to something specific in the passage. For example, if the choice says the author "draws an analogy in order to dispute a common view," ask yourself, *What's the analogy? Was it drawn to dispute something? What's the view it's disputing? Is that view common?* If there's anything that doesn't match, eliminate that answer.

Example: The use of drones, or unmanned aerial vehicles (UAVs), has become increasingly widespread in a variety of fields, including agriculture, conservation, and military operations. While UAVs offer many potential benefits, such as the ability to access difficult or remote areas and to gather data more efficiently and safely, they also raise a number of ethical and legal concerns. For example, the use of UAVs for surveillance or to collect data on individuals raises privacy issues, and the potential for UAVs to be used for malicious purposes or to cause accidents or injuries raises concerns about safety. As a result, there is ongoing debate about the appropriate regulations and guidelines that should be put in place to ensure the responsible and ethical use of UAVs.

Which choice best describes the overall structure of the text?

A) It describes both the benefits and the drawbacks of the use of UAVs, then describes the current state of the issue.
B) It argues on behalf of the use of UAVs, then explores the counterargument.
C) It presents a similarity between multiple uses of UAVs, then supports that claim with examples.
D) It illustrates the potential harm of UAVs, then suggests that they should be banned.

Start with choice A. Does the text describe the benefits of UAVs? Yes: the ability to access difficult or remote areas and to gather data efficiently and safely. Does it describe the drawbacks? Yes, in the next sentence. Does it describe the current state of the issue?
Yes, there is ongoing debate. Everything matches up, so choice A is looking good.

Now choice B. Does the text argue on behalf of the use of UAVs? No—this text maintained a neutral tone, exploring both sides of the issue without ever making an argument. Eliminate choice B.

As for choice C, the text does mention multiple uses of UAVs, but it doesn't present any particular similarity between them. And choice D is much too strong: the text never suggests that UAVs should be banned. The best answer is **A**.

Try It   2)   The US Postal Service relies on several types of automated sorting machines to efficiently process mail. Optical character recognition machines use optical sensors to scan the addresses on letters and packages and translate them into a digital format that can be interpreted and processed by the sorting machine. Additionally, advanced video coding systems are employed for the sorting of irregularly shaped or oversized mailpieces. These machines use cameras and image recognition software to capture images of the mail and analyze their characteristics. The system can identify the type, shape, and dimensions of the mailpiece, enabling accurate sorting based on predetermined criteria.

Which choice best describes the overall structure of the text?

Predict: _____

A) It presents a claim about the postal service, then offers several examples to illustrate the claim.
B) It describes the advantages of postal sorting technology, then notes some disadvantages.
C) It explains how the postal service sorts irregularly shaped packages, then provides additional detail.
D) It explores the current state of postal machine technology, then advocates for a change.

Reading: Information, Ideas, and Structure

Practice Set 1: Easy-Medium

The following text is from O. Henry's 1902 short story "The Duplicity of Hargraves."

When Major Pendleton Talbot, of Mobile, Alabama, and his daughter, Miss Lydia Talbot, came to Washington to reside, they selected for a boarding place a house that stood fifty yards back from one of the quietest avenues. It was an old-fashioned brick building, with a portico upheld by tall white pillars. The yard was shaded by stately locusts and elms, and a catalpa tree in season rained its pink and white blossoms upon the grass. Rows of high box bushes lined the fence and walks. It was the Southern style and aspect of the place that pleased the eyes of the Talbots.

1

Which choice best states the main purpose of the text?

A. To explore the character and background of Major Talbot
B. To explain in detail how the Talbots came to reside in the Washington boarding house
C. To describe the boarding house physically and suggest what the Talbots liked about it
D. To hint at Major Talbot's interest in architectural detail

Scholars of Greek and Roman maritime history have traditionally believed that the range of ancient trading vessels was sharply limited by the shipmasters' fears of the open sea. Unlike war ships, which had better navigational capacities and were free of the heavy cargo that increased the risk of capsizing, nonmilitary vessels were thought to follow a coast-hugging route whenever possible. Archaeologist Brendan Foley argues that the recently discovered wrecks of ancient Greek trading ships at the bottom of the eastern Mediterranean, many miles away from shore, call this belief into question. On the other hand, nautical expert Jeffrey Royal asserts that these wrecks might have occurred during a period of turbulent weather, when mariners might have chosen to head for deeper water to avoid being pushed onto rocks by the storm.

2

Which choice best describes the function of Royal's assertions in the overall structure of the text?

A. They summarize the disagreement between Foley's argument and the traditional view.
B. They reinforce Foley's theory that trading ships usually avoided the open sea.
C. They disprove Foley's statements about the wrecks found in the eastern Mediterranean.
D. They provide a possible alternative explanation for the evidence that Foley cites.

Structure and Purpose

The CRISPR-Cas9 gene editing system, first developed in 2012 by Jennifer Doudna and Emmanuelle Charpentier, is a revolutionary tool for genetic engineering that allows researchers to make precise edits to the DNA of living cells. The system consists of two components: a guide RNA molecule that recognizes and binds to a specific target sequence in the DNA, and a Cas9 protein that acts as molecular scissors to cut the DNA at the target site. By introducing synthetic guide RNA molecules that are programmed to recognize specific genes, researchers can use the Cas9 protein to make precise cuts in the DNA and introduce desired changes, such as deleting or inserting specific genes.

3

Which choice best describes the function of the first sentence in the overall structure of the text?

A. It explains how RNA molecules can be used to bind to specific DNA targets.
B. It describes the background of the invention of the CRISPR-Cas9 system.
C. It presents the rationale for experiments that involve deleting or inserting specific genes.
D. It introduces the CRISPR-Cas9 system and summarizes its function.

In David Armitage's view, the sweeping rights language of the Declaration of Independence is far less important than the way it sought to establish America's political sovereignty. As support, Armitage points to <u>18th century letters by Richard Henry Lee</u>, who argued that America would never be recognized by other European powers until it officially declared itself separate from Great Britain. In 1776, America's most pressing need was not a recitation of fundamental principles, but a formal announcement of a new political entity that could as a result contract alliances, conduct war, and conclude peace.

4

Which choice best describes the function of the letters by Richard Henry Lee in David Armitage's argument?

A. They provide corroborating evidence.
B. They represent a contradictory example.
C. They invoke authoritative sources.
D. They compare specific viewpoints.

In May of 1989, over 100,000 protesters converged on the city of Beijing in the People's Republic of China to protest the policies of the Communist Party of China. The protestors marched. They went on hunger strikes. They demanded political reform. They were met with rigid opposition and violence from the Chinese government. At the same time, forces of liberalization were sweeping Europe. The citizens of countries across Communist East Europe petitioned their governments for changes. The fall of the Berlin wall that year provided a strong symbol of the fall of Communist U.S.S.R.

5

Which choice best states the main purpose of the text?

A. To provide a history of Chinese politics
B. To analyze the collapse of communism
C. To describe a sequence of events
D. To detail various methods of protest

Reading: Information, Ideas, and Structure

In 2013, researchers collected leaf samples from multiple populations of flowering dogwood trees across the southeastern United States and analyzed the genetic markers of the samples. The study revealed significant genetic diversity within flowering dogwood populations, indicating the presence of diverse genetic variants and alleles within the species. Furthermore, the researchers identified distinct genetic clusters or groups within the populations, suggesting the existence of population structure. This indicates that certain populations of flowering dogwood may have unique genetic characteristics and adaptations based on their geographical locations.

6

Which choice best describes the function of the last sentence in the overall structure of the text?

A. to summarize the study's chief finding
B. to present an example that illustrates a challenge faced by the researchers
C. to describe part of the methodology used in the study
D. to explain the significance of one of the study's findings

While ancient Greece is often associated with a high regard for learning and intellectual pursuits, it is estimated that the overall literacy rates were relatively low by modern standards. However, this varied by time period and region. During the 5th and 4th centuries BCE, known as the Classical period, the city-state of Athens had a notable focus on education and intellectual pursuits. Athenian citizens, particularly the upper class, received an education that included reading, writing, and arithmetic. The Athenian playwright Aristophanes, in his comedies, often made references to a literate audience. Additionally, inscriptions and graffiti found in Athens and other urban centers suggest a relatively higher literacy rate among the general population compared to other regions of ancient Greece.

7

Which choice best describes the function of the reference to Aristophanes's comedies in the overall structure of the text?

A. It supports the text's central claim about literacy rates in Athens.
B. It introduces a potential counterargument to the point made in the preceding sentence.
C. It suggests that the audience for comedies might not be representative of Athens as a whole.
D. It indicates that Athens is less like other urban centers than its graffiti might suggest.

Structure and Purpose

Practice Set 2: Medium-Hard

The following is the full text of writer and civil rights activist James Weldon Johnson's 1917 poem "To America," which addresses America directly in order to pose a series of questions about the African American experience.

> How would you have us, as we are?
> Or sinking 'neath the load we bear?
> Our eyes fixed forward on a star?
> Or gazing empty at despair?
>
> Rising or falling? Men or things?
> With dragging pace or footsteps fleet?
> Strong, willing sinews in your wings?
> Or tightening chains about your feet?

1

Which choice best describes the function of the underlined portion in the text as a whole?

A. It implies that African Americans are heavily burdened.
B. Together with the next line, it offers America a dichotomy of choices.
C. It questions whether African Americans should continue to pursue progress.
D. It challenges America to confront its history of injustice.

The following text is adapted from Frank Norris's 1903 novel *The Pit*.

Suddenly the meaning and significance of it all dawned upon Laura. The Great Grey City, brooking no rival, imposed its dominion upon a reach of country larger than many a kingdom of the Old World. For, thousands of miles beyond its confines was its influence felt. Out, far out, far away in the snow and shadow of Northern Wisconsin forests, axes and saws bit the bark of century-old trees, stimulated by this city's energy. Her force turned the wheels of harvester and seeder a thousand miles distant in Iowa and Kansas. Her force spun the screws and propellers of innumerable squadrons of lake steamers crowding the Sault Sainte Marie. For her and because of her all the Central States, all the Great Northwest roared with traffic and industry; sawmills screamed; factories, their smoke blackening the sky, clashed and flamed; wheels turned, pistons leaped in their cylinders; cog gripped cog; beltings clasped the drums of mammoth wheels; and converters of forges belched into the clouded air their tempest breath of molten steel.

2

Which choice best describes the function of the underlined portion in the text as a whole?

A. It sets up a more detailed example indicating the true purpose of Laura's force.
B. It highlights important information about Laura's personal background.
C. It serves as part of a series of examples that demonstrate the breadth of the city's influence.
D. It illustrates the evils of industry due to its dependence on human labor.

Reading: Information, Ideas, and Structure

In accepting her 1993 Nobel prize, Toni Morrison examined in parable form the perils faced by generations coming of age in the late twentieth century. She told the story of a wise elderly woman being confronted by clever and mischievous youths. "Is there no context for our lives," they ask, ". . . no song, no literature, no poem full of vitamins?" Through a deep, meditative dialogue, the youths find the poetry in their despair. Morrison's sage then affirms the youths' character and ability to navigate the world, saying, "I trust you now."

3

Which choice best describes the function of the underlined portion in the text as a whole?

A. It underscores the point that the written word is nourishing.
B. It mocks the old woman's health.
C. It illustrates the cruelty of human beings.
D. It exposes an implicit political argument.

The traditional economic models assume that people take all available information and make consistent and informed decisions that are in their best interest. But a new group of economists, known as behavioral economists, argue that the traditional method leaves out something important: state of mind. For example, one can think differently about money if one is feeling vengeful, optimistic, or sorrowful. And what's more, actions under these conditions are indeed predictable, if the underlying environment is better understood. So, behavioral economics seeks to enrich the understanding of decision-making by integrating the insights of psychology into economics.

4

Which choice best describes the overall structure of the text?

A. A theory is put forward, a controversial definition is discussed, and a debate is begun.
B. A school of thought is introduced and a clarifying example is discussed.
C. A revolutionary viewpoint is distinguished from the more traditional theory and endorsed by the author.
D. A methodology is referenced and a question is posed.

In a 2021 article published in the *Journal of High Energy Physics*, authors Stefano Giusto and Raffaele Savelli used a holographic approach to investigate the dynamics of a three-dimensional gravitational theory. The holographic principle, a key concept in string theory, suggests that the information about a volume of space can be encoded on its boundary. The authors used this principle to relate the gravitational theory in the bulk of space to a quantum field theory on the boundary. They then used this relationship to study the dynamics of the gravitational theory and investigate its properties.

5

Which choice best describes the function of the second sentence in the overall structure of the text?

A. It presents the central finding reported by Giusto and Savelli.
B. It defines a term that helps explain the structure of the article written by Giusto and Savelli.
C. It provides context that clarifies the question that Giusto and Savelli sought to answer.
D. It states a generalization challenged by Giusto and Savelli.

In the 2020 New Zealand general election, prime minister Jacinda Ardern secured a resounding victory that far exceeded the expectations of many polls. Several factors may have contributed to the divergence between the polls and the actual outcome. First, Ardern's handling of various crises, including the response to the Christchurch mosque shootings and the COVID-19 pandemic, generated significant public support and a surge in popularity; some polls may have underestimated the extent of the "Jacinda Effect" on voter preferences. Second, in the weeks leading up to the election, some voters were swayed by the growing momentum and success of Ardern's leadership, resulting in a last-minute shift in support that the polls did not fully capture. Third, the 2020 New Zealand election witnessed a significant increase in youth voter turnout compared to previous elections; young voters are typically underrepresented in polls.

6

Which choice best describes the function of the second sentence in the overall structure of the text?

A. It provides a transition between the election outcome discussed in the first sentence and the possible causes analyzed in the rest of the passage.

B. It explains why the polling for the 2020 New Zealand general election was inaccurate.

C. It emphasizes the unexpected nature of Jacinda Ardern's victory by providing an example.

D. It reveals the significance of the role played by young voters in the 2020 New Zealand general election.

The J-curve hypothesis is a conceptual framework used to understand the dynamics of social movements. The theory suggests that after a period of gradual progress and resistance at the beginning of a movement, there comes a tipping point where the movement experiences a sudden surge in momentum and significant progress. In the context of the US civil rights movement, the J-curve theory suggests that while progress may have been slow and incremental initially, the cumulative impact of grassroots mobilization, nonviolent protests, legal challenges, and public advocacy ultimately led to a transformative phase in the mid-twentieth century. This era saw landmark events and legislation that moved the trajectory of the civil rights movement sharply upward, <u>resembling the shape of a "J" on a graph</u>.

7

Which choice best describes the function of the underlined portion in the text as a whole?

A. It suggests a potential problem with the traditional interpretation of the civil rights movement.

B. It clarifies the history and theoretical background of the term "J-curve."

C. It explains why the civil rights movement was able to make such significant progress in the mid-twentieth century.

D. It helps illustrate the meaning of the term "J-curve."

Compare and Contrast

Preview Quiz

1) The best approach to a Compare and Contrast question consists of several distinct steps. Put the steps below in the right order.

    1st: _____   Read Text 1.

    2nd: _____   Read Text 2.

    3rd: _____   Read the question.

    4th: _____   Summarize.

    5th: _____   Predict an answer.

    6th: _____   Evaluate the choices.

Choose the best answer.

2) **Text 1**

    The human brain is wired to seek comfort in the familiar, and habits provide a sense of predictability and security. As a result, habits play an important role in purchase decisions. Understanding and leveraging the power of habits can be a valuable marketing strategy for businesses to attract and retain customers.

    Text 2

    While habits can influence purchase decisions, they are not the sole determining factor. Consumers are increasingly becoming more conscious and intentional about their purchases, considering factors such as sustainability, ethics, and social responsibility. In addition, the rise of e-commerce and online shopping has provided consumers with more options and opportunities to explore new products and brands.

    Based on the texts, how would the author of Text 2 most likely respond to the claims of the author of Text 1?

    A) By disputing the idea that habits provide a sense of security.
    B) By agreeing that businesses should focus their marketing strategies on leveraging the power of habits.
    C) By denying the importance of the rise of e-commerce and online shopping.
    D) By arguing that habits may be a less powerful influence on purchase decisions than Text 1 claims them to be.

These questions ask you to compare or contrast two different passages on a related theme. Remember, no matter how these questions are phrased, *the answers are in the text.* You don't have to guess how the author of Text 2 would probably respond to the author of Text 1; instead, find the place in Text 2 where the author addresses the point.

Common **wrong answer choices** will

- confuse one passage's point of view for the other's
- include a statement that an author would probably agree with but that the passage never directly addressed
- be phrased in a way that's too broad, too narrow, or too extreme

As usual, our process begins with the **question**. Read carefully! You may be asked about the overall relationship between the two passages, but sometimes the question is more specific: for example, you may be asked how the authors of Text 2 would respond to a specific sentence or claim from Text 1 rather than the text as a whole.

Next, read the entire first text. Stop and summarize the big idea that the question is focused on (whatever Text 2 is being asked to respond to). **Write it down**.

Then, read the entire second text and consider its relationship to what you wrote. Does Text 2 agree with that position overall? Does it disagree? Is there a specific objection made? Are the claims quite similar, but with one important difference? Whatever you notice, that's your prediction. Move on to the answer choices and look for the best match.

> **TIP:**
> Always read *all* of Text 1, even if the question is only asking you to respond to a single underlined claim. The context matters.

> **TIP:**
> You don't have to answer the questions in the order they appear on the test. Feel free to skip the more time-consuming question types (like Compare and Contrast questions) at first and return to them at the end of the section. If you'd like to flag a question to remind yourself to come back to it, click the ⏷ symbol next to the question number.

Let's take a look at an example.

Example: **Text 1**

The human brain is wired to seek comfort in the familiar, and habits provide a sense of predictability and security. As a result, habits play an important role in purchase decisions. Understanding and leveraging the power of habits can be a valuable marketing strategy for businesses to attract and retain customers.

Text 2

While habits can influence purchase decisions, they are not the sole determining factor. Consumers are increasingly becoming more conscious and intentional about their purchases, considering factors such as sustainability, ethics, and social responsibility. In addition, the rise of e-commerce and online shopping has provided consumers with more options and opportunities to explore new products and brands.

Based on the texts, how would the author of Text 2 most likely respond to the claims of the author of Text 1?

A) By disputing the idea that habits provide a sense of security.
B) By agreeing that businesses should focus their marketing strategies on leveraging the power of habits.
C) By denying the importance of the rise of e-commerce and online shopping.
D) By arguing that habits may be a less powerful influence on purchase decisions than Text 1 claims them to be.

On the next page, we'll rearrange this wall of words so we can approach it in the right order.

TIP:

There's no need for panic if you encounter an unfamiliar vocab word in the passage. Often, you'll be able to figure it out from the context anyway. At other times, it will be a word that doesn't end up mattering, because you can answer the questions without needing it. If you do happen to get a question that asks about the word, just use your knowledge of the general tone and big themes of the passage as a whole and that section in particular to see if you can knock out answer choices, and then go with your gut.

We need the question first.

> *Based on the texts, how would the author of Text 2 most likely respond to the claims of the author of Text 1?*

Now we know our task: in this case, we're going to be focusing on how Text 2 would respond to Text 1 as a whole. So next, we'll read Text 1 and summarize its claims.

> **Text 1**
>
> *The human brain is wired to seek comfort in the familiar, and habits provide a sense of predictability and security. As a result, habits play an important role in purchase decisions. Understanding and leveraging the power of habits can be a valuable marketing strategy for businesses to attract and retain customers.*

What's the big idea here, in a few words? Keep it simple: maybe something like "habits are a big deal and businesses should make use of them."

> **Text 2**
>
> *While habits can influence purchase decisions, they are not the sole determining factor. Consumers are increasingly becoming more conscious and intentional about their purchases, considering factors such as sustainability, ethics, and social responsibility. In addition, the rise of e-commerce and online shopping has provided consumers with more options and opportunities to explore new products and brands.*

This author takes a more nuanced view of habits: "Sure, they play a role, but they're not the only thing that matters." That's our prediction. Now we evaluate the choices.

> A) By disputing the idea that habits provide a sense of security.
> B) By agreeing that businesses should focus their marketing strategies on leveraging the power of habits.
> C) By denying the importance of the rise of e-commerce and online shopping.
> D) By arguing that habits may be a less powerful influence on purchase decisions than Text 1 claims them to be.

Choice A is wrong: Text 2 did dispute some of Text 1's ideas, but not that specific one.

Choice B is wrong too: this puts Text 2 too much in agreement with Text 1. And anyway, Text 2 never took a position on how businesses should focus their marketing strategies.

Choice C is just backwards: Text 2 is the one arguing for the importance of these things, not denying their importance.

That leaves Choice **D**, which is the right answer.

> **TIP:**
>
> Remember to consider language strength. A choice may have the right general idea but be written too strongly to be correct.

Reading: Information, Ideas, and Structure

Try It   Based on the texts, how would the author of Text 2 most likely respond to Text 1's claims about the potential health benefits of red wine?

1) Analyze the question. What are we being asked to respond to from Text 1?

_____

Text 1

Numerous studies have suggested that moderate red wine consumption can have positive effects on heart health due to the presence of antioxidants, particularly resveratrol. Resveratrol has been linked to improved cardiovascular function, reduced inflammation, and increased levels of HDL cholesterol, known as the "good" cholesterol. Additionally, red wine has shown potential in protecting against age-related cognitive decline and certain types of cancer.

2) Summarize the relevant claims of Text 1.

_____

_____

Text 2

The health benefits attributed to red wine can often be obtained through other means, such as a healthy diet and regular exercise. Excessive consumption of alcohol, even in the form of red wine, can have detrimental effects on health, including liver damage, increased risk of addiction, and various negative impacts on physical and mental well-being. Moreover, the potential benefits of red wine must be weighed against the associated risks, such as an increased risk of certain cancers, adverse interactions with medications, and potential harm to pregnant women or individuals with specific health conditions.

3) Predict. How would Text 2 respond to what you wrote in #2 above?

_____

4) Choose the best answer:
   A) By denying that red wine consumption can have positive effects on heart health.
   B) By suggesting that the risks associated with red wine may outweigh its potential benefits.
   C) By disputing the idea that resveratrol increases levels of HDL cholesterol.
   D) By arguing that it is too risky for healthy individuals to consume even moderate amounts of red wine.

Practice Set 1: Easy-Medium

Text 1

Carbon markets—trading systems in which polluting companies can buy or sell carbon emissions credits—are an essential tool for combating climate change. By putting a price on emissions, carbon markets incentivize companies to reduce their carbon footprint. This market-based approach allows for emissions reductions to be achieved in a cost-effective and efficient manner. Moreover, carbon markets have the potential to drive innovation and investment in low-carbon technologies, ultimately leading to a more sustainable future.

Text 2

Carbon markets merely perpetuate environmental injustices. They allow companies in wealthy nations to continue polluting while buying credits from developing countries, which can hinder their development. Worse, carbon markets do not address the root causes of climate change, such as the reliance on fossil fuels and the overconsumption of resources.

1

Based on the texts, how would the author of Text 2 most likely respond to the claims of the author of Text 1?

A. By arguing that carbon markets are not as beneficial to businesses as they might appear.
B. By disputing the need for countries to work together to combat climate change.
C. By contending that carbon markets are a poorly conceived idea that may lead to unjust outcomes.
D. By agreeing that investment in low-carbon technologies is an important and necessary step.

Text 1

The controversy surrounding the use of genetically modified organisms (GMOs) in agriculture is largely based on misconceptions and misinformation. <u>GMOs have been extensively tested and have been shown to be safe for human consumption and the environment.</u> Furthermore, GMOs have the potential to increase crop yields and reduce the need for harmful pesticides and herbicides.

Text 2

While evidence of GMO safety in the short term certainly exists, the long-term effects of their use are still unknown. In addition, the use of GMOs often involves the patenting of living organisms, which can have negative impacts on farmers' livelihoods and which concentrates power in the hands of a few large corporations.

2

Based on the texts, how would the author of Text 2 most likely characterize the underlined claim in Text 1?

A. It is completely baseless and factually incorrect.
B. It is at least partially true, but it fails to address an important issue.
C. It is likely biased and intended to curry favor with large corporations.
D. It is a compelling argument but ultimately irrelevant to the point at issue.

Text 1

Did the Ancient Greeks see the color blue? According to linguist Guy Deutcher, this has been a topic of some controversy for well over a century. British politician and classicist William Gladstone noticed that Homer's epics, the *Iliad* and the *Odyssey*, contain no reference to the color blue. Famously, Homer refers to the sea as being "wine dark" instead.

Text 2

Retinal cones take information from the various wavelengths of visible light and convert it into a chemical signal. While humans have only three types of cones, the mantis shrimp has 16 and can detect wavelengths from ultraviolet to infrared. But even though these significant discoveries tell us something about how different the experience of color can be among different species, they do not shed any great psychological light on whether or not two humans can share anything as simple as our perception of the color red.

3

How would the author of Text 2 most likely respond to the question posed in the first sentence of Text 1?

A. The Greeks didn't see blue because all humans have the same types of retinal cones.
B. The Greeks saw blue because seeing is physiological and not linguistic or psychological.
C. The Greeks didn't see blue, because they weren't aware of how brains worked.
D. We don't know whether the Greeks saw blue as we do.

Text 1

In F. Scott Fitzgerald's *The Great Gatsby*, the character of Jay Gatsby represents the American dream and its ultimate failure. Through Gatsby's tragic downfall, Fitzgerald critiques the American dream and its emphasis on materialism and the pursuit of wealth. Gatsby's character serves as a cautionary tale against the dangers of blindly pursuing success without considering the cost to oneself and others.

Text 2

Gatsby's pursuit of wealth and status is driven not just by materialism, but also by his desire to win back the love of his life, Daisy. This is a manifestation of his desire for a deeper connection and a sense of belonging, which are also important aspects of the American dream. Gatsby's tragic downfall can also be attributed to the corrupt society in which he lives, which values wealth and social status above all else.

4

Based on the texts, how would the author of Text 2 most likely respond to Text 1's claim regarding the theme of the American Dream in *The Great Gatsby*?

A. By agreeing that Jay Gatsby is driven in part by the American dream but arguing that this drive consists of more than a mere desire for wealth.
B. By conceding that Jay Gatsby's failure to achieve financial success is tragic and suggesting that Daisy is to blame.
C. By challenging the idea that materialism is a concern for Jay Gatsby and arguing that his real interest is social status.
D. By taking offense to the notion that F. Scott Fitzgerald intended a large-scale critique of the American way of life.

Text 1

Food irradiation involves the application of ionizing radiation to food products in order to target microorganisms, including bacteria, viruses, and parasites. Supporters of the process claim it enhances food safety. However, food irradiation may lead to the formation of harmful byproducts, such as free radicals, which can have negative health implications. Additionally, many critics have expressed concern about the potential loss of essential nutrients and the impact of irradiation on the overall quality and taste of the food. Alternative methods of food safety, such as improved hygiene practices throughout the food production and handling chain, provide the same benefits without the potential drawbacks.

Text 2

Food irradiation is a valuable tool that significantly reduces the risk of foodborne illnesses by effectively eliminating or reducing harmful pathogens and pests present in food products. The process has been extensively studied and proven to be effective in reducing microbial contamination without causing significant changes to the nutritional value, taste, or texture of the food. It provides an additional layer of protection against foodborne pathogens, ensuring that consumers can enjoy safer and healthier food options.

5

Based on the texts, how would the author of Text 2 most likely respond to the claims expressed by the critics in the underlined sentence of Text 1?

A. Taste and nutrient loss are less important issues than protection against food-borne illnesses.

B. Extensive research has proven the critics' concerns to be unfounded.

C. Improved hygiene practices are not sufficient to mitigate the risks posed by harmful pathogens.

D. The critics have not considered the negative impact of free radicals.

Practice Set 2: Medium-Hard

Text 1

The suprachiasmatic nuclei (SCNs) are a cluster of cells in the hypothalamus that act as the primary circadian pacemaker in humans and other animals. These nuclei are responsible for controlling the body's internal clock, which regulates a wide range of biological processes, including sleep-wake cycles, hormone secretion, and body temperature. Research has shown that SCNs receive input from light-sensitive cells in the retina, which helps to synchronize the body's circadian rhythms with the 24-hour day-night cycle. Additionally, disruptions to the SCNs, such as damage to the hypothalamus or exposure to prolonged periods of darkness, can result in sleep disorders, mood disturbances, and other negative health outcomes.

Text 2

While SCNs undoubtedly play an important role in controlling human circadian rhythms, other factors may also contribute to this complex biological process. Some research has suggested that environmental factors, such as social cues or meal timing, may have a stronger influence on circadian rhythms than previously thought. Furthermore, certain genetic mutations have been found to affect circadian rhythms in humans, suggesting that there may be other molecular pathways involved in circadian regulation.

1

Based on the texts, how would the author of Text 2 most likely respond to the claim made in the first sentence of Text 1?

A. By arguing that Text 1's own statements about the effect of exposure to prolonged darkness act to undermine the claim.

B. By agreeing that SCNs may play a significant role in circadian regulation but adding that other factors may also be involved.

C. By distinguishing between the function of SCNs in humans with genetic mutations and the function of SCNs in non-human animals without such mutations.

D. By conceding that disruptions to SCNs can result in sleep disorders but suggesting that other evidence is needed before any conclusion about the role of SCNs can be drawn.

Text 1

Traditional physics theory holds that high temperatures and pressures are required to initiate nuclear fusion reactions. But this view is far too limited. The evidence that "cold fusion" is possible has existed for decades. In 1989, Martin Fleischmann and Stanley Pons conducted a simple electrolysis experiment using heavy water and palladium electrodes. Despite the standard air pressure and room temperature, evidence of nuclear reaction products was recorded.

Text 2

There is no theoretical basis for the concept of cold fusion. While it's certainly a tempting idea—if valid, it could have significant implications for the future of clean energy production—it simply flies in the face of our understanding of nuclear physics. The so-called evidence is in fact inconclusive, as many of the results cited can be explained by more conventional processes. In addition, numerous scientists have tried and failed to replicate the results reported by experimenters in the 1980s, suggesting that their results may have been due to experimental error.

2

Based on the texts, how would the author of Text 2 most likely respond to the "traditional physics theory" discussed in Text 1?

A. By arguing that it fails to recognize the other factors that are capable of initiating nuclear fusion reactions.
B. By asserting that no convincing evidence exists to challenge its claim about the requirements of nuclear fusion.
C. By disputing the relevance of the Fleischmann-Pons experiment, since it was conducted at standard air pressure and room temperature.
D. By advocating an alternative theory that could lead to better progress in the production of clean energy.

Text 1

According to 17th century alchemist Johann Joachim Becher, a key component of any combustion reaction is a substance called "phlogiston." Becher argued that when a combustible material burns, it releases phlogiston into the air, leaving behind the "ash" or "residue" of the original material. Many scientists of his era, noting that a piece of wood becomes less heavy when it burns (perhaps due to the release of some substance) found the theory extremely compelling.

Text 2

While the phlogiston theory enjoyed a period of popularity, it was ultimately replaced by the combustion theory put forward by Antoine Lavoisier in 1777. Lavoisier showed that when a substance burns, it combines with oxygen from the air, forming new compounds (some of which have lower mass than that of the original material) and releasing heat and light.

3

Based on the texts, how would the author of Text 2 most likely respond to the piece of evidence for the phlogiston theory noted in the underlined portion of Text 1?

A. By disputing the idea that a piece of wood becomes less heavy when it burns.
B. By positing that such observations do not account for the mass of the phlogiston released during combustion.
C. By arguing that the mass change of wood during combustion occurs because the products of the reaction weigh less than the original material.
D. By suggesting that phlogiston release may explain mass changes for only some materials and not others.

Text 1

The 21st century is witnessing the birth, or at least the rebirth, of American culture. To be sure, America has always produced great ideas and entertainment: jazz, Constitutionalism, alien movies, cheeseburgers, rock and roll. But in the large, these triumphs have been attributed to our distant heroes—a genius entrepreneur here or a revolutionary statesman there. Perhaps it's the stripping away of our national identity as a nation of consumers, but Americans are feeding, nourishing, and entertaining ourselves in ways that are more meaningfully profound and authentically American than those of generations past.

Text 2

Not long ago, cultural trends took months or years to travel across the United States. In our frenzied era of smart phones, we think this unacceptable, as though waiting two weeks for a hot new item to hit stores were some kind of federal emergency. But this seeming inconvenience allowed trends to settle in and absorb a modicum of local character. Our demand for plentiful and immediate content destroys the meaningful context of cultural trends. The breakneck pace of American life will be the end of culture.

4

Based on the texts, how would the author of Text 2 most likely characterize the argument presented in Text 1?

A. As questionable, because it offers too many different theories for the source of the rebirth of American culture.
B. As wrongheaded, because it ignores the cultural context lost by the speed of communications in the modern era.
C. As overly optimistic, because there is not yet enough evidence to determine whether the new cultural trends are here to stay.
D. As potentially correct, but lacking a clear explanatory context.

Text 1

The tuatara, an ancient reptile species endemic to New Zealand, can live to be over 100 years old. Its long lifespan can be attributed to its slow metabolic rate and negligible senescence, meaning the animals show little or no signs of aging as they grow older. The tuatara's slow metabolism minimizes cellular damage and reduces the accumulation of age-related issues. Furthermore, the phenomenon of negligible senescence allows tuataras to maintain their reproductive capabilities and physiological functions over extended periods without significant decline. These factors, coupled with efficient DNA repair mechanisms and low reproductive rates, support the idea that their longevity is a result of their unique biological adaptations.

Text 2

While metabolic rate and negligible senescence may contribute to tuataras' extended lifespan, other factors cannot be ignored. One such factor is their isolated and predator-free environment in the islands of New Zealand, which reduces external threats and allows them to live longer. Additionally, their low reproductive rates may enable better resource allocation for individual survival rather than reproduction.

5

Based on the texts, how would the author of Text 2 most likely respond to the claims made by the author of Text 1?

A. By agreeing that low reproductive rates are the most important reason why tuataras are able to live such long lives.
B. By disputing the notion that tuataras' lifespans are unusually long.
C. By contending that tuataras' metabolic rates are irrelevant to the length of their lifespans.
D. By arguing that the causal factors leading to tuataras' long lifespans may not be limited to their biological adaptations.

Reading: Evidence and Logical Reasoning

For these questions, the author will be making some kind of argument—it might be an interpretation of a work of art, a scientific hypothesis, a theory about a historical event, or any other kind of claim. You'll be asked to demonstrate your understanding of the author's reasoning.

Strategy in Brief

Read the question. Evaluate exactly what your task is for this question. Are you looking to strengthen an argument here? Are you supposed to take the next logical step? Something else?

Isolate the claim. Read the text carefully. What is the author's overall point? Make sure you can identify the individual sentence (or part of a sentence) in which the author makes this clear. If the question asked about a specific claim that was not the overall point of the passage, find that claim and highlight it in the text.

Consider the evidence. In most of these arguments, the text will already provide at least partial support. How convinced are you? What else is needed?

Predict. Read the question carefully and form a prediction in your mind of the kind of answer you're looking for. What does the right answer need to accomplish?

Evaluate the choices. Analyze the answers carefully, keeping your overall task in mind. Remember, you're not being asked to decide *whether this answer choice is true*—for purposes of this test, you have to assume that it is. The question is simply this: if the choice *is* true, what does that do to the argument?

Command of Evidence – Illustrate the Claim

Preview Quiz

Fill in your answer:

1) What is the difference between "illustrate the claim" questions and "strengthen/weaken" questions?

2) In answering these questions, it generally (is / is not) helpful to already be familiar with the topic or work of literature that the question discusses.

Choose the best answer:

3) "We Wear the Mask" is an 1896 poem by Paul Laurence Dunbar that explores the ways in which individuals mask their true selves in order to conform to societal expectations. The poem presents the mask as a kind of living entity that conceals the true identity of the wearer: _____

Which quotation from the poem most effectively illustrates the claim?

A) "We wear the mask that grins and lies, / It hides our cheeks and shades our eyes,"

B) "This debt we pay to human guile; / With torn and bleeding hearts we smile,"

C) "Why should the world be over-wise, / In counting all our tears and sighs? / Nay, let them only see us while / we wear the mask."

D) "We sing, but oh the clay is vile / Beneath our feet, and long the mile; / But let the world dream otherwise, / We wear the mask!"

Reading: Evidence and Logical Reasoning

The "command of evidence" questions are designed to test your understanding of how authors can support their claims. For some of these questions, the evidence is **quantitative** data presented in a chart or graph, as we'll see in the chapter beginning on p. 87. For now, we'll be focusing on the questions that use **textual** evidence.

In the "illustrate the claim" variety of these questions, there will be no doubt what claim the author is making. Your job is to consider what research findings, quotations, or other textual evidence would give the best example of the author's position.

Many of these questions involve literary analysis of an excerpt of poetry or prose. You are not expected to already know the work you're analyzing! The text will provide all the background information you need. Read through the text and then **highlight the claim** that you're being asked to illustrate. Then carefully review the choices to **find the best match**.

> *TIP:*
> To highlight in the Bluebook app, select some text and click "Annotate" on the upper right corner of the screen.

Common **wrong answer types** include

- quotations that are relevant to the work as a whole but not to the specific claim
- quotations that are famous or impressive but have the wrong focus
- choices that are half right, half wrong

> *TIP:*
> You won't need to know any advanced literary terms for these questions, nor will you be expected to already be familiar with the poem or prose. Everything you need to know is right there in the text and the question.

Here's an example question to demonstrate the process.

Example: *"We Wear the Mask" is an 1896 poem by Paul Laurence Dunbar that explores the ways in which individuals mask their true selves in order to conform to societal expectations. The poem presents the mask as a kind of living entity that conceals the true identity of the wearer: _____*

Which quotation from the poem most effectively illustrates the claim?

The text has given us a title, author, and date, as well as a brief description of some of the poem's themes. But the actual claim we need to focus on is in the last sentence. Notice we have two requirements for the right answer: it should present the mask as a *living entity*; and it should present the mask as something that *conceals the true identity* of the wearer.

Now, let's take a look at the answer choices.

A) "We wear the mask that grins and lies, / It hides our cheeks and shades our eyes"
B) "This debt we pay to human guile; / With torn and bleeding hearts we smile"
C) "Why should the world be over-wise, / In counting all our tears and sighs? / Nay, let them only see us while / we wear the mask."
D) "We sing, but oh the clay is vile / Beneath our feet, and long the mile; / But let the world dream otherwise, / We wear the mask!"

Several of these choices (A, C, and D) suggest a mask that conceals the true identity of the wearer. But only choice A presents it as a living entity (something that can "grin" and "lie"). Though the other choices may be relevant to the background information that the text supplied about the poem, only choice A fulfills the specific task that has been set for us. Choice **A** is the answer.

> **TIP:**
>
> It's essential to focus on the specific claim that the question is asking about. Illustrating *that claim* is our only concern.

Reading: Evidence and Logical Reasoning

Try It Use the passage below to practice the steps discussed above.

In Kate Chopin's 1899 novel *The Awakening*, the open water serves as a powerful symbol of freedom, liberation, and self-discovery for the protagonist. The novel references the ocean to emphasize the profound connection between the natural world and the human spirit: _____

1) List the elements that the right answer must illustrate:
   - Element #1:
   - Element #2:

2) Evaluate the answer choices below by considering how well it satisfies each of the elements you listed.

	Element #1	Element #2
A) "The voice of the sea speaks to the soul."	_____	_____
B) "The bird that would soar above the level plain of tradition and prejudice must have strong wings."	_____	_____
C) "There are some people who leave impressions not so lasting as the imprint of an oar upon the water."	_____	_____
D) "There were strange, rare odors abroad—a tangle of sea smell and of weeds and damp, new-plowed earth, mingled with the heavy perfumes of white blossoms somewhere near, but the night sat lightly upon the sea and the land."	_____	_____

3) What is the best answer?

FROM THE BLOG

Brains need to be calm to be "reason-able." During a stress response, the amygdala (which initiates the freeze, fight, or flight response) is activated, and the prefrontal cortex (responsible for planning, organizing, problem-solving, motivation, and impulse control) is effectively shut down. Arm yourself with the things that help keep the prefrontal cortex in charge: regular exercise, mediation, and plenty of sleep.

Practice Set 1: Easy-Medium

"Nie Zheng, Man of Valor" is a story from *Records of the Grand Historian*, a history of China written in 91 BCE by Sima Quan. In the story, Yan Zhongzi comes to Nie Zheng's home to offer him a gift of gold, but Zheng turns it down out of pride. Later, Nie Zheng comes to regret refusing the gift, saying, _____

1

Which quotation from "Nie Zheng, Man of Valor" most effectively illustrates the claim?

A. "I have been content to humble my will and shame my body, living as a butcher here by the marketplace and well, only because I am fortunate enough to have my old mother to take care of."
B. "Though our family is poor and I am living in a strange land and earning my way as a common butcher, I am still able to find some sweet or tasty morsel with which to nourish my mother."
C. "Ah! I am a man of the marketplace and well, swinging a knife and working as a butcher, while Yan Zhongzi is chief minister to one of the feudal lords."
D. "Yan Zhongzi did not consider it too far to come a thousand miles, venturing far out of his way just to befriend me. I treated him very shabbily indeed!"

In Jane Austen's 1811 novel *Sense and Sensibility*, a widowed mother and her three daughters must adjust to life in a new home. Mrs. Jennings, their busybody neighbor, wears on their patience with her endless attempts to find suitable husbands for the teenaged girls. She means no harm in these efforts. For Mrs. Jennings, matchmaking is a source of amusement necessary to fill her days, as the novel makes clear: _____

2

Which quotation from *Sense and Sensibility* most effectively illustrates the claim?

A. "Mrs. Jennings was a good-humored, merry, fat, elderly woman, who talked a great deal and seemed very happy and rather vulgar."
B. "She was full of jokes and laughter, and before dinner was over had said many witty things on the subject of lovers and husbands."
C. "A widow with an ample fortune, Mrs. Jennings had only two daughters, both of whom she had lived to see respectably married, and she had now therefore nothing to do but to marry off all the rest of the world."
D. "She was remarkably quick in the discovery of attachments, and had enjoyed the advantage of raising the blushes and the vanity of many a young lady by insinuations of her power over such a young man."

- 69 -

TM and © 2023 PrepMatters, Inc. All rights reserved.

US Congresswoman Tammy Baldwin, one of the first openly gay individuals elected to Congress, is a longtime activist for LGBTQ rights. When she addressed the crowd at the Millennium March for Equality on April 30, 2000 on the National Mall, she made clear that her previous marches and other activism inspire her in her legislative work, including legislation not specifically related to LGBTQ rights: _____

3

Which quotation from Baldwin's speech most effectively illustrates the claim?

A. "If I close my eyes, I can remember being here in 1987 [for another LGBTQ rights march]. I marched to replace my fear with courage, my isolation with belonging, my anger with hope."

B. "If I close my eyes again, I can remember coming to this city, this historic place, these steps in January, 1999. Only this time, I climbed these steps to take the oath of office."

C. "And as I climbed those steps, I remembered all those who had marched and mobilized—those who helped pave the way for my election and the election of those who will come after me."

D. "The lessons learned from you, from my participation in this civil rights movement, and from organizing against AIDS are now being applied, empowering me as I fight every day the battle for health care for all, increasing educational opportunities, and fighting for many others who lack a voice in our democracy."

"Love Song," a 1917 poem by William Carlos Williams, uses contrasting imagery to describe love as an uplifting force with a profound effect: _____

4

Which quotation from the poem most effectively illustrates the claim?

A. "The stain of love / Is upon the world, / Yellow, yellow, yellow, / It eats into the leaves,"

B. "There is no light— / Only a honey-thick stain / That drips from leaf to leaf / And limb to limb, / Spoiling the colors / Of the whole world."

C. "I am alone. / The weight of love / Has buoyed me up / Till my head / Knocks against the sky."

D. "See me! / My hair is dripping with nectar— / Starlings carry it / On their black wings."

Margaret Fuller was an influential writer, feminist, and social reformer who played a significant role in the transcendentalist movement of 19th century America. Fuller emphasized the importance of sharing knowledge and empowering others when she wrote, _____

5

Which quotation from Margaret Fuller most effectively illustrates the claim?

A. "We have waited here long in the dust; we are tired and hungry; but the triumphal procession must appear at last."
B. "If you have knowledge, let others light their candles in it."
C. "Let every woman, who has once begun to think, examine herself."
D. "There are noble books but one wants the breath of life sometimes."

Charlotte Brontë's 1853 novel *Villette* explores themes of isolation, love, and the role of women in society. In the novel, Brontë suggests that reality rarely aligns with our preconceived notions and desires: _____

6

Which quotation from the novel most effectively illustrates the claim?

A. "Life is so constructed, that the event does not, cannot, will not, match the expectation."
B. "I believe in some blending of hope and sunshine sweetening the worst lots. I believe that this life is not all; neither the beginning nor the end."
C. "No mockery in this world ever sounds to me so hollow as that of being told to cultivate happiness. What does such advice mean?"
D. "To see and know the worst is to take from Fear her main advantage."

Paul Verlaine's 1866 Poem "Il Pleure Dans Mon Coeur" ("It Rains in My Heart") juxtaposes the external and internal world to underscore the speaker's melancholy: _____

7

Which quotation from a translation of the poem most effectively illustrates the claim?

A. "It rains in my heart / As it rains on the town, / What languor so dark / That it soaks to my heart?"
B. "Oh sweet sound of the rain / On the earth and the roofs!"
C. "It rains for no reason / In this heart that lacks heart. / What? And no treason? / It's grief without reason."
D. "By far the worst pain, / Without hatred, or love, / Yet no way to explain / Why my heart feels such pain!"

Practice Set 2: Medium-Hard

"A Valediction: of Weeping" is a 1633 poem by John Donne. The speaker, about to depart from his lover for a distant journey, uses a financial metaphor to suggest that her presence makes his sadness worthwhile: _____

1

Which quotation from the poem most effectively illustrates the claim?

A. "Let me pour forth / My tears before thy face, whilst I stay here, / For thy face coins them, and thy stamp they bear, / And by this mintage they are something worth"

B. "For thus they be / Pregnant of thee; / Fruits of much grief they are, emblems of more, / When a tear falls, that thou falls which it bore, / So thou and I are nothing then, when on a diverse shore"

C. "On a round ball / A workman that hath copies by, can lay / An Europe, Afric, and an Asia, / And quickly make that, which was nothing, all; / So doth each tear / Which thee doth wear"

D. "A globe, yea world, by that impression grow, / Till thy tears mix'd with mine do overflow / This world; by waters sent from thee, my heaven dissolved so"

"Song of Myself" is an 1892 poem by Walt Whitman. The poem uses joyful language to assert that every individual is worthy of praise, while also emphasizing humanity's interconnectedness: _____

2

Which quotation from the poem most effectively illustrates the claim?

A. "A child said *What is the grass?* Fetching it to me with full hands; / How could I answer the child? I do not know what it is any more than he."

B. "I celebrate myself, and sing myself, / And what I assume you shall assume, / For every atom belonging to me as good belongs to you."

C. "I think I could turn and live with animals, they're so placid and self-contained, / I stand and look at them long. / They do not sweat and whine about their condition. / They do not lie awake in the dark and weep for their sins."

D. "I am not an earth nor an adjunct of an earth, / I am the mate and companion of people, all just as immortal and fathomless as myself, / (They do not know how immortal, but I know.)"

In Henry James's 1903 novel *The Ambassadors,* an American character embarks on a voyage of self-discovery during a trip to Europe. The novel uses figurative language to describe Paris as a vibrant and alluring city that captivates the protagonist with its sophistication: _____

3

The quotations from the novel given below are all from a scene that takes place in Paris. Which quotation most effectively illustrates the claim?

A. "He came down the Rue de la Paix in the sun and, passing across the river, indulged more than once in a sudden pause before the bookstalls of the opposite quay."
B. "The prompt Paris morning struck its cheerful notes."
C. "He watched little brisk figures whose movement was as the tick of the great Paris clock."
D. "The air had a taste as of something mixed with art, something that presented nature as a white-capped master chef."

Man and Superman is a 1905 play by George Bernard Shaw. The play skewers societal norms and conventional morality with sharp and witty dialogue: _____

4

Which quotation from the poem most effectively illustrates the claim?

A. "Self-sacrifice enables us to sacrifice other people without blushing."
B. "You don't get tired of muffins. But you don't find inspiration in them."
C. "We live in an atmosphere of shame. We are ashamed of everything that is real about us; ashamed of ourselves, of our relatives, of our incomes, of our accents, of our opinions, of our experience, just as we are ashamed of our naked skins."
D. "We shall never be able to keep the secret unless everybody knows what it is."

In his 1925 poem "in Just-," e.e. cummings explores themes of childhood and whimsy on a carefree Spring day. In its description of the season, the poem displays an attitude of gleeful celebration: _____

5

Which quotation from the poem most effectively illustrates the claim?

A. "the little / lame balloonman / whistles far and wee"
B. "and eddieandbill come / running from marbles and / piracies and it's / spring"
C. "when the world is puddle-wonderful"
D. "and bettyandisbel come dancing / from hop-scotch and jump-rope"

The 17th century thinker Gottfried Wilhelm Leibniz emphasized the close connection between mathematics and other disciplines. He argued that a universal language of symbols and ratios underlies all knowledge and understanding, even when we are not aware of it. For example, he said, _____

6

Which quotation from Gottfried Wilhelm Leibniz most effectively illustrates the text's claim?

A. "Perceptions which are at present insensible may grow some day: nothing is useless, and eternity provides great scope for change."
B. "Imaginary numbers are a fine and wonderful resource of the divine intellect, almost an amphibian between being and non-being."
C. "Music is the hidden arithmetical exercise of a mind unconscious that it is calculating."
D. "There is nothing in the intellect which has not come from the senses, except the intellect itself."

William Makepeace Thackeray's 1848 satirical novel *Vanity Fair* explores the moral corruption and social climbing of its characters. The novel suggests that human beings are inherently subjective, perceiving their world through a self-centered lens that ultimately shapes their experiences: _____

7

Which quotation from the novel most effectively illustrates the text's claim?

A. "The moral world has no particular objection to vice, but an insuperable repugnance to hearing vice called by its proper name."
B. "Long brooding over lost pleasures exaggerates their charm and sweetness."
C. "Are not there little chapters in everybody's life, that seem to be nothing, and yet affect all the rest of history?"
D. "The world is a looking-glass, and gives back to every man the reflection of his own face."

Command of Evidence – Strengthen/Weaken

Preview Quiz

1) What should you read first, the passage or the question?

2) For these questions, an answer choice that uses weak language is generally (more / less) likely to be right than an answer choice that uses strong language.

3) To help decide on the right answer, it is a (good / bad) idea to rely on your own knowledge of the subject from outside the passage.

Choose the best answer.

4) The Mississippi kite, a bird of prey native to the prairies of North America, has adapted to living in areas of human settlement. When humans arrive in a previously uninhabited area, many other wild animals face steep declines in their populations, but the Mississippi kite flourishes. While some scholars point to the lower number of natural predators as the likely explanation, researcher Julie Savidge hypothesizes that nesting opportunities in urban areas were a key reason for the kites' success.

Which finding, if true, would most directly support Julie Savidge's hypothesis?

A) Grasshoppers, a major food source for Mississippi kites, thrive in urban and suburban areas due to the abundant grasses available on landscaped lawns.

B) Mississippi kites prefer to nest in trees, which are more plentiful in towns and urban areas than in the open prairie.

C) Owls, hawks, and falcons frequently prey on Mississippi kites in the prairie but are seldom seen in areas of human settlement.

D) The Mississippi kite is known for its aerobatic flight displays, which are performed during courtship and for territorial defense.

As always, our first step is to **read the question** carefully. It's crucial to identify **which claim** you are supposed to support. Usually, this will be the overall point of the text, but some questions are more subtle: there may be multiple points of view in the same text, and your job is to support just one of them. Next, read the text, **find the claim**, and either highlight it on the screen or jot it down on your scratch paper.

Now, consider the argument that you've just read. What **evidence** has the arguer provided for their claim? Do you see a **weakness** in their argument that you could help patch up with the right answer choice? Or is there just not enough evidence one way or the other? **Predict** your answer, to the extent that it's possible to do so. This may mean you know exactly what you're looking for, but maybe not. It's still helpful to have an idea of a general type of information that would be useful.

> *TIP:*
> To highlight in the Bluebook app, select some text and click "Annotate" on the upper right corner of the screen.

Now it's time to **attack the answer choices**. As you read each one, remember that you are *not* trying to decide whether or not the answer choice is true. Assume it is! The question to ask yourself is this: **does this make the claim more likely to be true**?

Common **wrong answer types** include choices that

- are irrelevant to the specific claim that the question asked about
- weaken the author's claim instead of strengthening it
- strengthen the author's position *slightly* but don't go far enough

The language strength of the choice can be a good tiebreaker. For the Central Ideas & Details questions, a choice using weaker language was more likely to be right, because it was easier to support. For these questions, the opposite is true! **A choice with *stronger* language is more likely to be right**, because it's more likely to have a real impact on the author's argument.

FROM THE BLOG

One of the best tools we have on the SAT is the ability to answer questions in the way that works best for us. Very often, students will spend 5-6 minutes answering a single challenging question, foregoing 2-3 other questions they could answer correctly and quickly. Nobody likes to feel that she's "quitting," but it is vital to congratulate yourself on making strategic choices, promising yourself you'll go back at the end, and moving on to more easily solved questions.

Command of Evidence – Strengthen/Weaken

Try It

A group of researchers conducted long-term field observations and data collection on a population of woolly monkeys in Yasuní National Park, Ecuador. They studied various aspects of their ecology and behavior, including population density, group size, home range, diet, and ranging patterns. The monkeys were observed to consume a wide variety of fruits as they ranged through large tracts of forest habitat. The researchers concluded that woolly monkeys play a crucial role in seed dispersal.

1) What is the researchers' conclusion?

2) What evidence do we have so far?

3) What kind of evidence might help?

Mbabaram is an extinct Aboriginal language that was spoken by the Mbabaram people in north Queensland, Australia. Although Mbabaram is completely unrelated to English, the two languages both happened to develop the word "dog" to refer to the same type of animal. This is an example of a "false cognate," a linguistic phenomenon in which a pair of words share similar sounds and meaning but different etymologies. However, although the Aragonese word "nueit" sounds similar to the English word "night," which has the same meaning, these terms should not be considered false cognates.

4) What is the central claim of the text?

5) Summarize the steps of the argument.

6) What kind of evidence might strengthen this text's claim?

Reading: Evidence and Logical Reasoning

Let's practice the whole process: analyzing an argument, predicting an answer, and then examining the answer choices.

Example: *The Mississippi kite, a bird of prey native to the prairies of North America, has adapted to living in areas of human settlement. When humans arrive in a previously uninhabited area, many other wild animals face steep declines in their populations, but the Mississippi kite flourishes. While some scholars point to the lower number of natural predators as the likely explanation, researcher Julie Savidge hypothesizes that nesting opportunities in urban areas were a key reason for the kites' success.*

Which finding, if true, would most directly support Julie Savidge's hypothesis?

Before we even see the answer choices, let's put some of the earlier steps into practice. First, what is the claim we need to support? Find Julie Savidge in the text and underline or highlight her hypothesis.

Now, what's the context? There's a bird that does well when humans arrive, and people wonder why. Julie Savidge's take is that they succeed because of nesting opportunities in urban areas.

Great, that's what we're looking for: something to support the idea that <u>nesting opportunities</u>, specifically, are the reason for the kites' success. Now we're ready to look at some answer choices.

A) Grasshoppers, a major food source for Mississippi kites, thrive in urban and suburban areas due to the abundant grasses available on landscaped lawns.
B) Mississippi kites prefer to nest in trees, which are more plentiful in towns and urban areas than in the open prairie.
C) Owls, hawks, and falcons frequently prey on Mississippi kites in the prairie but are seldom seen in areas of human settlement.
D) The Mississippi kite is known for its aerobatic flight displays, which are performed during courtship and for territorial defense.

TIP: Always be sure to read *all* the choices. You won't know which one best supports the claim until you've considered them all.

Choice A doesn't tell us anything about nesting opportunities. If anything, this choice might actually *weaken* the argument, because it gives us another possible reason for the kites' success: towns provide them with lots of food.

Choice B is about nesting! If this is true, this definitely helps support the argument: this tells us why *nesting* might be the reason that kites do well where people are. Hold on to this one.

Choice C is the opposite of what we want! This supports the other viewpoint in the passage (the "some scholars"), not Julie Savidge's viewpoint. Remember, we're not just looking to support the idea that kites do well in towns; we want to support the idea that *nesting opportunities are the reason why.*

Choice D is interesting but irrelevant. Oh well! It sounds like these birds put on a good show.

Of these answers, only one helps out our argument the way we need. Choice **B** is the clear winner.

Now let's return to the arguments you analyzed earlier. Consider all your previous work as you evaluate the answer choices.

Try It

7) A group of researchers conducted long-term field observations and data collection on a population of woolly monkeys in Yasuní National Park, Ecuador. They studied various aspects of their ecology and behavior, including population density, group size, home range, diet, and ranging patterns. The monkeys were observed to consume a wide variety of fruits as they ranged through large tracts of forest habitat. The researchers concluded that woolly monkeys play a crucial role in seed dispersal.

Which of the following, if true, would most directly support the researchers' conclusion?

Mark each answer choice with an "S" (if it strengthens the argument), a "W" (if it weakens the argument) or an "I" (if it is irrelevant).

____ A) Many plants have adaptations that allow their seeds to be carried away by the wind.
____ B) Woolly monkeys live in small groups consisting of several adult females, one dominant male, and their offspring.
____ C) An analysis of spatial distribution of tree species found greater tree diversity and more seedlings in areas where the woolly monkeys ranged than in areas where woolly monkeys were absent.
____ D) Human-caused disturbances, including hunting and habitat fragmentation, pose a significant threat to woolly monkey populations.

Which choice is the best answer? _____

Reading: Evidence and Logical Reasoning

Try It

8) Mbabaram is an extinct Aboriginal language that was spoken by the Mbabaram people in north Queensland, Australia. Although Mbabaram is completely unrelated to English, the two languages both happened to develop the word "dog" to refer to the same type of animal. This is an example of a "false cognate," a linguistic phenomenon in which a pair of words share similar sounds and meaning but different etymologies. However, although the Aragonese word "nueit" sounds similar to the English word "night," which has the same meaning, these terms should not be considered false cognates.

Which of the following, if true, would most directly support the claim?

Mark each answer choice with an "S" (if it strengthens the argument), a "W" (if it weakens the argument) or an "I" (if it is irrelevant).

____ A) Both "nueit" and "night" developed from the same Indo-European root word.

____ B) Aragonese is not an extinct language.

____ C) There is no linguistic relationship between Aragonese and the Mbabaram language.

____ D) In Aragonese, the words "nit" and "nuet" can also mean "night."

Which choice is the best answer? _____

CHALLENGE:

A variation of this question type asks you to **weaken** the text's claim instead of strengthening it. The process for these questions is almost exactly the same. Read the question, read the text, isolate the claim, consider what evidence has been supplied for it so far, and then look for any potential weaknesses. Only the final step is different: when forming your prediction, look for ways to make the conclusion *less* likely to be true rather than *more* likely to be true.

For both types of question, the best answer choices are strongly worded to have a significant impact on the argument. The wrong answers will either not go far enough, or they'll go in the wrong direction (strengthening rather than weakening), or they'll simply be irrelevant (neither strengthening nor weakening at all).

Practice Set 1: Easy-Medium

In the frigid waters of the Arctic Ocean, the Arctic cod (*Boreogadus saida*) is a critical source of food for marine mammals, birds, and other fish. This species is known for its unique adaptations to the harsh environment, including the ability to survive in water temperatures below 0°C. Scientists hypothesize that a specialized molecule in the Arctic cod's bloodstream may act as an antifreeze, allowing the fish to maintain fluidity in its body tissues even in subzero temperatures.

1 Which finding, if true, would most directly support the scientists' hypothesis?

A. A glycoprotein found in Arctic cod blood prevents freezing by binding to ice crystals and preventing them from growing.
B. The *nototheniidae*, a family of ray-finned fishes native to the waters near Antarctica, are believed to possess a similar antifreeze molecule.
C. The primary food source for Arctic cod is plankton and krill, both of which are found in abundance in the Arctic Ocean.
D. Arctic cod females lay their eggs under the sea ice in the spring; the eggs hatch and develop in the relative safety of the ice-covered water.

Teotihuacan was an ancient city in central Mexico that collapsed between the 6th and 8th centuries CE for mysterious reasons. Some historians believe that the collapse was caused by internal conflict, as the city was torn apart by social factors such as inequality and political instability. Others argue that Teotihuacan was invaded and conquered by a neighboring group, such as the Toltecs or the Chichimecs. However, archaeologist Michael E. Smith claims that the chief cause of the collapse was widespread famine due to uncontrollable environmental factors.

2 Which finding, if true, would most directly support Smith's claim?

A. Archaeological evidence shows significant changes in the material culture of the region during the 7th century CE, which could be indicative of a change in the ruling order.
B. The distribution of housing and other structures in the ruins of Teotihuacan suggest that by the 6th century CE, the city's ruling elite had become increasingly isolated from the rest of society.
C. Studies of sediment cores in the Valley of Mexico have revealed evidence of volcanic eruptions, though the dates of the eruptions remain uncertain.
D. An analysis of tree-ring data from the nearby Sierra Madre Mountains shows evidence of several severe droughts during the 5th and 6th centuries CE, which likely impacted the agricultural productivity of the region.

Dolley Madison, who held the title of First Lady of the United States from 1809 to 1817, was a woman of great intelligence, grace, and charm. Her popularity with the public played a key role in helping President Madison win office in the first place, which became clear early in the campaign when members of the opposing party attacked her viciously in the press. <u>Somehow, though, she never seemed bothered by the remarks: no matter what was printed, she would laugh it off and hold her head high.</u>

3

Which quotation from the 1800s would most directly support the underlined claim?

A. After losing to Madison, Charles Pinckney remarked, "I might have had a better chance had I faced Mr. Madison alone. I was beaten by Mr. and Mrs. Madison."
B. According to Margaret Bayard Smith, "It would be absolutely impossible for anyone to behave with more perfect propriety than she did."
C. On one occasion, when asked for her reaction to a nasty article, Dolley simply smiled and said, "It was as good as a play."
D. President Martin Van Buren later called Dolley "the most brilliant hostess this country has ever known."

A student is studying the ancient medical technique of "leeching," which involves the application of leeches to the skin for the purpose of bloodletting. The leeches would draw a significant amount of blood from the patient, which was believed to help remove toxins from the body and balance the humors. The physician would apply the leeches to specific areas of the body, usually the arms or the legs. The student argues that these locations were chosen in order to maximize the amount of blood drawn by the leeches.

4

Which finding, if true, would most directly support the student's claim?

A. In the period during which leeching was popular, the body was believed to be governed by a careful balance of four basic fluids, or "humors": blood, phlegm, yellow bile, and black bile.
B. The arms and legs feature a rich network of veins located close to the surface of the skin, which makes it easier for leeches to access the blood.
C. Leeching has fallen out of favor because the resulting blood loss increases the risk of infection and because of a lack of scientific evidence to support its effectiveness.
D. The use of leeches on other parts of the body, such as the face or torso, was considered more dangerous and potentially harmful to the patient.

Theory of Mind (ToM) refers to the ability to understand and attribute mental states to oneself and others, including beliefs, desires, intentions, and emotions. It plays a crucial role in children's social interactions and communication. In a 2011 study, researchers assessed a sample of 3- to 5-year-old children and collected information about their TV viewing habits, including the amount of educational TV programming they watched. They also evaluated the children's ToM skills using age-appropriate measures, such as understanding false beliefs and recognizing different perspectives. Children who watched more educational TV shows exhibited higher levels of ToM understanding compared to those who had lower exposure to educational content. The researchers concluded that exposure to educational TV programming could aid in ToM development in preschoolers.

5

Which finding, if true, would most directly support the researchers' conclusion?

A. Educational TV programs can enhance children's cognitive skills, such as attention, memory, and problem-solving abilities.
B. High-quality educational TV programs use engaging storytelling and visuals to effectively teach children literacy, mathematics, and science.
C. By presenting characters and scenarios that require understanding others' perspectives and emotions, educational TV programs help children develop empathy and perspective-taking skills.
D. Exposure to rich and diverse language through various media can contribute to language acquisition and communication abilities.

In a 2008 study, Anna Nowak-Wegrzyn and colleagues investigated the effects of extensively heated egg protein on egg-allergic children. The study involved a double-blind, placebo-controlled food challenge where participants consumed muffins containing baked egg. The researchers found that a significant number of participants with egg allergy demonstrated tolerance to the baked egg products, experiencing no allergic reactions. Nowak-Wegrzyn concluded that the heating process alters the allergenic properties of egg proteins, making them less likely to trigger an allergic response.

6

Which finding, if true, would most directly support Nowak-Wegrzyn's conclusion?

A. Not all individuals with egg allergies can tolerate baked egg products, and the level of tolerance can vary among individuals.
B. Heat denatures egg proteins, altering their shape and making them less likely to bind to the antibodies responsible for initiating allergic reactions.
C. When children with egg allergies are gradually introduced to small amounts of baked egg, the immune system can build a tolerance to egg proteins over time.
D. During baking, eggs undergo coagulation, a process by which proteins form a network of interconnected structures resulting in solidification and firmness.

Practice Set 2: Medium-Hard

A recent study of college students found that over 50% of students self-reported their GPAs as significantly higher than their official academic records indicated. Biometric evaluation indicated a lack of any of the physical markers of an attempt to deceive. Moreover, many of these same students later increased their GPAs the exact amount of the discrepancy in reporting. Researchers concluded that the students' inaccurate reporting represented not a desire to mislead but an optimistic expression of future academic intent.

1

Which finding, if true, would most directly support the researchers' conclusion?

A. Many of the students reported GPAs more than five-tenths of a point higher than their actual GPAs.
B. When the students reported false information about their disciplinary records, many displayed increased heart rates and other indicia of physical distress.
C. Some of the students who reported their GPAs accurately seemed uncomfortable with the interviewing process.
D. Several students lied about not only their GPAs, but their country of origin, age, and socioeconomic status.

In 1974, the US House of Representatives held hearings to determine whether then-president Richard Nixon's actions during the Watergate scandal merited his impeachment, the first step in a process that could ultimately result in his removal from office. The opening statement at the impeachment hearings, delivered by Congresswoman Barbara Jordan, denounced Nixon's behavior in forceful terms and made a powerful argument in favor of impeachment. <u>However, Jordan stopped short of calling for an end to Nixon's presidency; she did not state a conclusion as to whether Nixon should be removed from office, suggesting only that Congress needed to begin the process of exploring the evidence of his alleged offenses.</u>

2

Which quotation from Jordan's speech would most directly support the underlined claim?

A. "Impeachment must proceed within the confines of the constitutional term 'high crimes and misdemeanors.' Common sense would be revolted if we engaged upon this process for petty reasons."
B. "The President has engaged in a series of public statements and actions designed to thwart the lawful investigation by government prosecutors. Moreover, the President has made public announcements and assertions which the evidence will show he knew to be false."
C. "If the impeachment provision in the Constitution of the United States will not reach the offenses charged here, then perhaps that 18th-century Constitution should be abandoned to a 20th-century paper shredder!"
D. "Has the President committed offenses, and planned, and directed, and acquiesced in a course of conduct which the Constitution will not tolerate? That's the question. We know that. We know the question. We should now forthwith proceed to answer the question."

A physician hypothesized that practicing yoga several times a week could significantly improve patients' cardiovascular health. Two groups of patients were studied, none of whom had regularly practiced yoga prior to the start of the experiment. For one year, Group A attended yoga sessions every Monday, Wednesday, and Friday morning, while Group B did not. At the end of the year, Group B's health had not changed, but most members of Group A had lower blood pressure and a decreased resting heart rate, both of which are indications of improved cardiac function.

3 Which finding, if true, would most directly weaken the physician's hypothesis?

A. During the experiment, many members of Group A engaged in other activities known to improve cardiovascular health, while the members of Group B did not.
B. At the start of the experiment, the average blood pressure and resting heart rates for Group A were lower than those of Group B.
C. Both groups were provided with information about healthy eating practices and advised to exercise regularly.
D. None of the members of Group B expressed an interest in practicing yoga after the experiment was concluded.

Fever has long been regarded as a symptom of disease, a byproduct of the inflammation brought on by infection. A team of researchers at the University of Alberta hypothesized that fever in fact regulates and controls infection, speeding recovery from illness. To test their hypothesis, the scientists infected two groups of teleost fish with *Aeromonas veronii* bacteria, then administered antifever medication to one group while allowing fever to develop unimpeded in the other. A control group of uninfected fish was also observed.

4 Which finding from the study, if true, would most directly support the researchers' hypothesis?

A. The infected fish that did not receive antifever medication exhibited symptoms of fatigue and muscle weakness.
B. The infected fish that received antifever medication cleared their infection in about 14 days, while the infected fish that did not receive antifever medication cleared their infection in about 7 days.
C. The infected fish that did not receive antifever medication showed a higher capacity to heal *A. veronii*-associated wounds than did the infected fish that received antifever medication.
D. The uninfected fish did not exhibit any symptoms of illness and showed no change in their wound healing capacity.

The Aurignacians, a group of early modern humans who lived in Europe during the Upper Paleolithic period, created intricate cave paintings considered to be some of the earliest known examples of human art. While some scholars believe the paintings were chiefly practical in nature, perhaps intended to communicate information about hunting techniques or to identify important resources in the area, others argue that the paintings served a primarily spiritual or religious purpose. The paintings were clearly created with great care and attention, featuring detailed depictions of animals that were likely important to the Aurignacian culture and may have held significant symbolic meaning. Additionally, the cave environment may have been considered a sacred space, and the act of creating the paintings may have been seen as a way to communicate with the spiritual realm or to honor and pay tribute to the animals depicted.

5

Which finding, if true, would most directly weaken the claim made by the scholars who favor the view expressed in the underlined portion of the text?

A. Many of the paintings feature strange, otherworldly creatures that are not found in the natural world, such as half-human, half-animal figures or creatures with exaggerated features.
B. The paintings have generally been found deep within caves, often in areas that would have been difficult for the Aurignacians to access.
C. Some of the paintings show animals with arrows or spears sticking out of their bodies, or with bright arrow-shaped lines tracing a path to the heart.
D. The paintings have been found in several locations in Europe, including in the Chauvet-Pont-d'Arc Cave and the Lascaux Cave, both in France, and the Altamira Cave, in northern Spain.

The human body burns calories all the time, not just when we're engaging in cardiovascular activity. The rate at which the body uses energy to maintain vital bodily functions when at rest is called the resting metabolic rate (RMR). In a study at the University of Alabama at Birmingham, a group of researchers claimed to have demonstrated that strength training can increase the RMR. Before and after a group of ten women underwent a 16-week strength training program, researchers measured the amount of oxygen consumed and carbon dioxide produced by each participant when at rest, a technique known as indirect calorimetry. Because the rates of oxygen consumption and carbon dioxide production reflect the body's energy expenditure, this technique is a useful way to measure RMR.

6

Which finding, if true, would most directly support the researchers' claim?

A. By the end of the study, most of the participants in the study had lost a moderate amount of weight.
B. The average rate at which participants consumed oxygen during strength training was greater at the end of the 16-week program.
C. Muscles are metabolically active tissue, meaning they require energy to function even at rest.
D. The average rate at which participants produced carbon dioxide while at rest was greater at the end of the 16-week program.

Command of Evidence – Quantitative

Preview Quiz

1) The quantitative Command of Evidence questions (do / do not) test your math skills.

2) A background in science (is / is not) necessary to do well on these questions.

Choose the best answer.

3) The common bumblebee goes through several distinct life stages. A bumblebee larva is 0 to 14 days old and 0 to 15 millimeters (mm) in length. After a brief pupal stage in a cocoon, the bumblebee emerges as an adult. Adult bumblebees are more than 21 days old, and their size depends on their sex and their role in the colony: the queen is 17 to 22 mm in length, a worker is 10 to 14 mm in length, and a male is 13 to 16 mm in length. A student recorded information about four bumblebees and asserted that three are workers and one is a queen.

Bee	Age (days)	Length (mm)	Mass (milligrams)
A	27	13.2	140
B	32	12.9	113
C	75	19.4	681
D	39	13.9	174

Which choice best describes data from the table that support the student's assertion?

A) The ages of the bees range from 27 to 75 days, and D's length is 174 mm.

B) None of the bees are more than 22 mm in length, and B is 32 days old.

C) Each of the bees has a mass between 113 and 681 milligrams, and only A is less than 30 days old.

D) All the bees are more than 21 days old, and all except C have lengths ranging from 10 to 14 mm.

These questions are similar to the last two sets, in that your overall task is to use evidence to support the author's argument. The difference lies in what kind of evidence you'll be using: this time, the answers will come from tables, graphs, or other visual representations of data.

Don't panic—this isn't as hard as it seems. Although many of these texts are science-based, *you don't need to understand the science*. As always, no outside knowledge of the passage's topic is necessary; in fact, relying on that outside knowledge can be a quick trip to the wrong answer. Our task here is to use the information we've been given to support the specific claim that they've asked us about, and that's it.

Typical **wrong answer choices** will:

- get the numbers wrong
- accurately report the numbers but misinterpret their meaning
- accurately report the numbers and their meaning, but don't support the claim

It's that last bullet point that's usually the tough one. Just like for the other "command of evidence" questions, a crucial first step here is to **identify the claim** that the text is making. What are we trying to show? **Predict an answer** on that basis. What kind of evidence are we looking for? For instance, if the overall point is that two things are similar, we can probably eliminate answer choices that focus on a difference between them instead of a similarity.

For the remaining answer choices, first make sure they're accurately stating the data, and then consider what impact that information has on the specific claim you've been asked about. Does it support the claim? Does it undermine it? Or does it not necessarily do anything at all?

> ***TIP:***
> The data provided in the chart or graph will include some irrelevant information. Focus on what matters, mentally crossing out the rest. What's relevant to the specific claim referenced in the question?

Example: *The common bumblebee goes through several distinct life stages. A bumblebee larva is 0 to 14 days old and 0 to 15 millimeters (mm) in length. After a brief pupal stage in a cocoon, the bumblebee emerges as an adult. Adult bumblebees are more than 21 days old, and their size depends on their sex and their role in the colony: the queen is 17 to 22 mm in length, a worker is 10 to 14 mm in length, and a male is 13 to 16 mm in length. A student recorded information about four bumblebees and asserted that three are workers and one is a queen.*

Bee	Age (days)	Length (mm)	Mass (milligrams)
A	27	13.2	140
B	32	12.9	113
C	75	19.4	681
D	39	13.9	174

Which choice best describes data from the table that support the student's assertion?

Let's see what we can do before we examine the answer choices. First, what's the student's assertion here? It's right there at the end of the passage: the student is saying that three of these four are "worker" bumblebees and one is a "queen." Given what the rest of the text told us about these categories, we can conclude that the lengths of three of these bees (the workers) should be 10-14 mm, while the length of the remaining one (the queen) should be 17-22 mm. Moreover, since both workers and queens are adults, we also know that all four bees should be more than 21 days old.

Right off the bat, what do you notice about the data? There's a whole column that we don't need! You can mentally cross off the entire "mass" column, since there was nothing about mass in the passage. This also means that <u>any answer choices that even *mention* mass would have to be wrong</u>.

TIP:

Some wrong choices will get the data wrong—but not all. It's not enough that the choice accurately reports the data. It also has to be relevant! Keep your focus on *the task set for you in the question* above all else.

Now let's take a look at our choices.

- A) The ages of the bees range from 27 to 75 days, and D's length is 174 mm.
- B) None of the bees are more than 22 mm in length, and B is 32 days old.
- C) Each of the bees has a mass between 113 and 681 milligrams, and only A is less than 30 days old.
- D) All the bees are more than 21 days old, and all except C have lengths ranging from 10 to 14 mm.

We can already eliminate choice C, since it mentions mass. Eliminate choice A for getting the data wrong: 174 is D's mass in milligrams, not its length in millimeters.

Choices B and D both accurately report the data. But how relevant is B? The fact that the lengths are all under 22 mm doesn't help us distinguish between worker bees and queen bees, which is the point we're really trying to make. Choice D is the one that points out that exactly three of the four bees have lengths in the "worker" category, and its information about age supports the idea that they're all adults. Choice **D** is the winner.

TIP:
The right answer doesn't have to completely *prove* the claim we've been asked to support. It just has to make that claim *more likely to be true*.

Try It

Ice Cream Butterfat Contents and Price Ranges

Ice cream type	Butterfat content	Price range (per pint)
Regular	10-16%	$2.99-$4.99
Premium	14-18%	$4.99-$6.99
Low-fat	3-8%	$2.99-$4.99
Non-dairy	varies	$4.99-$6.99

Ice creams can vary widely in their butterfat content, which refers to the amount of fat derived from milk or cream used in the ice cream formulation. A higher butterfat content contributes to a richer, denser, and more indulgent ice cream, but customers pay for the privilege: _____.

Which choice most effectively uses data from the table to complete the text?

1) What is the claim we're trying to strengthen?

2) Which rows and/or columns from the table are the most relevant?

3) Predict an answer:

4) For each answer choice, consider two questions. First, does it accurately report the data? And second, what effect does it have on the claim (does it Strengthen it, does it Weaken it, or is it Irrelevant)?

Is it accurate? (Y/N)   What effect? (S/W/I)

____ ____ A) premium ice cream contains more butterfat than regular or low-fat ice cream, and it costs more per pint.

____ ____ B) non-dairy ice cream can cost as much as premium ice cream but its butterfat content varies.

____ ____ C) low-fat ice cream contains less butterfat than other ice cream types yet costs as much per pint as regular ice cream.

____ ____ D) the non-premium ice creams contain less butterfat than premium and cost less.

Which choice is the best answer? _____

Practice Set 1: Easy-Medium

INCIDENTS OF INCOMPLETE INACTIVATION
BY PATHOGEN IN THE US, 2003-2015

Bacillus anthracis	8
Brucella species	1
Burkholderia pseudomallei	1
Clostridium botulinum	1
Ebola and Marburg viruses	2
Equine encephalitis viruses	3
Francisella tularensis	5
Total	21

In May 2015, the Department of Defense (DOD) discovered that one of its laboratories inadvertently sent live *Bacillus anthracis*, the bacterium that causes anthrax, to almost two hundred laboratories worldwide over the course of twelve years. The laboratory in question incorrectly believed that the samples had been inactivated—that is, that the scientists had destroyed the hazardous effects of the pathogen while retaining characteristics of interest for future use. The accident was hardly unique: between 2003 and 2015, _____

1. Which choice most effectively uses data from the table to complete the text?

A. samples of *Bacillus anthracis* were not completely inactivated in at least 7 other incidents in the US.
B. *Bacillus anthracis* was the pathogen involved in fewer than half of the US cases of incomplete inactivation.
C. scientists failed to completely inactivate Ebola and Marburg viruses at least twice.
D. incomplete inactivation incidents in the US involved fewer than 10 types of pathogens.

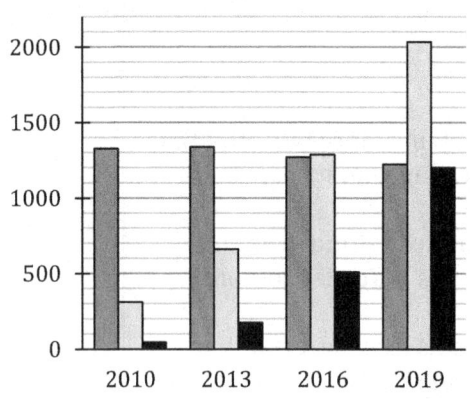

Trends in Movie Sales, 2010-2019

- Movie theater tickets sold (millions)
- Movies digitally downloaded (millions)
- Movies streamed at home (millions)

Some media analysts argue that trends in movie sales over time indicate a shift in movie-watching behavior away from movie theaters and towards more convenient and affordable options such as digital downloads and home streaming.

2. Which choice most effectively uses data from the graph to support the analysts' argument?

A. From 2010 to 2019, the change in the number of movie theater tickets sold was much smaller than the change in the number of movies streamed at home or downloaded.
B. The greatest number of digital downloads of movies occurred in 2019, while the greatest number of movie theater tickets sold occurred in 2013.
C. From 2010 to 2019, the number of movies downloaded or streamed at home increased, while the number of movie theater tickets sold decreased.
D. In 2016, the number of movies downloaded or streamed was greater than the number of movie tickets sold.

US DROWSY DRIVING FATALITIES

Year	Number of drowsy drivers in fatal crashes	Percent of all drivers in fatal crashes	Fatalities in crashes involving drowsy driving
2018	1,221	2.4%	785
2017	1,319	2.5%	697
2016	1,332	2.5%	803
2015	1,275	2.6%	824
2014	1,306	2.9%	851

Source: National Highway Traffic Safety Administration

Due to the enormous amount of evidence now available, there is a consensus in the scientific community about the hazards of sleep deprivation. Lack of sleep was a factor in some of the most serious accidents in recent memory, including the Exxon Valdez oil spill, the Chernobyl meltdown, and the disaster at Three Mile Island. Moreover, traffic statistics indicate that "drowsy driving"—the act of operating a motor vehicle when feeling fatigued or sleepy—is a significant threat on the roads.

3

Which choice best describes data from the table that support the claim made in the last sentence of the text?

A. The number of fatal crashes caused by drowsy driving increases every year.
B. Hundreds of people die each year in crashes involving drowsy driving.
C. Of all fatal crashes in the US, less than three percent involve drowsy drivers.
D. The number of drowsy driving fatalities was highest in 2014, but the number of drowsy drivers involved in fatal crashes peaked in 2016.

Value of U.S. Agricultural Exports to China

Product	2017 Export Value*	2018 Export Value*	Change in Export Value
Soybeans	$12,400	$3,100	−75%
Pork	$1,100	$550	−50%
Dairy products	$577	$281	−51%
Sorghum	$347	$4	−99%
Wheat	$430	$84	−80%

*in millions of dollars

In recent years, trade tensions between the US and China have resulted in the imposition of tariffs and other trade restrictions on agricultural products, limiting access to the Chinese market. This has had a significant impact on the profitability of U.S. agricultural businesses, particularly those that rely heavily on exports to China. For example, between 2017 and 2018, _____

4

Which choice most effectively uses data from the table to complete the example?

A. the decline in US exports of dairy products to China was very similar to the decline in US exports of pork.
B. the value of US exports of sorghum to China was almost completely wiped out.
C. the value of US exports of wheat to China decreased by more than $400 million.
D. US exports of soybeans to China maintained a value of more than $3 billion.

Carotenoid Mechanisms and Coloration Scores

Type of Animal	Carotenoid Signaling Mechanism	Average Coloration Score* for Males	Average Coloration Score* for Females
Birds	coloration of plumage	5.2	3.8
Fish	coloration of fins and skin	6.9	4.6
Reptiles	coloration of throat and skin	25.6	20.9

* a measure of intensity and brightness of color

In many species, males are more likely to compete for access to females than females are for males. As a result, the males of these species evolved to develop more elaborate and conspicuous traits than the females in order to attract mates. Carotenoids, a type of pigment found in many fruits and vegetables, are believed to indicate an individual's health and nutritional status, with brighter and more saturated colors indicating better health and greater access to high-quality food. Some researchers assert that carotenoids play an important role in mate selection.

5 Which choice best describes data from the table that support the researchers' assertion?

A. In all three animal types, males tend to have higher average coloration scores than females.
B. The average coloration score for male reptiles is approximately five times as high as the average coloration score for male birds.
C. The carotenoid signaling mechanism involves skin coloration for both fish and reptiles, but not for birds.
D. The difference between the average coloration score for males and the average coloration score for females was less than 5 for all three species.

Comparison of Outcomes of Laparoscopic and Open Appendectomies

	Laparoscopic technique	Open technique
Operating time	46.98 ± 2.99 minutes	53.02 ± 2.88 minutes
Length of hospitalization	4.38 ± 1.09 days	4.18 ± 0.77 days
Rate of surgical site infections	7 infections (10.77%)	18 infections (27.69%)

As a general rule, the longer a surgical patient must spend in the operating room, the greater the risk and the slower the recovery. In a 2019 study, 130 appendectomy patients at the Holy Family Hospital in Rawalpindi, Pakistan were randomly assigned either the laparoscopic or the open surgery technique. The findings demonstrated that laparoscopic appendectomy has several advantages over open appendectomy, including _____.

6 Which choice most effectively uses data from the table to complete the text?

A. longer operative times and a lower rate of surgical site infections.
B. longer hospital stays and similar operative times.
C. shorter operative times and significantly fewer surgical site infections.
D. hospital stays of similar length and a higher rate of surgical site infections.

Trends in Solid Waste Production
(millions of tons per year)

	2016	2030*	2050*
Middle East/ N. Africa	129	177	255
Sub-Saharan Africa	174	269	516
Latin America/Caribb.	231	290	369
North America	289	342	396
South Asia	334	466	661
Europe & central Asia	392	440	490
East Asia & Pacific	468	602	714

* projected

Rapid population growth, urbanization, industrialization, and changes in consumption patterns have contributed to a global increase in solid waste generation. While solid waste is a global issue, some regions and countries will face particularly dire waste management challenges in the coming years. For example, _____

7

Which choice most effectively uses data from the table to complete the text?

A. by 2050, the East Asia and Pacific region is projected to generate 714 million tons of solid waste per year.

B. in 2016, the amount of solid waste produced by Europe and central Asia was more than double that produced by the middle east and north Africa.

C. by 2030, nearly every region is projected to be generating more than 200 million tons of solid waste per year.

D. between 2016 and 2050, the amount of solid waste produced by North America is projected to increase by more than 100 million tons per year.

Body Temperatures (°C)

		Hours after sleep onset		
Participant	Sex	1	3	5
1	M	36.8	36.6	36.4
2	M	36.9	36.7	36.5
3	M	36.7	36.5	36.3
4	F	36.9	36.7	36.5
5	F	36.8	36.6	36.4
6	F	36.7	36.5	36.3

A study monitored the body temperature of six participants overnight. During sleep, the human body undergoes a natural fluctuation in body temperature. Throughout the night, the body's core temperature continues to decline gradually, reaching its lowest point during the early morning hours. After this thermal nadir, the body temperature gradually begins to rise, marking the transition from sleep to wakefulness.

8

Which choice best describes data in the table that support the claims made in the text?

A. The body temperatures of the male participants first decreased, then increased.

B. The body temperatures of the female participants first increased, then decreased.

C. The body temperatures of all participants gradually decreased during the first five hours of sleep.

D. The body temperatures of the participants varied with no general trend.

Practice Set 2: Medium-Hard

The Mediterranean diet, an eating plan that emphasizes plant-based foods and unsaturated fats, has been associated with numerous health benefits. It may even help stave off dementia. In the UK, a large cohort of participants submitted to genetic testing and completed questionnaires about their eating habits and lifestyles. Researchers used this information to calculate each participant's genetic risk of developing dementia and his or her Mediterranean Diet Adherence Screener (MEDAS) score, where a higher score indicates greater adherence to the diet. After tabulating the number of participants in each group who developed dementia during the 10-year study period, the researchers concluded that a Mediterranean diet may be protective against dementia regardless of an individual's genetic makeup.

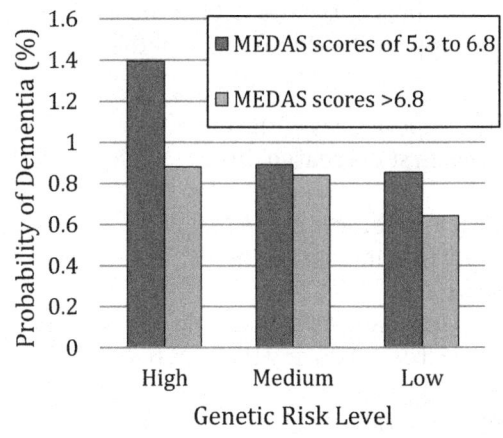

Probability of Developing Dementia

1

Which choice best describes data from the graph that strengthen the researchers' conclusion?

A. Greater adherence to the Mediterranean diet was associated with an increased probability of dementia across all categories of genetic risk.
B. Greater adherence to the Mediterranean diet was associated with a decreased probability of dementia across all categories of genetic risk.
C. Greater genetic risk was associated with an increased probability of dementia across both categories of adherence to the Mediterranean diet.
D. Greater genetic risk was associated with a decreased probability of dementia across both categories of adherence to the Mediterranean diet.

Galilean Moons

Moon	Orbital period (Earth days)	Eccentricity* of orbit	Average distance from Jupiter (km)
Io	1.77	0.0041	421,800
Europa	3.55	0.0094	671,000
Ganymede	7.16	0.0013	1,070,000
Callisto	16.69	0.0074	1,883,000

*A measure of how much the orbit deviates from a circular shape.

Io, Europa, Ganymede, and Callisto are four moons of Jupiter known collectively as the Galilean moons. Unlike the other three moons, Io generates a significant amount of electrical activity on its surface. A student asserted that this activity results from strong tidal forces caused by a highly elliptical orbit.

2

Which choice most effectively uses data from the table to weaken the student's assertion?

A. Of the four, Io's orbit is the closest to Jupiter.
B. The eccentricities of both Europa's and Callisto's orbits are higher than that of Io's.
C. Ganymede's average distance from Jupiter is greater than both Europa's and Io's.
D. Callisto's orbital period is greater than the sum of the other three orbital periods.

Group	pH	Light intensity (lux)	Average number of ephippia hatched
M	5.0	650	45
N	7.0	650	56
O	9.0	650	65
R	7.0	300	28
S	7.0	650	55
T	7.0	850	68

The *Moina micrura* is a species of microscopic aquatic crustacean. Under certain conditions, *M. micrura* will lay specialized eggs called ephippia that contain dormant embryos. Researchers prepared beakers of water that each contained 120 newly laid ephippia, then divided the beakers equally into six groups. The beakers in the first three groups were exposed to varying pH levels at a constant light intensity and a temperature of 27°C; the beakers in the other three groups were exposed to varying light intensities at a constant pH level and a temperature of 25°C. The results suggest that external environmental factors can significantly affect the hatching of dormant *M. micrura* embryos. For example, while in group R, the average number of ephippia hatched was 28, _____

3

Which choice most effectively uses data from the table to complete the example?

A. in group M, the average number hatched was 45.
B. in group O, the average number hatched was 65.
C. in group T, the average number hatched was 68.
D. the average number hatched in group N was very similar to the average number hatched in group S.

Depth below surface (cm)	CO_2 content of soil gas (% by volume)		Water content of soil (% by mass)	
	Nov 9	Dec 7	Nov 9	Dec 7
30	0.07	0.09	19.0	17.0
60	0.14	0.08	15.7	19.5
100	0.20	0.13	11.9	24.2
140	0.42	0.23	10.6	26.3

Carbon dioxide (CO_2) is produced in soil through respiration in plant roots. In a temperate forest in southern Ontario, a scientist hypothesized that the non-growing season would be characterized by temporally variable CO_2 emissions. He also claimed that the amount of moisture in the soil was an important factor controlling CO_2 variability.

4

Which choice best describes data from the table that support the scientist's claims?

A. On November 9, CO_2 content increased as water content decreased; on December 7, CO_2 content increased as water content increased.
B. At each depth, CO_2 content increased between November 9 and December 7, while water content decreased between November 9 and December 7.
C. On both November 9 and December 7, the lowest moisture and lowest CO_2 content were found at the shallowest depth.
D. The range of results for CO_2 contents at the various depths was smaller on December 7 than on November 9, and the average water content was greater on December 7 than on November 9.

Four Asteroids' Rotation Rates and Densities

Asteroid	Rotation period (hours)	Density (g/cm^3)
A	5.2	3.5
B	9.1	2.8
C	20.3	1.6
D	30.6	1.3

To determine whether an asteroid is a monolith (a solid, cohesive object) or a rubble pile (a collection of smaller rocks and debris held together by gravity), scientists look to the asteroid's rotation rate and density, among other features. A solid object is more dense and more likely to hold together under the stress of rapid rotation, while a rubble pile is less dense (containing more empty space between the individual rocks and debris) and is more likely to rotate slowly due to its loosely bound nature. If the four asteroids represented in the table above include two monoliths and two rubble piles, then asteroid C is most likely a rubble pile, because _____.

5

Which choice most effectively uses data from the table to complete the text?

A. its rotation period is relatively great, indicating less rapid rotation, and its density is relatively low, suggesting more internal empty space.
B. its rotation period is relatively great, indicating more rapid rotation, and its density is relatively low, suggesting less internal empty space.
C. its rotation period is relatively low, indicating less rapid rotation, and its density is relatively high, suggesting more internal empty space.
D. its rotation period is relatively low, indicating more rapid rotation, and its density is relatively high, suggesting less internal empty space.

Crude oil is a naturally occurring mixture of hydrocarbons, which are organic compounds primarily composed of hydrogen (H) and carbon (C) atoms. A study recorded the elemental composition, hydrocarbon (H/C) content, and density, in grams per milliliter (g/mL) of five petroleum crude oil samples.

Sample	C (%)	H (%)	H/C	Density (g/mL)
S1	84.84	13.08	1.84	0.8429
S2	85.24	12.76	1.78	0.8616
S3	83.15	10.30	1.49	1.0030
S4	83.94	13.69	1.94	0.7733
S5	86.18	13.00	1.80	0.8569

As the table indicates, the specific composition of a crude oil sample determines its physical properties. For example, _____

6

Which choice most effectively uses data from the table to complete the text?

A. The sample with the lowest hydrogen content had the greatest density, and the sample with the greatest hydrogen content had the lowest density.
B. The sample with the lowest carbon content had the greatest density, and the sample with the greatest carbon content had the lowest density.
C. The sample with the lowest hydrogen content had the lowest density, and the sample with the greatest hydrogen content had the greatest density.
D. The sample with the lowest carbon content had the lowest density, and the sample with the greatest carbon content had the greatest density.

Cigarette Use and Total Tobacco Use Among U.S. Middle School and High School Students

Year	Cigarette Use (percent)	Total Tobacco Use (percent)
2015	10.8	16.7
2016	8.0	12.2
2017	7.6	12.5
2018	6.1	10.5
2019	5.8	9.6

This table presents data from the National Youth Tobacco Survey, which tracks tobacco use among US middle and high school students. The results suggest that efforts to reduce tobacco use among young people (such as tobacco taxes, restrictions on advertising and sales, and public education campaigns) may be having a positive impact, given that _____

7

Which choice most effectively uses data from the table to complete the text?

A. the percent of young people who report using cigarettes decreased every year over the time period shown.
B. the data show a downward trend in reported tobacco use among young people from 2015 to 2019.
C. among young people who report using tobacco, the fraction who report using cigarettes decreased from 2015 to 2019.
D. the percent of young people who report using tobacco dropped over 4 percentage points in a single year.

Logical Inferences

Preview Quiz

1) For these questions, an answer choice that uses weak language is generally (more / less) likely to be right than an answer choice that uses strong language.

2) To help decide on the right answer, it is a (good / bad) idea to rely on your own knowledge of the subject from outside the passage.

Choose the best answer.

3) A 2014 study involving 176 adult participants aimed to examine how different forms of physical activity affect creative thinking. Participants were asked to complete creativity tasks while walking on a treadmill, while walking outside, or while sitting down. The tasks included the Guilford Alternate Uses Task, in which participants were asked to list as many possible uses for a given object as they could within a certain timeframe; the Compound Remote Associates Test, in which participants were asked to identify a word that was related to three other given words; and the Torrance Test of Creative Thinking, in which participants were asked to complete a series of drawing tasks. Whether the walking took place on a treadmill or outside, those who walked earned higher scores on all three tests than did those who remained seated, suggesting that _____

Which choice most logically completes the text?

A) the increased blood flow to the brain caused by moderate exercise stimulates creative thinking.
B) the meditative and calming effects of walking induce creativity regardless of the setting.
C) any benefits that walking may have on creativity are not limited to the experience of being outside.
D) word-association and drawing tasks are better suited for testing creativity in adult participants than in child participants.

Logical Inferences

While the previous three question types asked you to evaluate an argument that had already been made, these questions ask you to help create the argument in the first place: you're given the evidence, and your job is to pick the right conclusion. Read through the information in the passage so you have a full understanding of the author's evidence, and **predict** where you think the author is going.

Common **wrong answer types** include the following:

- choices that generally make sense but aren't directly supported by the text
- choices that are related to one aspect of the text but not the part emphasized in the fill-in-the-blank sentence
- answers that go too far

> *TIP:*
> For these questions, a choice that uses *weaker* language is more likely to be right.

Predicting an answer is particularly important for this type of question. Gather the evidence discussed in the text, taking notes if it's helpful to keep your thoughts organized, and decide where this seems to be headed. Then, evaluate those answer choices with a critical eye. The question is this: which of these *has* to be true?

Example: *A 2014 study involving 176 adult participants aimed to examine how different forms of physical activity affect creative thinking. Participants were asked to complete creativity tasks while walking on a treadmill, while walking outside, or while sitting down. The tasks included the Guilford Alternate Uses Task, in which participants were asked to list as many possible uses for a given object as they could within a certain timeframe; the Compound Remote Associates Test, in which participants were asked to identify a word that was related to three other given words; and the Torrance Test of Creative Thinking, in which participants were asked to complete a series of drawing tasks. Whether the walking took place on a treadmill or outside, those who walked earned higher scores on all three tests than did those who remained seated, suggesting that _____.*

Which choice most logically completes the text?

There's a lot of extra information in this text that is more detail than we really need. For example, how important is it that we know the exact way in which creativity was measured? For this particular question, not very, because the author isn't trying to cast doubt on the study. The last sentence is focusing on what we can draw overall from the results, so let's keep our eye on the big picture. What were the tests measuring? Creativity. The people who walked earned higher scores than the people who didn't walk, suggesting that the people who walked were *more creative* than the people who didn't. Also, the final sentence emphasizes that this outcome was observed in both groups of walkers, which suggests that it's the walking itself that's having this effect (if anything is), not the setting.

So that's our prediction: walking seems to aid creativity, whether you walk inside or outside.

But be careful not to go too far! We can't say that walking *causes* creativity based on this one study. Keep an eye out for those logical leaps as we examine the answer choices.

- A) *the increased blood flow to the brain caused by moderate exercise stimulates creative thinking.*
- B) *the meditative and calming effects of walking induce creativity regardless of the setting.*
- C) *any benefits that walking may have on creativity are not limited to the experience of being outside.*
- D) *word-association and drawing tasks are better suited for testing creativity in adult participants than in child participants.*

Let's start with choice A. If we can't say for sure that walking causes creativity, then we certainly can't say for sure that exercise in general (even "moderate" exercise) causes it. Plus, even if we could say that walking caused creativity, we can't say *how*. This choice is way too specific: we don't know anything about an increased blood flow to the brain.

Choice B gives us another possible way that walking might have an effect: maybe it's not the increased blood flow, but the meditative and calming effects. We still don't know if this is true! It's another possible way that walking *might* influence creativity, if it does. We can't say that this definitely happens, which is what we're looking for. Plus, "regardless of the setting" is too strong. The only settings we can compare are walking on a treadmill versus walking outside. For all we know, various types of outside settings might have very different effects.

Choice C is nice and weak, which is good. This isn't claiming that walking definitely affects creativity; it's just saying that if it does, those effects don't seem to be limited to being outside. That's a lot easier to support than the other choices so far. Hold on to choice C.

Choice D picks up on various details of the text, but not in a way we can justify. Just because this study used these tests for its adult participants, that doesn't necessarily mean that these tests would not be suited for child participants. We just have no way of knowing whether this is true.

Choice C was the best match for our prediction without taking it too far, so it's the winner. The answer is **C**.

> **TIP:**
> We're looking for what essentially *has* to be true. Any choices that assume **causation**, make a **prediction**, or describe a **hypothetical** are usually too speculative to be correct.

Logical Inferences

> ***Try It***   In a 2007 study, 1800 rats were divided into several groups and exposed to varying doses of the artificial sweetener aspartame throughout their lifespan. The findings suggested an association between aspartame consumption and the development of two types of cancers, lymphomas and leukemias, in female rats. However, the study faced criticism from the scientific community due to certain methodological limitations, including the rat strain used, the high dose levels tested, and the statistical analysis employed. If these criticisms are valid, _____
>
> 1) What would logically complete the text? Predict an answer:
>
> 2) Now evaluate each answer choice. For the ones that are wrong, what's wrong with them?
>
>   A) aspartame does not cause cancer in rats.
>
>   B) aspartame might be safer for consumption than the study's findings suggest.
>
>   C) no conclusion can be drawn about human consumption of aspartame because humans were not directly studied.
>
>   D) the study's findings are too dated to be useful.

FROM THE BLOG

Go for a walk in the woods. A 2012 University of Michigan study found that memory performance and attention spans improved by 20 percent after people "spent an hour interacting with nature." Our brains can be overwhelmed by the demands placed on them day to day; allowing our minds to wander aimlessly while we are engaged by beautiful surroundings can be hugely restorative.

Practice Set 1: Easy-Medium

Recycling conserves natural resources, diverts waste from landfills and incinerators, reduces greenhouse gas emissions, and can generate significant economic benefits for a community. In a recent study of 11,500 people across 28 countries, 82% of respondents indicated that they believe recycling makes a difference, but only 35% actually recycle regularly. The most commonly cited reasons for not recycling included a lack of convenient access and confusion as to what can and cannot be recycled, suggesting that _____

1 Which choice most logically completes the text?

A. recycling is better as a theory than as a practical solution to the world's problems.
B. a consistent and accessible recycling program with clear rules about recyclables could lead to substantial benefits for a community.
C. many people are aware of only the environmental benefits of recycling and do not consider the economic impact.
D. recycling centers should do a better job educating the community about the benefits of recycling.

In a 2018 study, economists analyzed the impact of minimum wage increases in six different US cities over a five-year period. The researchers found that minimum wage increases led to modest but statistically significant increases in wages for low-wage workers: specifically, a 10% increase in the minimum wage led to a 1.5% increase in wages for workers in the bottom 25% of the wage distribution. Importantly, the study found no significant harm to overall employment levels, suggesting that minimum wage increases _____

2 Which choice most logically completes the text?

A. can improve the economic well-being of low-wage workers without causing a significant increase in joblessness.
B. are the best way to improve the American economy.
C. may benefit middle-income workers more than minimum wage workers or other low-wage workers.
D. created overall beneficial effects in six US cities but may have detrimental effects in cities outside the US.

Studies on the use of health information technology (HIT) often use different definitions and measurements, making it difficult to compare results across studies. In addition, many studies use small sample sizes, which is particularly problematic when researching complex systems such as healthcare delivery. A large number of the studies also focus on only short-term outcomes rather than following patients over time. These problems indicate that the studies _____

3 Which choice most logically completes the text?

A. should be repeated with standardized measurements and other controls.
B. are useful for drawing conclusions about short-term outcomes but not long-term impacts.
C. may not provide reliable conclusions that can be generalized beyond the study participants.
D. faced significant challenges that would have been resolved if the research had concerned a less complex field.

Logical Inferences

Could astronauts really protect us from an asteroid locked into a collision course with Earth? In November 2021, NASA launched its Double Asteroid Redirection Test (DART) mission to find out. The mission's objective was to test the kinetic impactor technique, which involves hitting an asteroid with a spacecraft in order to change its trajectory. The target was a binary asteroid system consisting of a larger body, Didymos, orbited by a moonlet called Dimorphos once every 11 hours 55 minutes. NASA aimed its DART vehicle at Dimorphos with the goal of altering its orbital period by at least 73 seconds. After the impact, researchers announced that Dimorphos's orbit had been shortened to 11 hours 23 minutes, indicating that the kinetic impactor technique _____

4 Which choice most logically completes the text?

A. requires more study to fine-tune the targeting of the asteroid impact.
B. is in need of a re-design, since applying this technique to an asteroid that threatened Earth could actually place the planet in more danger rather than less.
C. may be incapable of inflicting a blow powerful enough to significantly affect the orbit of an asteroid.
D. might serve as a viable option to deflect potentially hazardous asteroids away from Earth.

We experience warmth when molecules of air strike our bodies and transfer their heat. On Earth, where we're surrounded by air, these transfers are happening constantly. But in the exosphere (an atmospheric layer that begins 500 to 1000 km above the Earth's surface), air is incredibly thin: air molecules might be separated by a kilometer or more of empty space. As a result, even though temperatures in the exosphere regularly rise to over 2000°C during the day, _____

5 Which choice most logically completes the text?

A. they can dip down to 0°C overnight.
B. the particle densities are similar to those found in the airless vacuum of space.
C. few gas molecules collide, and some fast-moving particles even escape earth's gravity.
D. if we were suddenly transported to the exosphere, we'd feel cold.

By the 19th century, it was well established in the scientific community that the Earth had once been a molten ball that cooled over time. The prominent physicist Lord Kelvin, assuming that the Earth had cooled uniformly at a constant rate and that there were no other sources of heat for the developing planet, used thermodynamics to estimate that the Earth was between 20 million and 400 million years old. However, later scientists argued that radioactive isotopes can generate heat and affect cooling rates. In the early 20th century, Arthur Holmes measured radioactive decay in rocks to show that the Earth was actually around 4.5 billion years old, an age more than 10 times greater than Kelvin's estimate. This implies that _____

6 Which choice most logically completes the text?

A. radioactive rocks on Earth are older than the Earth itself.
B. Lord Kelvin's estimate was inaccurate because it was based on faulty assumptions.
C. 19th century scientists were incorrect to believe that the Earth had once been a molten ball that cooled over time.
D. radioactive decay affects cooling rates differently on Earth than on other planets.

Practice Set 2: Medium-Hard

In a 2017 experiment, researchers synthesized a nanozyme (a nanoparticle made of cerium oxide) that could both detect and attack pollutants in water. The nanozyme targeted a common pollutant called bisphenol A, known as BPA. Within 30 minutes of exposure to the nanozyme, over 90% of the BPA was degraded; other materials, such as activated carbon and zeolites, were significantly less effective in removing BPA. In addition, the nanozyme was able to detect low concentrations of BPA in water, suggesting that _____

1

Which choice most logically completes the text?

A. nanozymes could be useful not only for the destruction of pollutants but for monitoring water quality as well.
B. BPA is particularly susceptible to short-term cerium oxide exposure.
C. zeolites are more effective at degrading pollutants in water than is activated carbon.
D. activated carbon required more than 30 minutes to detect low BPA concentrations.

Most people expect our national institutions to stand as exemplars for their local corollaries, displaying the acme of aesthetic and scientific achievement. Without the highest levels of funding, however, national institutions will not be able to outperform more localized institutions. Our national zoo, for instance, is continually hampered by real estate and financial constraints and therefore houses many animals in uncomfortably small concrete cages that in no way represent the highest modern zoological standards. It is obvious, then, that _____

2

Which choice most logically completes the text?

A. some of the people who visit the national zoo will be disappointed in the level of care of the habitats.
B. most of the animals in the national zoo are housed in habitats that reflect the current level of zoological habitat standards.
C. the national zoo should raise its standards of habitat development for all of its animals.
D. local zoos enjoy an unfair funding advantage that enables them to outperform the national zoo.

Bacterial species, though unicellular, exist in the natural world as part of a community of other bacterial cells. The individual cells maintain a type of communication with each other by emitting specific chemicals and detecting those emitted by others, a system known as quorum sensing. It is well established that this system affects the production of rhamnolipids, substances that are beneficial for the group as a whole, when the community reaches a certain size: quorum sensing enables the bacteria to determine whether rhamnolipids should be produced (and how many) based on the size of the local bacterial population. Researcher Kerry Boyle and colleagues have found that limiting the amounts of carbon, nitrogen, and iron present in the environment also affects the production of rhamnolipids, suggesting that _____

3

Which choice most logically completes the text?

A. in addition to quorum sensing, an additional system for bacterial communication must exist.
B. bacteria may use quorum sensing to integrate information about resource availability as well as population size.
C. resource availability plays a larger role in rhamnolipid production than does the size of the bacterial population.
D. all three resources are required to be present in sufficient quantities before any production of rhamnolipids can occur.

- 106 -

For centuries, a minority of scholars have argued that William Shakespeare was not the true author of all the works for which he is famous. Due to his relatively humble circumstances, he would have had little direct knowledge with the courtly setting of many of his plays, unlike contemporaries Christopher Marlowe and Francis Bacon. There are stylistic similarities between the work of these writers and the plays attributed to Shakespeare, as well as historical evidence establishing their connections to the theater world. Nonetheless, the fact that Marlowe and Bacon were so widely known may support the theory of Shakespeare's sole authorship: _____

4

Which choice most logically completes the text?

A. a personal familiarity with courtly life is no substitute for a gifted and creative mind.
B. there is no reason to think that Marlowe or Bacon were attempting to copy Shakespeare's style.
C. the similarities could merely be evidence that Shakespeare's writing style was influenced by that of the popular writers of his day.
D. neither one was more qualified than the other to write the Shakespearean sonnets alone.

There has been an undeniable increase in the number of reported cases of autism spectrum disorder (ASD) over the past few decades. In a 2018 study, Santhosh Girirajan and colleagues analyzed the genetic data of over 15,000 individuals with ASD and their family members, as well as a control group of over 10,000 individuals without ASD. The study found that the genetic factors underlying ASD are highly diverse and complex, with multiple mutations and variants contributing to the disorder. The researchers also found that changes in diagnostic criteria have only had a minor effect on the observed increase in ASD cases, and that other factors, such as increased awareness and reporting, are likely more important contributors to the increase. The study did note, however, that changes in diagnostic criteria may have led to an over-representation of individuals with certain genetic mutations in ASD cohorts used in other studies, which suggests that _____

5

Which choice most logically completes the text?

A. these studies may over-estimate the contribution of genetic mutations to ASD.
B. the apparent increase in ASD cases does not necessarily mean that the actual prevalence of the disorder has increased.
C. ASD is caused in greater part by environmental factors than by genetic factors.
D. greater societal awareness of ASD is a more likely explanation for the increase in reported cases than is a change in the way the disorder is defined.

Penguins' ability to survive in some of the coldest climates of the planet is thanks in part to a cluster of arteries and veins pressed against the flipper bone, or humerus. Especially important during long swims in icy waters, the humeral arterial plexus acts both to cool the blood leaving the heart and to warm the blood returning from the flipper tip, helping the penguin to _____

What drove the evolution of bones and teeth? Traditionally, scientists believed that when early vertebrates first evolved their bony scales (a type of external skeleton) about 420 million years ago, they did so purely as a defense mechanism. According to this view, vertebrates did not become predators until the first jawed vertebrates appeared about 20 million years later. But the study of conodonts, a group of extinct marine animals that lived more than 500 million years ago, has altered this picture. Conodont remains show evidence of bony tooth-like structures in the mouth that were likely used to grasp and shred prey, which may have driven other feeding adaptations. This suggests that _____

When two neutron stars collide, the result is a rare astronomical event called a kilonova. This causes a huge release of energy in the form of gravitational waves and a burst of electromagnetic radiation, including visible light, X-rays, and gamma rays. After the impact, both the gravitational waves and the electromagnetic radiation begin traveling away from the site at the speed of light, but some of the electromagnetic radiation is absorbed or scattered by dust and gas as it travels, slowing its progress. In August 2017, scientists detected gravitational waves from the collision of two neutron stars 130 million light-years away, and several hours later, a bright burst of light appeared. This suggests that _____

6

Which choice most logically completes the text?

A. maintain a stable body temperature by limiting heat loss through the flippers.
B. avoid the risk of overheating due to exertion.
C. increase its speed through the water.
D. enhance its survival chances during long winter nights on land.

7

Which choice most logically completes the text?

A. teeth could serve a predatory function in jawed vertebrates.
B. conodonts had no need for protection from either vertebrate or invertebrate predators.
C. the evolution of the vertebrate skeleton may have been driven in part by the need to adapt to different ecological niches.
D. an increase in predatory efficiency may have been one driver in the evolution of bones and/or teeth.

8

Which choice most logically completes the text?

A. any X-rays or gamma rays produced by the collision arrived several hours later than the burst of light.
B. the rate of travel of a gravitational wave is less affected by intervening matter than is the rate of travel of electromagnetic radiation.
C. the burst of electromagnetic radiation was generated several hours later than the gravitational waves.
D. if the collision had occurred less than 130 million light-years away, the burst of light would have preceded or coincided with the gravitational waves.

Writing: Standard English Conventions

These questions are about the mechanics of writing. Think of yourself as an editor reviewing someone else's work: are the commas in the right place? Does the verb agree with the subject? Does the sentence make sense? A mastery of the basic principles of standard English grammar and punctuation will be key here.

Strategy in Brief

Learn the rules. The trickiest part about these questions is that the correct answers don't always "sound" right because they're not the way most people speak on a daily basis, or even necessarily the way they write in informal situations. Remember that this is a test of formal written English, so the answers must be technically correct according to the grammar books.

Shorter is better. The SAT loves concise, clean writing. When in doubt, the choice with the fewest words is most likely to be right.

Trust your ear. As long as the sentence isn't violating a rule of grammar or punctuation, the one that sounds best is most likely to be correct. The test rewards your ability to identify good order, coherence, and unity within passages.

Read carefully. Read the sentence slowly to look for any errors, and be sure you're reading the sentence exactly as it appears on the screen (some of these sentences are so bad that our eye will "correct" them for us without our even noticing).

Re-read. Always take the time to reread the sentence in context with your choice plugged in so that you can make sure it works. ***Be careful not to select an answer choice that fixes one error but creates a different one.***

Sentence Structure

Preview Quiz

Fill in your answer:

1) What is the difference between a "clause" and a "phrase"?

2) What is an "independent clause"?

Correct the sentence fragments below.

3) Many students who use computers.

   _____

4) The doctor from Glasgow eating his breakfast.

   _____

5) Freddie broken a glass.

   _____

Choose the best answer.

6) Taking visual and thematic inspiration from classic film noir, director Ridley Scott—previously best known for the science fiction horror movie "Alien"—repurposed and updated the dark cityscapes of the 1930s genre _____ a grim vision of future Los Angeles perfect for 1982's dystopian "Blade Runner."

   A) in his creating of
   B) was the creator of
   C) to create
   D) created

A **clause** is a string of words that contains both a subject and a verb. Some clauses, known as **independent clauses**, can stand alone as complete sentences:

> *George walks.*
> *I like fish.*

Other clauses (**dependent clauses**) cannot stand alone as complete sentences:

> *Although I like fish...*

While a clause has both a subject and a verb, a **phrase** lacks one or both of those components:

> *...along with liking fish...*

In the punctuation sections coming up, we'll see a lot more about how to connect dependent clauses or phrases to independent clauses, as well as how to link more than one independent clause in the same sentence. But in order for any of that to make sense, you've got to be clear on how to decide whether a particular string of words can stand alone as a sentence or not. So let's jump into sentence structure with a review of some basics.

Verbs are words that express some kind of action: *talk, jump, sit,* and *explode* are all examples of verbs. However, not all actions are physical: *think, love, own,* and *recognize* are verbs as well. And note that for some verbs, the action expressed is merely that of existing, as in *is, seem,* or *become.*

To identify the **subject** of a verb, consider who or what is doing the action expressed by the verb.

    Example: George [walks].
                          subject verb

    Example: The band [rocked].
                          subject verb

Every valid sentence contains a subject and a verb. Some verbs also require an **object**, which is the person/thing *receiving* the action of the verb.

    Example: Everyone [likes] chocolate.
                          subject verb object

Writing: Standard English Conventions

We can use other types of words to add bells and whistles to a sentence. **Adjectives**, **adverbs**, and many kinds of **phrases** can modify and describe the various parts of the sentence.

Example: Everyone in my family really likes Belgian chocolate.
            subject   verb   object

In this sentence, "in my family" is a prepositional phrase modifying *Everyone*, the word "really" is an adverb modifying *likes*, and "Belgian" is an adjective modifying *chocolate*.

If the same subject is performing more than one action, we can connect the verbs with an "and."

Example: Beverly walked into the room and sat behind her desk.
            subject verb   verb

In a sentence like this, it's important to maintain **parallel structure**: the verbs must match each other. For example, this sentence would be incorrect if we replaced "sat" with "sitting" or "sits."

Try It   Correct each of the following sentences.

1) She enjoys studying vocabulary, solving geometry problems, and to diagram sentences.

   _____

   _____

2) Beverly decided to take a risk and opening her own business.

   _____

   _____

3) Before the start of the July 4th barbecue, the food had been laid out by Javier, the drinks chilled by Sue Ellen, and Barbara lit the grill.

   _____

   _____

To analyze whether or not a particular answer choice is a valid sentence, start by finding the **main verb**. But be careful! Verbs located inside a modifying phrase, such as a phrase starting with "who," "which," or "that," can never be the main verb of the sentence. These phrases are just the bells and whistles; they're not giving us an actual action. If the only verb you can find is locked into one of those phrases, then we have a **sentence fragment**, not a valid sentence. See how in the examples below, the incorrect versions still seem to be leading up to something?

Incorrect: The contribution that she made.

Correct: <u>The contribution that she made</u> [was] enormous.
                subject   verb

-or-

Correct: <u>Our family</u> greatly [appreciated] <u>the contribution that she made</u>.
   subject   verb   object

Incorrect: Many students who use computers.

Correct: Many <u>students</u> [use] <u>computers</u>.
      subject verb object

-or-

Correct: Many <u>students who use computers</u> [shop] at Mike's Electronics.
        subject   verb

If we find a verb that's not locked into one of those phrases, we next need to check what **form** it's in. The *–ing* form can be tricky, because these words can act as nouns or adjectives as well as verbs.

Example: <u>Laughing</u> [is] <u>the best exercise</u>.
    subject verb   object

Example: The laughing <u>child</u> [ran] down the street.
      adj.   subj. verb

Example: <u>The three of us</u> [were laughing] for hours.
     subject   verb

Notice that when the *–ing* form is acting as a verb, it must be preceded by some version of the verb "to be" (*is laughing, was laughing, has been laughing*, etc).

Writing: Standard English Conventions

If the only verb you can find in the answer choice is an *-ing* form alone, you have a sentence fragment. Look to fix it either by

- adding one of the "to be" words (*is, was,* etc.) before the *-ing* verb, or
- changing the *-ing* verb to a more active form (e.g., by changing "laughing" to "laughed.")

Incorrect: The doctor from Glasgow eating his breakfast.

Correct: The doctor from Glasgow [is eating] his breakfast.
           subject   verb   object

-or-

Correct: The doctor from Glasgow [eats] his breakfast.
           subject   verb   object

Try It   Turn the following sentence fragments into complete sentences.

4) Eduardo making the bed.   _____

5) The dogs rolling in the mud.   _____

6) Considering my options.   _____

Another verb form that can fool us is the **past participle**, which is the second word in many two-word verb tenses (for example, in the tense "has broken," the past participle is the word "broken"). Like the *-ing* form, a past participle needs an additional word before it in order to act as a verb.

Incorrect: Freddie broken a glass.

Correct: Freddie [has broken] a glass.
         subject   verb   object

-or-

Correct: Freddie [broke] a glass.
         subject   verb   object

> **TIP:**
> The past participle can also be used with the "to be" words, as in "A glass was broken."

Try It   Turn the following sentence fragments into complete sentences.

7) We all seen it happen.   _____

8) The weather been warm.   _____

9) It begun raining.   _____

Of course, the sentences we've seen so far are shorter and simpler than the ones you'll see on the SAT. But the process is still the same. Let's practice taking apart a longer, more complicated sentence to identify the right word for the blank.

Taking visual and thematic inspiration from classic film noir, director Ridley Scott—previously best known for the science fiction horror movie "Alien"—repurposed and updated the dark cityscapes of the 1930s genre _____ a grim vision of future Los Angeles perfect for 1982's dystopian "Blade Runner."

- A) in his creating of
- B) was the creator of
- C) to create
- D) created

To start, we'll try to find the main verb in the original sentence, and then we'll identify its subject. What action words do you see?

Taking both visual and thematic inspiration from classic film noir, director Ridley Scott—previously best known for the science fiction horror movie "Alien"—repurposed and updated the dark cityscapes of the 1930s genre _____ a grim vision of future Los Angeles perfect for 1982's dystopian "Blade Runner."

Well, *taking* is an *–ing* form without one of the "is"-type words before it, so it's not really a verb. The whole opening portion of this sentence (up to the comma) is just an introductory phrase. Similarly, *known* is a past participle without one of the "has"-type words before it, so it's not really a verb either. In this sentence, the entire portion that's set off by dashes is just a phrase modifying *director Ridley Scott*.

Let's try making the sentence simpler by cutting out the two modifying phrases we've identified so far.

Director Ridley Scott repurposed and updated the dark cityscapes of the 1930s genre _____ a grim vision of future Los Angeles perfect for 1982's dystopian "Blade Runner."

Now this is starting to make more sense. The words *repurposed* and *updated* are the main verbs. And *Director Ridley Scott* is doing the action of those verbs, so that's the subject.

Next, try plugging the choices in one at a time. Choices B and D would give us another main verb, meaning we'd need an additional "and" to join it with the two verbs we've got so far. Choices A and C turn the whole last section of the sentence into a phrase, one that makes perfect sense in the sentence. But choice A is awkward and much too wordy for what we need, so the correct answer is **C**.

TIP:

Cutting out the modifying phrases is a great way to simplify a sentence to make it easier to analyze the structure.

Try It   Turn the following sentence fragments into complete sentences.

10) The two students born in a distant country immigrating to the United States ten years ago.
    _____
    _____

11) The teacher, who brought 30 years of experience to the classroom, retiring in the spring.
    _____
    _____

12) Having lived and worked in Los Angeles for many years, unaccustomed to the lifestyle of the countryside.
    _____
    _____

13) Many critics that would have to admit that they misjudged the artist, having overlooked his important talents.
    _____
    _____

14) The author, known for his intricate plots, which often involve detailed knowledge of actual historical events.
    _____
    _____

15) Focusing intently on the details of the experiment right in front of her, the young chemist who didn't notice that anything was wrong with the one set up by her colleague on the other side of the room until the slowly accumulating smoke suddenly set off a blaring fire alarm.
    _____
    _____
    _____

Sentence Structure

Practice Set 1: Easy-Medium

Each generation seems to have its share of famous kidnappings, from Charles Lindbergh's baby in 1932 to Elizabeth Smart in 2002. However, despite the media attention directed at these high-profile cases, studies _____ the incidence of child abduction in the United States is extremely low.

1

Which choice completes the text so that it conforms to the conventions of Standard English?

A. indicating that
B. that indicate
C. having indicated
D. indicate that

The Venus Flytrap's leaves have modified lobes with sensitive trigger hairs. When an insect touches the hairs, the leaves snap _____ the prey and providing the plant with a unique mechanism for supplementing its nutrient intake.

2

Which choice completes the text so that it conforms to the conventions of Standard English?

A. shut. To trap
B. shut. Thus trapping
C. shut, trapping
D. shut. Trapping

Is video gaming a negative influence on children and on society as a whole? The popularity of this sentiment has led many parents to severely curtail their kids' "screen time," but in doing so, they may have overlooked some potential benefits of the habit. _____ games foster technological literacy and hand-eye coordination, according to their proponents.

3

Which choice completes the text so that it conforms to the conventions of Standard English?

A. Since video
B. While video
C. Because video
D. Video

In 1982, Eastside High School in Paterson, New Jersey was a low-performing school in a high-crime area. Principal Joe _____ an unconventional approach to turn the school around, combining strict disciplinary policies and a no-nonsense attitude with increased academic support for struggling students.

4

Which choice completes the text so that it conforms to the conventions of Standard English?

A. Clark, who used
B. Clark, which used
C. Clark with
D. Clark used

A community organization in tiny Beetle, California recently garnered a lot of attention for its grassroots effort to oust the deputy mayor after his controversial statements went viral. The group posted a petition online and blanketed social media with their requests for support. However, with fewer than 100 signatures as of today, one week from the _____ unlikely to succeed.

Compared to Robusta coffee beans, Arabica beans generally have a lower caffeine content and a milder, smoother taste. The cultivation of Arabica _____ specific conditions, including higher altitudes, adequate rainfall, and well-drained soil.

The Great Pyramids of Egypt were primarily built using limestone blocks, which were quarried and transported from nearby locations. Workers would level the terrain, lay out the foundation, and finally, under the watchful eye of the project overseer, _____ the pyramid's core using large, precisely cut stones. The outer casing stones were then added to create a smooth, polished surface.

Populations in Brunei, Indonesia, and Malaysia _____ durian, a tropical fruit known for its pungent odor, for hundreds of years. The fruit is rich in nutrients including vitamins B and C, and is believed to have a range of health benefits, such as reducing inflammation, aiding digestion, and promoting healthy skin.

5

Which choice completes the text so that it conforms to the conventions of Standard English?

A. deadline. Making the petition seem
B. deadline; the petition seeming
C. deadline. The petition seems
D. deadline, the petition seems

6

Which choice completes the text so that it conforms to the conventions of Standard English?

A. coffee often requiring
B. coffee often requires
C. coffee requiring
D. coffee, which often requires

7

Which choice completes the text so that it conforms to the conventions of Standard English?

A. they would construct
B. constructing
C. construct
D. constructed

8

Which choice completes the text so that it conforms to the conventions of Standard English?

A. have cultivated
B. to cultivate
C. having cultivated
D. cultivating

Practice Set 2: Medium-Hard

At Northwestern University, Dr. Chad Mirkin has been at the forefront of developing innovative nanoscale materials and technologies with a wide range of applications. Seemingly every day, _____ the science of nanotechnology.

1

Which choice completes the text so that it conforms to the conventions of Standard English?

A. as his team makes a new discovery that further advances
B. his team makes a new discovery that further advances
C. making a new discovery and further advancing
D. making a new discovery to further advance

To convince the town council of the wisdom of permitting the installation of a new parking garage, the businessman described the aesthetic benefits of moving parked cars indoors, _____ that no new taxes would need to be levied in order for the structure to be built.

2

Which choice completes the text so that it conforms to the conventions of Standard English?

A. details how the structure would be paid for, and indicated
B. detailing how the structure would be paid for, and indicating
C. detailed how the structure would be paid for, and indicated
D. he detailed how the structure would be paid for, and indicating

Louisa May _____ years crafting her stories and developing her skills as a writer only to face repeated rejection and discouragement from the male-dominated publishing industry of 19th century America. Despite these obstacles, she eventually succeeded in bringing *Little Women* to print and became one of the most celebrated authors of her era.

3

Which choice completes the text so that it conforms to the conventions of Standard English?

A. Alcott, who spent
B. Alcott, having spent
C. Alcott spent
D. Alcott will be spending

Corvids, the avian family that includes crows, jays, and ravens, have excellent reasoning skills. A study at the University Cambridge comparing corvids' puzzle-solving ability to that of human children demonstrated that corvids can analyze a difficult _____ still displaying a calm demeanor at all times.

4

Which choice completes the text so that it conforms to the conventions of Standard English?

A. problem, devise a unique solution, while
B. problem and devise a unique solution while
C. problem, devising a unique solution, and
D. problem, devise a unique solution, meanwhile

Commas

Preview Quiz

Add commas where necessary. (Some sentences are fine the way they are.)

1) The girl who won the state spelling bee lives next door to me.

2) Louise who studied engineering at MIT designed the city's largest bridge.

3) George described the process as "a miracle of modern science."

4) The truth however is that I never liked snowboarding.

5) The movies that I want to see are Spanish.

6) Noted physicist Albert Einstein sold my uncle this car.

7) Loretta always wanted to be on TV so she was thrilled when she heard about auditions for a new reality show.

8) The heavy ugly coat kept me extremely warm throughout the winter.

9) John looked around him and checked for spiders.

There are really only **three basic functions** that commas can serve in a sentence. Once you've mastered those, comma questions on the SAT become a lot easier.

1. **Setting off unnecessary information**

    Mark off unnecessary ("parenthetical") information with commas. Consider the differences between the two sentences below.

    The girl <u>who won the state spelling bee</u> lives next door to me.

    Louise, <u>who studied engineering at MIT</u>, designed the city's largest bridge.

    In the first sentence, the phrase in the middle is **necessary**: we need the information in the phrase to identify which girl we're talking about. In the second sentence, however, we'd know who we were talking about ("Louise") even without the phrase; the phrase gives us extra information, not something crucial to our understanding.

    Unnecessary information can be an entire phrase or a single word, and it can appear anywhere in the sentence:

    <u>Sleeping soundly in his bed</u>, Justin never heard Santa coming down the chimney.

    Every time I see that girl, <u>the one with the red hair</u>, she smiles at me.

    The father addressed the search party, <u>his emotions etched on his face</u>.

    The truth, <u>however</u>, is that I never liked snowboarding.

    > *TIP:*
    >
    > Remember, when you **DON'T** need the information, you **DO** need the commas.

    In each of these sentences, we could lift out the underlined portion without changing the meaning of the sentence. That's how we know to use commas there.

    CHALLENGE:

    Sometimes the number of items determines whether or not the information is necessary.

    My friend Jake told me a great joke the other day.

    My youngest sister, Kate, is attending medical school.

    In the first sentence, the name "Jake" is necessary information because it identifies *which* of the speaker's friends told a great joke. In the second sentence, however, the name is unnecessary—a person can only have one *youngest* sister, so we don't need the name to figure out who we're talking about.

Phrases that start with "that" are always necessary to the sentence, while phrases that start with "which" are always unnecessary. So, **"which" phrases always take commas; "that" phrases never take commas.**

Those movies, <u>which are all Spanish</u>, are my brother's favorites.

The movies <u>that I want to see</u> are Spanish.

You can sometimes use this rule even on phrases that don't use a "that" or a "which." If you can insert the word "that" at the beginning of the phrase and the sentence makes sense, don't use a comma.

Dad always said you have to spend money to make money.

In this sentence, there's an unspoken "that." After all, we could have written it as "Dad always said *that* you have to spend money to make money." Therefore, we can treat that whole section of the sentence as a "that" phrase: no commas.

CHALLENGE:

You don't always need a comma before a quotation.

George said, "The process is a miracle of modern science."

"The process is a miracle of modern science," said George.

George described the process as "a miracle of modern science."

When we set off a quote separately from the structure of the sentence with a phrase such as "he said" (as in the first two examples here), we mark that barrier with a comma. However, when the quote is incorporated into the grammar of the sentence (as in the third example), no commas are used.

Commas

> **Try It** Add commas where necessary.
>
> 1) The books that I wanted to buy were expensive.
> 2) My favorite tennis player is Roger Federer who won Wimbledon this year.
> 3) Although I really like chocolate ice cream vanilla is my favorite.
> 4) Because Maria enjoyed both writing and photography she decided to join the school's newspaper staff.
> 5) Joanne an expert in medieval architecture told us that the castle was built in the 1300s.
> 6) Nobody suspected that the quiet computer salesman was actually an accomplished sword swallower.
> 7) On the other hand avocados are high in healthful fatty acids.
> 8) I enjoy the challenge of learning a new language.
> 9) Dr. Phillips the best-known pediatrician in Chicago received an award from the governor last year.
> 10) After high school she attended a culinary academy in Paris led by the great chef Victor Richambaud.

TIP:

A clause that can stand alone as a sentence is **never** unnecessary information.

Incorrect: `Many dog breeds can be mixed, a Chihuahua and an Irish Wolfhound would be a bad combination.`

Neither side of this sentence can be considered unnecessary information, because each side is an independent clause: that is, each side forms a complete sentence on its own. This is called a **comma splice**, and it is always wrong.

To fix it, we could change the punctuation:

Correct: Many dog breeds can be mixed; a Chihuahua and an Irish Wolfhound would be a bad combination.

Or we could keep the comma but alter one of the clauses so that it can no longer stand on its own:

Correct: *Although* many dog breeds can be mixed, a Chihuahua and an Irish Wolfhound would be a bad combination.

Or we could simply add one of the FANBOYS after the comma, as we'll see in the next section.

Correct: Many dog breeds can be mixed, *but* a Chihuahua and an Irish Wolfhound would be a bad combination.

CHALLENGE:

When there are a few words before or after someone's name that tell us that person's occupation and/or place of origin (e.g., "Guatemalan author María Sanchez"), you can think of that entire description as a job title. To punctuate it correctly, there are two simple rules to keep in mind.

If the job title comes before the name, the job title is *never* unnecessary information. So there are really only two possibilities for this kind of sentence: either the *name* is unnecessary information, or nothing is. To check these sentences, lift out the name and see whether you still have a valid sentence.

> *Correct: The college's new provost, Marcel Ridley, will be arriving on Tuesday.*

Try it without the name: "The college's new provost will be arriving on Tuesday." That's a valid sentence, so the name is unnecessary information. Therefore, we set it off with commas.

> *Correct: Noted physicist Albert Einstein sold my uncle this car.*

Take out the name this time and we have this: "Noted physicist sold my uncle this car." That's not a valid sentence, so no commas.

However! The above only applies when the job title comes before the name. **If the name comes first**, then the job title *can* be unnecessary information.

> *Correct: Albert Einstein, the noted physicist, sold my uncle this car.*

Try It   Add commas where necessary.

11) Austrian mathematician Hannah Berg is scheduled to speak next.

12) The evening's top award went to Sally Martinez inventor of the Flybock maneuver.

13) My favorite English teacher Manny Kozlowski just published his first novel.

14) The study was conducted by renowned botanist Frederick Chang.

15) Chad Smith the drummer for the Red Hot Chili Peppers bears a striking resemblance to comedian Will Ferrell.

2. **Comma + FANBOYS = Period**

When a comma is paired with one of the coordinating conjunctions, also known as the "FANBOYS" (*for, and, nor, but, or, yet, so*), it acts just like a period: it separates two clauses that could each stand alone as a sentence.

> *Loretta always wanted to be on TV, so she was thrilled when she heard about auditions for a new reality show.*
>
> *I tried the restaurant that Lauren had recommended, but I wasn't impressed.*

If two independent clauses are separated by a comma alone (without one of the FANBOYS), the comma is wrong.

> Incorrect: ```Loretta always wanted to be on TV, she was thrilled when she heard about auditions for a new reality show.```

If two clauses are separated by the comma-plus-FANBOYS combination and either of the clauses *cannot* stand alone as a sentence, the comma is wrong.

> Incorrect: ```Loretta always wanted to be on TV, so was thrilled when she heard about auditions for a new reality show.```

Be on the lookout for words that seem very similar to FANBOYS trying to take their place. Common offenders include *however, therefore, also, furthermore,* and *nevertheless*.

> Incorrect: ```I tried the restaurant that Lauren had recommended, however I wasn't impressed.```

TIP:

Sometimes, the right answer choice will correct a sentence in a way that you weren't expecting. You may not have the option to either add FANBOYS or change the punctuation. Instead, one of the clauses that can stand on its own as a sentence may just be rewritten so that it can't stand on its own anymore.

Incorrect: ```He faced many obstacles in his early life, the child went on to become president of the United States.```

Correct: Having faced many obstacles in his early life, the child went on to become president of the United States.

Writing: Standard English Conventions

Try It Which version(s) of these sentences is/are correct? **Choose <u>all that apply.</u>**

16) Most new businesses fail in the first _____ the chef has high hopes for his new restaurant.

   A. year, but
   B. year, nevertheless

17) Rowing crew is the perfect _____ it works all the major muscle groups and provides a great cardiovascular workout.

   A. exercise,
   B. exercise because

18) Nancy participated in student government throughout high school, _____ was president her senior year.

   A. and she
   B. she

19) Elizabeth couldn't _____ she knew that Mr. Darcy had captured her heart.

   A. refuse, for
   B. refuse because

20) I might make the trip in the _____ might do it tonight.

   A. morning, on the other hand, I
   B. morning, or I

21) I have tried _____ of the items on the menu.

   A. all but one
   B. all, but one

22) _____ some people still prefer vinyl records.

   A. MP3s offer adequate quality of sound, but
   B. Although MP3s offer adequate quality of sound,

23) _____ was sure that it would run correctly.

   A. She had thoroughly bug-tested the program, so
   B. Having thoroughly bug-tested the program, she

24) Everyone I know loves Mr. _____ is by far the best teacher at my school.

   A. Williams, he
   B. Williams, who

3. Lists

Perhaps the most obvious use of commas is to separate items on a list.

> *I like apples, pears, and kumquats.*
>
> *The heavy, ugly coat kept me extremely warm throughout the winter.*

Just a few things to watch out for here. If the list consists of only two items and they're joined with an "and," don't use a comma.

> Incorrect: `The coat was heavy, and ugly.`

Also, make sure you don't use a comma to *introduce* a list.

> Incorrect: `I like, apples, pears, and kumquats.`

TIP:

When list items consist of whole actions or phrases, it's easy to confuse a two-item list joined with an "and" (which doesn't take a comma) with a FANBOYS sentence (which does).

Incorrect: `John looked around him, and checked for spiders.`

Correct: John looked around him and checked for spiders.

CHALLENGE:

When a list of two or more adjectives is used before a noun, see whether the sentence would still make sense if you swapped the order of the adjectives. If they would, you need a comma between them.

Try It   Add commas where necessary.

25) The sweet cold lemonade rushed down my throat.

26) The brochure features several colorful photographs.

27) The large Siamese cat purred happily in the corner.

28) Felicia is a happy witty child.

Try It Which version(s) of these sentences is/are correct? **Choose <u>all that apply.</u>**

29) She felt _____ hopeful.

    A. happy, and
    B. happy and

30) Chefs _____ of a new dish are as important as its taste.

    A. assert, that the presentation aroma and mouthfeel
    B. assert that, the presentation aroma and mouthfeel
    C. assert that the presentation, aroma, and mouthfeel

31) The best _____ or me.

    A. man will be Jim, Bobby,
    B. man, will be Jim, Bobby

32) Amy picked up a _____ began to read.

    A. magazine, and
    B. magazine and

33) _____ love hockey.

    A. Elliott, Maria, and the children
    B. Elliott, Maria and the children,

34) The garment's most popular _____

    A. colors include, turquoise, burgundy, and aubergine.
    B. colors include turquoise, burgundy, and aubergine.
    C. colors, include turquoise, burgundy, and aubergine.

35) He developed a taste for the finer _____ racked up a substantial amount of debt.

    A. things and soon
    B. things, and he soon
    C. things, and soon

36) The fascinating _____ remained at the Smithsonian for a month.

    A. exhibit, of prehistoric, hunting tools,
    B. exhibit, of prehistoric hunting tools,
    C. exhibit of prehistoric hunting tools,
    D. exhibit of prehistoric hunting tools

Common Comma Errors

Now that we've seen the three reasons to use a comma, let's take a look at some of the reasons *not* to.

- **Separating subject from verb or verb from object**

  You may have learned that a comma indicates a pause in a sentence. That's true! It's just not very helpful. The problem is that we pause for lots of reasons, and not all of them require a comma. If the only purpose the comma is serving is to allow for a breath of air between a lengthy subject and its verb, or between a verb and its object, that is not a good enough reason for the comma to be there.

  Incorrect: The only thing I could do, was wait.

  Incorrect: The necklace I was sure was lost forever, turned up in the bottom of my purse.

- **Commas before prepositional phrases** (phrases starting with "of," "in," "at," "with," "between," etc.)

  Commas before prepositions are usually incorrect.

  Incorrect: The dog sat, in the doorway.

  Incorrect: We knew that the entire group, of twenty, would be difficult to seat together.

> **TIP:** Don't start worrying about whether a prepositional phrase is necessary or unnecessary information. Just remember that as a general rule, you don't want a comma before a preposition.

- **Comma splices**

  A comma splice occurs when a comma is used alone (without one of the FANBOYS) to separate two clauses that could each stand alone as sentences.

  Incorrect: Amy knows me better than anyone, also she'd never betray a friend.

  Incorrect: I really like the new app, it makes budgeting much easier.

That's it! Those are the only reasons to ever use a comma. So, when trying to decide whether a particular comma belongs in a sentence, ask yourself what purpose it's serving.

- Is it setting off a phrase of unnecessary information?
- Is it separating two clauses that could be sentences (with one of the FANBOYS)?
- Is it separating items on a list?

If the answer to all three questions is no, the comma is **wrong**.

TIP: A good rule of thumb is that the choice with the fewest commas is most likely to be right.

TIP:

There are a few other functions for commas in English, but they're so easy that they won't be tested—and if they ever were, the answer would be so obvious that you wouldn't have to worry about asking yourself these questions.

Today is Monday, January 24.

I live in Bethesda, Maryland.

That office belongs to George Banks, Ph.D.

Try It In the blank, write the letter corresponding to the function that the comma or commas are serving in the sentence. If none apply, cross out the comma.

A: Unnecessary information   B: Comma + FANBOYS = period   C: Lists   X: None

37) Sitting in the next room were two students, their parents, and the principal. _____
38) That puppy, which belongs to my neighbor, loves to dig up my mother's azaleas. _____
39) The apparent chaos, is actually a well-ordered system. _____
40) Unfortunately, the weather was cloudy. _____
41) The books were perfectly arranged, in a row. _____
42) We knew a change was coming, and we weren't sure what to expect. _____
43) James no longer needed, my help. _____
44) Gandhi proved, that violence is not a prerequisite for social change. _____
45) My grandmother does not need a cookbook, for she knows all the recipes by heart. _____
46) Having established the crime's timeline, the detective turned his attention to the question of motive. _____

Practice Set 1: Easy-Medium

Computer programs can be designed to search for mathematical proofs automatically, without human intervention. This involves encoding mathematical statements and rules into a logical framework that the computer can _____ manipulate. While this approach has limitations, it has been used successfully to solve some challenging mathematical problems.

1

Which choice completes the text so that it conforms to the conventions of Standard English?

A. both understand, and
B. both, understand, and
C. both understand and
D. both understand and,

When dealing with older manuscripts, many publishers routinely update the spelling and punctuation to conform with modern standards. The "corrected" _____ and understand, is thereby made accessible to a wider audience. But professor Ruth Metlow opposes this practice, arguing the archaic spelling and punctuation can provide valuable insights into the historical context of the manuscript.

2

Which choice completes the text so that it conforms to the conventions of Standard English?

A. version, which is easier, to read
B. version, which is easier to read,
C. version which is easier to read,
D. version, which is easier to read

"Groupthink" is a psychological phenomenon that occurs when a group of individuals prioritize group harmony and consensus over critical thinking and independent decision-making. In a groupthink scenario, members of a group may feel pressure to conform to the majority opinion, _____ opinions or alternative ideas may be suppressed or ignored.

3

Which choice completes the text so that it conforms to the conventions of Standard English?

A. also dissenting
B. and dissenting
C. additionally, dissenting
D. dissenting

Garlic, a flavorful ingredient used in many cuisines around the _____ believed to have numerous health benefits. For example, garlic has been found to help lower total and LDL ("bad") cholesterol levels in the blood, which can reduce the risk of heart disease.

4

Which choice completes the text so that it conforms to the conventions of Standard English?

A. world, is
B. world is
C. world and is
D. world, being

Writing: Standard English Conventions

Any restaurateur will tell you that surging to the top of the competitive dining scene is no easy task. Despite the name, _____ actually years in the making.

5

Which choice completes the text so that it conforms to the conventions of Standard English?

A. every "overnight success" is
B. every "overnight success," is
C. every, "overnight success" is
D. every, "overnight success" is,

After months of negotiation between four countries in the region, a new trade partnership was announced. The agreement was instantly _____ protests from all sides of the political spectrum.

6

Which choice completes the text so that it conforms to the conventions of Standard English?

A. controversial, sparking
B. controversial, it sparked
C. controversial with it being the spark of
D. controversial, and sparking

In 1957, Wham-O, a toy company in California, began manufacturing plastic hula hoops and launched a marketing campaign to promote them. At the time, there was a growing interest in physical fitness and dance, and the hula hoop appealed to these trends. Its popularity was further fueled by endorsements from celebrities, including Lucille Ball and Jackie Kennedy. Their participation _____ the most popular toy in America.

7

Which choice completes the text so that it conforms to the conventions of Standard English?

A. helped solidify the hula-hoop's status, as
B. helped solidify, the hula-hoop's status as,
C. helped solidify, the hula-hoop's status as
D. helped solidify the hula-hoop's status as

Elementary education does not offer much freedom of choice. Children attend the classes picked out for them, complete the homework they are assigned, and follow many other one-size-fits-all rules. One exception is lunch: in many school _____ from a variety of options.

8

Which choice completes the text so that it conforms to the conventions of Standard English?

A. cafeterias, students are permitted to select their meals
B. cafeterias, students are permitted to select, their meals
C. cafeterias students are permitted to select their meals,
D. cafeterias, students are permitted to select their meals,

Practice Set 2: Medium-Hard

Stationery manufacturers _____ a variety of methods to generate a pure white color in the final result. One common method is to use bleaching agents, such as chlorine or hydrogen peroxide, which remove the natural color from the wood pulp used to make paper. Another method is to add fluorescent dyes or pigments to the paper. These colorants absorb ultraviolet light and emit a visible blue or violet light, which makes the paper appear brighter and whiter to the human eye.

1

Which choice completes the text so that it conforms to the conventions of Standard English?

A. attempting to produce saleable writing paper, may use
B. attempting to produce saleable writing paper may use
C. attempting, to produce saleable writing paper, may use
D. attempting to produce saleable writing paper, may use,

In her _____ innovative routines that blended traditional African styles with contemporary dance forms. Overton Walker was part of a generation of African-American performers who helped to break down racial barriers in the entertainment industry, paving the way for future generations.

2

Which choice completes the text so that it conforms to the conventions of Standard English?

A. performances Aida Overton Walker, a prominent African-American dancer and choreographer, showcased
B. performances, Aida Overton Walker, a prominent African-American dancer and choreographer, showcased
C. performances, Aida Overton Walker, a prominent African-American dancer and choreographer, showcased,
D. performances Aida Overton Walker a prominent African-American dancer and choreographer showcased

Over time, medical consensus on the use of hormone replacement therapy (HRT) in menopausal women has _____ between two opposing positions. In the 1990s, HRT was widely prescribed to help manage symptoms of menopause and prevent osteoporosis. However, in the early 2000s, large-scale studies suggested that HRT could increase the risk of breast cancer. This led to a significant shift in medical consensus, and many women stopped taking HRT. More recent studies have suggested that the risks of HRT may be lower than previously thought, leading some experts to argue that the benefits of HRT may outweigh the risks.

3

Which choice completes the text so that it conforms to the conventions of Standard English?

A. shifted back and forth
B. shifted back, and forth
C. shifted, back and forth
D. shifted back and forth,

Under Armour is a sports equipment and apparel company that is headquartered in Baltimore. The _____ comes from Maryland.

4

Which choice completes the text so that it conforms to the conventions of Standard English?

A. founder and executive chairman, Kevin Plank,
B. founder and executive chairman Kevin Plank,
C. founder, and executive chairman, Kevin Plank
D. founder and executive chairman, Kevin Plank

Typhlodromus mites are tiny predators that feed on the eggs, larvae, and adult stages of plant pests. One _____ is that the mites are highly specific in their feeding habits, targeting only certain types of pests and leaving beneficial insects unharmed.

5

Which choice completes the text so that it conforms to the conventions of Standard English?

A. advantage of using the *Typhlodromus* mite as a biological control agent
B. advantage, of using the *Typhlodromus* mite as a biological control agent
C. advantage, of using the *Typhlodromus* mite as a biological control agent,
D. advantage of using the *Typhlodromus* mite as a biological control agent,

Though information is safer when saved to the _____ security threats still exist. Cloud storage providers can be targeted by hackers, resulting in the exposure of sensitive data from thousands of users.

6

Which choice completes the text so that it conforms to the conventions of Standard English?

A. cloud, than it would be sitting in a physical file cabinet
B. cloud, than it would be sitting, in a physical file cabinet,
C. cloud than it would be sitting in a physical file cabinet,
D. cloud, than it would be sitting in a physical file cabinet,

Antilock brakes (ABS) are designed to help prevent skidding during hard braking. When a wheel begins to slow down more rapidly than the _____ that it may be about to lock up, the ABS system momentarily reduces the brake pressure to that wheel. This allows the wheel to continue rotating and maintain traction with the road, which can help the driver maintain control of the vehicle.

7

Which choice completes the text so that it conforms to the conventions of Standard English?

A. others, this indicates
B. others, indicating
C. others and indicating
D. others, the system indicates

Semicolons, Colons, Dashes, and Apostrophes

Preview Quiz

Choose the best punctuation.

1) The weather was terrible (, / ;) it rained all day.

2) I have traveled to Paris (, / ;) France (, / ;) Ireland (, / ;) where my mother was born (, / ;) and Japan.

3) The governor promised not to raise taxes (, / ;) however (, / ;) economists say some increases will be necessary.

4) Professor Westing's midterms are notoriously difficult. I'm not worried (, / ;) however (, / ;) my study group has come up with a solid review process that should put me in a great position to ace the exam.

5) Joe is scared of many things (, / ; / :) including getting attacked by lions, falling into swimming pools, and being buried alive.

6) There's only one thing that scares Joe (, / ; / :) lions.

7) Certain musical genres (; / : / —) classical and electronic, for instance (; / : / —) are often classified as "art music."

Fill in the best answer.

8) What is the difference between *its* and *it's*?

9) What is the difference between *your* and *you're*?

Add apostrophes where necessary. Some sentences may be fine the way they are.

10) Thelmas son bought the mayors wifes dog.

11) All three movies screenplays were well written.

12) The womens coalition also fought for childrens rights.

13) I dont think its wise to tell Gerry that he shouldnt play tennis.

14) The Morgans and the Stanleys meet for dinner on Tuesdays.

15) Both girls dresses are beautiful.

Semicolons

The semicolon, like the comma-plus-FANBOYS combination, separates two clauses that each could stand on its own as a sentence. So:

Semicolon = period

Incorrect: `The weather was terrible; raining all day.`

Correct: The weather was terrible; it rained all day.

TIP: If you can replace a semicolon in a sentence with a period, the semicolon is correct.

Semicolons do *not* need FANBOYS, so watch out for sentences that insert FANBOYS after a semicolon for no reason.

Incorrect: `The weather was terrible; for it rained all day.`

CHALLENGE:

A secondary use for semicolons is to separate items on a complicated list (a list in which some or all of the list items themselves contain commas).

Incorrect: `I have traveled to Paris, France, Ireland, where my mother was born, and Japan.`

The commas make it look like this person has traveled to five distinct places: the first is Paris, the second is France, the third is Ireland, the fourth is where their mother was born, and the fifth is Japan. Use semicolons to make it easier to find the divisions between the list items.

Correct: I have traveled to Paris, France; Ireland, where my mother was born; and Japan.

Try It — Choose the correct punctuation.

1) My favorite team is the Red Sox (, / ;) even though they disappoint me every year.

2) Theodore Roosevelt was the youngest president in U.S. history (, / ;) he was 41 when he took office.

3) Jim's parents completely approved of his decision (, / ;) and this approval allowed him to pursue his goal.

4) Mr. Wilson's tests are (, / ;) according to many students (, / ;) quite challenging (, / ;) they also tend to be extremely time-consuming.

5) I thought that the weather would be cloudy (, / ;) however (, / ;) I was wrong.

Why do we sometimes surround transitions like "however" with two commas, while at other times we need to use a semicolon and a comma?

The difference lies in **how many sentences you have** when you take the transition word/phrase out. If there's just one, use two commas. If there are two, use a semicolon (or colon, period, etc.) and a comma.

Example 1: The bearded dragon, however, is an expert climber.

Here, without the "however," we just have a single sentence: "The bearded dragon is an expert climber." So we can regard the "however" as unnecessary information and mark it off with a pair of commas.

Example 2: The governor promised not to raise taxes; however, economists say some increases will be necessary.

This time there are two sentences: "The governor promised not to raise taxes" and "Economists say some increases will be necessary." So, we use a semicolon to separate them. The comma after the "however" is there because the "however" is now unnecessary information in the second sentence.

Try It   Choose the correct punctuation.

6) The restaurant's food has been widely praised (, / ;) for example (, / ;) the *Tribune* called its poached salmon dish "a triumph."

7) Woodworking (, / ;) in conclusion (, / ;) is a rewarding hobby for senior citizens and younger people alike.

8) Belinda does well in all her classes (, / ;) however (, / ;) unlike her older brother.

9) Patrick is a talented musician (, / ;) moreover (, / ;) he's a skilled painter as well.

CHALLENGE:

We've already seen that the word "however" might have commas around it, or it might have a semicolon before it and a comma after it. But is it ever the other way around? Can we have a comma before the "however" and a semicolon after it?

Yes. We still need two independent clauses to make the semicolon work. In these sentences, though, the "however" is not contrasting the first half of the sentence from the second half of the sentence; it's contrasting the entire sentence from something that came before it.

Example: *Professor Westing's midterms are notoriously difficult. I'm not worried, however; my study group has come up with a solid review process that should put me in a great position to ace the exam.*

FROM THE BLOG

We love and crave the feeling of success, but the benefits are often distant and unknown, while the costs are near and certain. Many of us, for example, have had to weigh the benefits of eating a donut against making minute progress on our path to physical wellness. This is hardly a fair fight. (A donut!? Please!) We may get a different result, though, if success is reframed as putting on running shoes, drinking a glass of water and ignoring the donut. Instead of feeling daunted by a remote, difficult goal, we open the possibility of an ennobling victory.

It turns out, according to mounting social-science literature, that success is built on just these sorts of small wins. To get where you want to be on the SAT, the first step may be to commit to studying three punctuation rules a day, reviewing one Reading question type, or completing a single probability question. Once you start, there's a good chance that you'll keep working for 15-30 minutes. Even if you don't, reward yourself anyway. In a small way, you've already won.

Colons

The function of the colon is to ***introduce***. Most commonly, it introduces a list, but it can also introduce a single item or even a complete sentence.

Correct: Joe is scared of many things: getting attacked by lions, falling into swimming pools, and being buried alive.

Correct: There's only one thing that scares Joe: lions.

Correct: Joe has obviously conquered his fears: he went on an African safari last summer.

A sentence that uses a colon must follow these two basic rules:

- The part *before* the colon must be able to stand on its own as a sentence.

    Incorrect: `Joe is scared of many things, including: getting attacked by lions, falling into swimming pools, and being buried alive.`

- The part *after* the colon must consist **only** of whatever's being introduced, with nothing else added on.

    Incorrect: `Joe is scared of many things: such as getting attacked by lions, falling into swimming pools, and being buried alive.`

TIP:

For sentences that use connecting words like "including," choose a comma instead of a colon.

Correct: Joe is scared of many things, including getting attacked by lions, falling into swimming pools, and being buried alive.

The comma is valid because everything after the word "things" in this sentence is unnecessary information.

Writing: Standard English Conventions

Try It   Which choice completes the text so that it conforms to the conventions of Standard English?

10) The process of manufacturing a space _____ lengthy, expensive, and fascinating.

  A) suit is:
  B) suit: is
  C) suit is
  D) suit, is

11) There's only one kind of parking space _____ the rare kind.

  A) in Bethesda
  B) in Bethesda:
  C) in Bethesda, just
  D) in Bethesda, it's

12) Beyoncé made clear in her first solo _____ that she was trying to forge a new identity separate from that of Destiny's Child.

  A) album: *Dangerously in Love*
  B) album, *Dangerously in Love,*
  C) album *Dangerously in Love:*
  D) album *Dangerously in Love;*

13) _____ French, Polynesian, and modern American cuisine.

  A) Among the principal influences on the chef's menu were:
  B) The principal influences on the chef's menu were:
  C) There were several principal influences on the chef's menu, which included:
  D) Among the principal influences on the chef's menu were

Dashes

Dashes can take on many roles in a sentence. They may function as commas, as parentheses, or as colons.

> *Scarlett will wear a bold dress to the party—even if others are appalled.*
>
> *Certain musical genres—classical and electronic, for instance—are often classified as "art music."*
>
> *Some rights are inalienable—life, liberty, and the pursuit of happiness.*

Be on the lookout for **pairs**. A pair of dashes, like a pair of commas, can set off a phrase of unnecessary information in the middle of a sentence. But you can't have a dash on one end of the phrase and a comma on the other: it's two commas or two dashes, not one of each. Remember to look at the whole sentence, not just the underlined portion, before choosing an answer.

Incorrect: `Paella, a rice-based dish popular in Spain—is my mother's specialty.`

Correct: Paella, a rice-based dish popular in Spain, is my mother's specialty.

-or-

Correct: Paella—a rice-based dish popular in Spain—is my mother's specialty.

> **TIP:**
>
> To be clear, dashes don't *always* come in pairs. It's just a pattern that appears frequently on the SAT, so it's a good thing to watch out for.

Writing: Standard English Conventions

Try It Which choice completes the text so that it conforms to the conventions of Standard English?

14) Many celebrities—particularly _____ overwhelmed by too much exposure.

   A) those in the tabloids are
   B) those in the tabloids, are
   C) those in the tabloids—are
   D) those, in the tabloids, are

15) _____ was a major distribution point during the Gold Rush of the mid-19th century.

   A) Sacramento—the capital of California,
   B) Sacramento the capital of California
   C) Sacramento, the capital of California—
   D) Sacramento, the capital of California,

16) Twenty-six miles later, she glimpsed the finish line, and she felt her heart pound to the beat of a _____ victory.

   A) single, glorious word—
   B) single glorious word;
   C) single, glorious, word,
   D) single glorious word

Apostrophes

One of the two main uses of an apostrophe is to show **possession**. For singular nouns, this is pretty simple: just add an apostrophe and the letter "s" to the end of the word.

Thelma's son bought the mayor's wife's dog.

Phyllis's first priority was repairing her dress's broken zipper.

For plural nouns, you'll usually just add an apostrophe, without the additional letter "s."

All three movies' screenplays were well written.

There is one exception: when the plural noun does not already end in "s." For these, add an apostrophe and the letter "s," just as you would for a singular noun.

The women's coalition also fought for children's rights.

> **TIP:**
> The part of the word that comes BEFORE the apostrophe is what we're making possessive.
>
> the student's plans = one student with multiple plans
>
> the students' plan = multiple students who share one plan

Try It — Assuming the sentences below are correctly punctuated, evaluate whether the word in question is singular or plural.

		How many...	one	more than one
17)	The girl's dresses are over there.	girls?	___	___
18)	The men's pants are striped.	men?	___	___
19)	Max is the class's best student.	classes?	___	___
20)	The mice's cheese was hidden.	mice?	___	___
21)	I believed my sisters' story.	sisters?	___	___

The other function of the apostrophe is to form **contractions**. The apostrophe replaces the letters or numbers removed when the contraction is formed.

I don't think it's wise to tell Gerry that he shouldn't play tennis.

Wendy's unsure why the books she'd like to read haven't been available at the library.

The Berlin Wall fell in '89.

Common apostrophe errors

Don't use an apostrophe to make a pronoun possessive.

We make nouns possessive by attaching an apostrophe. But pronouns (*he*, *she*, *it*, *they*) don't work that way—when we want to make them possessive, we use an entirely different word instead. For example, we don't say, "This is *he's* book." We say, "This is *his* book." Words like *its* and *your* work the same way as *his*—they're just a bit tougher to remember because they each look or sound like a word that uses an apostrophe.

We can use apostrophes with pronouns only when we're making contractions. For example, "it's" is a contraction that stands in for the phrase "it is" (or "it has"). So when faced with an "it's" on the SAT, the easiest way to test it is to try replacing the "it's" with the complete phrase. You can use similar tests for "you're," "they're," and "who's."

> **TIP:**
> The **only** reason to attach an apostrophe to a pronoun is to make a contraction.

Try It   Use the stated rule to choose the correct word.

If "it is" makes sense, use "it's." Otherwise, use "its."

22) Our basketball team beat (its/it's) biggest rival in overtime.

23) The forecasters say (its/it's) going to rain tomorrow.

If "you are" makes sense, use "you're." Otherwise, use "your."

24) (Your/You're) going to love the new jacket I bought.

25) Is this (your/you're) backpack?

If "they are" makes sense, use "they're." Otherwise, use "their."

26) The students were curious about (their/they're) new classmates.

27) I think (their/they're) going to enjoy the field trip.

If "who is" makes sense, use "who's." Otherwise, use "whose."

28) (Whose/Who's) going to be the captain next year?

29) Everyone is wondering (whose/who's) gym bag that is.

> **TIP:**
> The following are **always wrong**:
>
> its'   their's
>
> your's   her's

Don't use an apostrophe to pluralize.

An apostrophe cannot make something plural. Unless you're making a contraction or showing possession, there's no need to involve an apostrophe.

Incorrect:	`The Morgan's and the Stanley's meet for dinner on Tuesday's.`
Correct:	The Morgans and the Stanleys meet for dinner on Tuesdays.

CHALLENGE:

The toughest apostrophe questions will have two words in a row that both contain apostrophes. The testmakers are trying to confuse you by throwing so much at you at once, so don't let them succeed. Focus on one word at a time. For that first word, first ask yourself this: *does this need an apostrophe at all?* If your answer to that question is yes, then move on to the second question: *where should the apostrophe go?* Use that information to eliminate as many answer choices as you can, and then start the process over with the second word.

Example: Which of these sentences is correct?

A) Both girl's dresses' are beautiful.
B) Both girls dresses are beautiful.
C) Both girls' dresses' are beautiful.
D) Both girls' dresses are beautiful.

First, does the word "girls" need an apostrophe? Yes: it indicates that these dresses belong to the girls. Cross out choice B. Second, where should that apostrophe go? The word "both" at the beginning of the sentence tells us that we're talking about multiple girls here, so we can cross out choice A.

Now, does the word "dresses" need an apostrophe? No: there's nothing owned by the dresses, and there's no contraction here. That lets us cross out choice C, so the correct answer must be **D**.

Writing: Standard English Conventions

> **Try It** Add apostrophes where necessary. (Some sentences are fine the way they are.)
>
> 30) Felicia claims that the phone is hers.
> 31) Is this Mr. Smiths book?
> 32) The suitcase and its contents were destroyed.
> 33) The problem is theirs, not mine.
> 34) Oak trees roots go deep beneath the soil.
> 35) The Smiths are friends of my parents.
> 36) Its beginning to look a lot like Christmas.
> 37) That old trees going to die soon.
> 38) Im not sure whos coming to the party.

FROM THE BLOG

It's a myth that the SAT is not "prep-able." Apart from playing the lottery, can you think of anything you don't get better at by practicing?

Practice Set 1: Easy-Medium

Nadia _____ when she became the first gymnast ever to be awarded a perfect score of 10.0 at the Olympic Games. Decades later, she is still considered one of the greatest gymnasts of all time.

1

Which choice completes the text so that it conforms to the conventions of Standard English?

A. Comăneci was 14 years old;
B. Comăneci was 14 years old,
C. Comăneci, was 14 years old
D. Comăneci was 14 years old

Karen Horn, a German economist and philosopher, has written extensively on the moral obligations of the modern employer. She argues that a business has a responsibility to provide _____ employees with a workplace culture that fosters dignity and respect.

2

Which choice completes the text so that it conforms to the conventions of Standard English?

A. its'
B. it's
C. its
D. they're

In wave-exposed rocky headlands, *Pisaster ochraceus* serves as a keystone _____ as one of the few predators capable of withstanding the harsh conditions, it controls the populations of the dominant prey species and thereby regulates the entire ecosystem. However, in the more complex intertidal communities found in wave-sheltered habitats, the impact of *P. ochraceus* is far less pronounced.

3

Which choice completes the text so that it conforms to the conventions of Standard English?

A. predator:
B. predator,
C. predator
D. predator, meaning:

The _____ in a criminal investigation is limited by one crucial factor: inadmissibility. Because polygraph results can be influenced by unrelated emotional factors as well as mental or physical disabilities, most jurisdictions do not allow them to be admitted into evidence.

4

Which choice completes the text so that it conforms to the conventions of Standard English?

A. usefulness of a polygraph ("lie detector") test,
B. usefulness, of a polygraph, or "lie detector" test
C. usefulness of a polygraph; or "lie detector" test
D. usefulness of a polygraph ("lie detector") test

Writing: Standard English Conventions

In 1883, at the age of 19, Anandi Gopal Joshi traveled from India to the United States to attend the Women's Medical College of Pennsylvania. A few years later, having become the first Indian woman ever to receive a medical degree, she returned home to Kolhapur to set up a clinic for women and children. Joshi was a pioneer for women's education and empowerment in _____ her legacy continues to inspire generations of women.

5

Which choice completes the text so that it conforms to the conventions of Standard English?

A. India with
B. India, and
C. India and;
D. India: and

It is now well established that children who are overscheduled may experience a range of negative impacts to their physical, emotional, and social well-being. Nonetheless, parents say that their kids' sports _____ more demanding than ever.

6

Which choice completes the text so that it conforms to the conventions of Standard English?

A. teams' schedules are
B. team's schedules are
C. team's schedule's is
D. teams' schedules' is

In 2018, the Amsterdam-based dealer Jan _____ the art world when he announced that a painting called "Portrait of a Young Gentleman" was in fact an authentic Rembrandt. The painting had been previously attributed to a follower of Rembrandt, but new research using X-ray and infrared technology confirmed that it had been created by the master himself.

7

Which choice completes the text so that it conforms to the conventions of Standard English?

A. Six's surprise announcement for
B. Sixs' surprised
C. Six's surprisingly announced to
D. Six surprised

To clean up an oceanic oil spill, several methods are available. One option is mechanical removal. Booms, skimmers, _____ and then separate it from the surface of the water.

8

Which choice completes the text so that it conforms to the conventions of Standard English?

A. sorbents and vacuums, are employed to contain the oil in one region,
B. sorbents, and vacuums are employed to contain the oil in one region
C. sorbents and vacuums are employed to contain the oil in one region;
D. sorbents, and vacuums, are employed to contain the oil in one region;

TM and © 2023 PrepMatters, Inc. All rights reserved.

Semicolons, Colons, Dashes, and Apostrophes

In 2008, a team led by Jakob Vinther of Yale University published the first analysis of fossilized dinosaur _____ possible full-color reconstructions of creatures that lived over 100 million years ago.

9 Which choice completes the text so that it conforms to the conventions of Standard English?

A. pigments; making
B. pigments; an achievement that made
C. pigments, this made
D. pigments, making

Musical instruments are often classified into families based on how they produce sound. For example, string instruments (such as guitars and violins) produce sound through the vibration of _____ by contrast, woodwinds (such as flutes and saxophones) produce sound through the vibration of a column of air.

10 Which choice completes the text so that it conforms to the conventions of Standard English?

A. strings,
B. strings; for
C. strings;
D. strings

Thermophotovoltaic (TPV) generators are a type of energy conversion device that convert thermal radiation into electricity. Although TPV technology is still in the research and development phase, it has been used successfully _____ military power systems, remote oil and gas exploration, and wireless monitoring of the structural health of bridges and other buildings.

11 Which choice completes the text so that it conforms to the conventions of Standard English?

A. in, at least, three contexts:
B. in at least three contexts:
C. in, at least, three contexts;
D. in at least three contexts,

Much of the lumber that is used commercially has been treated with chemicals to prevent decay and insect damage. This can significantly increase the life of a construction _____ that project is a playground, it is not without risks. Over time, chemicals such as arsenic, chromium, and copper can leach out of the wood and be absorbed by children who come into contact with the playground equipment or the soil around it.

12 Which choice completes the text so that it conforms to the conventions of Standard English?

A. project, but when
B. project when
C. project; although when
D. project but when,

Practice Set 2: Medium-Hard

Most biologists agree that the evolution of the bacterial flagellum, a complex structure that enables bacteria to swim, occurred through a gradual process of natural selection. Dr. Howard Berg has a different _____ he suggests that the flagellum evolved through a series of modifications to a pre-existing structure known as the bacterial rotary motor.

1

Which choice completes the text so that it conforms to the conventions of Standard English?

A. view; however,
B. view: however,
C. view, however,
D. view, however;

Although the game of chess is known to be over one thousand years _____ exact origins are unclear. The game is believed to have originated in northern India or central Asia, then spread over time to other parts of the world.

2

Which choice completes the text so that it conforms to the conventions of Standard English?

A. old; however, its
B. old, however, its
C. old, its
D. old; its

Famous for their incredible strength—at widths 10,000 times thinner than that of a human _____ carbon nanotubes offer a wide array of intriguing possibilities for the future of technology.

3

Which choice completes the text so that it conforms to the conventions of Standard English?

A. hair, they are stronger than steel—
B. hair, they are stronger than steel
C. hair—they are stronger than steel—
D. hair, they are stronger than steel,

Driving South Africa's Garden Route when _____ best, from February to April, is a truly spectacular experience. The scenic stretch of coastline is characterized by sandy beaches, picturesque villages, and a number of nature reserves.

4

Which choice completes the text so that it conforms to the conventions of Standard English?

A. its at its
B. its at it's
C. it's at its
D. it's at it's

A number of private companies now offer individuals the chance to fly beyond the Earth's atmosphere and experience space firsthand. However, the price tag for such "space tourism" puts it firmly out of reach for most would-be travelers: _____ $250,000 for the experience.

5

Which choice completes the text so that it conforms to the conventions of Standard English?

A. which is at a minimum
B. because it costs, at a minimum,
C. one must pay, at a minimum,
D. at a minimum,

When a company considers switching to a new computer system, the matter cannot be considered lightly. Although a wide variety of factors can impact the decision—price, memory capacity, ease of use, and many _____ the recommendation of a trusted information technology consultant is of primary importance.

6

Which choice completes the text so that it conforms to the conventions of Standard English?

A. others,
B. others—
C. others;
D. others

A funny movie can have a lasting cultural impact, perhaps to a surprising extent. According to Dr. _____ comedy that saves us: laughter transforms our mood, builds social connections, and helps us lead happier, more satisfying lives.

7

Which choice completes the text so that it conforms to the conventions of Standard English?

A. Mishkin, its
B. Mishkin, it's
C. Mishkin: it's
D. Mishkin its

The Tawahka people are an indigenous group who primarily live in the rainforests of the eastern Honduran region of La Mosquitia. Within the community, young people and old people _____ spiritual connection to their natural world, and their traditional practices and beliefs center around maintaining a harmonious relationship with the environment.

8

Which choice completes the text so that it conforms to the conventions of Standard English?

A. alike maintain a strong
B. alike, maintain a strong,
C. alike: maintain a strong
D. alike maintain: a strong,

As the _____ at LaRoche University, Elissa Scalise Powell has seen her share of family dramas. The institute aims to promote high-quality genealogical research and help genealogists of all levels improve their skills and understanding of family history.

9

Which choice completes the text so that it conforms to the conventions of Standard English?

A. director, of the Genealogical Research Institute of Pittsburgh (GRIP)
B. director—of the Genealogical Research Institute of Pittsburgh, (GRIP),
C. director of the Genealogical Research Institute of Pittsburgh (GRIP)—
D. director of the Genealogical Research Institute of Pittsburgh (GRIP)

The diffusionist theory, which posited that cultural similarities between different civilizations could be explained by the diffusion or spread of ideas and technologies from a single (usually European) source or culture, has been widely discredited by anthropologists. However, it is not hard to understand how it became so dominant. With their _____ diffusionists were unable to adequately comprehend the complex and multi-faceted nature of cultural interaction and change.

10

Which choice completes the text so that it conforms to the conventions of Standard English?

A. worldviews constrained by the Eurocentric societies in which they lived,
B. worldviews, constrained by the Eurocentric societies in which they lived,
C. worldviews (constrained by the Eurocentric societies in which they lived)
D. worldviews—constrained by the Eurocentric societies in which they lived—

The southern white rhino is a subspecies of white rhinoceros found in southern Africa. In 2021, thousands of southern white rhinos roamed the savannahs of Namibia, Zimbabwe, and neighboring countries. _____ their species had been nearly hunted to extinction a hundred years earlier: conservation efforts such as protected areas and anti-poaching measures helped their population rebound.

11

Which choice completes the text so that it conforms to the conventions of Standard English?

A. They did not—and still do not know—that
B. They did not know—and still do not, that
C. What they did not know—and still do not:
D. They did not—and still do not—know that

Some avian experts specialize in nest analysis. Based on _____ location and the materials from which it is constructed, they can determine what species of bird was responsible for its construction.

12

Which choice completes the text so that it conforms to the conventions of Standard English?

A. the nests
B. the nests'
C. a nests'
D. a nest's

A 1985 study evaluated methods for masking tinnitus, the phenomenon commonly referred to as a "ringing in the ears." Subjects were first subjected to continuous white noise at 20, 40, and 60 _____ followed, at 2, 4, 10, and 20 pulses per second. Because participants found the interrupted sounds to be more annoying than the continuous noise, the researchers concluded that interrupted noise is not suitable as a tinnitus masker.

13

Which choice completes the text so that it conforms to the conventions of Standard English?

A. decibels, interrupting sounds
B. decibels, interrupting the sounds'
C. decibels. Interrupted sounds
D. decibels' interrupted sounds

Verbs

Preview Quiz:

Choose the correct form of the verb.

1) Mammals, particularly those with thick fur, (is/are) well protected from the cold.

2) Angel is well suited to his new job in customer service, having an even temper and thick skin that (allows/allow) him to remain calm, cool and collected at all times.

3) The studies by the prominent professor (concludes/conclude) that change is inevitable.

4) The trauma team (was/were) the first to arrive.

5) Each of my siblings (works/work) after school.

6) Neither of the two chickens (has/have) been very well trained.

7) Although many people enjoy fly fishing, very few (studied/have studied) its unusual history.

| would have bought | will buy | would buy |

Match each of the sentences to the verb tense from the box above that best completes it.

8) If I win the game, I _____ a new shirt.

9) If I won the lottery, I _____ a house.

10) If I had won the bet, I _____ that new car.

Agreement

The subject of a sentence must **agree** with the verb: that is, if the subject of a sentence is singular, the verb must be singular, and if the subject is plural, the verb must be plural.

If you're not sure what the subject is, ask yourself who or what is doing the action of the verb. Don't be too limited in your answer—the subject could be a single word or a long, complicated phrase. To make it easier to "hear" which verb is right, say that subject immediately before the verb. If you're still not sure, try replacing that word with "it" (if the subject is singular) or "they" (if the subject is plural).

Example: *Mammals, particularly those with thick fur, (is/are) well protected from the cold.*

The subject here is "mammals." That's plural: the mammals **are** well protected from the cold.

Example: *Angel is well suited to his new job in customer service, having an even temper and thick skin that (allows/allow) him to remain calm, cool and collected at all times.*

This one's trickier. First, what's the subject of this verb? That is, who or what is doing the action of allowing Angel to remain calm, cool, and collected? Well, two things: his "even temper and thick skin." They **allow** him to remain calm, cool, and collected. Note that "Angel" is not the subject that we care about here! Angel is the subject of the sentence, but he's not the subject of this particular verb.

To make it easier to identify the subject, ***cross out any prepositional phrases***.

Example: *The studies by the prominent professor (concludes/conclude) that change is inevitable.*

The studies ~~by the prominent professor~~ **conclude** that change is inevitable.

Example: *The point of the lectures (was/were) difficult to grasp.*

The point ~~of the lectures~~ **was** difficult to grasp.

> **TIP:**
>
> ***Don't*** trust your ear on agreement questions. It's too easy for the test to hide the subject and trick you.

A noun indicating a group (such as *class, family*, or *herd*) is singular even though the group consists of more than one person/thing.

Example: *The trauma team (was/were) the first to arrive.*

There's just one team: it **was** the first to arrive.

Example: *The cast (was/were) nominated for an ensemble acting award.*

Again, just one cast. It **was** nominated.

These words are ***always singular***:

every	everyone	anyone	someone	no one
each	everybody	anybody	somebody	nobody
	everything	anything	something	nothing

Example: *Each of my siblings (works/work) after school.*

Cross out the prepositional phrase "of my siblings," and the subject we're left with is "each." That's singular. So change it to "it" or "he" to make it easier to hear the right verb: he **works** after school.

Example: *No one in either of the classes (know/knows) how to diagram a sentence.*

<u>No one</u> ~~in either of the classes~~ (know/knows) how to diagram a sentence.

He **knows** how to diagram a sentence.

If you're not sure whether a subject is singular, try inserting the word "one" after it. Does it still make sense?

Example: *Neither of the two chickens (has/have) been very well trained.*

"Neither one of the two chickens" makes sense. So, "neither" must be singular here. Change it to an "it" to make it easier to hear the right verb: It **has** been very well trained.

Example: *Many of the reasons for attending the event (remains/remain) difficult to understand.*

"Many one of the reasons" doesn't make sense. Therefore, "many" must be plural: They **remain** difficult to understand.

Try It   Choose the correct form of the verb.

1) The time and place for the meeting (has/have) yet to be determined.

2) The party is shaping up to be a good one; George will be attending with Susanna, and Felicia (is/are) going to perform with her band.

3) The entire herd (is/are) scheduled to be sheared tomorrow.

4) The Appalachian mountain chain, which is far older and flatter than the Rocky Mountains, (is/are) a popular destination for long range hikers.

5) Members of the school board, who meet monthly to discuss the policies of the school district, (is/are) now investigating the open campus policy for the high school seniors.

6) Several of the reporters (object/objects) to the coronation.

7) Who among the students (is/are) the tallest?

8) A fascinating and ingenious watercolor from Picasso's blue period and a laughably banal attempt at pseudo-cubism painted by one of his contemporaries (has/have) been displayed in the great hall.

9) Anna May Wong, whose varied career spanned film, television, stage and radio, (was/were) the first Chinese-American movie star.

10) A concise summary of both books (was/were) written by George.

11) The Scarlet Macaw, with its vibrant red, blue and yellow feathers, (eat/eats) the sodium-rich material available at so-called "clay licks."

12) Juju, a Nigerian musical style that draws on several percussion traditions, (was/were) created by Tunde King.

13) The entire group of students (is/are) to be suspended.

Tense

Make sure that any verbs in the sentence are conjugated correctly. For most questions, this just means "listening" for what sounds right or wrong in a sentence. Below are a few of the key things to watch out for.

The verb must **match** the rest of the sentence and the text as a whole. If there are other verbs nearby that are in the present tense, then the verb in the question should probably also be in the present tense. But the most important thing is to pay attention to the **context** and **meaning** of the sentence. The text will tell you what tense it needs to be in.

> *Example:*   *I went to the grocery store and (select/selected) my favorite brand of toothpaste.*
>
> The verb *went* is in past tense, and there's no indication in the sentence that the timeframe is changing. Therefore, we'll want the past tense again: I **selected** my favorite brand.

> *Example:*   *After Ann finishes her homework, she (will go / goes) to the movies.*
>
> This time, the word *after* tells us that the two verbs should not match. Although *finishes* is in present tense, going to the movies is what's going to happen after that, in the future. "She **will go** to the movies" is correct.

TIP: *Do* trust your ear on verb tense questions. You know what sounds right!

Simpler is better. Don't use a complicated tense (e.g., *had walked, has walked, will have been walking*) when a simple tense will do (e.g. *walks, walked*).

> *Example:*   *Jimmy stopped by the house because he (forgets/forgot/has forgotten) his wallet.*
>
> Keep it simple! He **forgot** his wallet.

TIP:

A good rule of thumb for the "Standard English Conventions" questions is that the choice with the fewest words is most likely to be right.

So when are the multi-word tenses correct? Use these when there's a complicated timeline: for example, two past actions, where one of them happened further in the past than the other.

Example: *The teacher (discussed/had been discussing) mitosis when the fight broke out.*

The fight *broke* out, past tense. We want to position the mitosis discussion as a background action that was already going on when the fight started, so **had been discussing** is correct. If we used *discussed* instead, we'd be putting both events in the same timeframe: as if, in response to a fight breaking out, the teacher discussed mitosis.

The multi-word tenses can also be useful for actions that started in the past but continue to the present day.

Example: *Although many people enjoy fly fishing, very few (studied/have studied) its unusual history.*

In this sentence, we're not trying to describe a specific time in the past when few people studied the history of fly fishing. Instead, we're saying that in general, few people studied it in the past *and* few people study it today. That makes **have studied** the right choice.

CHALLENGE:

Sometimes, the conjugation of a verb can tell us something about the attitude of the speaker. We call this the verb's **mood**.

The **subjunctive** most often shows up in dependent clauses that describe a wish, request, or command, or that use an "if" to talk about something that is not actually true. Notice the difference here:

Indicative:	Subjunctive:
The senator <u>listens</u> to us.	*We demand that the senator <u>listen</u> to us.*
I <u>am</u> not a tree.	*If I <u>were</u> a tree, I would be a maple.*
You <u>are</u> patient.	*Management asks that you <u>be</u> patient.*
Her mother says that she always <u>finishes</u> her vegetables.	*It is important that she <u>finish</u> her vegetables.*

The **conditional** tells us that whatever we're describing is in some way dependent on some condition. The kind of conjugation we choose tells us how likely or unlikely we think it is that the condition will be met.

Possible:	*If I win the game, I <u>will buy</u> a new shirt.*
Improbable:	*If I won the lottery, I <u>would buy</u> a house.*
Impossible:	*If I had won the bet, I <u>would have bought</u> that new car.*

> **TIP:**
> Notice that the "would" is never in the *if* part of the sentence. For example, it's never "If I would have won the game…"

> **TIP:**
> The constructions "would of" and "could of" are **always wrong.** It's would *have* and could *have*.

Try It   Choose the correct form of the verb.

14) The moving crate (bursted/burst) before I could duct tape it.

15) She devours the ice cream and then (drank/drinks) the soda.

16) The Everest climbers could (of/have) (froze/frozen) to death.

17) Cookie Monster (drank/has drank) too much milk and ate too many cookies.

18) The chess players who lost the game have (brought/brung) shame on their country.

19) I (felt/have felt) very ill after I ate the entire bag of cotton candy.

20) If I hadn't gotten in, I (would have/have) heard by now.

Practice Set 1: Easy-Medium

Educators have long used details about the personal lives of our political leaders to enrich the story and enhance learning. For example, legends about William Henry Harrison, who died from complications of pneumonia just a month into his presidency, _____ history books.

1

Which choice completes the text so that it conforms to the conventions of Standard English?

A. is often told in high school
B. is told often in high schools'
C. are often told in high school
D. which are often told in a high school's

Antimatter, a substance consisting of particles with charges opposite to those of regular matter, _____ for the first time by scientists at CERN in 2010. The experiment, which was led by Canadian physicist Jeffrey Hangst, managed to store 38 antihydrogen atoms for about 170 milliseconds.

2

Which choice completes the text so that it conforms to the conventions of Standard English?

A. were successfully stored
B. have been stored successfully
C. has successfully stored
D. was successfully stored

Human activity can have both positive and negative effects on the natural world. In the 19th century, human-caused pollution eradicated two plant diseases in English cities. The pollution from coal burning in the industrial cities _____ toxic to the fungi that caused the diseases.

3

Which choice completes the text so that it conforms to the conventions of Standard English?

A. was
B. were
C. being
D. it was

The *da capo* aria is a vocal form that emerged during the Baroque period in the early 18th century. George Frideric Handel, the renowned composer, created immensely popular *da capo* arias characterized by complex vocal lines that showcase the virtuosity of the singer. However, Handel's body of work, including his *da capo* arias, _____ as overly repetitive, with limited opportunity for improvisation or variation.

4

Which choice completes the text so that it conforms to the conventions of Standard English?

A. have been criticized by some musicians
B. have been criticized, by some musicians,
C. has been criticized by some musicians
D. has not made the criticism of some musicians

Writing: Standard English Conventions

While some countries are experiencing declining populations due to factors such as low fertility rates and aging populations, the population of our planet as a whole is still rapidly increasing. If current trends continue, the global population, estimated at around 7.9 billion in 2021, _____ 9.7 billion by 2050.

5

Which choice completes the text so that it conforms to the conventions of Standard English?

A. has reached
B. had reached
C. is reaching
D. will reach

For some crops, hybrid strains—strains created by cross-breeding two or more different varieties of a crop species—are consistently able to outperform non-hybrid strains. For example, hybrid corn strains such as Pioneer P1368AM _____ widely adopted by farmers due to their higher yields and improved resistance to disease and environmental stressors.

6

Which choice completes the text so that it conforms to the conventions of Standard English?

A. was
B. has been
C. is
D. have been

Under section 35 of the Canadian Constitution, Indigenous peoples in Canada have the right to practice their own customs, traditions, and ways of life, including their own systems of land tenure and resource management. As a result, the concept of collective ownership of land and resources _____ and may be protected under Canadian law.

7

Which choice completes the text so that it conforms to the conventions of Standard English?

A. is recognized
B. are recognized
C. recognize
D. recognized

In 1978, Richard F. Haines coined the term "indicator species" to describe a plant or animal whose presence or absence _____ important information about its local environment. In North America, the common loon (*Gavia immer*) is considered an indicator species because of its high degree of sensitivity to changes in water quality and habitat degradation.

8

Which choice completes the text so that it conforms to the conventions of Standard English?

A. have revealed
B. were revealing
C. reveals
D. reveal

Practice Set 2: Medium-Hard

The Union victory at Gettysburg in July of 1863 is generally considered to be the turning point of the US Civil War. According to one historian, if the south _____ the battle, the resulting boost in the Confederate Army's morale and momentum would have led to the capture of key Union cities, possibly including Washington, D.C.

1

Which choice completes the text so that it conforms to the conventions of Standard English?

A. would of won
B. would have won
C. won
D. had won

Supply chain problems, an unusually volatile crude oil market, and rampant market speculation have led to high rate of fluctuation in local gasoline prices. For the last six months, each of the gas stations in one town _____ price signs three times a day.

2

Which choice completes the text so that it conforms to the conventions of Standard English?

A. have been changing their
B. has been changing its
C. is going to change their
D. have changed their

Scientists are consistently puzzled as to why the polar bear, like many other animals, _____

3

Which choice completes the text so that it conforms to the conventions of Standard English?

A. eat their young.
B. eats its young.
C. will eat their young.
D. their young are eaten.

In 2016, the US implemented a near-total ban on the commercial trade of African elephant ivory, with limited exceptions for certain antiques and other items. The ban was aimed at curbing the illegal trade in ivory and protecting African elephant populations, which _____ by poaching and habitat loss.

4

Which choice completes the text so that it conforms to the conventions of Standard English?

A. have been threatened by
B. will have been threatened by
C. are threatening
D. is threatened by

A key step in embryonic development is the establishment of polarity: the embryo must define the orientation or axis along which different body parts and a significant amount of tissue _____ This will determine the position and orientation of specific structures and organs in the developing embryo.

5

Which choice completes the text so that it conforms to the conventions of Standard English?

A. have been formed.
B. is to be formed.
C. are to be formed.
D. is forming.

Pronouns

Preview Quiz

Choose the correct form of the pronoun.

1) The company is rightfully proud of (its/their) hardworking employees.

2) The success of new electronic devices is dependent on the strength of (its/their) marketing campaign.

3) The email was sent to Kenneth, Lydia, and (I/me).

4) I don't know the gentleman next to (who/whom) I am sitting.

What is wrong with these sentences?

5) The best teammates are those who fit in as a member of the family.

6) Everyone said that Betty had inherited her mother's good looks, but she privately believed that there was only one true beauty in the family.

7) When my husband looks at our daughter, he sees a younger version of myself.

Agreement

Look carefully at the sentence to identify which word the pronoun is standing in for. If you had to swap out the pronoun for one noun from elsewhere in the sentence, which one would make the most sense? That word is the pronoun's **antecedent**. If the antecedent is singular, the pronoun must be singular (e.g. *she, him, I*). If the antecedent is plural, the pronoun must be plural (*we, they, us*).

Example: *The company is rightfully proud of (its/their) hardworking employees.*

Try swapping out the pronoun: The company is rightfully proud of <u>the company's</u> hardworking employees. So "the company" is the antecedent. Since that's a singular word, we need the singular **its**, not the plural *their*.

Example: *The success of new electronic devices is dependent on the strength of (its/their) marketing campaign.*

Whose marketing campaign? The <u>devices'</u> marketing campaign. The word "devices" is plural, so **their** is correct.

Try It   Underline the antecedent and then choose the correct pronoun.

1) The Oglethorpe Bookstore buys thousands of books each year, most of (it/them) paperback novels.

2) Unlike (its/their) predecessors, which suffered from confusing interfaces and frequent crashes, the smartphone introduced by Boggle Corp. is easy to use and reliable.

3) Each of the most successful movies of the last twenty years, including *Avatar*, *Titanic*, and *The Lord of The Rings*, faced only middling reviews when (they/it) opened.

4) When the Supremes released the single "Baby Love" in 1964, (it/they) instantly established themselves as pop superstars.

5) As a student, (you/we) are responsible for planning (your/our) own schedule.

Agreement problems don't have to be limited to the subject-verb or pronoun-antecedent varieties. Any time you see a sentence involving a comparison, take a moment to check whether something singular is being compared to something plural.

Incorrect: `The best teammates are those who fit in as a member of the family.`

Correct: The best teammates are those who fit in as <u>members</u> of the family.

-or-

Correct: The best <u>teammate is one who fits</u> in as a member of the family.

Incorrect: `All the girls in the class want to be a ballerina.`

Correct: All the girls in the class want to be <u>ballerinas</u>.

-or-

Correct: <u>Each of</u> the girls in the class <u>wants</u> to be a ballerina.

Case

When a pronoun is standing in for a subject or an object, it takes one of these forms:

Subject	
Singular	**Plural**
I	we
you	you
he/she/it	they
who	who

Object	
Singular	**Plural**
me	us
you	you
him/her/it	them
whom	whom

For most pronoun questions, you can just trust your ear. For example, the sentence "Him hates asparagus" just sounds wrong, and indeed, it is.

When the pronoun is buried in a list, cross out everything on the list except for the pronoun to make it easier to "hear" what sounds right.

Example: *The email was sent to Kenneth, Lydia, and (I/me).*

Get rid of Kenneth and Lydia and it's much easier to hear it: "The email was sent to **me**."

TIP:

Do trust your ear for pronoun case questions.

To choose between *who* and *whom*, trusting your ear doesn't really help: we rarely use *whom* in day-to-day life, and so we don't have much of a sense for when it sounds right. However, there is a trick that can help. Try replacing the who/whom with *he* and then with *him*. Which one sounds right? If *he* sounds right, then "who" is correct. If *him* sounds right, then "whom" is correct. (To remember which is which, think about matching the m's: whoM goes with hiM).

> *Example:* The salesman (who/whom) sold me this computer must have made a hefty commission.
>
> Here, "he sold me this computer" sounds better than "him sold me this computer," so **who** is correct.
>
> *Example:* I don't know the gentleman next to (who/whom) I am seated.
>
> In this one, "next to him" sounds better than "next to he," so **whom** is correct.

> **TIP:**
> For plural subjects, you can plug in *they* instead of *he*, and *them* instead of *him*. Matching the m's still works.

TIP:

When a pronoun immediately follows a preposition, you always use the object case (e.g. *her, them, us*), instead of the subject case (e.g. *she, they, we*).

> *Example:* The proposal that was written by (he/him) and his partner failed to win the grant.
>
> Since "by" is a preposition, the correct word is **him**.
>
> *Example:* According to Cindy, there exists an easy friendship between Marcia and (her/she).
>
> Because it follows the preposition "between," **her** is the right choice.

You can use the **-self pronouns** (*myself, himself, herself,* etc.) only when the subject and the object are the same: that is, when the pronoun is referring back to the person doing the action of the sentence.

Correct: When I look at my daughter, I see a younger version of myself.

Incorrect: `When my husband looks at our daughter, he sees a younger version of myself.`

Try It   Choose the correct pronoun.

6) Did you give the marbles to Carlos and (he/him)?

7) At his wife's suggestion, Dr. Rodriguez made a note to remind (him/he/himself) to mail the letter on his way home.

8) (Who/Whom) lies buried in Grant's tomb?

9) You can contact Jeffries, Mitchelson or (I/me/myself) for more information.

10) The book that made the bestseller list, a book co-authored by Steven Wilson and (I/me), is a work of which both of (we/us) can be proud.

11) (Whose/Who's/Whom is) afraid of the big, bad wolf?

Ambiguity

If a pronoun has no clear antecedent (for example, if the sentence uses the word "he" when more than one man has been mentioned), it is incorrect. In these sentences, the error is not that the wrong pronoun was used; it's that a pronoun was used at all.

Incorrect: `Everyone said that Betty had inherited her mother's good looks, but `she` privately believed that there was only one true beauty in the family.`

When we say that Betty inherited "her mother's good looks," that's fine—at this point in the sentence, the word "her" could only be referring to Betty. But who exactly believed that there was only one true beauty in the family? The "she" could be referring to Betty, or it could be referring to Betty's mother. Since we have no way of knowing which one is right, the pronoun should not be used.

Incorrect: `In an effort to blend in with the locals, Carrie tried to avoid mispronouncing the complicated place names, but `it` failed.`

This time, the problem is not that the "it" could be referring to more than one noun. The problem is that it's not referring to anything! There's no specific noun in this sentence that this "it" could be pointing back to, so the "it" is incorrect.

Try It Circle any ambiguous pronouns.

12) Governor McAllister's son told us that he had decided not to run for reelection because he wanted to spend more time with his family.

13) Neither Jorge nor Edward believed that he would win the lottery.

14) We have been dependent on fossil fuels for decades, but now that the environmental impact has become clear, activists are urging citizens to change it.

Writing: Standard English Conventions

Practice Set 1: Easy-Medium

Trinidadian guppies are small, colorful fish found in rivers and streams in the Caribbean nation of Trinidad and Tobago. Among males, intense competition for mating opportunities has resulted in the evolution of elaborate courtship displays and ornament. When a male guppy has a larger tail and brighter coloration, _____ more successful in attracting mates and fathering offspring.

1

Which choice completes the text so that it conforms to the conventions of Standard English?

A. him being
B. they are
C. he is
D. it will be having

The health benefits of bicycling are undeniable, though many people just taking up the sport have something of a rough beginning. Experts agree that it's common for _____ when first learning to ride.

2

Which choice completes the text so that it conforms to the conventions of Standard English?

A. new cyclists to fall and hurt them
B. a new cyclist to fall and hurt themselves
C. new cyclists to fall and hurt themselves
D. a new cyclist to fall and hurt him

At the University of Bath, a multidisciplinary research center focuses on a range of social policy issues that includes the field of terrorism studies. The field _____ today has only existed for a short time. Initially, terrorism was studied primarily as a security or criminal justice issue, with a focus on understanding the motivations and tactics of terrorist groups and developing strategies to counter their activities. However, in recent years, scholars in the field have increasingly emphasized the need to examine the social and political contexts in which terrorism arises, as well as the broader social and psychological factors that may contribute to radicalization and violence.

3

Which choice completes the text so that it conforms to the conventions of Standard English?

A. as we know it
B. as it is known to we
C. as we know them
D. that those of us know

Jalāl ad-Dīn Muhammad Balkhī Rumi, known in the Western world simply as Rumi, was a Persian jurist, _____ works have been translated into many languages and read by people all over the world.

4

Which choice completes the text so that it conforms to the conventions of Standard English?

A. mystic, and poet, his
B. mystic, and poet whose
C. mystic, and he was a
D. mystic and a poet his

Practice Set 2: Medium-Hard

A 1990 study at the Massachusetts Institute of Technology found that adult schizophrenia was linked to a region on human chromosome number six. Some scientists even explored the possibility of using a patient's genetic information to aid in diagnosis. However, doctors soon found that all their sophisticated DNA information was meaningless if _____ with clinical examination and symptom analysis.

1 Which choice completes the text so that it conforms to the conventions of Standard English?

A. he or she didn't combine it
B. they didn't combine it
C. it wasn't combined by him or her
D. he or she wasn't to combine it

Type A lipid profile, also known as the "atherogenic" lipid profile, is characterized by high levels of low-density lipoprotein (LDL) cholesterol, and low levels of high-density lipoprotein (HDL) cholesterol. Both high LDL levels and low HDL levels can increase the risk of heart disease. Type B lipid profile, on the other hand, is characterized by an elevated level of another type of fat found in the blood called a triglyceride; _____ also associated with an increased risk of heart disease.

2 Which choice completes the text so that it conforms to the conventions of Standard English?

A. it is
B. they are
C. which is
D. high triglyceride levels are

The four papers that Einstein published in 1905 were so revolutionary that experts view _____ as watershed moments in the history of science.

3 Which choice completes the text so that it conforms to the conventions of Standard English?

A. this
B. them
C. him
D. it

The Russian journalist Sergei Shereshevsky had an extraordinary memory. Shereshevsky suffered from synesthesia, a condition in which sensory experiences are blended together. In his case, he saw every sound and every letter as having its own unique color and texture. This helped him to remember information in a very vivid and detailed way. In one experiment, Shereshevsky was recorded reciting a lengthy poem after listening to it only once. When researchers compared his recitation to the version he had listened to, they discovered that everything, including the word order, the emphases, and the pauses for breath, _____

4 Which choice completes the text so that it conforms to the conventions of Standard English?

A. was exactly as he remembered them.
B. were exactly as he remembered them.
C. was exactly as he remembered it.
D. being exactly as he remembered them.

Misplaced Modifiers

Preview Quiz

Consider the following sentence:

While riding his bicycle, Sam's dog barked at him.

1) What is wrong with the sentence above?

   _____

   _____

2) Write a corrected version of the sentence.

   _____

   _____

Consider the following sentence:

The ball was kicked by John.

3) The sentence above is written in "passive voice." What does that mean?

   _____

   _____

4) Rewrite the sentence in active voice.

   _____

   _____

Misplaced Modifiers

Sometimes, poor construction of a sentence will cause a phrase that is intended to modify one thing to either modify something else or modify nothing at all. That may sound a little dry, but this particular error actually has the side benefit of often creating some unintentional humor. When the SAT gives you a chance to laugh, you should grab it.

> Incorrect: `While riding his bicycle, Sam's dog barked at him.`

The problem here, of course, is that Sam's dog isn't riding the bicycle (we hope). *Sam* is. When a sentence begins with a phrase containing a –ing or –ed verb, like this one does, the phrase must modify the **very first noun that follows the comma**. So one easy way to fix a misplaced modifier is to change the wording in the independent clause so that the noun you want to modify comes first.

> Correct: While riding his bicycle, <u>Sam was barked at by his dog</u>.

The other major way to fix this kind of problem is to change the introductory phrase, usually by adding the subject to it.

> Correct: <u>While Sam was riding his bicycle,</u> his dog barked at him.

The hardest part about these questions is usually spotting the problem in the first place.

TIP: The overall rule here is that *grammar has a short memory*. You want to get the thing being described as close as possible to the thing describing it.

Try It — Each of the following is a common situation in which you should be on the lookout for misplaced modifiers, followed by an example. Write a corrected version of each sentence.

- **An introductory phrase using verbs in –ing or –ed form.**

1) `Having slept through my alarm, the school bus arrived before I was fully dressed.`

   _____

- **Passive voice** ("The ball was kicked by John" rather than "John kicked the ball") **in either the sentence or the answer choices.**

2) `Finding no evidence of guilt, the suspect was acquitted by the jury.`

   _____

- **Multiple prepositional phrases.** These are often easiest to fix by just changing the order of the phrases.

3) `I found a dress in a thrift store that I'd been looking for to wear to a party.`

   _____

TIP: In **passive voice**, the subject of the sentence is not the one doing the action. Since this affects the word order, a misplaced modifier can often be fixed (or caused!) by switching from passive to active voice.

- 173 -

Writing: Standard English Conventions

Practice Set 1: Easy-Medium

At Yoko Ono's 1966 exhibit at the Indica Gallery in London, a visitor noticed a painting on the ceiling on which something tiny was printed on an otherwise white canvas. After making his way up a ladder and picking up a provided magnifying glass, _____

1

Which choice completes the text so that it conforms to the conventions of Standard English?

A. the word "YES" surprised him.
B. it was the word "YES" that surprised him.
C. he was surprised to read the word "YES."
D. the word "YES" was a surprise to him.

The first new play from the acclaimed writer since he'd gone into seclusion over a decade earlier, _____

2

Which choice completes the text so that it conforms to the conventions of Standard English?

A. every performance of *The Cosmonaut*'s four-week run was sold out.
B. all four weeks of *The Cosmonaut*'s performances were sold out.
C. *The Cosmonaut*'s four-week run was completely sold out.
D. *The Cosmonaut* sold out every performance of its four-week run.

Professional gamer Nathan Kim is a proponent of mechanical keyboards, a type of computer keyboard that uses individual mechanical switches for each key rather than the rubber dome switches or membrane switches that are found on many standard keyboards. Arguing that that their durability and distinctive feel outweigh all other considerations, _____ that mechanical keyboards are worth their somewhat higher price.

3

Which choice completes the text so that it conforms to the conventions of Standard English?

A. Kim contends
B. Kim's contention is
C. it is contended by Kim
D. the contention of Kim is

Adobe, a building material made from a mixture of clay, sand, straw, and water, has been used for thousands of years in the construction of homes and other structures in arid regions of the world. _____ in the 13th century, the Great Mosque of Djenné in Mali, West Africa is the largest adobe building in the world.

4

Which choice completes the text so that it conforms to the conventions of Standard English?

A. Constructing it with their hands
B. A construction by hand
C. Constructed by hand
D. Due to constructing it by hand

Misplaced Modifiers

Practice Set 2: Medium-Hard

Since _____ in 2009, Adele's music has had ever-increasing commercial success. While her debut album "19" sold millions of copies, her second studio album, "21," became the best-selling album of the twenty-first century.

1

Which choice completes the text so that it conforms to the conventions of Standard English?

A. winning the Grammy for Best New Artist
B. her having won the Grammy for Best New Artist
C. she won the Grammy for Best New Artist
D. the Grammy for Best New Artist was won by her

Some scientists believe that the best approach to controlling cancer is to manipulate the body's own immune system rather than to try to attack the cancer cells directly. New medicines containing beta-glucan appear to work along these lines. Using this indirect approach, _____

2

Which choice completes the text so that it conforms to the conventions of Standard English?

A. cancerous growths are detected and destroyed by immune cells activated by the medicines.
B. the medicines activate immune cells to detect and destroy cancerous growths.
C. the detection and destruction of cancerous growths is caused by the medicines' activation of immune cells.
D. immune cells activated by the medicines detect and destroy cancerous growths.

_____ snake venom, researchers are hoping to build better medications for human snakebite victims by analyzing compounds in opossum blood.

3

Which choice completes the text so that it conforms to the conventions of Standard English?

A. Immune to
B. Since they are immune to
C. Because opossums are immune to
D. Being immune to

Julia Child was a beloved cookbook author and television personality known for hosting "The French Chef" on PBS. Her warm humor and distinctive physical presence endeared her to millions who didn't care about cooking, but she was also an accomplished chef. _____ at the famous Le Cordon Bleu cooking school in Paris, her detailed knowledge of French cuisine impressed even the most advanced culinary experts.

4

Which choice completes the text so that it conforms to the conventions of Standard English?

A. Trained
B. Having trained
C. She had trained
D. Thanks to her training

- 175 -

TM and © 2023 PrepMatters, Inc. All rights reserved.

Writing: Expression of Ideas

Transitions

Preview Quiz

Choose the most logical transition.

1) Smith's movies often receive glowing reviews. (For instance / Therefore / Similarly), I bought a ticket for his newest film as soon as I heard about it.

2) Smith's movies often receive glowing reviews. (Similarly / For instance / However), the *New York Times* called his newest film "an instant classic."

3) Smith's movies often receive glowing reviews. (For instance / However / In fact), it often seems that no filmmaker is more universally beloved.

4) Smith's movies often receive glowing reviews. (Therefore / Similarly / In fact), his paintings are widely respected by critics.

Write in your answer.

5) What is the difference between the words *subsequently* and *consequently*?

6) What is the difference between the words *accordingly* and *similarly*?

A well-written text should flow well from one topic to the next. Sometimes, this means making effective use of **transition** words and phrases such as *also, however, therefore, while, conversely, on the other hand,* and *in addition.*

Transitions can drastically change the meaning of a passage even when they don't create grammatical problems. Consider the difference in meaning in the examples below:

> *My sister, who just announced that she'd like to visit me this summer, is allergic to cats and dogs. <u>Unfortunately</u>, I bought a cat for my apartment last week.*

> *My sister, who just announced that she'd like to visit me this summer, is allergic to cats and dogs. <u>Therefore</u>, I bought a cat for my apartment last week.*

As these examples illustrate, the most important thing to consider when attacking transition questions is the *context*. When you work through transition questions on the test, be sure to ask yourself not just what is correct grammatically, but what makes the most sense in the context of the sentence and the paragraph. Consider the relationship between the ideas connected by the transition and ask yourself this: Is this a **continuation** in the same direction? Is it a **contrast**? Or is it something else?

Most transition words and phrases can be organized into the three broad categories shown on the next page: continuation words, contrast words, and sequence words.

CONTINUATION

Addition or Similarity	Cause & Effect	Emphasis	Examples	Summary or Conclusion
• moreover • similarly • likewise • furthermore • additionally • in addition • also • further • what's more • by the same token	To introduce the **cause**: • For • Because • since To introduce the **effect** or **result**: • therefore • thus • consequently • hence • as a result • accordingly • to these ends	• in fact • indeed	• for instance • for example • specifically • that is	• in other words • in sum • to conclude • in conclusion • in brief • therefore • thus

CONTRAST

- though
- although
- nevertheless
- nonetheless
- still
- instead
- meanwhile
- however
- regardless
- by/in comparison
- by/in contrast
- alternatively
- but
- whereas
- on the other hand
- on the contrary
- conversely
- after all
- despite
- yet

TIME OR SEQUENCE

- first
- second
- third
- next
- later
- last
- finally
- previously
- currently
- subsequently
- afterward

TIP:
This list is not exhaustive! The English language offers a wide variety of ways to connect sentences and ideas. This is just a glimpse of some of the transitions that are most commonly seen on the SAT.

The best way to handle a transition question is to follow a multi-part strategy.

Read.	Carefully read the first sentence or sentences (the part of the text that comes before the blank). Then, skip the blank—do NOT look at the answer choices yet—and read the second part of the text.
Summarize.	What was the big point of the first section? Try to summarize it in just a few words. Then, repeat: what was the big point of the second section?
Analyze and predict.	Consider what kind of relationship exists between those two big ideas. Is the second part continuing in the same direction? Is it a contrast? Or is it something else? Decide what transition word *you* might write into that blank if you didn't have answer choices.
Review the choices.	Go to the answer choices and find the best match for your prediction.
Re-read.	As a final step, read the whole text again with your answer choice plugged into the blank. Does it still make sense?

> ***TIP:***
>
> These questions are generally ***not about the grammar***. In most cases, all four answer choices will be grammatically correct.

Let's explore that "analyze and predict" step a bit further. The first task here is to decide whether we need a **continuation** word, a **contrast** word, or something else. The tough part often is choosing between the options within those categories, especially in the continuation category. Look closely at the relationship between the ideas. In some cases, the second part of the text is taking the claim made in the first part a step farther, perhaps by implying a **cause-and-effect** relationship. In that case, try "therefore," "thus," "consequently," "hence," "accordingly," or "as a result."

Example: *Smith's movies often receive glowing reviews. <u>Therefore,</u> I bought a ticket for his newest film as soon as I heard about it.*

In other cases, we're simply moving from a general claim to a specific **illustration** of that claim. For these sentences, "for example" or "for instance" might work.

Example: *Smith's movies often receive glowing reviews. <u>For instance,</u> the New York Times called his newest film "an instant classic."*

If we want to use the second part of the text to **emphasize** the point made in the first part, try "indeed" or "in fact."

Example: *Smith's movies often receive glowing reviews. <u>In fact,</u> it often seems that no filmmaker is more universally beloved.*

Another possibility might be that the second part of the text isn't extending the first point at all, but rather switching to a new topic that is similar to the first one. In these situations, some good options include "similarly," "likewise," "additionally," "also," "moreover," and "by the same token."

Example: *Smith's movies often receive glowing reviews. <u>Similarly,</u> his paintings are widely respected by critics.*

The flow chart on the next page gives one example of a process for identifying the exact relationship between the sentences so you can choose the right transition word.

> **TIP:**
> Yes, there is some overlap in some of these categories. Some transition words can work in more than one way. Don't worry: in an SAT question, there will only be one choice that logically fits the sentence.

Transitions Flow Chart

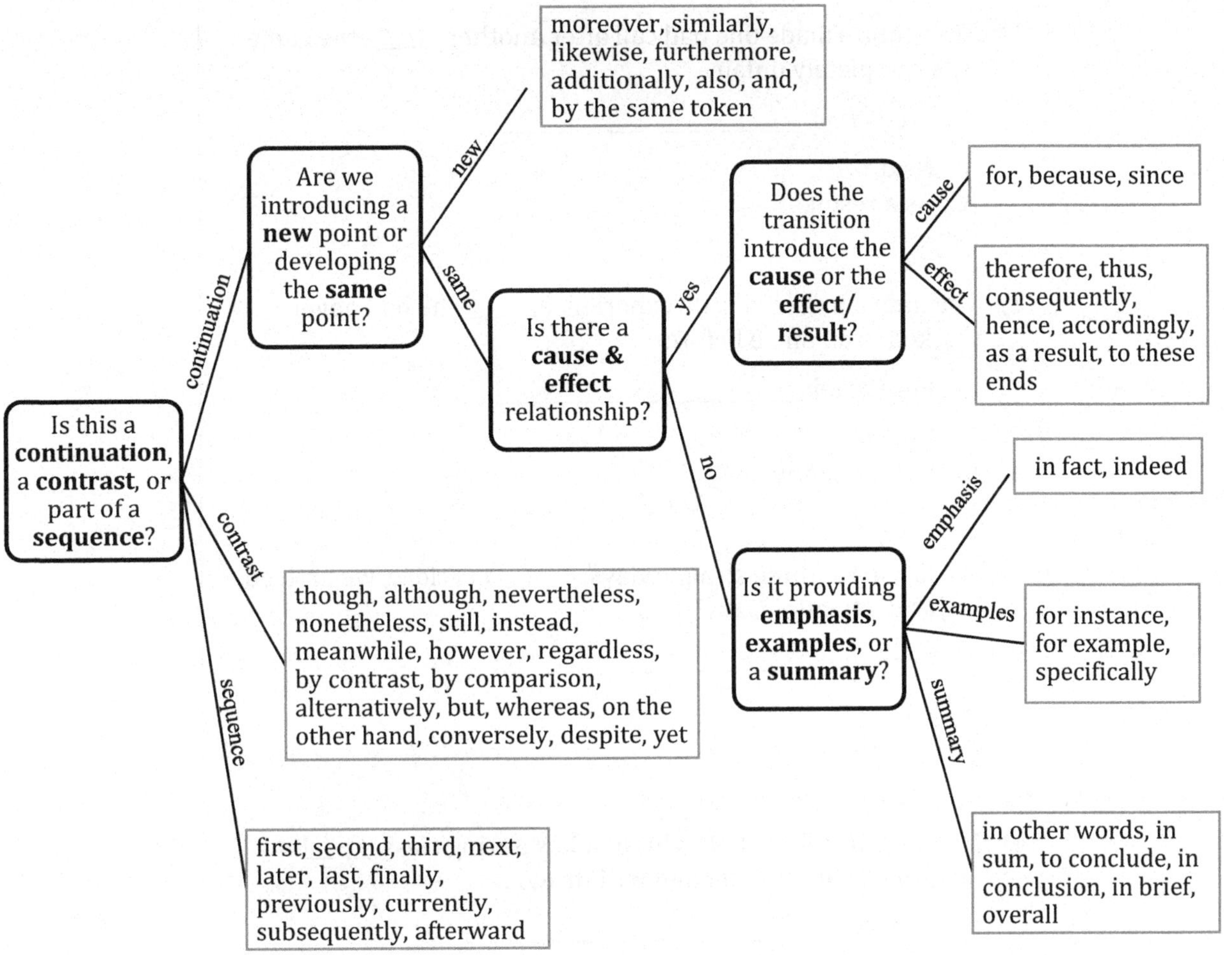

Is this a continuation, a contrast, or part of a sequence?

- **continuation** → **Are we introducing a new point or developing the same point?**
  - **new**: moreover, similarly, likewise, furthermore, additionally, also, and, by the same token
  - **same** → **Is there a cause & effect relationship?**
    - **yes** → **Does the transition introduce the cause or the effect/result?**
      - **cause**: for, because, since
      - **effect**: therefore, thus, consequently, hence, accordingly, as a result, to these ends
    - **no** → **Is it providing emphasis, examples, or a summary?**
      - **emphasis**: in fact, indeed
      - **examples**: for instance, for example, specifically
      - **summary**: in other words, in sum, to conclude, in conclusion, in brief, overall
- **contrast**: though, although, nevertheless, nonetheless, still, instead, meanwhile, however, regardless, by contrast, by comparison, alternatively, but, whereas, on the other hand, conversely, despite, yet
- **sequence**: first, second, third, next, later, last, finally, previously, currently, subsequently, afterward

TIP:

Although there can be many subtle differences that indicate a continuation in the same direction, the contrast keywords are extremely similar in meaning. Generally speaking, if you can use the word "however," you can probably use the word "nevertheless" as well. So in a transition question, if you see both of those words among your answer choices, neither one is likely to be the right answer.

Writing: Expression of Ideas

Try It — Which choice completes the text with the most logical transition? **Choose A, B, _or both_.**

1) The umpire made one bad call after another. _____ the game was completely unfair.

   Prediction: _____

   A. Next,
   B. As a result,

2) The intern had very little experience; _____ he had never worked in an office before.

   Prediction: _____

   A. Indeed,
   B. Subsequently,

3) We drove for three straight days. _____ on Friday, we arrived at our destination.

   Prediction: _____

   A. Finally,
   B. At last,

4) My English teacher tells a lot of jokes during class. _____ my history teacher is quiet and withdrawn.

   Prediction: _____

   A. Similarly,
   B. In contrast,

CHALLENGE:

The words "similarly" and "accordingly" are closely related but not exactly the same. Both indicate a continuation rather than a contrast. The difference lies in whether you're introducing a new example or just continuing/extending the same one you started with.

To introduce a new example that's like the one already mentioned, use "similarly":

Example: *Wearing a helmet should be a regular habit for everyone who rollerblades. <u>Similarly,</u> skaters should wear pads on their knees and elbows.*

Use "accordingly" to continue / expand on the same example rather than introduce a new one.

Example: *Wearing a helmet should be a regular habit for everyone who rollerblades. <u>Accordingly,</u> I bought a helmet on the same day I bought my skates.*

Writing: Expression of Ideas

Practice Set 1: Easy-Medium

When a beam of light passes through a medium containing small particles, such as dust, smoke, or mist, the light interacts with the particles and scatters in many directions. _____ the medium becomes visible, a phenomenon known as the Tyndall effect.

1

Which choice completes the text with the most logical transition?

A. Overall,
B. By the same token,
C. As a result,
D. Regardless,

Long-distance runners use two kinds of cognitive strategies to cope with the physical and mental challenges of their sport. "Associative" strategies involve focusing their attention on the internal sensations of running (such as breathing rate and muscle fatigue) in order to maintain a sense of control over their physical state and stay motivated. _____ "dissociative" strategies involve focusing on external stimuli (such as the scenery or other runners around them) to distract themselves from the physical discomfort and maintain a positive mental attitude.

2

Which choice completes the text with the most logical transition?

A. Similarly,
B. In contrast,
C. In other words,
D. Still,

Art scholars use semiotics, the study of signs and symbols, to analyze how visual elements are used to convey meaning and how cultural contexts can shape interpretation. _____ the use of certain colors or shapes might be associated with specific cultural or historical ideas, while the arrangement of elements within a painting might create a certain mood or convey a particular message.

3

Which choice completes the text with the most logical transition?

A. Meanwhile,
B. Additionally,
C. Therefore,
D. For example,

Although the word "heart" implies a complicated multi-chambered organ such as that found in the human chest, the word actually covers a wide variety of structures. The heart of the lancelet, a tiny sea creature found in shallow coastal waters, is nothing more than a single muscular tube that contracts rhythmically to circulate blood. Unlike in larger chordates, there is no complex network of blood vessels; lancelets rely instead on the movement of fluids within their body cavity to distribute nutrients and oxygen. _____ despite its simplicity, the lancelet must be said to possess a circulatory system due to its possession of a beating heart.

4

Which choice completes the text with the most logical transition?

A. Still,
B. Besides,
C. Consequently,
D. In sum,

Transitions

A recent study investigated the impact of aging on the flavor and tenderness of beef strip loins. The researchers found that aging the beef for a period of 14 to 21 days can significantly improve its tenderness, with the collagen in the meat breaking down over time. _____ the study also noted that prolonged aging beyond 21 days can lead to a decline in tenderness and a decrease in desirable flavor compounds.

5

Which choice completes the text with the most logical transition?

A. Moreover,
B. In conclusion,
C. However,
D. In fact,

The death of Nero in 68 CE left a power vacuum in the Roman empire, as there was no clear successor to the throne. _____ the ensuing chapter of Roman history was rife with political instability and conflict, marked by the rapid succession of four different emperors over the course of a single year.

6

Which choice completes the text with the most logical transition?

A. Despite this,
B. As a result,
C. Alternatively,
D. In other words,

Although the 1913 Bohr model of the atom was a significant advancement in atomic theory, it is now known to be inaccurate in several ways. First, the model suggests that electrons move in circular orbits, when in fact they orbit in complex patterns described by quantum mechanics. _____ the Bohr model assumes that electrons have a definite position and momentum, which is incompatible with the Heisenberg uncertainty principle. Despite these inaccuracies, however, the Bohr model provides a useful conceptual framework for understanding atomic structure and behavior, and as a result, it is still taught in introductory science courses today.

7

Which choice completes the text with the most logical transition?

A. Second,
B. For instance,
C. Thus,
D. Regardless,

In 2016, singer-songwriter Bob Dylan was awarded the Nobel Prize for Literature "for having created new poetic expressions within the great American song tradition." _____ some protested the idea of such a prestigious award going to a rock musician, for many others, it was a long-overdue recognition of the enduring influence of a true American original.

8

Which choice completes the text with the most logical transition?

A. Because
B. Although
C. Due to the fact that
D. Given that

Practice Set 2: Medium-Hard

Bipedalism (the ability to walk on two feet) has played a key role in the evolution of our species. Compared to other forms of locomotion, such as quadrupedalism or swimming, bipedalism is less stable and requires a more complex series of muscular and skeletal movements to maintain balance and motion. _____ bipedalism also offers unique advantages such as greater efficiency of energy expenditure and the ability to free up the hands for carrying objects or manipulating tools.

1

Which choice completes the text with the most logical transition?

A. Indeed,
B. However,
C. Moreover,
D. By comparison,

Purple loosestrife (*Lythrum salicaria*) is an invasive plant species that has had a significant impact on North American wetlands since its introduction from Europe in the early 19th century. The plant is highly adaptable, outcompetes native plants, alters the natural balance of the ecosystem, and impedes water flow. _____ it reduces biodiversity, impacting ecosystem functions and ultimately altering the physical structure of wetlands. This has been detrimental to the health of North American wetlands, causing long-term damage that is difficult to reverse.

2

Which choice completes the text with the most logical transition?

A. For example,
B. Nonetheless,
C. Finally,
D. Accordingly,

The use of limestone as a soil additive is a long-established practice that dates back centuries, with evidence of its use found in ancient Roman and Egyptian civilizations. However, while limestone has traditionally been employed by conventional large-scale farms to address issues such as soil acidity and erosion, evidence suggests a shift in usage. _____ small-scale farmers are turning to limestone as a natural and sustainable means of improving soil quality, while many organic farmers are using limestone to enhance soil structure and promote plant growth. As a result, the use of limestone is becoming more widespread and diverse, reflecting a growing awareness of the importance of soil health in modern agriculture.

3

Which choice completes the text with the most logical transition?

A. Similarly,
B. Increasingly,
C. In other words,
D. Furthermore,

Transitions

Andy Warhol was a prominent American artist and a leading figure in the Pop Art movement of the 1960s. His work, which often featured images of celebrities and everyday objects, sought to challenge traditional notions of art and to blur the lines between high and low culture. While Warhol's work was highly influential and his contributions to the art world are widely recognized, some critics contend that his popularity and commercial success may have overshadowed his artistic merit. _____ Warhol's impact on the art world and on popular culture more broadly remains undeniable, and his work continues to be celebrated and studied by art enthusiasts around the world.

4

Which choice completes the text with the most logical transition?

A. Nevertheless,
B. Accordingly,
C. Furthermore,
D. In other words,

The mandates of journalistic ethics require reporters to maintain impartiality and objectivity in their reporting, regardless of their personal beliefs or biases. Journalists must also strive to ensure that their reporting does not infringe on the privacy of individuals, particularly those who may be vulnerable or marginalized. In the digital age, the risks posed by rapidly-spreading misinformation only underscore the importance of accuracy and reliability in reporting. _____ journalists must remain vigilant in upholding ethical standards and commit to providing the public with truthful, unbiased information.

5

Which choice completes the text with the most logical transition?

A. Similarly,
B. In other words,
C. To this end,
D. Conversely,

Early sunscreens contained UV-B absorbers such as para-aminobenzoic acid, which was effective in preventing sunburn but did not provide protection against UV-A radiation. At the time, UV-B radiation was seen as the primary cause of sun-related skin damage, but later research established that UV-A radiation can also harm skin cells and increase the risk of skin cancer. _____ the development of sunscreens with broad-spectrum protection against both UV-B and UV-A radiation became a priority in the field of dermatology in the 1980s and 1990s. This led to the introduction of new sunscreen ingredients such as avobenzone, which blocks both types of radiation and thus significantly enhances the efficacy of modern-day sunscreens.

6

Which choice completes the text with the most logical transition?

A. Consequently,
B. In fact,
C. Instead,
D. Moreover,

Writing: Expression of Ideas

While both Neanderthals and Cro-Magnons are classified as members of the *Homo* genus, some researchers argue that they are separate species due to differences in physical characteristics and genetics. Neanderthals are known for their robust builds, large brow ridges, and prominent nasal cavities, while Cro-Magnons are characterized by their more gracile features and higher cranial capacity. _____ genetic analysis has shown that Neanderthals and Cro-Magnons interbred to some degree, suggesting that they may have been distinct but related groups rather than entirely separate species.

7

Which choice completes the text with the most logical transition?

A. Hence,
B. However,
C. By the same token,
D. In addition,

Avogadro's number, which is approximately 6.022×10^{23}, represents the number of particles in one mole of a substance. The number is significant because it provides a way to relate macroscopic properties of a substance, such as its mass, volume, and density, to the microscopic properties of its constituent particles. _____ knowing the molar mass of a substance allows us to calculate the number of particles present in a given mass of the substance, or the mass of a given number of particles.

8

Which choice completes the text with the most logical transition?

A. Besides,
B. Nevertheless,
C. For example,
D. Still,

For 160 million years, dinosaurs ruled the earth. Their success was due in part to evolutionary adaptations that allowed them to thrive in a variety of environments, and in part to the distinct geographic arrangement of the continents at the time, which allowed the animals to occupy a wide range of habitats, find new food sources, and avoid competition with other predators. These factors made the creatures ideally suited for the conditions around them, allowing them to outcompete countless other life forms. _____ were it not for the catastrophic environmental disruption that struck their world 65 million years ago, dinosaurs might have remained the dominant species on Earth to this day.

9

Which choice completes the text with the most logical transition?

A. Indeed,
B. Specifically,
C. Nonetheless,
D. On the other hand,

Rhetorical Synthesis

Preview Quiz:

1) When evaluating an answer choice for a rhetorical synthesis question, how important are the following considerations?

	very important	somewhat important	unimportant
Using proper grammar and punctuation	_____	_____	_____
Using sophisticated vocabulary words	_____	_____	_____
Satisfying the task set out in the question	_____	_____	_____

Choose the best answer.

2) While researching a topic, a student has taken the following notes:

- Burkina Faso is a country in western Africa.
- Its capital city is Ouagadougou.
- Ouagadougou is home to several important sculptures that reflect the region's cultural heritage.
- The Naba Koom statue is one the city's most famous sculptures.
- The statue is 6 meters tall and is located in front of the railway station.
- It depicts a woman holding a calabash full of water.
- A calabash is a type of gourd native to western Africa.
- The water is extended towards the rail station as a welcome for visitors to the city.

The student wants to emphasize the significance of the calabash in the Naba Koom statue. Which choice most effectively uses relevant information from the notes to accomplish this goal?

A) The Naba Koom statue is a 6-meter-tall sculpture in Ouagadougou, the capital of Burkina Faso.
B) In her hands, the Naba Koom statue holds a calabash—a type of gourd native to western Africa—which is filled with water.
C) The Naba Koom statue extends her calabash full of water towards the rail station as a welcome for visitors to Ouagadougou.
D) Several important sculptures in Ouagadougou reflect the region's cultural heritage, and the Naba Koom statue is one of the most famous of these.

All the other Writing question types ask you to evaluate someone else's work, but this one turns the tables on you: it's now your job to help create the writing yourself. You'll be placed in the position of a student writing a research paper, where the research has already been completed for you. Based on a list of bullet points that the research has yielded, you'll be asked to select the sentence that best satisfies a specific goal.

Read the question carefully. Your task is *not* just to pick the sentence that you think is the best written; in fact, the correct answer may be no more polished than any of the others. Instead, you must pick the sentence that does the best job of emphasizing some specific point, or making a comparison, or introducing an author to a new audience, or something else entirely—whatever goal was specified in the question.

You don't necessarily need to use all the bullet points. There may be some information provided that is irrelevant to the task set for you in the question. The longest answer is not necessarily the right one.

You don't necessarily need to use *any* of the bullet points. While the information in one or more of the bullet points will certainly be included in the right answer, it's not always essential to read them first. If you're pressed for time in this section, consider skipping the bullet points entirely and just picking the answer choice that best serves the goal laid out for you in the question. In many cases, there will only be one.

FROM THE BLOG

People can, effectively, be stressed out of their minds.
When brains are stressed, thinking is not clear, leaving us far from an optimal learning mood. Addressing your stress level – with breaks, with rest, with whatever you need – is a key part of preparing for the SAT.

Time to take a detailed look at an example.

Example: While researching a topic, a student has taken the following notes:

- *Burkina Faso is a country in western Africa.*
- *Its capital city is Ouagadougou.*
- *Ouagadougou is home to several important sculptures that reflect the region's cultural heritage.*
- *The Naba Koom statue is one the city's most famous sculptures.*
- *The statue is 6 meters tall and is located in front of the railway station.*
- *It depicts a woman holding a calabash full of water.*
- *A calabash is a type of gourd native to western Africa.*
- *The water is extended towards the rail station as a welcome for visitors to the city.*

The student wants to emphasize the significance of the calabash in the Naba Koom statue. Which choice most effectively uses relevant information from the notes to accomplish this goal?

A) The Naba Koom statue is a 6-meter-tall sculpture in Ouagadougou, the capital of Burkina Faso.
B) In her hands, the Naba Koom statue holds a calabash—a type of gourd native to western Africa—which is filled with water.
C) The Naba Koom statue extends her calabash full of water towards the rail station as a welcome for visitors to Ouagadougou.
D) Several important sculptures in Ouagadougou reflect the region's cultural heritage, and the Naba Koom statue is one of the most famous of these.

The question asks us to emphasize the significance of the calabash in the Naba Koom statue, so that's our main focus. Choices A and D can be quickly eliminated, as they don't mention the calabash at all. Choice B tells us what the calabash is, but not *why* it's present in the sculpture. Only choice C emphasizes the significance of the calabash: it's a gesture of welcome for visitors to the city. The right answer is **C**.

TIP:

For many of the Writing questions, a major consideration when evaluating an answer choice is how well-written its version of the sentence is. That is *not* a consideration for Rhetorical Synthesis questions. All we care about here is the task set for us in the question. The right answer is the one that does the best job of accomplishing *that specific task*; it won't necessarily be any better written than any of the other options.

Writing: Expression of Ideas

Notice that we really didn't need to have read the bullet points about the Naba Koom statute in order to pick the right answer.

Try It   It's often possible to pick the right answer choice *without reading the bullet points at all*. Use the question below to practice: try picking the right answer when you have no bullet points at all to read.

The student wants to explain, to an audience already familiar with DNA testing methods, why forensic scientists prefer STR analysis over RFLP.

1) List the elements that the right answer must contain:

   Element #1:

   Element #2:

2) Evaluate the answer choices below by considering how well it satisfies each of the elements you listed.

	Element #1	Element #2
A) Short Tandem Repeat (STR) analysis is a widely used technique in forensic DNA testing that has come to replace older methods such as Restriction Fragment Length Polymorphism (RFLP).	___	___
B) STR analysis offers a high degree of discrimination or resolving power, meaning it can differentiate between individuals with great accuracy.	___	___
C) RFLP analysis requires a larger amount of DNA for testing compared to STR, but it is still suitable for analysis if a large enough sample is available.	___	___
D) The advantages of STR analysis over RFLP include its higher sensitivity, its faster processing time, and its potential for automation.	___	___

3) What is the best answer?

Rhetorical Synthesis

Practice Set 1: Easy-Medium

While researching a topic, a student has taken the following notes:

- Hyperion is a coast redwood (*Sequoia sempervirens*) tree located in Redwood National Park in California.
- It measures 115.7 meters tall.
- Centurion is a mountain ash (*Eucalyptus regnans*) tree located in Tasmania, Australia.
- It measures 100.5 meters tall.
- Hyperion and Centurion are the two tallest known trees in the world.

1

The student wants to compare the heights of the two trees. Which choice most effectively uses relevant information from the notes to accomplish this goal?

A. Hyperion, which measures 115.7 meters tall, is a coast redwood tree located in Redwood National Park in California.
B. Some trees, including a *Sequoia sempervirens* tree in California and a *Eucalyptus regnans* tree in Australia, are more than 100 meters tall.
C. Hyperion, a coast redwood tree located in California, and Centurion, a mountain ash tree located in Australia, are the two tallest known trees in the world.
D. Hyperion measures 115.7 meters tall, while the slightly shorter Centurion measures 100.5 meters tall.

While researching a topic, a student has taken the following notes:

- Olafur Eliasson is a Danish-Icelandic artist.
- He created *The Weather Project* in 2003.
- *The Weather Project* is a large-scale installation consisting of a giant artificial sun, a misty atmosphere, and a reflective ceiling.
- These elements combined to create an illusion of a seemingly endless horizon.

2

The student wants to describe *The Weather Project* to an audience unfamiliar with Olafur Eliasson's work. Which choice most effectively uses relevant information from the notes to accomplish this goal?

A. Eliasson's 2003 installation *The Weather Project*, which created an illusion of a seemingly endless horizon, included such features as a giant artificial sun, a misty atmosphere, and a reflective ceiling.
B. Danish-Icelandic artist Olafur Eliasson created *The Weather Project* in 2003.
C. The components of *The Weather Project* jointly created an illusion of a seemingly endless horizon.
D. *The Weather Project*, a large-scale installation created by Danish-Icelandic artist Olafur Eliasson in 2003, used a giant artificial sun, a misty atmosphere, and a reflective ceiling to create an illusion of a seemingly endless horizon.

Writing: Expression of Ideas

While researching a topic, a student has taken the following notes:

- The viperfish is a marine animal in the genus *Chauliodus*.
- Viperfish are found in tropical and temperate waters, often at depths of 5,000 feet or more.
- The viperfish has a large mouth with hinged lower jaws and long, needle-like teeth.
- Extending from the viperfish's spine is a light-producing organ.
- Viperfish use the glowing organ to attract prey.

3

The student wants to explain the viperfish's predation habits while emphasizing prominent aspects of its appearance. Which choice most effectively uses relevant information from the notes to accomplish this goal?

A. The viperfish uses its long, needle-like teeth to trap prey lured by a light-producing organ extending from its spine.
B. Viperfish, of the genus *Chauliodus*, are equipped with long, needle-like teeth and hinged lower jaws.
C. Because viperfish dwell at depths of 5,000 feet or more, they need to use a light-producing organ to attract prey.
D. The viperfish is found in tropical and temperate waters, roughly 5,000 feet below the ocean surface.

While researching a topic, a student has taken the following notes:

- Claudio Monteverdi (1567-1643) was a prolific Italian composer of both secular and sacred music.
- He is credited with helping to develop the operatic form.
- He wrote the opera *L'Orfeo* in 1607.
- A madrigal is a type of secular vocal music.
- Monteverdi wrote the dramatic madrigal "Il Combattimento di Tancredi e Clorinda" in 1624.

4

The student wants to emphasize a difference between the two works. Which choice most effectively uses relevant information from the notes to accomplish this goal?

A. The musical works *L'Orfeo* and "Il Combattimento di Tancredi e Clorinda" were both completed by Claudio Monteverdi in the 1600s.
B. Monteverdi helped to develop the operatic form and composed a significant number of musical works, including *L'Orfeo* and "Il Combattimento di Tancredi e Clorinda."
C. While both works were composed by Monteverdi, *L'Orfeo* is an opera, while "Il Combattimento di Tancredi e Clorinda" is a madrigal.
D. "Il Combattimento di Tancredi e Clorinda" was a dramatic madrigal, a type of secular vocal music, written by Monteverdi in 1624.

While researching a topic, a student has taken the following notes:

- Historians use a variety of methods to construct historical narratives.
- Traditional methods include archival research and textual analysis.
- These methods do not always capture the stories of marginalized groups.
- Historians can also use digital history, which involves analysis with digital tools and technologies.
- This technique better represents the perspectives of marginalized groups.

5

The student wants to explain an advantage of the use of digital history. Which choice most effectively uses relevant information from the notes to accomplish this goal?

A. For historians aiming to capture the stories of marginalized groups, traditional methods are not always sufficient.
B. The use of digital history better positions historians to explore the perspectives of marginalized groups, whose stories may not have been fully represented in traditional historical narratives.
C. Historians can use digital tools and technologies, a method known as digital history.
D. As techniques for constructing a historical narrative, traditional methods and digital history vary in the degree to which they are able to represent the perspectives of marginalized groups.

While researching a topic, a student has taken the following notes:

- In 2015, the UK-based company Moggyblog.com coined the term "pawternity leave."
- The term is a combination of the terms "paternity leave" and "paw."
- "Pawternity leave" refers to time off work given to employees who have recently adopted a new pet.
- In India, the publisher Harper Collins offers its employees one week of paid leave following adoption of a pet.
- Mparticle, a data platform provider, offers two weeks of paid leave to employees who adopt a rescue dog.

6

The student wants to provide an explanation and example of the term "pawternity leave." Which choice most effectively uses relevant information from the notes to accomplish this goal?

A. The term "pawternity leave," coined by Moggyblog.com in 2015, is a combination of the terms "paternity leave" and "paw."
B. Harper Collins and Mparticle both offer forms of "pawternity leave," a term coined by the UK-based company Moggyblog.com.
C. "Pawternity leave" refers to time off work given to employees who have recently adopted a new pet; for instance, the data platform provider Mparticle offers two weeks of paid leave to employees who adopt a rescue dog.
D. In 2015, Moggyblog.com coined the term "pawternity leave" to refer to time off work given to employees who have recently adopted a new pet.

Writing: Expression of Ideas

While researching a topic, a student has taken the following notes:

- Numerical modeling is a key tool for the understanding of glacier dynamics.
- Numerical models are computer-based simulations that represent the physical processes occurring within and around glaciers.
- These models are based on mathematical equations that describe the physics of ice flow.
- A 2014 study used numerical modeling to simulate the behavior of the Jakobshavn Isbrae glacier in Greenland.
- Researchers inputted data and ran simulations with different scenarios.
- They found that water infiltrates the ice during the summer melt season.
- This reduces the friction between the ice and the bedrock.
- As a result, the glacier accelerates and flows more rapidly during this period.

7

The student wants to explain the findings of the 2014 study and mention the source of the information. Which choice most effectively uses relevant information from the notes to accomplish this goal?

A. The Jakobshavn Isbrae glacier flows more rapidly during the summer melt season, according to computer simulations performed as part of a 2014 study.
B. In 2014, researchers used mathematical equations to simulate the behavior of the Jakobshavn Isbrae glacier.
C. During the summer melt season, water infiltrates glacier ice, reducing the friction between the ice and the bedrock.
D. Glacier dynamics can be modeled with computer-based simulations, as researchers proved in a 2014 study of the Jakobshavn Isbrae glacier.

While researching a topic, a student has taken the following notes:

- The *mulieres Salernitanae* were a group of female physicians and authors in medieval Salerno, Italy.
- They were associated with *Schola Medica Salernitana*, which was one of the leading medical schools during the 11th to 13th centuries.
- One prominent figure associated with the group was Trotula.
- Trotula's works have had a significant impact on the field of medicine.
- One of her most famous treatises is *Trotula Major*.
- The work addressed various topics related to women's health and gynecology.

8

The student wants to introduce Trotula and her impact on the field of medicine to an audience already familiar with the *mulieres Salernitanae*. Which choice most effectively uses relevant information from the notes to accomplish this goal?

A. Trotula was a medieval medical practitioner associated with the renowned medical school *Schola Medica Salernitana*.
B. The *mulieres Salernitanae* of Salerno were female medical practitioners during the medieval period, known for their contributions to medical practice and the authorship of medical treatises.
C. Trotula, a medical practitioner who was associated with the famed *mulieres Salernitanae*, was a physician and author who wrote several influential works on women's health.
D. *Schola Medica Salernitana* flourished during the 11th to 13th centuries and was one of the leading centers of medical education at the time; one famous figure associated with the school was Trotula.

Practice Set 2: Medium-Hard

While researching a topic, a student has taken the following notes:

- The term "language loss" refers to the phenomenon of languages dying out due to a lack of living speakers.
- More than 6,900 languages exist on Earth.
- The number of speakers per language varies widely.
- The 20 languages with the most speakers account for 50% of the global population.
- The 100 languages with the most speakers account for 80% of the global population.
- A language is considered "critically endangered" if it is spoken by so few people that it is likely to be lost within a few years.
- More than 3,000 languages are critically endangered.

1 The student wants to emphasize the scope of the language loss problem. Which choice most effectively uses relevant information from the notes to accomplish this goal?

A. The term "language loss" refers to the phenomenon of languages dying out due to a lack of living speakers.
B. Although 6,900 languages exist on Earth, thousands of these languages are spoken by so few people that they are likely to be lost forever within the next few years.
C. 6,900 languages are spoken on Earth, but the number of speakers varies widely; the 20 languages with the most speakers account for 50% of the global population.
D. Many languages are considered "critically endangered," meaning that they are spoken by so few people that they are likely to be lost within a few years.

While researching a topic, a student has taken the following notes:

- A "quantum computer" is a type of computer that uses the principles of quantum mechanics to perform calculations.
- Classical computers use bits that can take one of two values (either 0 or 1).
- Quantum computers use quantum bits (or "qubits"), which can exist in multiple states at the same time.
- In 2019, researchers conducted an experiment with a quantum computer called Sycamore in an effort to demonstrate the ability of a quantum computer to perform a task that is beyond the reach of classical computers.
- Sycamore was given a calculation task that would have taken a classical supercomputer thousands of years to complete.
- Sycamore completed the task in 200 seconds.

2 The student wants to emphasize the significance of the experiment involving Sycamore. Which choice most effectively uses relevant information from the notes to accomplish this goal?

A. The computer involved in the 2019 experiment used quantum bits, each of which could exist in multiple states at the same time.
B. Sycamore is a quantum computer—a computer that performs calculations using the principles of quantum mechanics—that was involved in a 2019 experiment.
C. By completing in only 200 seconds a task that a classical supercomputer would have taken thousands of years to complete, Sycamore demonstrated the ability of a quantum computer to perform a task that is beyond the reach of classical computers.
D. If the task given to Sycamore in the 2019 experiment had been given to a computer using bits that can take one of two values (0 or 1), that computer would have required thousands of years to complete the task.

Writing: Expression of Ideas

While researching a topic, a student has taken the following notes:

- The relationship between blood pressure and cognitive decline in older adults has been the subject of considerable research.
- Research on this topic has been primarily conducted on white populations.
- A 2017 study investigated whether the conclusions of previous research would hold true for black populations.
- The researchers analyzed data from a large, ongoing cohort study.
- They found that high blood pressure was associated with cognitive decline in both black and white individuals.
- They also found that black individuals were at greater risk for both conditions.

3

The student wants to emphasize the aim of the study. Which choice most effectively uses relevant information from the notes to accomplish this goal?

A. Researchers wanted to determine whether previous conclusions about the relationship between blood pressure and cognitive decline, which were based on research primarily conducted on white populations, would also hold true for black populations.
B. After analyzing data from a large, ongoing cohort study, researchers determined that high blood pressure was associated with cognitive decline in both black and white individuals.
C. Researchers concluded that black individuals are at greater risk than white individuals for both high blood pressure and cognitive decline.
D. Researchers analyzed data from a large, ongoing cohort study of both black and white individuals.

While researching a topic, a student has taken the following notes:

- Tardigrades are exceptionally hardy creatures known for their ability to survive in extreme environments.
- In 2015, a study exposed tardigrades and several other small invertebrates to extreme temperatures and radiation.
- Most of the species tested were not able to survive.
- Tardigrades survived exposure to temperatures as low as −272°C (one degree above absolute zero) and as high as 151°C.
- The tardigrades also survived ionizing radiation doses of up to 5700 gray (Gy).
- A dose of 10-20 Gy usually lethal for humans.

4

The student wants to emphasize how hardy the tardigrade is relative to other small invertebrates. Which choice most effectively uses relevant information from the notes to accomplish this goal?

A. A 2015 study determined that tardigrades can survive temperatures ranging from −272°C to 151°C and ionizing radiation doses of up to 5700 Gy.
B. Most of the species tested in the 2015 study were not able to survive the extreme temperatures and radiation to which they were exposed.
C. While most small invertebrates are not able to survive exposure to ionizing radiation doses of 5700 Gy, tardigrades were shown to survive these conditions in a 2015 study.
D. Compared to other small invertebrates, tardigrades are exceptionally hardy: they can survive temperatures ranging from −272°C to 151°C and ionizing radiation doses of up to 5700 Gy.

While researching a topic, a student has taken the following notes:

- Teatro Campesino was a Chicano theater group founded in 1965 in Delano, California by Luis Valdez.
- Its primary goal was to use theater as a tool for political activism.
- Performances incorporated elements of traditional Mexican culture.
- The plays focused on issues of importance to the Chicano community, such as the exploitation of farmworkers and the importance of union organizing.
- Performances often took place in the fields where farmworkers were laboring.
- The plays energized farmworkers and drew attention to their plight.
- Luis Valdez was closely connected to labor leader César Chávez and his United Farm Workers union.

5

The student wants to explain how the Teatro Campesino used theater as a tool for political activism. Which choice most effectively uses relevant information from the notes to accomplish this goal?

A. Teatro Campesino's performances, which often took place in fields where Chicano farmworkers were laboring, focused on issues such as the exploitation of farmworkers and the importance of union organizing.
B. Luis Valdez, who was closely connected to labor leader César Chávez and his United Farm Workers union, founded Teatro Campesino in 1965.
C. Founded in 1965 in Delano, California, Teatro Campesino performed plays that incorporated elements of traditional Mexican culture.
D. The performance settings, cultural influences, and subject matter of Teatro Campesino's plays energized Chicano farmworkers and drew attention to their plight.

While researching a topic, a student has taken the following notes:

- An ant foraging for food leaves behind a trail of pheromones.
- Other ants detect the pheromones and follow the same path.
- Ants can adjust the strength and direction of the trail based on changing conditions.
- Ants are one of many species that solve problems by working in parallel.
- This strategy involves a large number of creatures performing simple actions whose collective impact can solve a complex problem.

6

The student wants to make and support a generalization about animal behavior. Which choice most effectively uses relevant information from the notes to accomplish this goal?

A. Many species are capable of working in parallel: a large number of creatures performs simple actions whose collective impact can solve a complex problem.
B. Large groups of animals can work in parallel to solve a complex problem: ants can collectively establish a trail to a food source and adjust the trail based on changing conditions.
C. Ants can adjust the strength and direction of a food trail based on changing conditions; thus, though the individual ants are performing simple actions, their collective impact can solve a complex problem.
D. An ant foraging for food leaves behind a trail of pheromones; other ants detect the pheromones and follow the same path.

Writing: Expression of Ideas

While researching a topic, a student has taken the following notes:

- The parathyroid glands are small endocrine glands located in the neck.
- They produce and release parathyroid hormone (PTH).
- PTH helps maintain the balance of calcium in the blood, bones, and other tissues.
- It acts on the bones, kidneys, and intestines to increase calcium absorption, reabsorption, and mobilization.
- PTH also acts on the kidneys to reduce the reabsorption of phosphorus.
- This helps maintain the balance of phosphorus in the body by preventing excessive buildup.

7

The student wants to explain what parathyroid glands are and describe their effect on the body. Which choice most effectively uses relevant information from the notes to accomplish this goal?

A. Parathyroid glands, which produce and release parathyroid hormone, are located in the neck.
B. By reducing the reabsorption of phosphorus, parathyroid hormone prevents excessive phosphorus buildup.
C. The parathyroid glands are small endocrine glands that produce parathyroid hormone to regulate calcium and phosphorus levels in the body.
D. Parathyroid hormone acts to increase calcium absorption, reabsorption, and mobilization.

While researching a topic, a student has taken the following notes:

- Workers renovating houses with lead-based paint should always wear personal protective equipment (PPE).
- PPE includes disposable coveralls, gloves, shoe covers, and face masks.
- This equipment protects workers from lead dust.
- Lead is a toxic metal that can affect various organs and systems.
- When lead dust is inhaled, it can enter the bloodstream and accumulate over time, leading to lead poisoning.
- In children, lead exposure can result in learning disabilities, reduced IQ, and behavioral issues.
- In adults, lead exposure can cause cognitive impairment and mood disorders.
- Prolonged exposure to lead dust can contribute to the development of respiratory conditions, including bronchitis and pneumonia.
- Lead can cause increased blood pressure and an increased risk of heart attacks and strokes.

8

The student wants to explain why workers should wear protective equipment when working in homes with lead-based paint. Which choice most effectively uses relevant information from the notes to accomplish this goal?

A. Protective equipment prevents workers from inhaling lead, a toxic chemical that can lead to harmful neurological, respiratory, and cardiovasculatory effects.
B. The acronym PPE refers to personal protective equipment, which can include disposable coveralls, gloves, shoe covers, and face masks.
C. Exposure to lead dust can lead to lead poisoning, which can cause cognitive impairment and respiratory conditions over time.
D. Lead buildup in the bloodstream is associated with an increased risk of cardiovascular problems such as high blood pressure, heart attacks, and strokes.

Math Section Overview

There are four general categories of math topics covered on the test.

- **Algebra**

    These questions focus on interpreting, manipulating, and solving linear equations. Make sure your algebra skills are strong and that you understand what each piece of a linear equation represents.

- **Advanced Math**

    Sort of next-level algebra, these problems will ask you to work with quadratic and other non-linear equations such as exponential functions and higher-order polynomials. You may be asked to characterize parts of these equations as well as to work with and solve them.

- **Problem Solving and Data Analysis**

    This category covers topics such as ratios, percentages, unit conversions, and working with charts/tables of data.

- **Geometry and Trigonometry**

    Problems in this category involve finding area or volume; using your knowledge of SOH-CAH-TOA; and working with similar triangles and other polygons.

Section Breakdown

Algebra
13-15 per section
≈ 35%

Advanced Math
13-15 per section
≈ 35%

Problem-Solving and Data Analysis
5-7 per section
≈ 15%

Geometry and Trigonometry
5-7 per section
≈ 15%

Strategy in Brief

Because the SAT is very different from most tests you take in school, the best method for solving SAT Math problems is often not the way you were taught in the classroom. The strategies we present in this introductory section are tailored to standardized testing and can be helpful in raising your score.

It is often helpful to ask yourself a series of questions when confronted with a difficult math problem.

- What specifically am I being asked to solve? Can I simplify the problem?

- Can I approximate? Is there a shortcut that will eliminate some complicated calculations?

- Do I know a formula?

Many find going through this checklist takes some of the mental burden off answering math questions, since the first moments are spent reacting instead of thinking. If you know a formula that's relevant to the question, be sure to get it down on your scratch paper. Simply writing out a formula will often help clarify what a question is asking for.

If you don't know how to get to the answer, start by writing down what you *do* know. Perhaps the question is asking for the measure of angle A, and all you can see how to figure out is the measure of angle B. Go ahead and fill that in. Once it's on the page, you may find that angle B actually helps you determine angle C, and the sum of angles B and C is supplementary to angle A, and so on… and before you know it, you've solved the problem. The key is to get your pencil moving—it's sitting and staring at the problem that's the enemy.

Back-solving and Substitution

Preview Quiz

Solve each of the following.

1) If the product of three consecutive odd integers is 1,287, what is the middle integer?

    A) 11
    B) 13
    C) 15
    D) 17

2) During a certain leap year, the number of non-rainy days is 30 more than half the number of rainy days. How many of this year's days are rainy? (Note: A leap year has 366 days.)

    A) 168
    B) 198
    C) 213
    D) 224

3) If $8^b + 8^b + 8^b + 8^b = a$, then which of the following expresses a in terms of b?

    A) 2^{6b}
    B) 2^{3b+2}
    C) 32^b
    D) 8^{4b}

4) The base of a triangle is decreased by 20%, while the height of the triangle is increased by 50%. What is the ratio of the triangle's new area to its old area?

    A) 6:5
    B) 3:10
    C) 10:3
    D) 25:3

Back-solving means trying the given answers until you find the one that works. This strategy takes advantage of the fact that most math problems on the SAT are multiple-choice.

Start in the middle.	Focus on either choice B or choice C. Substitute this value for the number that answers the question.
Plug in.	Use this number to evaluate all other unknowns in the question. If you've gone back through the entire question and everything works, select this answer and move on. You're done!
Cross it out.	If the number doesn't work, cross out the choice and consider whether the one you tried was too large or too small. Eliminate the other choice or choices that will have the same problem.
Continue.	If there's only one choice left, select it and move on. If there are two, try one of the remaining choices to see which one is your answer.

Let's walk through the process with a few examples.

Example: *If the product of three consecutive odd integers is 1,287, what is the middle integer?*

  A) 11
  B) 13
  C) 15
  D) 17

This problem tells us that there is a set of three consecutive odd numbers (three odds in a row, such as *3, 5, 7* or *5, 7, 9*) that multiply together to result in the number 1,287. We could set up some algebra to solve this, but it's difficult and time-consuming. Instead, we'll work backwards from the answer choices.

Let's start with choice B. If 13 is the middle number, then our set of three odd numbers would have to be *11, 13, 15*. So, turn to the calculator. Does it work?

$$11 * 13 * 15 = 2145$$

We didn't get 1287, so this is the wrong answer. Eliminate choice B.

And there's more. More specifically, choice B was wrong because it was too *big*. Choices C and D are even bigger, so they must be wrong as well. We're already done: choice **A** must be the right answer. You can double-check it to be sure:

$$9 * 11 * 13 = 1287$$

Back-Solving and Substitution

Let's try another.

Example: During a certain leap year, the number of non-rainy days is 30 more than half the number of rainy days. How many of this year's days are rainy? (Note: A leap year has 366 days.)

   A) 168
   B) 198
   C) 213
   D) 224

Start with choice B again. If 198 is the number of rainy days, then "half the number of rainy days" is 198/2 = 99. The number of non-rainy days must be 30 more than that amount, so 99 + 30 = 129. Okay: now we know that if there are 198 rainy days, then there are 129 non-rainy days. That gives us a total of 198 + 129 = 327 days in the year. But the problem told us that the total number of days should be 366, not 327. Therefore, this answer is too small. Eliminate choice B and choice A (which is even smaller).

Now we go to choice C. If 213 is the number of rainy days, then "half the number of rainy days" is 213/2 = 106.5. Uh-oh—this isn't going to work! We need a whole number of days in both categories.

The answer must be **D**, but let's double-check it to be sure:

$$\text{rainy} = 224$$
$$\text{non-rainy} = 224/2 + 30 = 142$$
$$\text{Total} = 224 + 142 = 366$$

Try It — Solve each of the following.

1) If $0 < x - \dfrac{1}{x} < 1$, which of the following could be x?

   A) $\dfrac{7}{8}$
   B) $\dfrac{11}{8}$
   C) $\dfrac{17}{8}$
   D) $\dfrac{19}{8}$

2) Marta owns 3 more than half the number of rare coins that Brigitta owns. If Brigitta owns 18 more rare coins than Marta, how many does Marta own?

   A) 24
   B) 33
   C) 36
   D) 42

TIP:

When you back-solve, as soon as you get an answer that works, you can stop. There's no need to check all the remaining choices.

- 205 -

Math: Strategy

Many math problems contain variables or other unknown quantities. **Substitution** is the practice of replacing these unknowns with numbers, so that you can solve the problems using arithmetic instead of algebra.

Choose a number or numbers.	Substitute on the side where there's more "action"—e.g., for the equation $x = 3y$, substitute a simple number for y. If there are multiple equations, start with the variable that the equations have in common. Pick easy numbers like 2 or 3 (or 100 for percentage problems, 60 for mph problems, etc). Avoid using 0 or 1.
Write it down.	Don't skip this step! It's easy to lose track of what you started with when you're several steps in.
Solve.	Use your number(s) to work through the problem on your scratch paper. When you reach an answer, circle it on the page.
Check.	Plug your original number(s) into **every** choice, crossing out all choices that do not match your circled answer.
Repeat as needed.	If more than one answer choice remains, pick a different number and try again with only the remaining choices.

FROM THE BLOG

You don't want to end up with a mistake on your admission ticket that you only discover on the day of the test. So take your time when registering. Don't register when you are in a rush. Don't register late at night when you are tired. Don't register on a smartphone. And above all else, double-check to make sure everything is accurate before the morning of the SAT.

Again, we'll walk through a few examples to see how it works.

Example: If $8^b + 8^b + 8^b + 8^b = a$, then which of the following expresses a in terms of b?

A) 2^{6b}
B) 2^{3b+2}
C) 32^b
D) 8^{4b}

This ugly-looking exponents problem becomes a lot easier if we can get rid of some of the abstraction by using actual numbers in place of the letters. To begin, pick a number you'd like to use for b. It should be a nice, small number that's easy to work with, but not zero or one. How about two? Write it down:

$$b = 2$$

Next, plug that value into the original equation to get a value for a.

$$8^2 + 8^2 + 8^2 + 8^2 = a$$
$$64 + 64 + 64 + 64 = a$$
$$256 = a$$

Okay, so if $b = 2$, then $a = 256$. Now, what was the question asking us? We want to identify the choice that "expresses a in terms of b." The phrase "in terms of b" doesn't mean anything! All that tells us is what the choices will look like: they'll each have a b in them. For our purposes, we can mentally cross that part of the question out. All we really need to do is find the answer choice that equals a.

Well, we already know that if $b = 2$, then a must equal 256. So next, plug 2 in for b in each answer choice. The one that comes out to 256 is our winner.

A) $2^{6b} = 2^{6(2)} = 2^{12} = 4096$

Nope, too big. Eliminate choice A.

B) $2^{3b+2} = 2^{3(2)+2} = 2^8 = 256$

Hey, that works! But wait: we're not done. It's still possible that another answer choice will also equal 256, so we have to check the remaining options.

C) $32^b = 32^2 = 1024$
D) $8^{4b} = 8^{4(2)} = 8^8 = 16777216$

Only choice **B** works, so that's the right answer.

> **TIP:**
> When you use the substitution strategy, always be sure to check **all** the choices in case there's more than one that works.

That first problem featured **variables in the answer choices**, which is one of the big tip-offs that a problem might be a good candidate for the substitution strategy. But in general, this is a good approach for any problem that is all about the **relationships** between numbers instead of the numbers themselves: for example, a problem that asks for an average or a ratio of two values. Let's look at another example.

Example: The base of a triangle is decreased by 20%, while the height of the triangle is increased by 50%. What is the ratio of the triangle's new area to its old area?

A) 6:5
B) 3:10
C) 10:3
D) 25:3

Draw a triangle and assign it a base and height. You can use any numbers you want, but you can make life easier by picking values that work well with the problem. Since we're dealing with percent here, let's use 10.

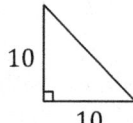

Now, 20% of 10 is $0.20(10) = 2$. The base should be decreased by that much, so the new base is $10 - 2 = 8$. And what about the height? 50% of 10 is $0.50(10) = 5$. The height should be *increased* by that much, so the new height is $10 + 5 = 15$.

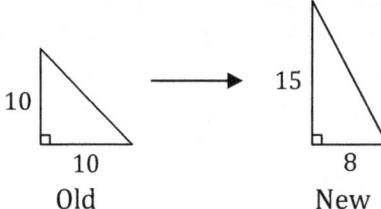

Old   New

The question was about the areas of these triangles, so we next need to calculate the area for each.

$$\text{Area of a triangle} = \frac{1}{2}bh$$

$$\text{Old area} = \frac{1}{2}(10)(10) = 50$$

$$\text{New area} = \frac{1}{2}(8)(15) = 60$$

Therefore, the ratio of the new area to the old area is 60/50, which simplifies to 6/5. The answer is **A**.

> **TIP:**
> A ratio is just a fraction. The ratio 60:50 is equivalent to the fraction 60/50, which simplifies to 6/5, which is equivalent to the ratio 6:5.

Try It Solve each of the following.

3) In a certain class, there are b boys and twice as many girls as boys. If four girls leave this class, then, in terms of b, how many girls remain in the class?

   A) $\dfrac{b-4}{2}$

   B) $\dfrac{b}{4} - 2$

   C) $2b + 4$

   D) $2b - 4$

4) If the average of x and y is 10 and the average of y and z is 6, what is the average of x and z in terms of y?

   A) $\dfrac{2y+8}{3}$

   B) $\dfrac{y+8}{2}$

   C) $16 - y$

   D) $8 - y$

Math: Strategy

Each strategy you just learned is specific to certain math problems on the SAT. One of the keys to mastering them is knowing which technique to use for which problems. Here are some tips that will help you to make this important distinction:

You should use **back-solving** for:

- questions with only numbers (no variables) in the answer choices
- tricky word problems that would be difficult to set up with algebra
- "could be" questions

You should use **substitution** for:

- questions with variables in the answer choices
- problems focused on ratios, percentages, or other *relationships* between unknown quantities
- "must be" questions

You should **NOT** use back-solving for:

- answer choices with unknown variables
- indirect questions (e.g., "Which of the following is NOT...?")

You should **NOT** use substitution for:

- problems with all fixed numerical values in the choices

For each of the problems in the practice sets that follow, first decide which of the two strategies is more suitable, and then use that method to solve the problem.

Practice Set 1: Easy-Medium

1

If $(x-1)(x-2) = (x+4)(x+8)$, what is the value of x?

A. -2
B. -1
C. 0
D. 1

2

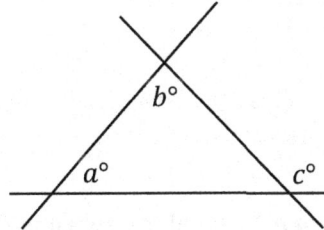

Three lines intersect to form a triangle as shown above. Which of the following expresses the value of c?

A. $a + b$
B. $180 - a$
C. $180 - b$
D. $90 - b$

3

Within a certain calling region, a telephone company charges 15 cents per minute for the first hour and 10 cents per minute beyond the first hour. If a telephone call within this region cost $23.00, how long was the conversation?

A. 1 hour, 8 minutes
B. 2 hours, 33 minutes
C. 3 hours, 20 minutes
D. 3 hours, 50 minutes

4

If $0 < c < d < 1$, then which of the following has the greatest value?

A. d^2
B. cd
C. c
D. d

5

Each side of a square has length s. When all side lengths are doubled, the area of the square increases by 108 square centimeters. What is the value of s in centimeters?

A. 4
B. 5
C. 6
D. 8

6

What number is 3 greater than twice the square root of itself?

A. 1
B. 3
C. 4
D. 9

7

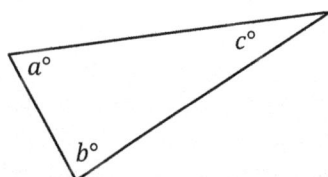

Note: Figure not drawn to scale

In the figure above, if $a + b = c$, then what is the value of c?

A. 10
B. 30
C. 60
D. 90

8

A certain store sold 40% more books on Saturday than it sold on Friday. If the store sold 35 books on Saturday, how many books did the store sell on Friday?

A. 14
B. 21
C. 25
D. 49

Math: Strategy

Practice Set 2: Medium-Hard

1

If the ratio of Gena's age to Sally's age is 2:3, and the ratio of Tim's age to Sally's age is 3:4, what is the ratio of Tim's age to Gena's age?

A. 8:9
B. 9:8
C. 1:2
D. 2:1

2

Which of the following is a solution set for $9z + 5 = 2z^2$?

A. $\left\{-\frac{1}{2}, \frac{1}{2}\right\}$
B. $\left\{-5, \frac{1}{2}\right\}$
C. $\left\{-\frac{1}{2}, 5\right\}$
D. $\left\{\frac{1}{2}, 5\right\}$

3

Let a and b be nonzero numbers such that a is $\frac{2}{3}$ of b. What is the ratio of b^2 to a^2?

A. 16 to 9
B. 9 to 4
C. 3 to 4
D. 2 to 3

4

If $2p = 3q = 4r$, what is the average of $p, q,$ and r in terms of r?

A. $\frac{3r}{2}$
B. $\frac{13r}{18}$
C. $\frac{13r}{9}$
D. $\frac{4r}{9}$

5

On a certain 25-question test, students receive 1 point for each correct answer and lose $\frac{1}{3}$ point for each incorrect answer. If Tyrrell answered every question on this test and earned a total of 17 points, how many questions did Tyrrell answer correctly?

A. 17
B. 18
C. 19
D. 21

6

If 20% of m is equal to n, what is 20% of $4m$ in terms of n?

A. $8n$
B. $4n$
C. $2n$
D. $\frac{n}{4}$

7

Penny needs to buy two hundred 6-inch nails for a construction project. If the pre-tax price of n 6-inch nails is p dollars, which of the following represents the total pre-tax price of Penny's order in terms of n and p?

A. $\dfrac{200n}{p}$
B. $\dfrac{n}{200p}$
C. $\dfrac{200p}{n}$
D. $\dfrac{p}{200n}$

8

Michael is five years older than James will be in three years. James is now j years old. In terms of j, how old will Michael be in three years?

A. $j + 3$
B. $j + 5$
C. $j + 8$
D. $j + 11$

9

If $x = 4y^2$ and $z = 2y - 6$, which of the following expresses x in terms of z?

A. $2z^2 + 9$
B. $(z + 8)^2$
C. $(z + 6)^2$
D. $2z^2 + 3z + 9$

10

A certain brand of tea is sold for d dollars per ounce. If z ounces are needed to make a single cup of tea, which of the following expresses how many dollars it would cost to make s cups of tea?

A. sdz
B. $\dfrac{dz}{s}$
C. $\dfrac{sz}{d}$
D. $\dfrac{d}{sz}$

11

Fred originally had $2 more than two-thirds the amount of money that Barney had. After Barney gave $5 to Fred, they both had the same amount of money. How much money did Barney originally have?

A. $36
B. $30
C. $26
D. $24

12

A passenger train departs for a 450-mile journey and travels at a rate of 75 miles per hour. A second train departs the same station x hours later for the same destination and arrives at the same time as the first train. What was the average speed, in terms of x, of the second train?

A. $150(6 - x)$
B. $150x$
C. $\dfrac{450}{x}$
D. $\dfrac{450}{6 - x}$

13

If $a = 2x^{-2}$ and $b = 2x^{\frac{1}{2}}$, then which of the following is equivalent to $a^2 b^2$?

A. $\dfrac{1}{8x^3}$
B. $\dfrac{16}{x^3}$
C. $4x^2$
D. $16x^2$

14

A biologist will use the partially completed table below to provide information about a sample of 62 moths.

	Male	Female	Total
Spotted		18	
Non-spotted	11		
Total	?		62

Which of the following could be the total number of male moths in the collection?

A. 43
B. 48
C. 55
D. 62

Math: Strategy

Mastering the Calculator

Preview Quiz

Choose the best answer(s).

1) What is the calculator policy on the SAT? <u>Choose all that apply.</u>

   A) You can use an on-screen calculator that's built into the testing software.
   B) You can use your own calculator.
   C) You can use a calculator on some math problems but not all.
   D) You can use a calculator on all problems in the math section.
   E) You are not permitted to use a calculator.

Solve.

2) Which of the following (x, y) points is a solution to $3x - y \leq 4$ and $x > 2$?

   A) $(-1, 0)$
   B) $(0, -5)$
   C) $(3, 7)$
   D) $(4, 1)$

3) If $-1 < a < 0$, which of the following values is the greatest?

   A) a^2

   B) $0.5a$

   C) $\dfrac{2}{a}$

   D) $\left|\dfrac{1}{a+1}\right|$

Mastering the Calculator

The SAT permits you to use a calculator on as many math problems as you choose. You can use your own calculator that you bring from home, or you can use the on-screen graphing calculator that's built into the testing software. Trust us on this: no matter how much you like your trusty TI-84, **the built-in calculator is better**.

If you've ever used the Desmos calculator in a math class before, congratulations: you already know how to use this. If you haven't, don't worry, because it's very easy to learn.

When you click on the calculator icon, you'll see a screen like this.

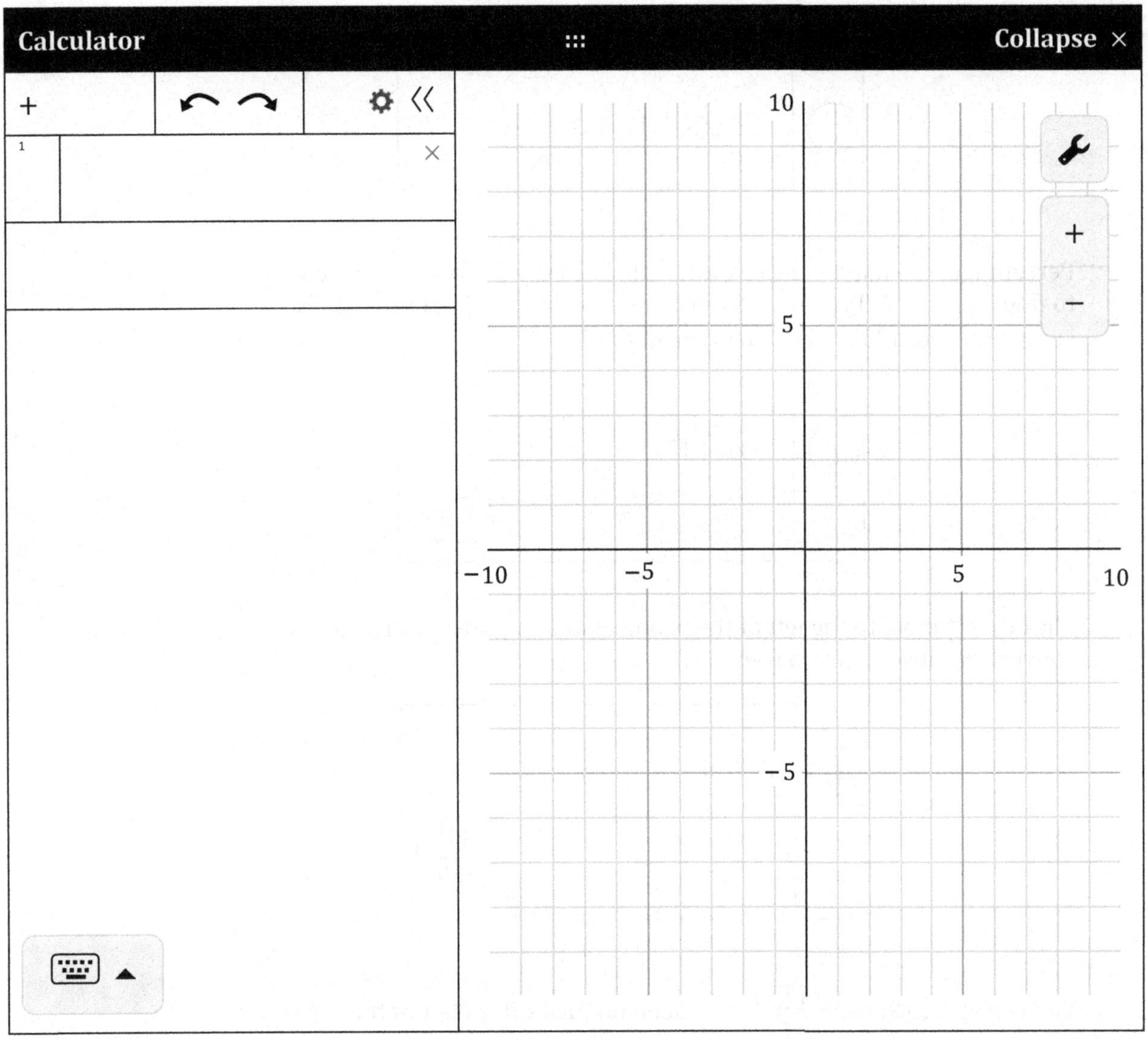

Type whatever expression you want into the window on the left, and the answer will display automatically.

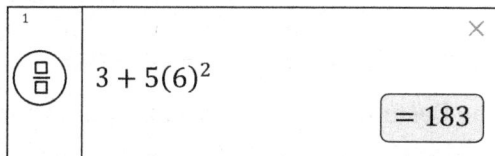

There are many intuitive keyboard shortcuts. For example, to find the square root of something, type `sqrt`, and those letters will automatically convert to a radical. To enter π, type `pi`. To apply an exponent, use the ^ symbol on your keyboard (press shift, 6). To calculate absolute value, type `abs(`. And here's how you find the average (the arithmetic mean) of the numbers 5, 8, 12, and 13:

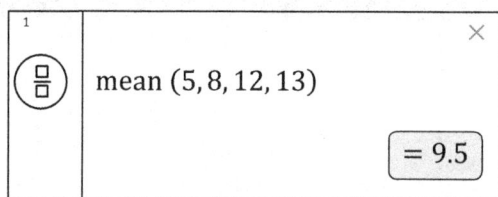

Percentages are maybe the easiest of all. Let's say a problem asks you to find 35% of 17. Type in 35%, and the calculator will automatically supply the word "of." Then just type in the 17.

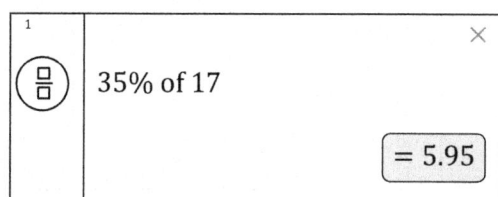

Click that symbol to the left of the problem and the calculator will convert the answer into a fraction:

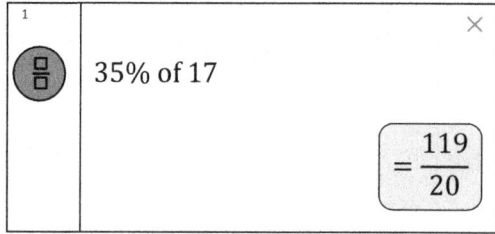

You can also click the ⌨▲ icon on the bottom left of the screen to access these and other functions by clicking buttons on a traditional calculator screen.

Try out the problems below using the calculator in the SAT's Bluebook™ app (or go to desmos.com/calculator).

Try It $3, 10, 1, -4, 6, 2$

1) What is the positive difference between the mean and the median of the given data set?

2) A circle has a radius of 3.5 inches. Which of the following is closest to the area of the circle, in square inches? (Note: the area of a circle with radius r is given by $A = \pi r^2$.)

   A) 7.0
   B) 12.3
   C) 22.0
   D) 38.5

3) The expression $\sqrt{27} + \sqrt{12}$ is equivalent to which of the following?

   A) $5\sqrt{3}$
   B) $4\sqrt{6}$
   C) $6\sqrt{3}$
   D) $9\sqrt{2}$

To **graph** an equation, type it into that box on the left. If you want to graph more than one equation at a time, press ENTER and type in the next equation in the box below it. The equations can be in any format: you do not have to isolate y in the equation to solve.

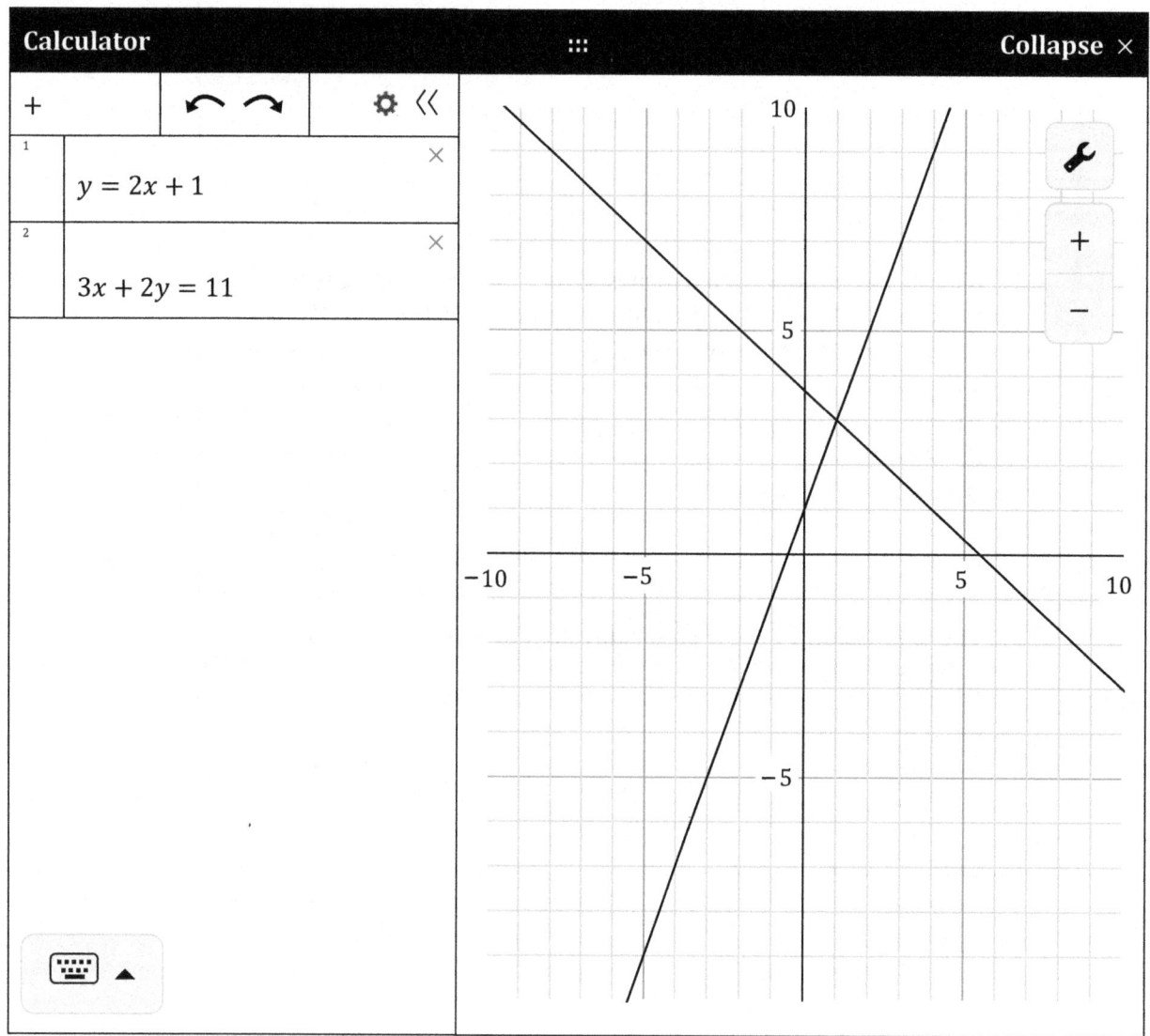

Hover over or click on the lines and the calculator will automatically display the coordinates of helpful points, such as an x-intercept, a y-intercept, or the point of intersection. In addition, although you can't see it in this image, the lines are color-coded to make it easier to tell which graph matches which equation.

The controls on the upper right of the screen help you control how much of the graph you see. Use the $+$ and $-$ buttons to zoom in and out, or click on the wrench icon to zoom to a specific interval by setting the minimum and maximum values for the x-axis and/or the y-axis.

There's more. See that little ⚙ symbol above the equations? Click on that to get an automatic table of points.

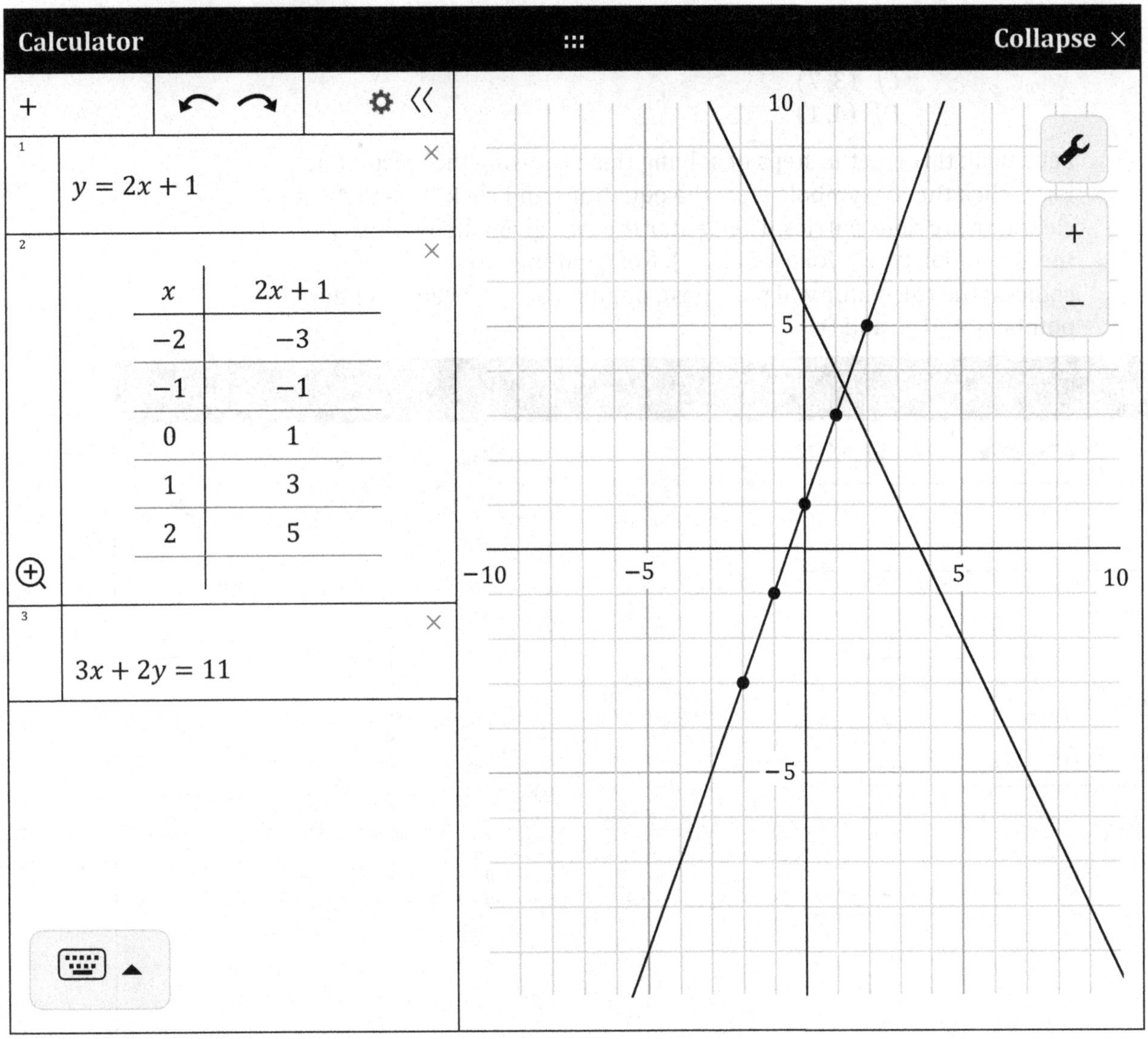

Calculator		
1	$y = 2x + 1$	✕
2		✕

x	$2x + 1$
-2	-3
-1	-1
0	1
1	3
2	5

| 3 | $3x + 2y = 11$ | ✕ |

The graph will automatically highlight those points, and you can type in whatever additional x values you want to see the corresponding y values. And, see that little ⊕ icon to the left of the table? Clicking on that will automatically zoom the window in or out so that you have the best view of the important features of the graph.

You can use these features to solve a wide variety of problems.

Example: Which of the following (x, y) points is a solution to $3x - y \leq 4$ and $x > 2$?

A) $(-1, 0)$
B) $(0, -6)$
C) $(3, 7)$
D) $(4, 1)$

Let's walk through the steps of solving this one using the calculator. First, click the ⚙ symbol above the equations and click "Delete All" to clear our previous entries. Then enter the two given inequalities (for the ≤ symbol, type < followed by =). Next, enter all four answer choices; the calculator will plot those points. You can even label the points as A, B, C, and D.

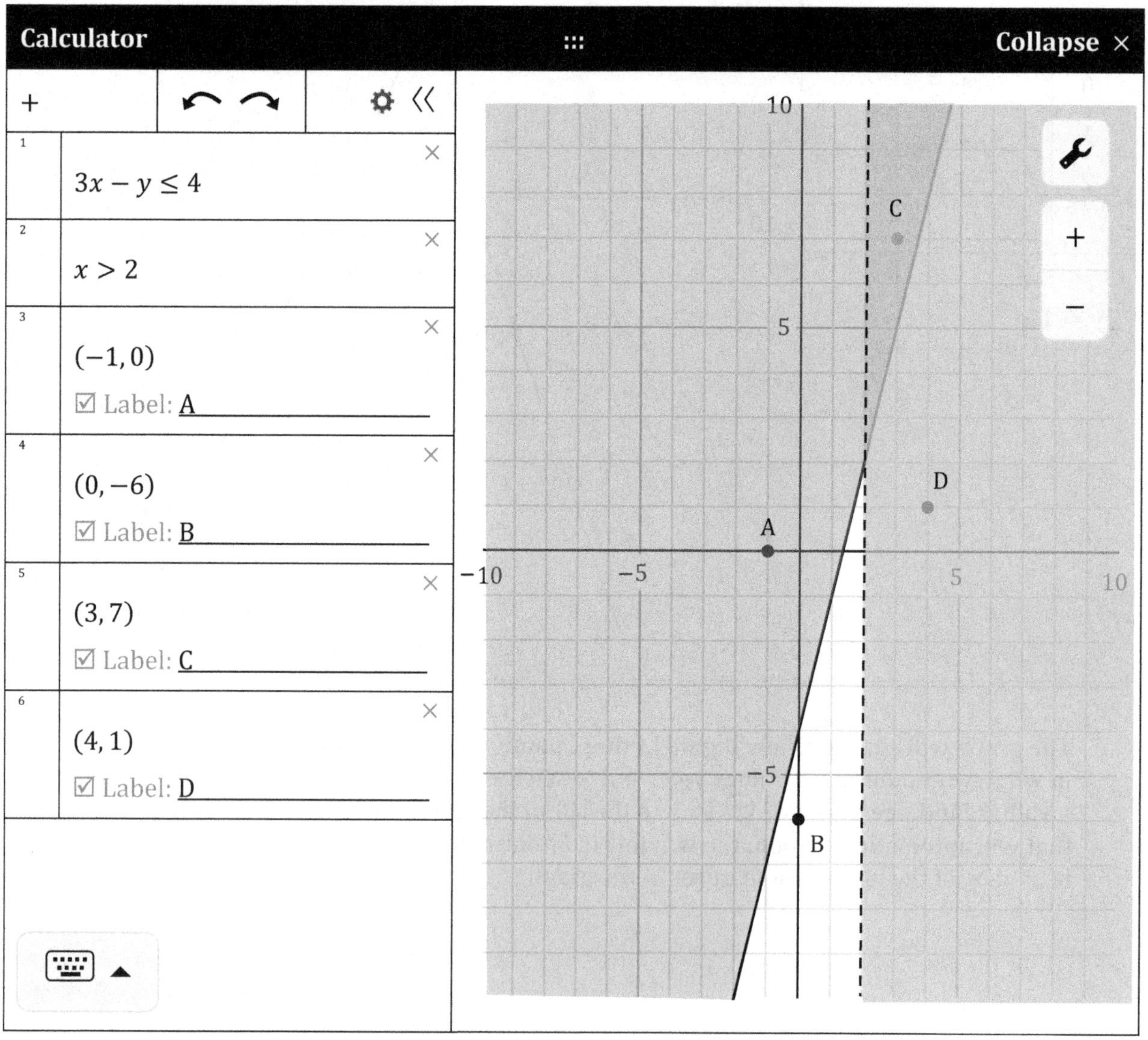

Choice C is the only point in the overlapping portion of the shaded regions, so the answer is **C**.

Try It   Solve the problems below by graphing them on the built-in calculator.

$$3x + 2y = 8$$
$$x - y = 4$$

4) What is the solution (x, y) to the system of equations above?

5) On the xy-plane, what are the x-intercepts of the graph of $f(x) = 2x^2 + x - 15$?

6) What is the diameter of the circle given by $(x - 3)^2 + y^2 = 9$, in coordinate units?

The calculator is also helpful for **back-solving** and **substitution**.

Example: If $-1 < a < 0$, which of the following values is the greatest?

A) a^2

B) $0.5a$

C) $\dfrac{2}{a}$

D) $\left|\dfrac{1}{a+1}\right|$

To solve this, first pick a number for a that falls within the boundaries set for us by the problem. Let's use $a = -0.2$ for our example. Enter that into the calculator, and then enter each answer choice exactly as it appears. The calculator will automatically plug in -0.2 for a in each answer choice and calculate the result.

1. $a = -0.2$, slider from -10 to 10	
2. a^2	$= 0.04$
3. $0.5a$	$= -0.1$
4. $\dfrac{2}{a}$	$= -10$
5. $\text{abs}\left(\dfrac{1}{a+1}\right)$	$= 1.25$

TIP:
You don't have to use "a" as your constant: almost any letter will work the same way. However, there are a few exceptions: the letters $x, y, t, e,$ and i all have other mathematical meanings, so the calculator won't interpret them in this way.

Of these options, 1.25 is the greatest, so the answer is **D**.

We can also use this approach to try a range of different values. Take another look at that first entry again, the one where we set the value of a. See the long horizontal line with a circle in the middle of it? That's called a **slider**, and it will let us change the value of a to whatever we want. Try dragging that slider to the left and right and watch the results of all the other entries change.

If you only want to test whole number values for a, click in that top row and change the "Step:" value to 1. If you like, you can fill in a minimum and maximum value for a as well.

You can also let the calculator show you the results of changing the value. Click the ⊙ button on the left side of that top row and the calculator will automatically cycle through different values for a.

> ### TIP:
> The built-in calculator is a powerful aid for this test, but it can't do everything. It's still in your interest to learn the algebraic way to solve these problems so that you have *both* methods at your disposal and can choose the best one to solve a particular problem.
> **Let the calculator be a tool, not a crutch.**

Practice Set 1: Easy-Medium

1

$$f(x) = 2x^2 + 13x - 7$$

The quadratic function f is defined above. Which of the following is an x-intercept of the graph of $y = f(x)$ in the xy-plane?

A. $(-7, 0)$
B. $(-1, 0)$
C. $(1, 0)$
D. $(7, 0)$

2

At the Robinson School, 24% of fifth-graders ride the bus to school. If there are 75 fifth-graders at the Robinson School, how many of them ride the bus to school?

3

$$12, 10, 5, 39, 8$$

What is the median of the list of data shown above?

A. 5
B. 10
C. 11
D. 14.8

4

What is the solution (x, y) to the system of equations below?

$$6x - y = 1$$
$$4y - x = 19$$

A. $(-9, -55)$
B. $(0, 4.75)$
C. $(1, 5)$
D. $(21, 10)$

5

$$f(x) = -2(x-1)(x+3)$$

Which table gives three values of x and their corresponding values of $f(x)$ for the given function?

A.
x	1	2	3
$f(x)$	-16	-20	-28

B.
x	1	2	3
$f(x)$	0	-10	-24

C.
x	1	2	3
$f(x)$	0	10	24

D.
x	1	2	3
$f(x)$	6	0	-10

6

The graph of $2x + y < -4$ includes NO points in which of the following quadrants of the xy-plane?

A. Quadrant I
B. Quadrant II
C. Quadrant III
D. Quadrant IV

7

$$y = x^2 + 2x$$
$$y = x^2 - 2x + 2$$

In the xy-plane, the graphs of the equations shown intersect at $(m, 1.25)$. What is the value of m?

Practice Set 2: Medium-Hard

1

In the equation $2x^2 + bx + 8 = 0$, b is a constant. For which of the following values of b does the equation have no real solutions?

A. -10
B. 5
C. 8
D. 9

2

$$f(x) = 1500(1.07)^x$$

The exponential function $f(x)$ gives the value of an investment account, in dollars, x years after it was opened. Which of the following is closest to the value of the account 6 years after it was opened?

A. $2000
B. $2104
C. $2127
D. $2251

3

The function f is defined by the equation $f(x) = x^2 + 2x - 3$. The function $g(x)$ is the result of shifting the graph of $f(x)$ up 3 units and right 2 units on the xy-plane. Which of the following could be the equation of $g(x)$?

A. $g(x) = 2(x - 0.5)^2 - 2$
B. $g(x) = (x - 2)^2 - 3$
C. $g(x) = (x - 1)^2 - 1$
D. $g(x) = 3(x + 1)^2 - 4$

4

In the linear function f, $f(0) = 6$ and $f(1) = 9$. Which equation defines f?

A. $f(x) = x + 3$
B. $f(x) = 3x + 6$
C. $f(x) = 6x + 9$
D. $f(x) = 9x + 1$

5

$$x^2 - 6x + y^2 + 8y = -16$$

In the xy-plane, what are the coordinates of the center of the circle given by the equation above?

A. $(3, -7)$
B. $(3, -4)$
C. $(0, -4)$
D. $(2, -1)$

6

$$3x - 5y = 8$$
$$y = x^2 - 1$$

How many solutions exist to the system of equations shown?

A. 0
B. 1
C. 2
D. infinitely many

7

In the xy-plane, the graph of the equation $ax + by = c$ is a vertical line. Which of the following could be the values of a, b, and c?

A. $a = 0, b = 1, c = 1$
B. $a = 0, b = 1, c = 0$
C. $a = 1, b = 0, c = 1$
D. $a = 1, b = 1, c = 0$

8

How many (x, y) pairs of real numbers satisfy the equations $xy = 1$ and $x^2 + y^2 = 9$?

Math: Strategy

Approximating and Measuring

If you're not sure how to even start a math problem, don't panic! You can often use simple methods to eliminate choices and make an educated guess.

It's okay to round. It's possible to solve all of the problems on the SAT exactly, but you can often save time by approximating. If you're told to square the number 4.9, try thinking of it as a little bit less than 5^2: almost 25.

Trust your eyes. All figures are drawn to scale unless you are told otherwise. Use that to eliminate choices: if an angle looks like less than 90°, it is. (You can double-check by holding up a piece of scratch paper to the screen and measuring the angle against the corner).

Choose something. There is no guessing penalty on the SAT, so there's no reason to ever leave anything blank. Once you've crossed out a few choices using the strategies above, go with your gut and select the choice that makes the most sense to you.

TIP:

Use the built-in calculator to help you approximate. Many questions about equations become a lot easier if you can take a look at the graph.

FROM THE BLOG

Sleep is crucial to consolidation of learning, test performance, and lowered anxiety. So make sleep a priority. The week before the test, punt on socializing and save that for a well-deserved post-test celebration.

Practice Set 1: Easy-Medium

1

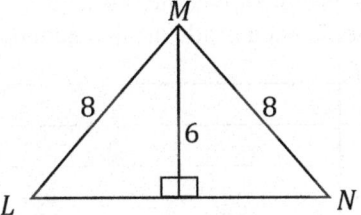

In the figure above, what is the length of $\overline{LN}$?

A. $2\sqrt{7}$
B. 7
C. $4\sqrt{7}$
D. $10\sqrt{2}$

2

A chemist mixed 30 milliliters (mL) of solution A with 40 mL of solution B. The next day, she created another batch of the mixture. If she used 25 mL of solution B in the second batch, how much of solution A did she use?

A. 15 mL
B. 18.75 mL
C. 33.33 mL
D. 35 mL

3

In the xy-plane, the line given by the equation $2x + y = 1$ is perpendicular to the line given by which of the following equations?

A. $-2x + \frac{1}{2}y = 1$
B. $x + 2y = 3$
C. $x - 2y = 1$
D. $2x + y = 3$

4

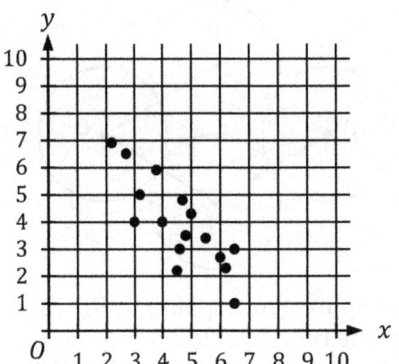

Which of the following equations is the most appropriate linear model for the data shown in the scatterplot above?

A. $y = -8.5x + 1$
B. $y = -x + 8.5$
C. $y = x - 8.5$
D. $y = 8.5x - 1$

5

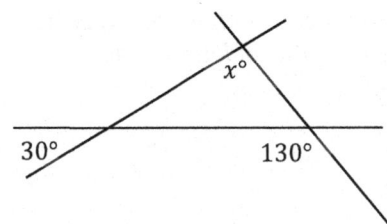

What is the value of x?

A. 30
B. 50
C. 80
D. 100

6

In the xy-plane, which of the following points lies on the line that passes through $(2, 5)$ and $(4, 8)$?

A. $(-3, 3)$
B. $(-2, -1)$
C. $(1, 0)$
D. $(5, 11)$

Practice Set 2: Medium-Hard

1

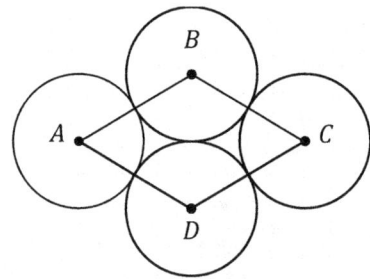

In the figure above, points $A, B, C,$ and D are the centers of four congruent circles, each of which has an area of 9π and is tangent to all adjacent circles. What is the area of rhombus $ABCD$?

A. $9\sqrt{3}$
B. $18\sqrt{3}$
C. $27\sqrt{3}$
D. $9\pi\sqrt{3}$

2

$$f(x) = x^3 + 2x^2 + 5$$

For the function f, defined above, what is a possible value of k such that $f(2k) = 8$?

3

$$g(x) = \frac{x-1}{\sqrt{5-x}}$$

What is the domain of the function $g(x)$, defined above?

A. $x < 1$
B. $x \geq 1$
C. $x < 5$
D. $x \geq 5$

4

The bar graph shows the number of students in each grade at Glen School.

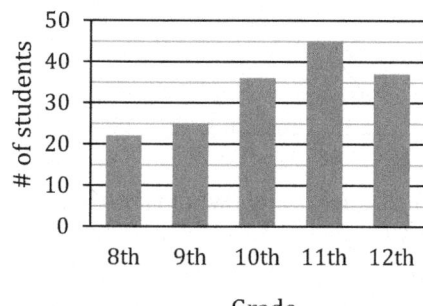

Which of the following is the greatest?

A. The number of 11th and 12th graders
B. The number of 9th and 10th graders
C. The number of 8th and 12th graders
D. The number of 10th and 12th graders

5

School	# of votes	% votes for Site A	% votes for Site B
1	3200	50	50
2	2000	30	70
3	4100	50	50
4	1900	70	30
5	5800	40	60

The table above shows the results of a vote among five high schools as to which site to select for the end of year party. Which high school had the greatest number of votes for the winning site?

A. 1
B. 2
C. 3
D. 5

Algebra

Algebra Essentials

Preview Quiz:

Simplify each of the following:

1) $3(2x + 4) =$

2) $5x + 6 - (2x - 4) =$

3) $\dfrac{8x - 10}{2} =$

4) $3(4x + 2x) - 5x =$

Solve:

5) $x - 10 = 13$

6) $\dfrac{2x}{3} = \dfrac{2x + 4}{5}$

7) $2x + 4 = 12$

8) $2(3x - 5) + 2 = 6x + 1$

9) What is the value of $3(x - y) + xy$ if $x = 2$ and $y = -4$?

10) If $\dfrac{1}{2}x - 3y = 5$, what is x in terms of y?

Math: Algebra

A **term** is a number, a variable, or the product of numbers and variables.

Example: $3xy$ is a single term.

We can use addition and subtraction to combine **like terms**, which are terms that have the exact same variables with the exact same exponents.

Example: The sum of $3n$ and $2n$ is $5n$.

If the terms have different variables *or* if the variables have different exponents, they're not like terms and we can't combine them that way.

Example: The sum of $3n$ and $2n^2$ is just $3n + 2n^2$.

Try It — **Simplify** each expression by combining like terms. If the expression is already in simplest terms, write *simplified*.

1) $3x - 2 + x + 5$

2) $x + x^2 + x^3$

3) $x^2 - 0.7x^2$

4) $2x + 3x - 4y - y$

5) $3xy + 2xy - x + 4x$

6) $-3 + y - x + xy$

TIP:

Remember, a variable without a coefficient written in front of it really has a coefficient of 1. You can always write in the "1" to remind yourself that it's there.

Example: $x + x = 1x + 1x = \mathbf{2x}$

When an expression is placed inside parentheses, we may need to **multiply** the whole expression by something that's outside the parentheses. To do this, make sure to multiply *each individual term* by whatever is outside.

Example: $3(2x + 4)$
$= 3(2x) + 3(4)$
$= \mathbf{6x + 12}$

Similarly, to **divide** an entire expression by some number, be sure to divide each individual term by the number that's in the bottom of the fraction.

Example: $\dfrac{8x - 10}{2} = \mathbf{4x - 5}$

When **subtracting** an expression in parentheses, it's important to remember to **distribute** that minus sign to each individual term in the expression. You can think of it as multiplying the whole expression by -1.

Example: $5x + 6 - (2x - 4)$
$= 5x + 6 + (-1)(2x - 4)$
$= 5x + 6 + (-1)(2x) + (-1)(-4)$
$= 5x + 6 - 2x + 4$
$= \mathbf{3x + 10}$

Use the acronym **PEMDAS** to remember the order of operations: first, simplify any expression in Parentheses; next, apply any Exponents; third, perform any Multiplication or Division; fourth, perform any Addition or Subtraction.

Example: $3(4x + 2x) - 5x$
$= 3(6x) - 5x$ ⟵ first handle the **P**arentheses
$= 18x - 5x$ ⟵ then **M**ultiply
$= \mathbf{13x}$ ⟵ then **S**ubtract

TIP:

To check your work, try plugging in a value for x and evaluating both the original expression and the result in the calculator. If they match, you simplified the expression correctly. For example, if we decide that $x = 2$, then the original expression above is $3(4(2) + 2(2)) - 5(2) = 26$, and the result is $13(2) = 26$.

For a review of how to use the SAT's built-in calculator to plug in values, see p. 222.

Algebra Essentials

- 231 -

TM and © 2023 PrepMatters, Inc. All rights reserved.

Try It   **Simplify** each expression by combining like terms. If the expression is already in simplest terms, write *simplified*.

7) $2x - (3x + 5) + 2$

9) $\frac{1}{2}(4x + 2) - 3$

8) $1 + 3(2x - 6)$

10) $2(3x - 8) + (1 - 4x)$

Some algebra problems will simply ask you to **evaluate** an algebraic expression given certain numeric values for the variables. Plug in carefully, follow PEMDAS, and *write out your steps*, especially where negative numbers are involved. Remember, subtracting a negative number is the same thing as adding a positive number.

Example: If $x = 2$ and $y = -4$, what is the value of $3(x - y) + xy$?

$$3(2 - (-4)) + 2(-4)$$
$$3(2 + 4) - 8$$
$$10$$

TIP:
You can also use the built-in calculator to solve these problems. See pp. 222-223 to learn how.

Try It   Find the value of each of the following if $x = -1$ and $y = 3$.

11) $2(3x - 8) + (1 - 4y)$

12) $2y - |x + y|$

TIP:

Absolute value bars are like specialized parentheses. To follow PEMDAS, first simplify the expression inside the absolute value bars, then take the absolute value of that result.

An **equation** is an algebra statement that has an equals sign in it. We can solve equations by doing the same thing to both sides (e.g., adding something, subtracting something, multiplying something, etc).

Example: If $x - 10 = 13$, what is the value of x?

$$\begin{aligned} x - 10 &= 13 \\ +10 & +10 \end{aligned} \quad \longleftarrow \text{ add 10 to both sides}$$

$$x = 23$$

Some equations require more than one step to solve. To determine what to do first, follow PEMDAS *backwards*—first any addition/subtraction, then the multiplication/division, and so on.

Example: If $2x + 4 = 12$, what is the value of x?

$$\begin{aligned} 2x + 4 &= 12 \\ -4 & -4 \end{aligned} \quad \longleftarrow \text{ subtraction first}$$

$$\begin{aligned} 2x &= 8 \\ \div 2 & \div 2 \end{aligned} \quad \longleftarrow \text{ then the division}$$

$$x = 4$$

For equations in which two fractions are set equal to each other, there's a shortcut: **cross-multiply** to solve. Multiply the bottom of one fraction by the top of the other one, and vice versa; set the results equal to each other and proceed to combine like terms as usual.

Example: $\dfrac{2x}{3} = \dfrac{2x+4}{5}$

$5(2x) = 3(2x + 4)$

$10x = 6x + 12$
$-6x -6x$

$4x = 12$
$\div 4 \div 4$

$x = 3$

TIP:

If an equation has a lot of fractions in it, try multiplying both sides of the equation by the bottoms of the fractions as a first step. This should eliminate all the fractions and make life easier.

Example: If $\dfrac{3}{4}x + 2 = x - \dfrac{5}{4}$, what is the value of x?

$$4\left(\dfrac{3}{4}x + 2\right) = 4\left(x - \dfrac{5}{4}\right)$$
$$3x + 8 = 4x - 5$$
$$8 = x - 5$$
$$13 = x$$

To solve an equation using the built-in calculator, enter it on two separate lines: the left side of the equation on one line, and the right side of the equation on the other. The x-coordinate of the intersection of those two graphs is your solution. Here's that last example again:

$$\text{If } \frac{2x}{3} = \frac{2x+4}{5}, \text{ what is the value of } x?$$

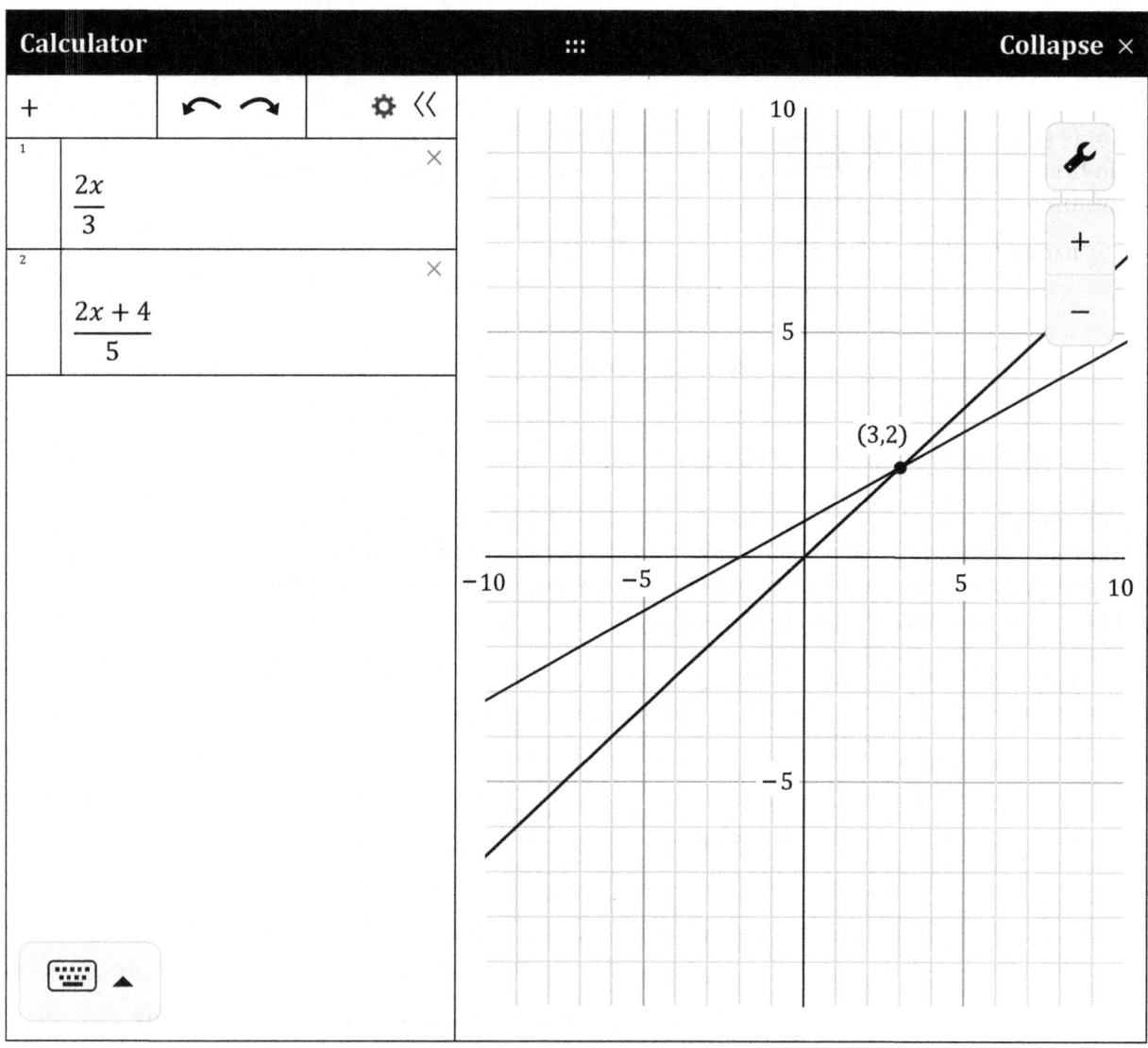

The lines intersect where $x = 3$, so the answer is **3**.

TIP:

This approach will only work if the variable is x. If the problem uses a different letter, change it to x when entering it into the calculator.

Try It Solve for x in each of the following:

13) $4x - 3 = 17$

16) $3x + 2 = 20$

14) $3.4 = 0.2x + 6$

17) $1 - 2x = \dfrac{1}{5}$

15) $\dfrac{x - 3}{2} = 9$

18) $6 = \dfrac{3x}{2} + 8$

TIP:

Whether or not you want to use the graphing approach from the last page, you should certainly be using the calculator to handle messy arithmetic (e.g., dividing by 0.2 in #14 above). There is no reason to do this stuff in your head; it's not what the SAT is trying to test you on, and it's too easy to make a test-day "hasty error" that ends up losing you points on a problem you actually know how to do.

Math: Algebra

Not all algebra problems ask you to find the value of a variable. Other problems will give you an equation involving two or more different variables and ask you to **solve for one variable**. (These may also be phrased as finding one variable "in terms of" the others). These problems may seem intimidating because they're more abstract, but you already know how to solve them. Use the same algebra skills you used on the last set: do the same thing to both sides of the equation, follow PEMDAS, etc.

Example: If $\frac{1}{2}x - 3y = 5$, what is x in terms of y?

$$\frac{1}{2}x - 3y = 5$$
$$+3y \quad +3y \quad \leftarrow \text{addition first}$$
$$2\left(\frac{1}{2}x\right) = 2(5 + 3y) \leftarrow \text{then multiply}$$
$$x = 10 + 6y$$

TIP:

When multiplying or dividing both sides of the equation by something, make sure you multiply or divide *each individual term* by that number.

Try It Solve for x in each of the following:

19) $x + 2y = 5$

22) $10x + 20y = 45$

20) $2x - 6 = 8y$

23) $3 - 4x = 12y + 1$

21) $\frac{3x - 9y}{2} = 4$

24) $6x = \frac{y}{4} + 12$

CHALLENGE:

All the equations we've seen so far have had exactly one solution. But occasionally, the SAT will ask us about equations with an infinite number of solutions, or about equations that have no solutions at all.

In both cases, the key is that when you combine the like terms in the equation, you find that *all the variables cancel out*. If what's left at that point is a *true* statement, then the equation had **infinitely many solutions**.

Example: $3x - 4 = 3(x - 2) + 2$
$3x - 4 = 3x - 6 + 2$
$-4 = -4$

This is <u>true</u>, so the equation has **infinitely many solutions**.

If what's left after the variables cancel out is a *false* statement, then the equation had **no solutions**.

Example: $2(3x - 5) + 2 = 6x + 1$
$6x - 10 + 2 = 6x + 1$
$-8 = 1$

This is <u>false</u>, so the equation has **no solutions**.

TIP:

If you use the technique on p. 234 to solve an equation using the built-in calculator, a graph where the lines never intersect means there are **no solutions**, while a graph that shows both equations as the same line has **infinitely many solutions**.

Algebra Essentials

Math: Algebra

Practice Set 1: Easy-Medium

1. If $x = 5$ and $y = -3$, what is the value of $x(x + y) - y$?

A. 1
B. 7
C. 13
D. 37

2. Which of the following expressions is equivalent to $3(2a - b) + 4(-5a + b)$?

A. $-14a - 2b$
B. $-14a + b$
C. $a + 7b$
D. $a + b$

3. For what value of x is the equation $3(x - 2) + x = 14$ true?

4. For $x = 6$, what is the value of $|2 - x|$?

A. -8
B. 2
C. 4
D. 8

5. The equation $p = 3n - 16$ can be used to find Max's profit p, in dollars, from selling n cupcakes. How many cupcakes does Max need to sell in order to obtain a profit of $20?

A. 7
B. 8
C. 10
D. 12

6. The real number n is defined such that $-2(n - 3) - 3(4 - n) = 5n + 6$. What is the value of $1 - 2n$?

A. -2
B. 0
C. 4
D. 7

7.
$$\frac{15}{q - 6} = \frac{24}{16}$$

What value of q makes the proportion above true?

A. 10
B. 12
C. 16
D. 32

8. For all real values of x, which of the following expressions is equivalent to $2(4x - 3) + 5(-3x + 6) - 3(4 - 2x)$?

A. $-19x + 30$
B. $-13x + 12$
C. $-x + 12$
D. $6x - 18$

9. If $\dfrac{3 + 2k}{7} = \dfrac{k}{3}$, what is the value of k?

10. If $a = 3, b = 5$, and $c = -2$, what is the value of $(a + b - c)(b + c)$?

A. 18
B. 30
C. 42
D. 54

Practice Set 2: Medium-Hard

1. What value of n satisfies the equation below?

$$\frac{9}{2n} = 0.15$$

2. If $a + b = c$ and $c = 10$, what is the value of $a + b + c$?

A. 10
B. 15
C. 20
D. 30

3. If $14n + jn = 22n$ for all nonzero values of n, what is the value of j?

A. 6
B. 8
C. 12
D. 28

4. A beaker currently contains 3 mL of solution A and 5 mL of solution B. After a scientist adds n mL of solution A to the beaker, the mixture will be p percent solution A by volume, where p is defined by the following equation:

$$p = \frac{100(3 + n)}{8 + n}$$

What is n in terms of p?

A. $n = 8p - 300$
B. $n = \dfrac{8p}{300}$
C. $n = \dfrac{300 - 3p}{800}$
D. $n = \dfrac{300 - 8p}{p - 100}$

5. $5x - 6 + (2 - x) = 2(2x + 7)$

Which of the following best describes the solution(s) of the equation above?

A. $x = 2$ is the only solution.
B. $x = 0$ is the only solution.
C. The equation has infinitely many solutions.
D. The equation has no solutions.

6. If $2n - m = 14$, then the value of which of the following expressions is -28?

A. $m - 2n$
B. $2m - 4n$
C. $-4n - m$
D. $n + 2m$

7. The equation $d = vt + 0.5at^2$ gives the distance d, in meters, traveled by a machine that accelerates at a constant rate, where v is the machine's initial velocity, in meters per second; a is its acceleration, in meters per second per second; and t is the time, in seconds. If the machine travels 108 meters in 60 seconds, with an initial velocity of 0.3 meters per second, what is its rate of acceleration, in meters per second per second?

8. If $\dfrac{3a + 2}{12} = \dfrac{2x}{9}$, which of the following expressions is equivalent to x?

A. $\dfrac{9a + 6}{8}$
B. $6a - 9$
C. $27a - 12$
D. $18a$

Word Problems

Preview Quiz:

Choose the best answer.

1) The word "product" refers to the result of (adding / multiplying).

2) When you divide one number by another, the result is called the (quotient / difference).

Translate and solve.

3) 27 is three-fourths of the sum of 13 and what number?

4) Early in her life, a baby gained 30 grams per day. If she weighed 3200 grams at birth, how much did she weigh after ten days?

5) George and Sal started their new jobs on the same day. George received a signing bonus of $300, after which he earned $20 per hour. Sal received a signing bonus of $500, after which he earned $18 per hour. After how many hours of work had George and Sal each earned the same amount?

6) A baby weighed 3200 grams when she was born two weeks ago. Since then, she has gained 30 grams each day. Her doctor says that by her first birthday, her weight should be triple her birth weight. To meet this goal, the baby will need to gain an average of x grams per day for the remaining 351 days of the year. What is the value of x, rounded to the nearest gram?

One of the goals of the SAT is to highlight practical applications of math reasoning. What that means in practice is lots of word problems. Here's a step-by-step approach.

Read slowly.	Read the first sentence slowly. What have they told you, and what does it mean?
Write down values.	Clarify your variables (e.g., write "a = number of apples" as well as "$a = 15$"). You can also jot down simple reminders of relationships to help avoid confusion later: for example, "a is bigger than b."
Jump in.	Work as you go. If you can put two pieces of information together, do it now. For example, if you're given the rate a car is moving and the time, go ahead and calculate the distance before you even finish reading.
Talk to yourself in sentences.	Your brain doesn't necessarily think linearly. If you talk yourself through your process, though (e.g., "now I'm finding how much a crate of melons cost...") you force yourself to be linear and think at a measured, efficient rate.
Track your units.	If a question is asking for dollars, but you have a unit that would be gallons per square dollars... something has gone sideways.
Focus on the question.	Re-read, if necessary, to make sure you know exactly what the test is asking for.

> ***TIP:***
> Thrown off by a long problem with a ton of words? Try breaking the problem into smaller pieces and solving one piece at a time.

Math: Algebra

Word Problem Translation

Word Problem	Math equivalent
sum	+
product	*
difference	−
quotient	÷
is	=
of	*

Many word problems can be translated directly into algebra using the conversions given above.

Example: *27 is three-fourths of the sum of 13 and what number?*

We have the number 27, followed by the word "is": that's an equals sign. Then we have "three-fourths," so just 3/4. Next is the word "of," which always means multiply. But multiply by what? By "the sum of 13 and" some unknown number. Use x to represent the unknown value; the sum of 13 and that value is $(13 + x)$. Putting it all together, we get this:

27 is three-fourths of the sum of 13 and what number?

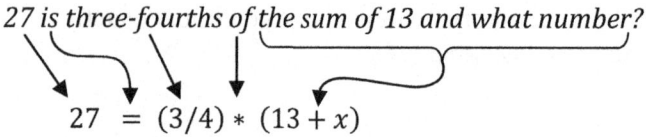

$$27 = (3/4) * (13 + x)$$

Now solve:

$$27 = \frac{3}{4}(13 + x)$$
$$27 = 0.75(13) + 0.75(x)$$
$$27 = 9.75 + 0.75x$$
$$17.25 = 0.75x$$
$$\mathbf{23 = x}$$

Try It Translate each of these into algebra:

1) The width is 3 inches greater than the height.

2) When n is subtracted from 5, the result is 2.

3) The sum of three consecutive integers is 15.

4) The product of a and b is 4 more than twice the value of c.

Rates

Many word problems on the SAT involve *rates*. Look for words like "per" or "each" to identify them: for example, a problem may involve a speed of "35 kilometers per hour," or you may be told that a store sells "1000 books each week."

The simplest of these problems can be solved simply by **multiplying** or **dividing**. Just be sure to write out the equation first so that you know which one to do.

Example: Early in her life, a baby gained 30 grams each day. How many grams did she gain in the first five days?

$x = 30(5)$
$x =$ **150 grams**

Example: If George earns $20 per hour, how long does it take him to earn $60?

$20(x) = 60$
$x =$ **3 hours**

Try It

5) A group of 5 employees contributed $8 each to buy a joint gift for their coworker. What was the total amount contributed?

6) A market sells 12 eggs for $9.36. What is the price per egg? (No sales taxes apply.)

Often, the problem will give you a *starting value* of some kind. This should typically be either added to or subtracted from the rest of the equation. Again, the first step is to **write out the equation**, plugging in what you know from the problem, so that you can see what steps you need to take to solve it.

Example: Early in her life, a baby gained 30 grams per day. If she weighed 3200 grams at birth, how much did she weigh after ten days?

$x = 3200 + 30(10)$
$x = $ **3500 grams**

Example: When he started at his current job, George received a signing bonus of x dollars. George earns 20 dollars per hour. If he earned a total of 1100 dollars in his first forty hours, what is the value of x?

$1100 = x + 40(20)$
$1100 = x + 800$
$x = $ **300 dollars**

Try It

7) A group of 5 employees decided to pool their money to buy a joint gift for their coworker. Their boss started the pool with a $50 donation. If the employees then contributed $8 each, what was the total amount contributed?

8) At a market, the price of 12 eggs and 1 bottle of soda is $11.61. If the eggs sell for $0.78 each, what is the price of the bottle of soda? (No sales taxes apply.)

The next level of difficulty is when you are given **multiple relationships** to deal with in the same problem. For some of these, each relationship might consist of a starting value and a rate, and you'll need to set the two expressions equal to each other to solve.

Example: *George and Sal started their new jobs on the same day. George received a signing bonus of $300, after which he earned $20 per hour. Sal received a signing bonus of $500, after which he earned $18 per hour. After how many hours of work had George and Sal each earned the same amount?*

$300 + 20x = 500 + 18x$
$300 + 2x = 500$
$2x = 200$
$x = \mathbf{100\ hours}$

Try It

9) Two departments at a company competed in a charity drive. In the sales department, the manager contributed $50, and five of his employees contributed $8 each. In the accounting department, the manager declined to contribute, but six employees contributed $n each. If the amount raised by the accounting department was the same as the amount raised by the sales department, what is the value of n?

10) At a market, the price of 12 eggs and 7 pints of yogurt is equal to the price of 30 eggs and 1 pint of yogurt. If the eggs sell for $0.78 each, what is the price of 1 pint of yogurt? (No sales taxes apply.)

Math: Algebra

Other problems may require more than one equation. For these **multi-step** problems, focus on breaking the problem into smaller chunks and doing one thing at a time, writing it all out as you go.

Example: *A baby weighed 3200 grams when she was born two weeks ago. Since then, she has gained 30 grams each day. Her doctor says that by her first birthday, her weight should be triple her birth weight. To meet this goal, the baby will need to gain an average of x grams per day for the remaining 351 days of the year. What is the value of x, rounded to the nearest gram?*

Current weight = $3200 + 30(14) = 3620$ grams
Goal = $3(3200) = 9600$ grams
must gain $9600 - 3620 = 5980$ grams
$351(x) = 5980$
$x = 17.04$

Rounded to the nearest gram, the value of x is **17 grams per day**.

> **TIP:**
> If you're having trouble setting up the algebra for a word problem, consider using the back-solving or substitution strategies instead.

Practice Set 1: Easy-Medium

1 A taxicab company charges passengers $3.50 for the first mile of a trip, then $2.25 for each additional mile. What is the charge for a 10-mile trip?

A. $20.25
B. $23.75
C. $26.00
D. $35.00

2 Mollie operates a juice stand. She charges $1.75 for a cup of carrot juice and $1.25 for a cup of grapefruit juice. Which of the following represents the amount, in dollars, that Mollie will receive if she sells c cups of carrot juice and g cups of grapefruit juice?

A. $1.25c + 1.75g$
B. $1.75c - 1.25g$
C. $1.75c + 1.25g$
D. $0.75(c + g)$

3 The height of one tree is 2 inches less than 3 times the height of a shorter tree. If the height of the taller tree is 64 inches, what is the height, in inches, of the shorter tree?

4 To operate his retail store, Sylvan pays an employee $15.75 per hour. His other costs come to $75 per day. For a day on which the employee works for 8 hours, how much must Sylvan receive from the sale of his products to cover all of his costs, including the employee's pay?

A. $50.75
B. $110.25
C. $143.50
D. $201.00

5 A gym charges a $19.50 monthly membership fee. There is an additional fee of $4.75 to attend a fitness class. If Jessie's fee was $33.75 this month, how many fitness classes did she attend?

A. 1
B. 2
C. 3
D. 4

6 It currently takes Nancy 12 minutes to run 1 mile. Nancy's goal is to run a mile in 8 minutes, and she believes that with practice, she will be able to reduce her 1-mile running time by 30 seconds every week. If Nancy is correct, which of the following represents the number of minutes that it will take Nancy to run 1 mile w weeks from now, where w is an integer less than 8?

A. $8w - 30$
B. $12 - 0.5w$
C. $0.5w + 8$
D. $12 + 8w$

7 For the use of its high-speed internet service, Hotel A charges each guest an initial $4 fee plus $7 an hour. Hotel B charges each guest an initial fee of $14 plus $5 an hour. A guest at Hotel A will have paid the same total amount for internet as a guest at Hotel B after how many hours?

A. 5
B. 6
C. 8
D. 9

Math: Algebra

Practice Set 2: Medium-Hard

1

In a certain bag of marbles, $\frac{1}{4}$ of the marbles are red. Of the marbles that aren't red, $\frac{3}{5}$ are green and the remaining 12 are blue. No marble is more than one color. How many marbles are in the bag?

A. 30
B. 40
C. 54
D. 60

2

A math team earned a total of 155 points by answering e easy questions and h hard questions. The equation $2e + 5h = 155$. Which of the following is the best interpretation of $5h$ in this context?

A. The number of points earned per hard question answered
B. The total number of points earned by answering hard questions
C. The number of points earned per easy question answered
D. The total number of points earned by answering easy questions

3

Michael can text 50 words in 1 minute. Which of the following equations represents the total number of words, w, that Michael can text in h hours?

A. $w = 50(60h)$

B. $w = \dfrac{50}{60h}$

C. $w = 60 + 50h$

D. $w = \left(\dfrac{60}{50}\right)h$

4

At an arcade, Bill starts out with t tokens and loses 4 tokens each time he plays a game. If Bill plays 5 games and has 4 tokens left, what is the value of t?

5

The side lengths of a certain pentagon are consecutive odd integers. If the longest side has length s inches, which of the following gives the perimeter of the pentagon, in inches, in terns of s?

A. $5s - 20$
B. $5s - 10$
C. $5s + 10$
D. $5s + 20$

6

The current population of a certain flamingo colony is 1,258 birds, which is 523 more than half the number of birds in the colony last year. If the number of birds in the colony decreases by the same amount from this year to next year as it did from last year to this year, then the population of the colony next year will be closest to which of the following?

A. 1046
B. 1098
C. 1123
D. 1207

7

Sarah is triple Andy's age, and Andy is double Melissa's age. If Sarah is 30 years old and Melissa is m years old, which of the following equations is true?

A. $\dfrac{m}{6} = 30$

B. $3m = 30$

C. $3m + 2 = 30$

D. $6m = 30$

Coordinate Geometry

Preview Quiz:

1) Label Quadrants I, II, III, and IV:

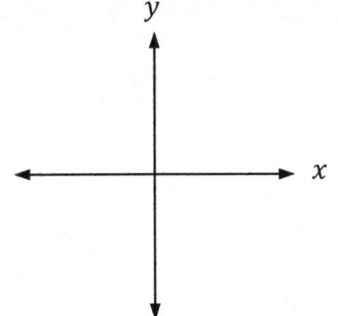

2) What is a y-intercept? _____

3) What is an x-intercept? _____

4) How do you find the slope of the line between two points?
_____

5) What is the most commonly used form of an equation of a line? _____

6) This form is called (standard form / slope-intercept form / point-slope form).

What is the relationship between:

7) the slopes of parallel lines? _____

8) the slopes of perpendicular lines? _____

9) What is the slope of a horizontal line? _____

10) What is the slope of a vertical line? _____

Solve:

11) On the xy-plane, the graph of $y = 4(3)^x$ passes through the point (2, ___)

12) What is the y-intercept of $y = -2x^2 + 5x + 17$ on the xy-plane?

13) The equation $y = 4x + k$, where k is a constant, represents a line on the xy-plane. If the line passes through the point (2, 11), what is the value of k?

14) What is the slope of the line given by $8x - 2y = 5$?

15) On the xy-plane, line t has a slope of 3 and passes through the point (2, 10). What is the equation of line t?

Each point on **the xy-plane** has both an x-coordinate and a y-coordinate. The points are written in the order (x, y), where the x value is represented horizontally and the y value is represented vertically. The center point is $(0, 0)$, also called the **origin**, which is where the x-**axis** and the y-**axis** intersect. These two lines divide the xy-plane into four **quadrants**, as shown below.

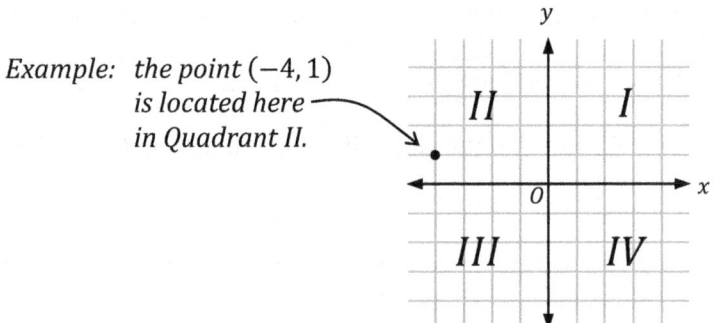

Example: the point $(-4, 1)$ is located here in Quadrant II.

When an equation is **graphed** on the xy-plane, the result is a visual representation of the x and y values that satisfy the equation. For example, in the equation $y = 2x + 3$, when the value of x is 1, the value of y must be 5, because $2(1) + 3 = 5$. Therefore, the graph of $y = 2x + 3$ must pass through the point $(1, 5)$ on the xy-plane.

This works for all kinds of equations, not just linear ones.

Example: On the xy-plane, the graph of $y = 4(3)^x$ passes through a point with an x-coordinate of 2. What is the y-coordinate of this point?

$$y = 4(3)^2 = 4(9) = \mathbf{36}$$

You can use this relationship to identify an equation based on its graph. Just pick one or more (x, y) points on the graph and plug those values into the equations in the answer choices.

Try It

1) The figure shows the graph of which of the following?

A) $y = -\dfrac{3}{2}x + 2$

B) $y = -\dfrac{2}{3}x + 2$

C) $y = \dfrac{2}{3}x + 3$

D) $y = \dfrac{3}{2}x + 3$

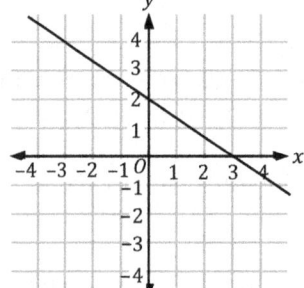

Any point at which the graph of an equation intersects the y-axis is called a **y-intercept**. The x-coordinate of this point will always be zero. Therefore, you can always find the y-intercept of an equation by plugging in zero for x.

Example: What is the y-intercept of $y = -2x^2 + 5x + 17$ on the xy-plane?

$y = -2(0)^2 + 5(0) + 17$
$y = -0 + 0 + 17$
$y = 17$

The y-intercept is the point $(\mathbf{0, 17})$.

TIP:
You can also solve these problems by graphing them on the built-in calculator: see pp. 218-219.

Similarly, any point at which a graph intersects the x-axis is called an **x-intercept**. Because the y-coordinate of this point will always be zero, we can find the x-intercept(s) by plugging in zero for y.

Try It

2) On the xy-plane, what is the x-intercept of the line given by $y = 3x - 6$?

3) On the xy-plane, what is the x-intercept of the horizontal parabola given by $x = 2(y+1)^2 - 5$?

In all of these equations, x and y are **variables**, meaning they can take on many different values. Some equations on the SAT may also contain a **constant**, which is a letter that represents some specific unknown value. Unlike a variable, a constant cannot take on multiple different values; it has exactly one value no matter what. To find out what that value is, come back to the same rule as before: plug in the coordinates of a point on the graph for x and y.

Example: The equation $y = 4x + k$, where k is a constant, represents a line on the xy-plane. If the line passes through the point $(2, 11)$, what is the value of k?

$11 = 4(2) + k$
$11 = 8 + k$
$\mathbf{3 = k}$

Try It

4) On the xy-plane, the point $(3, 22)$ lies on the graph of $y = ax^2 + 4$, where a is a constant. What is the value of a?

5) The figure below shows the graph of $y = x^3 - 3x^2 + 3x + k$, where k is a constant. What is the value of k?

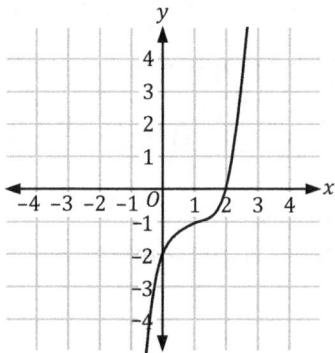

A **linear equation** gives the graph of a straight line on the xy-plane. The equation typically uses the form $y = mx + b$ (known as **slope-intercept form**), where m and b are constants. The constant m gives the **slope**, or rate of change, of the line; the farther the value of m is from zero, the steeper the line. The constant b gives the y-coordinate of the line's y-intercept.

Example: The line $y = 2x - 5$ has a slope of 2 and a y-intercept of $(0, -5)$.

TIP:
The slope of a perfectly horizontal line is 0. The slope of a perfectly vertical line is undefined.

If the test gives you the equation of a line written in some other format (such as $ax + by = c$), use algebra to rearrange the equation into slope-intercept form. It will likely be easier to work with that way.

Example: What is the slope of the line given by $8x - 2y = 5$?

$$-2y = -8x + 5$$
$$y = 4x - \frac{5}{2}$$

The slope of the line is **4**.

To calculate the slope of the line between two known points, use the **slope formula**:

$$m = \frac{y_2 - y_1}{x_2 - x_1}$$

Example: What is the slope of the line between the points $(0, 3)$ and $(-2, 1)$ on the xy-plane?

First, label the points. It doesn't matter which point you call (x_1, y_1) and which (x_2, y_2), as long as you're consistent.

$$\begin{array}{cc} x_1 \ \ y_1 & x_2 \ \ y_2 \\ (\ 0\ ,\ 3\ ) & (-2\ ,\ 1\ ) \end{array}$$

Now plug those values into the formula.

$$m = \frac{1 - 3}{-2 - 0}$$

$$m = \frac{-2}{-2}$$

$$m = 1$$

Try It

6) On the xy-plane, what is the slope of the line that passes through the points $(7, -4)$ and $(3, 2)$?

7) What is the slope of the line shown in the graph below?

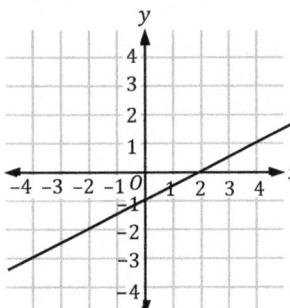

Math: Algebra

If two lines are **parallel**, their slopes are always equal. If two lines are **perpendicular**—that is, they intersect at a 90° angle—their slopes are *opposite reciprocals*. This means you can take the slope of one line, flip that number upside down, and make it the opposite sign: the result is the perpendicular slope. For example, a slope of $\frac{3}{4}$ is perpendicular to a slope of $-\frac{4}{3}$.

Try It

On the xy-plane, line l is represented by $y = 2x + 5$. Line q is parallel to line l, and line p is perpendicular to line l.

8) What is the slope of line q?

9) What is the slope of line p?

If you are given the slope of a line and one point that it passes through, you have enough information to find the equation of the line. Just use the form $y = mx + b$: plug in the slope for m and the coordinates of the point for x and y.

Example: On the xy-plane, line t has a slope of 3 and passes through the point (2, 10). What is the equation of line t?

$y = mx + b$
$y = 3x + b$
$10 = 3(2) + b$
$10 = 6 + b$
$4 = b$

Therefore, the equation of the line is $\boldsymbol{y = 3x + 4}$.

Try It

10) When graphed on the xy-plane, line l passes through the point $(-1, 6)$. If the slope of line l is 2, what is the equation of the line?

11) On the xy-plane, what is the equation of the line that passes through the points $(4, 2)$ and $(0, 6)$?

Coordinate Geometry

Practice Set 1: Easy-Medium

1

Which of the following points in the standard xy-plane lies on the line given by $y = -2x + 5$?

A. $(-1, 3)$
B. $(0, 2)$
C. $(1, -7)$
D. $(2, 1)$

2

In the xy-plane, the point $(-6, 2)$ is translated right 2 units and up 6 units. What are the coordinates of the point after the translation?

A. $(-8, 8)$
B. $(-4, -4)$
C. $(-4, 8)$
D. $(0, 2)$

3

In the xy-plane, the graph of the line given by $y = 2x - 5$ passes through the point $(k, 9)$, where k is a constant. What is the value of k?

4

x	-1	0	1	2
y	-9	-6	-3	0

The table above shows some values of the linear equation y. Which of the following gives the equation?

A. $y = -\dfrac{3}{4}x - 6$
B. $y = \dfrac{1}{3}x + 2$
C. $y = x + 2$
D. $y = 3x - 6$

5

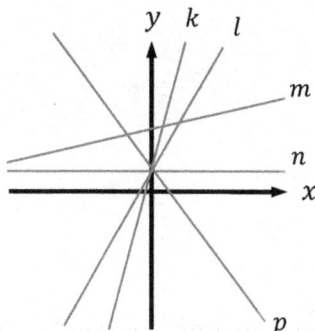

Which line in the figure above has the smallest positive slope? (Assume that line n is perfectly horizontal.)

A. l
B. m
C. n
D. p

6

In the xy-plane, the line that passes through the origin and $(4, -1)$ has a slope that is which of the following?

A. zero.
B. negative.
C. positive.
D. undefined.

7

What is the equation of the line graphed in the xy-plane plane below?

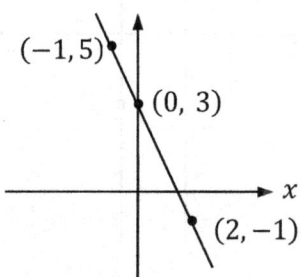

A. $y = -2x + 3$
B. $y = -3x + 2$
C. $y = -x + 3$
D. $y = 2x - 1$

Math: Algebra

8

When the equation $y = 8x - 24$ is graphed in the xy-plane, what is the x-coordinate of the line's x-intercept?

9

In the xy-plane, what is the slope of the line that passes through the points $(-1, 5)$ and $(6, 2)$?

A. $-\dfrac{7}{3}$

B. $-\dfrac{3}{7}$

C. $\dfrac{3}{7}$

D. $\dfrac{7}{3}$

10

In the figure below, line l is graphed in the xy-plane. Which of the following gives the equation of line l?

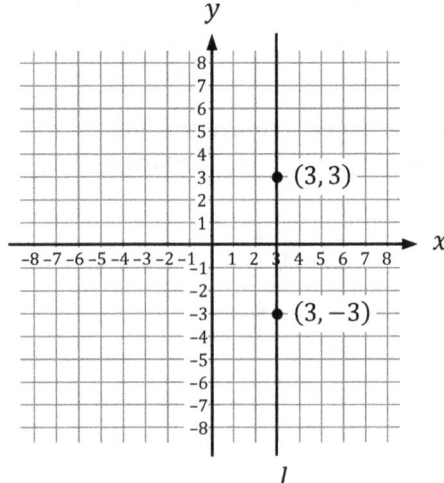

A. $y = x + 3$
B. $y = 3x$
C. $y = 3$
D. $x = 3$

11

In the xy-plane, the line that passes through the points $(1, 1)$ and $(4, -5)$ must also pass through which of the following points?

A. $(0, 3)$
B. $(0, 4)$
C. $(-2, 0)$
D. $(3, 0)$

12

Which of the following is the equation of a line that is perpendicular to the line graphed in the xy-plane below?

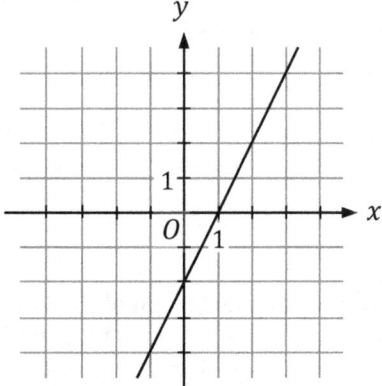

A. $y = 2x - 2$

B. $y = -\dfrac{1}{2}x + 2$

C. $y = \dfrac{1}{2}x - 2$

D. $y = -2x + 2$

13

In the xy-plane, what is the slope of the line given by the equation $3x - 2y = 5$?

Coordinate Geometry

Practice Set 2: Medium-Hard

1

In the xy-plane, the line given by the equation $5x - 2y = 8$ is perpendicular to the line given by which of the following equations?

A. $2x - 5y = 3$
B. $2x + 5y = 4$
C. $5x - 2y = 6$
D. $-5x + 2y = -1$

2

The shaded region below is bounded by the lines $y = 0$, $x = 0$, and $y = 4 - 2x$. What is the area of the shaded region?

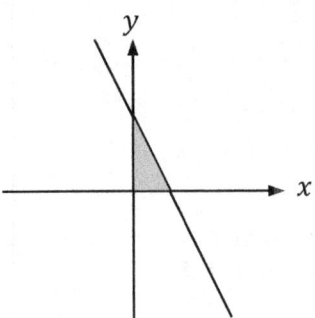

A. 1
B. 2
C. 4
D. 8

3

In the xy-plane, line l is parallel to the line $y = \frac{2}{3}x - 5$ and passes through the point $(6, 7)$. What is the y-coordinate of the y-intercept of line l?

4

In the xy-plane, the equation of line l is $2x - 5y = 7$. Which of the following values is the greatest?

A. the slope of line l
B. the x-coordinate of the x-intercept of line l
C. the y-coordinate of the y-intercept of line l
D. the slope of a line that is perpendicular to line l

5

In the xy-plane, the graph of the equation $y = ax + b$, where a and b are constants, is a horizontal line. Which of the following could be the values of a and b?

A. $a = -1$ and $b = 0$
B. $a = 0$ and $b = 1$
C. $a = 1$ and $b = -1$
D. $a = 2$ and $b = 0$

6

The figure below shows the average revenue per user for a social media company from 2003 to 2019.

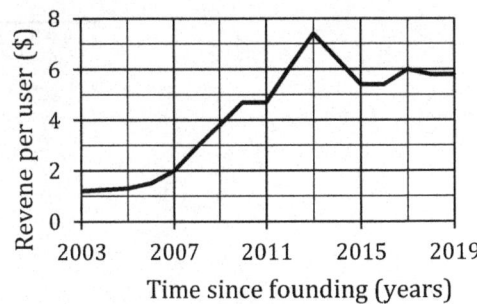

Time since founding (years)

From 2007 to 2010, the company's average revenue per user increased at a rate of $\$m$ per year. Based on the graph, which of the following is the best estimate for the value of m?

A. 0.9
B. 1.5
C. 1.9
D. 2.5

Systems of Equations

Preview Quiz:

Solve each of the following.

1) A small fruit stand sells apples for $1 each and bananas for $0.60 each. If the fruit stand sells a total of 45 apples and bananas for a total of $37.80, how many bananas were sold?

2) If $x - 2y = 5$ and $3x + y = 8$, what is the value of x?

3) The equations $y = 2x - 3$ and $y = -x + 3$ are shown graphed in the xy-plane below. What is the solution to this system of equations?

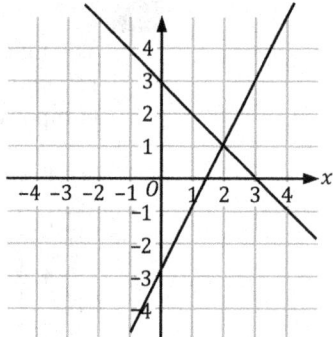

Choose **all that apply**.

4) It is possible for a system of two linear equations to have (zero / one / two / three / infinitely many) solutions.

5) The system of equations $y - x = 2$ and $2y - 2x = 4$ has (zero / one / two / three / infinitely many) solutions.

Systems of Equations

Some word problems involve two different properties of the items represented by the variables: for example, perhaps one property is *how many* of the items there are, while the other property is the *dollar value* of the items. In this situation, look to set up a **system** of two equations, one for each property.

Example: A small fruit stand sells apples for $1 each and bananas for $0.60 each. If the fruit stand sells a total of 45 apples and bananas for a total of $37.80, how many bananas were sold?

$$\text{Number:} \quad a + b = 45$$
$$\text{Price:} \quad (1)a + (0.6)b = 37.80$$

TIP: If all the problem is asking you to do is to pick out the correct system of equations from the choices, save yourself some time by looking for the easier equation (e.g., $a + b = 45$) first.

To **solve**, there are two main methods. One is to solve one of the equations for one variable, then plug that into the other equation.

$$a + b = 45$$
$$a = 45 - b$$

$$(1)(45 - b) + (0.6)b = 37.80$$
$$45 - b + 0.6b = 37.80$$
$$-0.4b = -7.2$$
$$b = \mathbf{18}$$

The other (and usually easier) way is to stack the equations and then add or subtract straight down to eliminate one of the variables.

$$\begin{aligned} a + b &= 45 \\ a + 0.6b &= 37.80 \end{aligned} \quad -$$
$$0.4b = 7.2$$
$$b = \mathbf{18}$$

In some cases, you may need to multiply one of the equations by something first to make the coefficients match up.

Example: If $x - 2y = 5$ and $3x + y = 8$, what is the value of x?

$$2(3x + y = 8) \rightarrow 6x + 2y = 16$$
$$x - 2y = 5 \quad +$$
$$7x \quad\quad = 21$$
$$x = \mathbf{3}$$

The elimination method is especially useful if the question is asking for the value of an **expression** instead of the value of an individual variable.

Example: If $x - 2y = 5$ and $3x + y = 8$, what is the value of $4x - y$?

$$\begin{aligned} x - 2y &= 5 \\ 3x + y &= 8 \end{aligned} \quad +$$
$$4x - y = \mathbf{13}$$

Math: Algebra

$$3x + 4y = 7$$
$$2x + 4y = 3$$

Try It 1) What value of x satisfies the system of equations above?

$$4p - j = -2$$
$$3p + 2j = 26$$

2) What value of p satisfies the system of equations above?

When a system of linear equations is graphed, the point where the two lines intersect is the solution to the system.

Example: *The solution to the system of equations $y = 2x - 3$ and $y = -x + 3$ is $x = 2, y = 1$.*

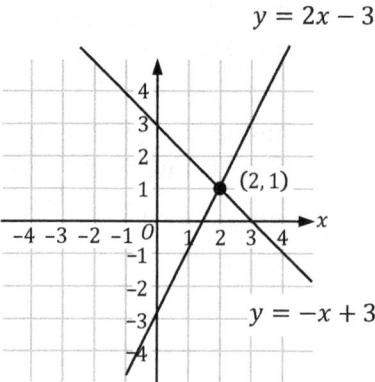

For this reason, the fastest way to solve a system of equations is often simply to graph both lines on the built-in calculator. If you're not sure how, check pp. 218-219 from the Mastering the Calculator section for more information.

Not all graphs of two lines will intersect exactly once. For a system of two linear equations, there are in fact three possible situations: the system can have **one solution** (the lines intersect), **no solutions** (the lines are parallel), or **infinite solutions** (they are both the same line).

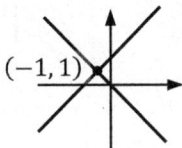 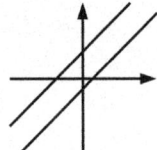 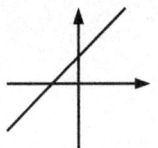

The system
$$\begin{cases} y - x = 2 \\ y + x = 0 \end{cases}$$
has one solution:
$x = -1, y = 1$

The system
$$\begin{cases} y - x = 2 \\ y - x = -1 \end{cases}$$
has no solutions.

The system
$$\begin{cases} y - x = 2 \\ 2y - 2x = 4 \end{cases}$$
has infinitely many solutions.

In both of the latter two situations, the slopes of the two lines are the same. This means that in systems with either no solutions or infinitely many solutions, **the coefficients of the variables all match**. If we were to use the elimination method on these systems, the variables would all cancel out. Just as with single-variable equations that have infinite solutions versus no solutions (see p. 237), the distinction between them is what's left after the variables cancel.

If what's left at that point is a *true* statement, then the system had **infinitely many solutions**. If what's left is a *false* statement, then the system had **no solutions**.

Example: $y - x = 2$
$y - x = -1$

What are the solutions to the system of equations above?

$$\begin{array}{r} y - x = 2 \\ -\quad y - x = -1 \\ \hline 0 = 1 \end{array}$$

This is <u>false</u>, so the system has **no solutions**.

Example: $y - x = 2$
$2y - 2x = 4$

How many solutions exist to the system of equations above?

$2(y - x = 2) \rightarrow \quad \begin{array}{r} 2y - 2x = 4 \\ -\quad 2y - 2x = 4 \\ \hline 0 = 0 \end{array}$

This is <u>true</u>, so the system has **infinitely many solutions**.

Math: Algebra

$$2a + 4b = 3$$
$$a + 2b = 0$$

Try It   3) What are the solutions, if any, to the system of equations above?

4) If $3x + 2y = 10$ and $3x + 2y = 2n$ have infinitely many solutions, where n is a constant, what is the value of n?

FROM THE BLOG

"My parents told me I shouldn't take away time from studying to exercise." That may be the *worst* advice I've heard this year. Why?

- **Faster feet, faster thinking.** New nerve cells are constantly being created in your brain. When you exercise regularly, the neurons created by the hippocampus react more quickly. In essence, they are "smarter."
- **Faster thinking, calmer brains.** You might think that neurons that react quickly would also stress more easily. But studies show that the brains of runners (unforced aerobic exercise) have a greater amount of a specific neurotransmitter that actually "shushes" neurons, thereby calming the brain.
- **Calmer brains, stress resistance, and finding solutions.** Scientists studying brain activation and stress reactions in sedentary and active mice noticed this advantage in the exercisers: "They didn't freeze or cling to dark spaces in unfamiliar situations. They explored. They appeared to be 'stress-resistant.'"

The ideal brain state for learning (and testing!) is relaxed alertness. Physical activity is, well, activating! (Ever fall asleep and run into a tree while out for a jog? Me neither). And, exercise is relaxing, both short-term and long-term.

Mens sano in corpere sana: A sound mind in a sound body.

Practice Set 1: Easy-Medium

1

What value of x satisfies the system of equations below?

$$x - 2y = 4$$
$$3x + 2y = 6$$

A. $\dfrac{1}{2}$

B. $\dfrac{2}{3}$

C. $\dfrac{5}{2}$

D. 10

2

If $3x + 4 = a$ and $2a = 20$, what is the value of x?

3

In the xy-plane, the graphs of the equations $y = 2x - 5$ and $y = -x + 7$ intersect at which of the following (x, y) points?

A. $(1.5, -2)$
B. $(2, -1)$
C. $(4, 3)$
D. $(4, 6)$

4

What is the solution (x, y) to the system of equations below?

$$2x + 3y = 10$$
$$3y - 7x = -8$$

A. $(0, 2)$
B. $(2, 2)$
C. $(4, 3)$
D. $(1, -9)$

5

$$8x + 6y = 25$$
$$4x - 9y = 17$$

If (x, y) is a solution to the system of equations above, what is the value of $12x - 3y$?

6

Yesterday, a food truck sold a total of 79 hamburgers and hot dogs. Let x represent the number of hamburgers sold and y represent the number of hot dogs sold. Each hamburger costs $7 and each hot dog costs $5. The food truck earned a total of $489 yesterday from its sale of hot dogs and hamburgers. Which of the following systems of equations represents the number of each food item sold?

A. $7y = 5x$
   $35x = 489$

B. $7x + y = 489$
   $x + 5y = 79$

C. $x + y = 489$
   $5x + 7y = 79$

D. $x + y = 79$
   $7x + 5y = 489$

7

Cory has 5 more first cousins than his friend James has. If they have a total of 23 first cousins, how many cousins does Cory have?

A. 9
B. 11
C. 14
D. 18

8

Main Street Theater sells two types of tickets: adult tickets and student tickets. For a recent Sunday matinee, Main Street Theater sold a total of 150 tickets. If the theater sold 40 fewer student tickets than adult tickets, how many student tickets were sold?

A. 55
B. 80
C. 95
D. 100

9

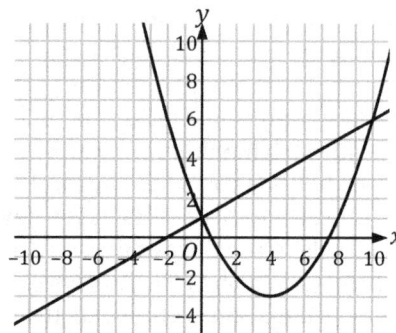

The xy-plane above shows the graphs of the equations $y = \frac{1}{4}x^2 - 2x + 1$ and $y = \frac{1}{2}x + 1$. Which of the following (x, y) points is a solution to this system of equations?

A. $(-2, 0)$
B. $(0.5, 0)$
C. $(6, 4)$
D. $(10, 6)$

10

What are the coordinates of the point of intersection between the lines represented by the equations $y = 3x - 2$ and $x - y = 4$?

A. $(1, 5)$
B. $(5, 1)$
C. $(-1, -5)$
D. $(-5, -1)$

11

If $10x + y = 8$ and $7x - y = 9$, what is the value of $3x + 2y$?

12

$$y = 3x - 4$$
$$y = 3x + 2$$

How many (x, y) solutions exist to the system of equations above?

A. 0
B. 1
C. 2
D. Infinitely many

13

In a math competition, teams earn 2 points for each easy question solved and 5 points for each difficult question solved. There are no other types of questions. If a team solved a total of 25 questions and earned a total of 71 points, how many difficult questions did the team answer?

A. 7
B. 9
C. 13
D. 18

14

$$3y = 6$$
$$x - 4y = 5$$

What is the solution (x, y) to the system of equations above?

A. $(-3, 2)$
B. $(2, -1.75)$
C. $(2, -0.75)$
D. $(13, 2)$

Practice Set 2: Medium-Hard

1

If the sum of two integers is 6 and the sum of twice the first integer and 3 times the second integer is 9, find the sum of the first integer and twice the second integer.

2

A family's change jar contains only nickels, dimes, and quarters. There are twice as many dimes as nickels. If the jar contains 20 coins with a total value of $2.50, how many quarters are in the jar?

A. 5
B. 6
C. 7
D. 8

3

Bob's Party Rentals charges a fixed amount for assembly plus an hourly rate for the rented equipment. If the total pre-tax charge for a five-hour party is $190 and the total pre-tax charge for a two hour party is $100, what is the total pre-tax charge for a three-hour party?

(Note: assume the same quantity of equipment is rented at all three parties).

A. $130
B. $140
C. $150
D. $170

4

If k is a constant, for what value of k will the system of equations below have no real solutions?

$$4x - 3y = 10$$
$$kx - 6y = 12$$

A. -4
B. 0
C. 8
D. 10

5

In triangle ABC, the degree measure of the largest angle is equal to the sum of the degree measures of the other two angles. If the degree measure of the smallest angle is added to the degree measure of the largest angle, the result is twice the degree measure of the remaining angle. What is the degree measure of the smallest angle in the triangle?

A. $15°$
B. $25°$
C. $30°$
D. $60°$

6

$$4x + b = 3x - 11$$
$$4y + c = 3y - 11$$

In the equations above, b and c are constants. If b is c plus $\frac{1}{4}$, which of the following is true?

A. y is x plus $\frac{3}{4}$
B. y is x minus $\frac{1}{4}$
C. y is x plus $\frac{1}{4}$
D. y is x minus $\frac{5}{4}$

Math: Algebra

7

Leslie has a box of c chocolate bars to sell to her neighbors for a school fundraising project. If each of her neighbors buys 2 chocolate bars, there will be 10 bars left in the box. Leslie would need 40 additional chocolate bars if each neighbor were to buy 4 chocolate bars. How many neighbors does Leslie have?

A. 20
B. 25
C. 50
D. 60

8

Abbott owns x hats. Becky owns three more hats than Abbott does. Costello owns two fewer hats than Becky. If the total number of hats owned by these three individuals is twice as great as the number of hats owned by Becky, what is the value of x?

9

In the system of equations below, k is a constant. If the system has infinitely many solutions, what is the value of k?

$$3x + ky = 15$$
$$2x + 5y = 10$$

A. $\dfrac{7}{2}$
B. 5
C. $\dfrac{15}{2}$
D. 9

10

Esther and Frances together have 20 grandchildren, Esther and Gertrude together have 13 grandchildren, and Frances and Gertrude together have 17 grandchildren. How many grandchildren does Frances have?

11

A survey was conducted among 197 families who own *either* one cat *or* one dog (none of the families own both). Each of these families was asked to report whether they live in a house or an apartment. There are three times as many cat-owning families as dog-owning families among apartment residents, and there are four times as many dog-owning families as cat-owning families among house residents. If a total of 129 of the families own dogs and a total of 68 own cats, which of the following is closest to the probability that a dog-owning family selected at random lives in an apartment?

		Type of Pet	
		Dog	Cat
Type of Residence	Apartment		
	House		
	Total	129	68

A. 0.403
B. 0.305
C. 0.282
D. 0.101

Inequalities and Absolute Value

Preview Quiz:

Solve each of the following.

1) $3 - 2x < 9$

2) $0 \leq x + 5 \leq 9$

3) $|4x + 1| = 7$

Sketch the graph for each of the following.

4) $y \geq x + 2$

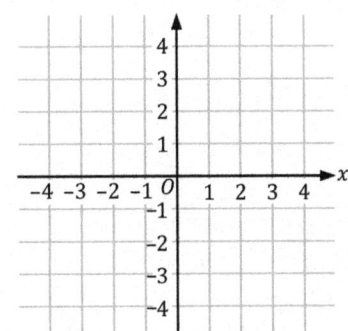

5) $y = |x|$

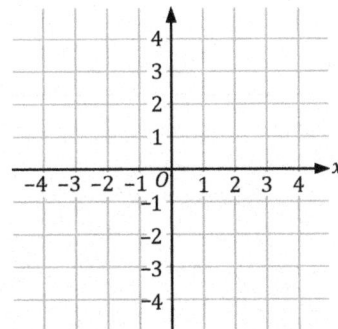

Solving an **inequality** such as $3 - 2x < 9$ is just like solving a regular equation with an equals sign, with one extra twist: when you multiply or divide by a negative number, you flip the "greater than" or "less than" sign.

$$3 - 2x < 9$$
$$-3 \quad\quad -3$$
$$-2x < 6$$
$$\div(-2) \quad \div(-2)$$
$$\boldsymbol{x > -3}$$

If the variable is between two inequalities, just make sure that whatever you do to one part of the equation, you do to *all three* parts.

$$0 \leq x + 5 \leq 9$$
$$-5 \quad -5 \quad -5$$
$$\boldsymbol{-5 \leq x \leq 4}$$

Try It

1) Simplify $x + 2 - 3(x + 2) > 4$

2) Simplify $2 < 1 - 2x < 5$

Make sure you know how to translate **inequality word problems** into algebra. A vague statement such as "x is greater than y" translates into an inequality symbol, but a specific statement such as "x is 5 greater than y" does not.

Examples:

p is less than one-half of q. $p < \frac{1}{2}(q)$

x is 7 less than y. $x = y - 7$

a is at least as great as b. $a \geq b$

Try It   Translate each of the following into algebra:

3) The value of x is no greater than 10.

4) The juniors raised $500 more than the seniors did.

5) A container holds a minimum of 5 liters.

6) The rectangle's length is more than 6 inches greater than twice its width.

Graphing an inequality is very similar to graphing regular equations, except that after you draw the lines, you *shade* either above the line (for $y >$) or below it (for $y <$). A solid line means the line itself is included, while a dashed line means it's not.

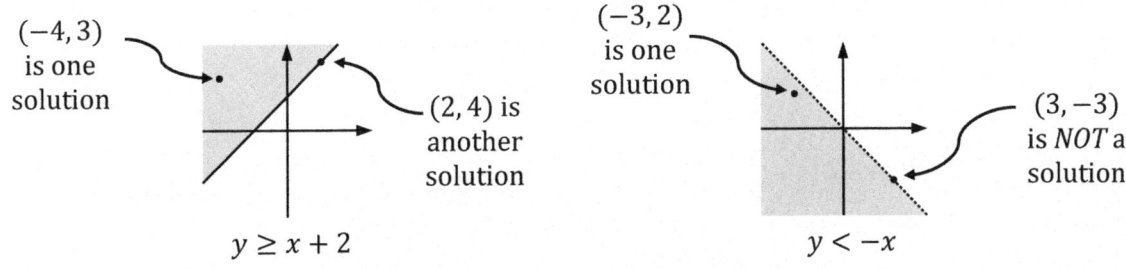

TIP:

In the built-in calculator, type > = for the $\geq$ symbol.

Math: Algebra

The **absolute value** of a number is its distance from zero on a number line. Just as you can never have a negative distance, you can never have a negative absolute value.

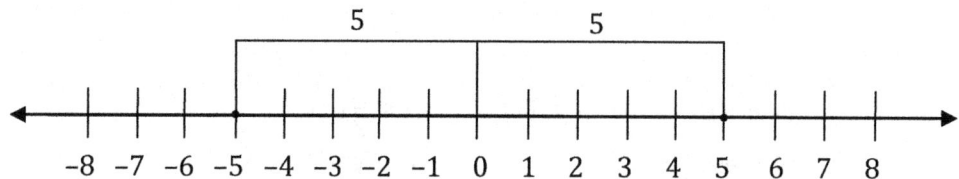

$|5| = 5$ because 5 is five units from zero.

$|-5| = 5$ because -5 is also five units from zero.

Absolute value equations that contain a variable within the absolute value bars are really two equations in one.

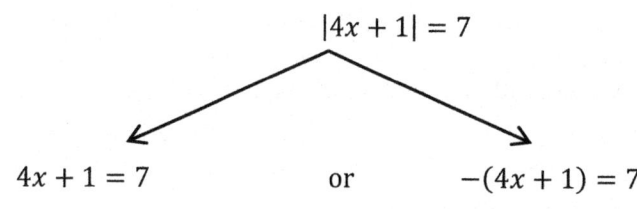

$|4x + 1| = 7$

$4x + 1 = 7$ or $-(4x + 1) = 7$

Solve both: $4x = 6$ or $-4x - 1 = 7$

$x = \dfrac{6}{4}$ or $-4x = 8$

$x = \dfrac{3}{2}$ or $x = -2$

TIP:

Think of absolute value as "math on sale": it's two for one.

TIP:

Be sure to plug your answers back in to make sure they work.

Try It Solve:

7) $|2x - 5| = 1$

8) $|3x + 8| = -2$

Inequalities and Absolute Value

Now, let's apply all that to **absolute value inequalities**. Remember to flip the inequality if you multiply or divide by a negative number.

Try It Simplify:

9) $|x - 6| \leq 4$

10) $|x - 6| \geq 4$

Absolute value **graphs** have a distinctive shape because absolute values are always nonnegative.

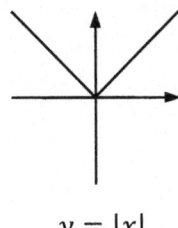

$y = |x|$

TIP:

To graph an absolute value equation on the SAT's built-in calculator, use the command `abs()`.

Math: Algebra

Practice Set 1: Easy-Medium

1

Which of the following is a solution to the equation $|1 - 2x| = 11$?

A. $x = -4$
B. $x = 3$
C. $x = 5$
D. $x = 6$

2

What is the maximum possible value of q, given that $-2q - 12 \leq -5q$?

3

A scientist tabulating her data finds that all her results fall within the range indicated by the number line below.

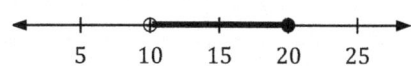

Which of the following best represents the scientist's data?

A. $x < 10$ or $x > 20$
B. $10 < x < 20$
C. $10 < x \leq 20$
D. $10 \leq x < 20$

4

Two stores sell the same item for two different prices: one sells the item for $\$x$, the other for $\$y$. While both prices vary, the positive difference between the two prices is always between $\$5.00$ and $\$7.50$, inclusive. Which of the following must be true?

A. $5 \leq x - y \leq 7.5$
B. $5 \leq |x - y| \leq 7.5$
C. $5 \leq |x + y| \leq 7.5$
D. $5 \leq x \leq 7.5$ or $5 \leq y \leq 7.5$

5

If $y < 0$ and $|x + y| = 6$, then which of the following could be the value of y when $x = 5$?

A. -11
B. -3
C. 3
D. 7

6

Which of the following numbers is a solution to the inequality $3 - 4n > 11$?

A. -3
B. -2
C. -1
D. 1

7

Which of the following could show the graph of $y \leq 2x - 1$ on the xy-plane?

A.
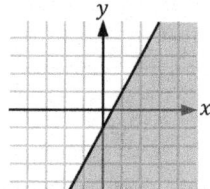

B.
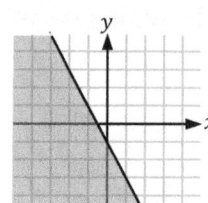

C.
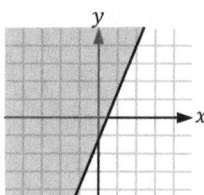

D.
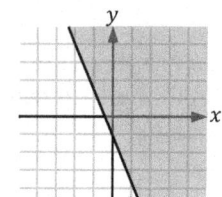

Practice Set 2: Medium-Hard

1

On the xy-plane, the graph of $y > -x + 3$ contains NO points in which of the following quadrants?

A. Quadrant I
B. Quadrant II
C. Quadrant III
D. Quadrant IV

2

Which of the following is always equal to $|y - x|$ for all real values of x and y?

A. $|x - y|$
B. $-(y - x)$
C. $x - y$
D. $|x + y|$

3

If $b = 2a$, where a is an integer such that $5a - 6 \leq 9 + 3a$, what is the maximum possible value of b?

A. 2
B. 7
C. 14
D. 15

4

A thermometer indicates that the current outside temperature is a degrees. The actual current outside temperature is b degrees. If the temperature indicated by the thermometer is within 3 degrees of the actual temperature, which of the following best represents this situation?

A. $a + b < 3$
B. $a > b - 3$
C. $-3 < b - a < 3$
D. $b + 3 > a$

5

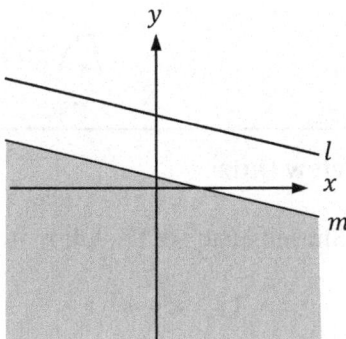

In the xy-plane above, lines l and m are parallel. If line l passes through the points $(-1, 5)$ and $(3, 4)$, which of the following could be the equation of the shaded area (the inequality that includes line m)?

A. $y \leq -\dfrac{1}{4}x + 1$

B. $y \leq 2x + \dfrac{3}{4}$

C. $y \geq \dfrac{3}{4}x + \dfrac{3}{4}$

D. $y \geq -\dfrac{1}{4}x + \dfrac{1}{2}$

6

Nine people weighing a total of 1,400 pounds (lbs) enter an elevator that has a weight limit of 1,500 lbs. One of the nine people is rolling a dolly weighing 15 lbs. On the dolly are b boxes, each weighing 18 lbs. What is the maximum possible value for b that will keep the combined weight of the people, the dolly, and the boxes under the elevator's weight limit?

Advanced Math
Exponents and Roots

Preview Quiz:

Simplify each of the following.

1) $a^b * a^c =$

2) $\dfrac{a^b}{a^c} =$

3) $(a^b)^c =$

4) $a^{-b} =$

5) $a^{1/b} =$

6) $a^c * b^c =$

7) $\dfrac{a^c}{b^c} =$

8) $\sqrt{a} * \sqrt{b} =$

9) $\dfrac{\sqrt{a}}{\sqrt{b}} =$

10) $a^1 =$

11) $a^0 =$

Solve.

12) If $x^2 = 36$, then $x =$ _____

13) If $y = 36$, then $\sqrt{y} =$ _____

Simplify each of the following.

14) $3x(x^4) =$

15) $3^{-2} =$

16) $\sqrt{p^4 q^{12}} =$

17) $\sqrt{9x^8} =$

Solve.

18) If $16^5 * 4^3 = 4^x$, what is the value of x? _____

As you already know, raising a number to an **exponent** means multiplying the number by itself that number of times.

Example: $2^4 = 2 \times 2 \times 2 \times 2 = \mathbf{16}$

You can simplify many ugly-looking exponent problems by simply rewriting them in this way.

Example: Simplify $x^3 * x^4$.

$$\underbrace{x * x * x}_{} * \underbrace{x * x * x * x}_{} = \boldsymbol{x^7}$$

This example illustrates an important rule: when you **multiply** the same base, you **add** the exponents.

Example: $n^5 * n^3 = \boldsymbol{n^8}$

Something similar happens when you divide.

Example: $\dfrac{x^5}{x^3} = \dfrac{\cancel{x} * \cancel{x} * \cancel{x} * x * x}{\cancel{x} * \cancel{x} * \cancel{x}} = \boldsymbol{x^2}$

See the relationship? When you **divide** the same base, you **subtract** the exponents.

Example: $n^{12} \div n^2 = \boldsymbol{n^{10}}$

We can use the same technique to illustrate problems that involve raising an exponent to another exponent.

Example: $(x^3)^2 = (x^3)(x^3) = (x * x * x)(x * x * x) = \boldsymbol{x^6}$

So when you raise an exponent to another exponent, you **multiply** the exponents.

Example: $(n^5)^3 = \boldsymbol{n^{15}}$

Try It   Simplify each of the following:

1) $a^4 * a^2 =$

2) $a^9 \div a^3 =$

3) $(a^7)^4 =$

Math: Advanced Math

Raising a value to the exponent 1 does nothing to it: the result is the same as the original value. This means whenever you see a variable that has no exponent written, you can always write in a 1 to remind yourself that it's there.

Example: Simplify $3x(x^4)$.
$$3 * x^1 * x^4 = \mathbf{3x^5}$$

By definition, when you raise any nonzero value to the exponent zero, the result is one.

Example: $7^0 = \mathbf{1}$

Try It   Solve for x:

4) $4^5 * 4^5 * 4^5 * 4^5 = 4^x$

5) $3^6 * 3^4 = 3^x$

6) $\dfrac{3^6}{3^4} = 3^x$

7) $(3^6)^4 = 3^x$

8) Simplify $2x(5x) - 4x^2$.

9) If $a = 2$ and $b = 3$, what is the value of $3(a^0) + 2(b^0)$?

Exponents and Roots

The key to many tricky exponent problems is to rewrite one or more of the expressions so that the bases match.

Example:
$$16^5 * 4^3 = 4^x$$
$$(4^2)^5 * 4^3 = 4^x$$
$$4^{10} * 4^3 = 4^x$$
$$4^{13} = 4^x$$
$$x = 13$$

Try It Solve for x:

10) $9^2 = 3^x$

11) $4^5 * 4^5 * 4^5 * 4^5 = 2^x$

12) $\dfrac{4^5}{2^2 * 2^3} = x$

13) $(4^3)^2 = 2^x$

Negative exponents are all about fractions. If the value with a negative exponent is in the numerator, move it to the denominator and make the exponent positive. If the value with a negative exponent is in the denominator, move it to the numerator and make the exponent positive.

Examples: $\dfrac{x^{-5}}{2} = \dfrac{1}{2x^5}$ $\dfrac{5a^{-3}b}{c^2} = \dfrac{5b}{a^3c^2}$

TIP: Be sure to move *only* the value that the exponent is attached to.

You can apply this rule to non-fraction values by simply rewriting them as fractions first.

Example: $3^{-2} = \dfrac{3^{-2}}{1} = \dfrac{1}{3^2} = \dfrac{1}{9}$

Try It 14) What is the value of 2^{-3}?

Roots can be written as fraction exponents: $x^{\frac{1}{2}}$ indicates the square root of x, and $x^{\frac{1}{3}}$ is the cube root of x, and so on. This notation helps illustrate the effect of a root on an expression that contains an exponent: taking the square root means multiplying that exponent by $\frac{1}{2}$.

Example: Simplify $\sqrt{a^6}$.
$$(a^6)^{\frac{1}{2}} = a^{6*\frac{1}{2}} = \boldsymbol{a^3}$$

Example: Simplify $\sqrt{p^4 q^{12}}$.
$$(p^4 q^{12})^{\frac{1}{2}} = (p^4)^{\frac{1}{2}} * (q^{12})^{\frac{1}{2}} = \boldsymbol{p^2 q^6}$$

Try It 15) Simplify $\sqrt{x^8 y^2}$, where x and y are positive numbers.

Both positive numbers and negative numbers become positive when squared. Therefore, an expression with an even-numbered exponent has two answers: plus and minus.

Example: If $x^2 = 36$, what is the value of x?
$$x = 6 \text{ or } x = -6$$

However, a square root expression has only one answer.

Example: If $y = \sqrt{36}$, what is the value of y?
$$y = 6 \text{ only}$$

TIP:

Think of the radical as a function that means "give me the positive root of this number."

Exponents and Roots

When multiplying or dividing two values that have been raised to the **same exponent**, you can squish them together in parentheses and keep the exponent outside.

Example: $4^5 * x^5 = (4x)^5$

You can also go the other way, eliminating parentheses by distributing the exponents that are attached to them.

Example: $(5n)^2 = 5^2 * n^2 = 25n^2$

These rules apply to roots too.

Example: $\sqrt{9x^8} = \sqrt{9} * \sqrt{x^8} = 3x^4$

To **simplify** a square root, use the rules above to break it up into factors that are perfect squares.

Example: $\sqrt{12} = \sqrt{4*3} = \sqrt{4} * \sqrt{3} = 2\sqrt{3}$

An important note: the rules on this page apply only to problems involving multiplying or dividing. This does *not* work when adding or subtracting!

Example: $(x+3)^2$ is NOT the same thing as $x^2 + 9$.

Try It   Simplify each of the following.

16) $\sqrt{16y^8} =$

17) $\sqrt{45} =$

18) $\sqrt[3]{8n^6} =$

19) $\sqrt[3]{-64} =$

TIP:

To enter a square root on the built-in calculator, just type `sqrt`. For other roots, type `nthroot`. Or, click the keyboard icon on the bottom left of the screen, then click the "functions" button, and then scroll down to the Number Theory category and click the $\sqrt[n]{\square}$ button.

Math: Advanced Math

Practice Set 1: Easy-Medium

1

$$\frac{8.0 * 10^6}{4.0 * 10^2}$$

The fraction above is equivalent to which of the following?

A. $4.0 * 10^{12}$
B. $2.0 * 10^{12}$
C. $2.0 * 10^4$
D. $4.0 * 10^3$

2

Given that a and b are positive integers, which of the following is equivalent to $\frac{-18a^9b^3}{(-3a^4)(2b)}$?

A. $-3a^5b^2$
B. $-\frac{3a^5}{b^2}$
C. $\frac{3a^5}{b^2}$
D. $3a^5b^2$

3

Which of the following represents the product of $2x^3$ and $3x^2$ for all real values of x?

A. $5x^5$
B. $5x^6$
C. $6x^5$
D. $6x^6$

4

Which of the following is equivalent to the expression $x^{\frac{3}{5}}$?

A. $\sqrt[5]{x^3}$
B. $\sqrt[3]{x^5}$
C. $\frac{x^3}{5}$
D. $\frac{3x}{5}$

5

If $7^{3x+5} = 7^8$, what is the value of x?

6

Given that x is a nonzero number, which of the following is equivalent to the expression $6x^4 - 9x^3 + 3x^2$?

A. $3x^2(2x^2 - 3x + 3)$
B. $6x^4(1 - 3x^2 + 2x)$
C. $x(6x^3 - 9x^2 + 3)$
D. $3x^2(2x^2 - 3x + 1)$

7

On the xy-plane, what is the y-intercept of the graph of $y = 2(4)^x$?

A. $(0, 1)$
B. $(0, 2)$
C. $(0, 4)$
D. $(0, 8)$

8

Let the function f be defined by the equation $f(x) = x^{-\frac{1}{2}}$ for all real values of x. What is the value of $f\left(\frac{9}{4}\right)$?

A. $-\frac{3}{2}$
B. $-\frac{2}{3}$
C. $\frac{3}{2}$
D. $\frac{2}{3}$

Practice Set 2: Medium-Hard

1. If $x > 0$ and $y > 0$, which expression is equivalent to $\sqrt{\dfrac{56x^3y^9}{7(xy)^5}}$?

A. $\dfrac{2y^2\sqrt{2}}{x}$

B. $2xy^2\sqrt{2}$

C. $\dfrac{8y^4}{x^2}$

D. $8x^2y^4$

2. If $x^{-\frac{1}{2}} = \dfrac{1}{4}$, then which of the following could be the value of x?

A. $\dfrac{1}{16}$

B. $\dfrac{1}{4}$

C. 4

D. 16

3. Which expression is equivalent to $(2xy)^3 * 3x^{-2}y$?

A. $6xy^4$

B. $6x^2y$

C. $\dfrac{24y^3}{x}$

D. $24xy^4$

4. Which expression is equivalent to the product of $\sqrt[4]{144a^6}$ and $2\sqrt{3a}$?

A. $12a^2$
B. $24a^2\sqrt{3a}$
C. $24a^4$
D. $12a^4\sqrt{3a}$

5. If $\dfrac{x^2y}{3x} = \dfrac{5}{2}$, where $x \neq 0$, then what is the value of xy?

A. $\dfrac{3}{5}$

B. $\dfrac{5}{6}$

C. $\dfrac{15}{2}$

D. 30

6. Let $x, y,$ and z be positive numbers such that $\sqrt{x} = y$ and $\sqrt{y} = z$. If $z = 4$, what is the value of x?

7. Which of the following is equivalent to $\dfrac{4n^6 - 8n^5}{2n^2 + (2n)^2}$, where $n \neq 0$?

A. $\dfrac{2}{3n^3}$

B. $\dfrac{2n^4 - 4n^3}{3}$

C. $\dfrac{2n^2 - 4n}{3}$

D. $3n^4 - 2n^3$

8. If the cube root of a negative integer is multiplied by the square of a positive integer, the result must be which of the following?

A. zero
B. positive
C. negative
D. imaginary

Factoring, FOILing, and Fractions

Preview Quiz

Distribute and simplify each of the following:

1) $3x(2 + y) =$

3) $(n + 2)(n - 3) =$

2) $x^3(2x^2 + y) =$

Factor completely:

4) $2ab + 4a =$

6) $x^2 - 2x - 35 =$

5) $x^2 - y^2 =$

7) $a^4 - 36 =$

Solve:

8) $x^2 - 11x + 18 = 0$

9) $\sqrt{x - 2} = x - 4$

Factoring, FOILing, and Fractions

When a term is multiplied by a quantity in parentheses, you can **distribute** that term by multiplying it by each item inside the parentheses.

Example: $3x(2 + y) = 3x(2) + 3x(y)$
$$= 6x + 3xy$$

TIP:
Remember, a **term** is a number, a variable, or the product of numbers and variables (e.g., $3xy$). **Like terms** are terms with the same variable and the same exponent. $3x$ and $2x$ are like terms; $3x$ and $2x^2$ are not. See p. 230 for more on this topic.

Try It   Simplify each of the following.

1) $2(a + 3b) =$ _____

2) $x(4 - y) =$ _____

3) $3a(b + 2c - d) =$ _____

If the term outside the parentheses and the terms inside the parentheses have any variables in common, use the exponent rules to combine them.

Example: $x^3(2x^2 + y) = x^3(2x^2) + x^3(y)$
$$= 2x^5 + x^3y$$

Try It   Simplify each of the following.

4) $3x(2x - 4x^2y) =$

5) $2n^3p(np^4 - 5n^2 + 3np) =$

6) $3(x - 2) + 5 =$

7) $4x(0.5) + 2\left(\dfrac{x}{2}\right) - x$

8) $2(2x) - 4(3x) =$

9) $9x - 3x(2 - y) =$

- 283 -

TM and © 2023 PrepMatters, Inc. All rights reserved.

Try It Solve for x:

10) $-2(x+5) = 3(-1-x)$

11) $2[4-(3+2x)] = 5$

The previous examples all involved multiplying a quantity in parentheses by a single term. But what if you're multiplying it by another quantity in parentheses?

To multiply two **binomials**, we **FOIL** them: multiply the
    First terms together, then the
    Outer terms, then the
    Inner terms, then the
    Last terms.

Then, add those products together and combine like terms.

TIP:

A **binomial** is an expression with exactly two terms, such as $(x+5)$.

Example: $(n+2)(n-3) = \underline{\underset{\underset{\mathbf{F}}{n \times n}}{n^2}\underset{\underset{\mathbf{O}}{n \times -3}}{-3n}\underset{\underset{\mathbf{I}}{2 \times n}}{+2n}\underset{\underset{\mathbf{L}}{2 \times -3}}{-6}}$

$= n^2 - 3n + 2n - 6$

$= \boldsymbol{n^2 - n - 6}$

Try It Simplify each of the following.

12) $(x-4)(x+2) =$

13) $(p+5)(q-6) =$

Factoring, FOILing, and Fractions

Factoring is just the opposite of distributing. To factor an expression, look to see whether all the terms in the expression can be divided by the same thing. This "thing" could be just a number, like 2, or a more complicated term such as $2x^2y$.

Example: $2ab + 4a$ *can be factored as* $2a(b + 2)$.

Try It   Factor completely:

14) $6x - 3 =$

15) $8n^2 - 4n =$

Factoring a **trinomial** (an expression with three terms) such as $n^2 - n - 6$ is a little more tricky. On the last page, we got to this trinomial by multiplying together two binomials, so that's where we'll end up when we factor it: $(n - 3)(n + 2)$.

Notice that -3 and 2 will *multiply* together to be -6 and *add* together to be -1. That's what we're looking for each time: try to find a pair of numbers that will multiply together to be the last term and add together to be the middle term.

Example: Factor $x^2 - 2x - 35$ *completely.*

Step One: List the possible pairs of numbers that could multiply together to be the last term.

$(1 \text{ and } -35); (-1 \text{ and } 35); (5 \text{ and } -7); (-5 \text{ and } 7)$

Step Two: Check each of those pairs to see which one adds up to the middle term.

$$
\begin{aligned}
1 + (-35) &= -34 \\
(-1) + 35 &= 34 \\
\boxed{5 + (-7) = -2} \\
(-5) + 7 &= 2
\end{aligned}
$$

TIP:
Don't forget to consider negative numbers!

Step Three: Plug those numbers into the parentheses.

$(x + 5)(x - 7)$ is the answer.

Try It   Factor completely:

16) $x^2 - 3x - 4 =$

17) $x^2 - 10x + 9 =$

Math: Advanced Math

The **difference of squares rule** says that any binomial of the form $a^2 - b^2$ can be factored as $(a + b)(a - b)$. This works whether a and b are variables, numbers, or some combination of both.

Examples:
$$x^2 - y^2 = (x + y)(x - y)$$
$$n^2 - 25 = (n + 5)(n - 5)$$
$$a^4 - 36 = (a^2 + 6)(a^2 - 6)$$
$$= (a^2 + 6)(a + \sqrt{6})(a - \sqrt{6})$$

Try It — Factor completely:

18) $x^2 - 81 =$

19) $p^2 - r^6 =$

TIP:
Here are a few other factoring patterns that are handy to know:
$$a^2 + 2ab + b^2 = (a + b)(a + b)$$
$$a^2 - 2ab + b^2 = (a - b)(a - b)$$

When a factorable expression starts out set equal to zero, you can often **solve by factoring**. Factor the expression completely, and then set each factor equal to zero. Then solve both.

Example:
$$x^2 - 11x + 18 = 0$$
$$(x - 9)(x - 2) = 0$$
$$x - 9 = 0 \text{ or } x - 2 = 0$$
$$x = 9 \text{ or } x = 2$$

TIP:
Take care to check whether the problem is asking for a factor or a solution. A **factor** of this equation is $(x - 9)$. A **solution** is positive 9.

Try It — Solve for x:

20) $x^2 - 3x - 4 = 0$

21) $2x^2 - 6x = 0$

CHALLENGE:

You know how to factor an expression of form $ax^2 + bx + c$ when there is no coefficient on the x^2 term (that is, when $a = 1$). But what about otherwise?

Example: Factor the expression $2x^2 + 13x + 15$.

To start, multiply the first coefficient (a) by the last value (c): in this case, that gives us $2 * 15 = 30$. Our task now is to find a pair of numbers that will multiply together to be 30 and add together to be the middle coefficient (13). In this case, 10 and 3 would work. So now, we rewrite the expression, breaking up the middle term into those two pieces:

$$2x^2 + 10x + 3x + 15$$

Next, **factor by grouping**: factor whatever you can out of the first two terms, and then factor whatever you can out of the last two terms. Here, we can factor $2x$ out of the first two terms, and we can factor a 3 out of the last two. That gives us this:

$$2x(x + 5) + 3(x + 5)$$

We now have two big, ugly terms, and they have something in common: they each have $(x + 5)$ as a factor. So, factor that out of both.

$$(x + 5)(2x + 3)$$

And that's it! The expression is now fully factored.

Try It   22) Solve the equation $2x^2 + 7x - 4 = 0$.

TIP:
You can also solve this problem by graphing it on the built-in calculator. The x-intercepts of the graph are the answers.

Some equations can be solved simply by taking the square root of both sides of the equation. Just remember that even-numbered exponents have *two* solutions: plus and minus.

Example: $(x-4)^2 = 100$

$$x - 4 = 10 \text{ or } x - 4 = -10$$
$$x = 14 \text{ or } x = -6$$

If you can solve an equation by square rooting both sides, you can also solve an equation by *squaring* both sides. However, be careful to square the *entire side*.

Example: $\sqrt{x-2} = x - 4$

Incorrect: $\cancel{(\sqrt{x-2})^2 = x^2 - 4^2}$
$\cancel{x - 2 = x^2 - 16}$

Correct: $(\sqrt{x-2})^2 = (x-4)^2$
$x - 2 = (x-4)(x-4)$

Next, simplify and combine like terms, then solve by factoring if possible. Once you have your solutions, plug them back into the original equation to check that they work.

$$(\sqrt{x-2})^2 = (x-4)^2$$
$$x - 2 = (x-4)(x-4)$$
$$x - 2 = x^2 - 8x + 16$$
$$0 = x^2 - 9x + 18$$
$$0 = (x-3)(x-6)$$
$$x = 3 \text{ or } x = 6$$

Now plug these values back in:

$x = 3$:
$\sqrt{3-2} = 3 - 4$
$\sqrt{1} = -1$
Not true!

$x = 6$:
$\sqrt{6-2} = 6 - 4$
$\sqrt{4} = 2$
True!

In this case, 3 was an **extraneous solution**, meaning it was a value that appeared to satisfy the equation but actually didn't. The only answer to this equation is $x = 6$.

TIP:

You should always check for extraneous solutions if the original equation contained an x either inside a square root or on the bottom of a fraction. That means it's usually quickest to back-solve these problems, if possible. After all, if you do all the algebra, you'll just have to plug those values in at the end anyway to double-check that they're not extraneous. So you may as well skip the extra work and go straight to the plugging-in step.

You can also use the built-in calculator to solve these equations. Enter the left side of the original equation on one line and the right side on another. For the $\sqrt{x-2} = x - 4$ example, we'd get this:

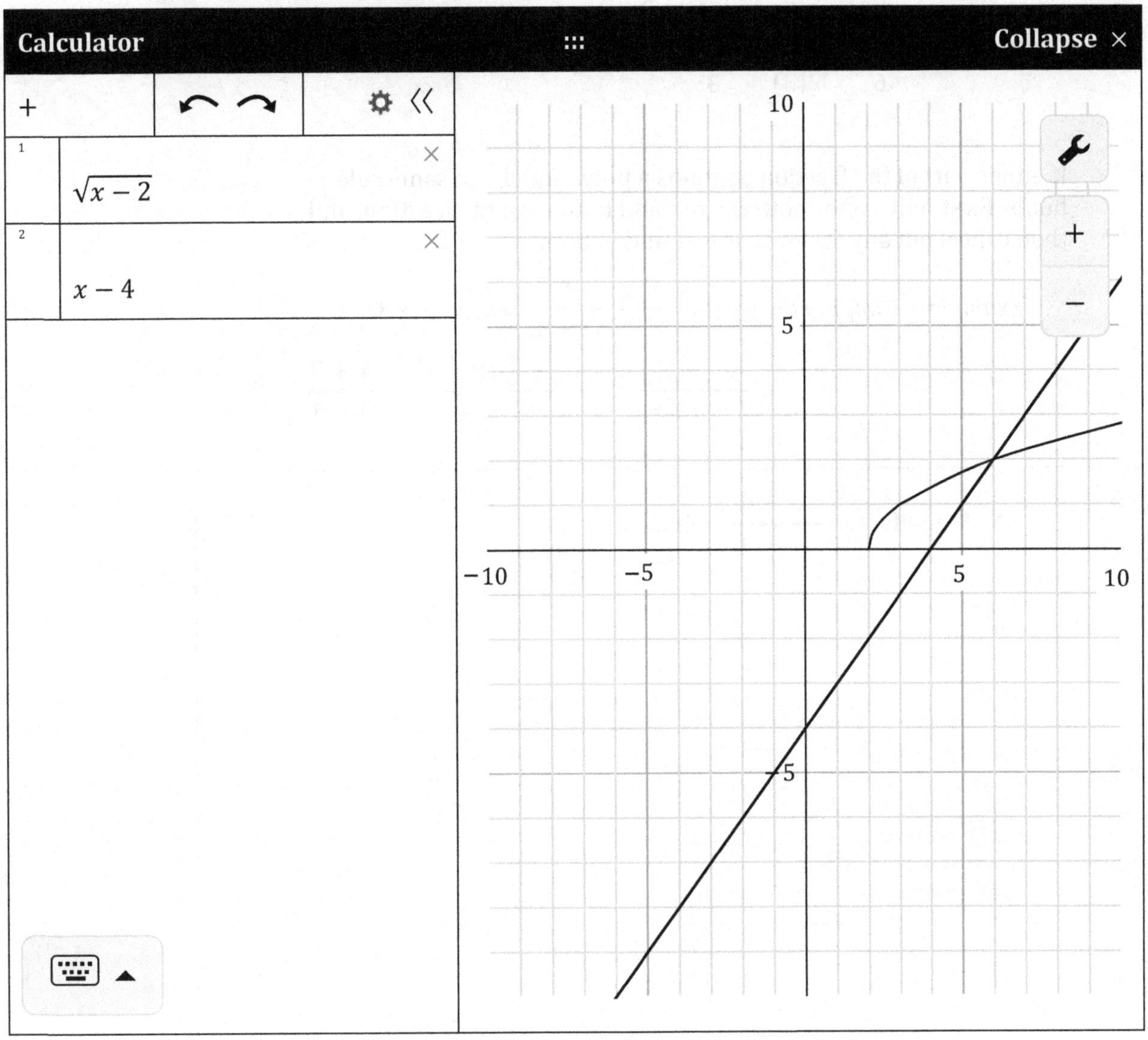

There's only one point of intersection: at the point $(6, 2)$. Therefore, the only solution to this equation is $x = 6$.

Try It Solve:

23) $\sqrt{x+23} = 3 + x$

Math: Advanced Math

As you know, you can simplify a fraction by canceling out any factor that the numerator and denominator have in common.

Example: Simplify the fraction $\frac{4x}{6}$.

$$\frac{4x}{6} = \frac{2(2x)}{2(3)} = \frac{2x}{3}$$

If either part of the fraction contains a polynomial, the same rule holds. First fully factor both the top and bottom of the fraction, and then cancel out any factor that you find in both.

Example: Simplify the fraction $\frac{x^2-9}{x^2-4x+3}$, where $x > 3$.

$$\frac{x^2-9}{x^2-4x+3} = \frac{(x+3)(x-3)}{(x-1)(x-3)} = \frac{x+3}{x-1}$$

Try It

24) Simplify $\frac{x^2-x-6}{x^2-2x-8}$, where $x > 4$.

TIP:

A common factor is the **only** thing you can cancel out from the top and bottom of a fraction. Other features that the two parts have in common don't count. For example, the expression $\frac{x+3}{x+5}$ **cannot** be simplified as $\frac{3}{5}$.

CHALLENGE:

A **rational expression** is an algebraic expression that takes the shape of a fraction. Remember, to add or subtract fractions, we need a common denominator. Once we have that, we add or subtract straight across the top, leaving the bottom the same.

$$\text{Example:} \quad \frac{1}{3} + \frac{5}{6} = \frac{2}{2} * \frac{1}{3} + \frac{5}{6} = \frac{2}{6} + \frac{5}{6} = \frac{7}{6}$$

We can do the same thing when the numerator and/or denominator contains variables instead of (or in addition to) numbers.

$$\text{Example:} \quad \frac{1}{x} + \frac{5}{6x} = \frac{6}{6} * \frac{1}{x} + \frac{5}{6x} = \frac{6}{6x} + \frac{5}{6x} = \frac{11}{6x}$$

Try It 25) Simplify $\frac{3}{x} + \frac{2}{y}$, where $xy \neq 0$.

If the numerator and/or denominator contain more than one term, no problem—the steps are the same. It's just that in order to find the common denominator (and simplify the result) we'll need to use some of the distributing, factoring, and FOILing skills we've just reviewed.

$$\text{Example:} \quad \frac{1}{x+2} + \frac{5}{x-1} = \frac{(x-1)(1)}{(x-1)(x+2)} + \frac{5(x+2)}{(x-1)(x+2)}$$

$$= \frac{x-1}{(x-1)(x+2)} + \frac{5x+10}{(x-1)(x+2)}$$

$$= \frac{x-1+5x+10}{(x-1)(x+2)}$$

$$= \frac{6x+9}{x^2+x-2}$$

Try It 26) Simplify $\frac{3}{x-4} + \frac{2}{x+4}$, where $x^2 \neq 16$.

Math: Advanced Math

Two expressions are equivalent if the coefficients of the like terms are equal. So, many abstract-looking problems can be solved by simplifying both sides of the equation and then **matching up the like terms**.

Example: If $2x^3 + 5(3x - 4) + 6 = 2x^3 + px + q$, where p and q are constants, what is the value of $p - q$?

$2x^3 + 5(3x - 4) + 6 = 2x^3 + px + q$
$2x^3 + 15x - 20 + 6 = 2x^3 + px + q$
$2x^3 + 15x - 14 = 2x^3 + px + q$

For these expressions to be equal, $15x$ must be the same thing as px, and -14 must be the same thing as q. Therefore, $p = 15$ and $q = -14$. So:

$p - q = 15 - (-14) = \mathbf{29}$

Try It

27) If $(qx - r)(2x + 5) = 8x^2 + 14x - 15$, where q and r are constants, what is the value of $q + r$?

TIP:

For these problems, it's important to be precise about exactly what the coefficient is. If you're told that $2kx + 5 = mx + b$, you might be tempted to think that m is 2. But it's not: it's $2k$.

Factoring, FOILing, and Fractions

Practice Set 1: Easy-Medium

1 Which expression is equivalent to $(2x - 1)(x + 3)$?

A. $2x^2 + 7x - 3$
B. $2x^2 + 7x + 3$
C. $2x^2 + 5x - 3$
D. $2x^2 + 5x + 3$

2 $(4x^3 - 3x^2 + 5) - (6 + 2x^2 - 3x^3)$ is equivalent to which of the following?

A. $x^3 - 5x^2 - 1$
B. $x^3 - x^2 - 11$
C. $7x^3 - 5x^2 - 1$
D. $7x^3 - x^2 - 11$

3 Which of the following is a factor of $x^2 + 2x - 24$?

A. $x - 4$
B. $x + 4$
C. $x - 6$
D. $x - 12$

4 What are the solutions to the quadratic equation $x^2 - 3x - 28 = 0$?

A. -7 and 4
B. -4 and 7
C. 4 and 7
D. -4 and -7

5 The expression $(5p + 6q)(7r - 8s)$ is equivalent to which of the following?

A. $35pr - 48rs$
B. $35pq^2 + 42qr - 48rs^2$
C. $30pr + 35ps - 48qr + 56qs$
D. $35pr - 40ps + 42qr - 48qs$

6 Which of the following is equivalent to $3x^2 - 12$?

A. $3(x - 2)(x + 2)$
B. $3(x - 2)^2$
C. $(3x - 2)^2$
D. $(x - 4)(x + 3)$

7
$$\frac{x^2 + 5x - 14}{x^2 - 4}$$

Where $x > 2$, the expression above is equivalent to which of the following?

A. $\dfrac{x + 7}{x + 2}$

B. $\dfrac{5x - 14}{-4}$

C. $\dfrac{2.5x - 7}{2}$

D. $\dfrac{x + 7}{x - 2}$

8 What is one solution to the equation $x^2 + 5x - 36 = 0$?

9 The expression $(x^2 - 1) - (2x^2 + 1)$ is equivalent to which of the following?

A. $-2x^4 + x^2 + 1$
B. $-x^2 - 2$
C. $-x^2$
D. 1

Practice Set 2: Medium-Hard

1

Which of the following expressions is equivalent to $\dfrac{d^2 + 6d + 9}{d^2 - 9}$, where $d^2 \neq 9$?

A. $-6d$
B. $d + 3$
C. $\dfrac{d - 3}{d + 3}$
D. $\dfrac{d + 3}{d - 3}$

2

$$y = (x - 5)^2$$
$$y = x + 1$$

Which of the following (x, y) points is a solution to the system of equations above?

A. $(-1, 0)$
B. $(5, 0)$
C. $(3, 4)$
D. $(2, 3)$

3

If $(a + b)^2 = (a - b)^2$, which of the following must be true?

A. $a + b = a - b$
B. $a = -b$
C. $ab = 0$
D. $|ab| = 1$

4

If $g + h = 2$ and $gh = -8$, what is the value of $\dfrac{g}{h} + \dfrac{h}{g}$?

5

When a price of d dollars is squared, the result is 4 dollars more than triple the value of d. Which of the following could be the value of d?

A. 1
B. 2
C. 3
D. 4

6

If $r - s = 10$ and $r^2 + s^2 = 20$, what is the value of rs?

7

Which expression is equivalent to $\dfrac{3}{x + 1} - \dfrac{1}{x + 3}$?

A. $\dfrac{1}{(x + 3)(x + 1)}$
B. $\dfrac{2x + 8}{(x + 3)(x + 1)}$
C. $\dfrac{2x + 10}{(x + 3)(x + 1)}$
D. $\dfrac{2}{x - 2}$

8

If $y = 2\sqrt{x - 1}$, for what value of x does $y = 8$?

A. 2
B. 3
C. 16
D. 17

Factoring, FOILing, and Fractions

9

$$\frac{4}{3+x} - \frac{2}{1+x} = 5$$

How many possible real solutions exist for x in the equation above?

A. 0
B. 1
C. 2
D. 3

10

In the figure below, the length of rectangle B is 2 inches greater than the side length of square A, and the width of rectangle B is 5 inches greater than the side length of square A.

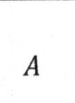

If the area of square A is x^2 square inches, which of the following represents the area, in square inches, of rectangle B?

A. $x^2 + 10$
B. $x^2 + 5x + 2$
C. $x^2 + 7x + 10$
D. $x^2 + 10x + 7$

11

If $ax^4y^2 + bx^3y^3 + cx^2y^4$ is equivalent to $(2x^2y - 6xy^2)^2$ for all real values of x and y, what is the value of $a + b + c$?

12

Suppose that the probability of a certain projectile object hitting its target is equal to $\frac{16t^2 - 40t + 125}{100}$, where t is the number of seconds for which the object has traveled. After how many seconds of travel is the object certain to hit its target?

A. 1.25
B. 1.5
C. 2.5
D. 4

13

$$3p(8x^2 - q) = 2x\left(4p^2x + \frac{9}{x}\right)$$

In the equation above, q and p are nonzero constants, x is a variable, and $x \neq 0$. What is the value of q?

14

If $\sqrt{x + 14} = x + 2$, which of the following could be the value of x?

A. -5
B. -2.7
C. 2
D. 3.7

15

$$\frac{6x^2 - 7x + 5}{kx - 3} = 3x + 1 + \frac{8}{kx - 3}$$

In the equation above, k is a constant and $x \neq \frac{3}{k}$. What is the value of k?

A. 1
B. 2
C. 3
D. 4

Math: Advanced Math

Function Essentials

Preview Quiz:

If $f(x) = 2x + 3$:

1) What is the value of $f(4)$? _____

2) For what value of x is $f(x) = 7$? _____

The table below gives values of the linear function $f(x)$.

x	−3	−2	−1	0	1	2	3
$f(x)$	−3	−1	1	3	5	7	9

3) What is the value of $f(1)$? _____

4) What is the value of $f(4)$? _____

In the graph of $y = f(x)$ shown below, each of the gridlines represents one coordinate unit.

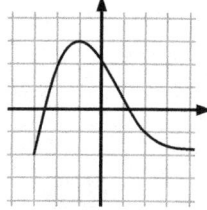

5) What is the value of $f(-1)$? _____

6) How would the graph of $y = f(x+3) + 2$ look different from the graph of $f(x)$?

_____

If $f(x) = 2x + 4$ and $g(x) = x - 5$:

7) For what value of x is $f(x) = g(x)$? _____

8) What is the value of $f(g(2))$? _____

Function Essentials

The definition of a **function** is that for all values of x, there is a unique value of $f(x)$. You can think of $f(x)$ as the y value: for example, the function notation $f(3) = 9$ tells you that when $x = 3$ on the graph of the function, $y = 9$.

Usually, functions will be defined by a given **equation**. To apply the equation, simply plug in whatever's inside the parentheses for x.

Example: *If $f(x) = 2x + 3$, what is the value of $f(4)$?*

$$f(4) = 2(4) + 3$$
$$= \mathbf{11}$$

If the problem gives you the value of $f(x)$ instead of the value of x, that just means you have to plug in your number on the other side of the equals sign.

Example: *If $f(x) = 2x + 3$, then for what value of x is $f(x) = 7$?*

$$7 = 2(x) + 3$$
$$4 = 2x$$
$$\mathbf{2 = x}$$

Try It

1) If $f(x) = 12 - 4x$, what is the value of $f(-2)$?

2) If $f(x) = 3x + 1$, then for what value of x is $f(x) = 19$?

3) Let $f(x) = 2x + k$, where k is a constant. If $f(4) = 1$, what is the value of k?

Math: Advanced Math

Functions can also be given as a **table** of values. You can use these values to find the equation, or in some cases, simply follow the pattern to find more values.

Example: The table below gives values of the linear function $f(x)$.

x	−3	−2	−1	0	1	2	3
$f(x)$	−3	−1	1	3	5	7	9

- *What is the value of $f(1)$?*

    In the column where $x = 1$, the value of $f(x)$ is 5. Therefore, $f(1) = \mathbf{5}$.

- *What is the value of $f(4)$?*

    There is no column where $x = 4$. However, we were told this was a *linear* function, so the same pattern that we can see in the table will continue indefinitely. And in the table, when $x = 1, 2,$ and 3, respectively, we can see that $f(x) = 5, 7,$ and 9, respectively. So, continue the pattern: when $x = 4$, $f(x)$ must equal **11**.

A third way that the test may present functions is by showing you the function's **graph**. To answer these, remember that x is the x-coordinate and $f(x)$ is the y-coordinate for all points.

Example: In the graph of $f(x)$ shown below, each of the gridlines represents one coordinate unit.

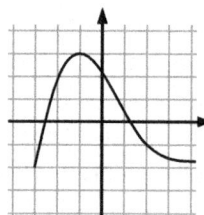

What is the value of $f(-1)$?

The graph passes through the point $(-1, 3)$. Therefore, $f(-1) = \mathbf{3}$.

> **TIP:**
> A point on the graph of a function f can be represented as (x, y) or as $(x, f(x))$. For example, the point in this problem could be written as $(-1, 3)$ or as $(-1, f(-1))$.

Another useful thing about function notation is that it allows us to define several different functions at the same time.

Example: If $f(x) = 2x + 4$ and $g(x) = x - 5$, for what value of x is $f(x) = g(x)$?

$$2x + 4 = x - 5$$
$$x + 4 = -5$$
$$x = -9$$

To find the value of a composite function such as $f(g(x))$, find the innermost value first and then work your way out.

Example: If $f(x) = 2x + 4$ and $g(x) = x - 5$, what is the value of $f(g(2))$?

First, we need the value of $g(2)$. So, start by plugging 2 into the g function:

$$g(2) = 2 - 5 = -3$$

Now that we know that $g(2) = -3$, we can rewrite $f(g(2))$ as just $f(-3)$. So that's all we need now:

$$f(-3) = 2(-3) + 4 = -2$$

The answer is -2.

Try It   If $f(x) = 12 - 4x$ and $g(x) = 2x - 3$, then:

4) What is the value of $f(g(2))$?

5) What is the value of $g(f(2))$?

6) What is the x-coordinate of the point on the xy-plane where the graphs of $y = f(x)$ and $y = g(x)$ intersect?

The limitations of a function are defined by its **domain** (all the possible x values) and **range** (all the possible y values). One way to determine the domain and range of a function is by looking at its graph.

Example: The graph of $f(x) = -x^2 - 4x - 3$ is shown below. What is the domain and what is the range of the function?

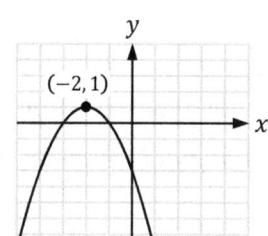

> **TIP:**
>
> **Interval notation** is a way of expressing domain, range, and other sets of numbers. The notation $(2, 5)$ represents all the values from 2 to 5, not including the 2 or the 5: for example, a domain of $2 < x < 5$. By contrast, the notation $[2, 5]$ represents all the values from 2 to 5, *inclusive*: for example, a domain of $2 \leq x \leq 5$.

This graph extends forever to the left and right, so **the domain is all real numbers**: from negative infinity to positive infinity. In interval notation, that's $(-\infty, \infty)$.

However, the range of this function is more limited. Although the graph extends forever downward (so its minimum value is negative infinity), it has a definite maximum point: it will never reach a point higher than the vertex of the parabola. As we can see from the graph, the y-coordinate of that point is 1. Therefore, **the range is $y \leq 1$**: that is, from negative infinity up to and including positive 1. In interval notation, that's $(-\infty, 1]$.

You can also use algebra to test the domain of a function. Any x value that would make the algebra impossible (for example, that would cause you to have to divide by zero, or to take the square root of a negative number) is excluded from the domain, and any y value that would do so is excluded from the range.

Example: Is 3 in the domain of $g(x) = \sqrt{1-x}$?

No: plugging in 3 for x would require us to take the square root of a negative number.

Example: Is -2 in the range of $h(x) = |x + 4|$?

No: the absolute value of any expression will always be greater than or equal to zero.

You may also be tested on the basic rules of **transformations** and **translations**. Remember, changes *inside* the parentheses affect the graph *horizontally*; changes *outside* the parentheses affect the graph *vertically*.

Vertical transformations:

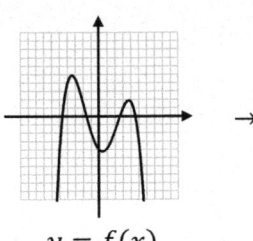 → 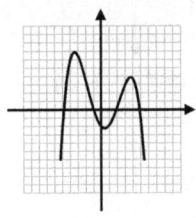 shifted **up** 2 units

$y = f(x)$ $y = f(x) + 2$:

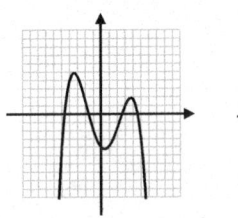 → 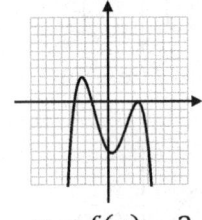 shifted **down** 2 units

$y = f(x)$ $y = f(x) - 2$

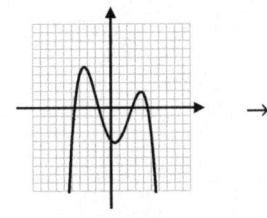 → 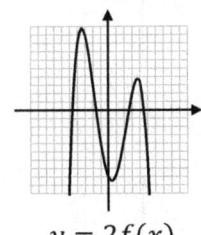 **stretched** vertically by a factor of 2

$y = f(x)$ $y = 2f(x)$

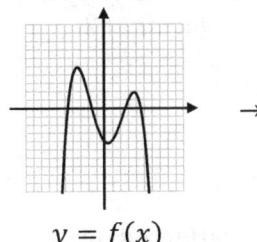 → 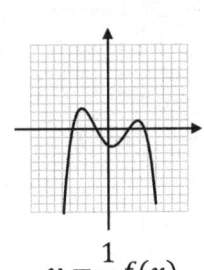 **compressed** vertically by a factor of 2

$y = f(x)$ $y = \frac{1}{2}f(x)$

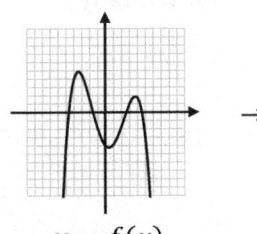 → 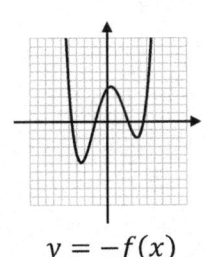 **reflected** over the *x*-axis (flipped upside down)

$y = f(x)$ $y = -f(x)$

Horizontal transformations:

TIP:
Inside the parentheses, everything works a bit backwards from what we'd expect. For example, +2 moves the graph *left*, not right.

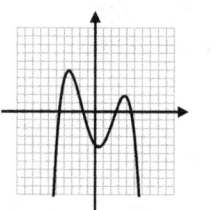 → 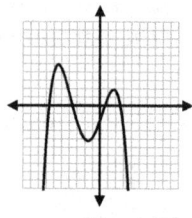   shifted **left** 2 units

$y = f(x)$ $y = f(x + 2)$

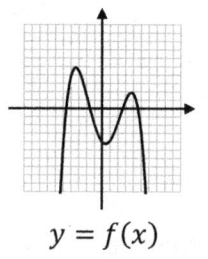 → 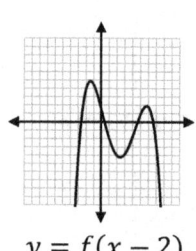   shifted **right** 2 units

$y = f(x)$ $y = f(x - 2)$

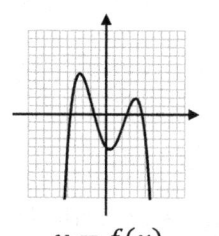 → 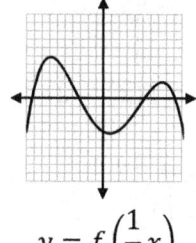   **stretched** horizontally by a factor of 2

$y = f(x)$ $y = f\left(\dfrac{1}{2}x\right)$

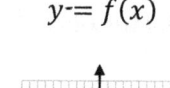 → 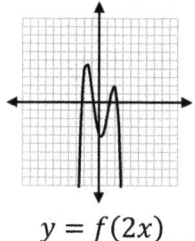   **compressed** horizontally by a factor of 2

$y = f(x)$ $y = f(2x)$

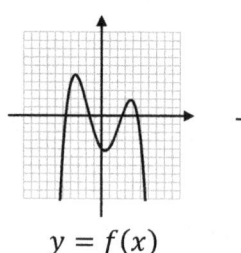 → 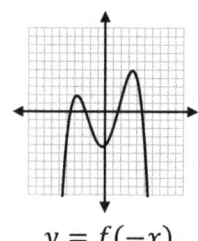   **reflected** over the y-axis (flipped horizontally)

$y = f(x)$ $y = f(-x)$

Try It

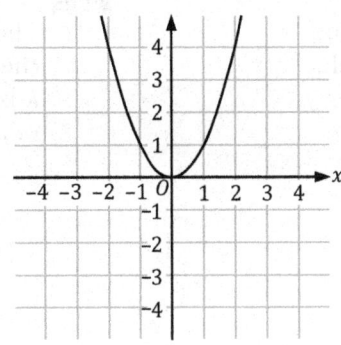

7) If the figure above shows the graph of $y = g(x)$, sketch the graph of $y = -g(x-2) + 1$:

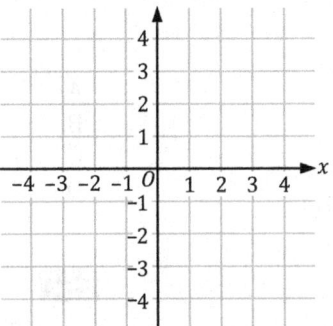

FROM THE BLOG

The literature on sleep deprivation is pretty darned stark: nearly everything one can measure from verbal retrieval to emotional control to blood pressure can be roughed up by sleep deprivation. Even worse, self-analysis suffers too. In one study, researchers found that their sleep-deprived subjects thought they had done great on the tasks they'd been given, when in fact their performance had tanked. They simply didn't realize it – their self-analysis was way off.

I encourage you to file that nugget away. If you were surprised by a test score that came back lower than you expected, it may be that on that test, it was your post-test assessment that missed the mark. Doing better next time may involve nothing more than taking the test again after you've caught a few more Z's.

Math: Advanced Math

Practice Set 1: Easy-Medium

1

A function f is defined by the equation $f(x) = 2x^2 - 3x + 5$. What is the value of $f(-2)$?

2

If $f(x) = x^2 + 3$ and $g(x) = 2x + 2$, then what is the value of $f(3) - g(2)$?

A. 3
B. 4
C. 6
D. 8

3

The total profit, p, that a manufacturer makes from selling x units of a certain product is equal to $p(x) = 27x - k$, where k is a positive constant. If the manufacturer makes a total profit of $19,850 when it sells 800 units, what is the value of k?

A. 1750
B. 2625
C. 9082
D. 15,225

4

The table below gives values of the function $f(x)$.

x	0	1	2	3
$f(x)$	−4	−3	0	5

If $f(x)$ is a quadratic function, then which of the following could be the equation of $f(x)$?

A. $f(x) = x^2 + 2$
B. $f(x) = x^2 - 4$
C. $f(x) = x - 4$
D. $f(x) = x^2 + x - 2$

5

The quadratic function f is graphed in the xy-plane below. If $f(4) = k$, where k is a constant, then what is the value of $f(k)$?

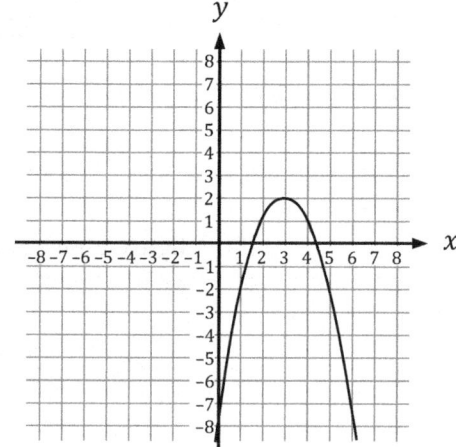

A. −2
B. −1
C. 1
D. 2

6

A ball is thrown straight up in the air from a height of 5 feet. Its height in feet above the ground after t seconds is expressed by $h(t) = 5 + 40t - 16t^2$. In this context, what is the best interpretation of $h(1) = 29$?

A. After 1 second, the ball has traveled 29 horizontal feet from its starting point.
B. After 1 second, the ball is 29 feet above the ground.
C. The ball reaches a height of 1 foot above the ground after 29 seconds.
D. The ball reaches a height of 1 foot above its starting point after 29 seconds.

7

If $f(x) = 1 - x$ and $g(x) = x - 1$, find $f(g(3))$.

Practice Set 2: Medium-Hard

1

Given the tables of values for the functions f and g shown below, what is the value of $g(f(2))$?

x	$f(x)$		x	$g(x)$
0	−3		0	−8
1	0		1	−6
2	3		2	0
3	6		3	10

A. −3
B. 1
C. 6
D. 10

2

Given the function f defined by the equation below, what is $f(1)$?

$$f(x) = \begin{cases} 2x - 1, x \leq 0 \\ x^2 + 1, x > 0 \end{cases}$$

A. 1
B. 2
C. 3
D. 4

3

Let $g(x)$ be defined by the equation $g(x) = |2x| - 6$. Which of the following is an x-intercept of the graph of g in the xy-plane?

A. $(-6, g(-6))$
B. $(-1, g(-1))$
C. $(0, g(0))$
D. $(3, g(3))$

4

The function $g(x)$ is defined by $g(x) = 2x^2$. If $r > 0$ and $g(r) = 36$, what is the value of $g(2r)$?

5

The figure below shows the graphs of the functions $f(x) = -x - 1$ and $g(x) = -x^2 - 6x + 5$ in the xy-plane. For what values of x is $f(x) < g(x)$?

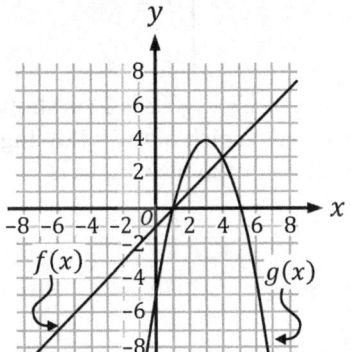

A. $x < 1$ or $x > 4$
B. $1 < x < 4$
C. $0 < x < 3$
D. $x < 0$ or $x > 3$

6

Let the function $g(x)$ be defined by the equation below:

$$g(x) = \frac{x - 4}{x - 3}$$

Which of the following values is NOT included in the domain of $g(x)$?

A. 0
B. 1
C. 3
D. 4

7

Let $f(x) = 3x^2$ and $g(x) = 2x + 1$. Which of the following expressions represents $f(g(x))$?

A. $12x^2 + 12x + 3$
B. $12x^2 + 6x$
C. $6x^3 + 3x^2$
D. $6x^2 + 1$

8

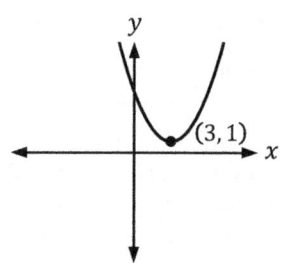

The graph of $y = -f(x-1)$ is shown in the above. Which of the following could be the graph of $y = f(x)$?

A.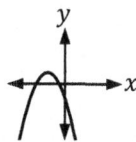

B.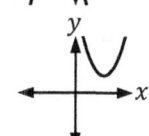

C.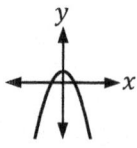

D.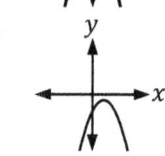

9

The function $f(x) = 24(1.15)^x$ gives a country's approximate population, in millions, at any time x years after the year 2000. Which of the following is the best interpretation of $f(0) = 24$?

A. The country's population in 2000 was approximately 24,000,000.
B. The country's population in 2024 was zero.
C. The country's population in 2000 was approximately 24.
D. Since 2000, the country's population has increased by 24 million per year.

10

Let $f(x)$ be a linear function such that $f(2) = 7$ and $f(4) = 11$. What is the value of $f(6)$?

11

If $g(x) = 2(x-1)^2 - x$, then which of the following is equivalent to $g(x+2)$?

A. $2x^2 + 7x + 6$
B. $2x^2 + 3x + 4$
C. $2x(x+1)$
D. $x(2x+3)$

12

$$f(x) = 2x^3 - 5x^2 + 6x - 1$$
$$g(x) = x^3 - 3x^2 - 2x + 8$$
$$h(x) = f(x) - 2g(x)$$

Which of the following defines the polynomial function $h(x)$?

A. $h(x) = 4x^3 - 2x^2 + 4x - 9$
B. $h(x) = 4x^3 - 11x^2 + 2x + 15$
C. $h(x) = x^2 + 10x - 17$
D. $h(x) = x^2 + 8x + 7$

13

x	0	1	2	3	1
y	1	4	5	9	2

Given the table of values above, the relationship between x and y could best be described as which of the following?

A. a linear function
B. an exponential function
C. a polynomial function
D. a relation that is not a function

Linear Functions

Preview Quiz:

The equation $f(x) = -15x + 750$ gives the amount owed, in dollars, on an interest-free loan after x months of payments.

1) What is the best interpretation of the y-intercept of the graph of $y = f(x)$ in the xy-plane?

   _____

2) What is the best interpretation of the slope of the graph of $y = f(x)$ in the xy-plane?

   _____

3) What is the best interpretation of $f(10) = 600$?

   _____

Solve:

4) Paul finds that the relationship between his semester grade point average, $g(s)$, and the number of hours per week he spends studying, s, can be modeled by $g(s) = 0.12s + 1$. Increasing his studying from 18 hours per week to 19 hours per week should raise his semester grade point average by how much?

   _____

Most of the time, the equation of a **line** will have a y term, an x term, and a standalone number: for example, $y = 4x - 1$. These terms may appear in a different order (e.g., $x - y = 3$ is still a line), and it's possible that one or more of these elements may be missing (e.g., $y = 7$, $x = 2$, and $y = x$ are all lines). But the ironclad rule is that the equation can't have any *other* types of terms in it. If an equation has a variable with an exponent (e.g., $y = x^2$) or puts one of the variables on the bottom of a fraction (e.g., $y = 1/x$), etc., the graph cannot be a line.

When equations are defined as functions, the y term is sometimes swapped for a **function notation** such as $f(x)$. All the rules above are the same: for example, $f(x) = 4x - 1$ is a line, as is $g(x) = 7$, while $h(x) = x^2$ is not.

You can also recognize a linear equation by its points. In a linear equation, the rate of change is constant. This means that each time the value of x increases by 1, the value of y must increase or decrease by a specific amount that does not change. That amount is the **slope** of the line.

Example: Given the values below, is $f(x)$ a linear function? Is $g(x)$ a linear function?

x	1	2	3	4
$f(x)$	2	6	10	14

x	1	2	3	4
$g(x)$	2	6	12	36

For the f function, as x increases by 1, y increases by exactly 4 each time. Because this rate of change does not change, **$f(x)$ is a linear function**.

But for the g function, as x increases by 1, y increases by a different amount each time: first by 4, then by 6, then by 12. Because there is no constant rate of change, **$g(x)$ is non-linear.**

Try It

1) If $f(x)$ is a linear function, which one of the following could define $f(x)$?

   A) $f(x) = \sqrt{x+3}$
   B) $f(x) = 5^x$
   C) $f(x) = -6$
   D) $f(x) = 2x^{-1}$

Do the scenarios below describe linear growth or nonlinear growth?

2) a salary increases by $200 per year   _____

3) a salary increases by 2% per year   _____

Linear Functions

A **linear function** usually takes the form $f(x) = mx + b$, where m and b are constants. As we've already seen in the Coordinate Geometry chapter (see p. 249), when a linear function takes the form $f(x) = mx + b$, the constant m gives the slope of the line, while the constant b gives the y-coordinate of the graph's y-intercept. To interpret these values in the context of a word problem, think of the y-intercept as the **starting point**, while the slope is the **rate of change**.

For example, say a botanist wants to use a linear function to model the height of a plant over the course of a multi-year study. If the plant was 5 centimeters tall at the beginning of the study and it grows at a rate of 3 centimeters per year, then we can use the equation $y = 3x + 5$: the starting point is a height of 5 centimeters, and the rate of change is 3 centimeters per year. In this equation, x represents the time that has passed, in years, and y represents the plant's height at that time. (Note that we could create the same equation in function notation by writing it as $f(x) = 3x + 5$.)

Try It

4) It costs a toy company a total of $250 to manufacture a batch of toys. Create a linear function to model the company's profits from selling x toys at $10 each.

TIP:

For this line, should the slope be positive or negative? What about the y-intercept?

The test will often ask you about the meaning of specific numbers or letters in a linear equation. Start by identifying the piece they're asking about: is it the slope, the y-intercept, or something else? Next, write down the appropriate definition, and then fill in the meanings with the context of the problem. For y-intercept questions, the definition to use is this: **y-intercept is the value of y when $x = 0$.**

Example: The equation $f(x) = -15x + 750$ gives the amount owed, in dollars, on an interest-free loan after x months of payments. What is the best interpretation of the y-intercept of the graph of $y = f(x)$ in the xy-plane?

y-intercept = value of y when $x = 0$.

750 = value of <u>amount owed</u> when <u># of months</u> = 0. That's our answer: $750 is what was owed before any payments had been made. So **$750 is the original amount of the loan.**

As for slope, the key thing to remember is that slope is the rate of change: every time you increase x by 1, you increase y by the amount of the slope. (For example, in the plant example, every time the number of years increases by 1, the height increases by 3 centimeters.) So the definition to use is this: **slope is the change in y as x increases by 1.**

> **TIP:**
> When a problem asks you to interpret the slope, look for answer choices that contain rate words such as "per" or "each."

Example: The equation $f(x) = -15x + 750$ gives the amount owed, in dollars, on an interest-free loan after x months of payments. What is the best interpretation of the slope of the graph of $y = f(x)$ in the xy-plane?

slope = change in y as x increases by 1.

-15 = change in <u>amount owed</u> as <u># of months</u> increases by 1. So the meaning of the -15 is that with each month that passes, the amount owed on the loan is decreasing by $15. The most likely interpretation? **The loan payments are $15 per month.**

Try It   After Sam has driven for x miles, the number of gallons of gasoline remaining in his car's tank is given by $g(x) = 12 - 36x$.

5) What is the best interpretation of the number 12 in the equation?

6) What is the best interpretation of the number 36 in the equation?

This understanding of slope can help you avoid a lot of unnecessary calculation.

Example: Paul finds that the relationship between his semester grade point average, $g(s)$, and the number of hours per week he spends studying, s, can be modeled by $g(s) = 0.12s + 1$. Increasing his studying from 18 hours per week to 19 hours per week should raise his semester grade point average by how much?

In this equation, $g(s)$ is our y value and s is our x value. Paul has increased the x value by 1. Therefore, the y value must increase by the amount of the slope: **0.12**.

For other problems, you may just need to use the meanings of each of the variables that the problem provided.

Example: The equation $f(x) = -15x + 750$ gives the amount owed, in dollars, on an interest-free loan after x months of payments. In this context, what is the best interpretation of $f(10) = 600$?

When $x = 10$, $f(x) = 600$.

When <u># of months</u> = 10, <u>amount owed</u> = 600. So the best interpretation is that **after 10 months of payments, the amount still owed will be $600.**

> **TIP:**
> Focus on the **units** to help move quickly through the answer choices. If x is measured in months, you can immediately eliminate any choices that define x as some number of dollars (or any other unit).

FROM THE BLOG

Here's my test prep advice. First, breathe. Second, breathe some more. Third, a quiz. One question, multiple choice.

Standardized tests are:

A) a measure of intelligence
B) a measure of acquired knowledge or skills
C) a measure of luck
D) a measure of height

Well, I am inclined to go with D since, on average, older kids (13+) do better on such tests than do younger kids (under 13) and, research shows, that, on average, older kids (13+) are taller than younger kids (under 13). But, I reckon you can recognize that I've conflated correlation with causality.

So, on to answer C. If you believe these are a measure of luck, then my advice about preparation likely won't matter. (Does one get better at the lottery with practice?)

If you believe that these are tests of intelligence, pure and simple, well, then sit back and relax or panic wildly, depending on what you think your IQ is. But, as in C, there's not much to do.

I am sticking with B. Standardized tests, perhaps imperfectly, test reading skills. They test facts and reasoning. They test grammatical rules and conventions. These are tests of acquired knowledge and skills. So build the knowledge and sharpen the skills, and you *can* conquer these tests.

Math: Advanced Math

Practice Set 1: Easy-Medium

1

The total cost C, in dollars, to produce the yearbooks at Greenville High School is modeled by the function $C(n) = 500 + 20n$, where n is the number of yearbooks printed. Which of the following is the best interpretation of the number 500 in this equation?

A. At least 500 yearbooks will be printed.
B. It costs 500 dollars to print 20 yearbooks.
C. The initial cost is 500 dollars regardless of the number of yearbooks printed.
D. After every 20 yearbooks printed, the cost rises by 500 dollars.

2

The profit, in dollars, that Jeremy will make selling cookies in today's bake sale can be modeled by the function $P(x) = 0.25x - 50$, where x represents the number of cookies sold. Which of the following best describes the meaning of the number 0.25 in the equation?

A. Jeremy's total profit will be $0.25.
B. The average selling price of Jeremy's cookies is $0.25 per cookie.
C. The difference between Jeremy's initial costs and total profit is $25.
D. Jeremy will sell a total of 25 cookies.

3

$$C(w) = 17.5 + 4.75w$$

The function above is used to calculate the cost $C(w)$ of shipping a certain package overnight, where w represents the weight of the package in pounds. By how much will the cost change if the weight of the package increases by 6 pounds?

A. The cost will increase by 17.5 dollars.
B. The cost will increase by 22.5 dollars.
C. The cost will increase by 28.5 dollars.
D. The cost will increase by 50.75 dollars.

4

$$f(x) = -0.5x + 2$$

Which table gives three values of x and their corresponding values of $f(x)$ for the given equation?

A.

x	0	1	2
$f(x)$	1.5	1	0.5

B.

x	0	1	2
$f(x)$	2	1.5	1

C.

x	0	1	2
$f(x)$	2	2.5	3

D.

x	0	1	2
$f(x)$	1	1.5	2

5

On Tuesday, Ben was on the second day of a multi-day road trip. The function $d(t) = 58t + 65$ models Ben's distance from home, in miles, after t hours of driving on Tuesday. Based on the model, what was Ben's average driving speed on Tuesday, in miles per hour?

6

Which of the following scenarios could best be modeled by a linear function with a positive slope?

A. Overnight, the outside temperature decreases by 2°F per hour.
B. An investment loses 4% of its value each month.
C. An online newspaper increases its readership by 1000 people per year.
D. A city's population increases steadily for 10 years and then levels off.

7

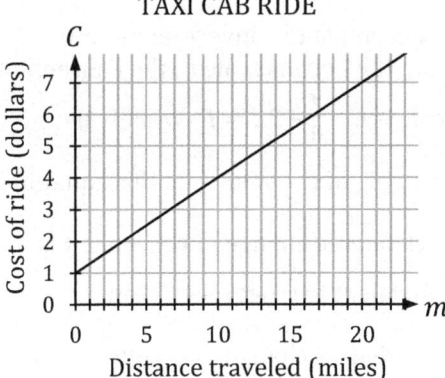

TAXI CAB RIDE

The graph above displays the total cost C, in dollars, of a taxi cab ride that travels a distance of m miles. What does the C-intercept of the graph represent?

A. The number of taxi cabs used
B. The initial number of miles
C. The increase in cost to ride the taxi for each additional mile
D. The initial cost to travel 0 miles

8

$$p = 750n + 3750$$

Gross domestic product per capita (PPP) is a measure of a country's total output on a per-person basis. An economist uses the model above to estimate the PPP p of a country, in US dollars, in terms of the number of years n that have passed since the country gained independence. Based on the model, what is the estimated increase, in US dollars, of the country's PPP each year?

9

$$f(x) = 150 + 14.75x$$

The linear function f, defined above, models the total cost of installed fencing from a local hardware store, where x represents the number of linear feet of fencing purchased and $f(x)$ represents the cost, in dollars. What is the best interpretation of $f(100) = 1625$ in this context?

A. The total cost for 100 linear feet of installed fencing is $1625.
B. The total cost of 1625 linear feet of installed fencing is $100.
C. The cost of fencing is $1625 per 100 linear feet, before installation.
D. The cost of fencing is $100 per 1625 linear feet, before installation.

10

The table shows four values of x and their corresponding values of $f(x)$. What is the y-intercept of the graph of $f(x)$ on the xy-plane?

x	-1	0	1	2
$f(x)$	0	2	4	6

A. $(-1, 0)$
B. $(0, -1)$
C. $(0, 2)$
D. $(2, 0)$

11

The function $f(t)$ gives the attendance at an annual music festival t years after 1990. During the period from 2002 to 2008, the graph of the function approximates a line with a positive slope. What is the best interpretation of the slope?

A. The rate of increase in attendance per year from 2002 to 2008
B. The festival's attendance in 1990
C. The total attendance from 2002 to 2008
D. The festival's maximum attendance in any year

Math: Advanced Math

Practice Set 2: Medium-Hard

1

Samuel receives a $50 weekly allowance, which he uses to buy equally priced packs of baseball cards (assume no sales tax). The amount of allowance money, A, Samuel has left at the end of the week can be estimated with the function $A(p) = 50 - \left(\frac{25}{4}\right)p$, where p represents the number of packs of baseball cards purchased. What is the meaning of the fraction $\frac{25}{4}$, which is equivalent to the decimal 6.25, in this function?

A. Each pack of baseball cards costs $6.25.
B. Samuel has $25 of allowance money to spend over 4 days.
C. Samuel purchases 6.25 packs of baseball cards.
D. Samuel will buy 25 packs of baseball cards, each costing $4.

2

An area's "water table" is the level below which the ground is saturated with water. A scientist studying a local wetland recorded CO_2 emissions of 10 mol C/m² (moles of carbon per square meter) in areas where the water table was exactly at the surface. She also found that for every 1 centimeter increase in the depth of the water table below the surface, CO_2 emissions increased by 2 mol C/m². Which of the following equations models the amount of CO_2 emissions y, in mol C/m², where x represents the depth of the water table in centimeters below the surface?

A. $y = -2x + 10$
B. $y = -10x + 2$
C. $y = 10x - 2$
D. $y = 2x + 10$

3

The formula to convert temperatures from the Celsius scale to the Fahrenheit scale is $C * \frac{9}{5} + 32 = F$. What is the meaning of the value $\frac{9}{5}$ in this equation?

A. Each degree change in Fahrenheit is equivalent to $\frac{9}{5}$ degrees Celsius.
B. Each degree change in Celsius is equivalent to $\frac{9}{5}$ degrees Fahrenheit.
C. Each Fahrenheit temperature reads $\frac{9}{5}$ degrees higher than its corresponding Celsius temperature.
D. Each Celsius temperature reads $\frac{9}{5}$ degrees higher than its corresponding Fahrenheit temperature.

4

MEDIAN OHIO HOME PRICES, 1940-2000

Year	Median Price
1940	$22,900
1950	$41,000
1960	$57,800
1970	$58,300
1980	$91,200
1990	$96,800
2000	$107,600

The table above represents the median home prices in Ohio between 1940 and 2000. The relationship between time and home price can be modeled by the linear equation $y = 1,600x + 24,000$, where x represents the number of years since 1940 and y represent the median home price. What does the number 1,600 represent in the equation?

A. the average yearly increase in the median home price
B. the average price of one home
C. the decrease in median home price from 1960 to 1970
D. the increase in number of homes sold from one decade to the next

Quadratic Functions

Preview Quiz:

Solve each of the following.

1) $x^2 - 5x + 4 = 0$
2) $x^2 - 7x - 3 = 0$

3) A quadratic has (at least / at most / exactly) ___ roots.

4) A quadratic has (at least / at most / exactly) ___ x-intercepts.

5) What are the coordinates of the x-intercepts of the parabola with equation $y = -4(x - 1)(x - 3)$?

For the parabolas given by the quadratic functions below, what are the coordinates of the vertex? What is the axis of symmetry?

6) $f(x) = 2(x + 3)^2 + 1$
7) $g(x) = x^2 + 2x - 10$

8) Sketch a parabola that has:

2 distinct real roots   1 distinct real root   no real roots

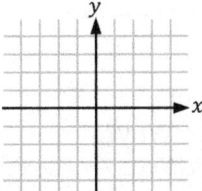 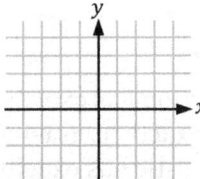 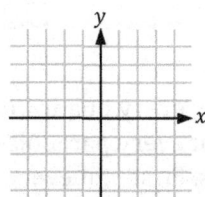

9) What is the product of the roots of $y = 2x^2 + 4x + 6$?

Math: Advanced Math

A **quadratic** is an equation of the form $y = ax^2 + bx + c$. On the xy-plane, this produces the graph of a **parabola**. If a is positive, the parabola points up, so that the **vertex** is the lowest point on the graph. If a is negative, the parabola points down, and the vertex is the highest point on the graph. Either way, the value of c is the y-coordinate of the graph's y-intercept.

$y = x^2$:

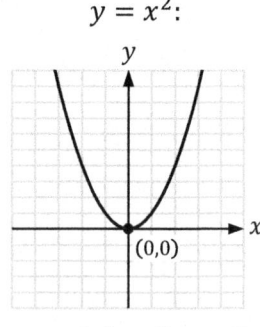

$a = 1, b = 0, c = 0$

$y = -x^2 - 4x - 3$:

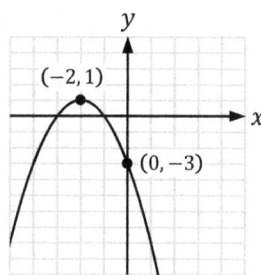

$a = -1, b = -4, c = -3$

The graph of a quadratic may have one, two, or zero x-intercepts. Each of these points represents a distinct real **root** of the equation. Because they are the **solutions** to the equation $ax^2 + bx + c = 0$, they are sometimes also called the **zeros** of the function.

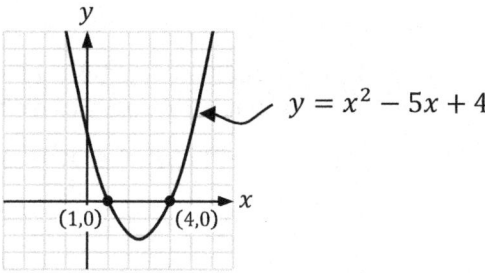

Example: The figure above is the graph of $y = x^2 - 5x + 4$ on the xy-plane. The graph has x-intercepts at $(1, 0)$ and $(4, 0)$ because the solutions to the equation $x^2 - 5x + 4 = 0$ are $x = 1$ and $x = 4$.

TIP:

By definition, every quadratic function has exactly two roots. However, not every parabola has exactly two x-intercepts. Why? Two reasons. First, not every quadratic has exactly two *distinct* roots. For example, the roots of $f(x) = (x - 3)(x - 3)$ are 3 and 3, so the graph has only one x-intercept: at $x = 3$.

And second, not every quadratic has *real* roots. When the roots of a quadratic function are imaginary numbers, the parabola has no x-intercepts at all.

Quadratic Functions

There are several ways to find the solutions to a quadratic equation. If possible, **factor** the quadratic and then set each factor equal to zero.

Example: $x^2 - 5x + 4 = 0$
$(x - 1)(x - 4) = 0$
$x - 1 = 0$ or $x - 4 = 0$
$\mathbf{x = 1}$ or $\mathbf{x = 4}$

TIP: For a review of these skills, check the Factoring, FOILing, and Fractions chapter on p. 282.

Not all quadratics can be factored. For the rest, one approach is to use the **quadratic formula**, which says that the solutions to any quadratic of the form $ax^2 + bx + c = 0$ are

$$x = \frac{-b \pm \sqrt{b^2 - 4ac}}{2a}$$

Example: $x^2 - 7x - 3 = 0$

In this equation, $a = 1, b = -7,$ and $c = -3$. So:

$$x = \frac{7 \pm \sqrt{(-7)^2 - 4(1)(-3)}}{2(1)} = \frac{7 \pm \sqrt{49 + 12}}{2} = \frac{7 \pm \sqrt{61}}{2}$$

$$x = \frac{7 + \sqrt{61}}{2} \quad \text{or} \quad x = \frac{7 - \sqrt{61}}{2}$$

TIP: A quicker way to find the solutions to a quadratic is to graph it. The built-in calculator will automatically highlight the zeros for you.

Try It 1) Solve $2x^2 + 3x - 1 = 0$.

TIP:

For any quadratic written in standard $y = ax^2 + bx + c$ form:

- the **sum** of the roots is equal to $-b/a$, and
- the **product** of the roots is equal to c/a.

This is true **whether or not the quadratic is factorable.**

Example: $y = 2x^2 + 4x + 6$
sum of roots is $-4/2 = -2$
product of roots is $6/2 = 3$
actual roots $= -1 + \sqrt{2}i$ and $-1 - \sqrt{2}i$

If you're asked to find the **vertex** of the parabola, the easiest method depends on the form the quadratic is written in. If the equation is given in **vertex form**, $y = a(x - h)^2 + k$, you can just read the vertex directly: it's (h, k).

Example: The parabola given by $f(x) = 2(x + 3)^2 + 1$ has its vertex at the point $(-3, 1)$.

If the equation is in factored form, the x-coordinate of the vertex is just the average of the x-coordinates of the zeros. Once you have that, plug it back into the equation to find the y-coordinate.

Example: What is the vertex of $f(x) = -4(x - 1)(x - 3)$?

The zeros are $x = 1$ and $x = 3$, so the x-coordinate of the vertex is $x = 2$. The y-coordinate is $y = -4(2 - 1)(2 - 3) = 4$. Therefore, the vertex is located at $(2, 4)$.

And if the equation is in standard form, you can use this formula to find the x-coordinate of the vertex:

$$x = \frac{-b}{2a}$$

Example: What is the vertex of $f(x) = x^2 + 2x - 10$?

$$x = \frac{-2}{2(1)} = -1$$

$$y = (-1)^2 + 2(-1) - 10 = -11$$

The vertex is $(-1, -11)$.

TIP: You can also type a quadratic into the built-in calculator in any of these forms. The software will automatically highlight the vertex for you.

Questions about the **minimum value** or **maximum value** of a quadratic function are asking for the y-coordinate of the vertex.

Try It

2) For what value of x does the function $g(x) = -3x^2 + 12x + 2$ reach its maximum value?

3) What is the minimum value of $f(x) = 2x^2 - 4x - 1$?

Quadratic Functions

The **axis of symmetry** of an upward-facing or downward-facing parabola with vertex (h, k) is $x = h$.

Example: The axis of symmetry for the parabola given by $y = (x - 2)^2 + 1$ is the vertical line $x = 2$.

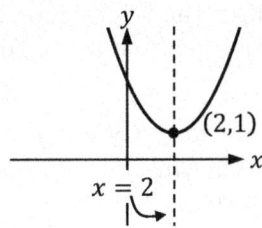

When a quadratic is written in standard $y = ax^2 + bx + c$ form, the expression $b^2 - 4ac$ is called the **discriminant**. Because it is the part of the quadratic formula that is found under the square root, it can be used to determine how many real solutions exist for a particular quadratic. After all, if the value of $b^2 - 4ac$ turns out to be less than zero, then the quadratic formula will require us to take the square root of a negative number, resulting in only imaginary solutions. And because the real solutions are also the x-intercepts of the graph, the graph of such a quadratic will not touch the x-axis at all.

In fact, the discriminant gives us three possible outcomes:

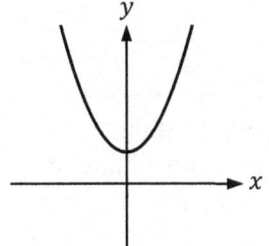 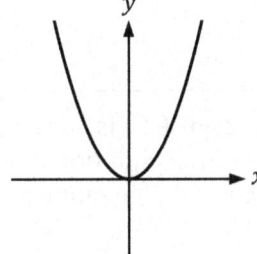 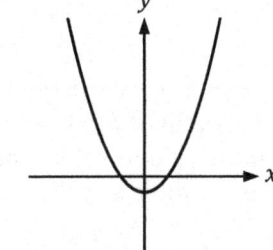

$b^2 - 4ac < 0$:　　　$b^2 - 4ac = 0$:　　　$b^2 - 4ac > 0$:
No real roots　　　　One real root　　　　Two real roots

Try It

4) The equation $x^2 + 2x + 3 = 0$ has how many distinct real solutions?

5) When the equation $y = x^2 + 3x + k$, where k is a constant, is graphed on the xy-plane, the graph has two x-intercepts. If k is an integer, what is the greatest possible value of k?

CHALLENGE:

The SAT will sometimes ask you to choose an alternate form of a quadratic equation that highlights some specific information by using those values as constants or coefficients. To highlight the y-intercept, choose standard form. To highlight the x-intercepts, choose factored form. To highlight the vertex, choose vertex form.

Example: The figure shows the graph of $y = f(x)$ on the xy-plane. The equation of $f(x)$ is given below in standard form, factored form, and vertex form.

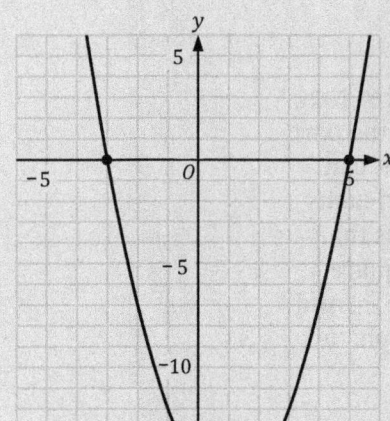

- $f(x) = x^2 - 2x - 15$: shows the y-intercept is $(0, -15)$
- $f(x) = (x + 3)(x - 5)$: shows the x-intercepts are $(-3, 0)$ and $(5, 0)$
- $f(x) = (x - 1)^2 - 16$: shows that the vertex is $(1, -16)$

Try It

6) The graph of $f(x) = (2x + 2)(x + 5)$ is shown. In which of the following equivalent forms of the equation does the y-coordinate of the parabola's vertex appear as a constant or coefficient?

A. $f(x) = 2x^2 + 12x + 10$
B. $f(x) = 2(x + 1)(x + 5)$
C. $f(x) = (2x + 10)(x + 1)$
D. $f(x) = 2(x + 3)^2 - 8$

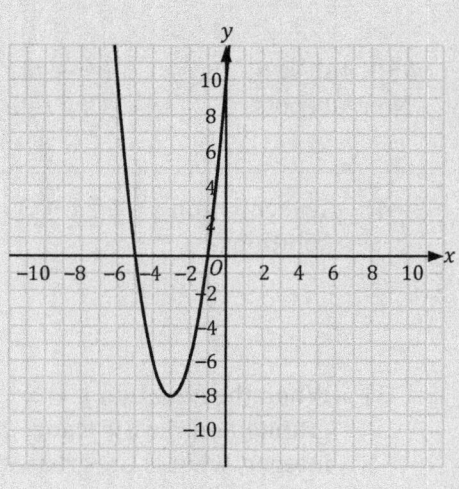

Practice Set 1: Easy-Medium

1

$$f(x) = 2x^2 - x + 5$$

Which table gives three values of x and their corresponding values of $f(x)$ for the given equation?

A.
x	0	1	2
$f(x)$	1	5	11

B.
x	0	1	2
$f(x)$	1	8	19

C.
x	0	1	2
$f(x)$	5	6	11

D.
x	0	1	2
$f(x)$	5	8	19

2

$$f(x) = -2(2x - 2)(x + 3)$$

What is the maximum value of the function defined above?

A. 0
B. 1
C. 8
D. 16

3

The equation $y = 2x^2 - 3x - 7$ has how many distinct real roots and how many imaginary roots?

A. 0 distinct real roots and 2 imaginary roots
B. 1 distinct real root and 0 imaginary roots
C. 2 distinct real roots and 0 imaginary roots
D. 2 distinct real roots and 1 imaginary root

4

$$f(x) = (x - 1)^2 + 3$$

The quadratic function $f(x)$ is defined above. Which of the following gives the axis of symmetry for the graph of $y = f(x)$ on the xy-plane?

A. $x = -1$
B. $x = 1$
C. $y = -1$
D. $y = 1$

5

The figure below gives the graph of the function $f(x) = (x - 3)^2 + 1$ in the xy-plane.

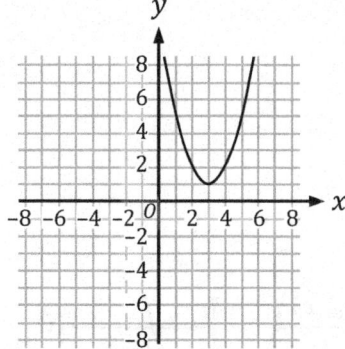

If the parabola is shifted 4 units down, the resulting parabola is the graph of the function $g(x)$. Which of the following defines $g(x)$?

A. $g(x) = (x - 7)^2 + 1$
B. $g(x) = (x + 1)^2 + 1$
C. $g(x) = (x - 3)^2 - 3$
D. $g(x) = -4(x - 3)^2 + 1$

6

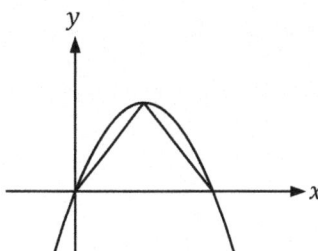

The figure above shows a triangle inscribed in the graph of the quadratic function f whose maximum value is $f(3) = 4$. What is the area of the triangle?

A. 6
B. 10
C. 12
D. 20

Math: Advanced Math

Practice Set 2: Medium-Hard

1

If $x = 4$ and $x = -1$ are the roots of the equation $y = x^2 - 3x + k$, where k is a constant, what is the value of k?

2

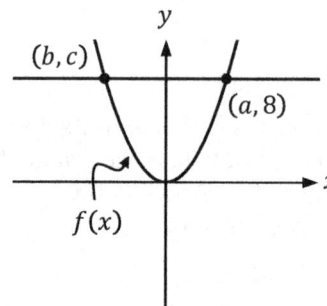

The figure above shows the graph of the equation $f(x) = \frac{1}{2}x^2$. Line l is parallel to the x-axis and intersects the graph of $f(x)$ at the points (b, c) and $(a, 8)$. What is the value of $a + b + c$?

3

For how many distinct values of n is the product of $2n + 3$ and $2n - 5$ equal to -16?

A. None
B. One
C. Two
D. Infinitely many

4

The equation $y = mx + 3$, where m is a constant, gives the graph of a line on the xy-plane. If the line intersects the graph of $y = x^2 + 3$ at the point $(1, a)$, what is the value of m?

5

Which of the following could be the graph of $f(x) = ax^2 + bx + c$, if $a, b,$ and c are all positive constants?

A.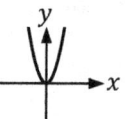

B.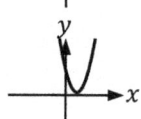

C.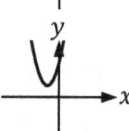

D.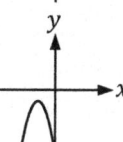

6

In the xy-plane, the graph of $y = g(x)$ is symmetrical across the y-axis. Which of the following could be the equation that defines $g(x)$?

A. $g(x) = x^2 + 1$
B. $g(x) = (x + 2)^2$
C. $g(x) = x^3 + 3$
D. $g(x) = x^3$

7

$$y = 1$$
$$y = ax^2 + b$$

In the system of equations above, a and b are constants. For which of the following values of a and b does the system of equations have exactly two real solutions?

A. $a = -2, b = -3$
B. $a = -2, b = 4$
C. $a = 1, b = 4$
D. $a = 3, b = 1$

8

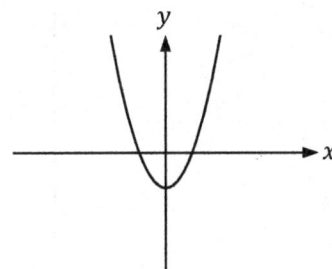

The figure above shows the graph of the equation $f(x) = x^2 - 3$. A square (not shown) is situated so that two consecutive vertices lie at the intersection of $f(x)$ and the x-axis. What is the area of the square?

9

What is the sum of the two solutions to the equation $x^2 - 5x - 24 = 0$?

A. -24
B. 0
C. 1
D. 5

10

The figure below shows the graph of the equation $f(x) = 4x - x^2 - k$, where k is a constant.

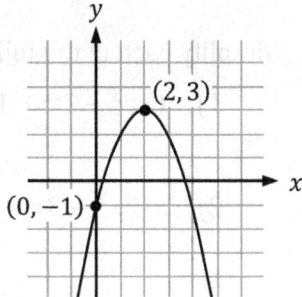

What is the value of k?

A. -1
B. 1
C. 2
D. 3

11

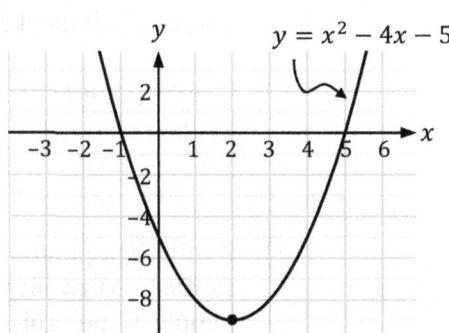

Which of the following is an equivalent form of the equation of the graph shown in the xy-plane above from which the coordinates of the parabola's vertex can be identified as constants in the equation?

A. $y = x(x - 4) - 5$
B. $y = (x - 2)^2 - 9$
C. $y = (x + 1)(x - 5)$
D. $y = (x + 5)(x - 3)$

Math: Advanced Math

Polynomial, Exponential, Radical, and Rational Equations

Preview Quiz:

Simplify each of the following polynomials:

1) $(3x^3 - 2x + 1) + (2x^2 + 5x - x^3) =$

2) $x(2x^2 - 3x + 4) - 2(3x^2 - x^3 + 1) =$

The polynomial function f is defined by $f(x) = (x + 1)(x + 2)(x - 5)$.

3) What are the x-intercepts of $y = f(x)$? _____

4) What is the y-intercept of $y = f(x)$? _____

Circle the right answer and/or fill in the blanks.

5) The graph of a 4th-degree polynomial function has
(at least / at most / exactly) _____ x-intercepts.

6) The graph of $f(x) = (x - 3)^2(x + 1)$ has
(at least / at most / exactly) _____ x-intercepts.

Solve.

7) A town's population is projected to increase by 7% per year for the next twenty years. The current population is 5000 people. If the projection is accurate, what will the town's population be in 15 years? (Round your answer to the nearest whole number.)

8) What is the domain of $f(x) = \sqrt{2x + 10}$?

The rational function g is defined by the equation below:
$$g(x) = \frac{x - 3}{(x - 3)(x - 2)}$$

9) What is the domain of $g(x)$?

10) What are the vertical asymptotes, if any, of the graph of $y = g(x)$ on the xy-plane?

A **polynomial** function is a function with multiple distinct x terms, such as $f(x) = x^3 - 2x^2 + 5x - 1$. Some polynomial problems will simply ask you to **combine like terms**.

TIP:
Don't assume the terms in both expressions will be presented in the same order.

Example: Simplify $(3x^3 - 2x + 1) + (2x^2 + 5x - x^3)$.
$$3x^3 - x^3 + 2x^2 - 2x + 5x + 1$$
$$\mathbf{2x^3 + 2x^2 + 3x + 1}$$

If the problem requires multiplying a polynomial by a monomial or by another polynomial, use the rules of FOILing and/or the exponent rules to simplify the expression.

Example: Simplify $x(2x^2 - 3x + 4) - 2(3x^2 - x^3 + 1)$.
$$x(2x^2 - 3x + 4) - 2(3x^2 - x^3 + 1)$$
$$(2x^3 - 3x^2 + 4x) - 2(3x^2 - x^3 + 1)$$
$$2x^3 - 3x^2 + 4x - 6x^2 + 2x^3 - 2$$
$$\mathbf{4x^3 - 9x^2 + 4x - 2}$$

Many polynomials can be **factored**. The relationship between the factors of the equation and the x-intercepts of the graph is the same as it is for quadratics.

TIP:
If $x + 1$ is a **factor**, then $x = -1$ is a **zero**.

Example: The graph of $f(x) = (x + 1)(x + 2)(x - 5)$ intersects the x-axis at the points $(-1, 0), (-2, 0),$ and $(5, 0)$.

Factors that appear in the equation an odd number of times indicate points where the graph **crosses** the x-axis. Factors that appear in the equation an even number of times indicate points where the graph simply **touches** the x-axis without crossing it.

Example:

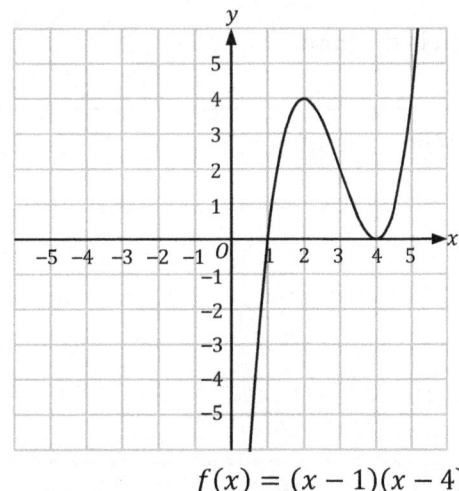

$$f(x) = (x - 1)(x - 4)^2$$

Math: Advanced Math

Try It

$$f(x) = -(x+1)(x-2)(x-3)$$
$$g(x) = -(x+1)(x-2)^2(x-3)$$

The polynomial functions f and g are defined by the equations above.

1) What are the x-intercepts of $y = f(x)$?

2) What are the x-intercepts of $y = g(x)$?

3) What is the difference between these two graphs?

The **y-intercept** of a polynomial function, like the y-intercept of any other graph, is just the value of y when $x = 0$.

Example: On the xy-plane, what is the y-intercept of the graph of $f(x) = (x+1)(x+2)(x-5)$?

To solve, find $f(0)$.

$$f(0) = (0+1)(0+2)(0-5)$$
$$= (1)(2)(-5)$$
$$-10$$

The y-intercept is the point $(\mathbf{0, -10})$.

Try It

4) What is the y-intercept of $g(x) = -(x+1)(x-2)^2(x-3)$?

TIP:
Don't forget to consider using the built-in calculator to solve these problems. You can often quickly get an answer just by looking at the graph.

CHALLENGE:

Polynomials: factors, zeros, and remainders

If $(x - 2)$ is a factor of polynomial function $f(x)$, then $x = 2$ is a solution of the equation. Because a solution is the same thing as a zero, this means that $f(2) = 0$. The reverse is also true: if $f(2) = 0$ for polynomial function f, then $(x - 2)$ is a factor of f.

This also means that once you know that $(x - 2)$ is a factor of f, you can plug in 2 for x and set the whole thing equal to zero.

Example: If $(x - 3)$ *is a factor of the function* $g(x) = x^3 - 3x^2 - kx + 12$, *where k is a constant, then what is the value of k?*

$$g(3) = (3)^3 - 3(3)^2 - k(3) + 12 = 0$$
$$27 - 3(9) - 3k + 12 = 0$$
$$12 = 3k$$
$$4 = k$$

If $(x - 2)$ is *not* a factor of a polynomial equation, then when we plug in 2 for x we will get a nonzero result. Let's say that in our unknown function f, $(x - 2)$ is not a factor, and specifically, that when we plug it in, the result is 1. In other words, $f(2) = 1$. Another way of saying this is that when the function f is divided by $(x - 2)$, the remainder is 1.

Example: *What is the remainder when* $h(x) = 2x^3 - 6x + 1$ *is divided by* $(x + 1)$?

$$h(-1) = 2(-1)^3 - 6(-1) + 1$$
$$= 2(-1) + 6 + 1$$
$$= 5$$

This same concept can be expressed through polynomial division.

$$f(x) = x^3 - 3x^2 + 5x - 5$$

All of these statements are true:

- $(x - 2)$ is not a factor of $f(x)$
- 2 is not a solution to $f(x) = 0$
- 2 is not an x-intercept on the graph of $f(x)$
- $f(2) = 1$
- The remainder when $f(x)$ is divided by $(x - 2)$ is 1
- $\dfrac{f(x)}{x - 2} = x^2 - x + 3$ with a remainder of 1
- $\dfrac{f(x)}{x - 2} = x^2 - x + 3 + \dfrac{1}{x - 2}$

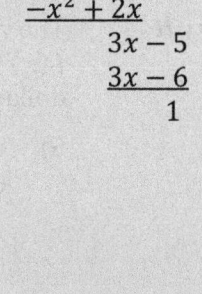

The standard form of an **exponential function** is $f(x) = a(b)^x$, where b is a positive number and $b \neq 1$. These functions model increases or decreases that are not linear: for example, a population that increases at a rate of 15% per year, or a bad investment that loses 5% of its value each month.

In the equation, the constant a gives the y-coordinate of the y-intercept of the graph (the starting population, or the original value of the investment). The constant b is equal to 1 plus the rate of change, represented as a decimal. (For the population example, b would equal $1 + 0.15 = 1.15$. For the investment, b equals $1 + (-0.05) = 0.95$.)

It may be helpful to think of these equations as following this form:

$$A = P(1 + r)^t$$

In this form, A is the final amount, P is the initial amount, r is the rate of change expressed as a decimal, and t is time.

Example: A town's population is projected to increase by 7% per year for the next twenty years. The current population is 5000 people. If the projection is accurate, what will the town's population be in 15 years? (Round your answer to the nearest whole number.)

The starting value of the population is 5000, so that's P. The population is increasing by 7% per year, so the value of r is 0.07. That gives us this:

$$A = 5000(1.07)^t$$

Now rewrite that in function notation:

$$f(x) = 5000(1.07)^x$$

In this equation, x represents the number of years that have passed. So we can solve this problem by finding $f(15)$:

$$f(15) = 5000(1.07)^{15} = 13795.16$$

In fifteen years, the town's population will be approximately **13,795** people.

TIP:

A constant percent increase is *not* a constant rate of growth. If we start with 5000 people and increase by 7% per year, then in the first year, the population will grow by 7% of 5000, which is 350. In the second year, the population must grow by 7% of 5350, which is 374.5. That's more than 350! The amount by which the population is changing is itself increasing every year.

Try It   The value of an investment account over time can be modeled by $f(x) = 2000(1.04)^x$, where $f(x)$ represents the value of the account, in dollars, x years after the account was opened.

5) What is the best interpretation of the number 2000 in this equation?

6) What was the value of the account 6 years after it was opened, rounded to the nearest cent?

The graph of an exponential function does not change direction: it either increases forever or it decreases forever.

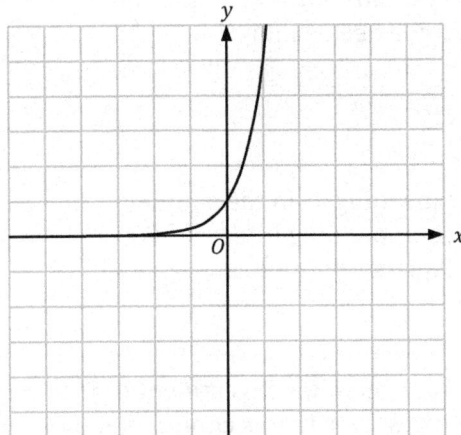 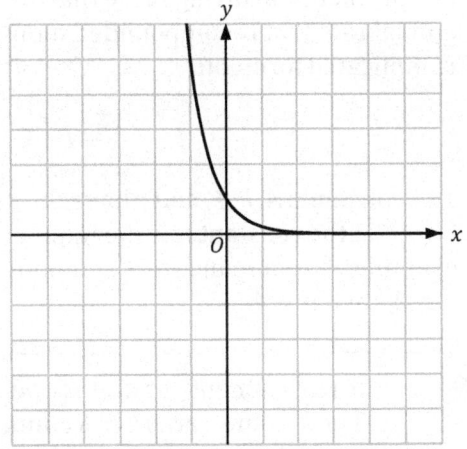

$f(x) = a(b)^x$ where $b > 1$:
exponential **growth**

$f(x) = a(b)^x$ where $0 < b < 1$:
exponential **decay**

TIP:

For an exponential function of form $f = a(b)^x$, the amount by which b differs from 1 is the rate of change.

Try It For each of the equations below, indicate whether the equation represents exponential growth, exponential decay, or neither. If the equation does represent exponential growth or decay, indicate the rate of change, expressed as a percent.

	growth, decay, or neither?	rate
7) $f(x) = 0.9(1.5)^x$	_____	_____
8) $f(x) = 12(-2.3)^x$	_____	_____
9) $f(x) = 2.7(0.6)^x$	_____	_____

CHALLENGE:

For problems involving more than one unit of time—for example, an annual rate that is compounded monthly—we need a more complicated formula:

$$A = P\left(1 + \frac{r}{n}\right)^{nt}$$

The constants A, P, r, and t have the same meaning as in the simpler formula; the constant n is the number of compounding intervals. For example, if an annual rate is compounded quarterly (four times per year), then $n = 4$.

Try It

An investment account is opened with an initial investment of $1000. The account earns a 6% annual interest rate that is compounded monthly.

10) Write an exponential equation that models this situation, where $f(x)$ represents the value of the account, in dollars, x years after it was opened.

11) According to the model, what was the value of the account 18 months after it was opened? Round your answer to the nearest cent.

Polynomial, Exponential, Radical, and Rational Equations

A **radical function** takes the form of a square root: for example, $f(x) = \sqrt{2x + 10}$.

To find the domain of a radical function, take the portion that's under the square root and set it greater than or equal to zero.

Example: What is the domain of $f(x)$, defined above?

$2x + 10 \geq 0$
$2x \geq -10$
$x \geq -5$
The domain is all real numbers greater than or equal to -5. In interval notation, that's $[-5, \infty)$.

A **rational function** takes the form of a fraction: for example, $f(x) = \dfrac{5}{2x - 6}$.

To find the domain of a rational function, take the bottom of the fraction and set it "unequal to" zero.

Example: What is the domain of $f(x)$, defined above?

$2x - 6 \neq 0$
$2x \neq 6$
$x \neq 3$
The domain is all real numbers except 3. In interval notation, that's $(-\infty, 3) \cup (3, \infty)$.

To find the **range** of a function, the easiest technique is usually just to graph the function on your calculator.

Example: What is the range of $p(x) = \sqrt{x - 4}$?

The graph starts abruptly at the x-axis (where $y = 0$) and continues to the right, heading gradually upwards with no apparent upper limit. Therefore, the range is **all real numbers greater than or equal to zero**: $[0, \infty)$.

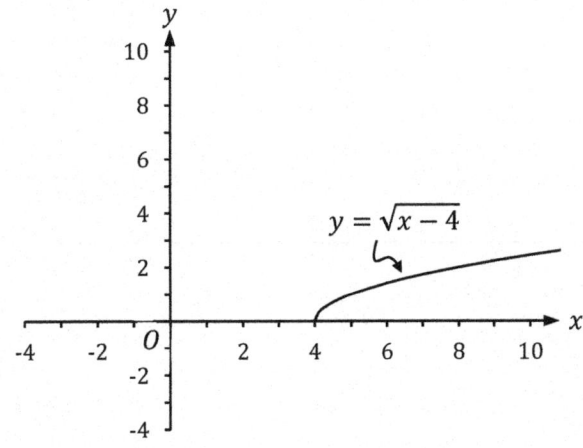

Try It

$$f(x) = 5 - \sqrt{3x+4}$$
$$g(x) = \frac{x+2}{3x+4}$$

The functions f and g are defined by the equations above.

12) What is the domain of $f(x)$?

13) What is the y-intercept of $y = f(x)$, if any?

14) What is the domain of $g(x)$?

15) What is/are the x-intercept(s) of $y = g(x)$, if any?

CHALLENGE:

A value that is not included in the domain of a rational function may show up in the graph as a vertical **asymptote**, which is an imaginary line that the graph approaches but does not reach.

Example:

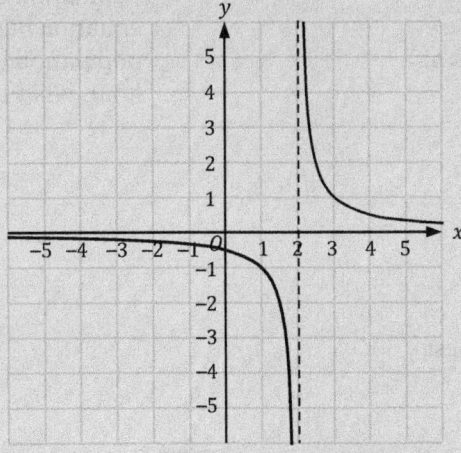

The graph of $f(x) = \dfrac{1}{x-2}$ has a vertical asymptote at $x = 2$.

A factor that appears in both the numerator and the denominator of a rational function appears in the graph as a **hole** rather than an asymptote.

Example:

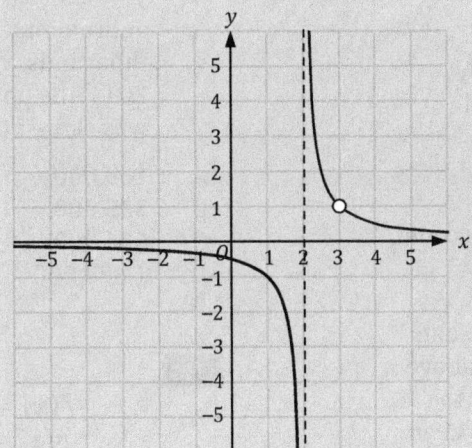

The graph of $g(x) = \dfrac{x-3}{(x-3)(x-2)}$ has a vertical asymptote at $x = 2$ and a hole at $x = 3$. It is identical to the graph of $f(x) = \dfrac{1}{x-2}$ where $x \neq 3$.

> **TIP:**
> A factor that cancels out from the top and bottom is still excluded from the domain.

Math: Advanced Math

Practice Set 1: Easy-Medium

1

In Earth's atmosphere, as altitude decreases, air pressure increases exponentially. The table below gives the approximate average air pressure $p(a)$, in pascals, at several altitudes a, in kilometers, above the Earth's surface.

a	$p(a)$
0	14.7
1	12.8
2	11.2

Which of the following equations best models the data in the table?

A. $p(a) = 12.8(0.998)^a$
B. $p(a) = 12.8(1.15)^a$
C. $p(a) = 14.7(0.873)^a$
D. $p(a) = 14.7(12.8)^a$

2

$$h(t) = -2t^4 + 13t^3 - 28t^2 + 23t + 1.9$$

To become accustomed to weightlessness, astronauts must fly training flights that make repeated ascents and descents in order to simulate the feeling of free-falling. During the first three minutes of one such flight, the motion of the plane could be modeled by the function above, where t represents the time since takeoff, in minutes, and $h(t)$ represents the plane's altitude, in kilometers above sea level. Which of the following is the best interpretation of the number 1.9 in the equation?

A. The flight lasted at least 1.9 minutes.
B. The flight's average rate of ascent was 1.9 kilometers per minute.
C. The plane made a maximum of 1.9 changes of direction during the first three minutes of the flight.
D. The plane took off from an altitude of 1.9 kilometers above sea level.

3

The population of a bacteria colony starts at 1,000. After t hours its population can be expressed by the equation $p(t) = 1,000r^t$. If the population increases by 20% each hour, what is the value of r?

4

In 2000, a census determined that the town of Benderberg had a population of approximately 126,000 people. Ever since, the population has grown at a rate of 7% per year. The equation $y = 126(1.07)^x$ gives Benderberg's approximate population y, in thousands, x years after the census. In 2014, the population of Benderberg was closest to which of the following?

A. 189,000
B. 325,000
C. 514,000
D. 1,887,000

5

$$f(x) = 2x^3 - 5x^2 + 8x - 1$$
$$g(x) = -x^3 + 2x^2 - x + 3$$

For the functions f and g defined above, which of the following gives $f(x) - g(x)$?

A. $x^3 - 7x^2 + 7x - 4$
B. $x^3 - 3x^2 + 7x + 2$
C. $3x^3 - 7x^2 + 9x - 4$
D. $3x^3 - 3x^2 + 9x + 2$

6. If $f(x) = 3.2(0.5)^x + 1$, which of the following is the y-intercept of the graph of $y = f(x)$ on the xy-plane?

A. $(0, 1)$
B. $(0, 2)$
C. $(0, 3.2)$
D. $(0, 4.2)$

7. For a toy company that experienced exponential growth, the function $T(x) = 1200(1.15)^x$ gives the number of toys sold per year, $T(x)$, at any time x years after 2015. What is the best interpretation of the number 1200 in this equation?

A. The toy company sold 1200 toys in 2015.
B. The number of toys sold per year increased by 12% per year.
C. The number of toys sold per year increased by 1200 per year.
D. The maximum number of toys sold in any one year was 1200.

8. If $f(x) = \sqrt{x + 30}$ and $g(x) = \frac{x}{2} - 9$, for which of the following values of x does $f(x) = g(x)$?

I. $x = 0$
II. $x = 6$
III. $x = 34$

A. I only
B. I and III only
C. II and III only
D. III only

9. The function f is defined as follows:

$$f(x) = \frac{(x + 1)(x - 3)}{(x - 3)(x - 1)}$$

For what value or values of x is the function f undefined?

I. -1
II. 1
III. 3

A. I only
B. I and III only
C. II and III only
D. I, II, and III

10. The value of an investment decreases by 11% per year. If the initial value of the investment is $24,000, which of the following exponential functions models the value of the investment, $A(t)$, in dollars, after t years?

A. $A(t) = 24{,}000(1.11)^t$
B. $A(t) = 24{,}000(0.11)^t$
C. $A(t) = 24{,}000(0.89)^t$
D. $A(t) = 0.89(24{,}000)^t$

11. $f(x) = -2(x - 3)(2x - 3)(3x + 5)$

Which of the following is an x-intercept of the graph of the function above on the xy-plane?

A. $(-3, 0)$
B. $\left(\frac{2}{3}, 0\right)$
C. $\left(\frac{3}{2}, 0\right)$
D. $\left(\frac{5}{3}, 0\right)$

Math: Advanced Math

Practice Set 2: Medium-Hard

1

The total amount of money in Kathy's bank account can be calculated by the expression $P\left(1+\frac{r}{n}\right)^{nt}$, where the initial amount P was deposited at an annual rate of r for t years, with interest compounded n times per year. If Kathy noticed that the total amount of money in her bank account was increasing every two months rather than quarterly, the value of which of the following would change?

A. P
B. r
C. n
D. t

2

The graph of which of the following functions must have points in all four quadrants of the xy-plane?

A. a linear function with a nonzero rate of change
B. an exponential function with a nonzero y-intercept
C. a polynomial function with four real zeros
D. a quadratic function with both positive and negative zeros

3

If $g(x) = 2\sqrt{x+1}$ and $g(k) = 50$, where k is a positive constant, what is the value of k?

4

$$f(x) = 3256(1.02)^{4x}$$

Since 2010, the value of a university's endowment has increased at an annual rate of $p\%$, compounded quarterly. The function f models this situation, where $f(x)$ is the value of the endowment x years after 2010. What is the value of p?

A. 8
B. 2
C. 0.08
D. 0.02

5

For the function $h(x) = a\sqrt{x-1} + b$, $h(1) = 2$, $h(5) = 10$, and $h(k) = 18$, where a, b, and k are constants. What is the value of k?

6

If the functions f and g are defined by $f(x) = 80(10)^x$ and $g(x) = f(x-1)$, which of the following gives $g(x)$?

A. $g(x) = 7(10)^x$
B. $g(x) = 8(9)^x$
C. $g(x) = 8(10)^x$
D. $g(x) = 80\left(\frac{1}{10}\right)^x$

7

$$f(x) = px^3 - 3x^2 + 2x + 5$$
$$g(x) = 3x^3 + 5x^2 - qx + 2$$

In the functions $f(x)$ and $g(x)$ defined above, p and q are constants. Given that $f(x) - g(x) = -x^3 - 8x^2 + 6x + 3$, what is the value of $p - q$?

8

The half-life decay model can be expressed as $A = A_0 \left(\frac{1}{2}\right)^{\frac{t}{h}}$, where A_0 is the initial amount of a substance at time $t = 0$, A is the amount remaining at time t, and h is the half-life (the amount of time it takes for half of the substance to decay). Based on the equation, which of the following must be true?

A. After three half-lives, $\frac{1}{8}$ of the substance will remain.
B. 50% of the substance will remain when $t = 2$.
C. $A > A_0$ for $0 < t < 2$.
D. As the value of t increases, the value of A_0 decreases exponentially.

9

In the xy-plane, the graphs of linear function $f(x)$ and exponential function $g(x)$ intersect a total of n times. Which of the following is NOT a possible value of n?

A. 0
B. 1
C. 2
D. 3

10

In the xy-plane, the x-intercepts of $y = f(x)$ include 2 and 5. The function has a y-intercept at 4. If f is a third-degree polynomial function, which of the following CANNOT be true of $f(x)$?

A. The graph of $y = f(x)$ has exactly two x-intercepts.
B. $(x + 5)$ is a factor of $f(x)$.
C. The remainder when $f(x)$ is divided by $(x - 2)$ is 5.
D. The function is increasing over the interval $-\infty < x \leq 0$.

11

$$f(x) = 4\sqrt{x}$$
$$g(x) = \frac{x+2}{x-9}$$

The functions f and g are defined above, and the function h is defined by $h(x) = g(f(x))$. Which of the following is the best description of the domain of $h(x)$?

A. $x > 0$
B. $x > 0$ and $x \neq 9$
C. $x \geq 0$ and $x \neq \frac{3}{2}$
D. $x \geq 0$ and $x \neq \frac{81}{16}$

12

The data in the scatterplot below could most appropriately be modeled by which of the following exponential functions, where a, b, and c are all positive constants?

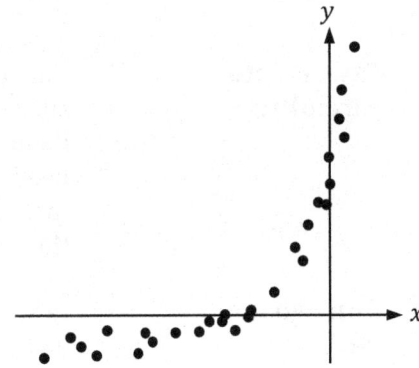

A. $f(x) = a^{(x+b)} + c$
B. $f(x) = a^{(x+b)} - c$
C. $f(x) = a^{(x-b)} + c$
D. $f(x) = a^{(x-b)} - c$

Problem Solving and Data Analysis

Charts and graphs are abundant on the SAT. When answering math questions that accompany a chart or graph, you'll need to put your critical reading skills to work by carefully analyzing the given data and drawing appropriate conclusions.

Focus on what matters.	It's common for the test to present you with a lot more information than you actually need. Always be sure that you're looking at the data that are relevant to the question being asked. (Beware of superfluous data intended solely to distract you!)
Double-check.	If more than one chart or graph is provided, verify that you're consulting the right one before you choose your answer. Check as well that you're not confusing one axis for the other, or one line for another, if multiple lines are graphed in the same figure.
Watch the scale.	The *x*-axis and the *y*-axis are not necessarily measured in the same way: for example, there may be a vertical gridline every 5 units and a horizontal gridline every 10. Also, do you need to multiply? Charts will often show you data in "thousands of dollars" instead of simply in dollars.
Extrapolate carefully.	The test may give you a chart that shows the results of a survey of 100 students and then ask you to make a deduction about the student body at large. If so, you'll need to set up a proportion—don't just circle the answer that shows the number of students *in the survey* that fit the category.
Don't go too far.	In some cases, you'll need to decide whether a certain deduction can be drawn from the data in front of you—that is, not whether the deduction is mathematically valid, but whether it can be appropriately drawn at all. Consider issues like **sample size**, **representativeness**, and **potential bias** as you make your decision.

Data Interpretation

Preview Quiz:

1) For a summer academic program in Washington, DC, the fifty participants were chosen from school districts in Maryland (MD), Virginia (VA), West Virginia (WV), or Washington, DC (DC). Based on the circle graph, which school district represents approximately 25% of the participants?

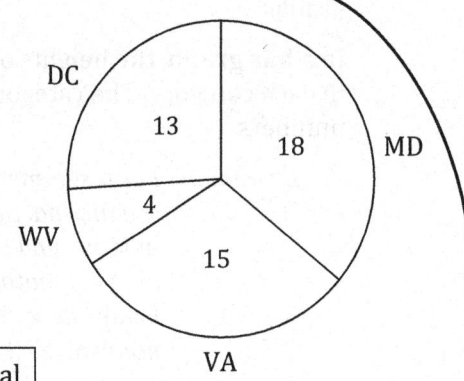

	Red	Green	Blue	Other	Total
Cleo	7	12	5	18	42
Harrison	9	4	13	22	48
Total	16	16	18	40	90

2) The table above shows the number of marbles of various colors owned by Cleo and Harrison. What fraction of Harrison's marbles are green?

3) What is the sum of the prices represented by the frequency distribution shown?

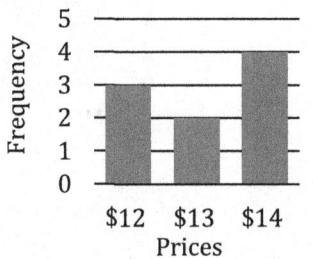

4) The scatterplot shows the relationship between two variables, x and y. Which of the following equations is the most appropriate linear model for the data?

A) $y = -x + 7$
B) $y = x - 7$
C) $y = 7x - 1$
D) $y = 7x + 1$

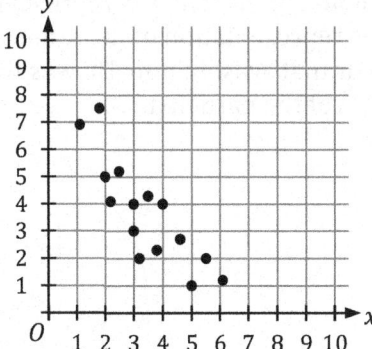

5) What is the median of the data set represented by the box-and-whisker plot below?

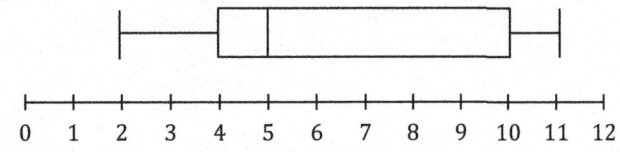

You'll see plenty of **1-variable data distributions** on the SAT, including tables, bar graphs, dot plots, and box-and-whisker plots, as well as **2-variable data distributions**, such as scatterplots and line graphs.

In a **bar graph**, the heights of the bars indicate how many there are in each category. The categories themselves may or may not be numbers.

Example: *For a summer academic program in Washington, DC, the fifty participants were chosen from school districts in Maryland (MD), Virginia (VA), West Virginia (WV), or Washington, DC (DC). Based on the bar graph below, how many of the participants come from a home district that is NOT Washington, DC?*

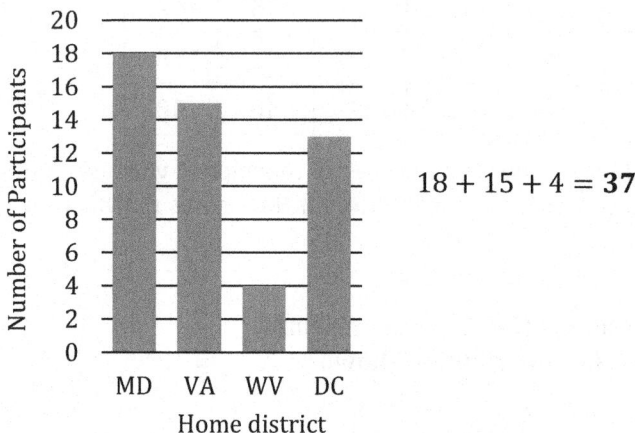

$18 + 15 + 4 = \mathbf{37}$

A **pie chart**, also called a **circle graph**, makes it easy to see what fraction of the whole is represented by each category. For example, this representation of the same summer academic program makes it clear that Washington, DC was the home district for approximately 25% of the participants.

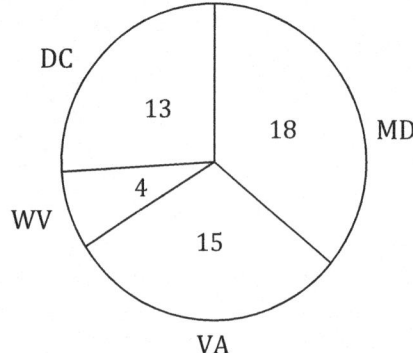

Many questions will be based on a **table** of data. These will often be **part over whole** problems. For these, be very careful to line up which category is the "part" and which is the "whole" (it may not be the total represented by the entire table).

Example:

	Red	Green	Blue	Other	Total
Cleo	7	12	5	18	42
Harrison	9	4	13	22	48
Total	16	16	18	40	90

The table above shows the number of marbles of various colors owned by Cleo and Harrison. What fraction of Harrison's marbles are green?

$$\frac{\text{Harrison's green marbles}}{\text{All of Harrison's marbles}} = \frac{4}{48} = \frac{1}{12}$$

Try It For the questions below, use the table shown in the example above.

1) Of all the marbles represented in the table, what fraction are blue and owned by Cleo?

2) What fraction of the blue marbles are owned by Cleo?

(Hint: these two questions do <u>not</u> have the same answer.)

CHALLENGE:

In a **box-and-whisker plot**, each vertical line displays information about the set. The ends of the "whiskers" are the minimum and maximum values, respectively. The bar in the interior of the box is the median of the set (the center of all the data). To find the edges of the "box," divide the data into two equal sets: the lower half of the data and the upper half of the data. The left side of the box represents the median of the lower half; the right side represents the median of the upper half.

Example: The data set { 2, 4, 5, | 5, 10, 11 }:

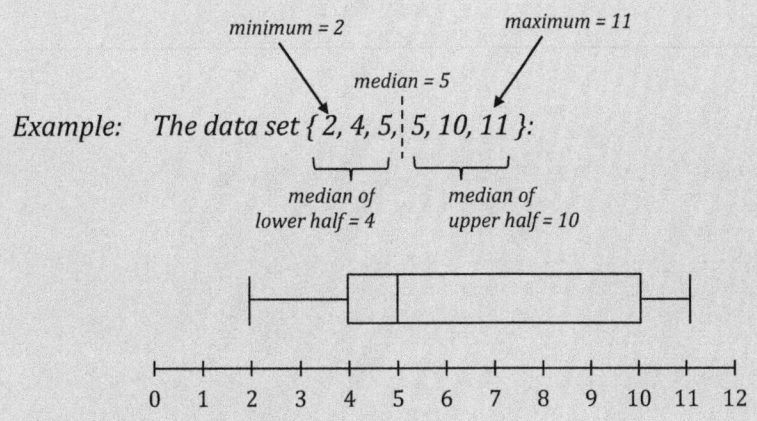

TIP:

For much more on mean, median, and mode, see p. 368.

A **frequency distribution** is a way of displaying two kinds of information at once: the values themselves and how many there are of each value.

Example: The price list $12, $12, $12, $13, $13, $14, $14, $14, $14 can be represented by any of the following frequency distributions:

Price ($)	Frequency
12	3
13	2
14	4

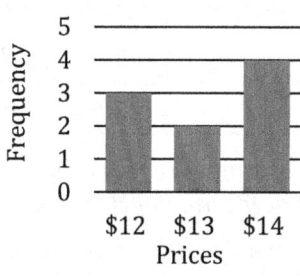 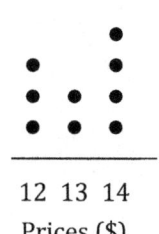

To calculate the sum of the prices, multiply each value by its frequency and add the results.

Example: The sum of the prices is 3($12) + 2($13) + 4($14) = $118.

Try It The bar graph below shows all the scores received on the AP European History exam at a local high school last year. Everyone who sat for the exam received a score.

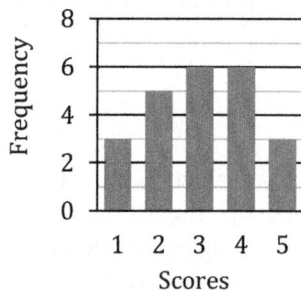

3) How many students sat for the exam?

A **scatterplot** is often used to present measurements of related variables. For example, if a scientist wants to measure the growth of an animal population over time, she might use the x-axis to represent the number of years that have passed and the y-axis to represent the population. Each (x, y) point on the scatterplot would then indicate an actual population measurement at a particular time: for instance, the point $(1, 340)$ would show that the population was 340 after 1 year.

Try It The scatterplot below shows the length, in feet, and the jaw width, in inches, of 15 great white sharks.

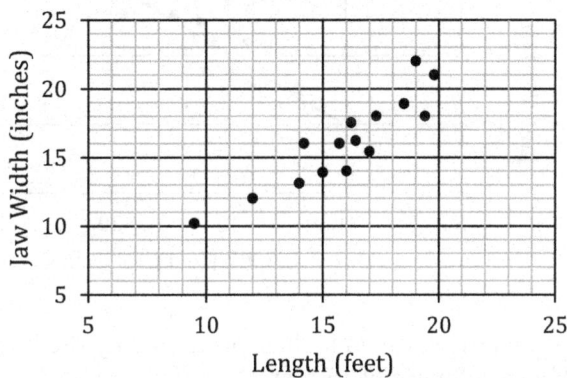

4) What is the length, in feet, of the shark with the greatest jaw width?

Some scatter plots also include a **line of best fit**, which is the line that comes closest to approximating the general trend of the data. Be sure to read carefully—questions about *predicted* values will be based on the line, while questions about actual *recorded* values will be based on the scatterplot points.

Try It   The scatterplot below shows the length, in feet, and the jaw width, in inches, of 15 great white sharks, along with a line of best fit.

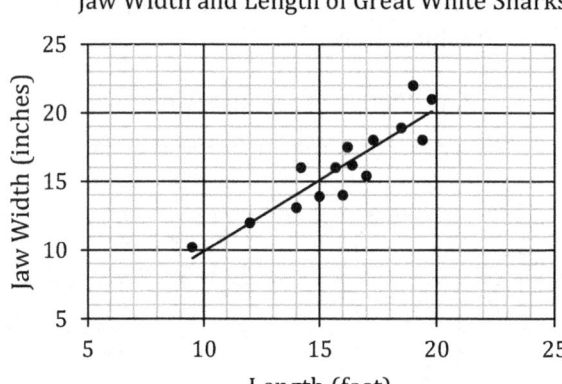

Jaw Width and Length of Great White Sharks

5) What is the jaw width, in inches, predicted by the line of best fit for a shark with a length of 15 feet?

FROM THE BLOG

One morning, a student arrived at her test center on a chilly morning of what proved to be a hot day. Dressed in long pants and a wool sweater, she discovered that, unlike her school, this school didn't have AC. As the temperature rose, so did her lethargy. Her performance, however, headed in the other direction.

When it's too warm, students' ability to reason is impaired. In fact, researcher Joshua Graff Zivin found that math performance decreased linearly at temperatures over 70 degrees Fahrenheit, with excessive heat (above 79° F) hurting performance by 1.6 percentile points.

The lesson? Dress in layers for the test. Science proves it's better to keep your cool!

The test will sometimes ask you to select the most appropriate "model" for the data shown in the scatterplot. If the data points appear to be roughly grouped along the path of a line, this just means finding an approximate line of best fit. Use your coordinate geometry skills to estimate the slope and/or y-intercept and start eliminating answer choices that can't be right.

> **TIP:**
> See the Coordinate Geometry chapter on p. 249 for a review of these skills.

Example: The scatterplot shows the relationship between two variables, x and y.

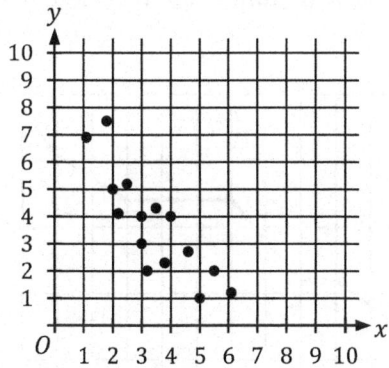

Which of the following equations is the most appropriate linear model for the data?

A) $y = -x + 7$
B) $y = x - 7$
C) $y = 7x - 1$
D) $y = 7x + 1$

Draw a line roughly through the points shown. Where would the line intersect the y-axis? Definitely closer to 7 than to -7, -1, or 1, so choice **A** must be the answer.

> **TIP:**
> Everything is drawn to scale on the SAT unless they tell you otherwise, but that doesn't mean they're not out to trick you. Always check the axes to make sure the scatterplot is really showing you what it seems to be showing you. Does the graph start at zero? Are the tick marks on the x-axis the same distance apart from each other as the tick marks on the y-axis? These are just a few of the ways the test will use "gotcha" questions to catch students who are moving too fast.

Another way to represent two-variable data is with a **line graph**. Pay close attention to what's being measured and how it's being measured (the units)—check both the description in the problem and the labels on the axes to be sure.

Try It

Ron recently took a road trip, leaving at noon and arriving at his destination at 6:00 pm. The graph below shows the relationship between time, in hours, and the distance Ron traveled, in miles.

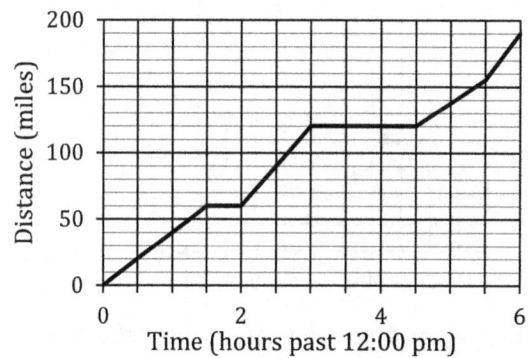

6) At some point during his journey, Ron stopped driving to take a 90-minute break. The break occurred during which of the following time intervals?

A) 12:00 pm – 1:30 pm
B) 1:00 pm – 2:30 pm
C) 2:00 pm – 3:30 pm
D) 3:00 pm – 4:30 pm

Practice Set 1: Easy-Medium

1

The table below gives the fees at a private shipping company for shipping packages that weigh 5 pounds or less.

Weight (lbs)	Fee ($)
0 – 1	12.50
1.01 – 2	13.20
2.01 – 3	13.60
3.01 – 4	13.85
4.01 – 5	14.10

On Wednesday, Seldon shipped two packages that each weighed 0.5 pounds and one that weighed 4.5 pounds. What was the total of Seldon's fees, in dollars?

2

2, 2, 2, 3, 3, 3, 3, 4, 4

Which frequency table correctly represents the data listed above?

A.
Number	Frequency
2	4
3	3
4	2

B.
Number	Frequency
2	2
3	3
4	4

C.
Number	Frequency
2	3
3	2
4	4

D.
Number	Frequency
2	3
3	4
4	2

3

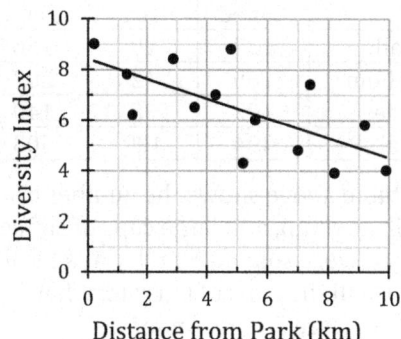

The Shannon-Wiener diversity index is a measure of species diversity within a given ecological community. A scientist calculated this index for 14 butterfly communities at various distances from an urban park. A line of best fit is also shown. Based on the figure, which of the following statements is true?

A. As distance from the park increases, the diversity index increases.
B. As distance from the park increases, the diversity index decreases.
C. As distance from the park decreases, the diversity index remains constant.
D. As distance from the park decreases, the diversity index decreases.

4

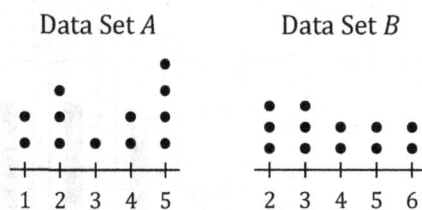

Based on the dot plots above, which of the following statements is true?

A. The least value in Data Set A is greater than the least value in Data Set B.
B. The greatest value in Data Set A is less than the greatest value in Data Set B.
C. The number of values in Data Set A is greater than the number of values in Data Set B.
D. The number of values in Data Set A is less than the number of values in Data Set B.

Math: Problem Solving and Data Analysis

5

Number of Cups of Coffee and Tea Sold

	Coffee	Tea	Total
Small	127	29	156
Medium	165	42	207
Large	102	38	140
Total	394	109	503

The table above shows the number of small, medium, and large cups of coffee and tea were sold on Monday at a local café. Of all the cups of tea sold, what fraction were size medium?

A. $\dfrac{42}{503}$

B. $\dfrac{42}{109}$

C. $\dfrac{207}{503}$

D. $\dfrac{165}{394}$

6

The bar graph below shows the number of new hybrid, plug-in hybrid, and all-electric vehicles sold in the US between 2015 and 2020.

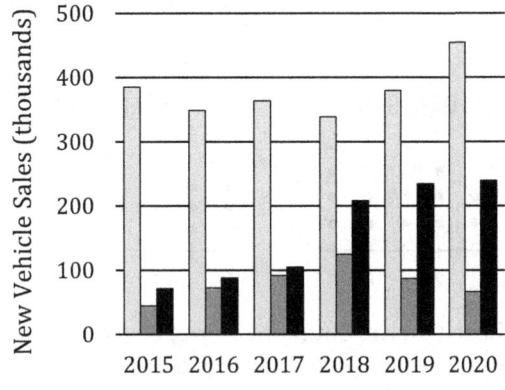

☐ hybrid   ▨ plug-in hybrid   ■ all-electric

The number of new all-electric vehicles sold in 2019 was approximately twice the number of new plug-in hybrid cars sold in what year?

A. 2015
B. 2016
C. 2018
D. 2019

7

On forty separate days over a six-year period, an economist recorded the price of crude oil and the average retail price of gasoline in her state. The scatterplot below shows these data and a line of best fit.

PRICES OF CRUDE OIL AND GASOLINE

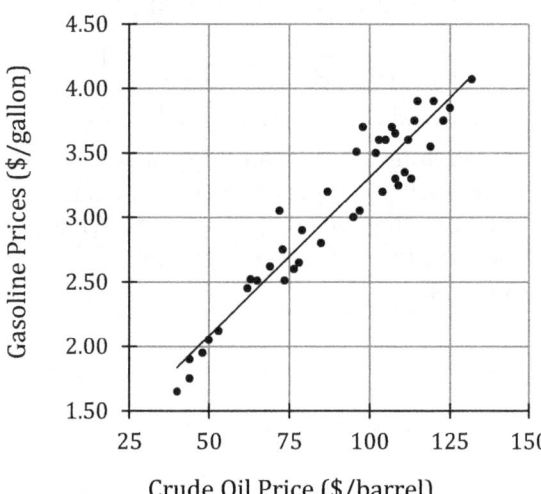

Crude Oil Price ($/barrel)

Consider the nine dates on which the crude oil price per barrel was more than $75 and less than $100. On how many of these dates was the actual gasoline price greater than the price predicted by the line of best fit?

Practice Set 2: Medium-Hard

1

The table below gives the price per ride, in dollars, for 14 attractions at a local amusement park, as well as the number of rides taken by Lupe on a recent visit. The park also sells a Fun Pass for $43.95 that covers unlimited rides on all the attractions listed except those marked with an asterisk.

Attraction	Price ($)	Rides
Teacups	6.00	0
Carousel	6.00	0
Kiddie copters	6.00	0
Mini-coaster	6.00	0
Bumper boats	8.00	0
Rock wall*	6.00	0
Laser tag*	9.00	0
Mini-golf	8.00	0
Ropes course	8.00	0
Parachuter*	25.00	1
Super slide	6.00	0
Tilt-a-whirl	8.00	0
Roller coaster	8.00	2
Go-karts	8.00	2

* Not included in the Fun Pass

Lupe bought individual tickets for all her rides. If she had bought the Fun Pass (plus individual tickets for any of her rides not included in that pass), how much more money or less money would she have spent?

A. She would have spent $13.05 less.
B. She would have spent $11.95 less.
C. She would have spent $11.95 more.
D. She would have spent $13.05 more.

2

The figure below shows the average US retail price of gasoline in June of each of the years from 1993 to 2021.

During which of the following three-year periods was the average rate of change of the retail price of gasoline the least?

A. 1993-1996
B. 1997-2000
C. 2003-2006
D. 2014-2017

3

The graph below gives the national minimum wage in the US, in dollars per hour, between 1930 and 2000.

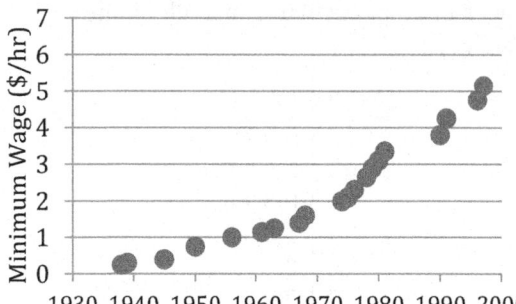

Assuming that a similar trend continued, which of the following was most likely the national minimum wage in the US in 2010?

A. $2.90 per hour
B. $5.00 per hour
C. $5.75 per hour
D. $8.00 per hour

4

At a carnival, a game was played in which each player scored a whole number of points between 0 and 50, inclusive. The scores of 22 players are displayed in the bar graph below. Each bar represents a group of players whose scores fell within a ten-point range: for example, the leftmost bar indicates that there were 4 players who each scored 0-10 points.

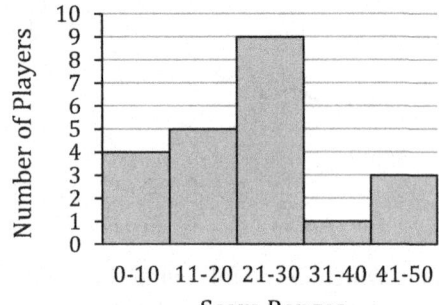

Which of the following could be the total number of players who scored fewer than 25 points?

A. 4
B. 5
C. 7
D. 11

5

The stem-and-leaf plot below gives the ages of 20 participants in a telephone survey.

Stem	Leaf
2	6 6 7
3	1 5 9 9 9
4	0 3 4 8
5	1 2 5 7
6	0
7	2 3 3

Key: 5 | 1 = 51 years

The oldest participant was how many years older than the youngest participant?

A. 35
B. 46
C. 47
D. 51

6

The scatterplot shows the relationship between two variables, x and y.

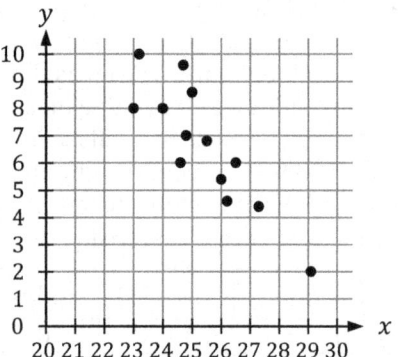

Which of the following equations is the most appropriate linear model for the data shown in the scatterplot?

A. $y = 45 - 1.5x$
B. $y = 18 + 3x$
C. $y = 18 - 3x$
D. $y = 45 + 1.5x$

7

As part of an experiment, a group of five students was asked to estimate each other's heights in feet (ft) and inches (in). For each student, the average (arithmetic mean) of the other students' estimates was recorded in the table below as the student's "estimated height"; the table also gives each student's actual height.

Student	Estimated height	Actual height
A	5 ft, 6 in	5 ft, 7 in
B	6 ft, 1 in	6 ft
C	5 ft, 9 in	5 ft, 10 in
D	5 ft, 4 in	5 ft, 2 in
E	6 ft, 3 in	6 ft, 1 in

The actual height of the tallest student was how many inches greater than the lowest estimated height?

(Note: 12 inches = 1 foot)

Ratios, Proportions, and Unit Conversions

Preview Quiz:

Solve each of the following.

1) On a certain map, 2 inches represents 30 miles. How long would a distance of 450 miles appear on this map?

2) Desiree's swimming pool contains 20,800 gallons of water. If one liter is equivalent to approximately 0.26 gallons, how many liters of water are in the pool?

3) Alicia jogs the same route every morning at an average rate of 5.1 miles per hour. If it takes her 25 minutes to complete her jog, how long is her jogging route, in <u>meters</u>?
(Note: 1 mile equals approximately 1.6 kilometers.)

4) An area of 1350 square meters is equivalent to an area of how many square kilometers?

5) If $2x = 3y$, what is the ratio of x to y?
(Hint: the answer is <u>not</u> 2 to 3.)

A **ratio** is defined as the size or number of one thing in relation to another. Ratios can simply be thought of as fractions: If a and b are in a ratio of 2:3, then the fraction $\frac{a}{b}$ is equivalent to the fraction $\frac{2}{3}$. So if $a = 2$, then $b = 3$; if $a = 4$, then $b = 6$; and so on.

The simplest ratio problems will set two ratios equal to each other (forming a **proportion**) and ask you to plug in the appropriate number.

Example: *On a certain map, 2 inches represents 30 miles. How long would a distance of 450 miles appear on this map?*

$$\frac{2}{30} = \frac{x}{450}$$

To make sure everything's in the right place, read your proportion back to yourself like an analogy. For example, we could read this one as "2 inches is to 30 miles as x inches is to 450 miles." Yep, that makes sense. Now just cross-multiply to solve:

$$900 = 30x$$

$$x = \mathbf{30\ inches}$$

TIP:

For a review of cross-multiplying, see p. 233.

Try It

1) If the wholesale price for 15 pounds of coffee is $28.50, what is the wholesale price, in dollars, for 24 pounds of coffee?

2) A rectangular photograph with a width of 4 inches and a height of 6 inches will be placed into a frame with a width of 7 inches. If the frame and the photograph are similar rectangles (their side lengths are proportional), what is the height of the frame, in inches?

Ratios, Proportions, and Unit Conversions

The SAT loves to test you on **unit conversions**. For straightforward problems in which only one unit is changing, you might choose to use a simple proportion.

Example: *Desiree's swimming pool contains 20,800 gallons of water. If one liter is equivalent to approximately 0.26 gallons, how many liters of water are in the pool?*

$$\frac{1}{0.26} = \frac{x}{20,800}$$

$$20,800 = 0.26x$$

$$x = 80,000 \text{ liters}$$

TIP:
The test may expect you to know the basic metric system conversions (e.g., there are 1000 grams in one kilogram; there are 100 centimeters in one meter) and a few other very easy conversion rates (e.g., there are 60 seconds in one minute). If any other conversions are necessary for a problem, the conversion rates will be given (e.g., there are 5280 feet in one mile).

For more complicated problems, though, the best approach is one you likely learned in chemistry class: set up a series of fractions so that all the extra units cancel out, and then multiply straight across.

Example: *Alicia jogs the same route every morning at an average rate of 5.1 miles per hour. If it takes her 25 minutes to complete her jog, how long is her jogging route, in <u>meters</u>? (Note: 1 mile equals approximately 1.6 kilometers.)*

$$\frac{25 \text{ min}}{1} \times \frac{1 \text{ hr}}{60 \text{ min}} \times \frac{5.1 \text{ mi}}{1 \text{ hr}} \times \frac{1.6 \text{ km}}{1 \text{ mi}} \times \frac{1000 \text{ m}}{1 \text{ km}}$$

$$= \frac{(25 \,\cancel{\text{min}})(1 \,\cancel{\text{hr}})(5.1 \,\cancel{\text{mi}})(1.6 \,\cancel{\text{km}})(1000 \text{ m})}{(1)(60 \,\cancel{\text{min}})(1 \,\cancel{\text{hr}})(1 \,\cancel{\text{mi}})(1 \,\cancel{\text{km}})}$$

$$= \frac{25(5.1)(1.6)(1000)}{60} \text{ m}$$

$$= 3400 \text{ meters}$$

Try It 3) At a local gourmet store, saffron sells for $1.71 per gram. At this rate, what is the price, in dollars, for three two-ounce tins of saffron? (Note: 1 ounce = 28 grams)

Be sure to carefully match up your units! If the units have different exponents, you have to keep multiplying those fractions enough times to cancel them all out. In other words, just because 1 foot equals 12 inches, that doesn't mean that 1 *square* foot equals 12 *square* inches.

Example: *An area of 1350 square meters is equivalent to an area of how many square kilometers?*

$$\frac{1350 \text{ m}^2}{1} \times \frac{1 \text{ km}}{1000 \text{ m}} \times \frac{1 \text{ km}}{1000 \text{ m}} = \frac{1350 \text{ km}^2}{(1000)(1000)} = 0.00135 \text{ km}^2$$

CHALLENGE:

If $2x = 3y$, what is the ratio of x to y?

Careful: the answer is <u>not</u> 2 to 3. Remember, the ratio we're looking for is the value of x/y. So, let's try working that out algebraically.

$$2x = 3y$$

First, divide both sides by 2:

$$x = \frac{3y}{2}$$

Next, we need to divide both sides by y. (If it's easier, you can think of this step as *multiplying* both sides by $1/y$). That gives us this:

$$\frac{x}{y} = \frac{3}{2}$$

So the ratio of x to y is backwards from what we first expected: it's **3 to 2**.

Another way to solve this problem would be to make up a value for one of the variables and plug it into the original equation. Let's say we decided to use $y = 6$:

$$2x = 3y$$
$$2x = 3(6)$$
$$2x = 18$$
$$x = 9$$
$$\text{ratio of } x \text{ to } y = \frac{9}{6} = \frac{3}{2}$$

Ratios, Proportions, and Unit Conversions

If there are multiple ratios in a problem, the best way to solve it may be to use substitution (plug in your own numbers).

Example: *If the ratio of a to b is 3:5 and the ratio of b to c is 3:7, what is the ratio of a to c?*

First, rewrite the ratios as fractions.

$$\frac{a}{b} = \frac{3}{5} \quad \text{and} \quad \frac{b}{c} = \frac{3}{7}$$

What makes this problem hard is the fact that b is a different number in the two equations: it's 5 in the first one and 3 in the other one. So, we plug in a new number for b so that it can be the same value in both fractions. Let's try $b = 15$:

$$\frac{a}{b} = \frac{3}{5} = \frac{9}{15} \quad \text{and} \quad \frac{b}{c} = \frac{3}{7} = \frac{15}{35}$$

This tells us that if $b = 15$, then $a = 9$ and $c = 35$. Therefore, the ratio of a to c is **9 to 35**.

> **TIP:**
> To plug in numbers, start with the letter the two equations have in common. In this case, that's b.

Try It 4) If the ratio of x to y is 3 to 4 and the ratio of x to z is 4 to 5, what is the ratio of y to z?

CHALLENGE:

If you're given a ratio of two variables and the value of their sum, you may want to use algebra to solve. For example, when two numbers in ratio 2:3 add up to 20, we can say that $2x + 3x = 20$.

Example: *At a zoo, the ratio of male reptiles to female reptiles is 3:5. There are 120 reptiles. How many male reptiles are there?*

We can't just use a proportion for this because the 120 doesn't match either category: it's not the number of male reptiles and it's not the number of female reptiles. So what do we do? Well, let's consider the possibilities. Based on the ratio, there could be exactly 3 males and 5 females (for a total of 8), or there could be exactly 6 males and 10 females (for a total of 16), and so on. Looking at that another way, there could be 3(1) males and 5(1) females, or there could be 3(2) males and 5(2) females, and so on. In other words, the number of males will be 3 times *something*, and the number of females will be 5 times *that same thing*. And we also know that the males and females have to add up to 120. We can represent that algebraically by doing this:

$$\text{\# of males} = 3x$$
$$\text{\# of females} = 5x$$

$$3x + 5x = 120$$
$$8x = 120$$
$$x = 15$$

$$\text{\# of males} = 3x = 3(15) = \mathbf{45}$$

Another way to handle this problem is to change up the relevant ratio. If hadn't been told that there are 120 total reptiles, what's the smallest total we might have? As we saw, it's eight: that's 3 males and 5 females. That means that out of every 8 reptiles, 3 of them are males. Therefore, while the ratio of males to *females* is 3 to 5, the ratio of males to *total reptiles* is 3 to 8. And now we can do a proportion!

$$\frac{3}{8} = \frac{x}{120}$$
$$x = \frac{3}{8}(120) = \mathbf{45}$$

Practice Set 1: Easy-Medium

1

Of the last 32 emails Joe received, 15 were spam. What is the ratio of non-spam emails to spam emails?

A. 15:32
B. 17:32
C. 15:17
D. 17:15

2

At a bake sale, the ratio of the number of cookies sold to the number of brownies sold is 3 to 4. If 24 brownies were sold at the bake sale, how many cookies were sold?

3

A mass of 0.28 kilograms is equivalent to a mass of how many grams?

(Note: 1 kilogram = 1000 grams)

4

A gardener needs to buy enough mulch to cover 6 cubic feet of her lawn. If 50 pounds of mulch can cover $2\frac{1}{2}$ cubic feet, how many pounds of mulch does the gardener need to buy?

A. 90
B. 100
C. 120
D. 130

5

In the line segment shown below, the ratio of the length of $\overline{FG}$ to the length of $\overline{GH}$ is 2:5.

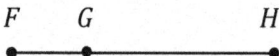

What is the ratio of the length of $\overline{GH}$ to the length of $\overline{FH}$?

A. 2:7
B. 3:5
C. 2:3
D. 5:7

6

In a recent survey, residents of counties A, B, C, and D were asked whether they plan to vote in an upcoming mayoral election. The numbers of "Yes" and "No" responses for each county are shown in the table below.

County	Yes	No	Total
A	25	92	117
B	78	61	139
C	45	18	63
D	51	24	75
Total	235	232	467

Based on the data in the table, in which county was the ratio of "Yes" responses to "No" responses the *greatest*?

A. A
B. B
C. C
D. D

7

At a bookstore, 30% of the books are currently on sale. What is the ratio of the number of books that are currently on sale to the total number of books at the bookstore?

A. 3:10
B. 3:7
C. 3:5
D. 7:3

Math: Problem Solving and Data Analysis

8. Bob will drive a distance of 180 miles at an average speed of 45 miles per hour. What is the total amount of time required for the journey, in *minutes*?

A. 60
B. 120
C. 180
D. 240

9. Yesterday, a university dining hall served 540 students, 36 of whom requested a vegetarian meal. At 1:00 yesterday, the study group for a physics class decided to take a lunch break and eat together at the dining hall. If all 15 students in the study group were served in the dining hall, and if the study group was a representative sample of all 540 students served at the dining hall that day, what is the most likely number of students in the study group who did NOT request a vegetarian meal?

A. 12
B. 14
C. 16
D. 18

10. On a recent Saturday, three friends split a "party sub" sandwich by cutting it into portions of unequal lengths. The lengths of the portions were in the ratio 1:2:3. If the original sandwich was 18 inches long, what was the length, in inches, of the largest portion?

11. In a garden, the ratio of azalea bushes to tulips is 2 to 5, and the ratio of tulips to marigolds is 5 to 8. If there are 24 marigolds in the garden, how many azalea bushes are there?

12. At Cirrus Tech, 3 out of every 5 employees are part-time, and 3 out of every 4 part-time employees work fewer than twenty hours per week. What fraction of Cirrus Tech employees are part-time employees who work fewer than twenty hours per week?

A. $\dfrac{3}{20}$
B. $\dfrac{9}{20}$
C. $\dfrac{7}{10}$
D. $\dfrac{4}{5}$

13. The ratio of the length of a rectangle, in inches, to the width of the rectangle, in feet, is 18 to 1. If the length of the rectangle is 3 <u>feet</u>, what is its width, in feet?

A. 1 foot
B. 1.5 feet
C. 2 feet
D. 3.6 feet

Practice Set 2: Medium-Hard

1

The ratio of x to 6 is the same as the ratio y to 10. What is the value of $\frac{x}{y}$?

2

In a bag of marbles, the ratio of red to green to blue marbles is 1:3:4. Which of the following could be the number of marbles in the bag?

A. 18
B. 24
C. 26
D. 36

3

Tim makes hot chocolate by combining 14 tablespoons of hot chocolate mix with 5 cups of milk. If this makes enough hot chocolate for 6 people, how many tablespoons of hot chocolate mix will Tim need to make enough hot chocolate for 21 people?

A. 9
B. 20
C. 36
D. 49

4

If $2x = 3y$ and $2y = 3z$, then what is the ratio of x to z?

A. 2:1
B. 2:3
C. 9:4
D. 4:9

5

Based on measurements made as part of an experiment for his physics class, Algernon determined the speed of sound to be 343 meters per second. Assuming this value to be correct, which of the following is closest to the speed of sound in miles per hour?

(Note: 1 meter = 0.001 kilometer, and 1 kilometer is equivalent to approximately 0.62 miles.)

A. 13
B. 128
C. 500
D. 766

6

Three legal partners are dividing $7,500 in a 4:5:6 ratio. How much more, in dollars, does the partner with the largest share make than the partner with the smallest share?

7

The ratio of sugar to flour in a recipe is 5:2. If the amount of sugar is decreased by 30% and the amount of flour is increased by 25%, what is the new ratio of sugar to flour?

A. 1:4
B. 7:5
C. 7:3
D. 3:1

Math: Problem Solving and Data Analysis

8

A saline solution is made up of 1.5 cups of salt and 5 cups of water. How many cups of water must be added so that the solution is 94% water?

9

After winning a grand prize of $60,000, Jim decides to save four times as much money as he will spend. How much money will Jim save?

A. $12,000
B. $24,000
C. $45,000
D. $48,000

10

The "escape velocity" of a planet is the minimum speed needed for an object launched from its surface to continue traveling away from the planet rather than either orbiting it or falling back down to its surface. The escape velocity from Earth's surface is about 11,186 meters per second. Which of the following is closest to is the escape velocity from Earth's surface in *miles per hour*?

(Note: 1000 meters = 1 kilometer; 1 mile = 1.609 kilometers.)

A. 417
B. 25,028
C. 40,270
D. 64,794

11

The length and width of a rectangle are in ratio 3:5. If the area of the rectangle is 135, what is the perimeter?

A. 24
B. 36
C. 48
D. 72

12

A library has 3 times as many fiction books as non-fiction books. If $\frac{1}{5}$ of all non-fiction books are biographies, what is the ratio of fiction books to biographies in this library?

A. 15:1
B. 5:3
C. 3:5
D. 1:15

13

A poll of a website's weekly visitors indicated the following data about the visitors' ages:

Age group	# of visitors
under 18	427
18-25	3,264
26-35	5,881
36-49	4,916
50-65	1,103
66 and older	812
Total	16,403

If this information was presented in a circle graph (pie chart), the degree measure for the sector representing the age group 36-49 would be closest to which of the following?

A. 30°
B. 54°
C. 72°
D. 108°

Percentages

Preview Quiz:

Solve each of the following.

1) What is 20% of 30? _____

2) 24 is what percent of 60? _____

3) 18 is 15% of what number? _____

4) What price is 10% less than $80? _____

5) 26 is 30% more than what number? _____

6) 51 is what percent less than 60? _____

7) 50 is what percent greater than 40? _____

Math: Problem Solving and Data Analysis

Both **percentages** and ratios deal with relationships between numbers. In fact, one way to solve percent problems is to think of a percentage as just another kind of ratio.

For "percent of" problems, the ratio is *part* to *whole* (or "is" to "of").

$$\frac{is}{of} = \frac{\%}{100}$$

Examples:

What is 20% of 30?
$$\frac{x}{30} = \frac{20}{100}$$
$$100x = 20(30)$$
$$x = 6$$

24 is what percent of 60?
$$\frac{24}{60} = \frac{x}{100}$$
$$24(100) = 60x$$
$$x = 40$$

18 is 15% of what number?
$$\frac{18}{x} = \frac{15}{100}$$
$$18(100) = 15x$$
$$x = 120$$

Another way to approach percentage problems is through word-for-word translation.

is	=
of	*
percent	$\frac{\square}{100}$
"what" or "what number"	x

TIP:
In the built-in calculator, you can simply type the % symbol.

Examples:

What is 20% of 30?
$$x = \frac{20}{100} * 30$$

24 is what percent of 60?
$$24 = \frac{x}{100} * 60$$

18 is 15% of what number?
$$18 = \frac{15}{100} * x$$

or write this as 0.2(30)

 or write this as $0.15x$

These two approaches are equally valid. Use whichever one makes the most sense to you.

Try It Solve each of the following (using either approach).

1) What is 18% of 50?

2) Ten is what percent of 80?

3) Thirty is 40% of what number?

Some percentage problems deal with the percent by which something has **changed.** For example, consider the question "What is 70% less than 200?" Here, it's not that the problem is asking us to find 70% *of* 200—it's asking us to find what the result is when 200 is *reduced* by that value.

To increase or decrease a number by p percent, you find $p\%$ of the number and then either add that to or subtract it from the original. In other words:

$$\text{Original} \pm \text{Percent}(\text{Original}) = \text{Final}$$

Examples:

What price is 10% less than $80?

$80 - 0.10(80) = x$
$80 - 8 = x$
$x = \$72$

26 is 30% more than what number?

$x + 0.30(x) = 26$
$x + 0.3x = 26$
$1.3x = 26$
$x = 20$

TIP:

The "Original" is the value after the word "than" in the problem.

TIP:

Percent increases and decreases, step by step:

1. Write the percent value as a decimal.

    $$25\% \rightarrow 0.25$$

2. For "percent more than," *add* that decimal value to 1; for "percent less than," *subtract* it from 1.

    "25% more than"   "25% less than"
    = 1.25   = 0.75

3. Multiply the result by the original number.

    "25% more than 40"   "25% less than 40"
    1.25(40)   0.75(40)
    = 50   = 30

Try It   Solve each of the following.

4) What is 20% more than 50?

5) If 34 is 15% less than x, what is x?

Math: Problem Solving and Data Analysis

You can also use the Original & Final formula for problems in which the percent is unknown.

Examples: *51 is what percent less than 60?* *50 is what percent greater than 40?*

$60 - x(60) = 51$ $40 + x(40) = 50$
$60x = 9$ $40x = 10$
$x = 0.15 = \mathbf{15\%}$ $x = 0.25 = \mathbf{25\%}$

CHALLENGE:

For a shortcut for the percent change problems in which the percent is unknown, you can use a ratio approach. This time, instead of *is* to *of*, set up your ratio as *amount of change* to the *base* (the number after the word "than").

Examples: *40 is what percent less than 64?* *50 is what percent greater than 40?*

$$\frac{64-40}{64} = \frac{x}{100}$$ $$\frac{50-40}{40} = \frac{x}{100}$$

$x = \mathbf{37.5\%}$ $x = \mathbf{25\%}$

For scenarios involving time, you can think of this as $\frac{|\text{new} - \text{old}|}{\text{old}}$.

Try It 6) A company had $800 in sales last year and $900 in sales this year. By what percent did sales increase?

TIP:

Many percent change problems are great for **back-solving**.

Practice Set 1: Easy-Medium

1 What is 30% of 15?

2 What is 0.4% of 800?
A. 3.2
B. 32
C. 320
D. 3,200

3 Fifteen is what percent of twenty?
A. 3%
B. 25%
C. 75%
D. 80%

4 Forty percent of what number is 24?

5 If 150% of x is 24, what is the value of x?
A. 16
B. 18
C. 20
D. 36

6 What number is 30% more than 40?
A. 43
B. 52
C. 64
D. 68

7 What number is 44% less than 60?
A. 16
B. 26.4
C. 33.6
D. 48

8 $36.00 is 120% of what price?
A. $22.00
B. $26.10
C. $30.00
D. $43.20

9 15 is what percent less than 20?
A. 25%
B. 30%
C. $33\frac{1}{3}\%$
D. 75%

10 20 is what percent greater than 15?
A. 25%
B. 30%
C. $33\frac{1}{3}\%$
D. 75%

11
If a price is $36 after a 25% discount, what was the price before the discount?

A. $45
B. $48
C. $52
D. $60

12
14 is 30% less than which of the following numbers?

A. 18.2
B. 20
C. 23.8
D. 26.4

13
If 70% of x is 42, what is 30% of x?

A. 3
B. 6
C. 12
D. 18

14
Of the 60 problems on a math test, a student answered 12 of the problems incorrectly and the rest correctly. If the student answered $p\%$ of the problems correctly, what is the value of p?

15
When 25% of x is rounded to the nearest whole number, the result is 55. Which of the following could be the value of x?

A. 215
B. 221
C. 222
D. 223.5

16
On Wednesday, 160 students took a standardized test consisting of multiple-choice questions with five possible responses (A, B, C, D, and E). The table below shows the distribution of responses for the first two questions on the test.

Choice	#1	#2	Total
A	12	117	129
B	10	5	15
C	125	9	134
D	6	3	9
E	7	26	33
Total	160	160	320

Out of all the responses recorded for the first two questions, approximately what percent of the answers were C?

A. 39%
B. 42%
C. 50%
D. 78%

17
The length of a circle's radius, in inches, is approximately what percent of the circle's circumference, in inches?

(Note: the circumference C of a circle with radius r is equal to $C = 2\pi r$).

A. 1.57%
B. 15.9%
C. 31.8%
D. It cannot be determined from the given information.

18
If Leslie has 20% more books than she had last week and she currently has 150 books, how many books did Leslie have last week?

A. 75
B. 120
C. 125
D. 200

Practice Set 2: Medium-Hard

1. Mike has 20 red shirts and 30 black shirts. 15% of the red shirts and 30% of the black shirts are striped. If p percent of all of Mike's shirts are striped, what is the value of p?

2. Daniel works as a waiter. He earns $3 an hour plus a 15% tip on all the food he sells. If he earns $45 in 6 hours, how many dollars' worth of food did he sell?

A. 180
B. 200
C. 280
D. 300

3. Kieran purchased several items at a wholesale price, then sold them all for $102.87. This amount was 35% greater than the wholesale price he paid for the items. What was the wholesale price?

A. $66.87
B. $76.20
C. $83.48
D. $183.87

4. What is 0.06% of $\frac{4}{5}$ of 3.2×10^5 ?

5. Ezekiel received some money for his birthday and decided to use part of it to buy a new pair of headphones. At the store, he handed 60% of his birthday money to the cashier and received $1.80 in change. If the change he received was 6% of the total amount of money he had handed to the cashier, how much money did Ezekiel receive for his birthday?

A. $30
B. $40
C. $50
D. $60

6. A leather jacket is sold at a 40% discount. After a 5% sales tax, the total price is $176.40. To the nearest dollar, what was the original pre-tax price of the jacket?

A. $120
B. $238
C. $280
D. $392

7. On Monday, a store received a delivery of b bushels of apples. The store sold 20% of the bushels on Monday and 20% of the remaining bushels on Tuesday. Which of the following represents the number of bushels from the delivery that were sold on Tuesday?

A. $0.2b$
B. $0.2(0.2b)$
C. $0.2(0.8b)$
D. $b - 0.2b$

Mean, Median, and Mode

Preview Quiz:

Define each term:

1) mean: _____

2) median _____

3) mode _____

4) range _____

Fill in the blank:

5) The standard deviation is a measure of _____
   _____

Solve:

6) What is the average (arithmetic mean) of 4, 9, and 5?

7) What is the median of the set $\{5, 1, 9, -7, 2\}$?

8) What is the median of the set $\{10, 2, 1, 4, 8, -3\}$?

9) What is the mode of the set $\{1, 3, 4, 4, 10\}$?

10) What is the range of the set $\{1, 3, 4, 4, 10\}$?

11) A squad of 5 soldiers has an average weight of 182 pounds. After a sixth soldier joins the squad, the new average weight is 179 pounds. How much does the sixth soldier weigh?

Mean, Median, and Mode

To find the **mean** of a set of numbers, add them up and divide by how many numbers there are. The result, commonly called the **average**, is technically the **arithmetic mean**.

Example: What is the average (arithmetic mean) of 4, 9, and 5?

$$\text{mean} = \frac{4+9+5}{3} = \frac{18}{3} = \mathbf{6}$$

The **median** is the center of the data. To find it, first put the numbers in order from smallest to largest, and then cross off the numbers from both ends. If the set had an odd number of values, the median is the number left standing in the middle. If the set had an even number of values, there will be two numbers left in the middle; the median is the average (the arithmetic mean) of those two.

Example: What is the median of the set $\{5, 1, 9, -7, 2\}$?

$\{-\cancel{7}, \cancel{1}, 2, \cancel{5}, \cancel{9}\}$: The median is **2**.

Example: What is the median of the set $\{10, 2, 1, 4, 8, -3\}$?

$\{-\cancel{3}, \cancel{1}, 2, 4, \cancel{8}, \cancel{10}\}$: $\text{median} = \dfrac{2+4}{2} = \mathbf{3}$

> **TIP:**
> Remember to put the terms in order first!

However, because of the SAT's built-in calculator, you'll rarely need to actually calculate the mean or median in this way. Just type in the word `mean` or `median`, and then follow that command with the list of numbers in parentheses:

```
1   mean (4, 9, 5)
                    = 6

2   median (5, 1, 9, −7, 2)
                    = 2
```

The **mode** is the number that repeats the most.

Example: In the set {1, 3, 4, 4, 10}, the mode is **4**.

To find the **range** of a data set, just subtract the smallest value from the biggest value.

Example: In the set {1, 3, 4, 4, 10}, the range is $10 - 1 = $ **9**.

Try It   A class of 9 students received the following scores on a recent exam:

82, 77, 65, 92, 97, 93, 82, 88, and 71

1) What is the mean of the scores?

2) What is the median?

3) What is the mode?

4) What is the range?

The SAT loves to trick you by taking a topic that you are very familiar with and asking you "backward" questions. For example, instead of giving you the sum of a group of numbers and asking you to solve for the average, they will generally give you the average and ask you to solve for the sum. When in doubt, just keep coming back to the same equation:

$$\text{mean} = \frac{\text{sum}}{\#}$$

Example: A squad of 5 soldiers has an average weight of 182 pounds. After a sixth soldier joins the squad, the new average weight is 179 pounds. How much does the sixth soldier weigh?

First, let's tackle the 182. Write out the mean equation and plug in what you know.

First five soldiers: $182 = \frac{\text{sum}}{5} \rightarrow \text{sum} = 182(5) = 910$

The problem then gives us another mean: 179. So we write out the equation again:

All six soldiers: $179 = \frac{\text{sum}}{6} \rightarrow \text{sum} = 179(6) = 1{,}074$

So the total weight of the squad is 1,074 pounds, and the weights of the first five soldiers added up to 910 pounds. Therefore, the weight of that last soldier must be $1074 - 910 =$ **164 pounds**.

Try It 5) The average budget for the last ten weddings held at the Astor Ballroom was $25,000. If the most recent wedding is excluded from the list, the average budget for the remaining nine weddings is $23,500. What was the budget, in dollars, for the most recent wedding?

TIP:

You can rearrange the formula for mean to make a handy acronym: **S**(um) = **A**(verage) ∗ **T**(hings)

You may be asked to find the mean, median, mode, or range based on a **frequency distribution**. Remember this example from p. 342?

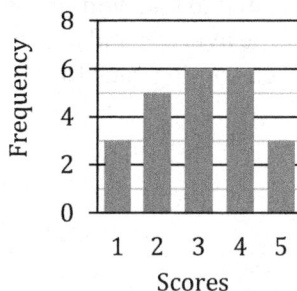

To find the mean, first multiply each value by its frequency and add up all those products: this gives you the sum of all the values. Next, add up all the frequencies: this gives you the total number of values in the set. Finally, divide the first sum by the second one.

$$\text{mean} = \frac{1(3) + 2(5) + 3(6) + 4(6) + 5(3)}{3 + 5 + 6 + 6 + 3} = \frac{70}{23}$$

To find the median, first consider how many values there are (add up all the frequencies). In this case, there are 23 values, so what's the term in the middle? Well, $23/2 = 11.5$, so the median is the 12th term (since that leaves 11 terms before it and 11 terms after it). Now look at the figure. There are a total of 8 terms in the first two bars, so that's not enough to get us to the median. But if we add in the third bar, we have a total of 14 terms. Therefore, the median is in that third bar: the median of this set is **3**.

TIP:

To find the median of an odd number of terms, divide the number of terms by 2 and round up. For example, say there are 47 terms. Since $47/2 = 23.5$, the median is the 24th term.

Try It — Fifty families were asked how many television sets they had in their homes. The responses are shown in the table below.

Number of TVs	Frequency
0	5
1	11
2	15
3	12
4	6
5	1

6) What is the average (arithmetic mean) number of TVs per family?

7) What is the median number of TVs per family?

CHALLENGE:

The **standard deviation** is a measure of how spread out a set of data is from the mean. The size of the numbers doesn't matter—all that matters is how far away they are, on average, from the mean of the set.

Example: Set A = {1, 5, 20}   Set B = {100, 101, 102}

The numbers in Set B are larger, but they're more closely grouped around the mean, so **Set A has the greater standard deviation**.

Example 2:   Set C = {20, 20, 80, 80}   Set D = {30, 50, 70}

Here, both sets have the same mean (50), and set C has some repeating terms, while set D doesn't. None of that matters. In set C, the terms are all 30 away from the mean, while the terms in D are all closer than that. It's the spread from the mean that matters, not the distance from the other terms. **Set C's standard deviation is greater**.

Try It   8) If Set E = {2, 9, 10} and Set F = {10, 11, 12}, which set has the greater standard deviation?

TIP:

In the built-in calculator, use the command `stddev()` to find the standard deviation.

Math: Problem Solving and Data Analysis

Practice Set 1: Easy-Medium

1

A group of friends recently contributed to a food drive. Youssef and Brian each donated 4 cans of food, Sal donated 8 cans of food, and Alysha and Lou each donated 7 cans of food. For these five friends, what was the average number of cans of food donated per person?

A. 5
B. 6
C. 7
D. 8

2

What is the positive difference between the median and the mean of the list of numbers below?

3, 17, 5, 2, 7, 7, 1

A. 1
B. 2
C. 3
D. 4

3

Jamal has an average test score of 92. What is the sum of his test scores if he has taken 5 tests?

4

The mean age of 10 infants in a research study is 8.6 months. If infant A were withdrawn from the study, the new mean of the remaining 9 infants would be 9 months. What is infant A's age, in months?

A. 4
B. 5
C. 6
D. 7

5

The table below lists the number of members of Reilly High's men's and women's swim teams who are 15, 16, 17, or 18 years old. No one on either team is below 15 or over 18 years of age.

Age	Men's Team: # of members	Women's Team: # of members
15	4	2
16	4	4
17	10	8
18	6	5

What is the average (arithmetic mean) age of the men's team?

6

If the 10 and 11 in the list below were replaced with 9 and 9, which of the following would increase?

8, 6, 9, 8, 7, 10, 11

A. the mean of the list
B. the median of the list
C. the mode of the list
D. the range of the list

7

If the average (arithmetic mean) of $x, x + 1$, and $2x - 5$ is 12, then what is the median of these three integers?

A. 10
B. 11
C. 12
D. 15

Practice Set 2: Medium-Hard

1

Ben has two brothers: a younger brother, Roger, and an older brother, Howard. Roger is three years younger than Ben. The range of the three siblings' ages, in years, is 5. If Howard is 15 years old, how old is Ben?

A. 10
B. 11
C. 12
D. 13

2

If Maya averages 0.6 goals per game during the first 10 games of the season, how many goals does she need to score in the 11th game in order to raise her average to 1 goal per game?

3

In a charity walkathon, 100 athletes each walked 1, 2, 3, 4, or 5 miles, as shown in the table below.

Miles Walked	Number of Athletes
1	10
2	13
3	18
4	35
5	24

If a represents the median number of miles walked and b represents the mode of miles walked, what is the value of $a - b$?

A. -1
B. 0
C. 1
D. 2

4

If $2z = 2x + 2y - 6$, then what is the average (arithmetic mean) of x and y?

A. $\dfrac{z+6}{2}$
B. $\dfrac{z+3}{2}$
C. $\dfrac{z+6}{3}$
D. $z+3$

5

Sets A and B are defined as follows:
$$A = \{2, 3, 5, 8, 9\}$$
$$B = \{2, 2, 10, 10, 300\}$$

Which of the following statements about sets A and B is true?

A. The range of Set A is greater than the range of Set B.
B. Set A has exactly one mode.
C. The median of Set A is one half the median of Set B.
D. The standard deviation of Set A is equal to the standard deviation of Set B.

6

At a certain gymnastics competition, the contestants receive scores from a panel of seven judges. To determine a contestant's final score, the computer deletes the highest and lowest of the seven scores and calculates the average (arithmetic mean) of the remaining scores. Felicia received the following scores from the panel: 15.73, 16.21, 19.34, 15.82, 18.14, 19.40, and 15.99. What was Felicia's final score?

A. 16.87
B. 17.10
C. 17.23
D. 17.78

Math: Problem Solving and Data Analysis

7. Mrs. Johnson's 1st period class has 21 students with an average grade of 84. Her 2nd period class has 28 students with an average grade of 91. What is the average of both classes combined?

8. The average (arithmetic mean) of a list of integers is 53. Three of the integers are 12, 108, and 36. If the average of the remaining integers on the list is 54, what is the total number of integers on the list?

A. 4
B. 5
C. 6
D. 7

9. Which of the following lists of numbers has the smallest standard deviation?

A. 2, 4, 6, 8, 10
B. 4, 4, 50, 90, 90
C. 5, 6, 7, 8, 9
D. 10, 20, 30, 40, 100

10. The average (arithmetic mean) of a, b, and c is 12. If a is increased by 1, b is decreased by 4, and c remains unchanged, what will be the new average of a, b, and c?

A. 11
B. 12
C. 13
D. It cannot be determined.

11. If $x + y = z$ and $z = 6$, what is the average (arithmetic mean) of x, y, and z?

12. Peng has 5 more marbles than Ali, Raj has twice as many marbles as Peng, and Kaimana has 16 fewer than triple the number of marbles that Raj has. If Kaimana has 26 marbles, then what is the average number of marbles per person for Ali, Peng, Raj, and Kaimana?

A. 12.25
B. 12.5
C. 13.25
D. 14

13. Data set A consists of 35 positive integers with a mean of 26.4. Data set B is created by adding 2 to each of the integers in data set A. Data set C is created by multiplying each of the integers in data set A by 2. Which of the following statements must be true?

A. The standard deviation of data set A is equal to the standard deviation of data set B.
B. The standard deviation of data set A is equal to the standard deviation of data set C.
C. The median of data set A is equal to the median of data set B.
D. The median of data set A is equal to the median of data set C.

Probability

Preview Quiz:

1) A box contains 32 oranges and tangerines. If Elsa picks a piece of fruit at random from the box, the probability that she will pick an orange is equal to $\frac{3}{4}$. How many oranges are in the box?

	Undergraduate students	Graduate students	Total
On campus	3562	184	3746
Off campus	986	671	1657
Total	4548	855	5403

2) The table above represents the number of undergraduate and graduate students in a particular program at Bethesda University and whether those students live on campus or off campus. What is the probability that a randomly chosen student who lives on campus is a graduate student?

3) If Adele flips a coin twice, what is the probability that the coin will land heads-up both times?

4) If Adele randomly selects two coins from a purse containing three quarters, three dimes, and three nickels, what is the probability that both of the coins she selects will be quarters?

The **probability** of a single event happening is defined as the ratio $\frac{part}{whole}$, where the "part" is the number of favorable outcomes (i.e., outcomes that give you what you're seeking) and the "whole" is the total number of possible outcomes.

Example: A box contains 32 oranges and tangerines. If Elsa picks a piece of fruit at random from the box, the probability that she will pick an orange is equal to $\frac{3}{4}$. How many oranges are in the box?

$$\frac{\text{oranges}}{\text{total fruits}} = \frac{x}{32} = \frac{3}{4}$$

$$x = \frac{3}{4}(32) = \mathbf{24}$$

Be sure to **read carefully** so that the numbers in the problem end up in the right spots in the fraction.

Example: A toy bag contains 3 red marbles, 4 green marbles, 6 blue marbles, and 7 other toys. If an object is drawn at random from the bag, what is the probability that the object is a marble that is NOT green?

$$\frac{\text{non-green marbles}}{\text{total \# of items}} = \frac{3+6}{3+4+6+7} = \frac{\mathbf{9}}{\mathbf{20}}$$

Try It

1) What is the probability that a card drawn at random from a standard deck of 52 playing cards is a face card? (Note: a standard deck of playing cards contains a total of 12 face cards: 6 red and 6 black.)

2) What is the probability that a card drawn at random from a standard deck of 52 playing cards is a seven that is NOT black? (Note: a standard deck of playing cards contains a total of four sevens: two red and two black.)

Many probability problems on the SAT will be based on a table of data. For these, be very careful to line up which category is the "part" and which is the "whole" (it may not be the total represented by the entire table).

Example:

	Undergraduate students	Graduate students	Total
On campus	3562	184	3746
Off campus	986	671	1657
Total	4548	855	5403

The table above represents the number of undergraduate and graduate students in a particular program at Bethesda University and whether those students live on campus or off campus. What is the probability that a randomly chosen student who lives on campus is a graduate student?

$$\frac{\text{on-campus grad students}}{\text{all on-campus students}} = \frac{184}{3746} = 0.0491$$

TIP: The word "given" indicates the *whole*. For example, the campus problem could have been rewritten this way: *If a student is chosen at random, what is the probability that she lives on campus, given that she is a graduate student?*

Try It For the questions below, use the table shown in the example above.

3) What is the probability that a student chosen at random is an undergraduate student who lives off campus?

4) If an undergraduate student is chosen at random, what is the probability that he lives off campus?

(Hint: these two questions do <u>not</u> have the same answer.)

Some probability problems involve **multiple events**. Solve "and" problems by multiplying the individual probabilities of each of the events.

Example: *If Adele flips a coin twice, what is the probability that the coin will land heads-up both times?*

Probability of heads on 1st flip = $\frac{1}{2}$

Probability of heads on 2nd flip = $\frac{1}{2}$

$$\frac{1}{2} * \frac{1}{2} = \frac{1}{4}$$

Be sure to consider whether the outcomes of early events will affect the probabilities of the later events.

Example: *If Adele randomly selects two coins from a purse containing three quarters, three dimes, and three nickels, what is the probability that both of the coins she selects will be quarters?*

The first time she selects a coin, there are 3 quarters out of a total of 9 coins, so the probability of selecting a quarter is 3/9. Now there are 2 quarters left out of 8 remaining coins, so the probability of selecting a quarter the second time is 2/8. Therefore:

$$\frac{3}{9} * \frac{2}{8} = \frac{6}{72} = \frac{1}{12}$$

Try It   A bag contains 3 green marbles, 2 red marbles, and 5 black marbles.

5) If Malik draws a marble at random, returns it to the bag, and then draws a marble again, what is the probability that he will select a green marble both times?

6) If Malik draws a marble at random and then draws a second marble at random (without replacing the first one), what is the probability that he will select a green marble both times?

CHALLENGE:

Solve "or" problems either by writing out all of the possibilities or by calculating the probability of the event not happening at all and then subtracting that probability from 1.

Example: *If Adele flips a coin twice, what is the probability that the coin will land heads-up at least once?*

There are only four possible outcomes for two flips of a coin: heads-heads, heads-tails, tails-heads, or tails-tails. In three of those four outcomes, the coin has landed heads-up at least once. So the answer is

$$\frac{\text{\# of outcomes with at least one heads}}{\text{total \# of outcomes}} = \frac{3}{4}.$$

Alternatively, we can take advantage of the rule that the probability of something happening and the probability of it *not* happening will always add up to 1. Start by calculating the probability of the opposite outcome from the one we want: that is, what is the probability that the coin never lands heads-up at all? Since she's flipping the coin twice, that's the same thing as asking this: what's the probability that the coin will land tails-up twice in a row? That's easy: $\frac{1}{2} * \frac{1}{2} = \frac{1}{4}$. Therefore, the probability that this outcome *doesn't* happen (that is, the probability that the coin *does* land heads-up at least once) is $1 - \frac{1}{4} = \frac{3}{4}$.

Math: Problem Solving and Data Analysis

Practice Set 1: Easy-Medium

1

At a teachers' conference, a committee consists of 3 Spanish language teachers, 2 French language teachers, 6 math teachers, 5 history teachers, and 4 science teachers. If a committee member is chosen at random, what is the probability that the member chosen is NOT a language teacher?

A. 0.05
B. 0.25
C. 0.60
D. 0.75

2

A gift store sells 12 t-shirts and x tote bags in one day. If one of these products is selected at random, what is the probability that the product selected is a tote bag?

A. $\dfrac{x}{x+12}$
B. $\dfrac{12}{x+12}$
C. $\dfrac{x}{12}$
D. $\dfrac{12}{x}$

3

A bowl contains red, yellow, and purple lollipops. There are 18 yellow lollipops and 22 red lollipops. The probability of choosing a purple lollipop is $\dfrac{3}{7}$. How many purple lollipops are there in the bowl?

4

There are 720 juniors and seniors at a certain high school. A representative from either the junior or senior class is to be chosen at random. If the probability that a junior is chosen is 5/16, how many <u>seniors</u> are there at this school?

A. 200
B. 225
C. 312
D. 495

5

Liam rolls two standard dice. What is the probability that he rolls a double six?

A. $\dfrac{1}{36}$
B. $\dfrac{1}{12}$
C. $\dfrac{1}{6}$
D. $\dfrac{1}{3}$

6

The table below gives the results of a study of two groups of mice, Group A and Group B. The scientist recorded how many mice in each group were able to solve a puzzle in 1-2 attempts, 3-5 attempts, or 6 or more attempts and how many never solved it.

	1-2	3-5	6+	Never
Group A	9	14	6	2
Group B	13	11	7	0

If a mouse is chosen at random from those that solved the puzzle in 3-5 minutes, what is the probability that the mouse belongs to Group B?

A. 0.23
B. 0.35
C. 0.44
D. 0.56

Practice Set 2: Medium-Hard

1

A fair six-sided die will be rolled three times. Which of the following gives the probability that the outcome of the rolls will be a 2, then a 3, then a 4?

A. $\left(\frac{1}{6}\right)\left(\frac{1}{6}\right)\left(\frac{1}{6}\right)$

B. $\left(\frac{2}{6}\right)\left(\frac{3}{6}\right)\left(\frac{4}{6}\right)$

C. $\left(\frac{1}{6}\right)\left(\frac{1}{5}\right)\left(\frac{1}{4}\right)$

D. $\frac{1}{6} + \frac{1}{6} + \frac{1}{6}$

2

The bar graph below shows the distribution of ages among the 50 participants in a summer pre-college program.

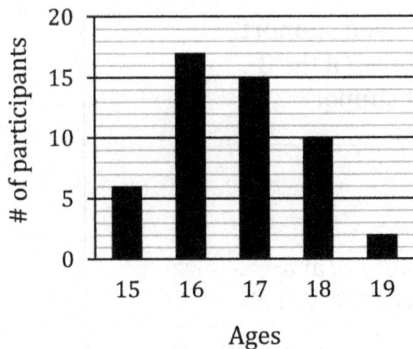

What is the probability that the age of a participant chosen at random was either 16 or 17?

A. $\frac{(15)(17)}{50}$

B. $\frac{(16)(17)}{50}$

C. $\frac{15 + 17}{50}$

D. $\frac{16 + 17}{50}$

3

If the probability that event X will occur twice is 0.84, what is the probability that event X will NOT occur twice?

A. 0
B. 0.16
C. 0.26
D. 0.71

4

Next year, Emma and Zoe will attend a school that has 4 different lunch periods. If each girl has an equal chance of being assigned to each lunch period, what is the probability that both will be assigned to the same lunch period?

5

Mr. Vega has to go through a certain intersection once a day on his way to work. Each time he goes through the intersection, the probability that he will hit a red light is 50%. What is the probability that Mr. Vega will hit a red light at least one day of a 5-day workweek?

A. 10%
B. 50%
C. 70%
D. 97%

Statistics

Preview Quiz:

Solve each of the following.

1) A random sample of 100 students was surveyed from a 500-student senior class. If 80 of the students surveyed planned to attend the homecoming dance, approximately how many seniors plan to attend?

2) In a random sample of 1000 dog owners in the United States, 75% were homeowners. Which of the following is an appropriate conclusion?

   A) Most US homeowners are dog owners.
   B) Most US dog owners are homeowners.
   C) Most people in the US own a dog, a home, or both.

3) A random sample of 500 voters was surveyed from a district of 2 million voters. 72% of those surveyed support Johnson for mayor, with a margin of error of 4%. Of the 2 million voters in the district, the percent that support Johnson for mayor is very likely to be between _____ and _____.

4) The mean GPA of a random sample of 200 students at a middle school was 3.1. The margin of error was 0.1. Which of the following is the best conclusion?

   A) It is likely that all students at the school have GPAs between 3.0 and 3.2.
   B) The mean GPA of the students at the school is likely to be between 3.0 and 3.2.
   C) No student at the school has a GPA below 3.0.

A common statistical technique when dealing with large populations is to study a smaller **sample** of the population and then extrapolate from those findings.

The simplest of these problems can be answered with a simple proportion.

Example: *A random sample of 100 students was surveyed from a 500-student senior class. If 80 of the students surveyed planned to attend the homecoming dance, approximately how many seniors plan to attend?*

$$\frac{80}{100} = \frac{x}{500}$$

$$x = 500\left(\frac{80}{100}\right)$$

$$x = \mathbf{400} \text{ seniors}$$

TIP:
For a review of proportions, see p. 352.

In order for the findings to be applicable to the larger group, the sample should be **random**. A **biased** sample is one that is not random.

What do we mean by random? Say we have a sample of 100 people. This sample is random if *every possible sample* of 100 people has an equal chance of being selected. Consider *who* was surveyed, *where* they were found, *how* they were approached, and any other methodology that might cause a particular subgroup to have a greater or lesser chance of inclusion than any other subgroup.

TIP:
The word "bias" in this context is distinct from its everyday usage. It simply means that the sample is not random; it does *not* imply that the people involved in the sampling have some sort of intentional prejudice against the group that's not adequately represented.

Try It   Are these random samples?

1) A mayor seeking information about his constituents puts a poll on the city website.

2) A company wants information about its workforce. Every worker whose employee ID number ends in 2 receives an interview.

3) A university wants to measure the level of interest its students have in the school's football team. It offers free tickets to the homecoming game to the first 100 students who volunteer to participate.

If the sample is random, we can draw a conclusion about the larger population that it's drawn from. But take care to identify precisely which group that is. That's the *only group* that we can use the sample to make reliable predictions about. Watch out for questions that apply the data to another population, even an apparently similar one.

Example: In a random sample of 1000 dog owners in the United States, 75% were homeowners. Which of the following is an appropriate conclusion?

A) Most US homeowners are dog owners.
B) Most US dog owners are homeowners.
C) Most people in the US own a dog, a home, or both.

The sample is drawn from dog owners in the United States, so that's the only population we can draw conclusions about. The answer is **B**.

Try It 4) A survey was mailed out to all 1200 people who earned a bachelor's degree from PM university in 2010. Two hundred of the responses came from physics majors, 146 of whom had gone on to grad school. If these 200 responses are a representative sample of the physics majors, what can be concluded?

A) Most PM graduates go on to grad school.
B) Most PM graduates from the class of 2010 went on to grad school.
C) Most PM graduates from the class of 2010 who majored in physics went on to grad school.

The **margin of error** is a way of estimating how close the sample's response is likely to be to the response of the population as a whole. The sample response, plus or minus the margin of error, is the range of the likely responses from the overall population.

Example: 60% of a sample answered "yes" to a survey question, where the margin of error was 3%. Therefore, the percent of the population as a whole who would answer "yes" to that question is very likely to be between 57% and 63%.

TIP:

When in doubt, check the strength of language of the answer choice. A choice that uses weaker language is more likely to be the right answer. For example, "X is associated with Y" is a better bet than "X causes Y," and "X *may* be associated with Y" is even better.

The smaller the sample size, the greater the margin of error.
Note that the size of the total population is *irrelevant* to the margin of error.

Example: *A random sample of 500 voters was surveyed from a district of 2 million voters. 72% of those surveyed support Johnson for mayor, with a margin of error of 4%.*

1. *Of the 2 million voters in the district, the percent that support Johnson for mayor is very likely to be between _____ and _____.*

    The actual percent should be 72 plus or minus 4: between **68%** and **76%.**

2. *If 1000 voters had been surveyed instead of 500, the margin of error would have been:*

    A) less than 4%.
    B) greater than 4%.
    C) equal to 4%.

    A *larger* sample size yields a *smaller* margin of error. The answer is **A**.

> **TIP:**
> Between sample size and bias, bias is generally the bigger deal. Think of it this way: if the sample is too small, the conclusion we can reliably draw about the larger population will be less precise than it could have been. But if the sample is not random, no reliable conclusion can be drawn at all.

The **type of conclusion** drawn from the sample also matters, because it's the only type of conclusion we can draw about the population as a whole. For example, if the result from the random sample was a mean, we can draw a conclusion about the mean of the larger population. Don't go beyond that to draw other kinds of conclusions.

Example: *The mean GPA of a random sample of 200 students at a middle school was 3.1. The margin of error was 0.1. Which of the following is the best conclusion?*

A) *It is likely that all students at the school have GPAs between 3.0 and 3.2.*
B) *The mean GPA of the students at the school is likely to be between 3.0 and 3.2.*
C) *No student at the school has a GPA below 3.0.*

The answer is **B**.

Math: Problem Solving and Data Analysis

Practice Set 1: Easy-Medium

1

A statistician interviewed a random sample of 200 Chesterton residents. Of those interviewed, 116 supported the proposed expansion of the community center. If there are a total of 35,700 Chesterton residents, which of the following is the most reasonable estimate for the number of residents who support the proposed expansion of the community center?

A. 11,600
B. 20,706
C. 23,200
D. 35,014

2

At a university, a researcher wants to evaluate the level of student satisfaction with the writing center. Which of the following study designs is most likely to result in a random sample of students at the university?

A. Survey the 100 students with the highest GPAs and the 100 students with the lowest GPAs
B. Survey 500 randomly selected English majors
C. Select 50 student ID numbers at random and then survey each student selected
D. On a randomly selected day, survey the first 200 students who enter the writing center

3

If a random sample of employees is selected from the shoe department of a Virginia department store and surveyed, which of the following is the largest population to which the results of the survey can be applied?

A. The employees in the sample
B. All shoe department employees at the department store
C. All employees at the department store
D. All shoe department employees in Virginia

4

In a survey conducted of a random sample of California residents, a researcher found that 19% of respondents had been born outside the state. The survey's margin of error was 3%. Which of the following is the best interpretation of these results?

A. The researcher is between 16% and 22% sure that the survey was accurate.
B. The percentage of California residents who were born outside the state cannot exceed 22%.
C. It is unlikely that the percentage of California residents who were born outside the state is less than 16% or more than 22%.
D. It is likely that between 16% and 22% of Americans were born outside the state in which they reside.

5

A statistician hypothesized that the general public's confidence in their own mathematics abilities varies widely from person to person. To test her theory, she surveyed 300 randomly selected pedestrians on the campus of an elite university. She found that 70% of those surveyed reported a moderate to high degree of confidence in their own mathematics abilities. Which of the following is the most accurate assessment of this survey?

A. The survey's results demonstrate that most people are at least moderately confident in their own mathematics abilities.
B. Because the survey's sample was not representative of the general public, it can be concluded that less than 70% of the general population are confident in their own mathematics abilities.
C. The survey design was inappropriate because the sample size was too small.
D. The survey's results may not be reliable because the sample was biased.

Practice Set 2: Medium-Hard

1

Holistic Healing Inc. wanted to research the effects of their new supervitamin, Supplement X, which is believed to reduce acne in young adults. A random sample of 1,200 young adults with acne was divided into two groups: half received Supplement X and half received a sugar pill. After six months, all participants from both groups were evaluated to measure any decreases in acne. Compared to the participants who had received the sugar pill, 60% more of the participants who had received Supplement X showed such a decrease. Which of the following is the most appropriate conclusion?

A. Supplement X decreases acne.
B. Supplement X decreases acne at least in young adults, but it may not have such an effect on other populations.
C. 60% of young adults with acne who take Supplement X are likely to experience a decrease in their acne within six months.
D. For young adults with acne, Supplement X use is associated with decreased acne, but it may not directly cause the decrease.

2

In a random sample of 50 action figures available for sale at a toy store, the mean selling price was $12.20, with a margin of error of $1.16. Which of the following can be inferred from these findings?

A. All action figures in the sample have a selling price between $11.04 and $13.36.
B. Most action figures at the store have a selling price between $11.04 and $13.36.
C. Any value between $11.04 and $13.36 is a plausible mean selling price of the action figures in the sample.
D. Any value between $11.04 and $13.36 is a plausible mean selling price of the action figures at the store.

3

A random sample of varsity athletes at Greendale High School was surveyed about their sleep habits. The sample included 50 soccer players, 65% of whom reported getting at least 8 hours of sleep per night. Which of the following can most reliably be inferred?

A. Most varsity athletes at Greendale High School get at least 8 hours of sleep per night.
B. Less than 35% of varsity soccer players at Greendale High School are sleep-deprived.
C. Most varsity soccer players at Greendale High School get at least 8 hours of sleep per night.
D. No students at Greendale High School get more than 8 hours of sleep per night.

4

In a survey of a random sample of 500 dog owners, 84% of respondents reported that they take their dog to the veterinarian once a year. Which of the following must be true?

I. 84% of dog owners take their dog to the veterinarian once a year.
II. If another randomly selected sample of 500 dog owners were surveyed, 84% would report that they take their dog to the veterinarian once a year.
III. If a random sample of 500 cat owners were surveyed, 84% would report that they take their cat to the veterinarian once a year.

A. None
B. II only
C. I and II only
D. I and III only

Geometry and Trigonometry
Area and Volume

Preview Quiz:

Solve each of the following.

1) A rectangle with a length of 4 centimeters has an area of 14 square centimeters. What is the width of the rectangle?

2) In the figure below, all edges intersect at right angles. What is the area of the shape?

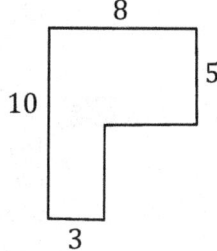

3) The figure below shows a rectangular prism with a length of 12 centimeters (cm), a width of 4 cm, and a height of 7 cm. What is the volume and what is the surface area of the prism?

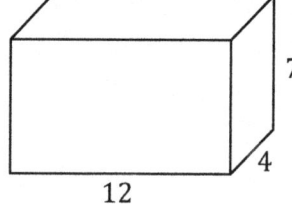

Area and Volume

Are you groaning at the thought of re-learning long-forgotten formulas? Good news: the SAT provides them for you at the beginning of each math module. Here's an advance look at the specific information that is provided:

REFERENCE

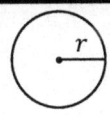 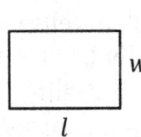 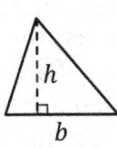 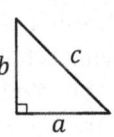 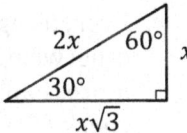

$A = \pi r^2$
$C = 2\pi r$ $A = lw$ $A = \frac{1}{2}bh$ $a^2 + b^2 = c^2$ Special right triangles

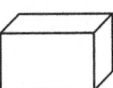 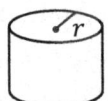  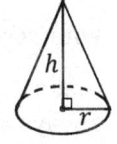 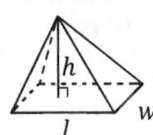

$V = lwh$ $V = \pi r^2 h$ $V = \frac{4}{3}\pi r^3$ $V = \frac{1}{3}\pi r^2 h$ $V = \frac{1}{3}lwh$

The number of degrees of arc in a circle is 360.
The number of radians of arc in a circle is 2π.
The sum of the measures in degrees of the angles of a triangle is 180.

FROM THE BLOG

The more you feel in control, the more confident you will be and the better you will do! As you go about your day and week and find yourself thinking about the SAT, try to imagine every scenario and every question and visualize HOW you will handle it. Don't imagine an easy test but rather some of the hard questions and weird things you have seen and what you would do: Plug in numbers? Speak up if the proctor makes an error. Move past a question that isn't clicking. Read purposefully S-L-O-W-L-Y to have a chance to figure things out.

Also, please do all you can to be excited for the test. Nerves are normal. We actually need some pressure to be at our best. Turning butterflies to a sense of nervous excitement harnesses that energy and puts it to work in a productive way.

Math: Geometry and Trigonometry

So how do you use it?

Draw it. If the problem hasn't provided a figure, draw one of your own. If the problem *has* provided a figure, jot down a quick copy on your scratch paper so you can draw and write on it as needed.

Trust the figures. Everything is drawn to scale unless the problem tells you otherwise, so trust what you see. If an angle looks like it's more than 90°, it is. You can often use that as a reality check for your answer, or as a way to eliminate choices if a problem really has you stumped.

Write out the formulas. In the testing software, look in the upper right corner of your screen for the $\boxed{\frac{x^2}{\text{Reference}}}$ button. You can click that at any time to see the list of geometry formulas, always a good place to start. When attacking a word problem, check that reference screen first, and write out any formulas you see that might be relevant to the problem. (Note that some problems may involve more than one formula.)

Fill in what you know. If the problem tells you that the height of a triangle is 5, jot that down on your sketch and plug 5 in for h in the equation you wrote down. Repeat that step for every measurement or value the problem has provided.

Take the next natural step. At this point, you will probably see something that you can calculate, even if it's not the value the question was ultimately asking for. Go ahead and calculate it! Then just see where it takes you. Often, you'll find that taking one step leads automatically to another step, which leads to another step, and before you know it you'll have solved the problem.

TIP:

On the SAT, everything is drawn to scale unless the problem tells you otherwise.

The **area** of a two-dimensional shape is a measure of how much space it takes up, while the **perimeter** is the length of the shape's outline. To find the perimeter of a polygon, simply add the lengths of all the sides. To find the perimeter of a circle (called the **circumference**), or to find the area of any simple two-dimensional shape, use the formulas shown in the reference section.

Example: In the figure below, the dimensions of the right triangle are given in inches (in). What is the perimeter and what is the area?

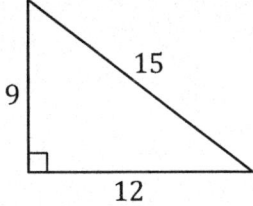

$$P = 9 + 12 + 15$$
$$P = 36 \text{ in}$$

The perimeter is **36 inches**.

$$A = \frac{1}{2}bh$$
$$A = \frac{1}{2}(12)(9)$$
$$A = 54 \text{ in}^2$$

The area is **54 square inches**.

Some problems will ask you to start with the area or perimeter and work backwards. Start by writing out the formula and plugging in whatever you know. Then use algebra to solve for the unknown values.

Example: A rectangle with a length of 4 centimeters has an area of 14 square centimeters. What is the width of the rectangle?

$$A = lw$$
$$14 = 4w$$
$$w = 14/4 = 3.5$$

The width is **3.5 centimeters**.

For other problems, you'll need to use algebraic expressions to represent the dimensions or other values. Start the same way: write out the formula, plug in what you know, and solve.

Example: *A certain rectangle has an area of 72. If the length is twice the width, what is the width of the rectangle?*

You might start this one by drawing a rectangle. Label the width as w and the length as $2w$. Then set up your equation:

$$A = lw$$
$$72 = (2w)(w)$$
$$72 = 2w^2$$
$$36 = w^2$$
$$\mathbf{6 = w}$$

TIP:
These types of problems are also good for back-solving.

Try It — Consult the formulas from p. 391 as needed as you solve. If your answer contains a π, include the π in your answer. (For example, an area of 10π should be given as 10π, not as 31.4159.)

1) What is the area, in square meters, of a circle with a radius of 9 meters?

2) A rectangle has a width of 4 inches and an area of 36 square inches. What is the perimeter of the rectangle, in inches?

3) What is the area of a square whose perimeter is 40?

Some problems ask how many of one shape can fit into another shape. Since area is a measure of how much space something takes up, you can solve these problems by **dividing** the area of the larger shape by the area of the smaller shape.

> **Try It**   4) How many squares of area 25 in² can be cut out of a rectangle with length 10 in and width 320 in?

The SAT will sometimes ask about a shape whose formulas are not provided in the reference section. To find the area, look to draw lines on the shape to split it into simpler shapes. Then find the areas of each of those and add them together.

Example: In the figure below, all edges intersect at right angles. What is the area of the shape?

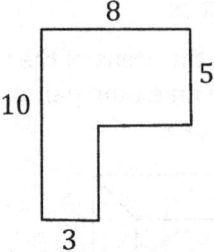

We can draw a single line on this figure to divide it into two rectangles. Draw it that way, and be sure to adjust the dimensions accordingly:

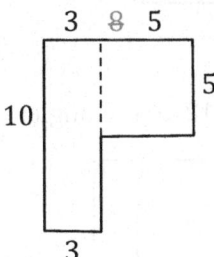

The area of the left rectangle is $10(3) = 30$. The area of the right rectangle is $5(5) = 25$. Therefore, the area of the shape is $30 + 25 = $ **55**.

> **Try It**   5) What is the perimeter of the shape used in the example above?

The **volume** of a three-dimensional shape is a measure of the three-dimensional shape it takes up. Its **surface area** is the sum of the areas of all its faces.

Example: The figure below shows a rectangular prism with a length of 12 centimeters (cm), a width of 4 cm, and a height of 7 cm. What is the volume and what is the surface area of the prism?

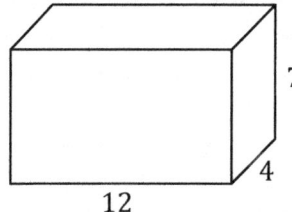

Start by writing out the formula for volume of a rectangular prism (provided in the reference section):

$$V = lwh$$
$$V = (12)(4)(7)$$
$$V = 336 \text{ cm}^3$$

The volume is **336 cubic centimeters**.

To find the surface area, we'll need the areas of the six rectangles that make up this prism. Take them one matching pair at a time. The front and the back are each a 12×7 rectangle:

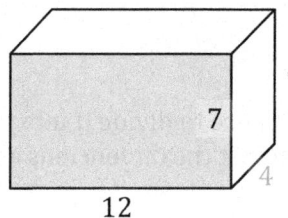

The top and the bottom are each a 12×4 rectangle:

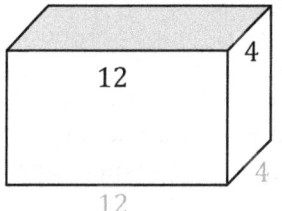

And the left and right ends are each a 7×4 rectangle:

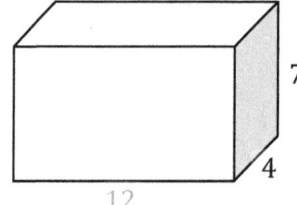

So the total surface area will be the sums of the areas of two 12×7 rectangles, two 12×4 rectangles, and two 7×4 rectangles:

$$SA = 2(12*7) + 2(12*4) + 2(7*4)$$
$$SA = 2(84) + 2(48) + 2(28)$$
$$SA = 320$$

The surface area is **320 square centimeters**.

Try It   Consult the formulas from p. 391 as needed as you solve.

6) What is the volume of a cylinder with a radius of 3 and a height of 10?

7) What is the surface area of a cube whose volume is 1000?

8) A cone with a volume of 32π has a height of 6. What is the radius of the cone's base?

9) How many cubes of side length 2 cm would fit into a rectangular prism with dimensions 6 cm by 4 cm by 10 cm?

Math: Geometry and Trigonometry

Practice Set 1: Easy-Medium

1

x ▭ 0.75

Note: figure not drawn to scale.

If the rectangle above has an area of 1, what is the value of x?

A. $\frac{1}{2}$

B. $\frac{3}{4}$

C. $\frac{4}{3}$

D. 12

2

A rectangle with a length of 8 meters has an area of 12 square meters. What is the width, in meters, of the rectangle?

A. 1.5
B. 2
C. 2.5
D. 4

3

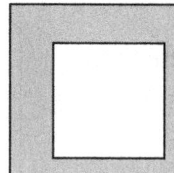

The picture above shows a square with side of length 3 completely enclosed within a square with side of length 4.5. What is the area of the shaded region?

4

What is the area of the pentagon shown below?

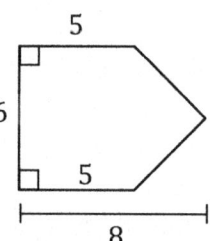

A. 25
B. 39
C. 41
D. 48

5

The volume of a certain rectangular prism is 120 cubic centimeters. If the width of the prism is 6 centimeters and the height is $\sqrt{50}$ centimeters, what is the length of the prism, in centimeters?

A. $\sqrt{7}$
B. $2\sqrt{2}$
C. 4
D. $2\sqrt{15}$

6

The figure below shows the foundation for a new building. All intersecting line segments are perpendicular, and all given dimensions are in meters.

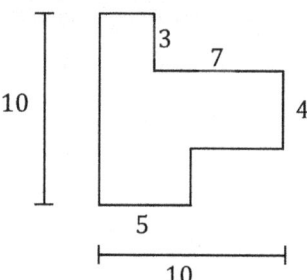

What is the perimeter of the foundation, in meters?

A. 20
B. 29
C. 34
D. 40

7

What is the area of a circle with a circumference of 16π?

A. 8π
B. 16π
C. 32π
D. 64π

8

On a garden wall, an artist creates a rectangular mosaic that is 20 feet long and 4 feet high. The mosaic is created using n individual square tiles, each 6 <u>inches</u> by 6 <u>inches</u>. What is the value of n?

(Note: 1 foot = 12 inches)

9

In the figure below, the height of the cylinder is 6 cm, and the radius of the base has length 4 cm. What is the surface area of the cylinder, in square cm?

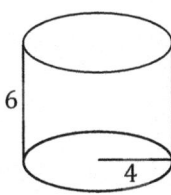

(Note: the surface area S of a cylinder with radius r and height h is given by the formula $S = 2\pi r^2 h + 2\pi r h$.)

A. 96π
B. 144π
C. 240π
D. 384π

10

In the figure below, a square is circumscribed about a circle.

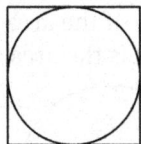

If the perimeter of the square is 24, what is the area of the circle?

A. 6π
B. 9π
C. 12π
D. 16π

11

Which of the following expressions gives the volume of a rectangular solid with length $x + 3$, width $x - 3$, and height 2?

A. $2x - 6$
B. $2x + 2$
C. $2x^2$
D. $2x^2 - 18$

12

In the figure below, three circles of equal size are inscribed in rectangle $ABCD$.

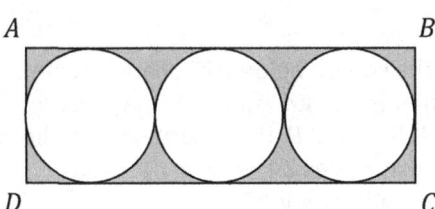

If rectangle $ABCD$ has a width of 2 and a length of 6, what is the area of the shaded region?

A. $12 - \pi$
B. $12 - 2\pi$
C. $12 - 3\pi$
D. $12 - 6\pi$

Math: Geometry and Trigonometry

Practice Set 2: Medium-Hard

1

Point O is the center of the circle pictured below. If the area of triangle MNO is 6, what is the area of circle O?

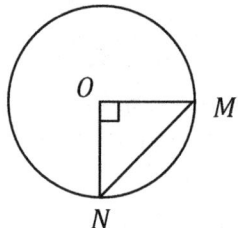

A. 3π
B. 6π
C. $4\sqrt{3}\pi$
D. 12π

2

How many small cubes with a surface area of 96 square inches can be cut from a solid wood cube whose surface area is 384 square inches?

3

In the square below, the shaded region is bounded by 4 equal arcs with centers at A, B, C, and D. If the perimeter of the square equals 24, what is the area of the shaded region?

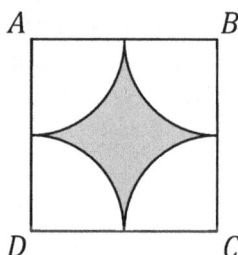

A. $36 - 6\pi$
B. $36 - 9\pi$
C. $24 - 6\pi$
D. $21 - 6\pi$

4

In the figure below, square $ABCD$ shares one vertex with triangle CEF. $\overline{AD}$ and $\overline{EF}$ are both congruent and collinear.

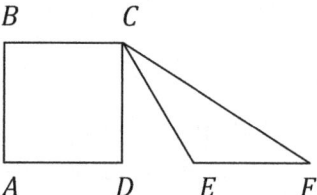

If the area of square $ABCD$ is 10, what is the area of triangle CEF?

A. 3
B. 5
C. 6
D. 12

5

An elementary school teacher has three geometric shapes: a blue rectangle, a green rectangle, and a yellow square. The blue rectangle has a length of 6 inches and a perimeter of 20 inches. The width of the green rectangle is twice the width of the blue rectangle, while the length of the green rectangle is the same as the side length of the yellow square. If the area of the yellow square is 25 square inches, what is the area of the green rectangle, in square inches?

6

A circle with diameter d has the same area as a square with side length 3. Which of the following is closest to the value of d?

A. 1.91
B. 2.86
C. 3.39
D. 5.73

7

The rectangular picture frame shown below has a width of x inches and a height of $x + 2$ inches. When a picture is placed in the frame, the edges of the picture are covered by the frame's border, which has a uniform width of 1 inch on all sides. Which of the following gives the area, in square inches, of the portion of the picture NOT covered by the border?

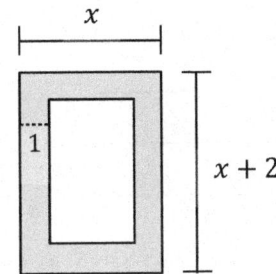

A. $x(x - 2)$
B. $x(x + 2)$
C. $(x - 2)(x + 1)$
D. $4x$

8

Rectangle $ABCD$ has length 8 and perimeter 22. If diagonal $\overline{AC}$ is drawn, the rectangle is split into two congruent right triangles. What is the area of right triangle ABC?

9

$ABCD$ is a square with sides of length 8. Point E is the midpoint of $\overline{AD}$, and point F is the midpoint of $\overline{BC}$.

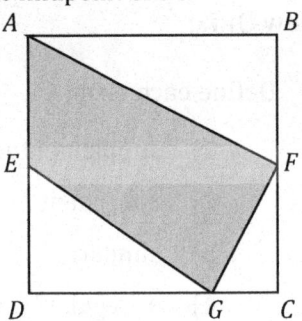

What is the ratio of the area of the shaded region to the area of the square?

A. 1:2
B. 3:4
C. 7:10
D. 9:16

10

A warehouse worker has to pack 100 small boxes of dimension 2 inches by 3 inches by 4 inches into one larger box. Which of the following could be the dimension of the larger box if all 100 boxes fit into the larger box perfectly with no space left over?

A. 20" × 30" × 40"
B. 10" × 12" × 20"
C. 10" × 15" × 24"
D. 8" × 27" × 64"

11

The side length of square A is 3 inches less than twice the side length of square B. If square B has an area of x in², which of the following gives the area of square A?

A. $0.25(x + 6\sqrt{x} + 9)$
B. $x - 6\sqrt{x} + 9$
C. $4x - 12\sqrt{x} + 9$
D. $x^2 - 6x + 9$

Angles, Lines, and Triangles

Preview Quiz:

Define each term:

1) supplementary: _____
2) congruent: _____
3) similar: _____
4) a "regular" polygon: _____
5) an isosceles triangle: _____
6) an equilateral triangle: _____

If two lines intersect, what is the relationship between:

7) the adjacent angles? _____
8) the vertical angles? _____

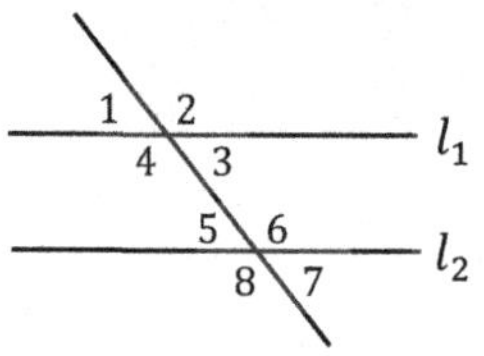

Lines l_1 and l_2 are parallel. Which angles are:

9) congruent? _____
10) supplementary? _____

Fill in the blanks:

11) The formula for the sum of the interior angles of an n-sided polygon is _____

12) The third side of the triangle rule is _____

Pick any point along a straight line, and that point can be defined as a 180-degree angle (also called a **straight angle**). If you draw new line segments out from that point, you're splitting that 180° angle into multiple pieces; thus, the newly created angles must add up to 180°.

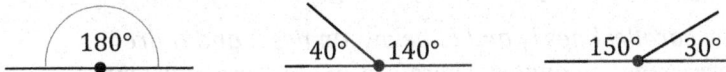

Angles that are next to each other on a straight line, such as in the examples above, are called **adjacent** angles. Adjacent angles are always **supplementary**, meaning their degree measures add up to 180°.

When two lines intersect, the angles that are across from each other are called **opposite angles** or **vertical angles**. Opposite angles are always **congruent** (equal) to each other.

Example: In the figure, angle A is congruent to angle D, and angle B is congruent to angle C.

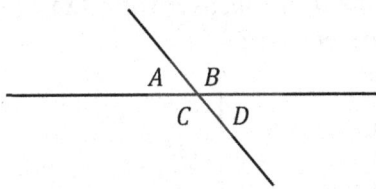

> **TIP:**
> Some other useful terms:
> - **perpendicular**: intersecting at a 90° angle
> - **bisect**: to divide into two equal parts

Parallel lines never intersect each other. When two parallel lines are intersected by another line (called a **transversal**), six angles are created; some of these are congruent to each other, while others are supplementary.

Example: If lines l_1 and l_2 are parallel in the figure below, then:
- *All the even-numbered angles are congruent.*
- *All the odd-numbered angles are congruent.*
- *Each even-numbered angle is supplementary to each odd-numbered angle.*

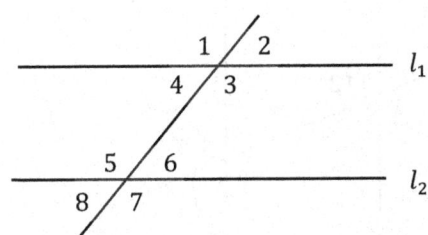

Math: Geometry and Trigonometry

At some point, you probably had to memorize a bunch of these angle relationships for a math class in school: *alternate exterior angles, same-side interior angles,* etc. There's no need for all that on the SAT. Make it simple: look for angles that are in the same position as each other relative to their respective lines. These are called **corresponding angles**, and they are always congruent.

Example: For parallel lines l_1 and l_2 below, angles A and B are corresponding angles. Therefore, angle A is congruent to angle B.

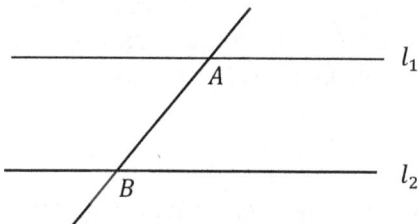

Once you find the corresponding angles, you can use them to determine lots of other angle relationships.

Example: In the figure below, $\overline{XZ}$ intersects parallel lines $\overline{AB}$ and $\overline{CD}$ at points X and Y. If the measure of ∠AXY is 112°, what is the measure of ∠DYZ?

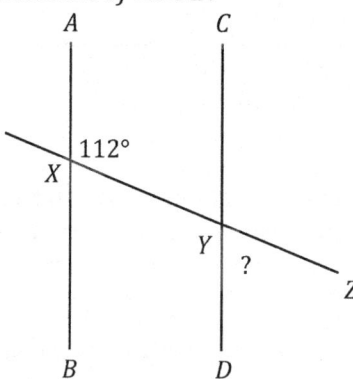

First, find the corresponding angle for the one we know. Here, that's ∠CYZ:

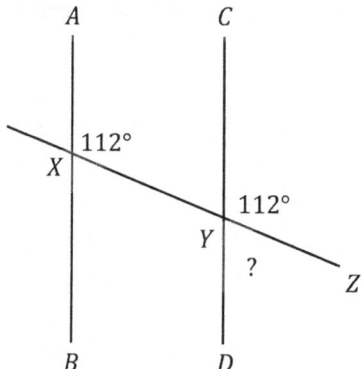

Now, what's the relationship of ∠CYZ and ∠DYZ? They're adjacent to each other, so they must add up to 180°. Therefore, the measure of ∠DYZ must be $180 - 112 = \mathbf{68°}$.

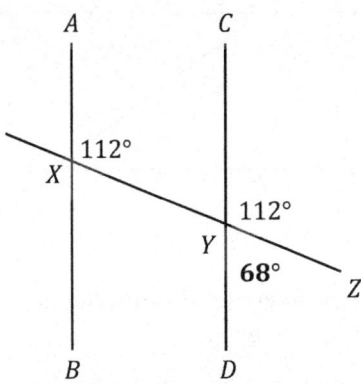

To make it easier to find those corresponding angles, try extending the lines of the figure.

Example: In parallelogram ABCD below, the measure of angle A is 155°, and point D lies on $\overline{EC}$. What is the measure of ∠ADE?

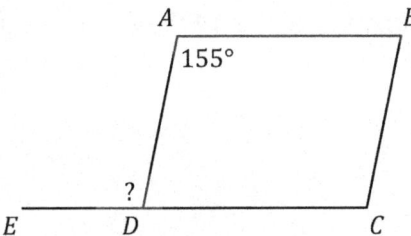

Start by redrawing the figure with lines $\overline{AD}$ and $\overline{EC}$ extended. Do you see a spot that corresponds to our 155° angle? Go ahead and fill it in.

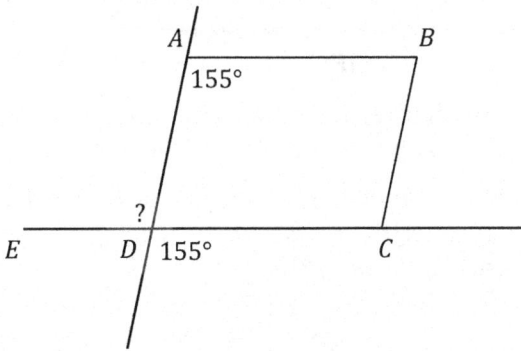

That angle is across from ∠ADE. So, since opposite angles are congruent, the measure of ∠ADE must also be **155°**.

Try It

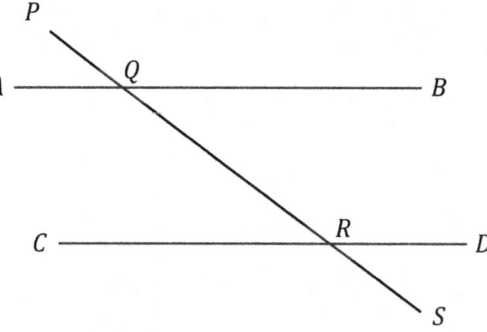

In the figure above, transversal $\overline{PS}$ intersects the parallel lines $\overline{AB}$ and $\overline{CD}$ at points Q and R, respectively.

1) Name three angles that are congruent to ∠AQP.

2) If the measure of ∠AQR is 144°, what is the measure of ∠SRD?

TIP:

Angles can be named with three letters or with one. In the three-letter format, the vertex is always the letter in the middle.

Example: The angle shown below could be referred to as ∠P, as ∠QPR, or as ∠RPQ. It <u>cannot</u> be referred to as ∠PQR.

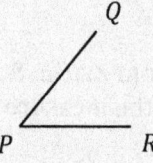

The interior angles of a triangle always add up to 180 degrees. For other polygons, the sum of the interior angles equals $180(n - 2)$, where n is the number of sides.

Example: What is the sum of the interior angles of a pentagon?
$180(5 - 2) = \mathbf{540}$

In a **regular polygon**, all sides have the same length and all angles have the same degree measure.

Try It Solve each of the following.

3) What is the sum of the interior angles of a hexagon?

4) What is the degree measure of one interior angle of a regular hexagon?

An **acute angle** measures less than 90 degrees, a **right angle** measures exactly 90 degrees, and an **obtuse angle** measures more than 90 degrees.

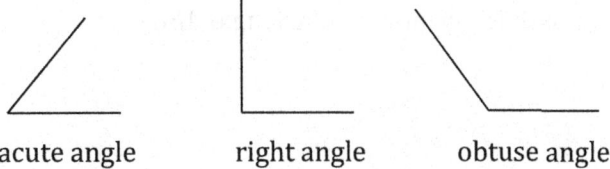

acute angle   right angle   obtuse angle

These terms also apply to triangles: an **acute triangle** contains only acute angles, a **right triangle** contains one right angle, and an **obtuse triangle** contains one obtuse angle.

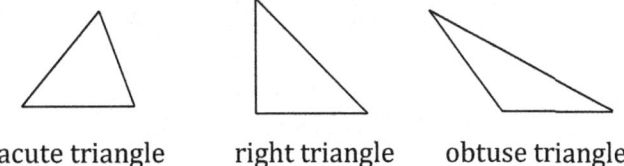

acute triangle   right triangle   obtuse triangle

> **TIP:**
> Because the interior angles of a triangle always add up to 180 degrees, these are the only possibilities. No triangle can ever have more than one obtuse angle or more than one right angle.

Math: Geometry and Trigonometry

In a **scalene** triangle, all three sides have different lengths, and all three angles have different degree measures. In an **isosceles** triangle, two of the side lengths are the same, and two of the angles are the same (the ones across from the matching sides). In an **equilateral** triangle, all three side lengths are the same, and all three angles are the same: each angle measures 180/3 = 60 degrees.

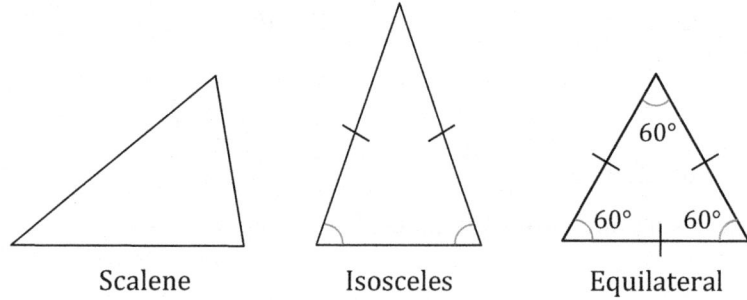

Scalene Isosceles Equilateral

You can make some inferences about triangle side lengths based on their angles. The sides go in order: the largest side of the triangle is always across from the largest angle, the second-largest side is across from the second-largest angle, and so on.

Try It Solve each of the following.

5) In isosceles triangle ABC, two of the side lengths are 5 and 6. What are the two possible perimeters of triangle ABC?

6) The hypotenuse of right triangle XYZ has a length of 10 inches. Which of the following could be the perimeter, in inches, of triangle XYZ? ***Choose all that apply.***

A) 10
B) 24
C) 30
D) 36

The **third side of the triangle rule** is a limit on the size of an unknown side length. Each side of a triangle must be *less* than the sum of the other two sides and *greater* than the positive difference of those other two sides.

Example: Triangle XYZ has side lengths 4, 6, and x. If x is an integer, what are the possible values of x?

$6 - 4 < x < 4 + 6$
$2 < x < 10$

The remaining side length must be greater than 2 and less than 10. Since x is an integer (a whole number), the only possible values for x are **3, 4, 5, 6, 7, 8, or 9**.

Congruent triangles are identical triangles: they have the same angle measurements as each other and the same side lengths as each other. **Similar triangles** have the same angle measurements as each other but different side lengths: specifically, their side lengths are **proportional**. Solve by setting up a proportion that matches up the corresponding sides.

TIP:
For a review of proportions, see p. 352.

Example: In the figure below, the smaller triangle is similar to the larger triangle. What is the value of x?

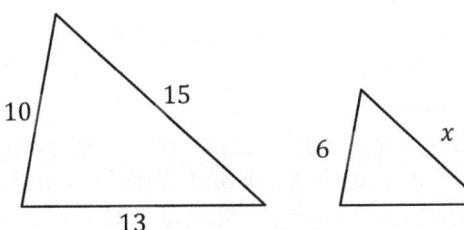

$$\frac{6}{10} = \frac{x}{15}$$

$$\frac{6}{10}(15) = x$$

$$9 = x$$

Many problems involving similar triangles will start off with a complicated diagram showing several overlapping triangles. Redraw the figure on your scratch paper and look for parallel lines, vertical angles, or any other hints that two or more angles match each other; indicate those on your drawing. Next, **redraw the figure as two separate triangles**. This will make it a lot easier to line up the sides correctly.

Example: In the figure below, $\overline{BD}$ is parallel to $\overline{AE}$. What is the value of x?

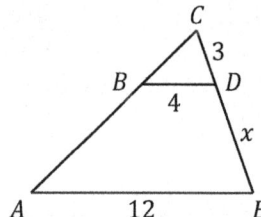

Redraw the figure as two separate triangles to make it easier to see the relationships.

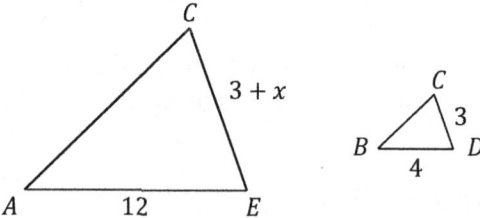

Because of the parallel lines, angle A in triangle ACE must be the same degree measure as angle B in triangle BCD, and angle E in triangle ACE must be the same degree measure as angle D in triangle BCD. Both triangles have angle C, so all the angles match: these are similar triangles. Therefore, we can set up a proportion to solve:

$$\frac{12}{4} = \frac{3+x}{3}$$
$$3(12) = 4(3+x)$$
$$36 = 12 + 4x$$
$$24 = 4x$$
$$\mathbf{6 = x}$$

Try It Solve each of the following.

7) Triangle PQR has side lengths of 5, 6, and 7 inches. Triangle XYZ also has side lengths of 5, 6, and 7 inches. Which of the following statements is correct?

    A) PQR and XYZ are congruent triangles.
    B) PQR and XYZ are similar triangles but not necessarily congruent.
    C) PQR and XYZ are not necessarily either similar or congruent.

In the figure below, $\overline{BE}$ and $\overline{AD}$ intersect at C, and $\overline{BA}$ is parallel to $\overline{DE}$.

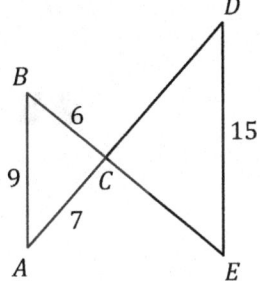

8) ∠BCA is congruent to ∠ _____

9) ∠BAC is congruent to ∠ _____

10) ∠ABC is congruent to ∠ _____

11) What is the length of $\overline{CE}$? _____

FROM THE BLOG

When reviewing missed questions, there are three big things to consider.

- **Content.** Did you honestly not know the necessary material to answer the question?
- **Process.** Is there a more strategic way you could have approached the problem?
- **Anxiety.** Upon review, does it seem that you really should have gotten that right? Was your mind occupied with other test-takers in the room? Were you concerned that you were "behind" and obsessing over catching up? Were you still stressing out over a previous question that you missed?

These factors can all impact your performance, and they can *all* be addressed. The important thing is to think strategically about how to attack the issues that have the greatest effect on *you*.

Math: Geometry and Trigonometry

Practice Set 1: Easy-Medium

1

In the figure below, a logo consists of two equilateral triangles that share one vertex. The given side lengths are in inches. What is the perimeter, in inches, of the entire logo?

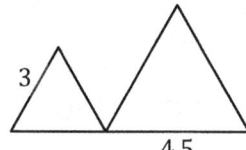

2

In the figure below, points K and L lie on line segment $\overline{JM}$.

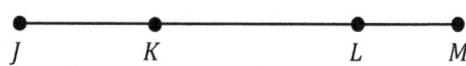

If $JL = 10$, $JM = 13$, and $JK = 4$, what is the length of $\overline{KM}$?

A. 7
B. 8
C. 9
D. 10

3

In the figure below, $\overline{XY}$ intersects parallel line segments $\overline{AB}$ and $\overline{CD}$ at points Q and R, respectively. If the measure of $\angle CRX$ is 42°, what is the measure of $\angle AQY$?

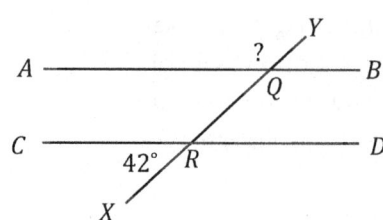

A. 42°
B. 126°
C. 138°
D. 142°

4

What is the length of $\overline{MQ}$ in triangle MPQ below?

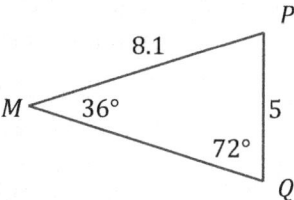

A. 5
B. 6.8
C. 7.5
D. 8.1

5

In the figure below, point R lies on $\overline{QS}$, $\angle QPR$ measures 66°, and $\angle PRS$ measures 153°. What is the measure of $\angle PQR$?

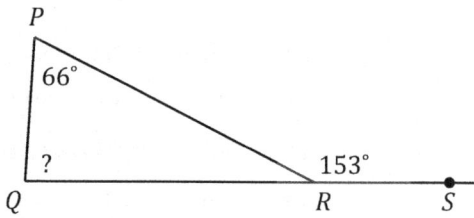

A. 24°
B. 72°
C. 87°
D. 114°

6

Andre uses a computer to draw a regular nonagon (a 9-sided polygon). What is the measure, in degrees, of one interior angle of the nonagon?

7. What is the perimeter of parallelogram WXYZ?

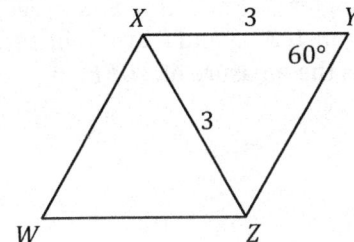

- A. 12
- B. $6\sqrt{3}$
- C. 9
- D. $3\sqrt{3}$

8. In the figure below, a circle has been divided into 8 congruent sectors by lines that all pass through the circle's center, creating 8 central angles that each measure $x°$. What is the value of x?

9. In the parallelogram below, what is the value of x?

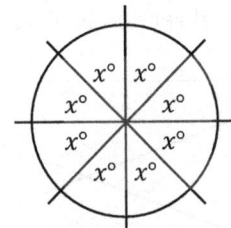

- A. 40
- B. 60
- C. 80
- D. 90

10. In the figure below, $\overline{BD}$ is parallel to $\overline{AE}$, point B lies on $\overline{AC}$, and point D lies on $\overline{CE}$. The lengths given are in centimeters. What is the length, in centimeters, of $\overline{CE}$?

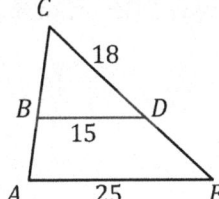

- A. 20
- B. 24
- C. 27
- D. 30

11. In triangle ACD, shown below, $\overline{AC} \cong \overline{AD}$, $\overline{AC} \perp \overline{AD}$, $\overline{BE}$ bisects $\overline{AD}$, and $\overline{BE} \parallel \overline{CD}$. What is the measure of $\angle BED$?

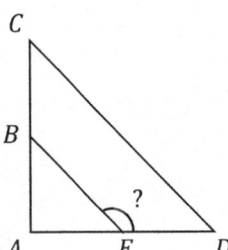

- A. 45°
- B. 75°
- C. 105°
- D. 135°

12. Points $A, B, C,$ and D lie on a line segment in that order, such that B bisects $\overline{AC}$ and C bisects $\overline{BD}$. If the length of $\overline{BC}$ is 4, what is the length of $\overline{AD}$?

- A. 4
- B. 6
- C. 8
- D. 12

Math: Geometry and Trigonometry

Practice Set 2: Medium-Hard

1

The town of Bellmore is 8 miles from the town of Cedarhurst and 2 miles from the town of Farmingdale. Which of the following could NOT be the distance between Cedarhurst and Farmingdale?

A. 5 miles
B. 6 miles
C. 7 miles
D. 9 miles

2

If line l is parallel to line m, what is the value of x?

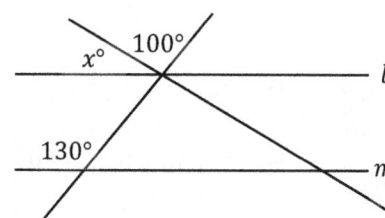

3

In the figure below, $\overline{BD}$ is a diagonal of trapezoid $ABCD$, where $\overline{AD}$ and $\overline{BC}$ are parallel. If $\angle BAD$ measures $43°$ and $\angle DBC$ measures $65°$, what is the measure of $\angle ABD$?

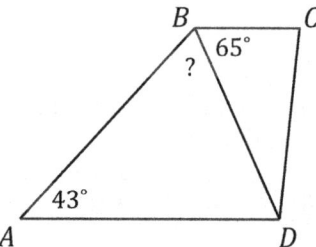

A. $25°$
B. $47°$
C. $65°$
D. $72°$

4

In the figure below, $ABCDE$ is a regular pentagon. If A, E, and F are collinear, what is the measure of $\angle DEF$, in degrees?

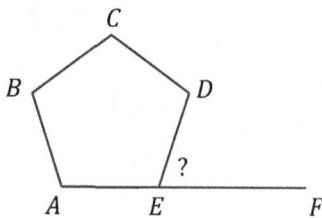

5

In the figure below, points P and Q lie on one side of rectangle $MNRS$.

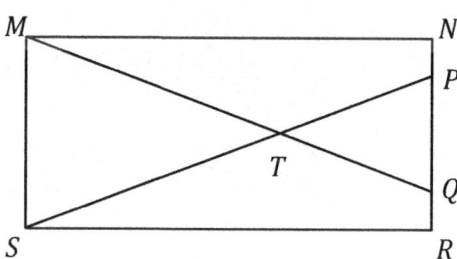

If the length of $\overline{MS}$ is 11, the length of $\overline{PQ}$ is 7, and the length of $\overline{MT}$ is 16, what else can be concluded?

A. The length of $\overline{TQ}$ is $\dfrac{112}{11}$.

B. The length of $\overline{TP}$ is $\dfrac{112}{11}$.

C. The length of $\overline{ST}$ is $\dfrac{77}{16}$.

D. The length of $\overline{ST}$ is $\dfrac{176}{7}$.

6

In the figure below, triangle ABC is similar to triangle DEF, where each side of triangle DEF is 3 times the length of the corresponding side of triangle ABC.

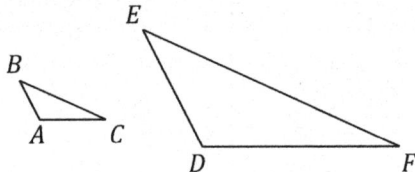

If the smallest angle in triangle DEF measures 24°, what is the measure of the smallest angle in triangle ABC?

A. 8°
B. 24°
C. 66°
D. 72°

7

In the figure below, the horizontal bases of the two triangles are parallel.

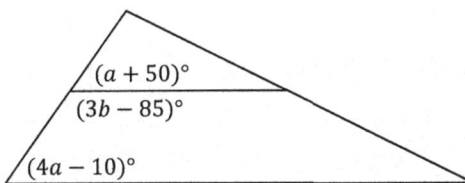

What is the value of $a + b$?

8

In the figure below, what is the average (arithmetic mean) of a and b?

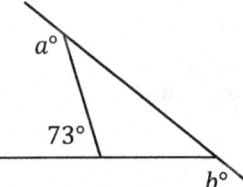

A. 36.5°
B. 86°
C. 107°
D. 143.5°

9

Which of the following statements, if true, is independently sufficient to prove that $l \parallel p$ in the figure below?

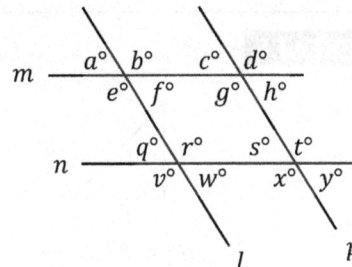

A. $c = h$
B. $f = w$
C. $q = s$
D. $d = y$

10

If two of the angles of a triangle measure 42° and 48°, the triangle must be which of the following?

A. scalene right
B. scalene acute
C. isosceles acute
D. isosceles obtuse

11

Skew lines are lines that neither intersect nor lie in the same plane. In the prism shown below, each of the six rectangular faces is perpendicular to both hexagonal bases. Which of the following line segments is skew to $\overline{AB}$?

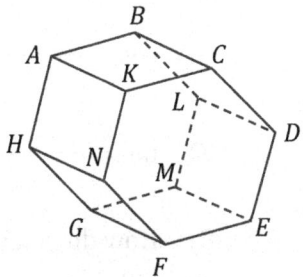

A. $\overline{AH}$
B. $\overline{GM}$
C. $\overline{FE}$
D. $\overline{ME}$

Right Triangles and Trigonometry

The relevant provided formulas:

REFERENCE

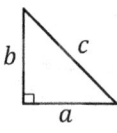
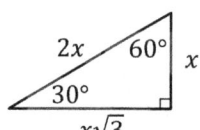

$a^2 + b^2 = c^2$ Special right triangles

Preview Quiz:

Solve:

1) A right triangle has the side lengths shown. What is the value of x?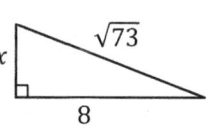

2) Name three common Pythagorean triples:

3) What is the length of the hypotenuse of a 45-45-90 triangle with a leg of length 5?

4) What is the perimeter of a 30-60-90 triangle with a hypotenuse of 8?

Fill in the blanks:

5) $\sin = \dfrac{O}{H}$ _____

6) $\cos = \dfrac{A}{H}$ _____

7) $\tan = \dfrac{O}{A}$ _____

8) How do you use the inverse trig functions $\sin^{-1}$, $\cos^{-1}$, and $\tan^{-1}$?

9) If $\cos 81° = 0.156$, then $\sin 9° =$ _____

A **right triangle** consists of two **legs**, each of which is across from an acute angle, and one **hypotenuse**, which is across from a right angle.

For any right triangle with legs of lengths a and b and a hypotenuse of length c, the **Pythagorean Theorem** states that $a^2 + b^2 = c^2$.

Example: What is the length of the shorter leg in the right triangle shown?

$(x)^2 + (8)^2 = (\sqrt{73})^2$
$x^2 + 64 = 73$
$x^2 = 9$
$x = \mathbf{3}$

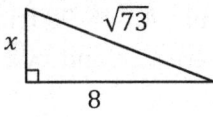

TIP:
Because the largest angle in a triangle is always across from the largest side, the hypotenuse is always the longest side in any right triangle.

Try It

1) What is the area of the right triangle shown?

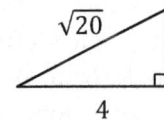

2) Which of the following gives the length of the hypotenuse of a right triangle with legs of length k and n?

A) $k^2 + n^2$
B) $\sqrt{k^2 + n^2}$
C) $k^2 - n^2$
D) $\sqrt{k^2 - n^2}$

You can save yourself some time by memorizing a few **Pythagorean triples**, which are sets of three whole numbers that happen to satisfy the Pythagorean theorem. For example, $\{3, 4, 5\}$ is a Pythagorean triple, because $3^2 + 4^2 = 5^2$. Some other helpful triples are $\{5, 12, 13\}$ and $\{8, 15, 17\}$. Note that multiples of these patterns work too.

Example: What is the hypotenuse of the triangle shown below?

This is a multiple of a 3-4-5 triangle. Because the legs are $4(3) = 12$ and $4(4) = 16$, the hypotenuse must be $4(5) = \mathbf{20}$.

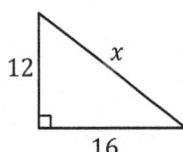

Included in the reference section are the unique patterns of side lengths for the **special right triangles**. You can use these as a shortcut to quickly answer many questions involving 30-60-90 triangles or 45-45-90 triangles.

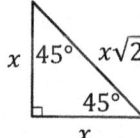

Example: What is the hypotenuse of the triangle shown?

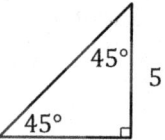

See the reference triangle on the left: the sides of a 45-45-90 triangle, from smallest to largest, are x, x, and $x\sqrt{2}$. Therefore:

$$x = 5$$
$$\text{hypotenuse} = x\sqrt{2} = \mathbf{5\sqrt{2}}$$

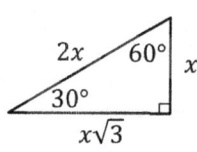

Example: What is the perimeter of the triangle shown?

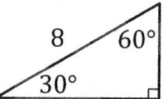

See the reference triangle on the left: the sides of a 30-60-90 triangle, from smallest to largest, are x, $x\sqrt{3}$, and $2x$. Therefore:

$$\text{hypotenuse} = 2x = 8$$
$$x = 4 = \text{shorter leg}$$
$$x\sqrt{3} = 4\sqrt{3} = \text{longer leg}$$
$$\text{Perimeter} = 8 + 4 + 4\sqrt{3} = \mathbf{12 + 4\sqrt{3}}$$

Try It

3) What is the area of an isosceles right triangle with hypotenuse $6\sqrt{2}$?

4) The equilateral triangle below has side length 4 and height h. What is the value of h?

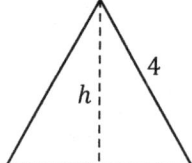

The trigonometric functions **sine**, **cosine**, and **tangent** can be defined as ratios of specific side lengths in a right triangle. The acronym **SOH-CAH-TOA** is a way to remember the relationships. For example, the TOA portion means that the <u>t</u>angent of any angle is equal to the length of the <u>o</u>pposite leg (the leg across from that angle) divided by the length of the <u>a</u>djacent leg (the other leg in the triangle).

Here are all the ratios:

SOH	CAH	TOA
$\sin = \dfrac{\text{opposite}}{\text{hypotenuse}}$	$\cos = \dfrac{\text{adjacent}}{\text{hypotenuse}}$	$\tan = \dfrac{\text{opposite}}{\text{adjacent}}$

Be careful to line up which leg is the *opposite* and which one is the *adjacent* for the particular angle the question is asking about.

Example: In the right triangle shown below:

$\sin x = \dfrac{4}{5}$ $\qquad\qquad$ $\sin y = \dfrac{3}{5}$

$\cos x = \dfrac{3}{5}$ $\qquad\qquad$ $\cos y = \dfrac{4}{5}$

$\tan x = \dfrac{4}{3}$ $\qquad\qquad$ $\tan y = \dfrac{3}{4}$

> **TIP:**
> The inverse trig functions $\sin^{-1}$, $\cos^{-1}$, and $\tan^{-1}$ allow you to use these values to find the degree measure of the angles.
>
> For example, since $\sin y = 3/5$:
>
> $y = \sin^{-1}(3/5)$
> $y = 36.87°$
>
> Make sure your calculator is in degree mode and not radians!

Try It

5) In the right triangle below, what is the value of $\cos a$?

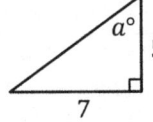

6) In the right triangle below, $\tan k = \dfrac{5}{4}$. What is the value of x?

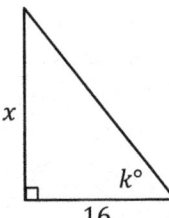

CHALLENGE:

The measures of the two acute angles in a right triangle will always add up to 90°. And as you can see in the examples on p. 419, the sine of one of those angles will always be equal to the cosine of the other one. This will always work: **if $a + b = 90°$, then $\sin a = \cos b$.**

Example: If $\cos 81° = 0.156$, what is the value of $\sin 9°$?

Because $81 + 9 = 90$, $\cos 81°$ must equal $\sin 9°$. The answer is **0.156**.

To convert degrees into **radians**, use this relationship:

$$180° = \pi \text{ radians}$$

Example: An angle measurement of 135° is equivalent to x radians. What is the value of x?

$$\frac{135}{x} = \frac{180}{\pi}$$

$$135\pi = 180x$$

$$x = \frac{135\pi}{180}$$

$$x = \frac{3\pi}{4}$$

Try It   7) Convert $\dfrac{5\pi}{2}$ radians to degrees:

CHALLENGE:

The **unit circle** is a circle with a radius of 1 centered at $(0, 0)$ on the xy-plane. The coordinates of any point (x, y) on the circle are $(\cos\theta, \sin\theta)$, where θ is the angle formed between the positive x-axis and the radius connecting to that point.

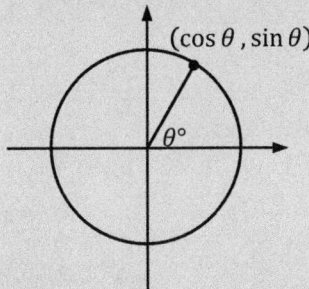

The unit circle is a convenient way to visualize and calculate trigonometric values for various angles. The quadrant that the angle falls in can quickly tell you whether the values of sin, cos, and tan will be positive or negative.

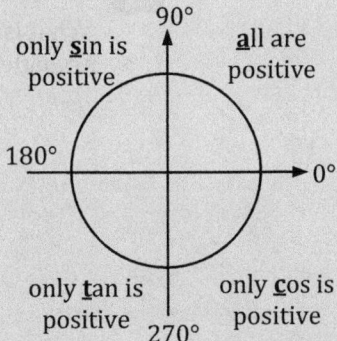

Starting in Quadrant I and moving in order through the quadrants, that sequence is **a**ll, **s**in, **t**an, **c**os. Use the mnemonic **A**ll **S**tudents **T**ake **C**alculus to remember the pattern.

Example: *If $\theta = 135°$, then the corresponding point on the unit circle lies in Quadrant II. Therefore, the value of cos 135 is negative, and the value of sin 135 is positive.*

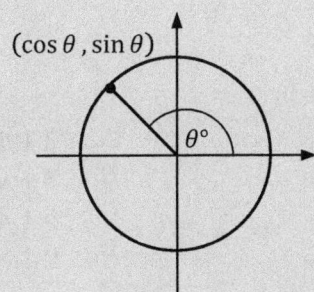

Math: Geometry and Trigonometry

Practice Set 1: Easy-Medium

1

What is the length of the hypotenuse of a right triangle with legs of length 5 and 8?

A. $\sqrt{13}$
B. $\sqrt{40}$
C. $\sqrt{75}$
D. $\sqrt{89}$

2

A circle with diameter $\overline{AB}$ of length 3 is tangent to $\overline{EF}$ as shown below. If the length of $\overline{EA}$ (not shown) is equal to 6 and the length of $\overline{AF}$ (not shown) is equal to 5, what is the length of $\overline{EF}$?

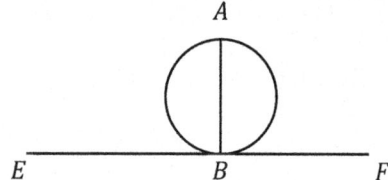

A. $4 + 3\sqrt{2}$
B. $4 + 3\sqrt{3}$
C. $7\sqrt{2}$
D. 9

3

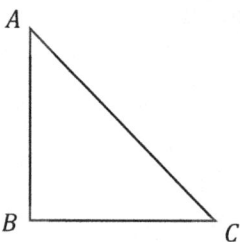

In the figure above, $\overline{AB} \perp \overline{BC}$ and $\overline{AB} \cong \overline{BC}$. If $AC = 5$, what is the area of $\triangle ABC$?

4

In the figure below, $\overline{CD}$ is a diameter of the circle, $\overline{BE}$ is a leg of right triangle ABE, and $BCDE$ is a square. What is the circumference of the circle?

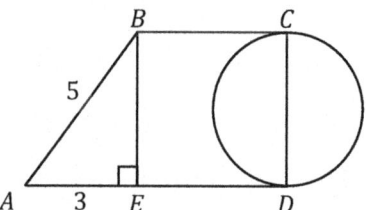

A. 2π
B. 4π
C. 12
D. 16

5

What is the value of $\cos x$ in the right triangle shown below?

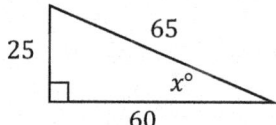

6

What is the perimeter of the isosceles right triangle shown below?

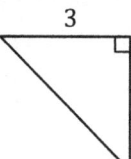

A. $3 + 3\sqrt{2}$
B. $3 + \sqrt{6}$
C. $6 + 3\sqrt{2}$
D. $6 + \sqrt{6}$

Right Triangles and Trigonometry

7 A ladder that is 8 feet long is positioned leaning against a wall such that the measure of the angle formed between the ladder and the level ground is 60 degrees. What is the distance (on the ground) between the ladder and the wall, in feet?

A. 0.5
B. 2
C. 4
D. $4\sqrt{3}$

8 In the right triangle shown below, which of the following statements is true about θ?

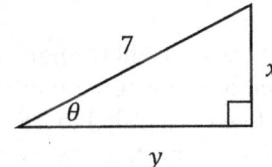

A. $\sin\theta = \dfrac{x}{y}$
B. $\cos\theta = \dfrac{7}{y}$
C. $\cos\theta = \dfrac{7}{x}$
D. $\sin\theta = \dfrac{x}{7}$

9 If B is the largest angle in right triangle ABC, what is the measure of angle B in radians?

A. 2π
B. π
C. $\dfrac{\pi}{2}$
D. $\dfrac{\pi}{4}$

10 What is the area of the triangle shown below?

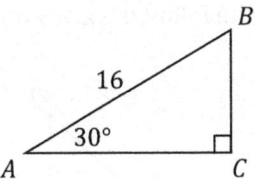

A. 8
B. $24\sqrt{2}$
C. $32\sqrt{3}$
D. 64

11 If a right triangle has a hypotenuse of length 14 and a shorter leg of length 5, what is the length of its longer leg?

A. $\sqrt{50}$
B. $\sqrt{75}$
C. $\sqrt{171}$
D. $\sqrt{221}$

12 Two ants were observed taking different routes from their anthill to a nearby food source. Ant A traveled due north for 0.8 meters, then due west for 1.5 meters, while ant B traveled in a straight line directly from the anthill to the food source. How many more meters were traveled by ant A than by ant B?

Math: Geometry and Trigonometry

Practice Set 2: Medium-Hard

1

In right triangle PQR shown below, which of the following gives the length of $\overline{QR}$?

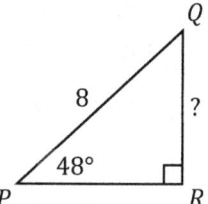

A. $\dfrac{\sin 48°}{8}$

B. $\dfrac{8}{\cos 48°}$

C. $8 \cos 48°$

D. $8 \sin 48°$

2

In quadrilateral $FGHJ$ below, angles G and J are right angles. If the lengths of $\overline{GH}$, $\overline{HJ}$, and $\overline{FJ}$ are 5, 4, and 6, respectively, which of the following is closest to the area of $FGHJ$?

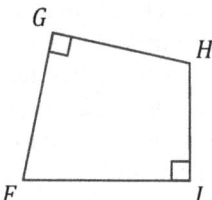

A. 20
B. 25
C. 28
D. 30

3

Equilateral triangle ABC has a perimeter of 12. What is the area of triangle ABC?

A. $2\sqrt{3}$
B. $4\sqrt{3}$
C. $6\sqrt{3}$
D. $8\sqrt{3}$

4

In a right triangle with side lengths $a, b,$ and c, where $a < b < c$, the smallest angle measures x degrees. What is the value of $\tan x$?

A. $\dfrac{a}{c}$

B. $\dfrac{a}{b}$

C. $\dfrac{b}{c}$

D. $\dfrac{c}{a}$

5

In the figure below, right triangle ABC is intersected by line l at points D and E such that line l is parallel to $\overline{AB}$. If $AB = 9, AC = 15$, the distance from line l to $\overline{AB}$ is 4, and the measure of $\angle CDE$ is $x°$, what is the value of $\cos x$?

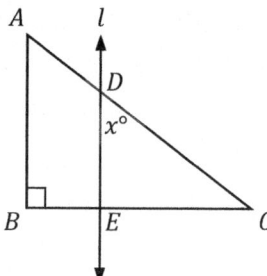

6

In triangle PQR, the lengths of $\overline{PQ}$, $\overline{QR}$, and $\overline{RP}$ are 7.5, 19.5, and 18, respectively. If the measure of angle Q is $q°$, what is the value of $\tan q$?

A. 0.417
B. 2.4
C. 2.6
D. It cannot be determined.

7

If $\cos P = \frac{r}{q}$, $q > 0$, $r > 0$, and $0 < P < \frac{\pi}{2}$, then $\tan P$ is equivalent to which of the following?

A. $\frac{q}{r}$

B. $\frac{\sqrt{q^2 - r^2}}{r}$

C. $\frac{\sqrt{q^2 - r^2}}{q}$

D. $\frac{q}{\sqrt{q^2 - r^2}}$

8

If $\cos \theta = 0.6$, what is the value of $\cos(90 - \theta)$?

9

The volume of a prism is equal to the product of its height and the area of its base. In the prism shown below, each of the bases is an isosceles right triangle with a hypotenuse of $6\sqrt{2}$. If the volume of the prism is 108, what is the height of the prism?

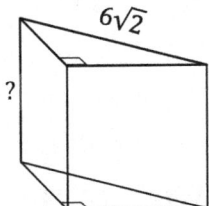

A. 3

B. $\frac{6}{\sqrt{2}}$

C. 6

D. $6\sqrt{2}$

10

If the value, to the nearest thousandth, of $\cos x$ is -0.707, which of the following could be true about x?

A. $0 \leq x \leq \frac{\pi}{6}$

B. $\frac{\pi}{3} \leq x \leq \frac{\pi}{2}$

C. $\frac{\pi}{2} \leq x \leq \frac{3\pi}{2}$

D. $\frac{3\pi}{2} \leq x \leq 2\pi$

11

If $\sin \theta = 0.45$ for the triangle shown below, then what is the value of x?

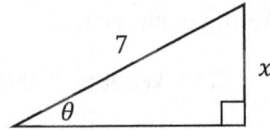

A. 0.064
B. 3.15
C. 3.52
D. 15.55

12

In the figure below, $\overline{YZ}$ is the hypotenuse of right triangle XYZ. If $\overline{YZ}$ has a length of 10 and the measure of angle Y is 70°, which of the following represents the length of $\overline{XZ}$?

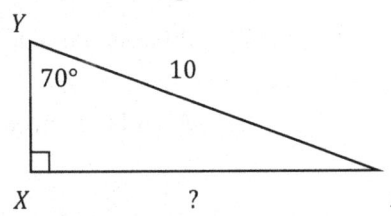

A. $10 \cos 70°$
B. $10 \tan 70°$
C. $10 \sin 20°$
D. $10 \cos 20°$

Circles

The relevant provided formulas:

REFERENCE

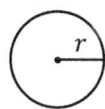

The number of degrees of arc in a circle is 360.
The number of radians of arc in a circle is 2π.

$A = \pi r^2$
$C = 2\pi r$

Preview Quiz:

Define each term:

1) What is an **arc**? _____
2) What is a **sector**? _____
3) What is a **chord**? _____
4) What does it mean for a line to be **tangent** to a circle?

_____

In the figure shown, points A, B, and C lie on the circle centered at point O, and the measure of $\angle AOC$ is 90°. The radius of the circle is 6.

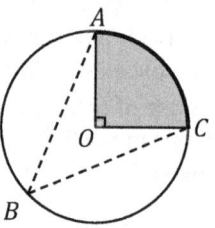

5) What is the degree measure of minor arc $\widehat{AC}$?

6) What is the degree measure of $\angle ABC$?

7) What is the length of minor arc $\widehat{AC}$?

8) What is the area of the shaded region?

If the circle given by $(x-2)^2 + (y+3)^2 = 49$ is graphed on the xy-plane:

9) What are the coordinates of the center?

10) What is the length of the radius?

11) What is the area of the circle?

Circles

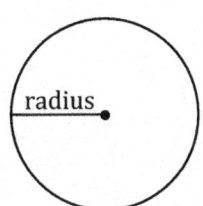

All points on a circle are the same distance from the circle's center. That distance is called the **radius**.

A **chord** is any line segment that intersects a circle in two places. If the chord passes through the center, it is called a **diameter**. The diameter is the longest chord that can be drawn in a circle. It is twice the length of the radius.

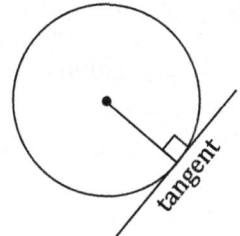

A line that is **tangent** to a circle intersects it in exactly one place. The tangent line is perpendicular to the radius at the point of intersection.

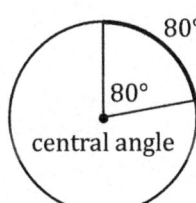

A **central angle** is an angle with its vertex at the center of a circle. Where the radii that form the sides of the angle intersect the circle, they mark off a portion of the circumference known as an **arc**. The degree measure of the arc is equal to the degree measure of the central angle.

An **inscribed angle** is an angle whose vertex lies on the circumference of a circle. The degree measure of the arc intercepted by an inscribed angle is twice the degree measure of the angle.

Because an arc is just a portion of the circumference of a circle, you can use the circumference, $2\pi r$, to calculate the **length of an arc**:

$$\text{Arc length} = \frac{\text{central angle}}{360}(2\pi r)$$

inscribed angle

Example: What is the length of minor arc AC in the circle shown?

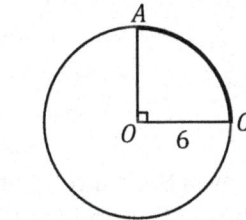

$$\text{Arc length} = \frac{90}{360}(2\pi(6))$$

$$\text{Arc length} = \frac{1}{4}(12\pi)$$

$$\text{Arc length} = \mathbf{3\pi}$$

Math: Geometry and Trigonometry

The region of a circle defined by two radii and an arc is called a **sector**. Because it is a portion of the circle's area, you can use something very similar to the arc length formula to calculate the **area of a sector** based on the area of the circle, πr^2:

$$\text{Sector area} = \frac{\text{central angle}}{360}(\pi r^2)$$

Example: *What is the area of the shaded region in the circle shown?*

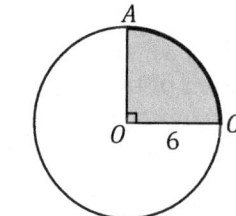

$$\text{Sector area} = \frac{90}{360}(\pi(6)^2)$$

$$\text{Sector area} = \frac{1}{4}(36\pi)$$

$$\text{Sector area} = \mathbf{9\pi}$$

Try It

1) What is the length of a 40° arc of a circle with radius 9?

2) In a circle, a sector with area 8π is intercepted by a central angle measuring $d°$. If the radius of the circle is 12, what is the value of d?

3) In the figure shown, points P, Q, and R all lie on the circle. If arc QR (shown in bold in the figure below) is a semicircle, then triangle PQR must be which of the following?

   A) an equilateral triangle
   B) a right triangle
   C) an obtuse triangle
   D) none of the above

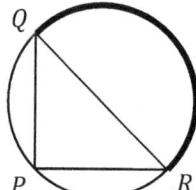

Circles

In the xy-plane, the graph of $(x-h)^2 + (y-k)^2 = r^2$ is a circle centered at the point (h, k) with radius r.

Example: What is the area of the circle defined by the equation $(x-2)^2 + (y+3)^2 = 49$?

This equation gives a circle centered at $(2, -3)$ with a radius of 7. Now use the formula for area of a circle:

$$A = \pi r^2$$
$$A = \pi(7)^2 = \mathbf{49\pi}$$

TIP:

Don't forget to switch the signs! A $(y+3)^2$ in the equation means the y-coordinate of the center is -3, not positive 3.

Try It

4) In the xy-plane, what are the coordinates of the center of the circle given by $(x+1)^2 + y^2 = 4$?

5) What is the equation of the circle centered at $(-9, 5)$ on the xy-plane, given that the radius of the circle is 4?

6) A circle with a radius of 5 is graphed in the xy-plane with its center at $(3, 1)$. The circle passes through the point $(k, -3)$, where k is a positive constant. What is the value of k?

CHALLENGE:

If the test gives you the equation of a circle that is not in standard form, the easiest way to handle the problem is to simply graph the equation in the built-in calculator.

Alternatively, you can solve the problem algebraically by **completing the square.**

Example: $x^2 + y^2 - 6x + 2y - 11 = 0$

First, group the x's together and the y's together. Stand-alone numbers (constants) go on the right side of the equation.

$$x^2 - 6x + y^2 + 2y = 11$$

The x's form the first two terms of a quadratic of form $ax^2 + bx + c$, and the y's form the first two terms of a different quadratic of the form $ay^2 + by + c$. Within each of those two sets, find $(b/2)^2$; add that to both sides of the equation. For example, the b term of the x quadratic here is -6, so $(b/2)^2$ is $(-6/2)^2 = (-3)^2 = 9$. On the y side, the b term is 2, so $(b/2)^2$ is $(2/2)^2 = (1)^2 = 1$. So:

$$x^2 - 6x + \mathbf{9} + y^2 + 2y + \mathbf{1} = 11 + \mathbf{9} + \mathbf{1}$$

Now, factor both quadratics and add up the numbers on the right.

$$(x - 3)^2 + (y + 1)^2 = 21$$

Therefore, this is a circle centered at $(3, -1)$, with a radius of $\sqrt{21}$.

Try It

7) On the xy-plane, what is the center of the circle given by $x^2 + 4x + y^2 - 10y = 2$?

Practice Set 1: Easy-Medium

1

When graphed in the xy-plane, the circle $(x+3)^2 + (y-1)^2 = 16$ is centered at which of the following points?

A. $(-3,-1)$
B. $(-3, 1)$
C. $(3,-1)$
D. $(3, 1)$

2

In the figure below, the chord shown does NOT pass through the center of the circle. If the area of the circle is 49π, which of the following must be true about x, the length of the chord?

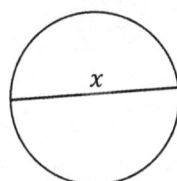

A. $x > 7$
B. $0 < x < 7$
C. $x > 14$
D. $0 < x < 14$

3

Which of the following gives the equation of a circle in the xy-plane?

A. $\dfrac{(x-2)^2}{4} + \dfrac{(y+8)^2}{6} = 1$
B. $(x-1)^2 + y^2 = 1$
C. $x^2 - y^2 = 1$
D. $x + (y+3)^2 = 1$

4

On the xy-plane, the point $(9, 0)$ lies on a circle with center $(6, -4)$. What is the radius of the circle?

5

Point C is the center of the circle of radius 18 pictured below. What is the length of arc DEF?

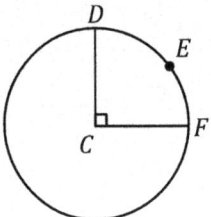

A. 6π
B. 9π
C. 12π
D. 18π

6

In the xy-plane, the graph of which of the following equations is a circle with center $(2, 5)$ and radius 9?

A. $(x-2)^2 + (y-5)^2 = 3$
B. $(x-2)^2 + (y-5)^2 = 81$
C. $(x+2)^2 + (y+5)^2 = 3$
D. $(x+2)^2 + (y+5)^2 = 81$

7

What is the length, in centimeters, of an 80° arc of a circle whose area is 81π square centimeters?

A. 2π
B. 3π
C. 4π
D. 9π

8

What is the circumference, in coordinate units, of the circle in the xy-plane given by the equation $x^2 + (y+9)^2 = 100$?

A. 10π
B. 20π
C. 81π
D. 100π

Math: Geometry and Trigonometry

Practice Set 2: Medium-Hard

1

On the xy-plane, the circle with radius 4 and center $(2, 4)$ intersects the line $y = 8$ at which of the following points?

A. $(-4, 8)$
B. $(2, 8)$
C. $(4, 8)$
D. $(8, 14)$

2

The shaded region in the circle below is bounded by minor arc AB and by radii $\overline{OA}$ and $\overline{OB}$. If the area of the shaded region is 20% of the area of the circle, what is the measure of $\angle AOB$, in degrees?

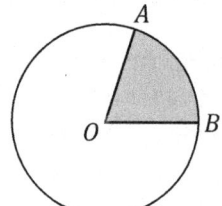

3

On the xy-plane, which of the following is an x-intercept of the circle with radius 5 and center $(3, 0)$?

A. $(-8, 0)$
B. $(2, 0)$
C. $(0, -2)$
D. $(8, 0)$

4

On the xy-plane, what is the center of the circle that has the equation $x^2 + 8x + y^2 + 18y = 10$?

A. $(3, 5)$
B. $(-5, 5)$
C. $(-4, -9)$
D. $(-8, 4)$

5

In the figure below, points A and B lie on the circle with center O, and the side lengths of triangle AOB are as shown. What is the area of the circle?

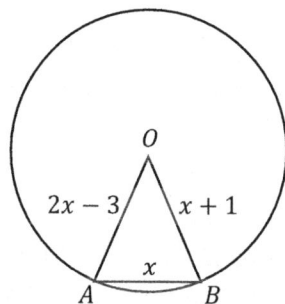

A. 4π
B. 9π
C. 16π
D. 25π

6

If all of the sides of the hexagon pictured below are congruent, and the radius of the circle is equal to 9, what is the length of arc XYZ?

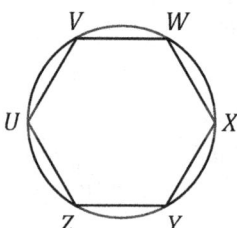

A. 3π
B. 6π
C. 9π
D. 18π

7

In the xy-plane, a circle with a radius of 4 is tangent to the lines $x = 2$ and $y = 3$. If the entire graph of the circle is located in Quadrant I, what are the coordinates of the circle's center?

A. $(6, 7)$
B. $(7, 6)$
C. $(10, 11)$
D. $(11, 10)$

Answers and Explanations

Reading: Information, Ideas, and Structure

Words in Context	435
Central Ideas and Details	437
Structure and Purpose	440
Compare and Contrast	443

Reading: Evidence and Logical Reasoning

Command of Evidence – Illustrate the Claim	446
Command of Evidence – Strengthen/Weaken	448
Command of Evidence – Quantitative	452
Logical Inferences	456

Writing: Standard English Conventions

Sentence Structure	460
Commas	463
Semicolons, Colons, Dashes, and Apostrophes	467
Verbs	472
Pronouns	474
Misplaced Modifiers	476

Writing: Expression of Ideas

Transitions	477
Rhetorical Synthesis	479

Math: Strategy in Brief

Back-Solving and Substitution	481
Mastering the Calculator	485
Approximating and Measuring	489

Math: Algebra

Algebra Essentials	491
Word Problems	496
Coordinate Geometry	498
Systems of Equations	503
Inequalities and Absolute Value	510

Math: Advanced Math

Exponents and Roots	514
Factoring, FOILing, and Fractions	518
Function Essentials	526
Linear Functions	529
Quadratic Functions	533
Polynomial, Exponential, Radical, and Rational Functions	536

Math: Problem Solving and Data Analysis
- Data Interpretation — 543
- Ratios, Proportions, and Unit Conversions — 546
- Percentages — 550
- Mean, Median, and Mode — 554
- Probability — 560
- Statistics — 562

Math: Geometry and Trigonometry
- Area and Volume — 564
- Angles, Lines, and Triangles — 571
- Right Triangles and Trigonometry — 579
- Circles — 585

WORDS IN CONTEXT (p. 18)
Words in Context: Try It

1) A
The New Yorkers in this sentence like to get away from crowded cities so they can be *alone* and *undisturbed*. We need a noun version of "alone" or "undisturbed" with a positive or neutral tone. "Companionship" does not work, because it means the opposite of being alone. "Cosmopolitanism" generally refers to large, diverse cities such as New York, so one wouldn't leave the city to find cosmopolitanism. Both "solitude" and "loneliness" require being by oneself, but loneliness has a negative connotation. If someone is lonely, they want company; the New Yorkers in this sentence don't. "Solitude" is therefore the right answer.

2) B
We're looking for a word to describe newly proposed theories, something that contrasts with *universally respected and accepted.* Theories that have just been proposed cannot be "well-established," so choice A is out. "Praised" and "endorsed" are both positive: they are consistent with *respected and accepted*, while we want the opposite. "Ridiculed" is the best fit.

3) C
People *believe* that diamonds are "rare," but the phrase "but they are actually" tells us that this belief is incorrect. We need something that is the opposite of rare. "Uncommon" is a synonym, so that's out. "Exquisite" means "beautiful," so while it's a word that could be applied to diamonds, it doesn't contrast with "rare." Similarly, "expensive" doesn't contrast with "rare;" it's also implied that diamonds are expensive *despite* the fact that they are not actually rare. "Common" is our answer.

4) A
Since the photographer "never posed" his subjects, we need a word that means "not posed." Candid is a word you might not know, but this can be solved by eliminating the other terms. "Unnatural" and "theatrical" both suggest something arranged or staged, which could well indicate something posed. "Brilliant" does not work either; the photographer's photographs can be very good no matter what the subject is doing.

Words in Context: Practice Set 1 (p. 23)

1) C
By the time we reach the blank, the recycled plastic has already been collected, sorted, cleaned, and melted. The blank expresses what happens to this melted plastic next: a good prediction might be that it is "shaped" into new products. Choice C matches that nicely. The other choices either don't make sense in the context, or don't work with the "into" that follows the word: for example, "they are completed into new plastic products" doesn't sound right.

2) A
The part of the sentence that follows the comma is about a relationship between humans and the world, so "interconnections" is a good fit. The word "fusions" indicates a literal connection, which doesn't match the figurative connection described in the sentence. "Articulations" refers either to the act of speaking, or the moving joint of an animal; neither definition makes sense here. And "illuminations," which refers to shedding light on something, is completely unrelated.

3) D
The structure of the last sentence gives us an important clue. The "While" at the beginning tells us that the first clause of the sentence is in contrast to the second part ("the precise nature of dark matter is still not understood"). So we're looking for a word that says we know *something* about dark matter, even if not everything. "Denied" does not work. "Construed" means "interpreted," which almost works but not quite. We are construing the evidence to conclude that dark matter exists; we're not construing the existence to conclude something else. "Insinuated" means "subtly suggested," which is a bit backwards: while it's true that the evidence suggests the existence of dark matter, this would say that the existence suggests the evidence, which doesn't make sense. "Inferred" means to conclude something from evidence, so it's the best fit.

4) C
In this context, "take" means "opinion" or "interpretation," so don't get tricked into choosing "steal." "End" doesn't work, and "agenda" means "plan" or "goal," so it does not work either. "Perspective" can mean "a way of looking at things," so that is our answer.

5) D
We need a word that indicates what scientists will do with greenhouse gases in order to get them to warm Mars: "releasing" them into the atmosphere makes sense. The words "asserting" or "suggesting" have to do with speech rather than action; these are not things we can do with gases. And while "inflicting" is more action-oriented, it has a negative connotation. In this sentence, placing the greenhouse gases into the atmosphere is intended to be a positive action, something that will help the terraforming effort. There's no evidence in the sentence that the author intends to criticize these ideas.

6) B
This passage suggests that it makes sense that migratory behavior is being studied extensively. "It is not outstanding" suggests that the behavior is ordinary, which does not work. "It is not surprising" suggests that the behavior expected, which is what we're looking for. "It is not unremarkable" suggests that the behavior *is* remarkable, which is the opposite of what we want.

Answer Explanations

"Conspicuous" means "especially visible," which is unrelated. "Surprising" is our answer.

7) C
"Transporting" almost works, but the "to move" after the word "magma" makes it incorrect. "Transporting magma to the surface" is correct, but "transporting magma to move to the surface" is not. "Rendering" means to create, but since the magma is being moved to the surface and not created there, it is incorrect. "Allowing" works; the tubes permit the magma to get up to the surface. "Bestowing" means to give an honor or a gift, so it makes no sense in this sentence.

8) A
We want a word that indicates the maize being modified will be less vulnerable to witchweed. "Resistant" and "adverse" are both possibilities: "resistant" means the witchweed won't affect the maize as much, and "adverse" means the maize will actually be harmful to the witchweed. Between them, "resistant" is the better choice; the goal isn't to hurt the witchweed, it is to protect the maize. "Insubordinate" means "disobedient," and does not fit; "tenacious" means "stubborn," and also does not work.

9) B
"Predict" does not work, because nothing is being predicted. "Date" can work, because one meaning of "date" is "to establish age." "Accompany" does not work; the process of thermoluminescence is not going anywhere with the artifacts. "Disinter" means "to dig up," but there is nothing suggesting that this phenomenon is used to get the artifacts out of the ground; it is only used to study them afterwards. "Date" is our answer.

Words in Context: Practice Set 2 (p. 25)
1) B
The passage suggests that this bird is different from other owls, so we need a word that expresses this. While other owls have a disk-shaped face, this particular owl does not. Our prediction for the blank, then, might be something like "does not have." Choices A and C are the opposite of what we want, because they would indicate that this owl *does* have a disk-shaped face (therefore, it's *similar* to other owls). "Distinguishes" means chooses, which makes no sense.

2) C
"Sustains" means strengthens or supports, which does not fit. The author of a drama may strengthen the dilemma, but a character within the drama will not. "Develops" means to cause something to grow or advance; again the author of a drama might develop the dilemma, but the character experiencing it will not. "Resolves" is a tempting choice, because to resolve something is to find a solution; however, when one considers the larger context, this portion of the sentence would mean "they find a solution to their problem and to their solution," which does not make sense. "Experiences" means the dilemma is something the character goes through, which is correct.

3) A
"Artfully" and "proficiently" both mean "skillfully," which does not apply here. "Durably" means something that can last a long time without damage, which also makes no sense in this context. "Tellingly" means "significantly;" since we are told that "Sullivan is hailed as something approaching a saint," the title of the play being *The Miracle Worker* is indeed significant.

4) D
This passage is talking about reluctance to get involved in conflicts, and contrasts the risks of "bold action" with the missing word. "Aggression," "imperialism," and "hostility" all suggest a readiness to get involved in conflict, whereas "inaction" refers to sitting the conflict out and therefore contrasts with "bold action." Inaction is our answer.

5) A
For this passage, trying to understand the overall context can be a hindrance, as there are a number of difficult vocabulary words that are not actually needed to answer the question. Let us simply look at the end of the passage: "bent on holding humanity back with set worldviews." The phrases "win worldviews" and "collection worldviews" are both completely meaningless and grammatically incorrect. "Group worldviews" also makes no sense in context. "Fixed" means "unchanging," and is our answer.

6) B
The tone of the overall passage makes it clear that this discovery was important; therefore, the phrase "It is difficult to ____ the importance" needs to emphasize this. "Downplay" does not work, because things that are very important are the easiest things to downplay. "Ascertain" and "evaluate" have a similar meaning, "to find out," which doesn't apply here—we know that this is very important. "Overstate" would mean that it was hard to express an undue degree of importance, which is an indication that it was very important indeed. "Overstate" is our answer.

7) C
In this study, there's a technique that is used to "produce clones of plants." The researchers use this technique "to ____ cumin." We need a synonym of "clone" to make this sentence work. "Circulate" and "diffuse" both can mean "to spread around," but that isn't really what we're looking for. "Publicize" can also mean to spread around, but applied specifically to information and not things in

- 436 -

general, so it does not work. "Propagate" means "to make new specimens," so that is our answer.

CENTRAL IDEAS AND DETAILS (p. 27)
Central Ideas and Details: Try It
1) Wood pulp was cheaper.
The passage mentions two negative aspects of rag papermaking: there was a limited supply of rags, and the process "required significant resources" (it was expensive). So, those are two possible motives for the switch: the cost and the limited supply. We don't know anything about the supply of wood pulp, but we do know that its processing had recently become more "cost-effective" (cheaper). Therefore, that's the best prediction for why the papermakers switched from rags to wood pulp: using wood pulp cost less.

2) The radif and the qafia.
Keep in mind that no prior knowledge about the topic is necessary to answer these questions. After all, how much did you know about rag papermaking before you answered #1 above? So if you've never heard of a ghazal before, no problem: everything we need is right here in the passage. The text tells us about several distinct elements of the ghazal, but only two are explicitly described as contributing to the rhyme scheme: the end of the second line of each couplet, called the *radif* (which is credited with "creating a distinctive rhyme scheme") and the end of the first line of each couplet, called the *qafia* (which is said to "further contribute to the rhyme pattern"). Therefore, the radif and the qafia are the two elements that most directly contribute to the rhyme scheme.

3)
  A) Researchers have developed a <u>revolutionary</u> new method for refining zirconium.
  B) Chlorination is <u>the most important step</u> in the zirconium refining process.
  C) A recent experiment has <u>proven</u> the criticisms of the new zirconium refining method to be <u>completely</u> unfounded.
  D) A new method of refining zirconium <u>appears to be</u> a <u>promising</u> alternative to the traditional approach.

  Most likely answer: <u>D</u>

Choice D refers to a "new method," while choice A calls it a *revolutionary* new method. That's substantially stronger language that would take much more specific information to support. Similarly, choice B doesn't just refer to chlorination as an important step in the process, but as *the most important* step. We'd need specific support for that from the text, something explicitly telling us that this step is more important than any of the others. In choice C, the word "proven" right away jumps out as problematic, as scientists will rarely claim that anything has been 100% "proven" or "disproven." And watch for adverbs like "completely" to add too much strength. Choice D uses the weakest language: the new method "appears to be " (not "is") a "promising" (not "revolutionary") alternative. That makes D the most likely answer.

4)
  A) He reads <u>at least part</u> of the reference book.
  B) He starts on his assignment to avoid an <u>inevitable</u> confrontation.
  C) He <u>uses the reference book</u> to complete his <u>entire assignment</u> three days early.
  D) He asks for help in using the reference book <u>after trying and failing to understand it</u>.

  Most likely answer: <u>A</u>

Here's an example of choices that build on each other. Note that if Alfred has tried and failed to understand the reference book, then he has read at least part of it. That means if D is right, then A would also have to be right! We can't have two right answers, so this eliminates choice D. Similarly, choice C says Alfred "uses the reference book," which also presumably means he has read at least part of it. Plus, this answer gives us the additional strong language of completing his "entire assignment," which goes farther than what choice B said. Eliminate choice C. Choice B also includes strong language: it describes not just a confrontation, but an "inevitable" confrontation. Choice A uses much weaker language to assert a claim that's much easier to support, so it's the most likely answer.

5)
  A) She <u>regrets</u> her life choices.
  B) She <u>thinks</u> her children ought to visit her more.
  C) She <u>sometimes argues</u> with her family members.
  D) She <u>privately believes</u> that the picnic is <u>sure</u> to be a disaster.

  Most likely answer: <u>C</u>

For this question, we've been told that the text consists of dialogue only. Based on what people *say* alone, we are unlikely to be able to infer anything about what they "think," "regret," or "privately believe." Choice C focuses only on the character's actions, not her thoughts, and it uses the weak language "sometimes." As long as the dialogue contains an argument between Susan and a family member, we'll have enough to support choice C, so it's the most likely answer.

6) D
Choice A may make sense, but there's no support for it in the passage. Choice B also isn't supported in the passage (and at any rate, we have no evidence to conclude that

Answer Explanations

rags weren't also "natural materials"). Choice C is partially supported, because we know there was a limited supply of rags, but we don't know anything about a change in popular fashion tastes. Choice D is the best match for our prediction.

7) C
The *takhallus* is the author's pen-name, which has nothing to do with the rhyme scheme. Eliminate choices B and D. The *bayt* is the name for the entire couplet, so it does indirectly contribute to the rhyme scheme—but only because it contains the radif and the qafia. It makes no sense to say that the bayt and the qafia contribute more directly to the rhyme scheme than the radif does, so choice A is out. Choice C is exactly what we predicted, so it's the winner.

Central Ideas and Details: Practice Set 1 (p. 34)
1) C
Be sure to limit your answers to what the passage specifically tells us. According to the text, tryptophan is transported into the brain, converted into something else, and then converted into serotonin. This would suggest that serotonin is synthesized inside the brain, not outside, so we can eliminate choice A. Choice B is much stronger than we can support from this passage. Choice D would be correct if the question was about tryptophan, but it's not: the text never said that *serotonin* is transported across the blood-brain barrier. That leaves C, which is correct: serotonin is derived from the "essential amino acid" tryptophan, and the passage told us that essential amino acids must come from the diet. Therefore, serotonin is a derivative of a substance (tryptophan) that is obtained from food.

2) B
Nothing in this passage addresses whether either kind of bee is more numerous than the other, so A is out. Nor is there anything about their sizes, or whether or not one is more likely to be imported, though you might get tricked into that one, since the one bee is called "native." Don't be fooled! It's possible that neither is imported at all. B is the right answer, though finding the evidence can be a bit tricky. The passage does not clearly mention honey bees as being more industrious; however, it does describe the native bee as "dozing" and "living from hand to mouth," which means it is *not* industrious. Since this description follows the contrasting transition "on the other hand," we can infer that the honey bee is different.

3) A
This passage could be summed up in this way: "Superconductivity was discovered as a phenomenon that takes place at extremely cold temperatures; later, it was found to be possible at much less cold temperatures." This makes A the clear choice. B and C do not work, because the passage tells us nothing about the materials used in 1986 being either "better" or "more efficient," only that they work at warmer temperatures. And in any case, we know nothing at all about the materials used in 1911. This also eliminates answer D.

4) C
In the first stanza, the poet talks about being dead and forgotten, such that even his grave has vanished. We can therefore eliminate answer A, because this indicates there is someone who remembers the poet's face; answer B, because a future student cannot ask advice of a poet who is dead; and answer D, because if the poet has been forgotten, he cannot have any fans. C is the only choice left, which fits: the stanza describes how this stranger "lights upon" the poet's work, which means "finding."

5) C
The text gives us a lot of information about ribbon microphones: how they worked (a vibrating aluminum ribbon), why they were popular (they captured audio with warmth and accuracy), when they were popular (the 1930s-1950s), why their popularity faded (new technology was less fragile), and why they're making a comeback (vintage appeal). Choice C does the best job of wrapping up as much as possible of that information in a single sentence.

Choice A is too strong: we know the microphones were valued for capturing vocals, but we don't know they were *ideally* suited for that task. Plus, this choice leaves out a lot of other important parts of the passage. Choices B and D are also too limited; they each focus on only a part of what was discussed rather than the big idea of the whole.

6) D
A might be a tempting choice because of the "bulbous-browed and pop-eyed" description, but that does not work both because it only describes *some* of the girls, and because it's not necessarily *Carol's* view. B might be tempting because of the bit about prayer-meetings, but there's no suggestion that Carol is "intimidated." C can be ruled out because we're looking for something negative about the girls, not something positive. D is our correct answer, as proven by the sentence "Neither sort tempted Carol."

7) D
Take a look at the sentence in the passage that first mentions Florey and Heatley. It says they overcame this obstacle by..." So, that's the effect of their method: it overcame an obstacle. What was the obstacle? It's described in the previous few sentences: the *Penicillium* mold was sensitive to oxygen, making it hard to efficiently produce penicillin on a large scale. If Florey and Heatley overcame that obstacle by inventing this new method, then the method must have helped make it easier to efficiently produce penicillin on a large scale.

That's choice D. Although the other choices certainly sound like they would be positive effects, none of them were directly mentioned in the passage, so they can't be right.

8) A
First, summarize the text. Some animals have evolved to be good at seeing moving objects. The dragonfly is one of these animals. They use specialized compound eyes to do it.

Choice B goes too far: we know dragonflies have these types of eyes, but we don't know that they're the *only* insects that do. Choices C and D are also too extreme for the passage. But choice A works: this is a nice summary of what we know, without going too far.

Central Ideas and Details: Practice Set 2 (p. 37)
1) A
The key phrase here is "he had nothing to do, and she had hardly anybody to love;" they are the only eligible people around, so A is our answer. "Mitigated" means "to make less severe," so "mitigated boredom" might work for Frederick, but not for Anne; therefore B is not correct. C and D do not work at all, because there is nothing about either "fearful obedience" or "carefree relief" in the passage.

2) B
The text tells us a lot about Otto Wagner and his functionalist design aesthetic: his buildings highlight the practical aspects of design and optimize functionality. Choice A is close, but it doesn't mention Otto Wagner. Since Wagner is mentioned in every sentence, he is the real focus of the passage; the concept of "functionalism" was only mentioned at the beginning. Choice C is *slightly* supported by the text's reference to Wagner as an "influential" architect, but it's still a step too far for us to say that many architects have followed him. And, more importantly, this is one tiny part of the passage, not the main idea. Choice D focuses too much on minor details about Wagner, like his country of origin and the "harmonious" relationship that was only mentioned in the end. Plus, the building never told us that Wagner designed homes! His architecture might never have been used for buildings that people "live in," which is enough by itself to eliminate D. Choice B is the best match for our prediction.

3) C
The first stanza describes the subject as "old and grey and full of sleep / And nodding by the fire." This context indicates that "full of sleep" means she is literally sleepy (thus "nodding" off to sleep). Eliminate choices B and D: though the poem as a whole may give us reason to suspect that these statements are true, neither one is communicated by this specific phrase. Since nothing in the poem directly tells us anything about an illness, we can also eliminate A. Given that "full of sleep" follows "old and grey" in the first line, the speaker seems to be suggesting that her sleepiness is linked at least in part to her old age. That makes choice C the best answer.

4) A
The question asks about Bilbao's *urban planners,* so focus on the part that talks about the urban planners: "Although urban planners derided early estimates of 500,000 visitors per year, after the first eight months, nearly 700,000 *turistas* had gaped in awe at Mr. Gehry's work." "Derided," meaning "mocked," is a somewhat difficult word, but even if you do not know that word specifically one can get that the urban planners were surprised at how many tourists came, and indeed A is our answer. Economic issues are mentioned at the end of the passage, but they are not connected to the urban planners and don't fit answer B regardless. C is incorrect because there isn't any suggestion that the urban planners were the ones who initiated the museum, and also because there is nothing suggesting that Bilbao is *the* "dominant economic power in Europe"—only that it has "a significant role." And nothing in this passage mentions "nationalistic pride."

5) D
Metaphysics is described as "the most abstract and theoretical;" this does not necessarily mean that it is the most "difficult," so A is not the best choice. B is out because there isn't anything saying that any answers have been found. The passage does not suggest that the other branches are based on metaphysics, so C can be eliminated. Since we are told that metaphysics is "the **most** abstract" branch, we know that the other branches, including epistemology, are *less* abstract, so D is our correct answer.

6) D
Several of the answer choices here accurately state one or more details from the text, which makes it especially important that we stay focused on the question we were asked: our task here is to state the overall main idea. In choice A, it's true that some electors violated their pledge, and this author might well agree that this action was inappropriate. But the point of the passage was not what the electors did; it was what the court did. Eliminate choice A. Choice B is tempting because of the point about election stability, but the passage didn't say it was the *unanimity* of the holding that was such a victory. And while choice C accurately states the issue before the court, it doesn't tell us the outcome, which was actually the author's point. Choice D gives us the outcome, plus a bit of the author's opinion (by calling it a "landmark" case, which matches the text's description of a "historic" holding). This is the best statement of the overall main idea.

Answer Explanations

7) D
This detail-heavy passage is tough to summarize, so let's jump right into the choices and use a process of elimination approach. Choice A is half-right, half-wrong. It's true that the UK is funded through a centralized system. But while Canada's system is decentralized in terms of its management ("healthcare is managed by each province and territory"), the system has "federal funding and standards." Thus, *funding* for the Canadian system is not decentralized.

Choice B also gets only the UK part right. The text told us that in Canada, service delivery "involves a mix of public and private providers," so it's not true that all healthcare professionals are privately employed.

The goal stated in choice C is shared by both countries: the text described both countries as "aiming for universal access to necessary services."

That leaves only choice D, which is the right answer.

8) A
The text begins with a strong, broad statement: the printing press was faster and more efficient than hand-copying texts. Then we get a lot of detail about how the printing press worked, plus a note at the end about how time-consuming it was: producing one book took from two weeks to several months. Since the opening sentence of the text told us that the printing press was faster than hand-copying, we can infer that producing a book via hand-copying must have taken *more* than two weeks. That's choice A.

Choice B is too extreme. All we can say for sure based on this passage is that a typesetter and a press operator were both involved in the process. But it's possible that there were others involved as well; in fact, if all we have to go on is the contents of this passage, it's still technically possible that the same person could serve both roles.

Choice C is not supported. Nothing in the text explicitly told us whether errors were more common in one method than in the other, so we can't say this for sure.

Choice D is like choice B: it goes too far. We know that oil-based inks were used by the printing press, but we have no idea whether they might also have been used in other types of book production.

STRUCTURE AND PURPOSE (p. 40)
Structure and Purpose: Try It
1) D
The question asks about the "kitchen scraps and yard trimmings," which is part of the second sentence. To form a prediction, start by looking at the context of the rest of the sentence. It is describing the first step of the composting process, where organic waste materials such as these are collected and layered. So, that's our prediction: the reference illustrates what is meant by the term "organic waste materials."

Now evaluate the choices. Choice A is wrong because this sentence is the only reference to this feature of the composting process; it is not explained in greater detail elsewhere. Nothing in the quote suggests a weakness, so choice B is out. Choice C describes what the passage as a whole is doing, but not what the specific reference to "kitchen scraps and yard trimmings" does. Choice D is a great match for our prediction, so it's the right answer.

2) A
The first sentence of the text introduces the topic: the USPS uses several types of automated sorting machines. The second sentence introduces one type (optical character recognition machines), and the rest of the text tells us about another (advanced video coding systems). So a good prediction might be something like "the text states that the USPS uses sorting machines and then provides two examples."

Based on that prediction, choice A looks like a winner. Choice B doesn't match the passage: there's nothing here about advantages and disadvantages. Choice C is too limited, as it only refers to the discussion of video coding systems. This choice leaves out the whole first half of the passage, so it's not a good description of the overall structure of the text. And choice D is half right, half wrong: while the passage does explore some postal service technology, it never advocates for a change. The best answer is A.

Structure and Purpose: Practice Set 1 (p. 46)
1) C
For this question, we're looking for the main purpose of the text as a whole. So what do you see in this text?

The first sentence introduces the two characters and tells us about the house they chose. The next few sentences describe the house in more detail, and the final sentence tells us which aspects of the house were the ones the Talbots particularly liked.

This text is much more focused on the house than on the people, so choices A and D are out. Nothing is explained in detail, so choice B is out too. Choice C is the best match: the text describes the house and tells us what the characters liked about it.

2) D
Now we're looking for the function of a piece of the passage in the context of the whole. Scan for "Royal's assertions" and you'll find them down at the end of the text. Highlight those assertions (the entire last sentence) and then go back up to the top to read the passage.

First, we get the traditional belief: people thought these ships stayed close to shore. Next, a new point of view:

Foley says they sometimes went further out to sea. As evidence, he points to some wrecks in the Mediterranean.

And finally, we get to the sentence we highlighted. It's introduced with the transition phrase "On the other hand," which is one big hint that there's a contrast happening: this must be a claim that goes against Foley's. Specifically, Royal is saying there's another possible explanation for the shipwrecks that Foley talked about.

Now check the choices. Royal's claims don't *summarize* the difference between two views; they're specifically working against one of them. Eliminate choice A. The assertions certainly don't reinforce Foley's theories, so B is out. But the word "disprove" is too strong for us to support: we don't know for sure that Royal is right and Foley is wrong. Even Royal used words like "might" when describing his theory, so to say he's disproved anything is going too far. On that basis, we can eliminate choice C.

That leaves choice D, which is the best match for our prediction: Royal is providing another possible explanation for the shipwreck evidence. The answer is D.

3) D
Don't get intimidated by the context. You don't have to understand the science! Focus instead on how the passage is put together. This whole passage consists of three long sentences, with this basic structure: "There's this DNA editing tool. This is what it's made of. This is how it's used." We're looking for the function of the first sentence, so "there's this DNA editing tool" is a pretty good prediction.

The sentence doesn't mention RNA, so choice A is out. Choice B is possible, if the year of its development and the names of the developers could be considered the background of the invention. It definitely doesn't give us a rationale, so we can eliminate choice C. Choice D is a neat match for our prediction: "there's this tool" sounds like an introduction, and "there's this *DNA editing* tool" summarizes its function. This is a better match than choice B, which leaves out the summarizing-its-function component, so D is the best answer.

4) A
The question is asking for the function of a specific phrase rather than a whole sentence, so look to the rest of the sentence for clues. In this case, the sentence tells us explicitly that the letters are used by David Armitage "as support." So that's their function in David Armitage's argument: the letters support his claim. That's choice A.

5) C
This time, the question is asking for the purpose of the text as a whole, not for the purpose of a specific element of it. So what do you see in the passage? The first few sentences describe a protest in China, and then the Chinese government's harsh response. Then we shift to a description of similar incidents in Europe, where other citizens protest against communist regimes.

Since half the passage is about places other than China, the overall purpose can't be limited to Chinese politics. Eliminate choice A. And while the passage does mention a few different methods of protest, that doesn't seem to be the main point, and at any rate, we're not given much detail. That's enough to cross off choice D.

The text definitely describes a sequence of events. Is that sequence intended to analyze the collapse of communism? Maybe, but we only get to that topic at the very end, and even there it was only about the collapse of one particular communist government, not the entire system. We'd have to take a couple of extra steps to justify choice B. And notice this: to the extent that this text is analyzing the collapse of communism, it's doing so by describing a sequence of events. In other words, if choice B is true, then choice C is also true. We can't have two right answers! Choice C is the answer that's most directly supported, so it's the right answer.

6) D
Summarize the passage one sentence at a time. The first sentence describes a study's methodology. The second sentence tells us a finding: the dogwoods were genetically diverse. The third sentence gives us another finding: a population structure. The final sentence explains what that finding means: some dogwood populations may adapt to their locations. Since the question is asking us for the function of the last sentence, that's our prediction: it explains what one of the findings means. That's choice D.

Choice A is wrong because this sentence doesn't summarize a finding; it only explains the import of a finding. Plus, we really can't justify calling one of these findings a "chief" finding. Choices B and C are not supported: the text does not describe a challenge faced by the researchers, and this sentence has nothing to do with methodology.

7) A
Summarize the passage. The first sentence asserts that literacy was generally low in ancient Greece. The second sentence backs off on that a bit, telling us that literacy varied. The next few sentences tell us several things about Athens during the classical period: the state focused on intellectual pursuits; citizens received an education; a playwright mentioned literate audiences; there was graffiti. These facts all support the point made in the last sentence: classical period Athens had a relatively high literacy rate. The question is asking about the reference to Aristophanes's comedies, which was one of the pieces of evidence supporting this central claim. That's choice A.

Answer Explanations

Structure and Purpose: Practice Set 2 (p. 49)

1) B

The basic structure of the poem is a series of either-or options. *How would you have us*, the poet asks of America. Rising or falling? As men or as things?

The first two lines form one of these either-or pairs. How would you have us: as we are, or sinking under the load we bear? Because this is set up as a contrast, the point of the underlined portion cannot be that African Americans are heavily burdened (sinking under a heavy load). Otherwise, the "or" at the start of the second line would make no sense. Eliminate choice A.

Choices C and D may describe other parts of the poem, or perhaps the purpose of the poem as a whole. But neither describes the function of this underlined piece, which is to serve as part of an either-or option (where the second line serves as the other part). Since a "dichotomy" is a pair, choice B is the best description of this purpose.

2) C

The underlined portion begins with the vague pronoun "her," so an important first step here is to figure out who or what this "her" is referring to. Let's walk through the passage.

Laura is realizing the extent of some city's power. Its influence is felt thousands of miles away. Way out in Wisconsin, things are stimulated by "this city's energy." This phrase is immediately followed by the underlined sentence, indicating that the "her" refers not to Laura, but to the city. This sentence, together with the next few sentences, is continuing to illustrate the extent of the city's power by describing its influence in widely distant places and contexts.

Choice A is wrong because it's not *Laura's* force we're talking about, but the city's. Laura's personal background isn't mentioned at all, so choice B is definitely out. And choice D goes too far. This passage is focused on the powers of this one city; it never goes beyond that to make some larger point about human industry. Choice C is the best match for our prediction.

3) A

In this passage, Toni Morrison tells the story of some young people talking to an elderly woman. They ask for a context for their lives, such as song, literature, or "poem full of vitamins."

There is no tone of mocking in this passage, so we can eliminate choice B. There's also no political argument (even an implicit one), so choice D is out as well. No one is being obviously cruel here, and even if they were, it's hard to see how the phrase "no poem full of vitamins" would illustrate that cruelty. Eliminate choice C.

That leaves choice A. The word "vitamins" certainly fits with the idea of nourishment. And the text describes these youths as finding poetry "in their despair": they are seeking a context for their lives, and they find the answer in poetry. So, poetry—one form of "the written word"—has served a nourishing function, helping them in their time of need.

4) B

This question is asking us to describe the structure of the full passage. We'll need to understand how all the different pieces of the text work together as a single whole.

So, let's go through it. The first sentence describes a traditional view: that people make good decisions. The next sentence tells us that behavioral economists disagree with this view, because it ignores the importance of state of mind. Then we get an example of how that works, followed by a statement of why it matters that we understand this (because it makes actions more predictable). Finally, there's a concluding sentence that summarizes what behavioral economists are seeking to do.

Now let's attack the choices, doing our best to match every abstract term from a choice with something specific in the passage.

Start with choice A. Is a theory put forward? Sure; the theory that state of mind matters. Is a controversial definition discussed? No. There is controversy here, in the sense that the two groups of economists disagree with each other, but there's no term that has been defined in a controversial way. Choice A is out.

Now choice B. Is a school for thought introduced? Yes: the behavioral economists' view. Is a clarifying example discussed? Yes, in the third sentence. Hold on to choice B.

Let's look at choice C. Is there a "revolutionary" viewpoint here? Not really. That's an awfully strong word that's just not supported by what we have in this passage. And anyway, skipping to the end of the choice, neither of these views is endorsed by the author: the author seems to be just neutrally describing the debate. Eliminate choice C.

Choice D is perhaps the easiest to get rid of. There's no methodology, and no question is posed!

That leaves B as the best answer.

5) B

The first sentence of this passage tells us these scientists used "a holographic approach" in their paper. The second sentence, which is the one we're asked about, tells us what the holographic principle is. The third and fourth sentences then explain how the scientists used this principle in their paper.

Don't understand what the holographic principle means? Don't worry—we don't have to. We're looking for the

function of the second sentence, so we have our prediction already: the second sentence tells us what the holographic principle is.

We have no idea what the scientists' findings were, so choice A is out. The passage tells us that the scientists used the principle, so they don't appear to have challenged it. That gets rid of choice D.

Let's look closely at choice B. Does the second sentence define a term? Yes, it defines the holographic principle. Does that term help explain the structure of the scientists' article? That question is a little harder to answer from this science-heavy passage, but it appears so.

Now go to choice C. Does the second sentence provide context? Sure: the definition could be considered context. Does that context clarify the question that they sought to answer? No, the passage isn't using the definition in that way. It describes how the scientists used the principle in their article, but no part of that discussion really clarifies any particular goal of their research. That leaves B as the best answer.

6) A
The first sentence tells us about an election outcome that defied the polls. The second sentence asserts that several factors may have contributed to this outcome. The rest of the passage then lists three of those factors. The question is asking about the function of the second sentence, so a good prediction might be that it sets up the list of factors that explain the outcome described in the previous sentence. That's a pretty good match for choice A.

By itself, this particular sentence doesn't "explain" or "reveal the significance" of anything; it just sets up the explanation that follows. Eliminate choices B and D. And since the sentence doesn't provide an example, choice C must be out too. Choice A is the winner.

7) D
The first half of this passage defines and explains the term "J-curve," while the second half applies the term to the civil rights movement. The last sentence continues the explanation of how the civil rights movement fits this hypothesis, ending with the underlined portion, which describes how such a pattern would look on a graph. In so doing, the passage returns to the earlier themes of the text, helping us to visualize why the term "J-curve" would be used to describe this pattern.

As you evaluate the choices, be sure to limit yourself only to the underlined portion, not to the sentence as a whole or other parts of the passage. This underlined portion does not suggest a problem with any particular interpretation, and anyway nothing has been defined as "the traditional interpretation" of the movement. Eliminate choice A. The underlined portion also gives us

no history or theoretical background, and it does not explain *why* the civil rights movement made a lot of progress in the mid-twentieth century (it only explains *that* the movement made such progress). Get rid of choices B and C. That leaves choice D: by giving us a visual, this part of the sentence helps us understand where the term "J-curve" gets its name, thus illustrating the meaning of the term.

COMPARE AND CONTRAST (p. 52)
Compare and Contrast: Try It
1) Any claims about the potential health benefits of red wine.
The question here is quite broad. Anything that Text 1 says about potential health benefits of red wine would be included.

2) Red wine is good for heart health due to antioxidants like resveratrol. Red wine may also protect against some cancers and against age-related cognitive decline.
The whole text is about the health benefits of red wine, so it's all relevant. The text makes several assertions, varying from broad to specific. First, numerous studies suggest that moderate red wine consumption is good for the heart. Second, the effects are due to antioxidants, particularly resveratrol. Third, the way resveratrol helps is by improving cardiovascular function, reducing inflammation, and increasing HDL cholesterol. Fourth, there are non-resveratrol-related benefits: red wine may help protect against cancer and against age-related cognitive decline.

3) Moderate consumption may have benefits, but you can get those benefits in other ways. Red wine also has risks.
Text 2 does not dispute that moderate consumption may have health benefits, though it doesn't exactly endorse the idea either. The main point here is that even if there are benefits, you can achieve those benefits in safer ways.

4) B
Choices A and C have Text 2 disputing points that it never disputed. Choice D goes too far: Text 2 spoke about the dangers of *excessive* consumption, not moderate consumption, and mentioned potential harm to individuals with specific health concerns, not healthy individuals. That leaves choice B, which lines up nicely with our prediction and doesn't go too far.

Compare and Contrast: Practice Set 1 (p. 57)
1) C
First, summarize the two texts. Text 1 defines carbon markets and tells us some good things about them; Text 2 tells us some downsides. So the overall relationship between the two texts is a contrasting one: Text 2 pretty clearly disagrees with Text 1.

Answer Explanations

But what is the nature of that disagreement? Text 2 never talks about whether carbon markets are good for businesses (choice A) or whether countries need to work together to combat climate change (choice B). It also never discusses investment in low-carbon technologies (choice D); even though it's not hard to imagine that Text 2 would agree with this, if it's not in the text, it can't be the right answer.

Choice C simply gives us a big, broad disagreement: Text 2 would say this is a bad idea that could lead to bad things. That's a good match for Text 2's overall attitude, so it's the best answer.

2) B

Text 1 is arguing that GMOs are not dangerous and can be good. The underlined claim is that they've been proven safe through extensive testing.

Text 2 says that GMOs have been proven safe only in the short term, and that we don't yet know about their long-term safety. The rest of Text 2 discusses another potential downside of GMOs, which is not strictly relevant to the claim we've been asked to focus on.

So, how would Text 2 respond to the idea that GMOs have been proven safe through extensive testing? We have our prediction already: "only in the short term."

Choice A goes too far. Text 2 does concede that GMOs have been proven safe at least in the short term, so they wouldn't say the claim is *completely* baseless.

Choice C is not something Text 2 said: they never addressed Text 1's motivations.

If choice A was too negative, choice D is too positive. Text 2's position toward this claim is overall disagreement; they don't seem to find the argument compelling.

Choice B is right. Text 2 would say that this claim is "at least partially true," since it's true with regards to the short-term effects. And Text 2 would also say that the claim "fails to address an important issue": the long-term effects. Choice B is the answer.

3) D

Text 1 asks whether the Ancient Greeks could see the color blue, then cites some evidence to suggest that perhaps they didn't. Text 2 describes the science behind color vision and points out the limits of that knowledge: it can't help us understand whether we perceive colors in the same way as each other. So, that's our prediction: if asked whether the Ancient Greeks could see the color blue, Text 2 would say something like "we have no way of knowing."

Choices A, B, and C are all much too definitive to fit. They're all lining up Text 2 on one side or the other of this debate, when all Text 2 said is that the science

doesn't really answer the question. That leaves D as the right answer.

4) A

Text 1 argues that Jay Gatsby represents the American dream, that his downfall represents its ultimate failure, and that the character therefore serves as a critique of a materialistic American dream and a cautionary tale.

Text 2 offers a more nuanced understanding of the character. This author says that Gatsby is driven by both materialism and love, and that the American dream is about both. Text 2 also argues for a different interpretation of Gatsby's downfall.

That's a pretty complicated take that's hard to summarize in a neat prediction, so let's go to the choices and see what we can eliminate.

Choice B is wrong because Text 2 never says Daisy is to blame for Gatsby's failure. Choice C is wrong because Text 2 agrees that materialism is a concern for Gatsby; the disagreement was just whether materialism was Gatsby's *only* concern. Choice D is wrong for several reasons, but the first few words are enough to eliminate it: nothing in Text 2 suggests that this author is offended, or would be offended, by anything that Text 1 said.

That leaves choice A, which is the right answer.

5) B

Text 1 first defines food irradiation and explains its purpose. The rest of the passage consists of several lines of attack on food irradiation: it may cause free radicals that are bad for our health; it may make the food less nutritious and less tasty; and safer methods, like improved hygiene, are available to achieve the same ends. It's that second line of attack that we're asked about: the idea that food irradiation can make food less nutritious and less tasty.

Text 2 argues that food irradiation is safe and effective. The second sentence of Text 2 is the one that's most relevant to the claim we've been asked about: according to Text 2, food irradiation "has been extensively studied" and has proved to be effective "without causing significant changes to the nutritional value, taste, or texture of the food." In other words, studies say that the critics in the underlined portion are wrong. That's what choice B says. It's pretty strongly worded, which is ordinarily a strike against it, but in this case the strong wording is justified. Text 2 did use the words "extensively" and "proven," so this matches up.

Choice A is wrong because Text 2 did not say anything about the relative importance of these different issues. Text 2 also did not directly address hygiene practices or free radicals (both of which were only mentioned in Text 1), so we can eliminate choices C and D.

Compare and Contrast: Practice Set 2 (p. 60)
1) B
Let's walk through the major points in each of these texts. Text 1 defines SCNs as the primary circadian pacemaker. It goes on to explain that SCNs control the internal clock by receiving light input, and that disruptions to the SCNs cause all kinds of bad things.

Text 2 concedes that SCNs are important for circadian rhythms, but says that other things matter too. According to Text 2, environmental factors and genetic mutations are also relevant. So our prediction here is that Text 2 would disagree with the claim that SCNs are "the primary circadian pacemaker," because there are other important factors.

Choice A is too specific. It's not clear how Text 1's statements would undermine its own claim, and nothing in Text 2 indicates that.

Choice C is wrong because Text 2 doesn't discuss non-human animals: the entire text is focused on humans.

Choice D is tempting because it's so weak, but it's not actually supported either. We just don't have the evidence to know what Text 2 would think about disruptions to SCNs or their relationship to sleep disorders.

That leaves choice B: Text 2 would agree in part (yes; Text 2 said that SCNs "undoubtedly play an important role") but point out that other factors exist (yes: for example, environmental factors).

2) B
According to Text 1, the "traditional physics theory" is that nuclear fusion requires high temperature and pressure. Text 1 disagrees with this view, pointing to a 1989 experiment as evidence that cold fusion is possible.

Text 2 denies that cold fusion is possible. The author says the very idea is incompatible with physics theory, and the evidence is inconclusive. It also says that results from 1980s experiments have not been replicated and thus are not reliable.

Be careful about the way the question is worded. This time, we're not being asked how Text 2 would respond to Text 1 (which would certainly be with disagreement). Instead, we're being asked how Text 2 would respond to *the traditional physics theory*, which was the idea that nuclear fusion requires high temperature; in other words, that cold fusion is impossible. Text 2 would agree with that!

Choice A is the opposite of what we want. This is how Text 1 would respond to traditional physics theory, not how Text 2 would.

Choice B says Text 2 would agree. That looks good.

Choice C is off for a couple of reasons. Text 2 never discussed the Fleischmann-Pons experiment specifically, so this is already looking wrong. But even without that problem, there's no reason for us to think that Text 2 would call the experiment irrelevant. Text 2 did have some objections to the 1980s experiments, but irrelevance wasn't one of them.

Choice D is way off, since Text 2 never advocates an alternative theory.

So choice B is the answer.

3) C
Text 1 tells us about an old alchemist who believed in a substance called "phlogiston." The underlined portion is the evidence for this view: when wood burns, it becomes lighter, suggesting that something (like phlogiston) is released during the burning.

Text 2 explains that the phlogiston theory was replaced by a different view: burning results in chemical compounds, not phlogiston release. The parenthetical in Text 2 suggests an alternate explanation for the underlined evidence: maybe wood becomes lighter during burning because the new compounds formed have lower mass than the original material. That's our prediction.

Text 2 never disputes the idea that wood becomes lighter, so choice A is out. Text 2 would definitely not argue on behalf of phlogiston, so choice B is out too. In fact, Text 2 seems completely unswayed by the phlogiston theory; this author doesn't appear to accept it even in part, so we can eliminate choice D.

That leaves choice C, which is a good match for our prediction.

4) B
Text 1 makes a rather abstract argument about American culture. It asserts that the great American ideas of the past were attributed to distant heroes, suggesting that today, these ideas are less distant. As a result, we are witnessing the rebirth of American culture.

Text 2 notes that cultural trends travel faster now than they did in the past. It regards this as a bad thing, since the speed destroys the context. As a result, Text 2 says the speed of our lives is the end of American culture.

So, the two texts end up on opposite sides of the issue: Text 1 thinks American culture is on the upswing, and Text 2 thinks it's doomed. Our prediction for how Text 2 would characterize Text 1? Let's keep it simple: Text 2 might just call it "wrong."

Choice D is the easiest to eliminate right off the bat, because Text 2 would definitely not call Text 1 potentially correct.

Choice A is half right, half wrong. The word "questionable" is a good characterization, but the

Answer Explanations

problem is not the number of theories offered; Text 2 was focused on something else.

Choice C is also focused on the wrong thing. For Text 2, the issue is not whether any of the new trends are here to stay; the issue was how quickly they spread.

Choice B gets everything right. The word "wrongheaded" definitely expresses the right attitude, and this one accurately conveys Text 2's objection: it's about the speed.

5) D

According to Text 1, tuataras live such long lives for two main reasons: their slow metabolisms and their negligible senescence. (For now, don't worry about what senescence means.) The passage explains why those factors matter so much, then makes a quick reference to a few additional biological factors (efficient DNA repair mechanisms and low reproductive rates) in order to make its overall point: tuataras' longevity is due to biological adaptations.

Text 2 accepts that slow metabolisms and negligible senescence are relevant. However, Text 2 says there's more to the story, including their isolated environment and low reproductive rates.

Choice A gets the tone and emphasis wrong. The two authors do agree that low reproductive rates are a factor, but neither one asserts that they are "the most important reason" for tuataras' longevity.

Choice B is wrong because the texts both accept that tuataras have very long lifespans. Choice C goes too far. Text 2 agrees that the metabolic rates may be relevant; the disagreement is only about whether other factors might also matter.

That leaves choice D, which matches up with Text 2's overall point, gets the tone right, and does not go too far.

COMMAND OF EVIDENCE – ILLUSTRATE THE CLAIM (p. 65)

Command of Evidence – Illustrate the Claim: Try It

1) Element #1: the quote must reference the ocean
   Element #2: the quote must emphasize the connection between the natural world and the human spirit

Note the two separate requirements here. First, the answer choice must include a reference to the ocean, or it cannot be right. And second, the answer choice must emphasize the connection between nature and the human spirit.

2)
	Element #1	Element #2
A)	Y	Y
B)	N	Y
C)	N	N
D)	Y	N

Choice A refers to the "voice of the sea," which is a reference to the ocean. And by saying that this voice "speaks to the soul," this choice emphasizes a connection between the natural world (the sea) and the human spirit (the soul).

Choice B does not mention the ocean or any other kind of water. It does include a connection between the natural world (birds) and the human spirit (tradition and prejudice). But because it failed to mention the water, it cannot be the answer.

Choice C mentions water, though not specifically the ocean. More importantly, the only connection made to the human spirit is the image of "an oar upon the water," which is more a reference to human activity (rowing) than to the natural world.

Choice D references a "sea smell" and mentions how "the night sat lightly upon the sea"—those are references to the ocean. But this choice is all about the natural world; it never connects that natural world to the human spirit.

3) A

The only answer to contain both of the elements we were looking for was choice A.

Command of Evidence – Illustrate the Claim: Practice Set 1 (p. 69)

1) D

The claim we need to illustrate is that Nie Zheng regrets refusing the gift from Yan Zhongzi. Choices A and B do not mention Yan Zhongzi or his gift. Choice C, on the other hand, does mention Yan Zhongzi; however, all the quote explicitly does is to compare the situations of the two men. Nothing in this quote directly expresses regret. Choice D mentions Yan Zhongzi traveling to see him, which presumably is a reference to the time the gift was offered. Moreover, "I treated him very shabbily indeed" is an expression of regret.

2) C

The claim here is that Mrs. Jennings fills her days with matchmaking as an amusement. Choices A and B give general information about the character but nothing directly related to this claim. Choice D gives us a clearer picture of the matchmaking efforts, but still doesn't tell us that the activity is "necessary" to fill Mrs. Jennings' days. Choice C is the most direct match.

3) D

Focus on the idea that previous activism inspires Baldwin in her legislative work. In choice D, the lessons learned from "participation in this civil rights movement" and other activism "are now being applied" to her current work: thus, they inspire her in her work as a Congresswoman (whose work would consist of "legislative work"). Choices A, B, and C give us more of

the background and context to understand her point, but choice D is the only one that directly makes the point stated in the claim.

4) C
The right answer here needs several components. It must use contrasting imagery, it must use that imagery to describe love, and it must specifically describe love as an uplifting force. Choices B and D don't specifically mention love. Choice A does, but there's no "uplifting force" component. But in choice C, love has buoyed (lifted) the speaker up to the sky. Plus, there's a contrast: weight usually pulls us down, but in this quote, the weight of love has pulled him *up*. Choice C has everything we're looking for, so it's the right answer.

5) B
For this question, we want to emphasize the importance of sharing knowledge and empowering others. Choice A focuses on waiting and fatigue, not sharing knowledge. Choice C is focused on a woman empowering herself, not empowering others. Choice D perhaps suggests the importance of inspiration from others, since it's saying that books are not enough, but we really have to stretch the quote to make that work. Choice B is the best match: letting others "light their candles" in your knowledge is pretty explicitly a reference to sharing your knowledge with others.

6) A
If life cannot match our expectations, then reality does not align with our preconceived notions. Choice A is a good match for the text. None of the other choices give us quite as direct a reference to this mismatch between expectations and reality.

7) A
There are two elements to satisfy here: the right answer must juxtapose the external and internal world, and this juxtaposition must underscore the speaker's melancholy, which means sadness. In choice A, the speaker juxtaposes the way it figuratively "rains in [his] heart" (the internal world) with the way it "rains on the town" (the external world). This is followed by a reference to "languor," or weakness, that "soaks to [his] heart," which sounds quite melancholy. Choice A looks good.

Choice B is only about the external world, and it's entirely too happy. Nothing here underscores melancholy.

Choice C is close, because "grief without reason" certainly sounds melancholic. But the quote only refers to the internal world (the way it figuratively "rains for no reason" in the speakers heart), so we're lacking the juxtaposition we need.

With its multiple references to terrible pain, choice D definitely satisfies the melancholy aspect of this question.

However, there is no juxtaposition of the external and internal world. The only answer to include everything we needed was A.

Command of Evidence – Illustrate the Claim: Practice Set 2 (p. 72)
1) A
The key phrase to seize upon in the text here is a financial metaphor. In choice A, the subject's face "coins" the speakers tears, the way a government coins metal (making it into currency by shaping and stamping it). This is also called *minting*, which connects to the next sentiment: "thy stamp they bear" (the tears bear your stamp), "and by this mintage they are something worth" (because of you, my tears are worth something). Thus, the whole quote is a financial metaphor indicating that the subject's presence makes his tears (his sadness) worthwhile. That's exactly what we needed, so the answer is A.

2) B
The text gives us several components to watch for. We need joyful language; we need an assertion that individuals are unique and praiseworthy; and we need a reference to the interconnected nature of humanity. Choice C praises animals, not other humans. Choice A doesn't suggest that anyone is particularly worthy of praise. Choice D is tough, because it certainly emphasizes the interconnectedness of humanity; however, the language is not particularly joyful.

Now consider choice B. Of all the lines quoted in the choices, "I celebrate myself" is the most joyful. This also indicates that an individual is worthy of praise (or at least that the speaker is). And the last line of the quote ties it all together. When the speaker says that every one of his atoms "as good belongs to you," he not only emphasizes the interconnectedness of human beings, but he also suggests that, since the speaker is worthy of praise, every other human must be too.

3) D
All four of the choices relate to Paris, as the wording of the question makes clear. But do all four use figurative language? A doesn't: it's a straightforward description of the character's actions. For the remaining three choices, consider the rest of our tasks for this question: the quote must describe Paris as a vibrant and alluring city that captivates the protagonist with its sophistication. B and C certainly describe the city in a positive tone, but neither specifically relate to sophistication. D, with its references to "art" and a "master chef," is the only one that accomplishes this final task.

4) A
Another multi-task question. The right choice should not only be witty, but should skewer social norms and

Answer Explanations

conventional morality. Choices B and D are funny, but nothing about them seems particularly related to norms or morality. Choice C is definitely related to norms and morality, but it's not particularly funny. Choice A is the only answer that succeeds on both counts.

5) C
Choices B and D both display an attitude of childhood glee, but they are not specifically descriptions of the season. Choice C's reference to the time "when the world is puddle-wonderful" is a description of Springtime itself. Because this is also a celebratory description, C is the best answer.

6) C
For this question, the right answer must argue that a universal mathematical language underlies our knowledge even when we're not aware of it. Choices A and D do not mention math, and choice B does not reference an underlying language that exists even when we're not aware of it. Only choice C fulfills both tasks.

7) D
The quote needs to show that human beings are inherently subjective, but in a specific way: it must present humans as perceiving their world through a lens that shapes their experiences. Choice A is about hypocrisy, which really only relates to the moral corruption mentioned as background information about the novel. Choice B suggests that our perspective can shape our experiences, but this is limited to brooding over lost pleasures: there's nothing about our perceptions of the world as a whole. Choice C is somewhat backwards, in that it suggests that we shape other people's experiences (affecting "the rest of history") when we want to say that we shape our own. Choice D is the best match: if the world is a "looking-glass" (a mirror), then when we look at the world, we are using a self-centered lens. And the fact that the world "gives back" to each of us a reflection of our own image means that by looking through this self-centered lens, we are ultimately shaping our own experiences.

COMMAND OF EVIDENCE – STRENGTHEN/ WEAKEN (p. 75)
Command of Evidence – Strengthen/ Weaken: Try It

1) Woolly monkeys play a crucial role in seed dispersal.
For this one, it's not hard to find the conclusion: it's directly stated in the last line of the text.

2) Woolly monkeys consume a wide variety of fruits and travel through a wide range of habitat.
There's a lot of background information about the study. But the key evidence for this conclusion is that the monkeys consumed "a wide variety of fruits," doing so as they "ranged through large tracts of forest habitat."

3) Something showing that the actions of the woolly monkey actually result in dispersal of seeds.
The researchers are presumably inferring that the monkeys disperse the seeds as they travel through their home range, most likely through their droppings (or perhaps carried on their fur or by some other means). Useful evidence would help confirm that this dispersal actually happened. For example, evidence of fruit seeds in the monkeys' droppings in various parts of the range would help. But we don't have to get too specific here: the general category of evidence we're looking for is something showing that the monkeys' actions actually do result in the dispersal of the fruit seeds.

4) The words "nueit" and "night" should not be considered false cognates.
This is a tougher argument, but focus on the overall point first. What is the author is trying to convince us of? It's in the last sentence: that these two words should not be considered false cognates.

5) False cognates occur when two words share similar sounds and meaning but different etymologies. The words "nueit" and "night" sound similar and have the same meaning.
Now let's examine how the argument got to that conclusion. Two unrelated languages, Mbabaram and English, happen to use the same word for "dog." The term for this type of coincidence is a "false cognate." Specifically, a false cognate occurs when two words share similar sounds and meanings but have different etymologies (linguistic histories). Next, the argument switches to a new pair of words: the Aragonese word "nueit" and the English word "night." The text tells us that these two words share similar sounds and meanings.

6) Something showing that the two words have related etymologies.
Consider what we're missing. As the text defined the term "false cognates," there are three elements that must be satisfied: similar sounds, similar meanings, and different etymologies. We already know that "nueit" and "night" share similar sounds and similar meanings. If they have different etymologies, they'd be false cognates. So to strengthen the idea that these are *not* false cognates, we need evidence that the words do *not* have different etymologies. In other words, look for evidence that the two words share a common linguistic root.

7) A. W
B. I
C. S
D. I
Best answer: C

Choice A slightly weakens this argument, because it provides another means by which the seeds might be dispersed. If the plants in this habitat have this type of adaptation, then we've just made it *less* likely that the monkeys are responsible for seed dispersal.

Choices B and D are irrelevant. While they certainly matter to the monkeys, neither answer impacts how likely it is that woolly monkeys help disperse seeds.

Choice C gives us evidence that there's an association between areas with monkeys and areas where seeds have been dispersed. This certainly doesn't *prove* that the monkeys are responsible, but we don't have to do that: we just have to make it slightly more likely that they do. Choice C is the only answer that has that effect, so it's the best answer.

8) A. S
   B. I
   C. I
   D. I
   Best answer: A

Choice A gives us just what we were looking for. If this is true, then the words do *not* have different etymologies, which means they fail to satisfy one of the requirements for false cognates. This strengthens the claim that the words should *not* be considered false cognates. None of the other choices are relevant to this claim, so choice A is the best answer.

Command of Evidence – Strengthen/ Weaken: Practice Set 1 (p. 81)
1) A
Summarize what we know. This particular kind of fish, the Arctic cod, can survive in very cold waters. The hypothesis that we're supposed to support is that there's a specialized molecule in the fish's bloodstream that acts as an antifreeze.

Choice B only tells us that other fish are "believed" to possess an antifreeze molecule as well. This is too weak to really help us, since the people who believe this might just be wrong. This choice would be a much better option if it simply told us that these other fish *actually possess* a similar molecule.

Choices C and D tell us nothing relevant to the question of whether the Arctic cod have an antifreeze molecule. At best, they explain why the cod need to swim in such cold waters; they don't tell us how they manage it.

Choice A tells us about a specific molecule, a glycoprotein, found in the Arctic cod bloodstream. According to choice A, this molecule prevents freezing. That directly supports the scientists' claim, so this is the best answer.

2) D
There's a lot of background information in this text, and several competing views. Isolate the view we're supposed to support: the collapse was caused by famine due to uncontrollable environmental factors.

Choices A and B go the wrong way, supporting the opposing views. A supports the idea that the city was conquered by a neighboring group, and B supports the idea that the city was torn apart by social inequality. Choice C is relevant to environmental factors, but it's not specific enough to give us much support for Smith's claim.

Choice D is much stronger. This is telling us about a series of severe droughts (environmental factors) during a time period overlapping that when the city is thought to have collapsed. And, more than that, they are droughts that likely impacted agricultural productivity, supporting the idea that these droughts may have led to famine.

3) C
Keep your eye on the claim we need to support: it's not just that Dolley Madison was interesting or awesome, but that she appeared unbothered by the nasty remarks printed about her and would simply laugh them off.

Choice A supports a different point about Dolley Madison: that she helped her husband win office. Although that was mentioned in the text, it wasn't the claim we're looking to support.

Choices B and D, at best, support another incidental claim made about Dolley Madison in the text (that she had great grace and charm). But they don't tell us how she reacted to vicious attacks in the press.

But choice C does. By saying that the negative article was "as good as a play," she was making clear that the story wasn't true, but without turning nasty herself; instead, she handled it with humor and grace. This gives us exactly the support we need.

4) B
The claim in this text is about why physicians who used leeches would apply them to the arms or legs in particular, rather than to other parts of the body. The specific claim is that physicians were trying to make sure the leeches got as much blood as possible. So, look for a choice that tells us why the arms and legs are a particularly good location for maximizing blood output.

Choice A tells us why leeches were used, and choice C tells us why they're not used anymore. Neither gives us information about *where* leeches were used or why doctors focused on the arms and legs.

Choice D is more relevant, because it's giving us a reason that doctors might not want to use other areas of the

body. But it's still not supporting the idea that the arms and legs would maximize the amount of blood drawn.

Choice B is the only one that gives us information about the arms and legs. Specifically, it explains why leeches can get more blood in this location: because of all the veins close to the surface. This one does the most to strengthen the student's specific claim.

5) C
The conclusion here is that educational TV programming can aid in Theory of Mind (ToM) development, which the text describes as "the ability to understand and attribute mental states to oneself and others." Choices A, B, and D tell us other positive things about educational TV, but none are quite relevant to the specific conclusion we're looking to strengthen: that this kind of programming helps with ToM development specifically. Choice C, however, tells us that educational TV helps children develop perspective-taking skills, which nicely matches ToM's "ability to attribute mental states to others." This is the best match for what we need.

6) B
Be careful about what we're looking to strengthen here. It's not just that heating eggs makes them less likely to trigger an allergic response: it's about *how* that happens. The claim is that the heating process does this by "altering the allergenic properties of egg proteins." Choice B is the only answer that directly relates to that claim, by explaining exactly how the proteins are altered.

Command of Evidence – Strengthen/ Weaken: Practice Set 2 (p. 84)
1) B
First, let's summarize the passage. A lot of students say they get better grades than they actually do. But there is no physical indication that these students were intentionally lying, and they did later improve their grades. The conclusion we're supposed to support is that when these students misstated their GPAs, they were just being optimistic rather than actually trying to deceive.

Choice A tells more us how big a discrepancy there was between the actual GPAs and what the students reported. But there's nothing here that tells us *why* these students misstated their grades at all.

Choice C doesn't do much, because it's only about "some" students. Plus, this statement is so vague that it might actually weaken the claim; maybe their misstatements were somehow related to their discomfort rather than their optimism.

Choice D is like choice A: it gives us more detail about the misstatements, but it doesn't help us understand *why*.

Choice B is the most relevant. Remember, the students in this study showed no "physical markers" of intentional deception when they misstated their GPAs. Based on choice B, it seems they *did* show these physical markers when they misstated their disciplinary records. This suggests that the two types of misstatements are qualitatively different: perhaps their misstatements about their disciplinary records were an attempt to deceive, while the misstatements about their GPA were simply optimism. This is a tough question because this choice certainly doesn't *prove* the author's point, but it doesn't have to; all we have to do is make the conclusion a little bit more likely to be true. Choice B goes the farthest towards doing that.

2) D
Be careful about which claim we're supposed to strengthen here. Although the passage tells us that Jordan denounced Nixon's behavior, that's not what we're looking for in the choices. The specific claim that we need to support is the idea that she did *not* state a conclusion about Nixon's removal from office, but rather emphasized the need for Congress to begin exploring the evidence.

Choice A gives us background information and suggests Congress has good reason (not a "petty" reason) to investigate. Choices B and C support the wrong claim: they're illustrations of Jordan denouncing Nixon's behavior. They do not support the specific claim we're working for here. Choice D is the winner: Jordan states that Congress has clarified "the question" (whether Nixon has committed offenses) and says that they should proceed to answer it. That illustrates that Jordan focused on the need to move forward with exploring the evidence rather than the need to remove Nixon from office, exactly what we want for this question.

3) A
The hypothesis here is pretty straightforward: yoga helps your heart. As evidence, we have the details of a study. After a year of yoga sessions, Group A had better heart health. The control group, Group B, had the same heart health that they started out with.

Do you see any weaknesses in this argument to begin with? One big one jumps out, which is that we don't know enough about this study. How similar are these two groups? How controlled were the conditions? If we want to weaken this physician's argument, we're looking to exploit those flaws and drive as big a wedge as we can between the evidence and the conclusion. One way to do this would be to point out some major difference between the two groups, indicating some possible alternate explanation for the difference in outcome.

Choices C and D aren't particularly relevant. Choice C gives us a similarity between the two groups rather than a difference, and we don't care about the group members' preferences (especially *after* the experiment was over).

Choices A and B both express a difference between the two groups, but consider the type of difference carefully. Choice B is essentially saying that Group A started out with better heart health than Group B. But the hypothesis we want to weaken is not that Group A was healthier than Group B at the end of the year; it was that Group A's health had improved over the course of the year while Group B's hadn't. For that comparison, it's not strictly relevant to know which one started out healthier.

Choice A, however, is giving us an important difference. This tells us that Group A, unlike Group B, was engaging in other heart-healthy activities (say, following a low-cholesterol diet). If that's the case, then these other activities might explain why Group A's heart health improved, suggesting that the yoga had nothing to do with it. This directly weakens the physician's claim, so it's the best answer.

4) B
The claim we want to support is that fever speeds recovery from illness by regulating and controlling infection. In the study, we have two groups of fish with bacterial infections, plus a third group that was not infected. Within the two groups of infected fish, we have a distinction: one received antifever medication (and thus presumably had no fever), while the other received no antifever medication (and thus presumably had fevers). For clarity, let's assign names to these groups: Group 1 has an infection and no fever; Group 2 has an infection and a fever; and Group 3 has no infection.

So, how can we support the idea that fever controls infection and speeds recovery? If this is right, then the fish with fevers (Group 2) should recover more quickly than the fish without fevers (Group 1). Note that Group 3 is entirely irrelevant.

Choice A tells us that Group 2 got sick. That's both unsurprising (since the fish were given a bacterial infection) and not particularly helpful: it's not telling us anything about how quickly the recovered. And, importantly, it's not comparing this group of fish to any other group. Eliminate choice A.

Choice B is all about speed. This tells us that Group 1 (the fish without fevers) recovered in 14 days, while Group 2 (the fish with fevers) recovered in 7 days. Thus, the fish without fevers recovered more slowly than the fish with fevers. That looks like exactly what we wanted, so hold on to choice B.

Choice C says that the Group 2 fish (the fish with fevers) were better able to heal from certain wounds than the Group 1 fish (the fish without fevers). That may support the idea that fever is useful, but it doesn't support the specific hypothesis we have in this passage, because it doesn't tell us how quickly they recovered. Eliminate choice C.

Choice D tells us that Group 3 didn't get sick. These fish never got an infection in the first place, so that's not surprising. But it certainly doesn't tell us anything about the role of fever, so we can eliminate choice D.

Choice B is the best answer.

5) C
Read the question carefully: we're being asked to *weaken* the claim, not strengthen it! This passage tells us about some ancient cave paintings created by the Aurignacians. Some scholars think the paintings were practical, while others interpret them as spiritual. It's that latter claim that's underlined, so that's what we're supposed to weaken.

The existence of supernatural characters would tend to undermine the idea that the paintings were merely practical in nature. Choice A thus *supports* the underlined claim rather than weakening it, so it goes the wrong way.

In choice B, the location of the paintings doesn't necessarily weaken this claim. We could even read this information as strengthening it, since you'd think that paintings with a practical purpose would be made easily accessible.

Choice C seems to strengthen the practical idea: maybe the paintings were illustrating where to strike the animal in order to get to the heart. In the text, the scholars who claimed the paintings were practical suggested that one purpose might have been to "communicate information about hunting techniques," which this would seem to support. If so, then it undermines the idea that the paintings were primarily spiritual in nature, so choice C looks good.

Choice D is irrelevant background information. The geographical location of the paintings tells us nothing about their original function, at least not without a lot of extra information about the Aurignacians that the passage doesn't supply. Thus we can eliminate choice D, leaving choice C as the best answer.

6) D
Carefully identify the claim: that strength training can increase the resting metabolic rate, or RMR. Given the explanation in the first few sentences of the text, this claim is saying that engaging in strength training can increase the rate at which we burn calories *while at rest*. We're not looking for a change in metabolic rates *during strength training*, so choice B is irrelevant. Choices A and C don't directly tell us anything about a change in metabolic rates. But choice D does. The text told us that carbon dioxide production reflects energy expenditure, which is why RMR can be assessed by measuring the amount of carbon dioxide produced at rest. Choice D tells us that the rate of carbon dioxide production *while at rest* is greater after 16 weeks of strength training, which

Answer Explanations

means the metabolic rate at rest is greater after 16 weeks of strength training. This supports the idea that strength training can increase the resting metabolic rate, which is exactly what we were trying to show.

COMMAND OF EVIDENCE – QUANTITATIVE (p. 87)
Command of Evidence – Quantitative: Try It
1) **Higher butterfat content makes ice cream taste better, but customers pay for the privilege.**
This passage isn't trying to hide the conclusion: it's right there in the last sentence. The claim is that butterfat makes ice cream taste great, but it costs more.

2) **The premium ice cream row**
The most relevant data would be the parts related to high-butterfat ice cream. That's the premium row. The right answer will most likely use this row and another one, perhaps the regular or low-fat ice cream row, so that it can make a comparison. The non-dairy row is the least useful because there is no fixed butterfat content.

3) **Premium ice cream has the most butterfat and costs more than other types**
Remember, the claim was that butterfat tastes better and costs more. The table can't tell us anything about tastiness, but it can tell us which types have more butterfat, and it can tell us about relative costs. The right answer will probably point out that premium ice cream has more butterfat than regular or low-fat ice cream, and that it also costs more than those types.

4) A. Y S
   B. Y I
   C. Y W
   D. N n/a
   Best answer: A

Choices A, B, and C all accurately report the data. Choice D doesn't, because it is worded too broadly: the "non-premium ice creams" would include the non-dairy row, and the table says that non-dairy ice cream costs the same as premium ice cream.

Choices B and C, though accurate, do not strengthen the claim. Choice B is irrelevant, focusing only on the unhelpful non-dairy ice cream row. Choice C actually weakens the claim slightly, since it shows that ice creams with different butterfat contents can cost the same.

Choice A is exactly what we predicted. It's also the only answer that is both accurate and has the effect of strengthening the claim, so it's the best answer.

Command of Evidence – Quantitative: Practice Set 1 (p. 92)
1) A
The text tells us that a government laboratory accidentally sent out samples of *Bacillus anthracis* that had not been completely inactivated. It goes on to say that this incident was "hardly unique." So, we're looking for evidence that such an incident had happened before. Check the table: the first row says there were 8 incidents in which *Bacillus anthracis* was incompletely activated. We already know about one (the May 2015 incident described in the text), so this row tells us that there were at least 7 more. That's what choice A says, so hold on to that choice.

Choice B focuses on how *atypical* the incident described in the text was: this particular type of pathogen was involved in fewer than half the cases. That makes the opposite point from the one we want to make.

Choice C tells us about a different pathogen that was incompletely activated. This does somewhat support the idea that the May 2015 accident was not unique, in that it's giving us another example of incompletely activated pathogens. But this was a different pathogen, so it's not as relevant as choice A. And the fact that it only happened twice for these viruses is less impressive than the fact that it happened at least 8 times for *Bacillus anthracis*, which makes this weaker support for the claim.

Choice D is irrelevant. The number of types of pathogens involved doesn't support the idea that the May 2015 incident wasn't unique.

The best answer is A.

2) C
In the text, the analysts argue that a shift in movie-watching behavior is occurring: specifically, that movies aren't seen in the theater as much anymore, and that instead they're either digitally downloaded or streamed at home. To support that claim, look for a choice about the overall trend of the data: either that the number of movies seen at the theater is going down, or that the number of downloaded and/or streamed movies is going up.

Choice A compares how big the change was in each category rather than which direction the change was headed in. Choices B and D don't tell us anything about the overall trend. But choice C gives us just the information we need: the bars representing downloaded and streamed movies show an increase over time, while the bars representing theater tickets sold (a fair indication for the number of movies seen at the theater) show a decrease over the same time period. That supports the trend we're looking for.

3) B
Highlight the specific claim made in the text: drowsy driving is a significant threat on the roads. Unlike in the last question, this isn't a claim about a trend over time, so we're not looking for a comparison of one year's data to

another's. Instead, we want evidence that drowsy driving is a major problem in general.

Choices A and D give us comparisons that we don't need, either comparing one year to the next (choice A) or contrasting one type of evidence with another (choice D). Both are irrelevant to this claim.

Choice C goes the wrong way. The fact that this percent is so small would tend to show that drowsy driving is *not* that big a deal, the opposite of what we're trying to show. Plus, this choice gets the data slightly wrong. The percentage column in the table tells us the percent *of drivers* involved in fatal crashes that were drowsy, not the percent *of fatal crashes* that involved drowsy drivers.

Choice B accurately reports the data, since the number of fatalities involving drowsy driving is in the "hundreds" for each year in the table. By pointing that out, this choice supports the idea that drowsy driving is a big deal, a major threat on the roads. Choice B is the best answer.

4) B
The text tells us that trade restrictions have significantly harmed the profitability of agricultural businesses in the US, particularly the ones that rely heavily on exports to China. We're supposed to provide an example of that phenomenon. Since this table is telling us about the values of US exports to China, we want something that shows a significant decrease in value (since that would likely result in a decrease in profitability for the business).

Choice A compares the declines in two categories but without particularly emphasizing an overall decrease in value. Choice C gives us a big decrease in value, but it gets the data wrong! According to the table, the value of wheat exports in 2017 was $430 million. If the value had decreased by more than $400 million, then the value in 2018 would have to be less than $30 million. Instead, it's $84 million.

Choice D points out that in 2018, the value of soybean exports was still more than $3,000 million (which is equivalent to $3 billion). This is accurate, but goes the wrong direction for what we want: it emphasizes that soybean exports still had a lot of value. We want to emphasize how much value was *lost*.

Choice B is strongly worded but accurate: according to the table, sorghum exports lost 99% of their value during this time period. It is reasonable to interpret such a dramatic change as the exports being "almost completely wiped out." That certainly goes the farthest to support the claim in the text, so choice B is the right answer.

5) A
The text tells us about carotenoids, a type of pigment found in certain foods. Based on the text and the table, it looks like the animals who consume a lot of carotenoids develop brighter and more saturated coloring in various parts of their body. The researchers at the end of the text indicate that this plays an important role in mate selection. Given the context in the rest of the text, the most likely interpretation is that animals who consume a lot of carotenoids (and thus develop brighter coloring) have more success in attracting mates. Since the text told us that attracting mates is typically of greater importance for male animals than for female animals, we would expect to see male animals showing brighter carotenoid-related colors than the female animals do.

Choice A gives us that exact comparison. Choices B and C focus on irrelevant comparisons by comparing one species to another rather comparing males to females. And choice D goes in the wrong direction, emphasizing how *similar* males' coloring is to females' coloring instead of how different they are.

6) C
Choices A and D are inaccurate: laparoscopic appendectomies had shorter operative times (eliminating choice A) and a lower rate of infections (eliminating choice D). While choice B is correct that the laparoscopic technique showed slightly longer hospitalization times, the difference is within the noted margin of error. And more importantly, this does not support the text's point: a longer hospital stay may indicate a slower recovery, so this is not an advantage of laparoscopic technique. Choice C focuses on the two clearest advantages supplied by the graph: laparoscopic appendectomies took less time (approximately 6 fewer minutes) and resulted in far fewer infections.

7) A
The claim we need to support is that some geographic areas will face especially big waste management challenges in the future. Since we have no information about population sizes or financial resources, all we can go by is the sheer amount of waste these regions are projected to produce. So, look for a choice focusing on the regions where those numbers appear to be getting particularly big, such as the South Asia region and the East Asia & Pacific region. Choice A focuses on the latter, emphasizing the enormous amount of solid waste that this region is expected to be producing each year.

Choice B is only about the past, not the future, so it can't be right. Choice C emphasizes that waste production will be a problem for all regions, which actually slightly weakens the text's claim (which was that while it's a problem for everybody, it's *especially* a problem for specific regions). Similarly, choice D only strengthens the idea that solid waste production is a significant problem generally, not the claim that it will be an especially big problem in certain regions (since, based on the table, North America does not appear to be one of those regions).

Answer Explanations

8) C

There's one whole column of the table that's irrelevant: the one giving the sex of each participant. Nothing in the passage distinguishes between male and female participants, so a choice that focuses on one or the other is unlikely to be right. The claim we want to strengthen is just the idea that for all of us, body temperature declines gradually during the night until it reaches a low point in the early morning hours, after which it begins to rise again.

Choices A and B are suspect right off the bat because they focus on the irrelevant "sex" column. Moreover, both choices are inaccurate! The table shows the same trend for all six participants: a gradual decrease in body temperature. That eliminates choice D as well, leaving C as the only possible answer.

Command of Evidence – Quantitative: Practice Set 2 (p. 96)

1) B

In the text, the researchers concluded that the Mediterranean diet protects against dementia. More specifically, they concluded that this effect is present regardless of an individual's genetic makeup.

In the figure, the height of the bars indicates the probability of dementia. The dark bars represent people with lower MEDAS scores, while the lighter bars are people with higher MEDAS scores. Based on the text, a higher MEDAS score indicates greater adherence to the Mediterranean diet. We want to show that people following the diet have less dementia, which on this figure should mean that the lighter bars are shorter than the dark bars. That's true. In fact, it's true three times. At each genetic risk level, the lighter bar is shorter than the dark bar: that is, people following the diet have a lower probability of developing dementia. That supports the researchers' claim that the protective effect of the diet exists regardless of individual genetics.

Choice A describes the opposite of what the figure shows. If greater adherence to the diet (represented by the lighter bars) was associated with increased probability of dementia, then the lighter bars would be taller than the dark bars. They're not.

Choice B is accurate: the lighter bars are shorter at each genetic risk level, indicating that the diet was associated with less dementia at each category of genetic risk. This accurately reports the data and supports the researchers' exact claim: following the diet helps protect against dementia regardless of genetics.

Choice C is accurate, but not helpful. That is, it's true that the two bars representing the "high" genetic risk level are taller than the two bars representing the "low" genetic risk level, so it's true that higher genetic risk is associated with a higher probability of developing dementia. But so what? That tells us nothing about whether the Mediterranean diet affects this probability or not.

Choice D is even less helpful, because it's not even accurate. As we just discussed, greater genetic risk is associated with a *higher*, not lower, probability of dementia. So it's still irrelevant to the conclusion we're looking to strengthen, but it's also getting the data wrong.

Choice B is the one that is both accurate and helpful, so it's the right answer.

2) B

The text tells us that Io, unlike the other Galilean moons, generates significant electrical activity on its surface. According to the student, this is caused by Io's highly elliptical orbit. Our task is to *weaken* that claim.

Choices A and C are accurate, based on the rightmost column of the table. But it's not obvious how that information would weaken the student's claim. Perhaps if we had some more information, this could help us identify some alternate cause for Io's electrical activity, which would weaken the idea that it's the elliptical orbit that causes it. But that information is not present in either the text or the table, so we really have nowhere to go with this.

Similarly, choice D is accurate based on the "orbital period" column, but it's not obvious what that has to do with this student's claim.

Choice B points out that two of the moons in the table have more highly elliptical orbits than Io's. That's both true and relevant. After all, if a highly elliptical orbit causes electrical activity, then wouldn't we see electrical activity on Europa and Callisto too? This does undermine the student's claim, and it's the only one that does. Therefore, the answer must be B.

3) C

Focus on the text's central claim first: external environmental factors can significantly affect the hatching of dormant embryos. The text explained that ephippia are specialized eggs that contain these dormant embryos, so we're looking for evidence that the number of ephippia that hatch varies significantly based on external environmental factors.

For groups M, N, and O, the researchers maintained a constant light intensity but changed the pH levels. As a result, the number of ephippia that hatched varied somewhat.

For groups R, S, and T, the researchers maintained a constant pH level but changed the light intensity. As a result, the number of ephippia that hatched varied significantly.

The text focuses on group R, which was the group with the lowest light intensity in the second round of the experiment and resulted in the smallest number of ephippia hatched. To emphasize how significantly these external factors can affect hatching, it would make the most sense to compare group R with group T, which had the *highest* light intensity in that second round and resulted in the *greatest* number of ephippia hatched. That's choice C.

But we don't need that level of detail to tackle this question. Focus on the goal: we're trying to show that the number of ephippia hatching varies significantly. Group R had the smallest number hatched, at 28. Choice C contains the group with the largest number hatched, at 68. That shows a more significant variance than choices A or B, so it's already a more likely answer. Meanwhile, choice D is focusing on the wrong thing entirely; it does not help support this claim at all. So the answer must be C.

4) D
The scientist makes several claims here: first, that we would see "temporally variable" carbon dioxide emissions in the non-growing season, and second, that the variability would be controlled (at least in part) by the amount of moisture in the soil.

Don't worry about trying to understand the science. Focus on the big themes: we're trying to show that CO_2 emissions vary in some way, and that moisture has something to do with how much they vary.

Choice A is accurate. The numbers in the first "Nov 9" column increase as the numbers in the second "Nov 9" column decrease: thus, on November 9, CO_2 content went up as water content went down. Also, the numbers in the first "Dec 7" column increase as the numbers in the second "Dec 7" column increase: thus, on December 7, CO_2 content went up as water content went up. But how relevant is all that? It gives us the overall trend of the data, but it doesn't tell us that the amount of moisture controls how much CO_2 emissions *vary*.

Choice B is not accurate. For example, at the 60 cm depth, the CO_2 content went *down* between November 9 and December 7, not up. That's enough to eliminate choice B.

Choice C is also not accurate. On December 7, the lowest CO_2 content was found at a depth of 60 cm, which was not the lowest depth. Eliminate choice C.

That leaves choice D, which is also the only answer to focus on how much the CO_2 content *varies*. Choice D points out that on December 7, the overall water content was greater (which it was: the numbers in the rightmost column are greater, on average, than the numbers in the second-to-last column). Thus, there was more moisture in the soil on December 7. And on that date, the CO_2 content found at different depths varied more: the December CO_2 measurements ranged from 0.09 to 0.23, while the November CO_2 measurements ranged from 0.07 to 0.42 (meaning both a smaller minimum value and a greater maximum value). This suggests that moisture may help control CO_2 variability, which is exactly what we need.

5) A
The text tells us that monoliths and rubble piles can be distinguished by their density and rotation speed: monoliths are more dense and rotate more rapidly, while rubble piles are less dense and rotate more slowly. The claim we need to support is that asteroid C is a rubble pile, so we want evidence showing that its density is low, that its rotation speed is great, or both.

Choice A correctly points out that a high rotation period indicates a *slower* rotation. After all, an asteroid that requires 20 hours to complete a single rotation is moving more slowly than an asteroid that can complete a rotation in only 5 hours. Therefore, the fact that asteroid C has one of the two higher rotation periods in the table supports the idea that C has one of the slower rotation speeds. Choice A also points out that the asteroid has one of the two lower densities in the table. Both these pieces of information support the idea that asteroid C is one of the two rubble piles rather than one of the two monoliths.

All of the other choices either inaccurately report the data or misinterpret it. C and D state that the asteroid's rotation period is relatively low, when it's one of the two highest in the table. These choices also assert that the asteroid's density is relatively high, when it's one of the greatest in the table. And choice B simply misinterprets everything: it reads a relatively great rotation period as evidence of more rapid rotation, and it reads a relatively low density as evidence of less internal empty space. Both of those interpretations are incorrect; the right answer is A.

6) A
Choice A is accurate: sample S3 had the lowest hydrogen content (10.30%) and the greatest density, while sample S4 had the greatest hydrogen content (13.69%) and the lowest density. This supports the text's point, because it shows that the composition of the sample (the relative amounts of carbon and hydrogen) affect a physical property (the sample's density).

The first half of choice B is accurate, but not the second half: sample S5 had the highest carbon content, but sample S4 had the lowest density.

Both halves of choice C are inaccurate. As we saw for choice A, sample S3 the lowest hydrogen content and the *greatest* density, not the lowest. And sample S4 had the greatest hydrogen content and the *lowest* density, not the highest.

- 455 -

Both halves of choice D are inaccurate as well. Sample S3 had the lowest carbon content and the *highest* density, not the lowest. And while sample S5 had the highest carbon content, it did not have the highest density.

7) B
The text describes efforts to reduce tobacco use among young people and asserts that these efforts are succeeding. So, that's what we need: evidence that *tobacco use* in general is decreasing. Note that the whole middle column of this table, which focuses specifically on *cigarette* use, is irrelevant. That eliminates choices A and C, both of which focus on changes in cigarette use rather than total tobacco use. Choice D is accurate and helps somewhat to support the point, but it is too limited, since it only focuses on one year. Choice B focuses on the overall trend over time, which is exactly what we needed.

LOGICAL INFERENCES (p. 100)
Logical Inferences: Try It
1) aspartame might not cause lymphomas or leukemias.

The text tells us about a study that found a link between aspartame consumption and cancer in rats. Next, it tells us about some criticisms the study has received. So if the critics are right, what can we conclude? That the study's findings aren't necessarily correct. That's about as far as we can go here, so watch out for answer choices that try to take this too far.

2) A is incorrect: the language is too strong.
   B is correct.
   C is incorrect: the criticisms of the study did not involve its use of non-human subjects.
   D is incorrect: the criticisms of the study did not involve its date.

All we can really say here is that aspartame *may* not cause cancer in rats; we can't say for sure that it doesn't. Choice A is too strong. Choices C and D attack the study on the wrong grounds: neither is a logical deduction to draw based on the specific criticisms made in the passage. Choice B uses nice, weak language and is the best match for the conclusion we predicted.

Logical Inferences: Practice Set 1 (p. 104)
1) B
Start by summarizing the text. Recycling is good, and most people know it. Yet most people don't recycle. According to the study, this is either because people find recycling inconvenient and/or because they're not sure what can be recycled.

So where do we think the text is going with this? Maybe something about how we should address those issues that were mentioned: for example, by making recycling more convenient and making sure everyone understands how to do it.

Choice A goes way too far. This author doesn't seem to be dismissing the idea of recycling as a practical solution.

Choice C isn't supported by the text. Based on the study, most people "believe recycling makes a difference." We have no way of distinguishing between the different types of benefits they might be talking about.

Choice D puts too much of the focus on the recycling centers in particular; maybe it's the government or someone else who should do this. And anyway, what's needed is not education about the benefits of recycling, since the study shows that most people already believe it makes a difference. Based on the text, what we need is increased convenience and education about *how* to recycle.

Choice B is the closest to what we were looking for. An "accessible" program sounds like a convenient one, and "clear rules about recyclables" should help people understand what can and cannot be recycled. This gets most directly to the issues expressed in the text, so it's the best answer.

2) A
In the study described in the text, increasing the minimum wage led to increases in wages for low-wage workers, while overall employment levels were not significantly harmed. Our prediction should just be a soft restatement of those findings: something along the lines of "increasing the minimum wage can increase income and not harm employment." That's a pretty good match for choice A.

Choice B goes too far. Based on this one study, we can't say that minimum wages are the *best* way to do anything.

Choice C gives us a comparison that's not supported in the text. We have no information about the benefits to middle-income workers.

The second half of choice D comes out of nowhere. We have no reason to suspect that the outcome would be so different outside the US. (We can't conclude the effect would be the *same* outside the US either—we lack enough information to make a prediction either way.)

3) C
The text offers several criticisms of health information technology studies. They use varying definitions and measurements. They use small sample sizes. And many of them focus on short-term outcomes. Overall, what do you think this text is trying to say about the studies? The direction is obvious: the studies are lousy.

That's the general idea for our prediction, but as we examine the answer choices, we'll have to be careful not to go too far.

Choice A takes an extra step by recommending a course of action. We can't say for sure that this author would

encourage repeating these studies with this change. Maybe the author has other problems with the studies and believes they were ill-conceived from the start; if so, repeating them with this one change wouldn't help.

Choice B gives the studies too much credit. Based on this text, we have no grounds to conclude that the studies are useful in any way, even for conclusions about short-term outcomes. After all, even those conclusions would be marred by the small sample sizes and other problems.

Choice D is like choice A: it takes an extra step that we can't justify. We have nowhere near enough information to conclude what would have been the case in some hypothetical situation.

Choice C is the best overall match for our general prediction: these studies are bad. Also important is that this choice uses the weakest language of the four, making this the easiest inference to support.

4) D
According to the text, NASA performed the DART mission in order to test its ability to change the trajectory of an asteroid by slamming into it with a spacecraft. Before the collision, the moonlet's orbital period was 11 hours, 55 minutes. Afterwards, the period was 11 hours, 23 minutes, indicating that the impact had shortened the orbital period by 32 minutes. This far exceeds NASA's original goal, which was to alter the orbital period by a little more than 1 minute (specifically, 73 seconds). So, what can we infer? It looks like the test was successful.

Choices A, B, and C all suggest that the test was unsuccessful. But given that NASA met its stated goal (in fact, surpassed it significantly), these don't match the information we have.

Choice D is the only one headed in the right direction. The fact that the test was successful means this "kinetic impactor" technique might actually work for the purpose it was designed for. And what was that purpose? Go back to the beginning of the passage: it was to protect Earth from asteroids headed our way.

5) D
According to the text, the sensation of warmth requires air. When molecules of air strike our bodies, they transfer their heat. In the exosphere, temperatures are extremely high, but there's much less air. So what's our prediction? The sensation of warmth doesn't exist (or at least is experienced massively less) in the exosphere. That's choice D.

6) B
First, summarize the text. 19th century scientists knew that Earth had cooled over time from a molten ball to its current state. Based on this knowledge and certain other assumptions, Kelvin estimated that the Earth was only 20-400 million years old. A later understanding of radioactivity changed this picture, and Arthur Holmes showed the Earth was actually 4.5 billion years old.

Where is this going? Given that the Earth turned out to be much, much older than 20-400 million years, it looks like Kelvin got it wrong.

That's our prediction, and it's a good match for choice B. Choices A and D are not supported by anything in the text. And choice C attacks the wrong theory. Based on the text, Kelvin and other 19th-century scientists were right that the Earth had been a molten ball that cooled over time; Kelvin just drew the wrong conclusions from that fact.

Logical Inferences: Practice Set 2 (p. 106)
1) A
Try not to get too thrown off by all the science in this passage. Focus on the big themes: scientists created a "nanozyme" that was capable of detecting and attacking pollutants in water. In an experiment, the nanozyme succeeded in massively degrading the pollutant BPA. Plus, it was able to detect low BPA concentrations.

A good prediction for this one? The experiment succeeded. Or the nanozyme achieved its objectives. Something along those lines. After all, the first sentence described the nanozyme as something that could both detect and attack pollutants in water. The next few sentences pointed out how good the nanozyme was at attacking, and this last sentence tells us it was good at detecting too.

Choice B is not supported by the text. The nanozyme in question is made of cerium oxide, but we don't know that it's that aspect of the nanozyme that made it so effective, nor that BPA is "particularly" susceptible to this exposure in the short term.

Choice C compares two other materials tested. We know that neither of them performed as well as the nanozyme did, but we have no grounds to compare these two materials to each other.

Choice D is about one of those other materials again. This time, we know even less. We have some information about how activated carbon performed at removing BPA from the water, but we know nothing about how effective it was at *detecting* BPA. The text only mentioned that the nanozyme could detect low BPA concentrations; it didn't tell us that the other two materials couldn't.

Choice A matches our prediction: the nanozyme can both destroy and detect. Plus, the wording is nice and weak ("could" be useful), making it easier to support.

2) A
The passage is trying to intimidate us with big vocabulary words, so don't let it: keep your focus on the

Answer Explanations

big ideas. People expect national institutions to be the best. But without high funding, they can't outperform local institutions. The zoo is one example: ongoing funding problems mean that animals are housed in substandard ways.

It's tougher to come up with a precise prediction for this one, so let's use a process-of-elimination approach. Choice A is weak, and there's nothing about it that's wrong. If "most" people expect that the national zoo will be the best, and funding problems mean that animal habitats are substandard, then at least some of the people who visit the zoo will find their expectations for the habitats to be unmet. In other words, they'll be disappointed. There's nothing terribly wrong with this answer, so hold on to it for now and move on to the next.

Choice B is flat wrong. The text says that many animals are housed in ways that do *not* reflect zoological standards. We have no grounds to say that most animals in the zoo are housed in ways that do.

Choice C goes too far. The author's point was that the national zoo is unable to meet the highest standards because of funding problems. The text isn't trying to argue that the zoo should fix this; that puts the blame on the zoo in a way that the text doesn't.

Choice D is not supported by the text. Since the national zoo is used as an example for the author's claim in the second sentence, it's probably fair to infer that the national zoo does not currently outperform local zoos. But that doesn't necessarily mean that local zoos outperform the national zoo; they could perform equally well. Plus, we don't know that local zoos have a funding advantage, and we certainly can't say that the funding advantage is "unfair."

That eliminates choices B, C, and D, leaving A as the only possible answer.

3) B
Summarize the text. In a bacterial community, individual bacterial cells use quorum sensing to detect each other's presence and communicate. Rhamnolipids, which are beneficial for the group as a whole, are only produced when enough bacteria are present for it to be worth it; the bacteria use quorum sensing to determine when this is the case. However, the scientists in the text found that the size of the community is not the only factor that controls whether rhamnolipids will be produced. According to the scientists, changing the amount of carbon, nitrogen, and iron present in the environment can also affect production.

So, what does this suggest? Maybe this tells us that carbon, nitrogen, and iron are required for rhamnolipid production. Or maybe this is another purpose for quorum sensing: the bacteria might use it not just to count how many bacterial cells are around, but also to sense how much carbon, nitrogen, and iron is present.

Choice A is too strongly worded ("must" exist rather than "may" or "might") and not supported by the text. We have no reason to conclude that bacteria are using any system other than quorum sensing.

Choice C gives us a comparison that we can't support. We know that both factors (resource availability and population size) matter; we have no grounds to say that one matters more than the other.

Choice D goes too far. While carbon, nitrogen, and iron may be relevant to rhamnolipid production, we can't say that there's a threshold amount for each that *must* be satisfied before *any* rhamnolipids can be produced.

That leaves choice B, which is a reasonable match for our prediction and is nice and weak: it only says that bacteria "may" use quorum sensing for this purpose, not that they definitely do.

4) C
The text lays out several pieces of evidence for the theory that Shakespeare didn't write his famous works. First, unlike Marlowe and Bacon, Shakespeare's lifestyle was too humble for him to be so familiar with the courtly setting of many of his plays. Second, there are stylistic similarities between the "Shakespearean" works and the works of Marlowe and Bacon. Third, there is historical evidence that Marlowe and Bacon had connections to the theater world.

But next, the passage takes a turn: the level of fame that both Marlowe and Bacon had at the time actually supports the idea that Shakespeare wrote the works himself. Why?

If no prediction is jumping out to you, go to the choices. Which one makes the most sense?

Choice A is perhaps another argument against the "minority of scholars" who think Shakespeare couldn't have written his works. If you're creative enough, this choice says, you don't need personal familiarity with a courtly setting. But while that supports the theory of Shakespeare's sole authorship, it doesn't explain why *the fact that Marlowe and Bacon were famous* supports Shakespeare's sole authorship.

Choice B doesn't make a lot of sense. The fact that they were famous may have meant they didn't need to bother copying anyone else, but no one so far has suggested that they did. Without more information, this doesn't do much to give us the link we need.

Choice C gives us a much clearer explanation. Sure, the styles were similar, says choice C, but of course they would be! Everyone knew Marlowe and Bacon. This directly attacks one of the pieces of evidence for the

Shakespeare-didn't-do-it scholars: the similarity might just be because Shakespeare was influenced by their style. After all, if the plays were remarkably similar to the works of an obscure author that Shakespeare had never heard of, that would be much stronger evidence that someone else (the obscure author) had written the plays. A similarity to very famous authors is much easier to explain, so the fact that Marlowe and Bacon were so famous makes the similarity of styles much weaker evidence against Shakespeare's sole authorship.

Choice D isn't helpful at all. Contrasting Marlowe and Bacon against each other isn't the point, and their ability to write sonnets seems completely unrelated to their level of fame. We can easily eliminate choice D, leaving C as the best answer.

5) A
As the text tells us, reported cases of ASD have increased over time. The text describes a study with several key findings. First, there are complex genetic factors underlying the disorder. Second, the increase in reported cases is likely *not* due to a change in diagnostic criteria. Third, the increase is more likely due to increased awareness and reporting. And fourth, while changes in diagnostic criteria have had only a minor effect on the increase in reported cases, they may have influenced the cohorts used in other studies; specifically, those cohorts may have oversampled patients with certain genetic mutations.

That's a lot of information. But it's that last sentence that leads to the inference we're asked for, so let's start there. What would be the implications if the cohorts were influenced in this way? Well, the studies that were based on those cohorts would be less reliable. That's a reasonable prediction, and it's a pretty good match for choice A.

Choice B is generally consistent with the information in the passage, but it doesn't fit into the last sentence. What connection does this have with the possible cohort problems? It's not clear that the cohort issue leads to this inference, which is enough to eliminate B.

Choice C is much too strong. We have nowhere near enough evidence to compare the relative importance of different causes for ASD.

Choice D is somewhat like choice B. The author of this text may agree with this sentiment, but it's not directly connected to the cohort issues discussed in the sentence. Therefore, the best answer is choice A.

6) A
According to the text, penguins have a cluster of arteries and veins called the "humeral arterial plexus" that help them survive cold climates. The text tells us that the cluster is pressed against the flipper bone and affects blood temperature in two ways: it cools the blood that is moving from the heart to the flippers, and it warms the blood that is moving from the flippers to the heart.

So, we're looking for something suggesting that this cluster *regulates* or *moderates* body temperature, something covering the fact that it both warms blood and cools it.

Choice B covers only one temperature direction, and not one that's likely a big problem for penguins in freezing climates.

Choice C isn't about temperature at all. Nothing in the text supports the idea that this cluster has anything to do with swimming speed.

Choice D is tempting, but it only covers the warming effect, not the cooling. Plus, note that the text referred to the cluster as being "especially important" during long swims. So its chief benefit should probably be evident when the penguins are in the water, not when they're on land.

Choice A says the cluster helps the penguins maintain a stable body temperature, thus covering both the warming and the cooling effects. This is the best answer.

7) D
The passage first lays out the traditional view about the evolution of bones and teeth: vertebrates developed bony scales purely as a defense mechanism, long before they were predators. Then we learn about conodonts, which probably used the bony structures in their mouths to grasp and shred prey. These conodonts existed 500 million years ago, earlier than the vertebrates that developed bony scales. So, what does this suggest? That the traditional view might be wrong: vertebrates might have been predators earlier than the traditionalists thought, and bones/teeth may have evolved for predatory as well as defensive reasons.

Choice A is wrong because the conodonts were not "jawed vertebrates." According to the passage, jawed vertebrates didn't show up until 20 million years after the early vertebrates developed their bony scales, so about 400 million years ago. Conodonts lived more than 500 million years ago, so they can't be part of that category.

Choice B goes too far. Just because the conodonts used their bony structures to shred prey, we can't conclude that they had *no* need for protection from *any* predators.

Choice C isn't supported by the text. We have no direct information about adaptation to different ecological niches.

Choice D is the best match for our prediction, and it's worded weakly enough for it to be easy to support. This is the right answer.

Answer Explanations

8) B

The text first describes a "kilonova," which occurs when two neutron stars collide. When this happens, both gravitational waves and electromagnetic radiation travel away from the impact at light speed, but some of the electromagnetic radiation is slowed by the dust and gas it encounters along the way. When a kilonova was observed in 2017, scientists detected the gravitational waves several hours before they detected the electromagnetic radiation (which appeared as bright burst of light). What can we predict? Well, we know they both started out at the same speed, and we know that the electromagnetic radiation was slowed down by gas and dust. So the best prediction is that gravitational waves are *not* slowed down by gas and dust—or at least not slowed down as much as the electromagnetic radiation is.

Nothing in the passage allows us to distinguish between the rates of travel of different types of electromagnetic radiation, so we can eliminate choice A. We also have no reason to believe that the electromagnetic radiation was released later than the gravitational waves; the passage just said that both were released "after the impact." Eliminate choice C. As for choice D, we should always be suspicious of answers that involve a hypothetical, and this one is no better than most: we just have no evidence in the passage that this is true.

That leaves choice B, which is a good match for our prediction: gas and dust are both forms of matter, so this is saying that the gravitational wave was slowed down less by that gas and dust than the electromagnetic radiation was. That's the answer.

SENTENCE STRUCTURE (p. 110)
Sentence Structure: Try It

1) **She enjoys studying vocabulary, solving geometry problems, and <u>diagramming</u> sentences.**
This is a list of three verbs, so each verb must be in the same format. To test it, try placing the subject individually before each verb. In the original sentence, that gave us "She enjoys studying," then "She enjoys solving," and finally "She enjoys to diagram." That last one doesn't work! To make it match, switch to an *-ing* form: use "She enjoys diagramming" instead.

2) **Beverly decided to take a risk and <u>open</u> her own business.**
As in #1 above, we have a list of verbs. This one is just a shorter list: there are only two items. But we can test it the same way. In the original sentence, we had "Beverly decided to take a risk" and then "Beverly decided to opening her own business." Nope. Make it "Beverly decided to *open* her own business" to make it match correctly.

3) **Before the start of the July 4th barbecue, the food had been laid out by Javier, the drinks chilled by Sue Ellen, and <u>the grill lit by Barbara</u>.**
The list is more complicated in this sentence, but we still need all three elements to follow the same pattern. The first element on the list is "the food had been laid out by Javier." That establishes the pattern: name the object first, then the action, then "by [person's name]." The second element, "the drinks chilled by Sue Ellen," follows this same pattern with one important changed: the "had been" has been omitted from the verb. That means the "had been" in the first element must apply to all three. Therefore, "the grill had been lit by Barbara" would be incorrect here; it's "the grill lit by Barbara" instead.

4) **Eduardo <u>makes</u> the bed**, or
Eduardo <u>is making</u> the bed
By itself, the word "making" cannot serve as the main verb of the sentence. Either change the *-ing* form to a more active form (such as "makes" or "made") or insert one of the "to be" words before it (e.g., changing it to "is making," "was making," etc).

5) **The dogs <u>rolled</u> in the mud**, or
The dogs <u>were rolling</u> in the mud
By itself, the word "rolling" cannot serve as the main verb of the sentence. Either change the *-ing* form to a more active form (such as "roll" or "rolled") or insert one of the "to be" words before it (e.g., changing it to "are rolling," "were rolling," etc).

6) **<u>I am considering</u> my options**, or
<u>I considered</u> my options.
By itself, the word "considering" cannot serve as the main verb of the sentence. Also, this sentence has no subject! Insert a subject ("I") and either change the *-ing* form of the verb to a more active form (such as "consider" or "considered") or insert one of the "to be" words before it (e.g., changing it to "am considering," "was considering," etc).

7) **We all <u>saw</u> it happen**, or
We <u>have</u> all <u>seen</u> it happen.
The word "seen" is a past participle and thus cannot serve as the main verb of the sentence by itself. Either change it to a more active form (such as "see" or "saw") or insert one of the "have" words before it (e.g., changing it to "have seen" or "had seen").

8) **The weather <u>has been</u> warm**, or
The weather <u>is</u> warm.
The word "been" is a past participle and thus cannot serve as the main verb of the sentence by itself. Either change it to a more active form (such as "is" or "was") or insert one of the "have" words before it (e.g., changing it to "has been" or "had been").

Writing: Standard English Conventions

9) It <u>began</u> raining, or
It <u>has begun</u> raining.

The word "begun" is a past participle and thus cannot serve as the main verb of the sentence by itself. Either change it to a more active form (such as "begins" or "began") or insert one of the "have" words before it (e.g., changing it to "has begun" or "had begun").

10) The two students born in a distant country <u>immigrated</u> to the United States ten years ago.

By itself, the word "immigrating" cannot serve as the main verb of the sentence. The best fix here is to change the *-ing* form to the more active form "immigrated."

11) The teacher, who brought 30 years of experience to the classroom, <u>will be retiring</u> in the spring.

By itself, the word "retiring" cannot serve as the main verb of the sentence. Either change the *-ing* form to a more active form (such as "will retire") or insert one of the "to be" words before it (e.g., changing it to "will be retiring").

12) Having lived and worked in Los Angeles for many years, <u>I was</u> unaccustomed to the lifestyle of the countryside.

The word "seen" is a past participle and thus cannot serve as the main verb of the sentence by itself. Also, this sentence has no subject! Insert a subject (e.g., "I") and insert one of the "have" words (e.g., changing it to "was unaccustomed").

13) Many critics <s>that would</s> have to admit that they misjudged the artist, having overlooked his important talents.

This sentence has no main verb. First, "having overlooked" is an *-ing* form and thus can't serve as a main verb without one of the "to be" words before it. And second, "would have to admit" is buried in a "that" phrase, so it's not the main verb either. The simplest fix is to simply delete the word "that" after "critics," transforming "would have to admit" into the main verb of the sentence.

14) The author <u>is</u> known for his intricate plots, which often involve detailed knowledge of actual historical events.

This sentence has no main verb. First, the word "known" is a past participle and thus cannot serve as the main verb of the sentence without one of the "have" words before it. And second, "involve" is buried in a "which" phrase, so it's not the main verb either. The simplest fix is to change "known" into an active verb by inserting the word "is" before it.

15) Focusing intently on the details of the experiment right in front of her, the young chemist <s>who</s> <u>didn't</u> notice that anything was wrong with the one set up by her colleague on the other side of the room until the slowly accumulating smoke suddenly set off a blaring fire alarm.

This sentence has no main verb. First, "focusing" is an *-ing* form and thus can't serve as a main verb without one of the "to be" words before it. And while the sentence contains several other verbs, each is buried in the long "who" phrase that follows "chemist." The simplest fix is to eliminate the word "who," allowing "didn't notice" to act as the main verb.

Sentence Structure: Practice Set 1 (p. 117)
1) D
Simplify the sentence by removing the transition word "however" and the introductory phrase that follows it. That leaves "studies" at the start, which is the subject of the sentence. Choice D gives a straightforward main verb: Studies indicate that the incidence is low. All the other choices are sentence fragments, because none give us a main verb. Choices A and C use an *-ing* form, which can't serve as a verb without one of the "to be" words before it (e.g., are indicating, have been indicating). In choice B, the verb "indicate" is locked in a modifying "that" phrase.

2) C
Make sure to read all the way to the end before deciding. Three out of these four choices give us the sentence "When an insect touches the hairs, the leaves snap shut." That's fine on its own, but what about the sentence after it? Choices A, B, and D all follow it with a sentence fragment: none contain both a subject and a main verb. Therefore, the best option is choice C, which wraps it all up into a single sentence: "the leaves snap shut" is the independent clause, and the part of the sentence that follows it is simply a modifying phrase.

3) D
There's nothing necessarily wrong with starting a sentence with the word "Because," or any other transition word, as long as it's just an introductory phrase. However, the independent clause can't start out that way. Choices A, B, and C here never get past that introductory phrase, so they can't stand as a sentence. Choice D eliminates the transition and just gives us a simple standalone independent clause: "Video games" is the subject, "foster" is the verb, "technological literacy and hand-eye coordination" are the objects, and the rest is a modifying phrase.

4) D
The subject of the sentence is Joe Clark. What's the main verb? In choice D, it's "used." In choices A, B, and C, there isn't one! Choices C uses no active verb at all, while the verbs in choices A and B are locked inside a modifying "who" or "which" phrase. After all, it's fine to say "Clark used an unconventional approach." But we can't say

- 461 -

Answer Explanations

"Clark, who used an unconventional approach." That's a sentence fragment.

5) D
The entire beginning of this sentence, up to and including the word "deadline," is nothing but modifying phrases. We still need both a subject and a main verb, so the answer choice will need to provide them both. Choices A and B fail to do that, since an -*ing* word needs some form of "to be" before it ("is," "was," etc.) to serve as a main verb. And choice C doesn't work because the sentence leading up to the word "deadline" can't stand on its own. That, by the way, is another problem with both choice A and choice B: both would need that part of the sentence to be an independent clause. The only choice that works is D.

6) B
The subject is the cultivation of Arabica coffee. Judging by the answer choices, we want some form of the verb *to require* as the sentence's main verb. But choice D locks it inside a modifying "which" phrase, and choices A and C each leave it in -*ing* form, which can't serve as a main verb unless it is preceded by some form of the word "to be" (for example, "is requiring" or "was requiring" instead of just "requiring"). Only choice B gives us the main verb we need.

7) C
This sentence contains a list: the three actions undertaken by the workers. So we have to make sure that the list maintains parallel structure, meaning that each of the verbs should be in the same form. The first item on the list is "would level," while the second item is just "lay," without the "would." This indicates that the "would" at the beginning of the list will apply to all three, meaning we won't need to repeat it. So we can test the list for parallelism by placing the list item right after the phrase "workers would." First, we have "workers would level the terrain": that's fine. Then, "workers would lay out the foundation": also fine. Choice C matches that pattern: "workers would construct the pyramid's core." By contrast, choice B gives us "workers would constructing the pyramid's core," which doesn't match (or even make sense). And choices A and D give us "workers they would construct" or "workers would constructed," neither of which make any sense at all.

8) A
The "populations" are the subject. Choice B doesn't conjugate the verb, and choices C and D leave it in an -*ing* form. As we've seen, we can't use form that as a main verb unless it's preceded by "is," "was," or some other form of the verb "to be." That leaves choice A, which works fine: Populations have cultivated durian for hundreds of years.

Sentence Structure: Practice Set 2 (p. 119)
1) B
To check the structure of each choice, we can simplify the sentence by eliminating "seemingly every day," which is just an introductory phrase. In choice A, we just launch into another modifying phrase. Seemingly every day, as his team makes a new discovery that advances the science... what? It's leading up to an independent clause that we never get to.

In choice C, the subject is "making a new discovery and further advancing the science." That would work if we followed it with an actual verb: for example, "Making a new discovery is awesome." But this choice never gets there, and choice D has the same problem.

That leaves choice B. The subject is "his team," the verb is "makes," and the rest is the object followed by a modifying phrase. "His team makes a discovery" is a perfectly valid sentence, so choice B is the right answer.

2) C
This sentence contains a complicated list, so we need to check for parallel structure. Just take care to identify what the list is that we're creating so we can match the forms correctly.

Choices A can be eliminated quickly because *details* doesn't match anything else in the sentence, including *indicated* later in the choice. And choice D has a similar problem: *detailed* and *indicating* don't match each other.

But in choice B, the forms *detailing* and *indicating* match. These also match the word *moving* in the sentence. But is that the list we want? With choice B's version, the businessman is describing the aesthetic benefits of three things: of moving cars indoors, of detailing how the structure would be paid for, and of indicating that no new taxes would be needed. But that's not right. We don't want the businessman to describe the aesthetic benefits of detailing how the structure would be paid for; we just want him to detail how the structure would be paid for. Choice B is creating the wrong list.

Choice C, however, matches the verbs *detailed* and *indicated* to *described* in the sentence, which creates a new list. The sentence is now telling us that the businessman did three things: he described the aesthetic benefits, he detailed how the structure would be paid for, and he indicated that no new taxes would be needed. That makes a lot more sense.

3) C
The sentence is long, but we can ignore most of it to pick the right beginning. In choice C, the subject is Louisa May Alcott, the verb is "spent," and the object is "years." That makes perfect sense and is the right answer. Choices A and B give us a sentence fragment, since they both set up the entire rest of the sentence as a (very long) modifying

- 462 -

TM and © 2023 PrepMatters, Inc. All rights reserved.

phrase, and hence we never get to a main verb. Choice D contains both a subject and a verb, but it is in the wrong tense.

4) B
This sentence contains a list, so we need to check for parallel structure. But although the sentence is describing three actions of corvids, the list can't be as simple as *analyze, devise,* and *display,* because the sentence has locked us into the form "displaying." So, hit the choices with an open mind to see what might work.

If we could change that "displaying" to "display," choices A or D would give us a list of three matching items. But since we can't, these choices don't work. We'll need the list to consist of just two things: *analyze* and *devise.* Choice B gives us exactly that, with its "while" turning the rest of the sentence into a separate modifying phrase.

Choice C tries to turn "devising a unique solution" into a modifying phrase. But that leaves us with the list *analyze* and *displaying.* Those don't match, so C is out too. The right answer is B.

COMMAS (p. 120)
Commas: Try It
1) (no commas)
Phrases that begin with the word "that" are always necessary information, so they never take commas.

2) My favorite tennis player is Roger Federer, who won Wimbledon this year.
Try reading the sentence without the "who" phrase: "My favorite tennis player is Roger Federer." That makes sense, it's grammatically correct, and we haven't lost anything we needed to identify someone, since we already have the player's name. Thus, the "who" phrase was unnecessary information and must be marked off by a comma. (On the other hand, if this sentence had been written as "My favorite tennis player is the guy who won Wimbledon this year," we would *not* use a comma, because we can't just say "My favorite tennis player is the guy.")

3) Although I really like chocolate ice cream, vanilla is my favorite.
Start with this: what's the subject of this sentence? It's not the word "I," because that's inside the introductory "although" phrase. In fact, the word "vanilla" is the subject, meaning "is" is the verb and "my favorite" is the object. That's the independent clause here: "vanilla is my favorite" is a perfectly valid standalone sentence. Everything before it was unnecessary information, so it must be marked off with a comma.

4) Because Maria enjoyed both writing and photography, she decided to join the school's newspaper staff.

The independent clause here is "she decided to join the school's newspaper staff." The fact that it doesn't contain the name "Maria" doesn't mean we need the first half of the sentence in order to identify who the "she" is: after all, "She walked" is a valid sentence even with no other context. As long as the independent clause makes sense (unlike the "My favorite tennis player is the guy" example in the explanation to #2 above), the rest of the information is unnecessary.

5) Joanne, an expert in medieval architecture, told us that the castle was built in the 1300s.
Lift out the middle portion: "Joanne told us that the castle was built in the 1300s." That makes sense, so the middle portion was unnecessary information and must be marked off by commas on both sides. No other commas are needed. Phrases beginning with the word "that" never require commas, because they're always necessary information.

6) (no commas)
Phrases that begin with the word "that" are always necessary information, so they never take commas.

7) On the other hand, avocados are high in healthful fatty acids.
The comma marks off "on the other hand" as unnecessary information.

8) (no commas)
You generally shouldn't put a comma before a prepositional phrase: here, "of learning a new language" is necessary information (it identifies which challenge we're talking about).

9) Dr. Phillips, the best-known pediatrician in Chicago, received an award from the governor last year.
Lift out the middle portion: "Dr. Phillips received an award from the governor last year." That makes sense, so the middle portion was unnecessary information and thus must be marked off by commas on both sides.

10) After high school, she attended a culinary academy in Paris led by the great chef Victor Richambaud.
The comma marks off "after high school" as unnecessary information.

11) (no commas)
"Austrian mathematician" is acting as the job title for Hannah Berg. Because the job title comes first, it can't be unnecessary information. But the name isn't unnecessary either, because "Austrian mathematician is scheduled to speak next" is not a valid sentence.

Answer Explanations

12) The evening's top award went to Sally <u>Martinez, inventor</u> of the Flybock maneuver.
This time, the job title ("inventor of the Flybock maneuver") comes *after* the name, which means it can be unnecessary information. In this case, it is: "The evening's top award went to Sally Martinez" works fine by itself.

13) My favorite English <u>teacher, Manny Kozlowski, just</u> published his first novel.
The job title comes before the name, so the job title can't be unnecessary information. What about the name? "My favorite English teacher just published his first novel" is a valid sentence, so we mark off the name as unnecessary information.

14) (no commas)
The job title comes before the name, so the job title can't be unnecessary information. Now try the sentence without the name: we get "The study was conducted by renowned botanist." That's not a valid sentence, so the name was necessary.

15) Chad <u>Smith, the</u> drummer for the Red Hot Chili <u>Peppers, bears</u> a striking resemblance to comedian Will Ferrell.
The job title for Chad Smith comes after his name. Check the sentence without it: "Chad Smith bears a striking resemblance to comedian Will Ferrell." That makes sense, so Chad Smith's job title was unnecessary information. What about Will Ferrell's? His job title comes *before* his name, so it can't be unnecessary. Could his name be unnecessary? No: "Chad Smith bears a striking resemblance to comedian" makes no sense. Therefore, the only unnecessary information in this sentence is "the drummer for the Red Hot Chili Peppers," so we mark off that portion—and only that portion—with commas.

16) A
Both choices involve two independent clauses. Choice A separates them with a comma plus one of the FANBOYS ("but"). Choice B uses the word "nevertheless," which is not one of the FANBOYS and thus cannot be used in this way.

17) B
Choice A is a comma splice: two independent clauses separated by a comma alone (without one of the FANBOYS). Choice B doesn't use a comma.

18) A
Choice A separates two independent clauses with a comma plus one of the FANBOYS ("and"). Choice B is a comma splice: two independent clauses separated by a comma alone.

19) A and B
Both are correct. Choice A separates two independent clauses with a comma plus one of the FANBOYS ("for"). Choice B doesn't use a comma.

20) B
Both choices involve two independent clauses separated by a comma, but only choice B pairs it with one of the FANBOYS ("for").

21) A
The word "but" only requires a comma when it is acting as one of the FANBOYS: that is, joining two independent clauses. Choice A correctly uses "but" for another purpose (as a synonym for "except"). Choice B incorrectly treats "but" as a FANBOYS conjunction, even though the second half of the sentence ("one of the items on the menu") could not stand alone as a complete sentence.

22) A and B
Both are correct. Choice A correctly separates two independent clauses with a comma plus one of the FANBOYS ("but"). In Choice B, the addition of the "although" means that the first half of the sentence can no longer stand alone as a sentence. It is now unnecessary information, so it is correctly set off with a comma.

23) B
Choice A looks like a comma+FANBOYS combination, but the second half of the sentence is not an independent clause: it is missing the subject ("she"), so it cannot stand on its own as a sentence. In B, the first part of the sentence is unnecessary, so it is correctly set off with a comma.

24) B
Choice A is a comma splice: two independent clauses separated by a comma alone (without one of the FANBOYS). In Choice B, the second half of the sentence cannot stand alone as a sentence; it is unnecessary information, correctly set off with a comma.

25) The <u>sweet, cold</u> lemonade rushed down my throat.
These two adjectives work in either order: we can have "sweet, cold lemonade" or "cold, sweet lemonade." Therefore, they require a comma to separate them.

26) (no commas)
Although "several" and "colorful" are both adjectives describing the photographs, we cannot change the order: "The brochure features colorful several photographs" makes no sense. Therefore, no comma should be used.

27) (no commas)
We can't change the order of the adjectives "large" and "Siamese": "The Siamese large cat" makes no sense. Therefore, no comma should be used.

28) Felicia is a happy, witty child.
Here, the sentence makes sense either as "Felicia is a happy, witty child" or as "Felicia is a witty, happy child." Therefore, a comma is required between the adjectives.

29) B
No comma is required in a list of two things separated by the word "and." This is not a FANBOYS usage of the word "and," because it is not joining two independent clauses. While "She felt happy" is an independent clause, the single word "hopeful" certainly is not.

30) C
This sentence contains a list of more than two things, so commas are required to separate the list items. Phrases that start with "that" are always necessary information, so there's no reason to add any other commas.

31) A
Choice A correctly uses commas to separate the items on a list of more than two things (or people, in this case). Choice B contains an incorrect comma after the word "man." (Note that the comma after "Bobby" is optional: this "Oxford comma" will never be the only difference between the right answer and the wrong one.)

32) B
This is a list of two things ("picked up" and "began") separated by an "and," so no comma is required. This is not a FANBOYS usage of "and," because "began to read" is not a full sentence.

33) A
Choice A correctly uses commas to separate the items on a list of more than two things. Choice B contains an incorrect comma after the word "children."

34) B
The only commas we need in this sentence are the ones separating the list items (the colors). Choice A contains an incorrect comma after "include," and choice C contains an incorrect comma after "colors."

35) A and B
Choice A contains a list of two things ("developed" and "racked") separated by an "and," so no comma is required. Choice B uses "and" as one of the FANBOYS, separating two complete sentences. In choice C, the second half is not a full sentence.

36) D
There is no reason for any commas in this sentence. Choices A and B incorrectly place a comma before the prepositional phrase "of prehistoric hunting tools." Choice C includes an incorrect comma after the word "tools."

37) C
This sentence correctly uses commas to separate the items on a list of more than two things.

38) A
The phrase "which belongs to my neighbor" is unnecessary information.

39) X
There is no list, and there are no FANBOYS. Moreover, neither half of the sentence can stand on its own as an independent clause, which means neither half can be cut out as unnecessary information. Therefore, the comma is incorrect.

40) A
The word "unfortunately" is unnecessary information.

41) X
This sentence incorrectly places a comma before the prepositional phrase "in a row."

42) B
This sentence correctly uses one of the FANBOYS ("and") to join two full sentences.

43) X
There is no list, there are no FANBOYS, and neither half of the sentence can stand on its own as an independent clause. Therefore, the comma is incorrect.

44) X
The word "that" never introduces unnecessary information. After all, try reading the sentence without that second half: "Gandhi proved." That is not a valid sentence on its own, so the information was necessary.

45) B
This sentence correctly uses one of the FANBOYS ("for") to join two full sentences.

46) A
The introductory phrase ("having established the crime's timeline") is unnecessary information.

Commas: Practice Set 1 (p. 131)
1) C
In general, you should favor the "no comma" choices, unless careful inspection shows that one or more commas is required. C correctly uses no commas in a list

Answer Explanations

of two things ("understand" and "manipulate") joined with an "and." Choice A incorrectly separates them with a comma. Choice B is wrong because when a list consists of only two items separated by an "and," no comma should be used. And choice D puts a comma after the "and" in a list, which is incorrect no matter how many items the list contains.

2) D
Choice D correctly inserts a comma after "version," which separates the unnecessary information ("which is easier to read and understand") from the independent clause. Choices A incorrectly places a comma before a prepositional phrase, while choices B and C incorrectly place a comma between two items on a list separated by the word "and."

3) B
In all four choices, the comma separates two independent clauses. Choice B correctly joins the two with one of the FANBOYS ("and"). Choices A and C use non-FANBOYS words, and choice D uses nothing at all.

4) A
Every comma in the sentence matters, including the ones in the non-underlined portion. Here, the comma after the word "garlic" can only be there to set off unnecessary information, which means we'll need another comma to mark off the other end of that unnecessary portion. With choice A, everything from "a flavorful" to "world" is marked off as unnecessary, which works fine: "Garlic is believed to have numerous health benefits" is a valid standalone sentence.

5) A
In choice B, there is no reason for the comma to be there after the word *success*, since neither half of the sentence could stand on its own as an independent clause. Choices C and D place a comma before the quotation, which is only correct when the quote is set off by a direct attribution (e.g., *Joe said, "It's an overnight success!"*). When the quote is incorporated into the grammar of the sentence, as it is here, no comma should be used.

6) A
Count your independent clauses. If we're going to use a comma without one of the FANBOYS, we can only have one independent clause; choice A has one, but choice B has two. Meanwhile, if we're going to use the comma-FANBOYS combination, we need *two* independent clauses; choice D only has one. Choice C has no punctuation problems but is terribly wordy and awkward. So choice A is the winner.

7) D
Choices B and C each incorrectly place a comma between a verb and its object (you wouldn't say "I liked, the book"). Choice A incorrectly places a comma before a prepositional phrase.

8) A
Choice A correctly uses a comma to mark off "In most school cafeterias" as unnecessary information. Choice B incorrectly places a comma between a verb and its object. Choices C and D each incorrectly place a comma before a prepositional phrase.

Commas: Practice Set 2 (p. 133)
1) B
No commas are needed. The complete subject of this sentence is "Stationery manufacturers attempting to produce saleable writing paper." That is, the subject is the entire noun phrase including "manufacturers" with its attached, necessary descriptors. Choices A and D incorrectly put a single comma between a noun and its verb. Simplified, you wouldn't write "manufacturers, may use." In choice C, "to produce saleable writing paper" is necessary (if we remove it, the sentence makes no sense) and so should not be set off with commas.

2) B
This is a tricky sentence because there are several pieces of unnecessary information: the introductory phrase "in her performances" and the descriptive phrase "a prominent African-American dancer and choreographer." After all, we already know that we are talking about Aida Overton Walker, so the information about her profession is unnecessary. Choice B correctly marks off both pieces of unnecessary information with commas.

3) A
Choice B incorrectly adds a comma to a list of two items ("back and forth"). C incorrectly puts a comma between a verb and its adverb. (How did it run? Back and forth.) D incorrectly puts a comma before a prepositional phrase ("between two opposing positions").

4) A
We already said "The founder and executive chairman," which indicates that we know who we are talking about. Thus, the name "Kevin Plank" is unnecessary and must be set off by commas. Choices B, C, and D don't set the name off correctly.

5) A
No commas are necessary. Choices B and C each incorrectly add a comma before a prepositional phrase. Choice D incorrectly adds a comma between the subject of the sentence and the main verb.

6) C
The lengthy introductory phrase here (everything up to and including the word "cabinet") is unnecessary information, so it must be set off by a comma.

- 466 -

7) B
Make sure you read all the way to the end of the sentence. Choices A and D run into trouble when we get to the comma after "lock up": now we have a comma splice! Because that second clause is a full sentence and we have no way to insert one of the FANBOYS before that comma, we have to make sure that the first clause is *not* a full sentence. That narrows our choices down to B and C. But in choice C, the "and indicating" sets up the word "indicating" as part of a list with the earlier verb "to slow down" but without the parallel verb form. We'd need "indicate" to make this work: *When a wheel begins to slow down… and <u>indicate</u> that it may be about to lock up.* In choice B, however, the comma sets off the entire phrase *indicating that it may be about to lock up* as unnecessary information, so the verbs don't have to match.

SEMICOLONS, COLONS, DASHES, AND APOSTROPHES (p. 135)
Semicolons, Colons, Dashes, and Apostrophes: Try It
1) ,
The clause "even though they disappoint me every year" cannot stand on its own as a sentence. The comma correctly marks it off as unnecessary information.

2) ;
Each side of this sentence is an independent clause that can stand on its own as a sentence.

3) ,
The semicolon would not require the use of the word "and," which is one of the FANBOYS.

4) , , ;
The two commas mark off the phrase "according to many students" as unnecessary information. The semicolon separates two clauses that can each stand as a sentence.

5) ; ,
This sentence contains two independent clauses: "I thought that the weather would be cloudy" and "I was wrong." The word "however" is not one of the FANBOYS, so we can't separate these two clauses with commas: that would be a comma splice. The semicolon before the "however" correctly separates the two sentences. The comma *after* the "however" marks the word "however" as unnecessary information in the second sentence.

6) ; ,
The restaurant's food has been widely praised is a full sentence. So is *the Tribune called its poached salmon dish "a triumph."* Therefore, we need a semicolon to separate the two independent clauses.

7) , ,
This sentence contains just one independent clause: Woodworking is a rewarding hobby for senior citizens and younger people alike. Therefore, no semicolons are needed.

8) , ,
Be sure to read the whole sentence before choosing your answer! In this one, *Belinda does well in all her classes* is a full sentence, but *unlike her older brother* is not.

9) ; ,
Patrick is a talented musician is a full sentence. So is *he's a skilled painter as well.* Therefore, we need a semicolon to separate the two independent clauses.

10) C
There is no reason for any additional punctuation in the sentence. In each of choices A and B, the part of the sentence that precedes the colon cannot stand on its own as a sentence. Choice D places an incorrect comma between a subject and its verb.

11) B
Choice B correctly has a complete sentence followed by a colon, which is then correctly followed by a single item. A incorrectly lacks any punctuation before "the rare kind." Choices C and D are both attempting to mark off the second half of the sentence as unnecessary information, but that's not quite right: the relationship between the two halves is that the first half is introducing the second half, which makes the colon the appropriate choice.

12) B
Once the sentence establishes that we are talking about Beyoncé's "first" solo album, the album title becomes unnecessary information: it's not like we need it to identify *which* first Beyoncé solo album we're talking about. Choice B therefore correctly marks off *"Dangerously in Love"* with commas. Choices A and C have colons following a sentence fragment rather than a complete sentence. In choice D, the parts of the sentence before and after the semicolon are not the required complete sentences.

13) D
This one is tricky because the verb ("were") comes *before* the subject ("French, Polynesian and modern American cuisine"). It could be written as "French, Polynesian and modern American cuisine were among the principal influences on the chef's menu." There are no commas here, and no commas if you flip the order as in the actual correct answer. Choices A, B, and C all have the same problem: the part of the sentence before the colon cannot stand on its own as a sentence.

Answer Explanations

14) C
This is a "mix and match" situation. Because the beginning of the unnecessary phrase is set off with a dash, the end must also be set off with a dash. A begins the unnecessary phase with a dash but leaves out the closing mark. Choice B starts with a dash but ends with a comma. Choice D does the same as B and adds an additional incorrect comma.

15) D
This is another "mix and match" situation. Choice D correctly sets off the unnecessary information ("the capital of California") with two commas. A opens the set-off with a dash then incorrectly closes with a comma. Choice B incorrectly has no commas to set off the unnecessary information. Choice C opens the set-off with a comma then incorrectly closes with a dash.

16) A
This sentence is a good reminder that while dashes *often* serve to mark off unnecessary information, that's not the *only* thing they can do. In choice A, the dash is working like a colon: it's placed after an independent clause in order to introduce something. Choice B's semicolon is incorrect because the single word "victory" is not a complete sentence. Choice C incorrectly places a comma between an adjective and the noun it describes (a "glorious, word"). And choice D is incorrect because we need *some* punctuation to indicate that the first part of the sentence is introducing the word "victory."

17) one
The part of the word before the apostrophe is the singular *girl*. Therefore, this is one girl with multiple dresses.

18) more than one
The part of the word before the apostrophe is the plural *men*, not the singular *man*.

19) one
The part of the word before the apostrophe is the singular *class*.

20) more than one
The part of the word before the apostrophe is the plural *mice*, not the singular *mouse*.

21) more than one
The part of the word before the apostrophe is the plural *sisters*. Therefore, this sentence is about multiple sisters who are jointly telling one story.

22) its
"The team beat it is biggest rival" makes no sense.

23) it's
"The forecasters say it is going to rain tomorrow" makes sense.

24) You're
"You are going to love the new jacket" makes sense.

25) your
"Is this you are backpack" makes no sense.

26) their
"The students were curious about they are new classmates" makes no sense.

27) they're
"I think they are going to enjoy the field trip" makes sense.

28) Who's
"Who is going to be the captain" makes sense.

29) whose
"Everyone is wondering who is gym bag that is" makes no sense.

30) (no apostrophes)
The word *hers* is a possessive pronoun, just like *its* or *your* or *their*. We never attach an apostrophe to a pronoun unless we're making a contraction (e.g., "it's" = "it is"). There's no contraction here, so no apostrophe is needed.

31) Is this Mr. Smith's book?
The pronoun shows possession: it indicates a book belonging to Mr. Smith.

32) (no apostrophes)
The word "it's" would only be correct if we were making a contraction ("it's" = "it is"). This sentence isn't doing that: after all, "'The suitcase and it is contents were destroyed" makes no sense. Therefore, no apostrophe is needed.

33) (no apostrophes)
The word *theirs* is another possessive pronoun. As explained in #30 above, pronouns do not use apostrophes to show possession.

34) Oak trees' roots go deep beneath the soil.
The pronoun shows possession: it indicates the roots that belong to the trees. Because we are talking about multiple trees, the apostrophe goes after the *s*.

35) (no apostrophes)
There are no contractions in this sentence, and nothing is being made possessive. (For example, there's nothing in

the sentence that belongs to the Smiths.) No apostrophes are needed.

36) It's beginning to look a lot like Christmas.
Remember, "it's" = "it is": if that phrase makes sense in the sentence, then we need the apostrophe. Here, "It is beginning to look a lot like Christmas" makes sense, so we do need the apostrophe.

37) That old tree's going to die soon.
There's no possession here, but there is a contraction: "That old tree is going to die soon." The apostrophe is correct.

38) I'm not sure who's coming to the party.
This sentence contains two contractions: "I am not sure who is coming to the party." Both contractions require apostrophes.

Semicolons, Colons, Dashes, and Apostrophes: Practice Set 1 (p. 147)
1) D
There's no need for any additional punctuation here. The semicolon in choice A is wrong because the second part of the sentence ("when she became the first gymnast...") is not an independent clause. Choice C incorrectly places a comma between a subject and its verb. In choice B, the comma attempts to set off the second part of the sentence as unnecessary information, but in fact it's necessary, because removing it would change the meaning: the sentence's point is not that this person was 14 years old, but that she was 14 years old when this particular incident happened.

2) C
Before you worry about apostrophe placement, always ask yourself whether we need an apostrophe at all. The only reason to use an apostrophe with a pronoun like "it" or "they" is to make a contraction, and we're not making a contraction here: the sentence would make no sense if we plugged "it is" or "they are" into the blank. Therefore, there's no need for an apostrophe. The possessive pronoun "its" is correct.

3) A
The first section of this sentence is an independent clause: "*Pisaster ochraceus* serves as a keystone predator." The second section is longer and more complicated, but it is also an independent clause. After a modifying transition phrase, we essentially get this: "it controls the populations and regulates the system." We need *something* to separate two independent clauses, so choice C is out. But that something can't be a comma without one of the FANBOYS, so B is out too. But choice A separates them with a colon, which is a valid choice. Choice D's placement of the colon is incorrect because with the addition of the word "meaning," the first section of the sentence is no longer a full sentence.

4) D
We can quickly eliminate choice C because neither side of the sentence is an independent clause. To choose between the remaining answers, carefully consider exactly which piece of this sentence is the unnecessary information. In choices A and D, the parentheses set off "lie detector" as unnecessary information, which is fine: the sentence works without that name. However, choice A adds an extra comma after the word "test," which serves only to separate the subject of the sentence from the verb. ("The usefulness, is limited.") In choice B, the commas mark off "of a polygraph" as the unnecessary portion, but the sentence doesn't work if we lift just that part out ("The usefulness or "lie detector" test is limited...").

5) B
Choice B correctly uses a comma with one of the FANBOYS ("and") to join two independent clauses. Choice C is wrong because the first clause is not independent once we stick the word "and" onto the end of it. Choice D is wrong because once we use the colon, the only thing following it should be whatever we're introducing; the "and" shouldn't be there. And choice A just makes a mess of the sentence once we get to the word "continues."

6) A
Start with the word "teams." Does this word need an apostrophe? Yes, to indicate possession: we're talking about the schedules belonging to the teams. Now, where should the apostrophe go? We're talking about parents and kids in general, so it's certainly multiple teams, meaning the apostrophe must go after the s. Eliminate choices B and C. Next, we go to the word "schedules." Does this word need an apostrophe? No: we're not making a contraction and there's no possession here (there's nothing belonging to the schedules). Choice A is correct.

7) D
Do we need an apostrophe on the name Six? Well, it depends on the choice. In B and C, no: there's no contraction and no possession (there's nothing belonging to Six). In choice A, yes: the apostrophe indicates possession, because we're talking about Six's announcement. However, choice A ends up giving us a sentence fragment. After all, if "Six's surprise announcement" is the subject, what is the verb? There isn't one, so this can't be right. Choice D avoids that problem by simplifying the sentence: now Six is the subject and "surprised" is the verb, and there's no need for any apostrophes at all.

Answer Explanations

8) B
The first few commas in this sentence are separating items on the list: we're referring to "booms, skimmers, sorbents, and vacuums" as the pieces of equipment used in the process of mechanical removal. The final comma on that list, the one before the "and," is optional. This is called the "Oxford comma," and because there is no universally agreed-upon rule about whether it's required or not, it will never be the difference between the right and the wrong answer on the SAT. So although two of our choices use that comma and two don't, we can't eliminate anything at this point.

Move on to the next comma difference: choices A and D both have a comma after "vacuums," while choices B and C do not. What purpose is this comma serving? None! This is just separating the subject of the sentence (the list of equipment) from the verb ("are employed"). That's not a valid reason to use a comma, so we can eliminate choices A and D.

Now move to the only difference between the two remaining choices: the semicolon after the word "region" in choice C. The part of the sentence to the left of this semicolon is an independent clause, but the part to the right is not. After all, "And then separate it from the surface of the water" is not a valid standalone sentence. Therefore, the semicolon in choice C is incorrect, meaning choice B must be the right answer.

9) D
In choices A and B, the part of the sentence to the left of the semicolon is an independent clause, but the part to the right is not. In choice C, we have the opposite problem: both the part of the sentence to the left of the comma and the part to the right *are* independent clauses, making this a comma splice. In choice D, the part on the right is not a full sentence; the comma is correctly used to mark off that section as unnecessary information.

10) C
Choice A is a comma splice: it separates two independent clauses with a comma without using one of the FANBOYS. In choice B, the "for" makes no sense. Choice D is incorrect because we need some kind of punctuation to separate these two independent clauses, such as the semicolon used in choice C.

11) B
Choice B correctly places a colon after an independent clause in order to introduce a list. Choices A and C each incorrectly add a comma before a prepositional phrase. In choice D, the second half of the sentence (the list) is not strictly unnecessary: the relationship between the two halves of the sentence is that the first half is introducing the second half, which makes the colon the appropriate choice.

12) A
Choice B is a comma splice, as it separates two independent clauses with a comma (after the word "playground") without using one of the FANBOYS. Choice C's use of the word "although" is incorrect: it needs to precede two complete thoughts in order to contrast them against each other (e.g., "Although treating lumber can be useful, it is not without risks"). Here, "when that project is a playground" is not a complete thought, and no contrast exists between that and "it is not without risks." Choice A correctly separates two independent clauses with a comma and the word "but," which is one of the FANBOYS. Choice D tries to do the same, but puts the comma in the wrong place.

Semicolons, Colons, Dashes, and Apostrophes: Practice Set 2 (p. 150)
1) D
The word "however" is not one of the FANBOYS, so we can't use it with a comma to separate two independent clauses. Eliminate choice C. Choice B can be quickly eliminated

as well: the purpose of a colon is to introduce, so it doesn't make a lot of sense to follow the colon with a contrast word.

To choose between choices A and D, we need to consider the context. The punctuation in A positions the "however" as the first word in the second independent clause in the sentence. That works when our goal is to contrast the first clause against the second clause. But that doesn't make sense here: the first clause tells us that Howard Berg has a different idea, and the second clause describes that idea. That's a continuation, not a contrast.

Choice D's punctuation for the however changes its meaning. For choice D, the word "however" is the *last* word in the *first* independent clause, which means it is contrasting the first clause against the previous sentence. The sequence goes something like this: "Biologists think the flagellum evolved gradually. Berg disagrees, however. He thinks it evolved in a different way." That makes a lot more sense, so choice D is the right answer.

2) C
The word "although" establishes the contrast for the sentence, so it would be redundant to use another contrast word (like "however"). Eliminate choices A and B. Choice D is wrong because the first clause is not a valid standalone sentence, so the answer must be C.

3) A
In this sentence, the entire phrase from "at" to "steel" is unnecessary information; since the sentence marked off one side with a dash, we need to add another dash to finish it off. What makes this trickier is that we have a

comma within that unnecessary portion, because "at widths 10,000 times thinner than that of a human hair" is unnecessary information as well.

4) C
Take this dizzying sentence one *its* at a time. Do we want an apostrophe for the first one? Yes: "Driving the route when *it is* at its best" makes sense. Eliminate choices A and B. Now, do we want an apostrophe for the second one? No: "Driving the route when it's at *it is* best" makes no sense. That eliminates choice D, so the answer must be C.

5) C
The colon's purpose is to introduce. The part before the colon must be an independent clause, which it is here. The part *after* the colon must be whatever we want to introduce, *and nothing else*. There should be no transition words or other connectors between the introducing sentence and the thing being introduced: the colon is the only connection we need. Thus, choice A's "which" and choice B's "because" are both wrong. Choice D doesn't have this problem, but it doesn't make as much sense as choice C. Because the independent clause followed the reference to a "price tag" with several other ideas, jumping right to the figure is confusing. Choice C gives us the clarity we want without sacrificing grammatical correctness.

6) B
The mix of commas and dashes is confusing here, but they are serving different purposes. The commas are separating items on a list, while the dashes are setting off the entire list as unnecessary information. Only choice B gets that right.

7) B
"According to Dr. Mishkin" is an introductory phrase. Because it is unnecessary information, it should be separated in some way from the independent clause, so choice D is wrong. But the phrase cannot stand on its own as a sentence, so choice C is wrong as well.

Choices A and B correctly use a comma to mark off the phrase. So now, we have to consider the apostrophe. Make sure you don't move too fast! Read the whole sentence to get the context. Mishkin isn't saying *its comedy* as a reference to the comedy contained in a funny movie. If he were, the next part of the sentence ("that saves us") would make no sense. Instead, Mishkin is saying that comedy is what saves us: in other words, *it is comedy that saves us*. That makes choice B the right answer.

8) A
Choices C and D each incorrectly place a colon after a clause that cannot stand on its own as a sentence. Choice B incorrectly places a comma between the subject of the sentence ("young people and old people alike") and its verb ("maintain"). Thus, we don't have to worry about whether "strong" and "spiritual" should be separated by a comma or not: the only possible answer is A.

9) D
In this sentence, the entire introductory phrase (from "As" to "University") is unnecessary information. Within that phrase, the acronym GRIP is also unnecessary, since the sentence still makes sense without it. We can mark that off with parentheses, commas, or dashes. Choice B uses both parentheses *and* commas to mark it off, which is incorrect. Choice A incorrectly places a comma before a prepositional phrase. Choice C attempts to mark off "at LaRoche University" as unnecessary, but this is wrong for two reasons: first, this is another prepositional phrase, and second, we can't mark off unnecessary information by placing a dash on one side and a comma on the other (we'd need either two commas or two dashes). Choice D marks off the correct piece of unnecessary information ("GRIP") and does so with one matching pair of parentheses.

10) A
This one comes down to understanding exactly which portion of the sentence is unnecessary. Choices B, C, and D are essentially the same thing (which is one hint that none of them are correct): they're all marking off "constrained by the Eurocentric society in which they lived" as unnecessary information. The problem is that the actual phrase of unnecessary information goes back farther than that, all the way back to the beginning of the sentence. Choice A marks off everything from "with" to "lived" as unnecessary, which is correct.

11) D
Choices B and C mix and match dashes with other punctuation when marking off unnecessary information, so we can eliminate both of those. To choose between A and D, focus on the precise boundaries of the unnecessary portion. If we remove the marked-off section from choice A, we get this: "They did not that their species had been nearly hunted to extinction." That doesn't make any sense. But choice D gives us this: "They did not know that their species had been nearly hunted to extinction." That's the one that works.

12) D
Take apostrophes one step at a time. First, consider whether we need an apostrophe on the word at all. Then, and only then, should we worry about its correct placement. So, do we want an apostrophe on the word *nests* here? Yes: the location and materials belong to the nest(s), so an apostrophe is needed to indicate possession. Eliminate choice A. Now, is the word singular or plural? Look later in the sentence: there's a reference

Answer Explanations

to "the materials from which *it* is constructed." We're talking about a singular nest here, so choices B and C are wrong. The answer is D.

13) C
Choices A and B each incorrectly separate two independent clauses with a comma without using one of the FANBOYS. Choice D looks okay on its own, but makes no sense when you read it into the sentence: for example, what is the word "followed" doing there immediately after it? That leaves choice C as the right answer.

VERBS (p. 153)
Verbs: Try It
1) have
The subject is "the time and place." That's two things, so make it a "they" to make it easier to hear the right verb: *They **have** yet to be determined.*

2) is
This is a more complicated sentence, but the only subject of the verb in question is "Felicia," which is singular. *Felicia **is** going to perform.*

3) is
Although the herd consists of more than one animal, there's just one herd. That's singular, so we can replace it with an "it" to make it easier to hear: *It **is** scheduled to be sheared.*

4) is
The "which" phrase is just an obstacle placed between the subject and the verb, so read the sentence without it: *The Appalachian mountain chain **is** a popular destination.*

5) are
Read the sentence without the "who" phrase or the prepositional phrase "of the school board": *Members **are** now investigating.*

6) object
Eliminate the prepositional phrase "of the reporters." The subject is "several," which is plural (to check, try placing the word "one" after it: "Several one of the reporters" doesn't make sense). So since the subject is plural, we can replace it with the word "they": *They **object** to the coronation.*

7) is
The subject is "who," which in this case is singular. After all, although the group may include several tall students, only one is the tallest. So, make it a "he": *He **is** the tallest.*

8) have
This is a tough one. What's the subject? That is, what's doing the action of being displayed in the great hall? Well, two things: one is a fascinating and ingenious watercolor from Picasso's blue period, and the other is a laughably banal attempt at pseudo-cubism painted by one of his contemporaries. In other words, there's a good painting (the Picasso) and a bad painting (the other one). Because there are two paintings, we can replace this whole first part of the sentence with "they." And it can't be *They has been displayed*, so *They **have** been displayed* is right.

9) was
Cut out the extra words in the middle and just put the name in front of the noun: *Anna May Wong **was** the first Chinese-American movie star.*

10) was
Eliminate the prepositional phrase "of both books." The subject here is the summary: *A summary **was** written by George.*

11) eats
Eliminate the prepositional phrase "with its vibrant red, blue, and yellow feathers." The subject here is the bird: *The Scarlet Macaw **eats** the material.*

12) was
The subject is "Juju," so cut out everything else: *Juju **was** created by Tunde King.*

13) is
Eliminate the prepositional phrase "of students." The subject here is the group, which is singular: *The group **is** to be suspended.*

14) burst
This is an irregular verb: the past tense of "to burst" is just "burst." The word "bursted" is never correct.

15) drinks
The first half of the sentence establishes that we're in present tense (since it uses "devours," not "devoured"), so we match it in the second half: *she **drinks** the soda.*

16) have frozen
To establish that something was possible, we say "could have," not "could of"—although they sound similar, the "of" is never correct in this type of tense. The correct past participle for the verb "to freeze" is "frozen," so *The climbers could **have frozen*** is correct. The word "froze" is used only in the simple past tense (without the "have": for example, "John froze his leftovers.")

17) drank
Keep it simple! The simple past tense "drank" matches the simple past tense "ate." There's no reason to use a multi-word tense here.

18) brought
For the irregular verb "to bring," both the simple past tense and the past participle are "brought." So, "they brought shame" would be correct, and so is "they have brought shame." The word "brung" is never correct.

19) felt
Keep it simple! The simple past tense "felt" matches the simple past tense "ate." There's no reason to use a multi-word tense here.

20) would have
The first half of the sentence establishes a conditional, so we need the "would" to describe that possibility.

Verbs: Practice Set 1 (p. 161)
1) C
In this question, the subject (the plural "legends") is separated from its verb ("are") by a lot of confusing junk. Choices A and B incorrectly use the singular "is," while choice D incorrectly inserts "which" between the subject and a verb. (If you cross out all the junk in the middle, choice D reads, "Legends which are told in a high school's history books.")

2) D
In choice D, the singular subject ("Antimatter") is correctly paired with the singular verb ("was stored"). Choices A and B use plural verbs, while choice C is missing "been" which tells us that the antimatter itself has been stored and is not doing the storing. For example, it would be correct to say, "scientists have stored antimatter," but not "antimatter has stored."

3) A
Choice A correctly pairs the subject ("pollution") with the singular verb ("was"). Choice B uses the plural "were," while choices C and D just make a mess of forming a complete sentence.

4) C
Be careful: the subject here is <u>not</u> the *da capo* arias. Those are inside the modifying phrase "including his *da capo* arias," which we can mentally eliminate from the sentence. That leaves "Handel's body of work" as the subject. Since "of work" is a prepositional phrase, the real subject is just the singular word "body." Thus, we need a singular verb, meaning choices A and B are out. Choice D makes no sense, so choice C must be the right answer.

5) D
The context of the text will always tell us which tense is the correct one. This sentence is talking about what will be the case in the future (in 2050), so we need the future tense. Choices A and B place the action in the past, while choice C is locked in the present.

6) D
The science context is irrelevant here: identify the subject of the verb and highlight or underline it. Here, the subject is the "hybrid corn strains." That's plural, so the verb must be plural. Choices A, B, and C are all singular, so the answer must be D. And remember that you don't have to identify whether a verb is singular or plural in the abstract. Just say the subject before each of the answer choices. Choice A: "strains was widely adopted." Choice B: "strains has been widely adopted." Choice C: "strains is widely adopted." Those all sound terrible! But try choice D: "Hybrid corn strains have been widely adopted." That's the only one that sounds right.

7) A
Strip away all the extra words and context. You don't have to understand the legal argument! All we care about is identifying the subject of this verb and checking the tense. In this sentence, "the concept" is the subject. Cross out the prepositional phrases that follow ("of collective ownership" and "of land and resources") and focus on the fact that "the concept" is singular. That's enough to get rid of choices B and C. Choice D doesn't make sense (the concept recognized what?), so A must be the answer.

8) C
What's the subject of this verb? That is, what's doing the action of revealing important information? It's "a plant or animal." Say that phrase before each of the answer choices; only choice C sounds right.

Verbs: Practice Set 2 (p. 163)
1) D
In choice A, "would of" is always incorrect. It's a mis-hearing of the contraction "would've." Choice B is wrong because it uses "would have" for both verb forms; the word "would" should never be in the "if" part of a conditional sentence.

Choice C is tempting, but it's not quite right. Strip away the extra words in the sentence, and C says this: "If the union lost, it would have led to X." But when we have the simple past tense ("lost") in the "if" part of a conditional, it needs to be matched with "would [present tense]" in the other verb. This pattern describes an unlikely hypothetical situation: for example, "If Joe completed his homework on time, he would get an A." Notice how this outcome seems less likely than a conditional with present tense in the "if" part ("If Joe completes his homework on time, he will get an A") but more likely than the version where the whole event is already over ("If Joe had completed his homework on time, he would have gotten an A"). In this sentence, we're locked into "would have led" for the second verb, which means we must be in that last version of the conditional statement. So, we need a verb that matches "had completed": that's D.

Answer Explanations

2) B
This is a tricky verb agreement question. The word "each" is always singular, as in, "each one of the chickens needs to get in the chicken house." That's the same as "it needs," not "they need." That means A and D, which both use the plural "have," are wrong. C uses the present tense "is," when context ("for the last six months") tells us that we should be using the past tense. Also, it incorrectly uses the plural pronoun "their" instead of the singular "its."

3) B
Here the species name ("the polar bear") is singular and so is matched with the singular verb and pronoun ("eats its"). Choices A, C and D all incorrectly treat "the polar bear" as plural.

4) A
Choice B is the easiest one to eliminate, because the future tense makes no sense here. C makes the elephant populations the subject, but we don't want to say that the elephants are threatening something; we want to say that the elephants are threatened *by* something. D is using the singular verb "is," which wouldn't match the elephants either: this is now saying that *the illegal trade* is threatened by poaching and habitat loss. Only choice A works both in terms of tense (the threatening started in the past and continues to the present) and agreement (directing the threat at the elephant populations).

5) C
This complicated sentence is describing how an embryo establishes polarity. To make it easier to follow, let's simplify the part after the colon by condensing some ideas: "The embryo must define the axis along which body parts ___." The subject of the verb we're analyzing is the body parts—or, more specifically, body parts and a significant amount of tissue. But because of the "and," that's still a plural, which is all we really care about for the verb. So we can use "body parts" as an easy test. That quickly eliminates B and D, since "body parts is" certainly doesn't work. To choose between A and C, consider the tense of the next sentence. It's describing what *will* happen in the future, meaning the verb tense we want for this blank should also describe something that hasn't yet happened. Choice A says these body parts etc. have already been formed, but choice C says they "are to be formed," meaning they haven't been formed yet. That's a better match for the tense we want, so choice C is the right answer.

PRONOUNS (p. 164)
Pronouns: Try It
1) thousands of books   them
The antecedent must be the books, since this phrase is saying that most of those books are paperback novels. The books are plural, so **them** is the right match.

2) smartphone   its
Although "predecessors" is plural, the pronoun is referring to the singular "smartphone" introduced later in the sentence. Test it by reading in the smartphone in place of the pronoun: *"Unlike the smartphone's predecessors, which suffered from…"* Therefore, the correct pronoun is the singular **it**.

3) Each   it
This is a tricky one. The antecedent here is not the movies: it's the phrase "each of the movies." Well, as we saw in the verbs chapter, the word "each" is always singular. What we're saying here is that each one of these movies, when **it** opened, faced only middling reviews.

4) the Supremes   they
Make sure you read the entire sentence before deciding! From the first half of the sentence, it's not 100% clear whether the pronoun is referring to the Supremes or to their single. But if it was the single, we'd need to say that it established *them* as pop superstars. Because the sentence uses *themselves* instead, the subject and the object must be the same: the Supremes established themselves as superstars. Therefore, the pronoun must be standing in for the Supremes, not for the single. Because "the Supremes" is plural, the right pronoun is **they**.

5) student   you … your
Pay attention to the rest of the sentence. The words "we" and "our" would work if we adjusted a few other things: "As *students*, we are responsible for planning our own *schedules*." As it stands, though, those words are singular: "As *a student*, **you** are responsible for planning **your** own *schedule*."

6) him
Eliminate Carlos from the sentence to make it easier to hear the right choice. It's not *Did you give the marbles to he?*; it's *Did you give the marbles to **him**?*

7) himself
Dr. Rodriguez is both doing the action (reminding someone) and receiving the action (he's the one being reminded), so the -self pronoun is correct.

8) Who
The sentence *Him lies buried in Grant's tomb* doesn't sound right, so "whom" is wrong. Instead, it's *He lies buried in Grant's tomb*: **who** is correct.

9) me
In this sentence, the person doing the contacting ("You") and the people being contacted are not the same, so "myself" is not correct. To choose between "I" and "me," eliminate Jeffries and Mitchelson. *You can contact I* sounds wrong; *You can contact **me*** sounds right.

10) me ... us
Eliminate Steven Wilson. *a book co-authored by I* sounds wrong; *a book co-authored by me* sounds right. The other pronoun follows the preposition "of," so we must use the object case **us**, not the subject case **we**. (Also, "*both of we*" sounds weird.)

11) Who's
The word "Whose" is wrong because we're making a contraction here: it's *Who/whom is afraid*. To choose between "Who" and "Whom," try substituting "he" and "him." *Him is afraid* sounds wrong; *He is afraid* sounds right. The word "he" matches with "who," so this sentence needs to say *Who is,* or the equivalent contraction *Who's*.

12) Governor McAllister's son told us that he had decided not to run for reelection because he wanted to spend more time with his family.
Assuming Governor McAllister is male, any of these pronouns could theoretically refer to either the governor or his son.

13) (no changes)
This sentence is applying the same sentiment to both Jorge and Edward. It's saying that Jorge doesn't believe that he (Jorge) will win the lottery, and Edward doesn't believe that he (Edward) will win the lottery. So it's not that we don't know whether the "he" refers to Jorge or Edward; it's that it actually refers to both. That's allowed.

14) We have been dependent on fossil fuels for decades, but now that the environmental impact has become clear, activists are urging citizens to change it.
There's no specific noun that we could point to in this sentence that the "it" is pointing back to.

Pronouns: Practice Set 1 (p. 170)
1) C
The pronoun refers back to "a male guppy," so we need a singular pronoun such as "he," "him," or "it." That eliminates choice B. The pronoun is the subject of the sentence, so the object pronoun "him" is wrong: eliminate choice A. In choice D, the verb tense doesn't match the rest of the sentence: when a male guppy *has* a larger tail etc., he/it *is* more successful. Choice D is a mess. Choice C is the best answer.

2) C
Here it is correct to use the plural reflexive pronoun "themselves" because the cyclists (plural) are both the ones doing the hurting and the ones being hurt. That is, "cyclists" are both subject and object. Choice A incorrectly uses the regular object pronoun "them" rather than the reflexive "themselves," which makes it sound like the cyclists are hurting the experts. Choice D has a similar problem, failing to use the reflexive. Choice B has an agreement issue: "a new cyclist" (singular) doesn't match with "themselves" (plural). Only choice C gets everything right.

3) A
"The field" is singular, so we must use "it" rather than "them." Eliminate choice C. Choice B uses "we" as the object of a preposition, which both is wrong and sounds wrong (we'd need to say "known to us," not "known to we"). Choice D doesn't make any sense. Choice A is simple, concise, and contains no agreement errors, so it's the best answer.

4) B
Be sure to look for more than one kind of problem in the choices. Choice A gives us a comma splice: two independent clauses separated by a comma without one of the FANBOYS (see the Commas chapter for more about this). Choices C and D give us a list that lacks parallel structure (see the Sentence Structure chapter). Choice B is correct.

Pronouns: Practice Set 2 (p. 171)
1) B
First, find the antecedent for the pronoun we're looking for. This one is tricky because the antecedent is separated from the pronoun by a lot of other stuff, but ultimately, it's the "doctors" that these pronouns must be pointing back to. That's a plural, so we need a plural pronoun like the "they" in choice B. Each of the other choices uses the wrong pronoun (e.g., the singular "he or she" doesn't match the plural "doctors"), among other problems.

2) D
This question deals with ambiguity. In choices A, it's not clear which word the "it" is referring to it could be pointing back to either "a triglyceride" or to the "type B lipid profile." Choice B doesn't work because there is no plural noun in the sentence, so the "they" doesn't have a match at all. Choice D supplies the noun, which is the most clear. And choice C has a punctuation problem: it uses a semicolon even though the second half of the sentence is not an independent clause.

3) B
This is a good reminder of the importance of reading the entire text before jumping to the answer choices. From the first half of the sentence, it's not 100% clear what the antecedent is going to be for this pronoun. Are the experts viewing *Einstein* ("him") as revolutionary? Are they viewing the *papers* ("them") as revolutionary? Or are they viewing the *publication* of these papers ("this" or "it") as revolutionary? Any of these could work. But in the next part of the sentence, we get the answer: only the plural "them" can be viewed as "watershed *moments*," plural. Choice B must be the answer.

Answer Explanations

4) C
Here, it's key that the subject of the sentence, "Everything," is singular. Thus the verb ("was") should be singular, and so should the pronoun ("it.") Choices A, B, and D all get the pronoun wrong; choices B and D get the verb wrong too.

MISPLACED MODIFIERS (p. 172)
Misplaced Modifiers: Try It

1) <u>Because I</u> slept through my alarm, the school bus arrived before I was fully dressed.

     or

   Having slept through my alarm, <u>I wasn't fully dressed when the school bus arrived.</u>

As written, this sentence is saying that the *school bus* slept through the alarm. We want to say that *I* slept through the alarm instead, so either add the "I" to the first part of the sentence or rearrange the second part so that the "I" comes first.

2) Finding no evidence of guilt, the <u>jury acquitted the suspect.</u>

     or

   <u>Because the jury found</u> no evidence of guilt, the suspect was acquitted.

As written, this sentence is saying that *suspect* found no evidence of guilt. We want to say that *the jury* found no evidence of guilt. The first option here simply changes the sentence from passive voice to active voice, thereby rearranging the second half of the sentence so that the jury comes first. The second option adds the jury to the first part of the sentence.

3) <u>In a thrift store,</u> I found a dress that I'd been looking for to wear to a party.

As written, this sentence is saying that the *thrift store* is what I'd been looking for to wear to a party. We want to say that the *dress* is what I'd been looking for. You might think you can accomplish this by moving the phrase "in a thrift store" to the end of the sentence, but that actually doesn't work! *I found a dress that I'd been looking for to wear to a party in a thrift store* just creates a new misplaced modifier problem: now it sounds like there's a party in a thrift store. Instead, move the "in a thrift store" phrase to the beginning of the sentence to get it out of the way.

Misplaced Modifiers: Practice Set 1 (p. 174)
1) C
The red flag here is the introductory phrase containing the -ing words "making" and "picking." We need the first noun or pronoun after the comma to be the person described by this phrase (the visitor who made his way up the ladder). In A and D, the word "YES" is making its way up the ladder. B makes even less sense, because "it" can't make its way up a ladder either. Only choice C puts the ladder-climber first.

2) D
The introductory phrase describes a play, so the play must be the first noun after the comma. In choices A, B, and C, the performances, the four weeks of performances, or the four-week run are described as "the first new play." None of those make sense. Choice D, however, positions *The Cosmonaut* as "the first new play." That works.

3) A
Note the introductory phrase with the -*ing* word "arguing." Who is doing the arguing? We don't want to say that Kim's contention is arguing anything, which is what choices B and D say. This idea makes more sense than some of the wrong answers to the previous questions, but if nothing else, it's redundant. It's much simpler to just say that Kim is the one arguing. That's choice A.

4) C
This time, we're choosing the modifier instead of the part of the sentence that's modified. Choice C creates an introductory phrase with an -ed verb ("constructed") which matches well with the first noun after the comma (the Great Mosque of Djenné). The other options are wordy, awkward, and make less sense.

Misplaced Modifiers: Practice Set 2 (p. 175)
1) C
The first noun after the comma is "Adele's music." Choice A is wrong because Adele's *music* didn't win the Grammy for Best New Artist; *Adele* did. (Her music may have won an award for best album, etc., but only a person can win an award for best artist). Choices B and D are wordy and awkward, so choice C is the best answer.

2) B
The introductory phrase "using this indirect approach" refers to the approach taken by the medicines: they manipulate the immune system rather than attack cells directly. So we need the medicines to be first, as in choice B. Choices A, C, and D place other nouns first: the cancerous growths, the detection and destruction, or the immune cells, respectively.

3) C
The first noun after the comma is the researchers. Choices A, B, and D all say that the researchers are immune to snake venom, which is not what the sentence is trying to say. After all, the rest of the sentence says that the researchers are analyzing compounds in opossum blood to make medicines for snakebite victims, which suggests that there's something special about the opossum blood. This only makes sense if opossums are the ones who have the immunity to snake venom, which is what choice C makes clear.

4) D
The first noun after the comma in this sentence is Julia Child's knowledge of French cuisine. But it was *Julia*, not her knowledge, who trained at Le Cordon Bleu. That eliminates choices A and B. Choice C is a comma splice (it separates two independent clauses with a comma without using one of the FANBOYS), so choice D is the correct answer.

TRANSITIONS (p. 176)
Transitions: Try It
1) B
Here, the unfairness of the game is the result of the bad calls, so we are looking for a cause-and-effect transition word such as "therefore" or "thus." The phrase "as a result" works here, too. "Next" indicates a sequence, which isn't quite right.

2) A
The second part of this sentence is restating the first, with the word "never" providing a little more punch, or emphasis. So emphasis transitions like "in fact" or "indeed" would be a good fit.

3) A and B
Here we have a sequence in time. First, they drove for three days. Then, they arrived. Both of the transitions offered here indicate the literal or metaphorical end of the road: "finally" and "at last."

4) B
This sentence provides a clear contrast between the English and history teachers.
"However" would be the classic prediction; "in contrast" works, too.

Transitions: Practice Set 1 (p. 184)
1) C
The first sentence explains a situation: what happens when light travels through air and scatters on colliding with suspended particles. The second sentence reveals the result: the medium becomes visible. Look for a cause-and-effect word or phrase, specifically one introducing the effect, such as "thus" or "therefore." In these choices, "as a result" is the best fit.

2) B
The sentences before and after the blank discuss the contrasting "associative" and "dissociative" strategies. Look for a contrast transition such as "however." Choices A and C both express similarity rather than difference. Choice D can be a contrast word, but is better suited to an argument (e.g., "Candidate X makes some good points; still, I prefer Candidate Y") rather than a description of a factual difference.

3) D
The sentence before the blank introduces the idea of semiotics, while the sentence after the blank gives an example of some of the signs and symbols (colors, shapes, elements in a painting) and how they might function to convey meaning. This requires an illustrative transition such as "for example" or "for instance."

4) A
Here the first sentence states the argument that organisms with complex and simple hearts should both be considered to have hearts. The next sentence introduces the simple heart of lancelet. The following sentence first introduces a contrast with larger chordates, then flips back to the simple circulatory system of the lancelet. The final sentence continues to emphasize the contrast. The blank at this final turning point should be a contrast transition, similar to the word "despite" that's already there. Choices B, C, and D here all imply continuation in the same direction rather than a contrast.

5) C
The sentences before the blank tell us that when beef is aged for 14 to 21 days, good things happen (it becomes more tender). The sentence after the blank tells us that when beef is aged for more than 21 days, bad things happen (tenderness and flavor both decrease). To connect these two ideas, then, we need a contrast word. Choice C is the only contrast transition offered.

6) B
Here, there is a clear cause and effect before and after the blank. Some good predictions would be "therefore" or "thus." Choices A and C are contrast words, so they don't work. Choice D suggests that the second sentence simply repeats the ideas of the first, but that's not the case here: the first sentence explained that there was a power vacuum, and the second sentence tells us how that vacuum was filled. That's an extra step, not a simple restatement, so choice B is a better fit than choice D.

7) A
This passage is about the inaccuracies inherent in the Bohr model. The first sentence suggests that a list is coming by stating that the model is inaccurate "in several ways." This suggestion is confirmed in the second sentence, which starts with the big clue word "First." That sentence goes on to tell us about one specific inaccuracy of the model: its circular orbits. The following sentence describes another inaccuracy: the assumption that electrons have a fixed position and momentum. Even if you're not sure you understand the science, the final sentence confirms that these are two separate issues with its reference to "these inaccuracies" (plural). That means the blank must be introducing a separate inaccuracy than the one described before it. Since the

Answer Explanations

first inaccuracy is introduced with the word "first," it makes sense for the second inaccuracy to be introduced with the word "second."

8) B
In this passage, the first sentence simply provides background information by telling us that Bob Dylan won the Nobel Prize. The second sentence has two clauses: the first clause describes those who opposed Dylan's award, while the second clause describes those who supported it. Look for a word contrasting those two ideas. Choices A and C instead suggest similarity (in fact, a cause-and-effect relationship, as if the people who supported Dylan did so *because* some other people opposed him). Choice D also suggests a continuation in the same direction. Choice B is the only option that gives us a contrast.

Transitions: Practice Set 2 (p. 186)
1) B
The first sentence defines bipedalism and states its importance. The second sentence then goes the other way, telling us some weaknesses of bipedalism (e.g., it's less stable than other forms). Finally, the last sentence describes the advantages of bipedalism. There's a contrast between those last two sentences, so we need a contrast word like "however." The phrase "by comparison" doesn't quite fit because we're not introducing a new topic to be compared; we're sticking to the same topic (bipedalism) and just noting its downsides rather than its strengths. A better fit for "by comparison" would be something like this: *Bipedalism is unstable and requires a complex series of movements. By comparison, quadrupedalism is simpler and more stable.*

2) D
The second sentence introduces some attributes of the purple loosestrife (it's adaptable, it alters, it outcompetes.) The third sentence expands on the impact of these same attributes. You are looking for a particular type of continuation word: one that sticks with the same topic and develops it further (in this case, by describing the effects of the attributes just described). Eliminate choice B, which is a contrast word, and choice C, which suggests a list. Choice A doesn't work either, because it indicates that the reduction of biodiversity described in the third sentence is an example of the attributes described in the second sentence rather than the result of those attributes. The best fit is the "accordingly" in choice D. (For more on this type of difference, see the challenge box on p. 183.)

3) B
This text takes a few twists and turns. The first sentence emphasizes how long limestone has been used as a soil additive. The second tells us that traditionally, limestone has been used by conventional large-scale farms. By starting with the word "however," this sentence alerts us that a shift is coming: the emphasis is on a recent change in direction. This is a big hint that the next sentence is going to tell us about how limestone is used differently now. And indeed, the third sentence describes how limestone is now being used by "small-scale" farmers (as opposed to the "large scale" farms described in the second sentence) and "organic" farmers (as opposed to the "conventional" farms from the second sentence). But we're not looking for a contrast word here, because this third sentence is continuing the ideas expressed in the second sentence (that there is a recent change in how limestone is being used). The final sentence summarizes the point: "the use of limestone is becoming more widespread and diverse." We need a continuation word that indicates this trend. A good prediction might be the phrase "more and more." The best match is choice B: "increasingly."

Choices A and D both indicate that the ideas in the third sentence are a new point that's similar to the "shift in usage" described in the second sentence, but that's not quite right: the ideas in the third sentence *are* that shift in usage. Simplified, choice A is giving us something like this: "Although limestone was traditionally used by big farms, it's being used differently now. Similarly, small farms are using it." That doesn't work.

Choice C implies that the third sentence is simply a restatement of the ideas in the second sentence, but it's not: it takes an extra step by clarifying *how* the usage of limestone has changed.

4) A
Focus on the big point of each part of the text. The first two sentences give us background information about Andy Warhol. The third sentence gives us the point of view of some critics: that his popularity overshadowed his merit. The fourth sentence supports Warhol, asserting that his impact is undeniable. To connect the third and fourth sentences, then, we need a contrast word like "still" or "however." Choice A, "nevertheless," is the best fit. Choices B, C, and D all suggest a continuation in the same direction, which is incorrect.

5) C
Here we have a cause-and-effect relationship: because of the current information climate, journalists must uphold ethical standards. The blank introduces the effect, so you are looking for an "effect" transition, like "therefore." Choice D goes in the wrong direction, giving us a contrast instead of a continuation. A and B are continuations, but not the type we want: B implies a restatement of the same point, while A suggests that we're switching to a new point that's similar to the previous one. But really, we're sticking with the same point and developing it further: the previous sentences give us the goal for

Writing: Expression of Ideas

journalists, and the final sentence tells us how that goal should be satisfied.

6) A
Another cause-and-effect question! Because of the discovery of the importance of protection from UV-A radiation, the development of that protection became a priority. The blank introduces the effect, so you are looking for an "effect" transition, like "therefore" or "thus."

7) B
The first sentence of the text establishes a point of view: some researchers argue that Neanderthals and Cro-Magnons are separate species. The second sentence provides some evidence for this view by describing some physical differences between the groups. The final sentence tells us that the two groups interbred, which is used as evidence for the idea that they were *not* separate species. Because this is a switch from the previous sentence, we need a contrast word like "however" or "nevertheless." Only choice B gives us the contrast we need.

8) C
Focus on the overall point. The sentence before the blank tells us why Avogadro's number is important: because it gives us a way to relate macroscopic properties to microscopic properties. The sentence after the blank gives an example of this kind of relating: based on a given mass of a substance (a macroscopic property), we can use Avogadro's number and the substance's molar mass to calculate the number of particles present (a microscopic property). The final sentence is an example of the sentence before it, so "for example" is the perfect fit.

9) A
The first several sentences of the text explain why dinosaurs were successful for so long. The last sentence repeats that point: it's telling us that dinosaurs were in fact *so* successful that they might *still* rule the earth if the environmental disruption hadn't occurred. So the big point of this last sentence is not the environmental disruption, but rather the strength of the dinosaurs. That's a continuation of the previous ideas, so we need a continuation word, not a contrast. Eliminate choices C and D. But choice B isn't quite right either, because the last sentence isn't giving us an example or restatement of the idea that dinosaurs were well-suited to their environment; it's going a step further to make a claim about what would have happened in an alternate timeline. The best fit is an emphasis word like "indeed."

RHETORICAL SYNTHESIS (p. 189)
Rhetorical Synthesis: Try It
1) Element #1: the sentence should be tailored for an audience that is already familiar with DNA testing methods
Element #2: the sentence should compare STR analysis to RFLP and explain why STR is preferred.

This question gives us two specific tasks to satisfy, both equally important. First, the intended audience should be already familiar with DNA testing methods, meaning we can eliminate choices that include too much background and explanation about those methods. And second, the choice should include a comparison between the two types of analysis that shows why STR is better than RFLP.

2)
	Element #1	Element #2
A)	N	N
B)	Y	N
C)	Y	N
D)	Y	Y

Choice A spends all its time explaining what these techniques are, thus failing to satisfy element #1. It states that STR has replaced RFLP but does not explain why; the vague reference to RFLP being "older" is not enough. Thus, it fails to satisfy element #2 as well.

Choices B, C, and D seem to be written for the right audience; they all satisfy element #1. But choice B only tells us about STR; there's no comparison between STR and RFLP. Choice C tells us about both but only indirectly explains a reason why STR might be preferred (the amount of DNA required). Choice C spends half the sentence telling us why RFLP might be okay after all, which is the wrong focus. So neither choice B nor choice C really fulfill element #2.

Choice D satisfies both. It wastes no time explaining what the two types of analysis are. And it explicitly lists the advantages of STR over RFLP, thus explaining why STR is preferred.

3) D
Choice D is the only answer that satisfied both criteria set out for us in the question, so it is the best answer.

Rhetorical Synthesis: Practice Set 1 (p.193)
1) D
We want to compare the two heights. Choice A only mentions one of the two trees, so it doesn't compare them. Choices B and C mention both trees but emphasize their similarities rather than their differences. Choice D is the one that maintains the best focus on our task.

2) D
The audience for this sentence is unfamiliar with the artist's work, so we'll need the sentence to include some kind of introduction to Olafur Eliasson. That eliminates A

Answer Explanations

and C. Choice B introduces the artist, but doesn't do much to describe the artwork; all this choice tells us is the year it was created. Choice D does everything we need.

3) A
We have two tasks here: explain the fish's predation habits and emphasize prominent aspects of its appearance. Choice B gives us the appearance but not the habits. Choice C gives us the habits but not the appearance. And choice D gives us neither! Only choice A satisfies both tasks we were given.

4) C
The goal here is to emphasize a difference between *L'Orfeo* and "Il Combattimento di Tancredi e Clorinda." Choices A and B focus on similarities instead, while Choice D only tells us about one of the two works. Choice C mentions both and focuses on a key difference between them: one is an opera, while the other is a madrigal.

5) B
For this question, we have to highlight an advantage of digital history. That eliminates choice A, which doesn't mention digital history at all. Choices C and D both do, but they're too neutral: they're not explaining an *advantage* of digital history over traditional methods. Choice B gives us the information and the attitude that we're looking for.

6) C
We need both an explanation of the term and an example. Choices A and D each give us an explanation without an example. Choice B gives us an example without an explanation. Only choice C supplies both.

7) A
We have two elements to satisfy: explain the findings and mention the source. Choices B and D don't explain the findings, while choice C fails to mention the source. Choice A is the only answer that does both.

8) C
This time, the question gives us three tasks. The right answer must introduce Trotula, it must mention her impact, and it must be tailored to an audience that's already familiar with the *mulieres Salernitanae*. Choice B doesn't mention Trotula and is not tailored to the right audience. Choice D mentions Trotula slightly, but it doesn't give us much of an introduction. Choice A introduces her, but it doesn't tell us much about her impact. Choice C tells us who Trotula was (so the choice introduces her), references the *mulieres Salernitanae* without explaining who they were (so the choice is tailored to the right audience), and tells us that she wrote several "influential" works (which was her impact on the field of medicine). That makes choice C the best answer.

Rhetorical Synthesis: Practice Set 2 (p. 197)

1) B
For this question, we don't just want to explain what language loss is: we want to emphasize the scope of the problem. Choice A is just a definition, so it's far too neutral for what we need. Choice C hints at the problem but doesn't directly tell us anything about languages dying out, which is how the term "language loss" was defined. Choice D most directly tells us that language loss is a problem, but it doesn't really emphasize the *scope* of this problem; it only tells us that "many" languages are likely to be lost. That's not specific enough to satisfy this task. By contrast, choice B tells us that "thousands" of the 6900 languages on Earth are likely to be lost soon. Not only does this give us a more specific idea of the number of at-risk languages, but it also emphasizes what a significant percentage this is of the whole (since "thousands" would be a pretty major portion of 6,900 languages). That gives us the best emphasis on the scope of the problem.

2) C
Choices A and B tell us nothing about the significance of the experiment, so they can be pretty quickly eliminated without even reading the bullet points. Choices C and D are better contenders, but choice D gives us only half of what we need. The point is not just that a classical computer would take thousands of years to do this. The point is that what a classical computer would take thousands of years to do, Sycamore could do in 200 seconds. Choice C mentions both elements and is the only one of the choices to articulate the significance: Sycamore demonstrated the ability of computers to perform a task that is beyond the reach of classical computers.

3) A
The bullet points give us a lot of information about the study, but all we care about for this question is the study's *aim*. We don't need to read the bullet points for this one: choice A is the only one that tells us about the researchers' goal. Choices B and C give us the outcome of the study, and choice D only gives us the methodology.

4) D
The right answer needs to focus on the idea that the tardigrade is hardier than other small invertebrates. Not sure what "hardy" means? We can still eliminate choices A and B off the bat: choice A doesn't give us a comparison (it tells us only about the tardigrades), and choice B focuses on similarity rather than difference (it tells us something that's true about "the species tested" in general). Now compare choices C and D. Both mention that tardigrades, unlike the other small invertebrates, were able to survive high doses of ionizing radiation. But choice D also mentions that tardigrades, unlike the other small invertebrates, were able to survive extreme temperatures. Already, that seems like a better

comparison than choice C. But more importantly, choice D gives us exactly the word we're looking for: tardigrades are exceptionally *hardy* compared to other small invertebrates. That must be the right answer.

5) D
We want to explain how this group used theater as a tool for political activism. Choice C tells us nothing about political activism, while choice B only hints at it; this gives us a connection to a political leader, but it doesn't tell us how Teatro Campesino used theater as a tool. Choices A and D are both tempting, but while choice A suggests that the group did use theater as a tool for political activism, choice D more explicitly tells us *how*: the plays energized farmworkers and drew attention to their plight.

6) B
Take the tasks from the question one at a time. First, we need a generalization about animal behavior. That easily eliminates choice D, which focuses only on ants. But it also eliminates choice C, which only hints at a generalization without explicitly making it.
Now move to the second task: we need to *support* the generalization about animal behavior we made. That eliminates choice A, which simply states a generalization without supplying any evidence for it. Choice B is the only answer to explicitly satisfy both tasks.

7) C
The right answer here must both explain what parathyroid glands are and explain their effect on the body. Choices B and D only explain the effect of parathyroid *hormone* on the body, not the parathyroid gland. Because these choices don't mention the gland, they certainly fail to explain what parathyroid glands are. Choice A explains what they are, but tells us nothing about their effect on the body (since the choice doesn't tell us what parathyroid hormone actually does). Choice C directly explains what parathyroid glands are and describes their effect: they regulate calcium and phosphorus levels by means of the parathyroid hormone.

8) A
Choice B is easy to eliminate because it focuses only on what protective equipment is, telling us nothing about *why* workers should wear it. Choices C and D are a bit more tempting, because each one accurately explains some of the risks of exposure to lead dust. But since neither mentions protective equipment, these do not directly explain why workers should wear such equipment when these risks are present. Remember, the right answer should not rely on any outside knowledge, even if it seems obvious: every connection must be made explicitly in the answer. Choice A is the only one to make that direct link.

Math Strategy

BACK-SOLVING AND SUBSTITUTION (p. 203)
Back-Solving and Substitution: Try It

1) B
Start with choice B. We need to plug in $11/8$ for x in the given expression; if the outcome is between 0 and 1, we have our answer.

To make this easier to handle, you might use the calculator to convert the fraction $11/8$ to the decimal 1.375. Now plug in:

$$x - \frac{1}{x}$$
$$1.375 - \frac{1}{1.375}$$
$$= 0.6477$$

That value is greater than 0 and less than 1, so this is our answer.

2) A
Start with choice B. If Marta owns 33 rare coins, and Brigitta owns 18 more than Martha, then Brigitta owns $18 + 33 = 51$ rare coins. We also know that Marta owns 3 more than half the number that Brigitta owns. But half of 51 wouldn't even be a whole number! So choice B won't work.

Now let's try choice A. If Marta owns 24 rare coins, then Brigitta owns $18 + 24 = 42$. Half of 42 is 21, and 3 more than 21 is 24. We got back to where we started, so this is the right answer.

3) D
Let's say there are 10 boys ($b = 10$). There are twice as many girls as boys, so that would give us 20 girls. If four girls leave the class, then $20 - 4 = 16$ girls remain. Now test the answer choices with $b = 10$; the one that comes out to 16 is our answer.

A) $(10 - 4)/2 = 3$
B) $10/4 - 2 = 0.5$
C) $2(10) + 4 = 24$
D) $2(10) - 4 = 16$

Only D gave us the 16 we were looking for, so D is the right answer.

4) C
The problem gives us two relationships: one between x and y, and one between y and z. So, start with the variable they have in common: y. To make this simple, pick a number for y that's in between 10 and 6. Let's split the difference and say $y = 8$. Since the average of x and y is 10, that means $x = 12$. And since the average of y and z is 6, this means that $z = 4$. Now, what was the question asking? It wanted the average of x and z. In our case, that's the average of 12 and 4:

Answer Explanations

$$\frac{12+4}{2} = \frac{16}{2} = 8$$

So our answer is 8. Now we go to the choices, plugging in the y we started with: $y = 8$. The one that comes out to 8 is the right answer.

A) $(2(8) + 8)/3 = 8$
B) $(8 + 8)/2 = 8$
C) $16 - 8 = 8$
D) $8 - 8 = 0$

Uh oh! The only choice we can eliminate is D. That means we'll need to pick another value for y and start again. What if $y = 6$? That makes z easy: it would also have to be 6. As for x, now we know that the average of x and 6 is 10:

$$\frac{x+6}{2} = 10$$
$$x + 6 = 20$$
$$x = 14$$

Okay, so if $y = 6$, then $z = 6$ and $x = 14$. In that case, the average of x and z is

$$\frac{14+6}{2} = \frac{20}{2} = 10$$

Let's return to the choices, plugging in $y = 6$ and looking for an outcome of 10.

A) $(2(6) + 8)/3 = 6.\overline{66}$
B) $(6 + 8)/2 = 7$
C) $16 - 6 = 10$

We already eliminated D, so we don't have to test that one again. Of the remaining choices, the only one that matched our 10 was choice C, so that's our answer.

Back-Solving & Substitution: Practice Set 1 (p. 211)
1) A
Start with choice B. If $x = -1$, then the left side of this equation is $(-1 - 1)(-1 - 2) = (2)(-3) = -6$, while the right side is $(-1 + 4)(-1 + 8) = 21$. Those aren't equal, so eliminate choice B.

It's not obvious which direction to go in, so let's try choice C.

Left side = $(0 - 1)(0 - 2) = 2$
Right side = $(0 + 4)(0 + 8) = 32$

These don't match either, and in fact they're farther apart from each other than what we had in choice B. That probably means we're going in the wrong direction, so let's go to choice A next.

Left side = $(-2 - 1)(-2 - 2) = 12$
Right side = $(-2 + 4)(-2 + 8) = 12$

Those match, so choice A is the right answer.

2) A
Pick some values for a and b that look roughly accurate based on the diagram: for example, perhaps $a = 60$ and $b = 80$. In that case, the degree measure of the remaining angle in the triangle is $180 - (60 + 80) = 40$. Because that angle is adjacent to c, we can now do this:

$$40 + c = 180$$
$$c = 140$$

Circle that 140 on your scratch paper and hit the choices, using $a = 60$ and $b = 80$.

A) $60 + 80 = 140$
B) $180 - 60 = 120$
C) $180 - 80 = 100$
D) $90 - 80 = 10$

The only one that matches the 140 we were looking for is choice A, so that's the right answer.

3) C
Let's back-solve this problem, starting with choice B. The cost for the first hour is $0.15(60) = $9.00. That leaves another 1 hour 33 minutes, or $60 + 33 = 93$ minutes, unaccounted for. The cost for that remaining time is $0.10(93) = $9.30. So choice B comes out to $9.00 + $9.30 = $18.30. This isn't enough, so eliminate choice B as well as choice A (which is even smaller) and try C.

The cost for the first hour is still $9.00. For this choice, the remaining time after the first hour is 2 hours 20 minutes, or $2(60) + 20 = 140$ minutes. The cost for that remaining time is $0.10(140) = $14.00. So choice C comes out to $9.00 + $14.00 = $23.00. That's what we were looking for, so this is the right answer.

4) D
Plug in values for c and d that satisfy the rule we've been given: $0 < c < d < 1$. For example, let's say $c = 0.2$ and $d = 0.3$. Now evaluate the choices:

A) $0.3^2 = 0.09$
B) $0.2 * 0.3 = 0.06$
C) 0.2
D) 0.3

The greatest of these is 0.3, so D is the right answer.

5) C
Start with B. If $s = 5$, then the original area of the square is $5 * 5 = 25$. Doubling the side length would give us a new side length of 10, in which case the area becomes $10 * 10 = 100$. The area has increased by $100 - 25 = 75$. But we need it to increase by 108, so this is not enough. Eliminate choice B and choice A (which is even smaller) and let's move on to choice C.

If $s = 6$, then the original area is $6 * 6 = 36$. Doubling the side length would give us a new side length of 12, in

which case the area becomes 12 * 12 = 144. The area has increased by 144 − 36 = 108, so this is the right answer.

6) D
To analyze each choice, we'll find the value that's 3 greater than twice the square root. For the right answer, the result will match the original number.

Right off the bat, choice B isn't going to work: the square root of 3 is not a whole number, so there's no way that doubling that and then adding 3 will get back to the 3 we started with. Let's try choice C instead.

Three greater than twice the square root of 4 would be $3 + 2\sqrt{4}$. That comes to $3 + 2(2)$, which is 7. This doesn't match the 4 we started with, so C is out.

Now try D. Three greater than twice the square root of 9 would be $3 + 2\sqrt{9}$. That's $3 + 2(3)$, which equals 9. We've ended up back where we started, so D is the right answer.

7) D
Back-solve starting with B. If $c = 30$ and $a + b = c$, then $a + b = 30$. We can make up values for a and b that satisfy this: for example, maybe $a = 20$ and $b = 10$. Does this work? Well, the angles in a triangle must add up to 180. But here, adding up our three angles would give us $20 + 10 + 30 = 60$: way too small. Eliminate choice B and choice A, which is even smaller. Since B wasn't even close, let's jump ahead to choice D. If $c = 90$, then $a + b = 90$. So let's say $a = 40$ and $b = 50$. Now the sum of the angles is $40 + 50 + 90 = 180$. That works!

8) C
Back-solve starting with choice B: the store sold 21 books on Friday. The store sold 40% more books on Saturday than on Friday. Well, 40% of 21 is $0.4(21) = 8.4$, so that would mean that the store sold 8.4 more books on Saturday than on Friday. It doesn't make sense to sell a fraction of a book, so we can eliminate choice B.

Try choice C. 40% of 25 is $0.4(25) = 10$, meaning the store would have sold 10 more books on Saturday than on Friday. For this choice, then, the number of books sold on Saturday is 10 more than 25: that's 35. That matches what we're looking for, so C is correct.

Back-Solving & Substitution: Practice Set 2 (p. 212)
1) B
First, write out the ratios as fractions.

$$\frac{g}{s} = \frac{2}{3} \quad \text{and} \quad \frac{t}{s} = \frac{3}{4}$$

This is really two equations, and s is the thing they have in common. So, plug in something for s. In this case, that basically means coming up with a common denominator that makes sense in both fractions. The easiest thing to use here is 12:

$$\frac{g}{s} = \frac{2}{3} = \frac{8}{12}$$

$$\frac{t}{s} = \frac{3}{4} = \frac{9}{12}$$

So if $s = 12$, then $g = 8$ and $t = 9$. Therefore, the ratio of t to g is 9 to 8.

2) C
The wording of this problem is a bit tricky. The right answer is a solution set for the equation, meaning each of the two values in the set is a solution to the entire equation. So to test choice B, we're not going to plug in -5 for z on one side of the equation and $1/2$ for z on the other side. Instead, we're going to plug in -5 for z on both sides, and if that works, then we'll plug in $1/2$ for z on both sides. In the right answer, both numbers should (separately) work on both sides of the equation.

But let's not start with that -5 from B. A better choice would be a number that appears in more than one answer, like positive 5 (which is in both C and D). That way, we know for sure we'll be able to eliminate two choices right off the bat: if 5 works, we can eliminate A and B, and if 5 doesn't work, we can eliminate C and D.

Let's try.

Left side = $9(5) + 5 = 50$
Right side = $2(-5)^2 = 50$

These match, so 5 is a solution to this equation. Eliminate choices A and B, which do not contain 5.

And what if we plug in $-1/2$?

Left side = $9(-1/2) + 5 = 0.5$
Right side = $2(-1/2)^2 = 0.5$

These match, so $-1/2$ is also a solution. C is correct.

3) B
Let's substitute 3 for b. That makes a two-thirds of 3, which is 2. Therefore, the ratio of b^2 to a^2 is the ratio of 3^2 to 2^2: in other words, 9 to 4. That's choice B.

4) C
We're told that $2p = 3q = 4r$. For this problem, it may be easiest to start by plugging in something that the whole chain equals. For example, let's try 12:

$$2p = 3q = 4r = 12$$

If $2p = 12$, then $p = 6$. And if $3q = 12$, then $q = 4$. Finally, if $4r = 12$, then $r = 3$.

What was the question asking? It wanted the average of p, q, and r. For us, that's the average of 6, 4, and 3, which is $(6 + 4 + 3)/3 = 13/3$. Now we check the answer choices one at a time, using $r = 3$. The one that comes out to 13/3 is the answer.

Answer Explanations

A) $3(3)/2 = 9/2$
B) $13(3)/18 = 13/6$
C) $13(3)/9 = 13/3$
D) $4(3)/9 = 4/3$

Only C gives us the 13/3 we were looking for, which makes it the right answer.

5) C

Back-solve starting with choice B. There are 25 questions, so if Tyrell answers 18 of them correctly, then he answers $25 - 18 = 7$ incorrectly. He earns 1 point for each of his 18 correct answers, and he loses 1/3 point for each of his 7 incorrect answers. Calculate his total points:

$$1(18) - \frac{1}{3}(7) = 15.\overline{66}$$

This doesn't match the 17 points we were looking for. It's too low, so eliminate choice B and choice A (which is even smaller) and move on to choice C.

If Tyrell answers 19 questions correctly, then he answers $25 - 19 = 6$ questions incorrectly. Now his total point value is this:

$$1(19) - \frac{1}{3}(6) = 17$$

That's exactly the right point total, so C is correct.

6) B

Pick a value for m. Since we're dealing with percents, let's make things simple and use $m = 100$. We're told that 20% of m is equal to n, which means that n must be 20% of 100: that's 20. Okay, so if $m = 100$, then $n = 20$.

But what is the question asking? It wants 20% of $4m$. For us, $4m$ is $4(100) = 400$, so we need to find 20% of 400. That's $0.2(400) = 80$. Circle the number 80 on your scratch paper and hit the choices, plugging in $n = 20$. The one that comes out to 80 is the winner.

A) $8(20) = 160$
B) $4(20) = 80$
C) $2(20) = 40$
D) $20/4 = 5$

The only one that matches the 80 we were looking for is choice B, so that's our answer.

7) C

The variables in the answer choices are a good signal that substitution might be a good strategy here. The problem has not defined a relationship between n and p—it's not like we were told that one is twice as great as the other, or something along those lines—so we can plug in whatever we want for both. So, let's say that $n = 10$ and $p = 2$: that is, the price of ten nails is $2. She needs to buy 200 nails. If the price of ten nails is $2, then the price of 20(10) nails is $20($2) = 40. So our answer is 40. Circle that on your scratch paper and evaluate the choices with $n = 10$ and $p = 2$.

A) $(200 * 10)/2 = 1000$
B) $10/(200 * 2) = 0.025$
C) $(200 * 2)/10 = 40$
D) $2/(200 * 10) = 0.001$

The only one that matches the 40 we were looking for is choice C, so that's our answer.

8) D

Plug in a number for j. Let's say $j = 10$: James is now 10 years old. Now, be careful: we're not told that Michael is 5 years older than James, but rather that Michael is 5 years older *than James will be in three years*. If James is currently 10, then in 3 years, he'll be 13. Thus, Michael is currently $5 + 13 = 18$ years old.

But we're still not done, because the question isn't asking how old Michael is today; it's asking how old he will be in 3 years. If he's currently 18 years old, then in 3 years he will be $18 + 3 = 21$ years old. So that's our answer: 21. Circle that number on your scratch paper, because that's what we want the right answer to come out to.

Now we go to the choices, plugging $j = 10$ into each one.

A) $10 + 3 = 13$
B) $10 + 5 = 15$
C) $10 + 8 = 18$
D) $10 + 11 = 21$

The answer is D.

9) C

We have two equations, so start by plugging in something for the variable they have in common: y. Let's say $y = 3$.

$$x = 4(3^2) = 36$$
$$z = 2(3) - 6 = 0$$

Check what the question is asking: it wants the value of x. For us, that's 36, so circle that number on your scratch paper. Now we check the choices, plugging in 0 for z in each one.

A) $2(0^2) + 9 = 9$
B) $(0 + 8)^2 = 64$
C) $(0 + 6)^2 = 36$
D) $2(0^2) + 3(0) + 9 = 9$

The answer is C.

10) A

Plug in numbers for one variable at a time, reading each one into the problem and using them to figure out whatever we can. Let's say $d = 2$: the tea is sold for 2 dollars per ounce. Next, let's say $z = 3$: that is, 3 ounces are needed for 1 cup. Do you see what we can calculate already? If the tea is $2 per ounce, and you need 3 ounces for one cup, then it costs $3($2) = 6 to make one cup of

tea. Now, keep reading. We have one more variable, so let's say $s = 4$: we want to know how much it costs to make 4 cups of tea. Well, if it costs $6 to make one cup, then it costs $4(\$6) = \$24$ to make 4 cups. So 24 is our answer. Circle that on your scratch paper and hit the choices with $d = 2$, $z = 3$, and $s = 4$.

A) $(4)(2)(3) = 24$
B) $(2*3)/4 = 1.5$
C) $(4*3)/2 = 6$
D) $2/(4*3) = 0.1\overline{66}$

The answer is A.

11) A
Start with choice B: Barney originally had $30. We know that Fred originally had $2 more than 2/3 of what Barney had. If Barney had $30, that's $2 + (2/3)\$30 = \$22$. After Barney gives Fred $5, Barney has $\$30 - 5 = \$25$ and Fred has $\$22 + 5 = \$27$. Those don't match, so we can eliminate choice B.

It's not obvious which direction to go in here, so let's pick at random and try choice A. If Barney originally had $36, then Fred originally had $2 + (2/3)\$36 = \$26$. After Barney gives Fred $5, Barney has $\$36 - \$5 = \$31$, while Fred has $\$26 + \$5 = \$31$. Those match, so A is correct.

12) D
The first sentence tells us a lot about the first train: we know the distance it traveled (450 miles) and its rate of speed (75 miles per hour). From that, we can calculate the amount of time it was traveling. Set it up like a unit conversion:

$$\frac{450 \text{ mi}}{1} \times \frac{1 \text{ hr}}{75 \text{ mi}} = 6 \text{ hr}$$

So the first train was traveling for 6 hours.

The second train also traveled a distance of 450 miles, but it traveled for a different amount of time. To use the substitution strategy here, pick a number for x. Let's say $x = 2$: the second train left 2 hours later than the first. If they arrived at the same time, that means the second train was traveling for only $6 - 2 = 4$ hours.

Since the second train traveled 450 miles in 4 hours, its rate of speed was:

$$\frac{450 \text{ mi}}{4 \text{ hr}} = 112.5 \text{ mi per hr}$$

So 112.5 is our answer. Circle that number on your scratch paper and go to the choices, plugging in $x = 2$:

A) $150(6 - 2) = 600$
B) $150(2) = 300$
C) $450/2 = 225$
D) $450/(6 - 2) = 112.5$

The answer is D.

13) B
The two equations have x in common, so begin by plugging in a number for x. Let's say that $x = 4$. Use the calculator to find the values of a and b:

$$a = 2(4^{-2}) = 0.125$$
$$b = 2(4^{1/2}) = 4$$

Now use the calculator to find the value of $a^2 b^2$:

$$a^2 b^2 = (0.125^2)(4^2) = 0.25$$

So 0.25 is our answer. Now plug $x = 4$ into each answer choice.

A) $1/(8*4^3) = 0.00195$
B) $16/(4^3) = 0.25$
C) $4(4^2) = 64$
D) $16(4^2) = 256$

The answer is B.

14) A
Back-solve starting with B. If the total number of male moths is 48, then the total number of female moths is $62 - 48 = 14$. But wait: just to account for the spotted female moths that we know about, there must be at least 18 female moths total, so choice B is wrong. Specifically, it's too big: it caused us to subtract too much from 62. Therefore, the right answer must be smaller than 43. That means the answer must be A, but let's check. If we fill in 43 for the total male moths and use that to work our way around the table, we end up with this:

	Male	Female	Total
Spotted	32	18	50
Non-spotted	11	1	12
Total	43	19	62

That works, so the answer is A.

MASTERING THE CALCULATOR (p. 214)
Mastering the Calculator: Try It
1) 0.5 or 1/2
Use the command `mean()`.

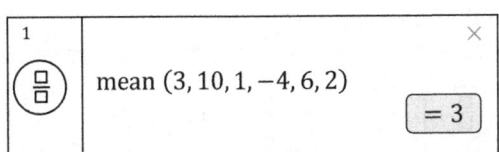

If you click on the ⚙ button, you can duplicate this entry to the next row. Then just change `mean()` to `median()`.

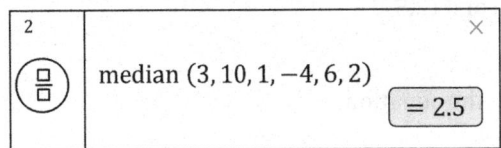

The positive difference is $3 - 2.5 = 0.5$.

Answer Explanations

2) D
Type `pi` to enter the number π. Use an asterisk (shift, 8) to multiply. Type in the radius, 3.5, and then use ^ (shift, 6) followed by a 2 for the exponent.

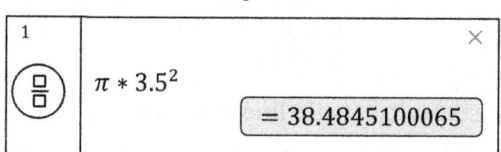

3) A
Type `sqrt` for the square root.

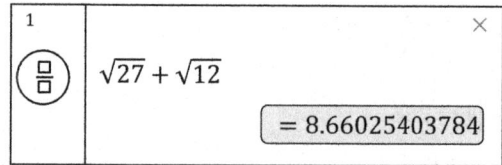

Choice D is obviously out, because that would be greater than 9. Try typing in choice A:

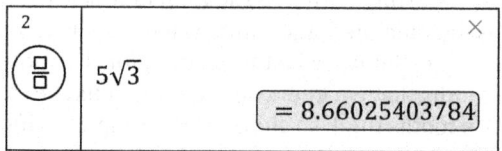

This matches, so A is the right answer.

4) $(3.2, -0.8)$
Type in both equations.

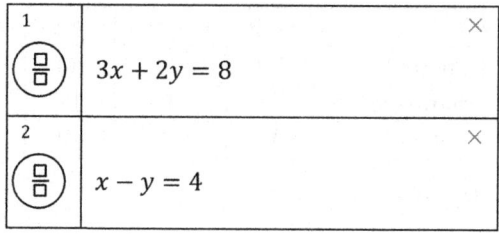

Click on the point of intersection and the calculator will show the coordinates: $(3.2, -0.8)$.

5) $(-3, 0)$ and $(2.5, 0)$
Type in the equation.

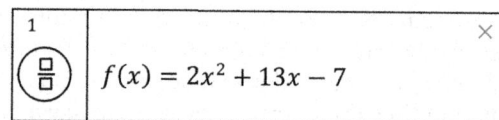

Click on each of the points where the graph intersects the x-axis and the calculator will show the coordinates: $(-3, 0)$ and $(2.5, 0)$.

6) 6
Type in the equation.

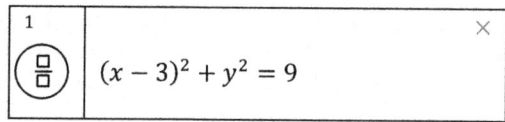

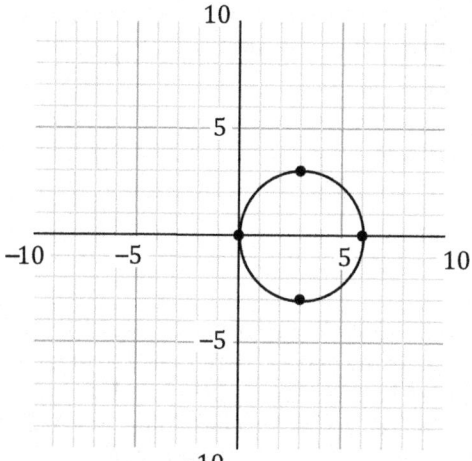

The points shown are directly across the circle from each other, so the distance between them is the diameter of the circle. The x-intercepts here are $(0, 0)$ and $(6, 0)$, so the diameter of the circle is 6.

Mastering the Calculator: Practice Set 1 (p. 224)
1) A
Type in the equation.

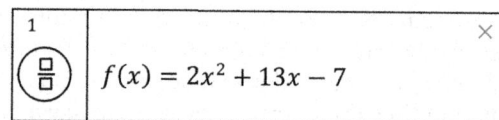

Click on each of the points where the graph intersects the x-axis and the calculator will show the coordinates: $(-7, 0)$ and $(0.5, 0)$. Only $(-7, 0)$ is included in the answer choices: the answer is A.

2) 18
We need to find 24% of 75. Type in `24%`, and the calculator will automatically supply the word "of." Then type in the `75`.

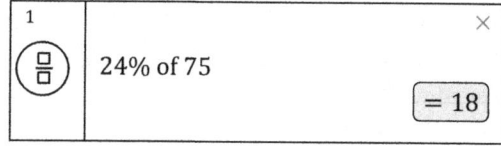

3) B
Use the command `median`. Then enter the list of numbers in parentheses.

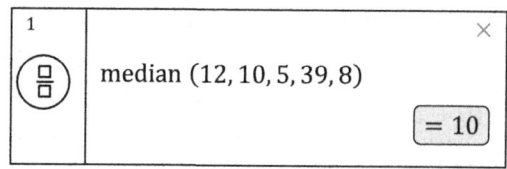

4) C
Type in both equations.

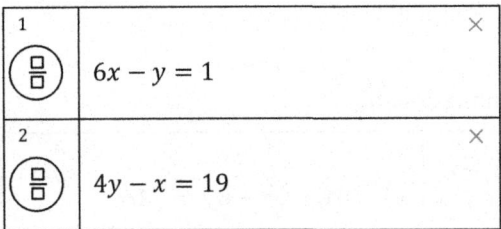

Click on the point of intersection and the calculator will show the coordinates: $(1, 5)$.

5) B
Type in the equation.

$$f(x) = -2(x-1)(x+3)$$

Now click the ⚙ icon above the equations, which will bring up several options. Click on the one that looks like a table. The calculator will automatically create a table of points for you.

x	$f(x)$
-2	6
-1	8
0	6
1	0
2	-10

The last two rows of this table tell us that when x is 1, $f(x)$ is 0, and when x is 2, $f(x)$ is -10. That's enough to eliminate choices A, C, and D, so B must be the answer. But if you'd like to confirm that, click on the empty row at the bottom of the table and type in an x value of 3. The calculator will fill in the corresponding $f(x)$ value: -24.

6) A
Type in the inequality.

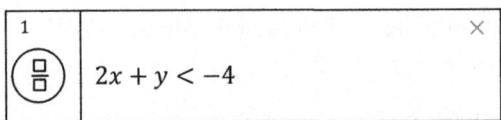

The shaded area of the graph includes parts of Quadrants II, III, and IV. The only quadrant not included is Quadrant I.

7) 0.5
Type in both equations.

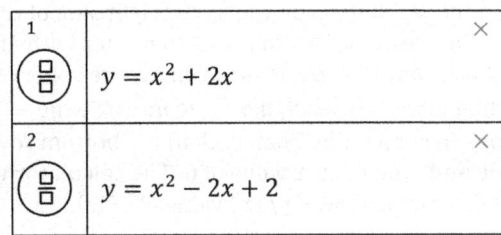

Click on the point of intersection and the calculator will show the coordinates: $(0.5, 1.25)$. The problem told us that the graphs intersect at $(m, 1.25)$, so the value of m must be 0.5.

Mastering the Calculator: Practice Set 2 (p. 225)
1) B
Type in the equation exactly as written in the problem, including the b. The calculator will automatically provide a slider for the b value.

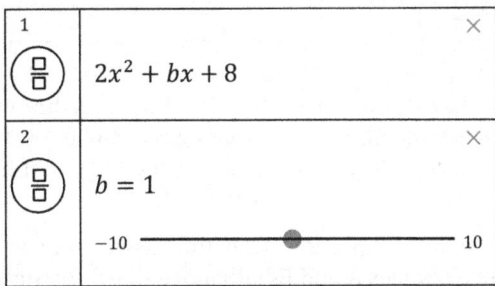

We can use the slider to check each of the answer choices in turn. Let's try choice A first. Drag the slider all the way to the left to check what happens when $b = -10$. The graph shows two x-intercepts, which means the equation now has two real solutions. We want the equation to have no real solutions, so choice A is not the answer.

Now let's try choice B. Drag the slider to the right until you reach $b = 5$. The graph now shows no x-intercepts, which means the equation has no real solutions. This is the right answer.

To confirm, drag the slider to $b = 8$ (choice C) and then to $b = 9$ (choice D). At $b = 8$, the equation has one real solution; at $b = 9$, it has two. The only choice that gave us no real solutions was B, so B is our answer.

2) D
Type in the equation.

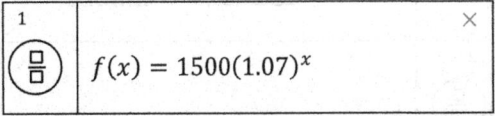

Uh oh—we don't see a graph! That's because this whole curve exists outside the window that's automatically set for us. We can adjust the window by zooming out (either use your mouse's trackball or click on the — button

Answer Explanations

on the upper right side of the screen) or by directly adjusting the minimum and maximum values for the axes (click on the 🔧 button on the upper right side of the screen). But we actually don't need to bother with any of that. All we want to know is this: what is the value of $f(x)$ when $x = 6$? So, click the ⚙ icon above the equations to get a table. Then click in the bottom row of the table and type in an x value of 6. The calculator will display the corresponding $f(x)$ value: 2251.0955.

Alternatively, we can skip the x altogether. Since the equation is $f(x) = 1500(1.07)^x$, what we're really looking for is the value of $1500(1.07)^6$. Type that expression in directly, and the calculator will dispay 2251.0955 as the answer.

3) C
Type in the equation.

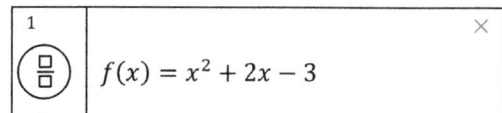

Click on the vertex of the parabola: it's at $(-1, -4)$. In the correct answer, the vertex must be 2 units further to the right, which means its x-coordinate should be $-1 + 2 = 1$. And the vertex should be 3 units up, meaning that its y-coordinate should be $-4 + 3 = -1$.

Now type in the equations from the answer choices one at a time. Choices A and B both move the graph up and to the right, but they don't go far enough: the vertex isn't where we need it to be. And choice D doesn't move the vertex at all! This is just making the graph more narrow, not translating it anywhere.

But choice C is perfect. The vertex is now at $(1, -1)$, so the graph has been moved 3 units up and 2 units to the right. C is the right answer.

4) B
The big rule of functions is that whatever's in the parentheses is your x value; the number on the other side of the equals sign is the corresponding value of y. So this problem is really giving us two (x, y) points: $(0, 6)$ and $(1, 9)$. Go ahead and type those points in directly.

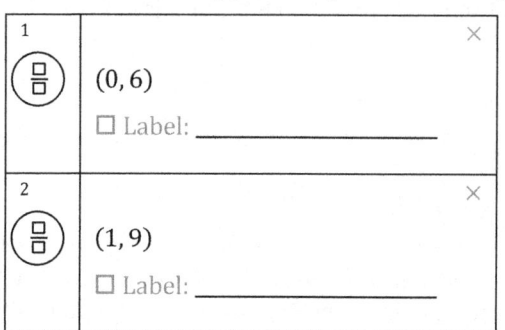

Now type in the answer choices one at a time. Only choice B gives us a line that passes through both points, so B is the right answer.

5) B
Type in the equation.

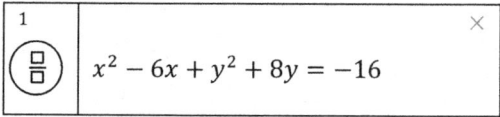

The calculator automatically highlights important points on the circumference of the circle, but it does not directly give us the center. However, we can hover the highlighted points on the top and bottom of the circle: they are $(3, -1)$ and $(3, -7)$. These points are directly across the circle from each other, so the center must be the point equidistant from the two of them: $(3, -4)$. That's choice B.

Alternatively, you could type in each of the answer choices. Click the "Label" checkbox under each point to add the answer choice letters.

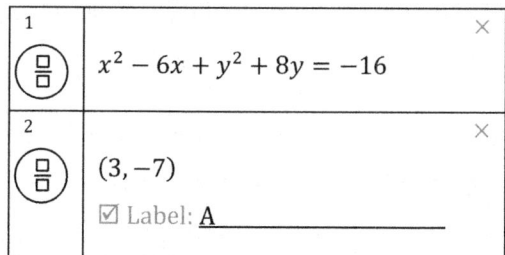

Repeating that process for the remaining choices gives us this:

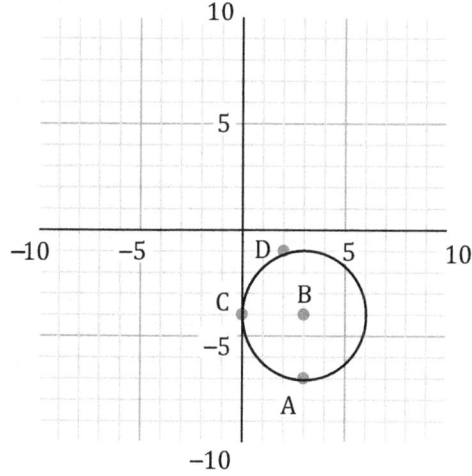

The only one that looks remotely correct is B.

6) A
Type in both equations.

| 1 | $3x - 5y = 8$ | ✕ |
| 2 | $y = x^2 - 1$ | ✕ |

The solutions to a system of equations are the points of intersection. The graphs of these two equations do not intersect, so there are zero solutions.

7) C
Type in the equation exactly as written in the problem, including the constants. The calculator will automatically provide sliders for the values of a, b, and c.

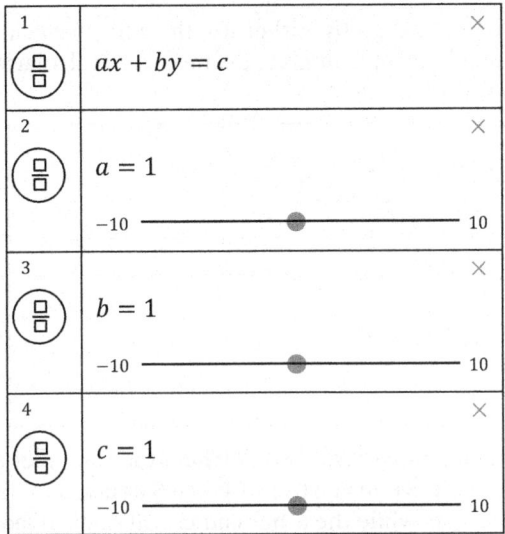

Now use the sliders to check the answer choices one at a time. Choices A and B each give us a horizontal line. Choice C gives a vertical line. Choice D gives us neither.

We were looking for the vertical line in this problem, so the answer is C.

8) 4
Here's a problem that can be quite ugly and time-consuming if you try to solve it algebraically. But on the calculator, it's simple. Type in both equations:

| 1 | $xy = 1$ | ✕ |
| 2 | $x^2 + y^2 = 9$ | ✕ |

The calculator automatically highlights the four points of intersection, which is all we needed to know: there are four solutions to the system.

Math Strategy

APPROXIMATING AND MEASURING (p. 226)
Approximating and Measuring: Practice Set 1 (p. 227)
1) C
In the figure, $\overline{LN}$ appears longer than $\overline{LM}$, which we know has length 8. Therefore, the answer must be greater than 8. That automatically eliminates choice B.

Type the other answer choices into the calculator to compare them. $2\sqrt{7}$ is just a little more than 5, so choice A is out. $10\sqrt{2}$ is a little more than 14, which is too big: that would make $\overline{LN}$ almost twice as long as $\overline{LM}$, and we can see that it isn't. Eliminate choice D.

The remaining choice, C, must be the answer.

2) B
The chemist used 40 mL of solution B in the first batch, and now she's using 25 mL. It makes sense that the amount of solution A should also decrease, so we need an answer that's less than 30. Get rid of choices C and D.

But choice A is too simple. To go from 40 to 25, we didn't just cut it in half, so we probably don't want to simply cut the 30 in half either. Choice B makes the most sense.

3) C
This one is easy to approximate once you know how to use the built-in calculator. Type in the original equation:

| 1 | $2x + y = 1$ | ✕ |

Now type in the equations from the answer choices one at a time.

Here's choice A:

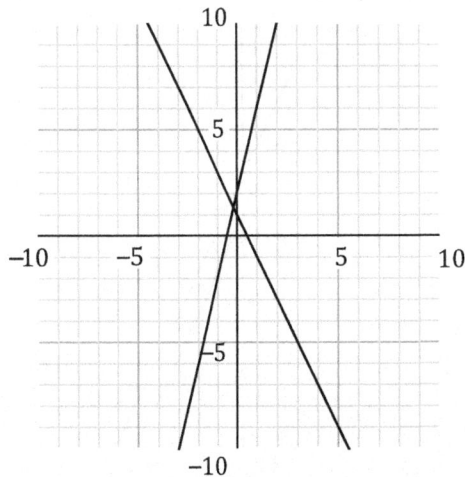

The lines intersect, but not at a right angle. These are not perpendicular lines.

Now delete the choice A equation and enter the choice B equation in its place.

Answer Explanations

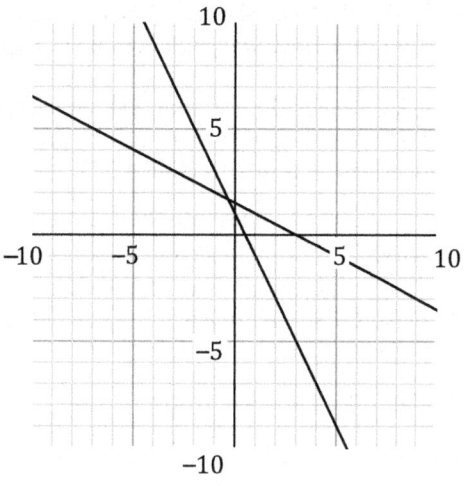

Again, they intersect, but they're not perpendicular. How about choice C?

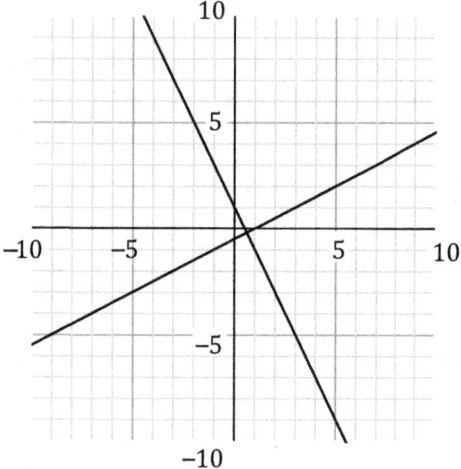

That one looks the most like a right angle. Choice C is looking good. But let's check choice D to be sure:

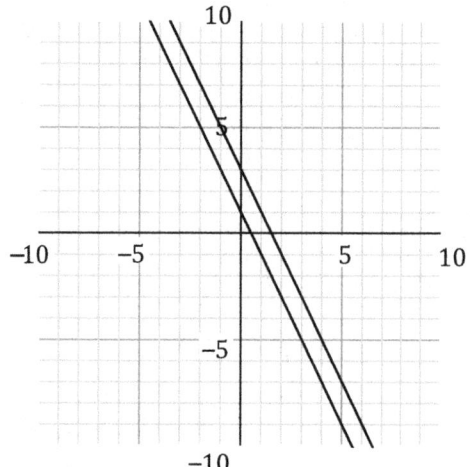

The graphs don't even intersect! These two lines are parallel, not perpendicular.

The best answer is C.

4) B
Imagine drawing a line of best fit through these points. Would it be pointing up or down? Clearly down, so this line must have a negative slope. Eliminate choices C and D. And roughly where would that line hit the y-axis? Certainly closer to 8.5, the y-intercept of choice B, than to 1, the y-intercept of choice A. Therefore, B must be the answer.

5) D
Hold the corner of your scratch paper up to the figure, trying to fit it as neatly as possible into the angle marked $x°$. That makes it clear that the angle shown is slightly greater than 90°, so the only possible answer is D.

6) B
Plot the points directly. Either use the built-in calculator in the Bluebook app, or go to desmos.com/calculator for the same tool.

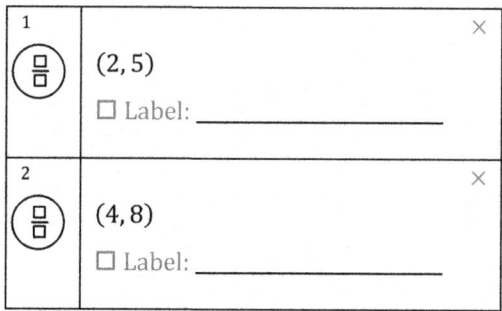

Now, leaving those two entries where they are, plot the answer choices one at a time. Choice B appears to be on the same line, while the other choices all seem at least a little off. The answer must be B.

Approximating and Measuring: Practice Set 2 (p. 228)
1) B
If the circles each have an area of 9π, then the radius of each circle is 3. Each side length of this rhombus is exactly two radii long, so the side length of the rhombus is 6.

Now, if this were a square, the area would be $6 * 6 = 36$. So that should give us at least a rough estimate of the area of this rhombus: it won't be exactly 36 since this isn't actually a square, but it should be reasonably close.

Evaluate each answer choice in the calculator. Choice A comes out to about 15.6, which is way too small. Choices C and D are roughly 47 and 49, respectively; those are big. But choice B comes out to about 31, which is the closest of these options to our estimate of 36.

2) 1/2 or 0.5
The big rule of functions is that whatever's in the parentheses is your x value; the number on the other side of the equals sign is the corresponding value of y. This time, what's in the parentheses is the expression $2k$,

which is a bit confusing. So let's focus on the other side instead. For this function, what input would give us an output of 8?

It's going to have to be pretty small, because all this cubing and squaring will increase the size rapidly. Try plugging in a number. What if the input is 2?

$$f(2) = (2)^3 + 2(2)^2 + 5$$

Nope. Just the first term of that, 2^3, already gets us to 8, and then the answer only gets bigger. So if 2 is too big, then how about 1?

$$f(1) = (1)^3 + 2(1)^2 + 5$$

That's $1 + 2 + 5$, which is 8! Perfect: now we know that $f(1) = 8$. Well remember, we also know that $f(2k) = 8$. So, try this:

$$1 = 2k$$
$$k = 1/2$$

3) C
The domain of a function is all its possible x values. This question is trying to intimidate us with an ugly equation, but we can solve this quite quickly just by graphing it. Enter the equation into the built-in calculator. What can we see about x?

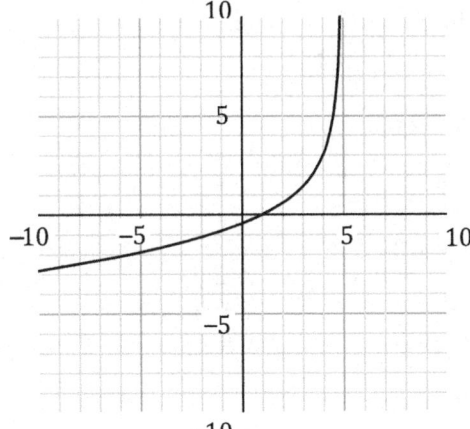

The curve certainly goes through points to the right of $x = 1$, so choice A is out. But it goes through points to the left of that as well, so we can also eliminate choice B.

To choose between C and D, don't worry about having to decide whether 5 is included in the domain or not. Focus on which direction the inequality should be going. Does this graph pass through points where x is greater than 5? Not that we can see. Does it pass through points where x is less than 5? Definitely yes. Therefore, choice C must be the right answer.

4) A
The height of each bar tells us the number of students in that grade. For example, the leftmost bar has a height of about 22, which means there are about 22 eighth graders at Glen School.

Notice that the first four bars are in increasing order. In other words, the number of 8th graders is less than the number of 9th graders, which is less than the number of 10th graders, which is less than the number of 11th graders. Based on that, choice C must be smaller than choice D, and choice D must be smaller than choice A. We're looking for the *greatest* choice, so we can already eliminate choices C and D.

Now compare choice A and choice B. There seem to be roughly as many 10th graders as there are 12th graders, but there are many more 11th graders than 9th graders. Therefore, choice A must be the answer.

Alternatively, you can just calculate all four answer choices, approximating as needed:

A) $45 +$ about $36 =$ about 81
B) $25 +$ about $36 =$ about 61
C) about $22 +$ about $36 =$ about 58
D) about $36 +$ about $36 =$ about 72

Choice A is the greatest.

5) D
This problem can be quite tedious to solve if we actually calculate everything. But let's look at it this way. We're looking for the *greatest* number of votes for something, so start with the school that has the most overall votes: School 5. That school had $0.4(5800) = 2320$ votes for Site A and $0.6(5800) = 3480$ votes for Site B. Without knowing which site won, then, we certainly know that neither School 2 nor School 4 could have had the most votes for the winning site, since neither of those schools had that many votes total. Eliminate choice B.

The next largest vote total was school 3, which had $0.5(4100) = 2050$ votes for each of Site A and Site B. Again, this is smaller than School 5's contribution to either site's vote total, so we can eliminate choice C.

Similarly, School 1 had $0.5(3200) = 1600$ votes for each of Site A and Site B. This is also less than School 5's votes for each site, so eliminate choice A.

The only choice remaining is D, so that must be the answer.

ALGEBRA ESSENTIALS (p. 229)
Algebra Essentials: Try It
1) $4x + 3$

$$3x - 2 + x + 5$$
$$3x + 1x + 5 - 2$$
$$4x + 3$$

2) simplified
There are no like terms to combine.

3) $0.3x^2$

$$1x^2 - 0.7x^2 = 0.3x^2$$

Answer Explanations

4) $5x - 5y$

$$2x + 3x - 4y - 1y$$
$$5x - 5y$$

5) $5xy + 3x$

$$3xy + 2xy - x + 4x$$
$$3xy + 2xy + 4x - 1x$$
$$5xy + 3x$$

6) simplified

There are no like terms to combine.

7) $-x - 3$

$$2x - (3x + 5) + 2$$
$$2x - 3x - 5 + 2$$
$$-x - 3$$

8) $6x - 17$

$$1 + 3(2x - 6)$$
$$1 + 6x - 18$$
$$6x - 17$$

9) $2x - 2$

$$\frac{1}{2}(4x + 2) - 3$$
$$2x + 1 - 3$$
$$2x - 2$$

10) $2x - 15$

$$2(3x - 8) + (1 - 4x)$$
$$6x - 16 + 1 - 4x$$
$$2x - 15$$

11) -33

$$2(3x - 8) + (1 - 4y)$$
$$2(3(-1) - 8) + (1 - 4(3))$$
$$2(-3 - 8) + (1 - 12)$$
$$2(-11) + (-11)$$
$$-22 - 11$$
$$-33$$

12) 4

$$2y - |x + y|$$
$$2(3) - |(-1) + (3)|$$
$$6 - |-1 + 3|$$
$$6 - |2|$$
$$6 - 2$$
$$4$$

13) 5

$$4x - 3 = 17$$
Add 3: $\quad 4x = 20$
Divide by 4: $\quad x = 5$

14) -13

$$3.4 = 0.2x + 6$$
Subtract 6: $\quad -2.6 = 0.2x$
Divide by 0.2: $\quad -13 = x$

15) 21

$$\frac{x - 3}{2} = 9$$
Multiply by 2: $\quad x - 3 = 18$
Add 3: $\quad x = 21$

16) 6

$$3x + 2 = 20$$
Subtract 2: $\quad 3x = 18$
Divide by 3: $\quad x = 6$

17) 2/5 or 0.4

$$1 - 2x = \frac{1}{5}$$
Subtract 1: $\quad -2x = -\frac{4}{5}$
Divide by -2: $\quad x = 2/5 = 0.4$

18) $-4/3$ or $-1.\overline{33}$

$$6 = \frac{3x}{2} + 8$$
Subtract 8: $\quad -2 = \frac{3x}{2}$
Multiply by 2: $\quad -4 = 3x$
Divide by 3: $\quad -4/3 = x$

19) $x = 5 - 2y$

$$x + 2y = 5$$
Subtract $2y$: $\quad x = 5 - 2y$

20) $x = 4y + 3$

$$2x - 6 = 8y$$
Add 6: $\quad 2x = 8y + 6$
Divide by 2: $\quad x = 4y + 3$

21) $x = 3y + 8/3$

$$\frac{3x - 9y}{2} = 4$$
Multiply by 2: $\quad 3x - 9y = 8$
Add $9y$: $\quad 3x = 9y + 8$
Divide by 3: $\quad x = 3y + 8/3$

22) $x = 4.5 - 2y$

$$10x + 20y = 45$$
Subtract $20y$: $\quad 10x = 45 - 20y$
Divide by 10: $\quad x = 4.5 - 2y$

23) $x = -3y + 1/2$

$$3 - 4x = 12y + 1$$
Subtract 3: $\quad -4x = 12y - 2$
Divide by -4: $\quad x = -3y + 1/2$

24) $x = y/24 + 2$

$$6x = y/4 + 12$$

Divide by 6: $\quad x = y/24 + 2$

Algebra Essentials: Practice Set 1 (p. 238)

1) C

Plug in the given values for x and y:

$$x(x+y) - y$$
$$5(5 + (-3)) - (-3)$$
$$5(2) + 3$$
$$13$$

2) B

Distribute and combine like terms:

$$3(2a - b) + 4(-5a + b)$$
$$3(2a) - 3(b) + 4(-5a) + 4(b)$$
$$6a - 3b - 20a + 4b$$
$$-14a + b$$

3) 5

Distribute, combine like terms, and solve:

$$3(x - 2) + x = 14$$
$$3x - 6 + x = 14$$
$$4x - 6 = 14$$
$$4x = 20$$
$$x = 5$$

4) C

Plug in the given value for x. Then follow the order of operations.

$$|2 - 6| = |-4| = 4$$

5) D

The p in this equation represents the profit, and the n represents the number of cupcakes sold. We know that Max's profit was $20, so $p = 20$. We want to know how many cupcakes he sold. So, plug 20 in for p in the equation and solve for n.

$$p = 3n - 16$$
$$20 = 3n - 16$$

Add 16 to both sides:

$$36 = 3n$$

Divide both sides by 3:

$$12 = n$$

6) D

Distribute, combine like terms, and simplify.

$$-2(n - 3) - 3(4 - n) = 5n + 6$$
$$-2n + 6 - 12 + 3n = 5n + 6$$
$$n - 6 = 5n + 6$$
$$-4n - 6 = 6$$
$$-4n = 12$$
$$n = -3$$

Now that we know that $n = -3$, we can plug that value into the expression the question asked us for, which was $1 - 2n$.

$$1 - 2(-3) = 1 + 6 = 7$$

Alternatively, we can solve this using the built-in calculator. Enter the left side of the original equation on one line and the right side on another, using x for the variable:

1	$-2(x - 3) - 3(4 - x)$
2	$5x + 6$

The graphs intersect where $x = -3$. That tells us that $n = -3$, so the value of $1 - 2n$ must be $1 - 2(-3) = 7$.

7) C

Whenever you see variables in fraction form, the best way to solve is probably to cross-multiply.

$$\frac{15}{q - 6} = \frac{24}{16}$$
$$15(16) = 24(q - 6)$$
$$240 = 24(q - 6)$$
$$10 = q - 6$$
$$16 = q$$

8) C

Distribute, combine like terms, and simplify.

$$2(4x - 3) + 5(-3x + 6) - 3(4 - 2x)$$
$$8x - 6 - 15x + 30 - 12 + 6x$$
$$-x + 12$$

If you got choice B, write out your steps when you distribute! That $-3(4 - 2x)$ should give us $-12 + 6x$, not $-12 - 6x$.

An alternative approach to this problem would be to use the built-in calculator. Enter the original expression on one line, and then enter the answer choices on the second line one at a time to check the resulting graphs. The one that matches the original is the right answer.

9) 9

Cross-multiply to solve.

$$\frac{3 + 2k}{7} = \frac{k}{3}$$
$$3(3 + 2k) = 7(k)$$
$$9 + 6k = 7k$$
$$9 = k$$

Answer Explanations

Alternatively, we can solve this using the built-in calculator. Enter the left side of the original equation on one line and the right side on another, using x for the variable:

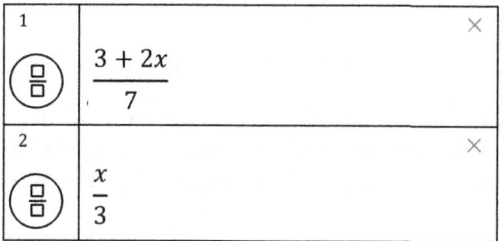

The graphs intersect where $x = 9$. Therefore, $k = 9$ is the answer.

10) B
Enter the expression into the built-in calculator and use the provided sliders to set values for $a, b,$ and c:

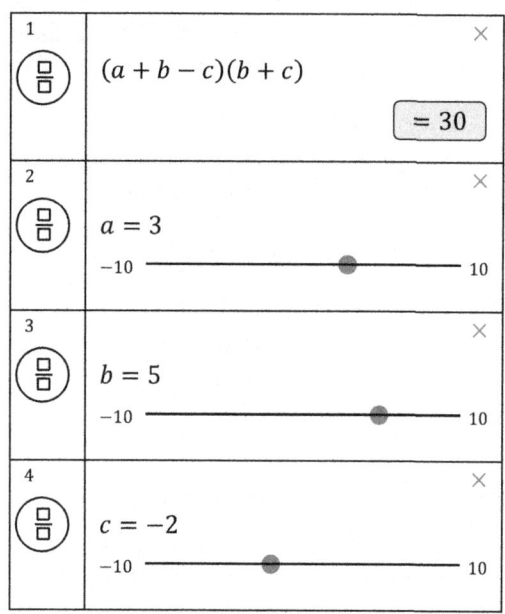

Alternatively, you can solve the problem algebraically. Plug in the given values for $a, b,$ and c. Then follow the order of operations to simplify the expression.

$$(a + b - c)(b + c)$$
$$(3 + 5 - (-2))(5 + (-2))$$
$$(10)(3)$$
$$30$$

Algebra Essentials: Practice Set 2 (p. 239)
1) 30
Just like the fraction problems in the last set, you can cross-multiply to solve. To make it easier to see it, try writing out 0.15 as a fraction. Then use your calculator to do the rest.

$$\frac{9}{2n} = \frac{0.15}{1}$$

$$9(1) = 2n(0.15)$$
$$9 = 0.3n$$
$$n = 9/0.3 = 30$$

2) C
We are given these relationships:
$$a + b = c$$
$$c = 10$$

From the above, we can deduce the following:
$$a + b = 10$$

Substitute in:
$$a + b + c = (a + b) + c = 10 + 10 = 20$$

Another approach is to plug in your own numbers. We already know $c = 10$, which means $a + b = 10$. So, let's say that $a = 5$ and $b = 5$.
$$a + b + c = 5 + 5 + 10 = 20$$

3) B
$$14n + jn = 22n$$

It's not immediately clear how to solve this since there are two variables in the equation. Conveniently, each term includes n, so the first step is to divide all terms by n. (This is allowed because we know n is not zero.)

$$14 + j = 22$$

Now just subtract 14 from both sides:
$$j = 8$$

4) D
We can ignore all the science context in this question. It actually doesn't matter at all what these variables represent! We can see from the answer choices what we are supposed to do: solve for x. Just as we did for #1 in this set, we can write this out as a fraction set equal to a fraction, then cross-multiply to solve.

$$\frac{p}{1} = \frac{100(3 + x)}{8 + x}$$
$$p(8 + x) = 1(100)(3 + x)$$
$$8p + px = 300 + 100x$$

Now, we need to isolate x. Get all the x terms on one side, and everything else on the other side.

$$px - 100x = 300 - 8p$$

Can we combine those x terms? We can! Think of it as factoring out an x.

$$x(p - 100) = 300 - 8p$$

Now just divide both sides by $(p - 100)$ to get x by itself:

$$x = \frac{300 - 8p}{p - 100}$$

Alternatively, we could use the built-in calculator to solve this problem. Enter the original expression, and then use the provided slider to set a value for n. Let's say we decide to use $n = 2$:

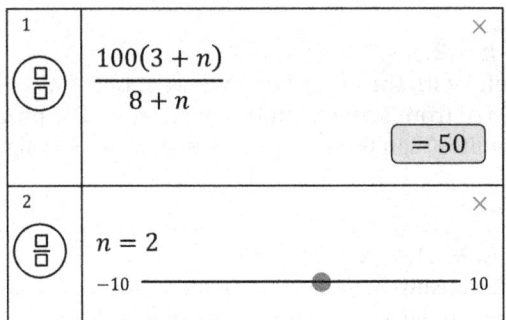

Now we know that when $n = 2$, the value of the original expression is 50. Since the original expression was equal to p, this means that when $n = 2$, $p = 50$.

Now, enter $p = 50$, and then enter each answer choice.

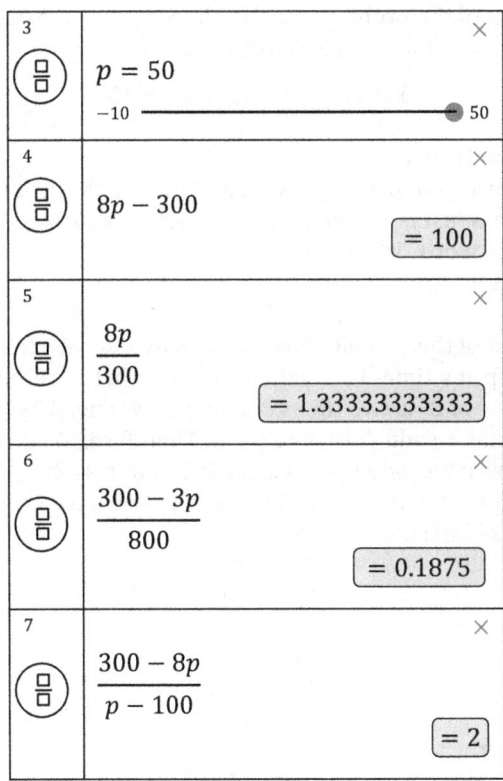

Each of these is supposed to be what n equals. Only the expression in choice D got us back to the $n = 2$ that we started with, so D is the right answer.

5) D
Distribute and combine like terms to simplify.
$$5x - 6 + (2 - x) = 2(2x + 7)$$
$$5x - 6 + 2 - x = 4x + 14$$
$$4x - 4 = 4x + 14$$
Now subtract $4x$ from both sides.

$$-4 = 14$$

Uh oh! That's not true. Since all the variables have cancelled out and what we're left with is a false statement, the equation has no solutions. (If we had been left with a true statement after all the variables cancelled out, the equation would have had infinitely many solutions.)

Alternatively, we can solve this using the built-in calculator. Enter the left side of the original equation on one line and the right side on another:

| 1 | $5x - 6 + (2 - x)$ |
| 2 | $2(2x + 7)$ |

The solution should be the x-coordinate of the point where the graphs intersect. But these graphs are parallel lines, meaning they never intersect. Therefore, the equation has no solutions.

6) B
If you notice that -28 is a multiple of 14, then this problem is straightforward.
$$2n - m = 14$$
$$-2(2n - m) = -2(14)$$
$$-4n + 2m = -28$$

Another possibility is to make up numbers for n and m. We'll need to make up a number for one variable then solve for the other:
$$n = 10$$
$$2(10) - m = 14$$
$$20 - m = 14$$
$$6 - m = 0$$
$$6 = m$$

Now plug $n = 10$ and $m = 6$ into all answer choices to see which one spits out -28.

A) $m - 2n = 6 - 2(10) = 6 - 20 = -14$
B) $2m - 4n = 2(6) - 4(10) = 12 - 40 = -28$
C) $-4n - m = -4(10) - 6 = -40 - 6 = -46$
D) $n + 2m = 10 + 2(6) = 10 + 12 = 22$

Only choice B gave us the -28 we were looking for.

7) 0.05
This is a wordy problem, but ultimately all it's asking us to do is to plug in the given numbers for the variables in the equation. Take one number from the problem at a time. The 108 is the number of meters traveled. Well, look at the first line of the problem: the equation "gives the distance, d, in meters, traveled by ..." So 108 is the value of d. What about the 60 seconds? At the end of that

Answer Explanations

sentence, the problem says, "t is the time, in seconds." Great: $t = 60$. Next is the "initial velocity of 0.3 meters per second." Earlier in that first sentence, we had this: "...where v is the machine's initial velocity, in meters per second." Therefore, $v = 0.3$. Now all we have to do is plug in what we know:

$$d = vt + 0.5at^2$$
$$108 = (0.3)(60) + 0.5(a)(60^2)$$

Don't worry about understanding the rest; the actual science behind this doesn't matter. We have an equation we can solve, with only one unknown value: the a. Now just use your calculator and the order of operations to simplify and solve:

$$108 = 18 + 0.5(a)(3600)$$
$$108 = 18 + 1800a$$
$$90 = 1800a$$
$$a = 90/1800 = 0.05$$

8) A
Cross-multiply to solve.

$$9(3a + 2) = 12(2x)$$
$$27a + 18 = 24x$$
$$x = \frac{27a + 18}{24}$$

Now divide the top and bottom of the fraction by 3:

$$x = \frac{9a + 6}{8}$$

You can also solve this one by plugging in a number for a. If we had chosen $a = 10$, then the original problem would look like this:

$$\frac{30 + 2}{12} = \frac{2x}{9}$$
$$9(32) = 12(2x)$$
$$x = \frac{9(32)}{24} = 12$$

Now plug $a = 10$ into each of the answer choices. Choice A is the only answer that works.

WORD PROBLEMS (p. 240)
Word Problems: Try It
1) $w = h + 3$
Let's use w for the width and h for the height. First translate "the width is": since the word "is" means an equals sign, that's

$$w =$$

Now consider the rest. The width is "3 inches greater" than the height. If you're not sure how to represent that, try plugging in some numbers. For example, if the height is 10 inches, and the width is 3 inches greater than that,

then the width would be 13 inches. Now it's clearer how to translate this: "3 inches greater than the height" means we add 3 to whatever the height is.

$$w = h + 3$$

2) $5 - n = 2$
Be careful with the order here: we want to show n subtracted from 5, not 5 subtracted from n. The phrase "the result is" can be represented with an equals sign.

$$5 - n = 2$$

3) $x + (x + 1) + (x + 2) = 15$
The relationship between consecutive integer is that each integer on the list is exactly one greater than the one before it. So if x is the smallest integer, the next one can be represented by $x + 1$, and the one after that as $x + 2$. We want the "sum," so add those values:

$$x + (x + 1) + (x + 2)$$

The rest of the problem was "is 15." Since "is" means an equals sign, that just gives us this:

$$x + (x + 1) + (x + 2) = 15$$

4) $ab = 2c + 4$
The word "product" means multiplying, so the product of a and b is just $a * b$, which we can write as ab. Next, we have the word "is": that's an equals sign.

$$ab =$$

The rest of this is a bit more complicated, so let's take it one step at a time. The "value of c" is c. Therefore, "*twice* the value of c" is two times c: that's $2c$. We need "4 more than" that, so add 4: that's $2c + 4$. Therefore, "4 more than twice the value of c" can be translated as $2c + 4$. So, "the product of a and b is 4 more than twice the value of c" looks like this :

$$ab = 2c + 4$$

5) $40

$$5(\$8) = \text{total}$$
$$\$40 = \text{total}$$

6) $0.78

$$12(x) = \$9.36$$
$$x = \$9.36/12$$
$$x = \$0.78$$

7) $90

$$\$50 + 5(\$8) = \text{total}$$
$$\$50 + \$40 = \text{total}$$
$$\$90 = \text{total}$$

8) $2.25

$$12(\$0.78) + 1(s) = \$11.61$$
$$\$9.36 + s = \$11.61$$
$$s = \$2.25$$

- 496 -

9) $15

$$\$50 + 5(\$8) = 6(\$n)$$
$$\$90 = 6(\$n)$$
$$n = \$90/6 = \$15$$

10) $2.34

$$12(0.78) + 7(y) = 30(0.78) + 1y$$
$$9.36 + 7y = 23.4 + y$$
$$7y = 14.04 + y$$
$$6y = 14.04$$
$$y = 2.34$$

Word Problems: Practice Set 1 (p. 247)

1) B
This is a linear relationship with a starting value ($3.50) and a rate ($2.25 per mile). The twist is that the rate only applies *after* the first mile. So the charge for a 10-mile trip is $3.50 for the first mile plus $2.25(9) for the nine additional miles:

$$3.50 + 2.25(9) = 23.75$$

2) C
Since c and $1.75 both refer to carrot juice, they should be in the same term: $1.75c$. Same goes for g and $1.25 for grapefruit juice: $1.25g$. Add those two terms to arrive at answer choice C.

3) 22
Let t stand for the tall tree and s stand for the short tree:

$$t = 3s - 2$$

We already know that $t = 64$. So:

$$64 = 3s - 2$$
$$66 = 3s$$
$$22 = s$$

4) D
Sylvan's costs are $75 per day plus $15.75 per hour, for 8 hours:

$$\text{costs} = 75 + 15.75(8) = 201$$

To cover all of his costs, then, he must receive $201.00 per day from the sale of his products.

5) C
The monthly fee is the $19.50 membership fee plus $4.75 per class taken. We could solve this problem algebraically by setting up the following equations, where x equals the number of classes:

$$33.75 = 19.50 + 4.75x$$
$$14.25 = 4.75x$$
$$3 = x$$

Alternatively, you could back-solve this problem. Say we started with choice B: if Jessie took two classes, she'd need to pay the $19.50 membership fee plus two classes at $4.75 each. That would come to a total of $19.50 + 2(4.75) = 29$ dollars. But her actual fee this month was 33.75 dollars, so that's too low. So we eliminate choice B, and while we're at it, we eliminate choice A, which would be even lower. Then test choice C: this would come to $19.50 + 3(4.75) = 33.75$ dollars, exactly what we need.

6) B
First note that we have minutes and seconds here. The correct expression should tell you Nancy's time (in minutes) to run one mile based on w weeks of training. One strategy is to try some values for w and determine the corresponding number of minutes. If $w = 0$, meaning Nancy has not yet done any training, it should take 12 minutes for her to run a mile. Choices A and C give us values other than 12 when we plug in 0 for w, so we can eliminate both.

To choose between choices B and D, try another number. What if $w = 1$? In that case, her time should be reduced by 30 seconds, or 1/2 a minute: the new time should be 11.5 minutes. Only choice B gets that right.

7) A
If h is the number of hours of use, then the charges for high-speed internet service at each hotel are as follows:

$$\text{Hotel A: } 4 + 7h$$
$$\text{Hotel B: } 14 + 5h$$

We want to know when the costs will be the same, so we just have to set them equal to each other. Then combine like terms and solve.

$$4 + 7h = 14 + 5h$$
$$4 + 2h = 14$$
$$2h = 10$$
$$h = 5$$

Alternatively, you can back-solve this problem. Start with choice B. If a guest has stayed for 6 hours, then the charges for high-speed internet service at Hotel A would be $\$4 + 6(\$7) = \$46$, and at Hotel B the charges would be $\$14 + 6(\$5) = \$44$. These don't match, so this is the wrong answer. Keep trying choices until you find the one that works: choice A.

Word Problems: Practice Set 2 (p. 248)

1) B
The easiest approach here is to back-solve. Start with choice B. If there are 40 marbles, then 10 are red and 30 are not red. Of the 30 not-red marbles, $(3/5)(30) = 18$ are green. We know from the problem that the remaining 12 marbles are blue. Now add those up to check the total. Here, 10 red marbles + 18 green marbles + 12 blue marbles = 40 total marbles, which is exactly the number we started with. Therefore, B is the right answer.

To solve algebraically (not recommended), start with the fact that 1/4 of the marbles are red, which means 3/4 of

Answer Explanations

the marbles are NOT red. Further, we know that 3/5 of the non-red marbles are green, meaning 2/5 of the non-red marbles are NOT green. According to the problem, that last category consists of 12 blue marbles. Therefore, the 12 blue marbles are 2/5 of the non-red marbles, which themselves are 3/4 of the total:

$$12 = \frac{2}{5}\left(\frac{3}{4}x\right)$$
$$12 = \frac{6}{20}x$$
$$240 = 6x$$
$$40 = x$$

2) B

In the equation, the terms $2e$ and $5h$ are added together and set equal to 155, which is the total number of points earned. The only way that makes sense is if $2e$ and $5h$ each represent some number of points. Since e represents the number of easy questions, $2e$ must represent the number of points earned on the easy questions, where each easy question is worth 2 points. And since h represents the number of hard questions, $5h$ must represent the number of points earned on the hard questions, where each hard question is worth 5 points.

Now let's check the choices. The $5h$ obviously has to do with the hard questions rather than the easy questions, so choices C and D are out. Choice A gives the best interpretation for the number 5 in the equation, which is not quite what we were asked: we wanted the best interpretation of $5h$. As discussed above, $5h$ must represent the total number of points the team earned from all the hard questions, so B is the best answer.

3) A

Michael can text 50 words per minute, but we need to convert that to hours. Here's one way to make that conversion:

$$h \text{ hrs} * \frac{60 \text{ min}}{1 \text{ hr}} * \frac{50 \text{ words}}{1 \text{ min}} = h(60)(50) \text{ words}$$

Alternatively, plug in a number for h. Let's say $h = 2$. Now our question is this: how many words can Michael text in 2 hours? Well, if he can text 50 words in 1 minute, then he can text 50(60) words in 1 hour. And if he can text 50(60) words in 1 hour, then he can text 2(50)(60) words in 2 hours. Now plug $h = 2$ into each answer choice, and you'll see that only one matches that result: choice A.

4) 24

Bill starts out with t tokens. After the first game, he has $t - 4$ tokens remaining. After two games, he has lost another 4 tokens, meaning he has $t - 4(2)$ tokens remaining. Continuing that pattern, we can see that after 5 games, Bill will have $t - 4(5)$ tokens remaining. Since we know he has 4 tokens left at this point, we now have the full equation:

$$t - 4(5) = 4$$
$$t - 20 = 4$$
$$t = 24$$

5) A

Since the side lengths are consecutive odd integers, if the longest side has length s, then the second-longest side must have length $(s - 2)$, the third-longest side must have length $(s - 4)$, and so on. The perimeter is the sum of those five quantities:

$$p = s + (s - 2) + (s - 4) + (s - 6) + (s - 8)$$
$$p = 5s - 20$$

6) A

There's a lot going on in this problem. Let's deal with this one sentence at a time. If we let L equal last year's population, the first sentence says the following:

$$1258 = 523 + \frac{1}{2} * L$$

Solve for L:

$$735 = \frac{1}{2} * L$$
$$1470 = L$$

If there were 1470 birds last year, and there are 1258 birds this year, then the number of birds has decreased by $1470 - 1258 = 212$. Therefore, next year's population must be 212 fewer than this year's population:

$$1258 - 212 = 1046$$

7) D

First, translate words into equations.

Sarah is triple Andy's age: $s = 3a$
Andy is double Melissa's age: $a = 2m$

Since Sarah is 30 years old, we can now plug $s = 30$ into the first equation:

$$30 = 3a$$
$$10 = a$$

Now plug $a = 10$ into the second equation:

$$10 = 2m$$
$$5 = m$$

Plug $m = 5$ into each of the answer choices, and only choice D works.

COORDINATE GEOMETRY (p. 249)
Coordinate Geometry: Try It
1) B

The line passes through the point (0, 2). Try plugging 0 in for x in each answer choice.

A) $y = -\dfrac{3}{2}(0) + 2 = 2$

B) $y = -\dfrac{2}{3}(0) + 2 = 2$

C) $y = \dfrac{2}{3}(0) + 3 = 3$

D) $y = \dfrac{3}{2}(0) + 3 = 3$

This tells us that in choices C and D, the line passes through the point $(0, 2)$ rather than $(0, 3)$. Eliminate both answers.

We also know that the line passes through the point $(3, 0)$. Try plugging 3 in for x in each remaining answer choice.

A) $y = -\dfrac{3}{2}(3) + 2 = -2.5$

B) $y = -\dfrac{2}{3}(3) + 2 = 0$

In choice A, the line passes through the point $(3, -2.5)$ rather than $(3, 0)$. Only choice B works for both of the given points, so it must be the right answer.

2) $(2, 0)$

$$y = 3x - 6$$
$$0 = 3x - 6$$
$$6 = 3x$$
$$2 = x$$

Alternatively, type the equation into the built-in calculator and click on the point where the graph intersects the x-axis.

3) $(-3, 0)$

$$x = 2(y + 1)^2 - 5$$
$$x = 2(0 + 1)^2 - 5$$
$$x = 2(1)^2 - 5$$
$$x = 2(1) - 5$$
$$x = 2 - 5$$
$$x = -3$$

Alternatively, type the equation into the built-in calculator and click on the point where the graph intersects the y-axis.

4) 2

$$y = ax^2 + 4$$
$$22 = a(3)^2 + 4$$
$$18 = a(3)^2$$
$$18 = a(9)$$
$$2 = a$$

5) -2

$$y = x^3 - 3x^2 + 3x + k$$

The graph passes through the point $(0, -2)$.

$$-2 = (0)^3 - 3(0)^2 + 3(0) + k$$
$$-2 = 0 - 0 + 0 + k$$
$$-2 = k$$

6) $-3/2$ or -1.5

$$m = \dfrac{y_2 - y_1}{x_2 - x_1}$$
$$m = \dfrac{2 - (-4)}{3 - 7}$$
$$m = \dfrac{6}{-4} = -\dfrac{3}{2} = -1.5$$

7) ½ or 0.5

The line passes through the points $(-2, -2)$ and $(2, 0)$.

$$m = \dfrac{y_2 - y_1}{x_2 - x_1}$$
$$m = \dfrac{0 - (-2)}{2 - (-2)}$$
$$m = \dfrac{2}{4} = \dfrac{1}{2}$$

8) 2

When the equation of a line is given in slope-intercept form, $y = mx + b$, the slope of the line is m. The equation of line l is $y = 2x + 5$, so the slope of line l is 2. Lines that are parallel have equal slopes. Line q is parallel to line l, so the slope of line q is also 2.

9) $-1/2$ or -0.5

When two lines are perpendicular, their slopes are opposite reciprocals. The slope of line l is 2, as explained above. The reciprocal of 2 is $1/2$; the *opposite* reciprocal, which is what we need here, is $-1/2$.

10) $y = 2x + 8$

When the equation of a line is given in slope-intercept form, $y = mx + b$, the slope of the line is m. Line l has a slope of 2, so the form of its equation is

$$y = 2x + b$$

Line l passes through the point $(-1, 6)$, so when the value of x is -1, the value of y must be 6. Therefore:

$$6 = 2(-1) + b$$
$$6 = -2 + b$$
$$8 = b$$

For line l, then, the value of m is 2 and the value of b is 8. The full equation of the line in $y = mx + b$ form is therefore $y = 2x + 8$.

11) $y = -x + 6$

The line passes through the points $(4, 2)$ and $(0, 6)$.

Answer Explanations

$$m = \frac{y_2 - y_1}{x_2 - x_1}$$

$$m = \frac{6 - 2}{0 - 4} = -1$$

In the form $y = mx + b$, the y-intercept is given by b. From the point $(0, 6)$, we know the y-intercept of this line is 6. Therefore, the full equation of the line is $y = -x + 6$.

Coordinate Geometry: Practice Set 1 (p. 255)
1) D
For each choice, plug the x-coordinate in for x in the equation and plug the y-coordinate in for y.

A) $3 = -2(-1) + 5$
$3 = 2 + 5$: FALSE

B) $2 = -2(0) + 5$
$2 = 0 + 5$: FALSE

C) $-7 = -2(1) + 5$
$-7 = -2 + 5$: FALSE

D) $1 = -2(2) + 5$
$1 = -4 + 5$: TRUE

Only choice D works.

Alternatively, we can solve this problem using the built-in calculator. Type in the equation and then click the ⚙ symbol above the equation-entering area. Click on the image that looks like a table, and the calculator will automatically generate a table of points:

x	$-2x + 5$
-2	9
-1	7
0	5
1	3
2	1

$y = -2x + 5$

Only choice D matches one of the rows in the table.

2) C
Any horizontal translation (left or right) will impact the x-coordinate value; any vertical translation (up or down) will impact the y-coordinate value. Going to the right adds to the x-value; going up adds to the y-value. So, here:

$$x = -6 + 2 = -4$$

$$y = 2 + 6 = 8$$

Thus the new coordinates will be $(-4, 8)$.

3) 7
To find the value of k, plug in the coordinates of the given point. Plug the x-coordinate in for x in the equation, and plug the y-coordinate in for y.

$$y = 2x - 5$$
$$9 = 2(k) - 5$$

Add 5 to both sides:

$$14 = 2k$$

Divide both sides by 2:

$$7 = k$$

4) D
Go to the built-in calculator. In the upper left corner of the screen, above the equation-entering area, you'll find a button that looks like this: ➕

Clicking that button will open up a dropdown menu of options. Click on the "table" option and you can type the whole table from this problem right into the calculator. It should look something like this:

x_1	y_1
-1	-9
0	-6
1	-3
2	0

The calculator will automatically plot those points. Now test the choices by entering the equations one at a time.

Here's choice A:

$$y = -\frac{3}{4}x - 6$$

The calculator will automatically graph this line, and we can see it does not come close to the points we entered. So now, delete that equation (keeping the table of points where it is) and enter the remaining choices one at a time. Choice D is the only one to give us a line that goes straight through the given points.

Alternatively, we can solve this problem algebraically. For example, we can see from the table that when $x = 0$, $y = -6$. So plug $x = 0$ into each of the answer choices.

Choices B and C come out to 2, while choices A and D come out to −6. Eliminate choices B and C.

We can also see from the table that when $x = 2, y = 0$. Plug $x = 2$ into the remaining choices; only D works.

5) B
A horizontal line has a slope of zero. A vertical line has an undefined slope. Diagonal lines pointing upward from left to right have positive slopes. For these, the "steeper" the line is (i.e., closer to vertical), the greater its slope; the smallest slope will be the one closest to horizontal. In this case, that would be line m.

6) B
The (x, y) coordinates of the origin are $(0, 0)$. In the built-in calculator, plot that point as well as the other point provided in the problem, $(4, -1)$:

1		×
	$(0,0)$	
2		×
	$(4,-1)$	

Now look at the graph. The line passing through those two points would be pointing down: that's a negative slope.

Alternatively, we can determine the slope algebraically by plugging the points into the slope formula:

$$m = \frac{y_2 - y_1}{x_2 - x_1}$$

$$m = \frac{-1 - 0}{4 - 0} = -\frac{1}{4}$$

7) A
Each of the answer choices is written in slope-intercept form, $y = mx + b$. In this form, the b is the y-intercept, which we can see from the figure is 3. Eliminate choices B and D.

Now we just need m, which represents the slope. Plug any two of the points provided, such as $(0, 3)$ and $(-1, 5)$, into the slope formula:

$$m = \frac{y_2 - y_1}{x_2 - x_1}$$

$$m = \frac{5 - 3}{-1 - 0} = \frac{2}{-1} = -2$$

Therefore, the equation of the line is $y = -2x + 3$.

Alternatively, we can solve this problem using the built-in calculator. Type in the equation for one of the choices, and then click on the line to find the coordinates of various points. Only choice A satisfies more than one of the points we were given.

8) 3
The x-intercept of a graph is the x-coordinate of the point where the line crosses the x-axis, or the value of x when $y = 0$. Graph the equation in the built-in calculator and click on the point where the line intersects the x-axis. The calculator will automatically display the coordinates of that point: $(3, 0)$. Therefore, the x-intercept is 3.

Alternatively, we can solve this algebraically by plugging in 0 for y.

$$y = 8x - 24$$
$$0 = 8x - 24$$

Add 24 to both sides:

$$24 = 8x$$

Divide by 8:

$$3 = x$$

9) B
Plug the given points into the slope formula.

$$m = \frac{y_2 - y_1}{x_2 - x_1}$$

$$m = \frac{2 - 5}{6 - (-1)} = -\frac{3}{7}$$

10) D
A vertical line is written in the form $x = c$, where c is a constant. As you move up and down the line, the y-value changes while the x-value remains the same. On this graph, the constant x-value is 3, so the equation of line l is $x = 3$.

Alternatively, you can solve this by graphing the given equations in the built-in calculator one at a time. Only choice D resembles the vertical line we're looking for.

11) A
Plot the two given points in the built-in calculator, along with the point given in choice A.

1		×
	$(1, 1)$	
2		×
	$(4, -5)$	
3		×
	$(0, 3)$	

Take a look at the resulting graph. Do all three points seem to lie on the same line? Yes, they do. That probably

Answer Explanations

means choice A is the answer, but just to be sure, let's check choice B. Replace $(0, 3)$ with $(0, 4)$, leaving the first two points where they are. Nope, that looks a little less linear. Choices C and D look even worse, so the right answer was choice A.

Alternatively, we can solve this problem algebraically. Begin by finding the slope between the two points given in the problem, $(1, 1)$ and $(4, -5)$:

$$m = \frac{y_2 - y_1}{x_2 - x_1}$$

$$m = \frac{-5 - 1}{4 - 1} = -\frac{6}{3} = -2$$

Any two points on the same line will have an identical slope. Thus, we can find the slope between one of the above points—let's go with $(1, 1)$—and each of the answer choices in turn until we find the one that also gives us a slope of -2. Here's how that works out for choice A:

$$m = \frac{y_2 - y_1}{x_2 - x_1}$$

$$m = \frac{3 - 1}{0 - 1} = -\frac{2}{1} = -2$$

None of the other points give a slope of -2, so choice A is the answer.

12) B
Let's start by identifying two points on the graph, such as $(0, -2)$ and $(1, 0)$. Use those to calculate the slope of the original line.

$$m = \frac{y_2 - y_1}{x_2 - x_1}$$

$$m = \frac{-2 - 0}{0 - 1} = \frac{-2}{-1} = 2$$

This line has a slope of 2. The slope of a perpendicular line would be the opposite reciprocal of 2: so, $-1/2$.

When the equation of a line is given in $y = mx + b$ form, the value of m is the slope. The only answer choice that has $-1/2$ in that spot is choice B.

13) 3/2 or 1.5
To clearly identify the slope of a line expressed in standard form ($ax + by = c$), convert it to slope-intercept form, which is $y = mx + b$.

$$3x - 2y = 5$$

Subtract $3x$ from both sides:

$$-2y = -3x + 5$$

Divide both sides by -2:

$$y = \frac{3}{2}x - \frac{5}{2}$$

Now that the line is in $y = mx + b$ form, the slope is m: in this case 3/2.

Coordinate Geometry: Practice Set 2 (p. 257)
1) B
One option would be to graph the original line in the built-in calculator, then graph each of the answer choice equations with it to see which one looks the most perpendicular.

Alternatively, we can solve this problem algebraically. First, convert the given equation into $y = mx + b$ form.

$$5x - 2y = 8$$
$$-2y = -5x + 8$$
$$y = \frac{5}{2}x - 4$$

We would then express the equations in the answer choices in slope-intercept form as well in order to determine which has the perpendicular slope. Remember, when lines are perpendicular, their slopes are opposite reciprocals, so for this problem, the right equation will have a slope of $-2/5$.

We can save some time by recognizing that in the correct answer, the x and y terms will have the same sign (either both positive or both negative): that way, when we subtract the x term to the other side and then divide by the coefficient of y, we'll end up with a negative slope. That seems to eliminate every option except B, but let's check it to make sure:

$$2x + 5y = 4$$
$$5y = -2x + 4$$
$$y = -\frac{2}{5}x + \frac{4}{5}$$

Yep, this matches what we were looking for. Choice B is the right answer.

2) C
The shaded region forms a triangle. So, a good way to start is to write out the formula for the area of a triangle:

$$A = \frac{1}{2}bh$$

That means we'll need to figure out the base and the height in order to solve this. Notice that for this triangle, the base is the horizontal line that extends from $(0, 0)$ to the x-intercept of the diagonal line ($y = 4 - 2x$). The height of the triangle is the vertical line that extends from $(0, 0)$ to the y-intercept of that diagonal line. Thus, if we can determine the x- and y-intercepts of the diagonal line, we will have found the base and height of the triangle.

Find the x-intercept by plugging in 0 for y in the equation of the diagonal line.

$$y = 4 - 2x$$

$$0 = 4 - 2x$$
$$2x = 4$$
$$x = 2$$

The base extends from $(0,0)$ to $(2,0)$, so the base is 2.

Now, find the y-intercept by plugging in 0 for x in the same equation.

$$y = 4 - 2x$$
$$y = 4 - 2(0)$$
$$y = 4$$

The height extends from $(0,0)$ to $(0,4)$, so the height is 4.

So, this is a triangle with a base of 2 and a height of 4. Now we can calculate the area:

$$A = \frac{1}{2}bh$$
$$A = \frac{1}{2}(2)(4) = 4$$

3) 3
Parallel lines will have the same slope. Thus, line l must have an equation of this form:

$$y = \frac{2}{3}x + b$$

To find the value of b, which is also the y-intercept of line l, plug the point $(6, 7)$ in for x and y in our equation.

$$7 = \frac{2}{3}(6) + b$$
$$7 = 4 + b$$
$$3 = b$$

4) B
Calculate the values one by one. Let's start with choices B and C, since we can calculate the x- and y-intercepts of this line with the equation in its current form.

To find the x-intercept, plug in 0 for y:

$$2x - 5(0) = 7$$
$$2x = 7$$
$$x = 7/2 = 3.5$$

So the value of choice B is 3.5.

To find the y-intercept, plug in 0 for x:

$$2(0) - 5y = 7$$
$$-5y = 7$$
$$y = -7/5 = -1.4$$

The value of choice C is -1.4. That's less than B's 3.5, so we can eliminate choice C.

Next, we need the slope of the line. For this, rearrange the equation into $y = mx + b$ form:

$$2x - 5y = 7$$
$$-5y = -2x + 7$$

$$y = \frac{2}{5}x - \frac{7}{5}$$

The slope of the line is $2/5 = 0.4$, so that's the value of choice A. That's less than B's 3.5, so we can eliminate A.

The slope of a perpendicular line would be the opposite reciprocal of $2/5$. So choice D is $-5/2 = -2.5$. Still lower than B's 3.5, so eliminate choice D. Choice B is the answer.

5) B
A horizontal line is written in the form $y = c$, where c is any constant number. As a horizontal line does not contain an x term, the coefficient in front of the x in the equation $y = ax + b$ must be zero. The only choice in which $a = 0$ is choice B, so that must be the answer.

Alternatively, you can solve this using the built-in calculator. Type in the equation exactly as given, including the constants a and b. The calculator will automatically provide sliders for both values.

1	$y = ax + b$
2	$a = 1$ -10 ——●—— 10
3	$b = 1$ -10 ——●—— 10

Now use the sliders to check the answer choices one at a time. Only choice B gives us a horizontal line.

6) A
The y-axis represents the user revenue in **dollars**. The x-axis represents the **years** since the company's founding. "Per" means division. Thus the rate of increase, in $m per year, from 2007 to 2010 represents the change in y over the change in x—also known as slope.

We can use the slope formula to find the rate of increase. Based on the graph, approximate the points for 2007 and 2010: they look like roughly $(2007, 2)$ and $(2010, 4.8)$.

$$m = \frac{y_2 - y_1}{x_2 - x_1}$$

$$m = \frac{4.8 - 2}{2010 - 2007} = \frac{2.8}{3} = 0.933$$

That's closest to choice A.

SYSTEMS OF EQUATIONS (p. 258)
Systems of Equations: Try It
1) 4
Subtract straight down:

Answer Explanations

$$\begin{array}{r} 3x + 4y = 7 \\ - \quad 2x + 4y = 3 \\ \hline x \qquad\quad = 4 \end{array}$$

Alternatively, we can solve this problem using the built-in calculator. Type in both equations:

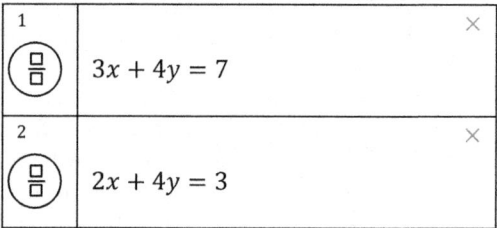

Click on the point of intersection and the calculator will show the coordinates: $(4, -1.25)$. The value of x is 4.

2) 2
First, multiply the top equation by 2:

$$2(4p - j = -2)$$
$$8p - 2j = -4$$

Now stack that with the other equation and add straight down:

$$\begin{array}{r} 8p - 2j = -4 \\ + \quad 3p + 2j = 26 \\ \hline 11p \qquad\quad = 22 \\ p = 2 \end{array}$$

Alternatively, we can solve this problem using the built-in calculator. Type in both equations, using x and y as the variables:

1	$4x - y = -2$
2	$3x + 2y = 26$

Click on the point of intersection and the calculator will show the coordinates: $(2, 10)$. The value of x is 2. Since we were using the variable x to stand in for p, the answer to this problem is $p = 2$.

3) There are no solutions
First, multiply the bottom equation by 2:

$$2(a + 2b = 0)$$
$$2a + 4b = 0$$

Now subtract straight down:

$$\begin{array}{r} 2a + 4b = 3 \\ - \quad 2a + 4b = 0 \\ \hline 0 = 3 \end{array}$$

All the variables cancel out and we are left with a *false* statement. Therefore, there are no solutions.

Alternatively, we can solve this problem using the built-in calculator. Type in both equations, using x and y as the variables:

1	$2x + 4y = 3$
2	$x + 2y = 0$

The lines do not intersect, so there are no solutions.

4) 5
If the equations have infinitely many solutions, then 10 must equal $2n$:

$$10 = 2n$$
$$5 = n$$

Alternatively, we can solve this problem using the built-in calculator. Type in both equations exactly as they appear on the page, including the constant "n." The calculator will automatically provide a slider for n values:

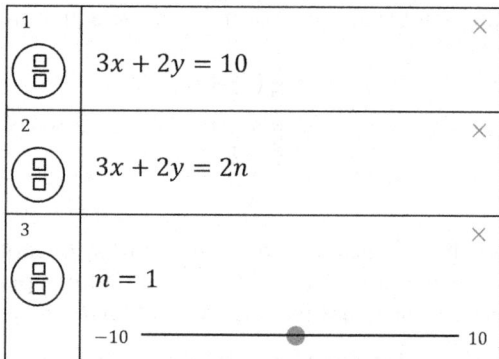

Drag the n slider to the right until the graphs overlap. When $n = 5$, these equations represent the same line, meaning the system has infinitely many solutions. Therefore, the answer is $n = 5$.

Systems of Equations: Practice Set 1 (p. 263)
1) C
Add the two equations together, combining like terms, and the y-terms will cancel out:

$$\begin{array}{r} x - 2y = 4 \\ + \quad 3x + 2y = 6 \quad + \\ \hline 4x \qquad\quad = 10 \\ x = 10/4 = 5/2 \end{array}$$

Alternatively, we can solve this problem using the built-in calculator. Type in both equations:

- 504 -

1	$x - 2y = 4$	×
2	$3x + 2y = 6$	×

The lines intersect at the point $(2.5, -0.75)$. The x value is 2.5, which is equivalent to the fraction 5/2.

2) 2

Take these equations one at a time, starting with the simpler one:
$$2a = 20$$
$$a = 10$$

Now that we have the value of a, we can plug it right into the other equation.
$$3x + 4 = 10$$
$$3x = 6$$
$$x = 2$$

3) C

You can solve this problem directly on the built-in calculator. Type in both equations:

1	$y = 2x - 5$	×
2	$y = -x + 7$	×

Click on the point of intersection and the calculator will show the coordinates: $(4, 3)$.

Alternatively, we can solve this problem algebraically. Set the two equations equal to each other.
$$2x - 5 = -x + 7$$
$$3x - 5 = 7$$
$$3x = 12$$
$$x = 4$$

Now we know the value of x is 4. Eliminate choices A and B, and plug this value back into either equation to find the value of y:
$$y = -(4) + 7$$
$$y = 3$$

4) B

Type in both equations:

1	$2x + 3y = 10$	×
2	$3y - 7x = -8$	×

Click on the point of intersection and the calculator will show the coordinates: $(2, 2)$.

Alternatively, we can solve this problem algebraically. But be careful: the x and y terms in these equations are switched! Once we put them in the same order, we have a system with a straightforward elimination method approach:

$$\begin{array}{r} 2x + 3y = 10 \\ --7x + 3y = -8 \\ \hline 9x = 18 \\ x = 2 \end{array}$$

We do not need to go any further, as only answer B has 2 as the x-value.

5) 42

Don't do more work than you have to! We don't need to find the values of x and y separately if there's a way to get directly to the value of $12x - 3y$. In this case, we can just add straight down:

$$\begin{array}{r} 8x + 6y = 25 \\ +4x - 9y = 17 \\ \hline 12x - 3y = 42 \end{array}$$

6) D

We know that 79 hamburgers and hot dogs in total were sold (though not how many of each), so in algebraic terms one of our equations is:
$$x + y = 79$$

This is enough to answer the question, because only answer D includes this equation.

The other equation is the total revenue. Each hamburger costs $7, so $7x$ dollars are earned by selling x hamburgers. Each hot dog costs $5, so $5y$ dollars are earned by selling hotdogs. Since total revenue is $489, our second equation must be:
$$7x + 5y = 489$$

Again, this equation alone is enough to answer the question, because only D includes it.

7) C

Let's say Cory has c cousins and James has j cousins. We know that Cory has 5 more cousins than James does:
$$c = j + 5$$

We also know that together, the two friends have 23 cousins:
$$c + j = 23$$

If we rearrange the first equation by subtracting j from both sides, we can use the elimination method:

Answer Explanations

$$\begin{aligned} c - j &= 5 \\ + \quad c + j &= 23 \\ \hline 2c &= 28 \\ c &= 14 \end{aligned}$$

8) A

Let's say that s is the number of student tickets and a is the number of adult tickets.

We know the theater sold 150 tickets total:
$$s + a = 150$$

And we know that there were 40 fewer student tickets than adult tickets:
$$s = a - 40$$

Solve the second equation for a by adding 40 to both sides. Then substitute and solve:
$$\begin{aligned} s + (s + 40) &= 150 \\ s + s + 40 &= 150 \\ 2s &= 110 \\ s &= 55 \end{aligned}$$

9) D

Don't overthink this one! On a graph, the solution to a system of equations will just be the coordinates of a point where they intersect. In the figure, we can see that these two graphs intersect at two points: $(0, 1)$ and $(10, 6)$. Only one of those is provided as an answer: choice D.

If you picked B, you found a solution to just one of the equations. The x-intercepts of quadratics are often referred to as "solutions," but specifically they're the solutions you get when you set that single equation equal to zero. The solution to a *system* is a point that exists on *both* graphs, and it won't necessarily be an x-intercept of either one. In other words, while B is a solution to the equation $0 = \frac{1}{4}x^2 - 2x + 1$, only D is a solution to the system of equations $y = \frac{1}{4}x^2 - 2x$ and $y = \frac{1}{2}x + 1$.

10) C

You can solve this problem directly on the built-in calculator. Type in both equations:

1	$y = 3x - 2$
2	$x - y = 4$

Click on the point of intersection and the calculator will show the coordinates: $(-1, -5)$.

Alternatively, we can solve this problem algebraically. Since one of these equations is already solved for y, the substitution is probably the easiest method for this one.

$$\begin{aligned} x - (3x - 2) &= 4 \\ x - 3x + 2 &= 4 \\ -2x + 2 &= 4 \\ -2x &= 2 \\ x &= -1 \end{aligned}$$

There's only one answer choice with an x-coordinate of -1, so we're done.

11) -1

It's tempting to use either the elimination method or the substitution method to find the values of x and y, but we do not actually *need* to find either value: we can find $3x + 2y$ directly. Just subtract straight down:

$$\begin{aligned} 10x + y &= 8 \\ - \quad 7x - y &= 9 \\ \hline 3x + 2y &= -1 \end{aligned}$$

Alternatively, we can solve this problem using the built-in calculator, though it takes a few more steps. Type in both equations:

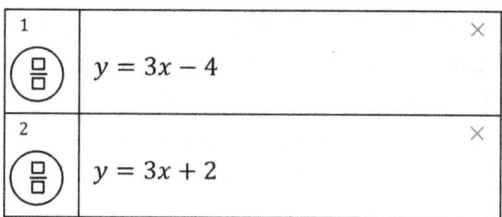

The lines intersect at the point where $x = 1$ and $y = -2$. Therefore, the value of $3x + 2y$ is $3(1) + 2(-2) = -1$.

12) A

Type both equations into the built-in calculator:

1	$y = 3x - 4$
2	$y = 3x + 2$

These two graphs do not intersect, so there are no solutions.

Alternatively, we can solve this problem algebraically. Try subtracting straight down:

$$\begin{aligned} y &= 3x - 4 \\ - \quad y &= 3x + 2 \\ \hline 0 &= \quad -6 \end{aligned}$$

All the variables cancel out and what we're left with is a false statement, so there are no solutions.

13) A

Let's say there are e easy questions and d difficult questions. If there are a total of 25 questions, we have this:

$$e + d = 25$$

Now, since each of the easy questions is worth 2 points, the e easy questions must be worth a total of $2e$ points. Similarly, since each of the difficult questions is worth 5 points, the d difficult questions are worth a total of $5d$ points. Those two point amounts must add up to 71 points:

$$2e + 5d = 71$$

We want to find the value of d, so we need to eliminate e. Therefore, multiply the top equation by 2:

$$2(e + d = 25)$$
$$2e + 2d = 50$$

Now stack and eliminate:

$$\begin{array}{r} 2e + 5d = 71 \\ - \quad 2e + 2d = 50 \\ \hline 3d = 21 \\ d = 7 \end{array}$$

14) D

First solve the simpler equation on top.

$$3y = 6$$
$$y = 2$$

Now plug that value into the second equation:

$$x - 4(2) = 5$$
$$x - 8 = 5$$
$$x = 13$$

Only one answer choice has an x-value of 13, so we don't have to go any further. Choice D must be the answer.

Alternatively, we can solve this problem using the built-in calculator. Type in both equations:

1	$3y = 6$
2	$x - 4y = 5$

Use your mouse to drag the viewing screen over until you can see where the lines intersect. Click on the point of intersection, and the calculator will display the coordinates: The lines intersect at the point (13, 2).

Systems of Equations: Practice Set 2 (p. 265)

1) 3

The first step is to get this into algebraic terms. Let's call our two unknowns x and y. We know the sum of the two integers is 6:

$$x + y = 6$$

Now consider the other piece of information: "the sum of twice the first integer and 3 times the second integer is 9." If the first integer is x, then twice the first integer is $2x$. And if the second integer is y, then 3 times the second integer is $3y$. So:

$$2x + 3y = 9$$

We're looking for "the sum of the first integer and twice the second integer": in other words, $x + 2y$.

$$\begin{array}{r} 2x + 3y = 9 \\ - \quad x + y = 6 \\ \hline x + 2y = 3 \end{array}$$

2) A

There are a total of 20 coins. If we have n nickels, d dimes, and q quarters, then we can say this:

$$n + d + q = 20$$

We also know there are twice as many dimes as nickels:

$$d = 2n$$

We can plug that into the first equation to get the number of variables down to two:

$$n + (2n) + q = 20$$
$$3n + q = 20$$

Now, the total value of the coins is $2.50. But to avoid having to deal with decimals, let's write all this in cents: the total value is 250 cents. Since each nickel is worth 5 cents, the value of the n nickels is $5n$ cents. And so on:

$$5n + 10d + 25q = 250$$

To reduce the number of variables, let's do the same thing to this equation that we did to the first equation:

$$5n + 10(2n) + 25q = 250$$
$$5n + 20n + 25q = 250$$
$$25n + 25q = 250$$
$$n + q = 10$$

We're looking for the number of quarters, so we'll want to eliminate the n's. So first, multiply that last equation by 3:

$$3(n + q = 10)$$
$$3n + 3q = 30$$

Then, use the elimination method:

$$\begin{array}{r} 3n + 3q = 30 \\ - \quad 3n + q = 20 \\ \hline 2q = 10 \\ q = 5 \end{array}$$

3) A

Let's use a for the fixed amount for assembly and h for the hourly rate. That gives us two different equations, which we can solve using the elimination method:

Answer Explanations

$$a + 5h = 190$$
$$-\quad a + 2h = 100$$
$$\overline{\quad 3h = 90\quad}$$
$$h = 30$$

Now plug h back into one of the equations to find a:

$$a + 2(30) = 100$$
$$a + 60 = 100$$
$$a = 40$$

We can now model the cost of renting party equipment for a 3-hour party this way:

$$c = a + 3h$$
$$c = 40 + 3(30)$$
$$c = 130$$

4) C

Multiply the top equation by 2 to get this system:

$$8x - 6y = 20$$
$$kx - 6y = 12$$

If kx was the same thing as $8x$, then subtracting straight down at this point would cancel out all the variables, leaving us with the false statement $0 = 8$. That's the situation we need for the system to have no real solutions. Therefore, kx must equal $8x$, meaning the value of k is 8.

Alternatively, we can solve this problem using the built-in calculator. Type in both equations exactly as they appear on the page, including the constant "k." The calculator will automatically provide a slider for k values:

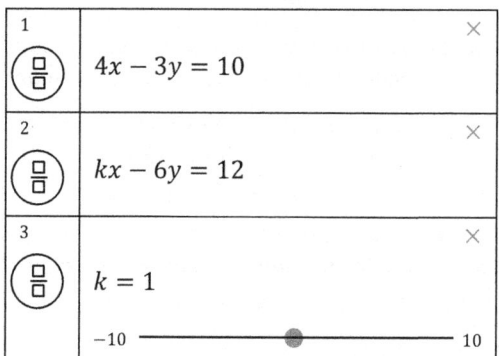

To test choice A, use the slider to set k equal to -4, or just click the $k =$ line and type in -4 directly. We're looking for the value of k that will give us no real solutions, which means the lines must not intersect. But we can see that the graphs intersect when $k = -4$, so this is not the answer. Now try $k = 0$, $k = 8$, and $k = 10$ to check the remaining answer choices. Only $k = 8$ gives us the parallel (and therefore non-intersecting) lines we're looking for.

5) C

First, we need to assign variables to the degree measures of the three angles of the triangle. For simplicity, let's use s, m, and l, for small, medium, and large. Here's what we know from the problem:

$$l = s + m$$
$$s + l = 2m$$

We can plug that first equation right into the second one:

$$s + (s + m) = 2m$$
$$s + s + m = 2m$$
$$2s + m = 2m$$
$$2s = m$$

The fact that this is a triangle gives us one other relationship: the angles must add up to 180°.

$$s + m + l = 180$$

Let's plug the first equation into this one too:

$$s + m + (s + m) = 180$$
$$2s + 2m = 180$$
$$s + m = 90$$

We figured out earlier that $2s = m$. So now, let's plug that into this:

$$s + (2s) = 90$$
$$3s = 90$$
$$s = 30$$

6) C

These equations are nearly identical; the only thing that changes is the variable. It's not possible to find the values of x, y, b, and c (because we do not have enough equations) but we can find the correct answer with a little thought. We know that $b = c + 1/4$, so let's substitute that in:

$$4x + c + \frac{1}{4} = 3x - 11$$
$$4y + c = 3y - 11$$

Now, what we want to know is how x and y relate to each other: we don't actually care about c. So, let's subtract the two equations to eliminate it:

$$4x + c + \frac{1}{4} = 3x - 11$$
$$-\quad 4y + c \quad\quad = 3y - 11$$
$$\overline{4x - 4y + \frac{1}{4} = 3x - 3y}$$

Now let's simplify. Subtract $3x$ from both sides:

$$x + \frac{1}{4} - 4y = -3y$$

Next, add $4y$ to both sides:

$$x + \frac{1}{4} = y$$

This tells us that y is equivalent to $x + 1/4$. That's choice C.

7) B

Let's focus on setting up one equation at a time. The number of bars in a box will be c, and the number of neighbors will be n. We know that if each of her neighbors buys 2 chocolate bars (a total of $2n$ chocolate bars), there will be 10 bars left in the box. So if we add those 10 to the $2n$ chocolate bars, the result equals the c bars we started with:

$$2n + 10 = c$$

We also know that if each neighbor were to buy 4 chocolate bars (for a total of $4n$ bars), Leslie would need 40 additional bars. So, $4n$ bars is 40 more than c:

$$4n = c + 40$$

Let's plug the first equation into the second one to solve.

$$4n = (2n + 10) + 40$$
$$4n = 2n + 50$$
$$2n = 50$$
$$n = 25$$

Alternatively, you could back-solve this problem. Start with choice B: Leslie has 25 neighbors. If they each buy 2 chocolate bars, they'd buy a total of 50 bars. At this point, there should be 10 bars left in the box, meaning the box originally held $50 + 10 = 60$ bars. If each of the 25 neighbors buys 4 chocolate bars, that's 100 bars: she'd need 40 more than her original 60 to cover this. That matches what we were looking for, which means B is the right answer.

8) 2

If Abbott owns x hats and Becky owns 3 more than Abbott, then Becky owns $x + 3$ hats. If Costello owns two fewer hats than Becky, then Costello must own $x + 3 - 2 = x + 1$ hats. The total number of hats should be twice as great as the number of hats owned by Becky. Since Becky owns $x + 3$ hats, the total number of hats must be $2(x + 3)$. So:

$$\text{Abbott} + \text{Betty} + \text{Costello} = \text{Total}$$
$$(x) + (x + 3) + (x + 1) = 2(x + 3)$$
$$3x + 4 = 2x + 6$$
$$x + 4 = 6$$
$$x = 2$$

9) C

If the system has infinitely many solutions, the coefficients of the variables must match. So, multiply the first equation by 2 and the second equation by 3: that way, both equations will start with $6x$.

$$2(3x + ky = 15)$$
$$6x + 2ky = 30$$

$$3(2x + 5y = 10)$$
$$6x + 15y = 30$$

Now we know that $6x + 2ky = 30$ must be the same equation as $6x + 15y = 30$, which means that $2k$ must be the same thing as 15:

$$2k = 15$$
$$k = 15/2$$

10) 12

Let's use e, f, and g as our variables. That gives us these three equations:

$$e + f = 20$$
$$e + g = 13$$
$$f + g = 17$$

There are multiple approaches one could take to solve this, and one could use either the elimination or the substitution method (or both). Here's one path, involving the elimination method in two steps:

$$\begin{aligned} e + f &= 20 \\ -\underline{e + g = 13} \\ f - g &= 7 \end{aligned}$$

And then:

$$\begin{aligned} f + g &= 17 \\ +\underline{f - g = 7} \\ 2f &= 24 \\ f &= 12 \end{aligned}$$

Another approach would be to use the substitution method twice. First, rearrange the first equation as $e = 20 - f$, then rearrange the third equation as $g = 17 - f$. Now plug both into the second equation:

$$e + g = 13$$
$$20 - f + 17 - f = 13$$
$$-2f = -24$$
$$f = 12$$

11) D

The system of equations we need to solve here is not obvious. But we've been given a table, so let's begin by filling that in. Start with the apartments. Among apartment residents, there are three times as many cat-owning families as dog-owning families. So if there are x apartment-dwelling families that own dogs, then there are $3x$ apartment-dwelling families that own cats.

	Dog	Cat
Apartment	x	$3x$
House		
Total	129	68

Now let's consider the houses. Among house residents, there are 4 times as many dog-owning families as cat-owning families. So if there are y house-dwelling families

Answer Explanations

that own cats, then there are $4y$ house-dwelling families that own dogs.

	Dog	Cat
Apartment	x	$3x$
House	$4y$	y
Total	129	68

Each column can be represented with its own equation, giving us this system of equations:

$$x + 4y = 129$$
$$3x + y = 68$$

Type both equations into the built-in calculator:

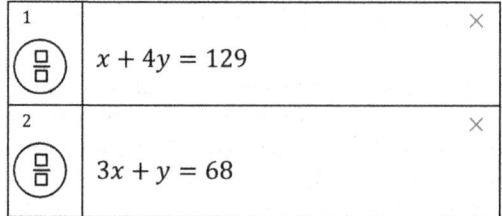

Zoom out (using either the — button or the trackball on your mouse) until you can see where the lines intersect. Click on the point of intersection and the calculator will display the coordinates: (13, 29).

In our equations, x represented the number of apartment-dwelling families that own dogs. Now we know that
$x = 13$. So, of the 129 dog-owning families, 13 of them live in apartments. The probability that a dog-owning family selected at random is therefore $13/129 = 0.101$.

INEQUALITIES AND ABSOLUTE VALUE (p. 267)
Inequalities and Absolute Value: Try It
1) $x < -4$

$$x + 2 - 3(x + 2) > 4$$
$$x + 2 - 3x - 6 > 4$$
$$-2x - 4 > 4$$
$$-2x > 8$$
$$x < -4$$

Alternatively, we can use the built-in calculator to simplify this. Type in the original expression:

[calculator: $x + 2 - 3(x + 2) > 4$]

The resulting graph shades all the points to the left of $x = -4$. Therefore, $x < -4$ is the answer.

2) $-2 < x < -\dfrac{1}{2}$

$$2 < 1 - 2x < 5$$
Subtract 1:
$$1 < -2x < 4$$

Divide by -2, which flips the <'s:

$$-\dfrac{1}{2} > x > -2$$

Rewrite to put it back in standard order:

$$-2 < x < -\dfrac{1}{2}$$

3) $x \leq 10$
Consider the possibilities if the value of x is "no greater than" 10. It could be equal to 10. It could be less than 10. It just can't be greater. Therefore, this phrase translates to the "less than or equal to" sign:

$$x \leq 10$$

4) $j = s + 500$
Let's start by defining our variables. Make j the number of dollars the juniors raised, and make s the number of dollars the seniors raised. In this problem, we're given the exact quantity of the difference between these two numbers. In other words, it's not just that the juniors raised more than the seniors (which we could express with the inequality $j > s$); it's that the juniors raised exactly $500 more. For that, we use an equals sign:

$$j = s + 500$$

5) $c \geq 5$
Let's make c the capacity of the container (in liters). Since we do not know exactly how many liters the container holds, we would express this statement as an inequality. The container holds "a minimum" of 5 liters, meaning it could hold exactly 5 liters, or it could hold more, but it definitely doesn't hold less. Therefore, the capacity is greater than or equal to 5 liters:

$$c \geq 5$$

6) $l > 2w + 6$
Let's make l the length of the rectangle and w the width of the rectangle. The phrase "more than 6 inches greater" is *not* a specific quantity (for example, the length might be 9 inches greater than twice the width, or 17 inches greater than twice width, or any number of other options). Therefore, we'll use the "greater than" inequality symbol here. Translate from left to right: the length (l) is more than ($>$) 6 inches greater than twice the width ($2w + 6$).

$$l > 2w + 6$$

7) $x = 2$ or $x = 3$
$$|2x - 5| = 1$$
$$2x - 5 = 1 \quad \text{or} \quad -(2x - 5) = 1$$
$$2x = 6 \quad \text{or} \quad -2x + 5 = 1$$
$$x = 3 \quad \text{or} \quad -2x = -4$$
$$x = 3 \quad \text{or} \quad x = 2$$

Alternatively, we can use the built-in calculator to solve this. Type in $y =$ [left side of the equation] on one line, and then type in $y =$[right side of the equation] on the other. Use `abs()` for the absolute value.

1		×
☐	$y = \text{abs}(2x - 5)$	

1		×
☐	$y = 1$	

The graphs intersect at two points: $(2, 1)$ and $(3, 1)$. The solutions are the x-coordinates of those points: $x = 2$ and $x = 3$.

8) No solutions
This is a classic SAT "gotcha" question: it's designed to catch students who are moving too fast and not looking before they leap. We don't have to bother with setting up the two equations here and then solving both, because the whole thing is impossible! Whatever the value of $3x + 8$ is, the absolute value of that quantity (or any other quantity) can never be negative. The problem has no solutions.

We can use the built-in calculator to confirm this. Type in $y =$ [left side of the equation] on one line, and then type in $y =$[right side of the equation] on the other. Use `abs()` for the absolute value.

1		×
☐	$y = \text{abs}(3x + 8)$	

1		×
☐	$y = -2$	

The graphs never intersect, which means there are no solutions.

9) $2 \leq x \leq 10$

$$|x - 6| \leq 4$$
$$x - 6 \leq 4 \quad \text{or} \quad -(x - 6) \leq 4$$
$$x \leq 10 \quad \text{or} \quad x - 6 \geq -4$$
$$x \leq 10 \quad \text{or} \quad x \geq 2$$
$$2 \leq x \leq 10$$

Alternatively, we can use the built-in calculator to simplify this. Type in the original expression. Use `abs()` for the absolute value and `<=` for the $\leq$ sign.

1		×
☐	$\text{abs}(x - 6) \leq 4$	

Drag the viewing screen to the right until you can see the whole graph. The graph consists of vertical lines $x = 2$ and $x = 10$, and the shading in between those lines. That's the graph of $2 \leq x \leq 10$.

10) $x \leq 2$ or $x \geq 10$

$$|x - 6| \geq 4$$
$$x - 6 \geq 4 \quad \text{or} \quad -(x - 6) \geq 4$$
$$x \geq 10 \quad \text{or} \quad x - 6 \leq -4$$
$$x \geq 10 \quad \text{or} \quad x \leq 2$$

Alternatively, graph the original expression in the built-in calculator, as in #9 above. This time, the graph consists of the same two vertical lines (at $x = 2$ and $x = 10$) but with shading to the left of $x = 2$ and to the right of $x = 10$. That's the graph of $x \leq 2$ or $x \geq 10$.

Inequalities and Absolute Value: Practice Set 1 (p. 272)
1) D
The easiest way to solve this problem is probably to back-solve. Plug the choices in one at a time.

A) $|1 - 2(-4)| = |1 + 8| = 9$
B) $|1 - 2(3)| = |1 - 6| = 5$
C) $|1 - 2(5)| = |1 - 10| = 9$
D) $|1 - 2(6)| = |1 - 12| = 11$

Alternatively, we can solve the problem algebraically. To solve an absolute value equation, remove the absolute value bars and write two separate equations, taking into account that the variable expression previously inside the absolute value bars could have been positive or negative:

$$|1 - 2x| = 11$$
$$1 - 2x = 11 \quad \text{or} \quad -(1 - 2x) = 11$$
$$-2x = 10 \quad \text{or} \quad -1 + 2x = 11$$
$$x = -5 \quad \text{or} \quad 2x = 12$$
$$x = -5 \quad \text{or} \quad x = 6$$

The only answer choice that contains one of those two solutions is D.

Another option would be to use the built-in calculator to solve this problem. Type $y =$ [left side of the equation] on one line, and then type in $y =$[right side of the equation] on the other. Use `abs()` for the absolute value.

1		×
☐	$y = \text{abs}(1 - 2x)$	

1		×
☐	$y = 11$	

The graphs intersect at two points: $(-5, 11)$ and $(6, 11)$. Thus, the solutions are $x = -5$ and $x = 6$.

2) 4
$$-2q - 12 \leq -5q$$

Add $5q$ to both sides:

Answer Explanations

$$3q - 12 \leq 0$$

Add 12 to both sides:

$$3q \leq 12$$

Divide both sides by 3:

$$q \leq 4$$

The value of q must be 4 or less, so the maximum possible value of q is 4.

3) C
On a number line, an open circle indicates that a certain number is excluded from a solution set, while a closed circle indicates that the number is included.

Here, though the bolded line extends from 10 to 20, the number 10 is excluded due to the open circle at that value. Thus, the solution set includes all values greater than 10 up to (and including) 20.

When expressing the answer using inequality notation, x would be **greater than** 10 and **less than or equal to** 20: $10 < x \leq 20$.

4) B
One way to solve is to plug in your own numbers. We are told that the positive difference (bigger number minus smaller number) of the two prices is always between $5 and $7.50, inclusive. Let's say that $x = 11$ (the higher price is $11) and $y = 4$ (the lower price is $4). Then the positive difference in price would be $11 - $4 = $7. Because this value is greater than $5 and less than $7.50, we have satisfied the criteria in the problem.

Now plug in $x = 11$ and $y = 4$ to check the choices.

A) $5 \leq 7 \leq 7.5$: TRUE
B) $5 \leq |7| \leq 7.5$: TRUE
C) $5 \leq |15| \leq 7.5$: FALSE
D) $5 \leq 11 \leq 7.5$ or $5 \leq 4 \leq 7.5$: FALSE

We can eliminate choices C and D. To choose between A and B, let's swap the values: that is, now $x = 4$ and $y = 11$. After all, we do not know which is the higher-priced item, so we've still satisfied all the rules of the problem.

Check the remaining choices with these new values.

A) $5 \leq -7 \leq 7.5$: FALSE
B) $5 \leq |-7| \leq 7.5$: TRUE

That eliminates choice A, so choice B is the answer.

Alternatively, we can solve the problem abstractly. Each of the choices involves the numbers 5 and 7.5, so what do we know about those values? According to the problem, it was a *positive difference* that must lie between those numbers. We don't know anything about the individual values of x or y, so choice D is out. Eliminate Choice C because it represents a sum, not a difference. And while choice A represents a difference, as we saw, it might end up being a difference that's negative. Absolute value bars are necessary to always yield the *positive* difference between two numbers.

5) A
As we are told that $x = 5$, we can plug that value in for x in the equation:

$$|x + y| = 6$$
$$|5 + y| = 6$$

We are also told that y is a negative number, so we can already eliminate choices C and D. At this point, rather than solving, we can just test out the remaining two answer choices to confirm which will give us a true statement.

A) $|5 + (-11)| = 6$: TRUE
B) $|5 + (-3)| = 6$: FALSE

The answer is A.

6) A

$$3 - 4n > 11$$

Subtract 3 from both sides:

$$-4n > 8$$

Now divide both sides by -4 (remember to flip the inequality!):

$$n < 8/-4$$
$$n < -2$$

The only value here that's *less* than -2 is -3, so the answer is A.

Alternatively, we can solve this problem using the built-in calculator. Type in the original inequality, using x for the variable so that it can be graphed.

$$3 - 4x > 11$$

The resulting graph shades everything to the left of $x = -2$. Thus, $x = -3$ (which is included in that shaded region) is a solution, while the other options are not.

7) A
The easiest way to solve this problem is to graph it on the built-in calculator. Type in the inequality (use < = to get the $\leq$ sign):

$$y \leq 2x - 1$$

The resulting graph best matches choice A.

Alternatively, we can solve this algebraically. Begin by identifying which is the correct graph of the line. The linear inequality has a positive slope of 2 and a negative y-intercept of –1. Choices B and D both have negative slopes, so we can eliminate them both.

Next, we can use the inequality symbol to determine the direction of the shading. If y is less than *or* less than or equal to the linear expression, the shaded region should be **below the line**. That eliminates C, so we're done.

If you're not sure whether shading should be above or below the line, you could test a point. Should $(0, 0)$ be included in the graph? Try it in the given equation.

$0 \leq 2(0) - 1$: FALSE

So no, $(0, 0)$ is not a solution. Therefore, it should not be part of the shaded region. That eliminates choice C, so the answer must be A.

Inequalities and Absolute Value: Practice Set 2 (p. 273)
1) C
The built-in calculator makes this problem easy. Type in the inequality:

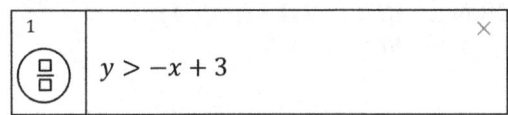

In the resulting graph, there is shading in all the quadrants except Quadrant III.

2) A
Plug in your own numbers for x and y. For example, let's say $x = 2$ and $y = 5$. Then $|y - x| = |5 - 2| = |3| = $ **3**.

We'll now want to plug 5 for x and 2 for y in every answer choice to see which one yields the same value.

A) $|2 - 5| = |-3| = 3$
B) $-(5 - 2) = -(3) = -3$
C) $2 - 5 = -3$
D) $|2 + 5| = 7$

Please note that when using the substitution strategy, we want to try out *every* answer to make sure that only one response gives us the value we're looking for. Had more than one choice given us 3, then we'd need to pick a new value for x and/or y, get a new solution, and only test out the choices that still worked from the round before to confirm the one true answer.

In this case, as it turned out, the first numbers we picked gave us only one possible answer: A was the only match.

3) C
One way to handle this problem is through back-solving. Since the question asks for the *maximum* possible value of b, start with the biggest option: $b = 15$. Plug that into the problem:

$$b = 2a$$

$$15 = 2a$$
$$a = 15/2 = 7.5$$

But wait: a must be an integer! So this choice doesn't work. Eliminate choice D and move on to choice C: $b = 14$.

$$14 = 2a$$
$$7 = a$$

This gives us an a that's an integer, so we're good so far. Now check it in the given inequality.

$$5a - 6 \leq 9 + 3a$$
$$5(7) - 6 \leq 9 + 3(7)$$
$$29 \leq 30$$

That's true, so this works: choice C is the answer.

Alternatively, we can solve the problem algebraically. If $b = 2a$, then $b/2 = a$. We can now replace a with $b/2$ in the inequality statement:

$$5a - 6 \leq 9 + 3a$$
$$5\left(\frac{b}{2}\right) - 6 \leq 9 + 3\left(\frac{b}{2}\right)$$
$$\frac{5b}{2} - 6 \leq 9 + \frac{3b}{2}$$

Multiply both sides by 2 to get rid of the fractions:

$$5b - 12 \leq 18 + 3b$$
$$2b - 12 \leq 18$$
$$2b \leq 30$$
$$b \leq 15$$

This seems to point to D as the answer. But remember, we were told that $b = 2a$, where a is an <u>integer</u>. If $2a = 15$, then a is 7.5. That doesn't work!

In order for a to be an integer, b must be an even number. Therefore, the maximum possible value of b is 14.

4) C
Plug in your own numbers. Let's say $a = 10$ (it's a very cold day). Since b must be within 3 degrees of this temperature, the value of b must be less than 13 but greater than 7: in other words, $7 < b < 13$.

Let's test the choices with $a = 10$.

A) $10 + b < 3 \rightarrow b < -7$. FALSE.

B) $10 > b - 3 \rightarrow 13 > b$. True, but too permissive: this would allow b to have values less than 7.

C) $-3 < b - 10 < 3 \rightarrow 7 < b < 13$. True.

D) $b + 3 > 10 \rightarrow b > 7$. True, but too permissive: this would allow b to have values greater than 13.

The only choice that matches exactly the relationship we were looking for is C.

Answer Explanations

Alternatively, we can solve this problem abstractly. The two temperatures are *less than* 3 degrees apart. If a is the higher temperature, we can express the inequality as $a - b < 3$. If b is the higher temperature, we can express the inequality as $b - a < 3$.

Since we do not know which of the two temperature readings was the higher one, we can account for *both* possible options by writing a single absolute value inequality statement:

$$|b - a| < 3$$

Note that this means the same thing as $|a - b| < 3$, as no matter which value comes first, the absolute value will only give us the *positive* difference between the two temperature readings.

For "less than" or "less than or equal to" absolute value inequalities, the variable expression can be sandwiched between the negative and positive versions of the value. This results in the three-part inequality $-3 < b - a < 3$.

5) A
One way to solve this problem is to use the built-in calculator. Plot the two given points and the inequality from choice A (use < = to get the ≤ sign):

1	$(-1, 5)$	×
2	$(3, 4)$	×
3	$y \leq -\dfrac{1}{4}x + 1$	×

On the graph, imagine the line that passes through the two points. Does it look like that line would be parallel to the line graphed? It does, so hang on to choice A.

Next, keeping the two points plotted, replace the choice A equation with the one from choice B. That's not parallel, and neither is choice C. Choice D is, but the shading is wrong: this shades above the line instead of below it. So the answer must be A.

Alternatively, we can solve this algebraically. As lines l and m are parallel, start by finding the slope of line l using the points provided:

$$m = \frac{y_2 - y_1}{x_2 - x_1} = \frac{5 - 4}{-1 - 3} = \frac{1}{-4} = -\frac{1}{4}$$

We know the slope of line m must be the same as the slope of line l, which eliminates choices B and C. As the shading is *below* the graph of solid line m, we are looking for an inequality where y is *less than or equal to* the linear expression, which eliminates choice D. Choice A is the only remaining answer.

6) 4
The weight of the nine people *and* the dolly is $1400 + 15 = 1415$ lbs. If each box weighs 18 lbs, then b boxes weigh $18b$ lbs. Thus, the combined weight of the nine people, the dolly, and the boxes is $1{,}415 + 18b$ lbs.

We are looking to keep the combined total weight under 1,500 lbs, so we can set up an inequality statement:

$$1{,}415 + 18b < 1{,}500$$

Now solve for b.

$$18b < 85$$
$$b < 85/18$$
$$b < 4.7\overline{22}$$

But the number of boxes must be a whole number, so the maximum number of boxes is 4.

EXPONENTS AND ROOTS (p. 274)
Exponents and Roots: Try It

1) a^6

$$a^4 * a^2 = a^{4+2} = a^6$$

2) a^6

$$a^9 \div a^3 = a^{9-3} = a^6$$

3) a^{28}

$$(a^7)^4 = a^{7*4} = a^{28}$$

4) 20

$$4^5 * 4^5 * 4^5 * 4^5 = 4^x$$
$$4^{5+5+5+5} = 4^x$$
$$4^{20} = 4^x$$
$$20 = x$$

5) 10

$$3^6 * 3^4 = 3^x$$
$$3^{6+4} = 3^x$$
$$3^{10} = 3^x$$
$$10 = x$$

6) 2

$$\frac{3^6}{3^4} = 3^x$$
$$3^{6-4} = 3^x$$
$$3^2 = 3^x$$
$$2 = x$$

7) 24

$$(3^6)^4 = 3^x$$
$$3^{6*4} = 3^x$$
$$3^{24} = 3^x$$
$$24 = x$$

8) $6x^2$
$$2x(5x) - 4x^2$$
$$2x^1 * 5x^1 - 4x^2$$
$$10x^2 - 4x^2$$
$$6x^2$$

9) 5
Plug in the given values for a and b:
$$3(a^0) + 2(b^0)$$
$$3(2^0) + 2(3^0)$$
$$3(1) + 2(1) = 5$$

10) 4
$$9^2 = 3^x$$
$$(3^2)^2 = 3^x$$
$$3^4 = 3^x$$
$$x = 4$$

11) 40
$$4^5 * 4^5 * 4^5 * 4^5 = 2^x$$
$$4^{5+5+5+5} = 2^x$$
$$4^{20} = 2^x$$
$$(2^2)^{20} = 2^x$$
$$2^{40} = 2^x$$
$$x = 40$$

12) 32
$$\frac{4^5}{2^2 * 2^3} = x$$
$$\frac{(2^2)^5}{2^5} = x$$
$$\frac{2^{10}}{2^5} = x$$
$$x = 2^5 = 32$$

13) 12
$$(4^3)^2 = 2^x$$
$$4^6 = 2^x$$
$$(2^2)^6 = 2^x$$
$$2^{12} = 2^x$$
$$x = 12$$

14) 1/8
$$2^{-3} = \frac{1}{2^3} = \frac{1}{8}$$

15) $x^4 y$
$$\sqrt{x^8 y^2}$$
$$(x^8 y^2)^{\frac{1}{2}}$$
$$x^4 y^1$$

16) $4y^4$
$$\sqrt{16y^8} = \sqrt{16} * (y^8)^{\frac{1}{2}} = 4y^4$$

17) $3\sqrt{5}$
$$\sqrt{45} = \sqrt{9} * \sqrt{5} = 3\sqrt{5}$$

18) $2n^2$
$$\sqrt[3]{8n^6} = \sqrt[3]{8} * (n^6)^{\frac{1}{3}} = 2n^2$$

19) -4
$$\sqrt[3]{-64} = \sqrt[3]{-4 * -4 * -4} = -4$$

Exponents and Roots: Practice Set 1 (p. 280)

1) C

First, divide the 8 by the 4: that's 2. Now divide 10^6 by 10^2. Since this is the same base, we just subtract the exponents: the new exponent should be $6 - 2 = 4$. Therefore, $2.0 * 10^4$ is the answer.

2) D
$$\frac{-18a^9 b^3}{(-3a^4)(2b)}$$
First, multiply out the bottom:
$$\frac{-18a^9 b^3}{-6a^4 b}$$
Divide the coefficients first: $-18/-6 = 3$.

Now divide the a's: $a^9/a^4 = a^{9-4} = a^5$.

Next, the b's: $b^3/b^1 = b^{3-1} = b^2$.

That's our answer: $3a^5 b^2$.

3) C
The word "product" means multiply:
$$(2x^3)(3x^2) = 2 * 3 * x^3 * x^2$$
$$= 6x^5$$

4) A
Since raising an exponent to another exponent means multiplying the exponents, we can rewrite $x^{\frac{3}{5}}$ as $(x^3)^{\frac{1}{5}}$. The exponent 1/5 means the fifth root, so $(x^3)^{\frac{1}{5}}$ is the same thing as $\sqrt[5]{x^3}$.

Alternatively, plug in your own number for x. Using your calculator, raise that value to the exponent 3/5. Write down the result and circle it. Then plug your original x value into each of the answer choices. The one that matches the result you circled is the right answer.

5) 1
If $7^{\wedge (\text{something})}$ equals $7^{\wedge (\text{something})}$, the only way that's going to work is if the somethings equal each other:
$$3x + 5 = 8$$
$$3x = 3$$
$$x = 1$$

Answer Explanations

6) D

To factor this expression, look for anything that all three terms have in common. Well, the coefficients are all divisible by 3, so we can do this:

$$3(2x^4 - 3x^3 + x^2)$$

Now let's see what happens if we take out an x. This means we're dividing the expression in the parentheses by x, so we'll need to subtract 1 from each of the exponents.

$$3x(2x^3 - 3x^2 + x^1)$$

Each of the terms in the parentheses still have something a common: an x. So we can do that again. Note that this will <u>not</u> make the last term in the parentheses disappear. We are dividing by x, not subtracting it, and anything divided by itself equals 1. So now we have this:

$$3x^2(2x^2 - 3x^1 + 1)$$

That's choice D.

Alternatively, we can back-solve this problem by distributing each of the answer choices. In choice A, the last term is wrong: this would end up with $9x^2$ in the last spot instead of $3x^2$. In choice B, the exponents quickly get too big. In choice C, the last term is wrong again: we end up with $3x$ in the last spot instead of $3x^2$. But choice D gets everything right, so it's the right answer.

You could also use the built-in calculator to solve this problem. Graph the original expression, and then graph the answer choices with it one at a time. Only choice D results in a matching graph.

7) B

The y-intercept of a graph occurs at the point where $x = 0$. So, plug in 0 for x in the equation:

$$y = 2(4)^0$$

Following PEMDAS, we have to apply the exponent before we do the multiplication. So first, calculate the value of 4^0. Anything raised to the zero power is 1, so:

$$y = 2 * 4^0$$
$$y = 2(1)$$
$$y = 2$$

The y-intercept is $(0, 2)$.

Alternatively, just graph the equation in the built-in calculator:

```
1
   y = 2(4)^x                    ×
```

Click on the point where the graph intersects the y-axis and the calculator will display the coordinates: $(0, 2)$.

8) D

The big rule of functions is that whatever's in the parentheses is your x value. Here, we have 9/4 in the parentheses. So, plug in 9/4 for x in the equation, and then use the calculator:

$$\left(\frac{9}{4}\right)^{-\frac{1}{2}} = \frac{2}{3}$$

Exponents and Roots: Practice Set 2 (p. 281)

1) A

$$\sqrt{\frac{56x^3y^9}{7(xy)^5}}$$

First, distribute that exponent in the bottom of the fraction:

$$\sqrt{\frac{56x^3y^9}{7x^5y^5}}$$

Divide the coefficients:

$$\sqrt{\frac{8x^3y^9}{x^5y^5}}$$

Next, divide the x's:

$$\sqrt{\frac{8y^9}{x^2y^5}}$$

Finally, divide the y's:

$$\sqrt{\frac{8y^4}{x^2}}$$

Now simplify.

$$\frac{\sqrt{8}\sqrt{y^4}}{\sqrt{x^2}}$$

We can break up $\sqrt{8}$ as $\sqrt{8} = \sqrt{4} * \sqrt{2} = 2\sqrt{2}$. For the variables, the radical just cuts the exponents in half. That leaves us with this:

$$\frac{(2\sqrt{2})y^2}{x}$$

That's choice A.

2) D

$$x^{-\frac{1}{2}} = \frac{1}{4}$$

We want the value of x^1. Well, when we raise an exponent to another exponent, we multiply those exponents. So, what do we need to multiply $-1/2$ by to get it to equal 1? That'd be -2, of course. So, raise both sides of the equation to the exponent -2.

$$\left(x^{-\frac{1}{2}}\right)^{-2} = \left(\frac{1}{4}\right)^{-2}$$
$$x^1 = (4)^2$$
$$x = 16$$

Alternatively, we can back-solve this problem using the built-in calculator. Change the variable to something other than x so that the calculator will provide a slider for values:

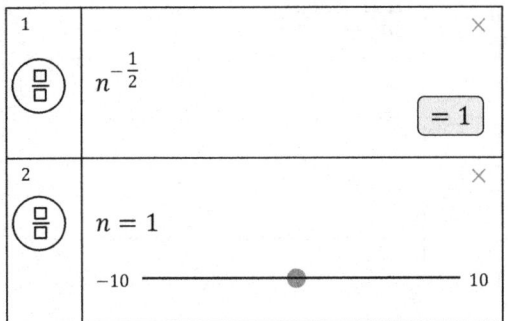

To test choice A, click on the $n =1$ line and type in 1/16.

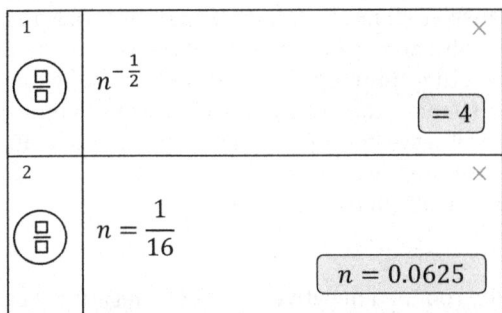

This tells us that when $n = 1/16$, the value of $n^{-1/2}$ is 4. We need it to be 1/4, so this is the wrong answer. Click in that $n =$ line again to type in the values of the other answer choices. The only value that works is 16, so the answer is D.

3) D

$$(2xy)^3 * 3x^{-2}y$$

First, distribute the exponent that's attached to the parentheses.

$$2^3 x^3 y^3 * 3x^{-2} y$$

Multiply the coefficients: $2^3 * 3 = 8 * 3 = 24$
Multiply the x's: $x^3 * x^{-2} = x^{3-2} = x^1 = x$
Multiply the y's: $y^3 * y^1 = y^{3+1} = y^4$

So the answer is $24xy^4$.

4) A

$$\sqrt[4]{144a^6} * 2\sqrt{3a}$$

First, break up each of the roots.

$$\sqrt[4]{144} * \sqrt[4]{a^6} * 2 * \sqrt{3} * \sqrt{a}$$

Now rewrite the roots as fraction exponents.

$$144^{1/4} * (a^6)^{1/4} * 2 * 3^{1/2} * a^{1/2}$$

Now, let's see what we can do with that first term. $144 = 12^2 = (2^2 * 3)^2 = 2^4 * 3^2$. So:

$$(2^4 * 3^2)^{1/4} * (a^6)^{1/4} * 2 * 3^{1/2} * a^{1/2}$$
$$= (2^4)^{1/4} * (3^2)^{1/4} * (a^6)^{1/4} * 2 * 3^{1/2} * a^{1/2}$$

Rearrange to group matching bases together:

$$= (2^4)^{1/4} * 2 * 3^{1/2} * (3^2)^{1/4} * (a^6)^{1/4} * a^{1/2}$$

Use the exponent rules to simplify. For example, we can rewrite $(a^6)^{1/4}$ as $a^{6/4}$, which is $a^{3/2}$:

$$= 2 * 2 * 3^{1/2} * 3^{1/2} * a^{3/2} * a^{1/2}$$
$$= 4 * 3 * a^{4/2}$$
$$= 12a^2$$

Alternatively, we can use the built-in calculator to solve this problem. First type in the original product. To get the 4th root, click the keyboard on the bottom left of the screen, then click the "functions" button, then scroll down to the Number Theory category, and then click on the $\sqrt[n]{\square}$ button. To get the square root, just type in `sqrt`.

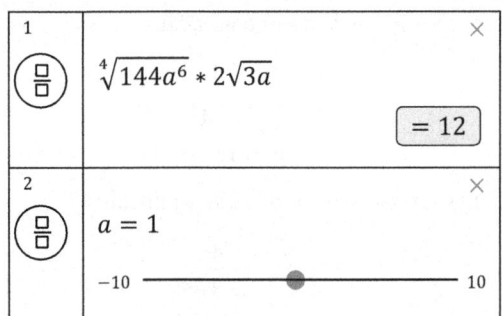

This tells us that when $a = 1$, the value of the original expression is 12. Now, leaving those rows in place, type in the answer choices, each in a separate row. Notice that choice A also comes out to 12, while all the other choices result in other numbers. That means A must be the answer. (If more than one of the choices had come out to 12, no problem—we'd just drag the a slider to a different value until there was only one choice that matched the value of the original expression.)

5) C

It's important to note that we don't need to find x and y to solve this; we only need to find xy. So let's see what we can do with this original equation.

$$\frac{x^2 y}{3x} = \frac{5}{2}$$

Cancel out an x from the top and bottom of the fraction on the left:

$$\frac{xy}{3} = \frac{5}{2}$$

Answer Explanations

Now multiply both sides by 3:
$$xy = \frac{5}{2}(3) = \frac{15}{2}$$

Alternatively, plug in your own value for x, use it to find a value for y, and then proceed from there. For example, if $x = 2$, we have this:
$$\frac{(2^2)y}{3(2)} = \frac{5}{2}$$
$$\frac{4y}{6} = \frac{5}{2}$$

Cross-multiply:
$$8y = 30$$
$$y = \frac{30}{8} = \frac{15}{4}$$

This tells us that if $x = 2$, then $y = 15/4$. Now we can find xy:
$$xy = 2\left(\frac{15}{4}\right) = \frac{15}{2}$$

6) 256
Plug in 4 for z in the second equation.
$$\sqrt{y} = 4$$
$$\left(\sqrt{y}\right)^2 = 4^2$$
$$y = 16$$

Now plug that value into the first equation:
$$\sqrt{x} = 16$$
$$\left(\sqrt{x}\right)^2 = 16^2$$
$$x = 256$$

7) B
$$\frac{4n^6 - 8n^5}{2n^2 + (2n)(2n)}$$
$$= \frac{4n^6 - 8n^5}{2n^2 + 4n^2}$$

Factor the top:
$$= \frac{4n^5(n - 2)}{6n^2}$$

Cancel out an n^2 from the top and bottom:
$$= \frac{4n^3(n - 2)}{6}$$

Divide top and bottom by 2:
$$= \frac{2n^3(n - 2)}{3}$$

Distribute:
$$= \frac{2n^4 - 4n^3}{3}$$

Alternatively, we can use the built-in calculator to solve this problem. Type in the original expression, and then use the slider provided by the calculator to set a value for n. Let's try $n = 3$:

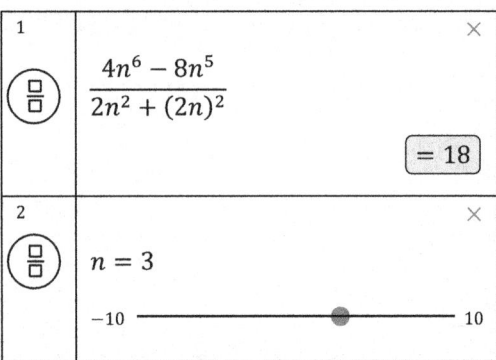

Now we know that when $n = 3$, the value of the original expression is 18. Now, leaving those rows in place, type in the answer choices, each in a separate row. Notice that choice B also comes out to 18, while all the other choices result in other numbers. That means B must be the answer. (If more than one of the choices had come out to 18, no problem—we'd just drag the n slider to a different value until there was only one choice that matched the value of the original expression.)

8) C
The cube root of a negative number is negative. The square of any number must be positive. So if we multiply those results, we're multiplying a negative number by a positive number: the answer must be negative.

Alternatively, plug in some easy numbers. For the cube root of a negative integer, let's use the cube root of -1: that's -1. For the square of a positive integer, let's use the square of 1: that's 1. Now multiply -1 by 1. The result is -1. That's a real number, so we can eliminate choice D. But it's not zero and it's not positive, so we can eliminate choices A and B. Choice C must be the answer.

FACTORING, FOILING, AND FRACTIONS (p. 282)
Factoring, FOILing, and Fractions: Try It
1) $2a + 6b$
$$2(a + 3b)$$
$$2(a) + 2(3b)$$
$$2a + 6b$$

2) $4x - xy$
$$x(4 - y)$$
$$x(4) + x(-y)$$
$$4x - xy$$

3) $3ab + 6ac - 3ad$
$$3a(b + 2c - d)$$

$$3a(b) + 3a(2c) + 3a(-d)$$
$$3ab + 6ac - 3ad$$

4) $6x^2 - 12x^3y$
$$3x(2x - 4x^2y)$$
$$3x(2x) + 3x(-4x^2y)$$
$$6x^2 - 12x^3y$$

5) $2n^4p^5 - 10n^5p + 6n^4p^2$
$$2n^3p(np^4 - 5n^2 + 3np)$$
$$2n^3p(np^4) + 2n^3p(-5n^2) + 2n^3p(3np)$$
$$2n^4p^5 - 10n^5p + 6n^4p^2$$

6) $3x - 1$
$$3(x - 2) + 5$$
$$3(x) + 3(-2) + 5$$
$$3x - 6 + 5$$
$$3x - 1$$

7) $2x$
$$4x(0.5) + 2\left(\frac{x}{2}\right) - x$$
$$2x + x - x$$
$$2x$$

8) $-8x$
$$2(2x) - 4(3x)$$
$$4x - 12x$$
$$-8x$$

9) $3x + 3xy$
$$9x - 3x(2 - y)$$
$$9x - 3x(2) - 3x(-y)$$
$$9x - 6x + 3xy$$
$$3x + 3xy$$

10) 7
$$-2(x + 5) = 3(-1 - x)$$
$$-2(x) - 2(5) = 3(-1) + 3(-x)$$
$$-2x - 10 = -3 - 3x$$
Add 10 to both sides: $-2x = 7 - 3x$
Add $3x$ to both sides: $x = 7$

Alternatively, we can solve this using the built-in calculator. Enter the left side of the original equation on one line and the right side on another:

1	$-2(x + 5)$
2	$3(-1 - x)$

The graphs intersect where $x = 7$.

11) $-3/4$ or -0.75
$$2[4 - (3 + 2x)] = 5$$
$$2(4 - 3 - 2x) = 5$$
$$2(1 - 2x) = 5$$
$$2(1) + 2(-2x) = 5$$
$$2 - 4x = 5$$
$$-4x = 3$$
$$x = -3/4$$

12) $x^2 - 2x - 8$
$$(x - 4)(x + 2)$$
$$x(x) + x(2) - 4(x) - 4(2)$$
$$x^2 + 2x - 4x - 8$$
$$x^2 - 2x - 8$$

13) $pq - 6p + 5q - 30$
$$(p + 5)(q - 6)$$
$$p(q) + p(-6) + 5(q) + 5(-6)$$
$$pq - 6p + 5q - 30$$

14) $3(2x - 1)$
$$6x - 3$$
$$3(2x) - 3(1)$$
$$3(2x - 1)$$

15) $4n(2n - 1)$
$$8n^2 - 4n$$
$$4n(2n) - 4n(1)$$
$$4n(2n - 1)$$

16) $(x - 4)(x + 1)$
$$x^2 - 3x - 4$$
What pair of numbers multiplies to -4 and adds to -3? It's -4 and 1. So:
$$(x - 4)(x + 1)$$

17) $(x - 1)(x - 9)$
$$x^2 - 10x + 9$$
What pair of numbers multiplies to 9 and adds to -10? Only -9 and -1. So:
$$(x - 9)(x - 1)$$

18) $(x + 9)(x - 9)$
$$x^2 - 81$$
Because 81 is a perfect square (it equals 9^2), we can use the difference of squares rule, which says that any binomial of the form $a^2 - b^2$ can be factored as $(a + b)(a - b)$.
$$(x + 9)(x - 9)$$

19) $(p + r^3)(p - r^3)$
$$p^2 - r^6$$
Factor using the difference of squares rule, where the square root of r^6 is r^3:
$$(p + r^3)(p - r^3)$$

Answer Explanations

20) $x = -1$ or $x = 4$
$$x^2 - 3x - 4 = 0$$

First, factor. What pair of numbers multiplies to -4 and adds to -3? Only -4 and 1. So:
$$(x - 4)(x + 1) = 0$$

Now set each factor equal to zero and solve:
$$x - 4 = 0 \text{ or } x + 1 = 0$$
$$x = 4 \text{ or } x = -1$$

21) $x = 0$ or $x = 3$
$$2x^2 - 6x = 0$$

To factor a binomial like this one, look at it this way: what can be factored out of both terms? Here, we can get a $2x$ out of both. So, we can do this:
$$2x(x - 3) = 0$$

Now set each factor equal to zero and solve:
$$2x = 0 \text{ or } x - 3 = 0$$
$$x = 0 \text{ or } x = 3$$

22) $x = 1/2$ or $x = -4$
$$2x^2 + 7x - 4 = 0$$

First, we need to factor. This time, the pair of numbers we're looking for must multiply to $2(-4) = -8$ and add to 7. So, 8 and -1. Now, rewrite the equation, breaking up the middle term into those pieces:
$$2x^2 + 8x - x - 4 = 0$$

Next, factor out whatever you can from the first two terms, and factor out whatever you can from the last two terms:
$$2x(x + 4) - 1(x + 4) = 0$$

Now factor the $(x + 4)$ out of both those pieces:
$$(x + 4)(2x - 1) = 0$$
$$2x - 1 = 0 \text{ or } x + 4 = 0$$
$$x = 1/2 \text{ or } x = -4$$

Alternatively, we can solve this problem using the built-in calculator. Type in the equation:

1	$2x^2 + 7x - 4 = 0$	✕

The graph intersects the x-axis at $(-4, 0)$ and $(0.5, 0)$, so the answers are $x = -4$ and $x = 0.5$.

23) $x = 2$ only
To solve using the built-in calculator, enter the left side of the original equation on one line and the right side on another. (Type `sqrt` for the square root.)

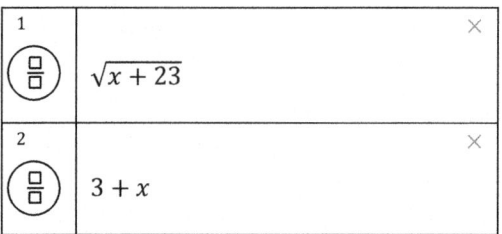

There is only one point of intersection: at the point $(2, 5)$. Therefore, there is only one solution to this problem: $x = 2$.

Alternatively, we can solve the problem algebraically. Write out the equation and carefully square both sides:
$$\sqrt{x + 23} = 3 + x$$
$$(\sqrt{x + 23})^2 = (3 + x)^2$$
$$x + 23 = (3 + x)(3 + x)$$
$$x + 23 = 9 + 6x + x^2$$
$$0 = x^2 + 5x - 14$$
$$0 = (x + 7)(x - 2)$$
$$x = -7 \text{ or } x = 2$$

Now we have to check for extraneous solutions. Check $x = -7$:
$$\sqrt{-7 + 23} \stackrel{?}{=} 3 - 7$$
$$\sqrt{16} \neq -4$$

This doesn't work, so $x = -7$ is an extraneous solution. Check $x = 2$:
$$\sqrt{2 + 23} \stackrel{?}{=} 3 + 2$$
$$\sqrt{25} = 5$$

This works, so $x = 2$ is the only solution.

24) $\dfrac{x - 3}{x - 4}$

$$\frac{x^2 - x - 6}{x^2 - 2x - 8}$$

$$\frac{(x - 3)\cancel{(x + 2)}}{\cancel{(x + 2)}(x - 4)} = \frac{x - 3}{x - 4}$$

25) $\dfrac{3y + 2x}{xy}$

$$\frac{3}{x} + \frac{2}{y}$$

To get a common denominator, multiply the top and bottom of the first fraction by y, and multiply the top and bottom of the second fraction by x.

$$\frac{y}{y} * \frac{3}{x} + \frac{2}{y} * \frac{x}{x}$$

Now add straight across the top:
$$\frac{3y + 2x}{xy}$$

26) $\frac{5x + 4}{x^2 - 16}$

$$\frac{3}{x-4} + \frac{2}{x+4}$$
$$\frac{(x+4)}{(x+4)} * \frac{3}{x-4} + \frac{2}{x+4} * \frac{(x-4)}{(x-4)}$$
$$\frac{3(x+4) + 2(x-4)}{(x+4)(x-4)}$$
$$\frac{3x + 12 + 2x - 8}{x^2 - 16} = \frac{5x + 4}{x^2 - 16}$$

27) 7

$$(qx - r)(2x + 5) = 8x^2 + 14x - 15$$
$$2qx^2 + 5qx - 2rx - 5r = 8x^2 + 14x - 15$$

Match up the coefficients of the like terms. For example, $2qx^2$ must be the same thing as $8x^2$, so $2q$ must equal 8:
$$2q = 8$$
$$q = 4$$

Now match up the non-x terms. The $-5r$ must be the same thing as -15, so:
$$-5r = -15$$
$$r = 3$$

So the value of $q + r$ is just the value of $4 + 3$: it's 7.

Factoring, FOILing, and Fractions: Practice Set 1 (p. 293)

1) C

$$(2x - 1)(x + 3)$$
FOIL: $2x(x) + 2x(3) - 1(x) - 1(3)$
Simplify: $2x^2 + 6x - x - 3$
$$2x^2 + 5x - 3$$

2) C

$$(4x^3 - 3x^2 + 5) - (6 + 2x^2 - 3x^3)$$

Distribute the minus sign:
$$4x^3 - 3x^2 + 5 - 6 - 2x^2 + 3x^3$$

Rearrange to group matching terms:
$$4x^3 + 3x^3 - 3x^2 - 2x^2 + 5 - 6$$

Combine like terms:
$$7x^3 - 5x^2 - 1$$

3) A

$$x^2 + 2x - 24$$

What's a pair of numbers that multiplies to -24 and adds to 2? Only -4 and positive 6. Those are the numbers that go into the factors:
$$(x - 4)(x + 6)$$
So the factors are $(x - 4)$ and $(x + 6)$. Only the first of those is in the answer choices, so that's our answer.

4) B

$$x^2 - 3x - 28 = 0$$

First, factor. What's a pair of numbers that multiplies to -28 and adds to -3? Only -7 and positive 4. Set up those numbers in the factors:
$$(x - 7)(x + 4) = 0$$

Now set each factor equal to zero and solve.
$$x - 7 = 0 \text{ or } x + 4 = 0$$
$$x = 7 \text{ or } x = -4$$

5) D

$$(5p + 6q)(7r - 8s)$$

We don't need to waste time FOILing the entire thing. We aren't multiplying anything containing the same variable together; there's no (for example) p-term times p-term, so we're not going to have p^2 anywhere. We can rule out answer B. And we know we're going to have four different terms ($pr, ps, qr,$ and qs), so we can rule out answer A. Let's start FOILing, but check along the way to see if we can learn more. The "F" part of FOIL, multiplying the first terms together, gives us:
$$(5p)(7r) = 35pr$$

Choice C has $30pr$ as a term, and choice D has $35pr$ as a term. We do not need to proceed any further; the answer has to be D.

6) A

$$3x^2 - 12$$

It's actually easier to factor a binomial, like this expression, than to factor a trinomial such as the ones we saw in #s 3 and 4 in this practice set. For this problem, just look for anything that can be factored out of our original two terms. What do the two terms have in common? Well, they're both divisible by 3. That means we can rewrite the expression like this:
$$3(x^2 - 4)$$

Now, the expression in parentheses is a difference in squares. Follow the difference of squares rule: $a^2 - b^2 = (a + b)(a - b)$. Following that rule, we can do this:
$$3(x + 2)(x - 2)$$

That's choice A.

Answer Explanations

Alternatively, you can back-solve this problem by multiplying out all the answer choices.

A) $3(x+2)(x-2) = 3(x^2 - 4) = 3x^2 - 12$

B) $3(x-2)^2 = 3(x-2)(x-2)$
$= 3(x^2 - 4x + 4)$
$= 3x^2 - 12x + 12$

C) $(3x-2)^2 = (3x-2)(3x-2)$
$= 9x^2 - 12x + 4$

D) $(x-4)(x+3) = x^2 - x - 12$

A is the only match for the $3x^2 - 12$ we were looking for.

7) A

First, factor the numerator. What two numbers multiply to -14 and add to positive 5? Only -2 and positive 7 do that. Therefore, the top of this fraction can be written as $(x-2)(x+7)$. Now, factor the denominator. This is a square minus a square, so we can follow the difference of squares rule: this is $(x+2)(x-2)$.

Therefore, the whole fraction can be written like this:

$$\frac{(x-2)(x+7)}{(x+2)(x-2)}$$

Cancel out the factor that the top and bottom of the fraction have in common:

$$\frac{\cancel{(x-2)}(x+7)}{(x+2)\cancel{(x-2)}}$$

$$= \frac{x+7}{x+2}$$

Alternatively, we can use the built-in calculator to solve this problem. First type in the original fraction, and then, leaving that first line in place, type in the answer choices one at a time. The choice that produces the same graph as the original fraction is the right answer.

8) 4 or −9

$$x^2 + 5x - 36 = 0$$

First, factor. What's a pair of numbers that multiplies to -36 and adds to 5? The only pair that works is -4 and positive 9. Set up those numbers in the factors:

$$(x+9)(x-4) = 0$$

Now set each factor equal to zero and solve.

$$x + 9 = 0 \text{ or } x - 4 = 0$$
$$x = -9 \text{ or } x = 4$$

Alternatively, we can use the built-in calculator to solve this problem. Type in the equation:

```
1
[⬚/⬚]  x² + 5x − 36 = 0      ×
```

The graph intersects the x-axis where $x = -9$ and where $x = 4$.

9) B

$$(x^2 - 1) - (2x^2 + 1)$$

Distribute the minus sign:

$$x^2 - 1 - 2x^2 - 1$$

Now combine like terms:

$$-x^2 - 1 - 1$$
$$-x^2 - 2$$

Alternatively, we can use the built-in calculator to solve this problem. First type in the original expression, and then, leaving that first line in place, type in the answer choices one at a time. The choice that produces the same graph as the original expression is the right answer.

Factoring, FOILing, and Fractions: Practice Set 2 (p. 294)

1) D

Factor both the numerator and denominator. Note that the numerator is a perfect square, and that the denominator is a difference of squares:

$$\frac{(d+3)(d+3)}{(d+3)(d-3)}$$

Cancel out the common factors from the numerator and denominator:

$$\frac{\cancel{(d+3)}(d+3)}{\cancel{(d+3)}(d-3)}$$

$$\frac{(d+3)}{(d-3)}$$

Alternatively, we can use the built-in calculator to solve this problem. First type in the original expression, and then, leaving that first line in place, type in the answer choices one at a time. The choice that produces the same graph as the original expression is the right answer.

2) C

Graph both equations in the built-in calculator. The points where the graphs intersect are the solutions to the system of equations.

Alternatively, solve algebraically by setting the two equations equal to each other:

$$(x-5)^2 = x + 1$$
$$x^2 - 10x + 25 = x + 1$$
$$x^2 - 11x + 24 = 0$$
$$(x-8)(x-3) = 0$$
$$x = 8 \text{ or } x = 3$$

Only one of the answer choices has an x value of 8 or 3, so C must be the answer. But if we want to double-check

- 522 -

the corresponding y value for that point, plug $x = 3$ into either of the original equations:

$$y = x + 1$$
$$y = 3 + 1$$
$$y = 4$$

3) C
Take the square root of both sides of the equation. Make sure to think about both the positive and the negative values of a square root!

$$a + b = a - b \quad \text{or} \quad a + b = -a + b$$

Now simplify both outcomes by combining like terms.

$$b = -b \quad \text{or} \quad a = -a$$
$$2b = 0 \quad \text{or} \quad 2a = 0$$
$$b = 0 \quad \text{or} \quad a = 0$$

Since either a or b must equal 0, the product of a and b must equal 0.

4) $-5/2$ or -2.5
There are several ways to solve this problem. You could solve it algebraically, by isolating g in the second equation and substituting that expression into the first equation:

$$gh = -8 \quad \rightarrow \quad g = -8/h$$
$$g + h = 2$$
$$-8/h + h = 2$$

To eliminate the fraction, multiply both sides of the equation by h. Then rearrange and solve the quadratic.

$$-8 + h^2 = 2h$$
$$h^2 - 2h - 8 = 0$$
$$(h - 4)(h + 2) = 0$$
$$h = 4 \quad \text{or} \quad h = -2$$

Now plug those values back into either equation to get the corresponding values of g. If $h = 4$, then $g = -2$, and if $h = -2$, then $g = 4$. Either way, the value of $g/h + h/g$ comes out to $-5/2$.

But wait. The problem didn't actually ask us for the values of g or h, so do we really need them? Maybe there's a way to get an answer directly.

Try squaring $g + h = 2$:

$$g + h = 2$$
$$(g + h)^2 = 2^2$$
$$(g + h)(g + h) = 4$$
$$g^2 + 2gh + h^2 = 4$$

Now plug the value of gh we were given in the problem into that equation:

$$g^2 + 2(-8) + h^2 = 4$$
$$g^2 + h^2 = 20$$

The problem asked for the value of $g/h + h/g$, which we can simplify as $\dfrac{g^2 + h^2}{gh}$. Now we have both pieces of that fraction: the answer is $20/-8 = -5/2$.

And there's a third way to solve this, using your factoring skills. After all, h and g are simply two numbers that multiply to be -8 and add to be 2. If you were trying to factor $y = x^2 + 2x - 8$, you would very quickly realize the numbers you are looking for are 4 and -2. Therefore, the solution is $4/-2 + -2/4 = -5/2$.

5) D
Translate one piece at a time. "When a price of d dollars is squared" can be written as d^2. "Triple the value of d" is just $3d$, and "4 dollars more than" that value would be $3d + 4$. So:

$$d^2 = 3d + 4$$

Now rearrange into standard quadratic form and solve by factoring.

$$d^2 - 3d - 4 = 0$$
$$(d - 4)(d + 1) = 0$$
$$d = 4 \quad \text{or} \quad d = -1$$

Of these two values, only $d = 4$ is offered as an answer choice (and the negative value doesn't make sense in this context anyway).

Another approach would be to simply back-solve this problem. For example, if B were the answer, then d is $2. If that price is squared, we get $4. Triple the value of $2 is $6, and four dollars more than $6 is $10. So B isn't the answer, because $4 ≠ $10. Repeat that process for each answer choice until you reach the one that works: D.

6) -40
Square both sides of the first equation:

$$(r - s)^2 = 10^2$$
$$(r - s)(r - s) = 100$$
$$r^2 - 2rs + s^2 = 100$$

We already know that $r^2 + s^2 = 20$, so now we can do this:

$$20 - 2rs = 100$$
$$-2rs = 80$$
$$rs = -40$$

7) B
To add or subtract fractions, we need a common denominator. Here, the easiest common denominator to use would be the product of the two original denominators: $(x + 1)(x + 3)$.

$$\frac{3}{x + 1} - \frac{1}{x + 3}$$

$$\frac{(x + 3)}{(x + 3)} * \frac{3}{x + 1} - \frac{1}{x + 3} * \frac{(x + 1)}{(x + 1)}$$

Answer Explanations

$$\frac{3(x+3)}{(x+3)(x+1)} - \frac{1(x+1)}{(x+3)(x+1)}$$

$$\frac{3(x+3) - 1(x+1)}{(x+3)(x+1)}$$

$$\frac{3x + 9 - x - 1}{(x+3)(x+1)}$$

$$\frac{2x + 8}{(x+3)(x+1)}$$

If you got answer choice C for this problem, be sure to distribute that minus sign carefully! Once we join these two fractions together, the top of the new fraction becomes $3x + 9 - x - 1$, not $3x + 9 - x + 1$.

An alternative approach to this problem would be to use the built-in calculator. First type in the original expression, and then, leaving that first line in place, type in the answer choices one at a time. The choice that produces the same graph as the original expression is the right answer.

8) D
Start by typing both original equations into the built-in calculator.

| 1 | $y = 2\sqrt{x-1}$ |
| 2 | $y = 8$ |

The graphs intersect where $x = 17$.

Alternatively, we could solve this problem by back-solving. Plug each answer choice in for x on the right side of the equation; the one that gives you a result of 8 is the right answer.

If you'd prefer to solve the problem algebraically, start by writing out the radical equation, then plugging in 8 for y:

$$y = 2\sqrt{x-1}$$
$$8 = 2\sqrt{x-1}$$

Divide both sides by 2:

$$4 = \sqrt{x-1}$$

Square both sides:

$$4^2 = \left(\sqrt{x-1}\right)^2$$
$$16 = x - 1$$
$$17 = x$$

9) A
A simple way of eliminating fractions from an equation is to multiply both sides of the equation by the bottoms of the fractions.

$$(3+x)(1+x) * \left(\frac{4}{3+x} - \frac{2}{1+x}\right) = 5 * (3+x)(1+x)$$
$$4(1+x) - 2(3+x) = 5(x^2 + 4x + 3)$$
$$4 + 4x - 6 - 2x = 5x^2 + 20x + 15$$
$$5x^2 + 18x + 17 = 0$$

Note that we don't need to know what the solutions are; we only need to know how many there are. So, use the built-in calculator to graph $y = 5x^2 + 18x + 17$. The solutions to this equation would occur where $y = 0$, so at the x-intercepts of the graph. This graph has no x-intercepts, which means this equation has no real solutions.

Alternatively, we can skip the algebra altogether and solve this using the built-in calculator from the start. Enter y = [left side of the original equation] on one line and y = [right side of the equation] on another:

| 1 | $y = \dfrac{4}{3+x} - \dfrac{2}{1+x}$ |
| 2 | $y = 5$ |

The graphs never intersect, so there are no solutions to the equation.

10) C
Since the area of square A is x^2 square inches, the sides of square A must be x inches long. The length of rectangle B is 2 inches greater than that side length, so $x + 2$. And the width of rectangle B is 5 inches greater than square A's side length, so $x + 5$. To find the area of rectangle B, then, we multiply its length, $x + 2$, by its width, $x + 5$:

$$A = (x+2)(x+5)$$
$$A = x^2 + 7x + 10$$

11) 16

$$ax^4y^2 + bx^3y^3 + cx^2y^4 = (2x^2y - 6xy^2)^2$$
$$ax^4y^2 + bx^3y^3 + cx^2y^4 = (2x^2y - 6xy^2)(2x^2y - 6xy^2)$$
$$ax^4y^2 + bx^3y^3 + cx^2y^4 = 4x^4y^2 - 24x^3y^3 + 36x^2y^4$$

Based on the coefficients of the matching terms, we can see that $a = 4$, that $b = -24$, and that $c = 36$. Therefore, $a + b + c = 4 - 24 + 36 = 16$.

12) A
When an event is certain to happen (that is, there is a 100% chance that the event will occur), the probability of the event is 1. So:

$$\frac{16t^2 - 40t + 125}{100} = 1$$

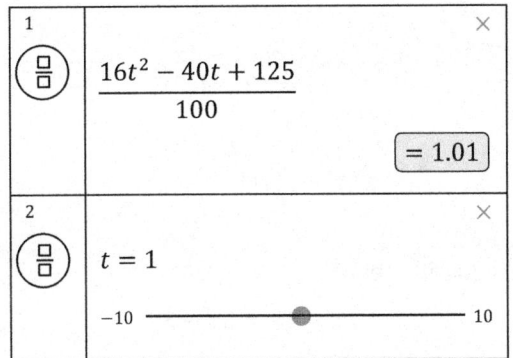

Click the $t = 1$ line to type in the values of t provided in the answer choices. Only choice A, $t = 1.25$, causes the original expression to come out to exactly 1.

Alternatively, we can solve the original equation algebraically. First, multiply both sides by 100 and combine like terms.

$$16t^2 - 40t + 125 = 100$$
$$16t^2 - 40t + 25 = 0$$

Factor by grouping:

$$16t^2 - 20t - 20t + 25 = 0$$
$$4t(4t - 5) - 5(4t - 5) = 0$$
$$(4t - 5)(4t - 5) = 0$$
$$4t = 5$$
$$t = 5/4 = 1.25$$

13) -2

$$3p(8x^2 - q) = 2x\left(4p^2x + \frac{9}{x}\right)$$
$$3p(8x^2) - 3p(q) = 2x(4p^2x) + \frac{2x}{1}\left(\frac{9}{x}\right)$$
$$24px^2 - 3pq = 8p^2x^2 + 18$$

We have two kinds of terms here: the x^2 terms and the non-x terms. Match up the coefficients of the like terms. First, $24px^2$ must be the same thing as $8p^2x^2$, so $24p$ must be the same thing as $8p^2$:

$$24p = 8p^2$$
$$8p^2 - 24p = 0$$
$$p(8p - 24) = 0$$
$$p = 0 \text{ or } 8p = 24$$
$$p = 0 \text{ or } p = 3$$

The problem told us that p is a nonzero constant, so the value of p must be 3. Next, match up the non-x terms: $-3pq$ must be the same thing as 18.

$$-3pq = 18$$

But now we know $p = 3$, so:

$$-3(3)q = 18$$
$$-9q = 18$$
$$q = -2$$

14) C

The easiest approach here is to back-solve. Start with choice C.

$$\sqrt{2 + 14} \stackrel{?}{=} 2 + 2$$
$$\sqrt{16} = 4$$

Yep, that works! Therefore, C is the answer.

Another option is to use the built-in calculator. Type the left side of the original equation into one line and the right side into another.

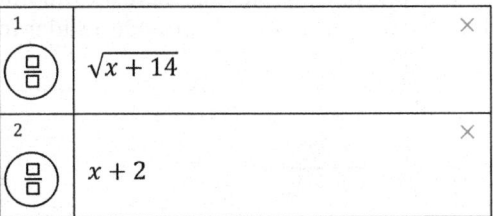

The graphs intersect where $x = 2$.

If you'd prefer to solve algebraically, write out the equation and then square both sides.

$$\sqrt{x + 14} = x + 2$$
$$\left(\sqrt{x + 14}\right)^2 = (x + 2)^2$$
$$x + 14 = (x + 2)(x + 2)$$
$$x + 14 = x^2 + 4x + 4$$
$$0 = x^2 + 3x - 10$$
$$0 = (x + 5)(x - 2)$$
$$x = -5 \text{ or } x = 2$$

It seems we have two solutions. But because we started out with an x under a square root, we're not done: we have to check for extraneous solutions.

Check $x = -5$:

$$\sqrt{-5 + 14} \stackrel{?}{=} -5 + 2$$
$$\sqrt{9} \neq -3$$

Nope. Now check $x = 2$:

$$\sqrt{2 + 14} \stackrel{?}{=} 2 + 2$$
$$\sqrt{16} = 4$$

True! So $x = 2$ is the only solution.

15) B

$$\frac{6x^2 - 7x + 5}{kx - 3} = 3x + 1 + \frac{8}{kx - 3}$$
$$\frac{6x^2 - 7x + 5}{kx - 3} - \frac{8}{kx - 3} = 3x + 1$$
$$\frac{6x^2 - 7x - 3}{kx - 3} = 3x + 1$$
$$6x^2 - 7x - 3 = (3x + 1)(kx - 3)$$

Answer Explanations

$$6x^2 - 7x - 3 = 3kx^2 - 9x + kx - 3$$

This looks worse than it is. All we have to do now is match up the coefficients of the like terms. Since $6x^2$ must be the same thing as $3kx^2$, we know that 6 must equal $3k$:

$$6 = 3k$$
$$2 = k$$

Alternatively, we could solve this problem using the built-in calculator. Type the left side of the original equation into one line and the right side into another. The calculator will automatically provide a slider for k values.

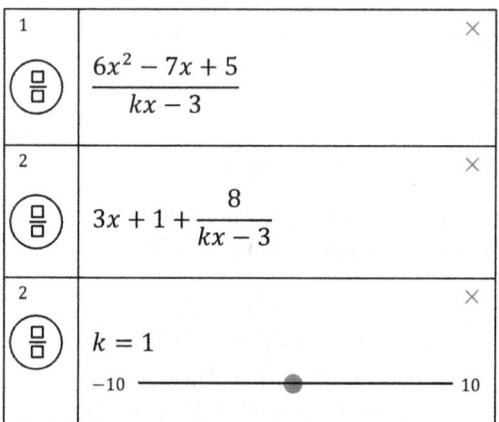

Use the slider to check the different values of k provided by the answer choices one at a time. Only choice B causes the two graphs to be the same.

FUNCTION ESSENTIALS (p. 296)
Function Essentials: Try It

1) 20
$$f(x) = 12 - 4x$$
$$f(-2) = 12 - 4(-2)$$
$$= 12 + 8$$
$$= 20$$

2) 6
$$f(x) = 3x + 1$$
$$19 = 3x + 1$$
$$18 = 3x$$
$$6 = x$$

3) −7
$$f(x) = 2x + k$$
$$1 = 2(4) + k$$
$$1 = 8 + k$$
$$-7 = k$$

4) 8
$$g(x) = 2x - 3$$
$$g(2) = 2(2) - 3$$
$$g(2) = 1$$
$$f(x) = 12 - 4x$$
$$f(1) = 12 - 4(1) = 8$$

5) 5
$$f(x) = 12 - 4x$$
$$f(2) = 12 - 4(2)$$
$$f(2) = 4$$
$$g(x) = 2x - 3$$
$$g(4) = 2(4) - 3 = 5$$

6) 5/2 or 2.5
Set the equations equal:
$$12 - 4x = 2x - 3$$
Subtract $2x$ from both sides:
$$12 - 6x = -3$$
Subtract 12 from both sides:
$$-6x = -15$$
Divide both sides by -6:
$$x = 2.5$$

7)

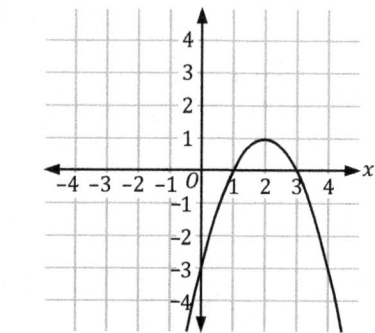

In the original function, the vertex of the parabola is located at $(0, 0)$. The -2 in the parentheses will shift this 2 units to the right, to the point $(2, 0)$. The $+1$ outside the parentheses will shift it 1 unit up, getting us to $(2, 1)$. Finally, the negative sign in front of the function will flip the whole thing upside down. So, this is a downward-pointing parabola with its vertex at $(2, 1)$.

Function Essentials: Practice Set 1 (p. 304)

1) 19
Plug in -2 for each x in the equation.
$$f(x) = 2x^2 - 3x + 5$$
$$f(-2) = 2(-2)^2 - 3(-2) + 5$$

Evaluate carefully, following PEMDAS. For example, to evaluate $2(-2)^2$, we must apply the Exponent first, *then* Multiply.

$$f(-2) = 2(4) + 6 + 5$$
$$= 8 + 6 + 5$$
$$= 19$$

2) C
First, find $f(3)$: plug in 3 for x in the $f(x)$ equation.
$$f(x) = x^2 + 3$$
$$f(3) = 3^2 + 3 = 12$$

Next, find $g(2)$: plug in 2 for x in the $g(x)$ equation.
$$g(x) = 2x + 2$$
$$g(2) = 2(2) + 2 = 6$$
Therefore:
$$f(3) - g(2) = 12 - 6$$
$$= 6$$

3) A
In this problem, x represents the number of units sold, and $p(x)$ represents the profit. The manufacturer sold 800 units, so $x = 800$. And the profit is $19,850, so $p(x) = 19850$. Plug those values into the equation.
$$p(x) = 27x - k$$
$$19850 = 27(800) - k$$

Now combine like terms to simplify and solve.
$$19850 = 21600 - k$$
$$-1750 = -k$$
$$1750 = k$$

Alternatively, we can use the built-in calculator to solve this problem. Enter the original function on one line, and then enter $y = 19,850$ on another line. The calculator will automatically provide a slider for k values.

1	$p(x) = 27x - k$
2	$y = 19850$
3	$k = 1$, slider from -10 to 10

Zoom out using either the — button or your mouse's trackball until you can see the intersection of the two lines.

We know from the problem that when $x = 800$, the value of $p(x)$ is 19,850. Therefore, for the right value of k, these lines should intersect at the point $(800, 19850)$.

To test choice A, click on the $k = 1$ line and type in 1750 as the value of k. Now click on the point where the two lines intersect. When $k = 1$, the point of intersection is $(800, 19850)$, so this is the right answer.

4) B
The table gives us a set of (x, y) points that satisfy the right equation. For example, according to the table, when $x = 0$, the value of $f(x)$ must be -4. So, plug $x = 0$ into each of the choices and eliminate any that don't come out to -4. That gets rid of choices A and D. Now move to another column in the table: for example, when $x = 2$, the value of $f(x)$ must be 0. Plug $x = 2$ into each of the choices and eliminate any that don't come out to 0. That gets rid of choice C, so B must be the answer.

Alternatively, we can use the built-in calculator to solve this problem. For each answer choice, type in the equation and then click the ⚙ symbol above the equation-entering area. Click on the image that looks like a table, and the calculator will automatically generate a table of points.

Here's what we get for choice A:

1	$f(x) = x^2 + 2$

x	$f(x)$
-2	6
-1	3
0	2
1	3
2	6

This doesn't match the table of points we were given, so A is the wrong answer. Repeat that process for the remaining choices and you'll find that B is the only match.

5) A
Based on the graph, what is the value of $f(4)$? That's just another way of asking this: for the point on the graph that has an x-coordinate of 4, what is the y-coordinate? We can see that the graph passes through the point $(4, 1)$, so $f(4) = 1$. The problem tells us that $f(4) = k$, so we can conclude that $k = 1$.

The question asked for the value of $f(k)$. But now that we know that $k = 1$, we can think of that question this way: what is the value of $f(1)$? Check the graph again. For the point on the graph that has an x-coordinate of 1, what is the y-coordinate? The graph passes through the point $(1, -2)$, so -2 is the answer.

6) B
To solve this problem, we need to identify the meaning for each variable, starting with the one in the parentheses (the t). In this problem, t is the number of seconds that have passed since the ball was thrown. The question is asking us to interpret $h(1) = 29$, which has the 1 in that t position. Therefore, $t = 1$: 1 second has passed since the ball was thrown. Already, we can eliminate choices C and D, because they use the wrong unit for the 1 (feet instead of seconds).

Answer Explanations

The other variable, h, represents the height of the ball above the ground, in feet. So the best interpretation of the 29 here is that the ball is 29 feet above the ground. That's choice B.

7) −1

The way to handle a composite function like this one is to start in the middle and work your way out. First, we find $g(3)$: plug in 3 for x in the $g(x)$ equation.

$$g(x) = x - 1$$
$$g(3) = 3 - 1 = 2$$

Since $g(3) = 2$, finding $f(g(3))$ is equivalent to finding $f(2)$. So, plug in 2 for x in the $f(x)$ equation.

$$f(x) = 1 - x$$
$$f(2) = 1 - 2 = -1$$

Function Essentials: Practice Set 2 (p. 305)
1) D

Start in the middle and work your way out. What's the value of $f(2)$? Check the table: when $x = 2$, the corresponding value of $f(x)$ is 3. Therefore, $f(2) = 3$, which means that finding $g(f(2))$ is equivalent to finding $g(3)$. So, what's the value of $g(3)$? Check the second table: when $x = 3$, the corresponding value of $g(x)$ is 10.

2) B

This is a "piecewise" function, which means it has a different equation for one interval (where $x \leq 0$) than it does for another (where $x > 0$). So first, we have to identify which interval applies. We're looking for the value of $f(1)$, so $x = 1$. That's a positive number, so the bottom equation applies:

$$f(x) = x^2 + 1$$
$$f(1) = 1^2 + 1 = 2$$

3) D

An x-intercept on a graph in the xy-plane is a point with a y-coordinate of zero. So this question is really asking this: what value of x will yield the result $g(x) = 0$?

To solve, plug in 0 for $g(x)$:

$$0 = |2x| - 6$$
$$6 = |2x|$$
$$6 = 2x \quad \text{or} \quad -6 = 2x$$
$$3 = x \quad \text{or} \quad -3 = x$$

Therefore, the x-intercepts of this graph occur at the points $(3, 0)$ and $(-3, 0)$, which can also be written as the points $(3, g(3))$ and $(-3, g(-3))$.

Alternatively, we find the x-intercepts using the built-in calculator. Type in the original equation (using `abs()` for the absolute value) and click on the points where the graph intersects the x-axis. The calculator will display the coordinates: $(3, 0)$ and $(-3, 0)$.

4) 144

The big rule of functions is that whatever's in the parentheses gets plugged in for x. We've been given $g(r) = 36$, which has an r in the parentheses. So, we plug in r for x.

$$g(x) = 2x^2$$
$$g(r) = 2r^2$$

We've been told that this is equal to 36. So:

$$2r^2 = 36$$
$$r^2 = 18$$
$$r = \sqrt{18} \quad \text{or} \quad r = -\sqrt{18}$$

The problem told us that $r > 0$, so only one of those two possible values of r can be correct: $r = \sqrt{18}$.

We're supposed to find the value of $g(2r)$. Since $r = \sqrt{18}$, that's equivalent to finding $g(2\sqrt{18})$. We now have $2\sqrt{18}$ in the parentheses, so we plug that in for x:

$$g(x) = 2x^2$$
$$g(2\sqrt{18}) = 2(2\sqrt{18})^2$$
$$= 2(2\sqrt{18})(2\sqrt{18})$$
$$= 2^3 * 18$$
$$= 144$$

5) B

In function notation, $f(x)$ represents the y-values of the graph of the f function, and $g(x)$ represents the y-values of the graph of the g function. So the places in the figure where $f(x) < g(x)$ occur where the graph of the f function is lower than the graph of the g function.

In the xy-plane shown in the figure, there are two points where the graphs of f and g intersect: at $(1, 0)$ and at $(4, 3)$. In other words, $f(x) = g(x)$ when $x = 1$ and when $x = 4$.

To the left of $(1, 0)$, the f graph is always above the g graph: that is, $f(x) > g(x)$ where $x < 1$. That also happens at points to the right of $x = 4$: in other words, $f(x) > g(x)$ where $x > 4$. But for points in between $x = 1$ and $x = 4$, the opposite is true. That's our answer, then: $f(x) < g(x)$ for $1 < x < 4$.

6) C

The domain of a fraction function excludes any values that would cause the denominator of the fraction to be equal to zero. The numerator of the fraction is irrelevant. Focus on the bottom of the fraction alone:

$$x - 3 \neq 0$$
$$x \neq 3$$

Alternatively, we can solve this problem using the built-in calculator. Type in the equation and then click the ⚙ symbol above the equation-entering area. Click on the

image that looks like a table, and the calculator will automatically generate a table of points:

1	$g(x) = \dfrac{x-4}{x-3}$	
2		
	x	$g(x)$
	-2	1.2
	-1	1.25
	0	1.3333333
	1	1.5
	2	2

We can already see that 0 and 1 are in the domain, because when x equals either of those numbers, there is a value indicated for $g(x)$. Based on that, we can eliminate choices A and B.

To test choice C, click on an empty line of the table and type in 3 for the x value. This time, the output for $g(x)$ is "undefined," indicating that 3 is not in the domain. By contrast, if we type in 4 for x, we do get a value for $g(x)$, so D is not the answer. The right answer is C.

7) A
The big rule of functions is that whatever's in the parentheses gets plugged in for x. Here, we have $g(x)$ in the parentheses, so we've got to plug that in for x.

$$f(x) = 3x^2$$
$$f(g(x)) = 3(g(x))^2$$
$$= 3(2x+1)^2$$
$$= 3(2x+1)(2x+1)$$
$$= 3(4x^2 + 4x + 1)$$
$$= 12x^2 + 12x + 3$$

8) D
Since the original function opens upwards, and we are taking the negative, it must open downwards. We can therefore eliminate B as a possibility. Transforming $f(x)$ to $f(x-1)$ shifts the function one unit to the right, meaning the x-coordinate of the original vertex must have been 2. That eliminates choices A and C, so the answer is D.

9) A
We have a zero in the parentheses, so that's the value of x. Check the context of the problem to see what x represents: it's the number of years that have passed since the year 2000. When $x = 0$, then, no years have passed: the year is 2000.

The other number here, 24, is the value of $f(x)$ when $x = 0$. So what does $f(x)$ represent? According to the problem, it's the population, in millions.

Therefore, the best interpretation of $f(0) = 24$ is that in the year 2000, the population of the country was 24 million. That's choice A.

10) 15
This is a linear function, so this problem is really just giving us two points on a line: $(2, 7)$ and $(4, 11)$. We could use these to calculate slope and find the equation of the line, but it's easier to just use the pattern that these points establish. Based on these points, when the value of x increases by 2, the value of y increases by 4. We're looking for $f(6)$, which is just increasing x by 2 again. Therefore, the y must increase by 4 again: the answer is $11 + 4 = 15$.

11) D
Here, we replace x with $(x + 2)$. The fact that we use x in both cases can be confusing, so be careful!

$$g(x+2) = 2[(x+2) - 1]^2 - (x+2)$$
$$= 2(x+1)^2 - x - 2$$
$$= 2(x^2 + 2x + 1) - x - 2$$
$$= 2x^2 + 4x + 2 - x - 2$$
$$= 2x^2 + 3x$$

This is not an answer choice, but if we factor out an x we get $x(2x + 3)$, which is choice D.

12) C
$$h(x) = f(x) - 2g(x)$$
$$= 2x^3 - 5x^2 + 6x - 1 - 2(x^3 - 3x^2 - 2x + 8)$$

Distribute the -2:

$$= 2x^3 - 5x^2 + 6x - 1 - 2x^3 + 6x^2 + 4x - 16$$

Rearrange to group the matching terms:

$$= 2x^3 - 2x^3 - 5x^2 + 6x^2 + 6x + 4x - 1 - 16$$

Combine like terms:

$$= x^2 + 10x - 17$$

13) D
By definition, a function must have exactly one output for each distinct input. In other words, each x value must be matched with one unique y value. In this table, when the input is $x = 1$, there are two different outputs: $y = 4$ and $y = 2$. Therefore, this is not a function.

LINEAR FUNCTIONS (p. 307)
Linear Functions: Try It
1) C
In a linear function, the x cannot have an exponent attached, as in choice D; it cannot be located under a

Answer Explanations

square root, as in choice A; and it cannot be an exponent, as in choice B. Only choice C is a linear equation: in the xy-plane, $y = -6$ is just a horizontal line.

To confirm, try graphing each of the answer choices using the built-in calculator. Only choice C looks like a line.

2) linear
This scenario has a constant rate of growth: the increase is $200 every year. That's linear.

3) non-linear
In this scenario, the rate of growth is not constant. Say someone starts with a salary of $100. The first year, the salary will increase by $0.02(100) = 2$ dollars, meaning the salary for the second year is $102. But what happens at the end of that year? Now the salary must increase by $0.02(102) = 2.04$ dollars, meaning the new salary is $104.04. The amount of the increase was only $2 the first year, but it was $2.04 the second year, and that amount will only continue to grow. Because the number of dollars added each year is not constant, this is non-linear growth.

4) $f(x) = 10x - 250$
Let's start by figuring out what the y-intercept of the line should be. In this scenario, the y value represents the company's profit, and the x value represents the number of toys sold. So, what is the company's profit when no toys have been sold? It's not just that they have no profits yet: they actually start out $250 in the hole (their profits are -250 dollars). So $b = -250$. Now, what is the slope? Each time the company sells another toy, they add $10 to their profits. Therefore, $m = 10$.

That gives us this equation:
$$y = 10x - 250$$

Now rewrite it in function notation by swapping the y for $f(x)$:
$$f(x) = 10x - 250$$

5) The tank held 12 gallons of gasoline when Sam began driving.
The equation $g(x) = 12 - 36x$ can be rewritten as $y = -36x + 12$. In this form, it's easier to see that 12 is the y-intercept. Write out the definition:

y-intercept = value of y when $x = 0$

Now plug in what x and y represent in this context:

12 = <u>gallons remaining</u> when <u># of miles</u> = 0

So, before Sam had driven any distance at all, there were 12 gallons in the tank.

6) The car uses an average of 36 gallons of gasoline per mile.
The slope of this line is -36. Write out the definition for slope:

slope = change in y as x increases by 1

So, here:

-36 = change in <u>gallons remaining</u> as <u># of miles</u> increases by 1

This tells us that with each mile driven, the amount of gasoline remaining in the tank decreases by 36 gallons. Therefore, the car uses 36 gallons per mile.

Linear Functions: Practice Set 1 (p. 312)

1) C
First, rearrange the terms in the given equation in order to rewrite it in $y = mx + b$ form:
$$C(n) = 20n + 500$$

Now it's easier to see that the 500 is the y-intercept. Write out the definition:

y-intercept = value of y when $x = 0$

Next, adjust that definition to use the variables from this problem:

y-intercept = value of $C(n)$ when $n = 0$

Now plug in the actual y-intercept and the meanings of the variables in this context:

500 = value of the <u>total cost</u> when the <u>number of yearbooks printed</u> = 0

In other words, before any yearbooks are printed at all, there are costs of $500 to pay. The best match for that interpretation is choice C.

2) B
$$P(x) = 0.25x - 50$$

When a linear equation is given in $y = mx + b$ form, the slope is m. Therefore, the slope of this line is 0.25. Write out the definition:

slope = change in y as x increases by 1

So, here:

slope = change in $P(x)$ as x increases by 1

Now plug in the actual slope and the meanings of the variables in this context:

0.25 = change in <u>profit</u> as <u>number of cookies sold</u> increases by 1

In other words, each time Jeremy sells an additional cookie, his profit increases by 0.25 dollars. The best interpretation is that the selling price is $0.25 per cookie.

3) C

First, rearrange the terms in the given equation in order to rewrite it in $y = mx + b$ form:

$$C(w) = 4.75w + 17.5$$

Now it's easier to see that the 4.75 is the slope. Write out the definition:

slope = change in y as x increases by 1

So, here:

slope = change in $C(w)$ as w increases by 1

4.75 = change in the <u>cost</u> as the <u>weight</u> increases by 1

In other words, every time we increase the weight of the package by 1 pound, we'll increase the cost by $4.75. In this problem, we're increasing the weight by 6 pounds. Therefore, the change in cost is

$$6(\$4.75) = \$28.5$$

4) B

Type the equation into the built-in calculator, and then click on the ⚙ icon. This will bring up several options. Click on the one that looks like a table, and the calculator will automatically create a table of points for you:

```
1
   f(x) = -0.5x + 2

2
   x    | f(x)
   -2   | 3
   -1   | 2.5
    0   | 2
    1   | 1.5
    2   | 1
```

That's choice B.

If you'd prefer to solve this algebraically, plug an x value from the tables into the equation and check the corresponding $f(x)$ value. First, what is the corresponding value for $f(x)$ when $x = 0$?

$$f(x) = -0.5x + 2$$
$$f(0) = -0.5(0) + 2$$
$$= 0 + 2$$
$$= 2$$

Eliminate choices A and D. Now let's try another value. What is the corresponding value for $f(x)$ when $x = 1$?

$$f(1) = -0.5(1) + 2$$

$$= -0.5 + 2$$
$$= 1.5$$

Choice C has 2.5 in this column, so choice B is the right answer.

5) 58

The fact that this question is asking us for a rate (Ben's driving speed) is a big hint that we're looking for slope here. To be sure, let's match up the definition:

slope = change in y as x increases by 1

So, here:

slope = change in $d(t)$ as t increases by 1

Now plug in the actual slope and the meanings of the variables in this context. Focus on the units:

58 = change in <u>distance from home, in miles</u> as <u>time, in hours</u> increases by 1

Or, more concisely:

58 = change in <u>miles</u> as <u>hours</u> increase by 1

That certainly matches a driving speed of 58 <u>miles</u> per <u>hour</u>, so 58 is the right answer.

6) C

Check one choice at a time. Keep in mind that we're looking for two things: the function must be *linear*, meaning the rate of change is constant, and the slope must be *positive*, meaning the direction of the rate of change is an increase rather than a decrease.

Choice A is linear, but it's a decrease rather than an increase. This would be a linear function with a *negative* slope, so it's not our answer.

Choice B is a decrease too. Also, this one isn't even linear!

Choice C is a steady, positive rate of growth: the readership increases by 1000 each year. Hold on to choice C.

Choice D is not linear, because after the first 10 years, it levels off. That means the rate of change does not stay the same after those first 10 years, so it can't be our answer.

7) D

The figure looks like a typical xy-graph, except the x-axis is labeled m and the y-axis is labeled C. The C-intercept of this graph would be the point where the line intersects the C-axis, which is at the point $(0, 1)$. This is the point where m, the distance traveled, is 0, while C, the cost, is 1. Therefore, this point tells us that the cost to travel 0 miles is $1.

8) 750

The problem is asking for the increase in dollars each year. Problems asking for a rate of increase or a rate of

Answer Explanations

decrease are usually asking for slope; also, the "each" in the phrase "each year" is another hint that slope is the relevant number here. Based on the equation, the slope is 750. (Specifically, using our slope definition, we could say that 750 is the change in PPP as the number of years increases by 1.)

9) A
The big rule of functions is that whatever's in the parentheses is the x value. Here, we have 100 in the parentheses, so $x = 100$. The other number, 1625, is the value of $f(x)$.

In the context of this problem, x is the number of installed linear feet of fencing purchased, and $f(x)$ is the cost in dollars. So, 100 is the number of installed linear feet of fencing purchased, and 1625 is the cost in dollars. In other words, 100 linear feet of fencing costs $1625. That's choice A.

10) C
This table is just giving us a set of points for the graph: the top row is the x-coordinates and the bottom row is the corresponding y-coordinates. We want the y-intercept, which is the value of y when $x = 0$. So, find the column in this table where $x = 0$:

x	−1	0	1	2
$f(x)$	0	2	4	6

The corresponding y value is 2.

11) A
Start with the definition for slope:

$$\text{slope} = \text{change in } y \text{ as } x \text{ increases by 1}$$

So in this case:

$$\text{slope} = \text{change in } f(t) \text{ as } t \text{ increases by 1}$$

Now replace those variables with what they represent in the problem:

slope = change in attendance as years increase by 1

That's choice A.

Linear Functions: Practice Set 2 (p. 314)
1) A
Rewrite the equation in slope-intercept form:

$$A(p) = -\frac{25}{4}p + 50$$

In this equation, the slope is $-25/4$ and the y-intercept is 50. It's the 25/4 that we care about in this problem, so start with the definition of slope:

$$\text{slope} = \text{change in } y \text{ as } x \text{ increases by 1}$$

Given the variables used in this problem, we can adjust that to this:

$$\text{slope} = \text{change in } A(p) \text{ as } p \text{ increases by 1}$$

Now plug in the actual slope and the meanings of each of those variables:

−25/4 = change in amount of money left as number of packs purchased increases by 1

Therefore, each time Samuel buys an additional pack, the amount of money he has left decreases by $25/4 = 6.25$ dollars. The most logical interpretation is that each pack costs $6.25.

2) D
In this problem, x represents the depth of the water table, while y represents the amount of CO_2 emissions. Let's plug those definitions into our slope definition.

$$\text{slope} = \text{change in } y \text{ as } x \text{ increases by 1}$$

slope = change in CO_2 emissions as depth increases by 1

According to the problem, for every 1 cm increase in depth, emissions increase by 2. Therefore, the slope must be positive 2. Only D can be the answer.

3) B
First, rearrange the terms in the given equation in order to rewrite it in $y = mx + b$ form:

$$F = \frac{9}{5}C + 32$$

Now it's easier to see that the 9/5 in the equation is the slope. Write out the definition:

$$\text{slope} = \text{change in } y \text{ as } x \text{ increases by 1}$$

So, here:

$$\text{slope} = \text{change in } F \text{ as } C \text{ increases by 1}$$

Now plug in the actual slope and the meanings of the variables in this context:

9/5 = change in °F as °C increases by 1

In other words, each time the temperature increases by 1°C, the temperature increases by 9/5°F. That's choice B.

4) A

$$y = 1{,}600x + 24{,}000$$

The equation is already in $y = mx + b$ form, so we can see that the 1,600 is the slope. Write out the definition:

$$\text{slope} = \text{change in } y \text{ as } x \text{ increases by 1}$$

So, here:

1,600 = change in median home price as number of years since 1940 increases by 1

In other words, with each year that passes, the median home price increases by $1,600.

QUADRATIC FUNCTIONS (p. 315)
Quadratic Functions: Try It

1) $x = \dfrac{-3 \pm \sqrt{17}}{4}$

$$2x^2 + 3x - 1 = 0$$

This equation is written in $ax^2 + bx + c$ form, where $a = 2$, $b = 3$, and $c = -1$.

$$x = \frac{-b \pm \sqrt{b^2 - 4ac}}{2a}$$

$$x = \frac{-(3) \pm \sqrt{(3)^2 - 4(2)(-1)}}{2(2)}$$

$$x = \frac{-3 \pm \sqrt{9 + 8}}{4}$$

$$x = \frac{-3 \pm \sqrt{17}}{4}$$

2) 2

The graph of this function is a downward-pointing parabola, so the maximum value will occur at the vertex. The equation, $g(x) = -3x^2 + 12x + 2$, is written in standard $ax^2 + bx + c$ form, where $a = -3$, $b = 12$, and $c = 2$. Therefore, we can find the x-coordinate of the vertex by using the formula:

$$x = \frac{-b}{2a}$$

$$x = \frac{-(12)}{2(-3)}$$

$$x = \frac{-12}{-6}$$

$$x = 2$$

Alternatively, graph the equation in the built-in calculator and click on the vertex. The calculator will automatically display the coordinates: (2, 14). This tells you two things: that the maximum value of the function is 14, and that the value of x for which the function reaches that maximum value is $x = 2$.

3) −3

The minimum value of this upward-pointing parabola is the y-coordinate of the vertex. The given equation, $f(x) = 2x^2 - 4x - 1$, is written in standard $ax^2 + bx + c$ form, where $a = 2$, $b = -4$, and $c = -1$. First, use those values to find the x-coordinate of the vertex:

$$x = \frac{-b}{2a}$$

$$x = \frac{-(-4)}{2(2)}$$

$$x = \frac{4}{4}$$

$$x = 1$$

Now plug that x value back into the equation to find the corresponding y value:

$$f(1) = 2(1)^2 - 4(1) - 1$$
$$= 2(1) - 4 - 1$$
$$= 2 - 4 - 1$$
$$= -3$$

Alternatively, graph the equation in the built-in calculator and click on the vertex. The calculator will automatically display the coordinates: (1, −3).

4) none

The number of distinct real solutions to a quadratic written in standard $ax^2 + bx + c$ form is determined by the value of the discriminant, which is $b^2 - 4ac$. This equation, $x^2 + 2x + 3 = 0$, is written in standard form: $a = 1, b = 2$, and $c = 3$.

$$\text{discriminant} = b^2 - 4ac$$
$$\text{discriminant} = 2^2 - 4(1)(3)$$
$$= 4 - 12$$
$$= -8$$

Because the value of the discriminant is less than zero, the equation has no real solutions.

Alternatively, graph the equation in the built-in calculator. The parabola has no x-intercepts, so the equation has no real solutions.

5) 2

The equation $y = x^2 + 3x + k$ is written in standard $ax^2 + bx + c$ form, where $a = 1, b = 3$, and $c = k$. Since the graph has two x-intercepts, the value of the discriminant, $b^2 - 4ac$, must be positive.

$$b^2 - 4ac > 0$$
$$(3)^2 - 4(1)(k) > 0$$

Simplify:

$$9 - 4k > 0$$

Subtract 9 from both sides:

$$-4k > -9$$

Now divide both sides by −4. Remember, when you multiply or divide by a negative number, you flip the inequality:

$$k < 9/4$$
$$k < 2.25$$

Answer Explanations

All this tells us for sure is that the value of k must be less than 2.25. But the problem told us that k must be an integer. Therefore, the greatest possible value for k would be the greatest integer that is less than 2.25: so, 2.

Alternatively, we could solve this problem using the built-in calculator. Enter the equation as written, including the constant k. The calculator will automatically provide a slider for k values:

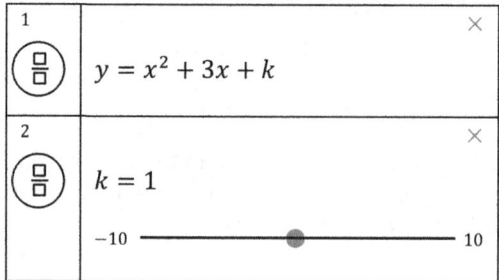

The problem said k was an integer. So, use the slider to check $k = 1$, $k = 2$, and so on. The largest integer value for which the parabola has two x-intercepts is $k = 2$, so that's the answer.

6) D
Read the question carefully. We don't just want any equivalent form of the equation. (In fact, all four answer choices here are equivalent to the original equation!) What we're looking for is a specific equivalent form: one in which the y-coordinate of the vertex is visible as a constant or coefficient. From the graph of the equation, we can see that the vertex of the parabola is located at the point $(-3, -8)$. Therefore, -8 must be one of the numbers used in the equation. Only choice D has a -8 in it, so D must be the answer.

Quadratic Functions: Practice Set 1 (p. 321)
1) C
Type the equation into the built-in calculator, and then click on the ⚙ icon above the equations. This will bring up several options. Click on the one that looks like a table:

x	$f(x)$
-2	15
-1	8
0	5
1	6
2	11

with $f(x) = 2x^2 - x + 5$

That's choice C.

If you'd prefer to solve this algebraically, plug an x value from the tables into the equation and check the corresponding $f(x)$ value. First, what is the corresponding value for $f(x)$ when $x = 0$?

$$f(x) = 2x^2 - x + 5$$
$$f(0) = 2(0)^2 - 0 + 5$$
$$= 0 - 0 + 5$$
$$= 5$$

Eliminate choices A and B. Now let's try another value. What is the corresponding value for $f(x)$ when $x = 1$?

$$f(1) = 2(1)^2 - 1 + 5$$
$$= 2 - 1 + 5$$
$$= 6$$

Choice D has 8 in this column, so choice C is the right answer.

2) D
This is a downward-pointing parabola, so the "maximum value of the function" is the y-coordinate of the parabola's vertex. Graph the equation in the built-in calculator and click on the vertex. The calculator will automatically display the coordinates: $(-1, 16)$. Therefore, the maximum value is 16.

Alternatively, we can solve this problem algebraically. Because this function is given in factored form, we can see that the zeros occur at $x = 1$ and $x = -3$. Average those values to find the x-coordinate of the vertex:

$$x = \frac{-3 + 1}{2} = \frac{-2}{2} = -1$$

Now plug that value for x back into the function to find the corresponding value for y:

$$y = -2\big((2 * -1) - 2\big)(-1 + 3)$$
$$y = -2(-4)(2)$$
$$y = 16$$

3) C
No quadratic has more than 2 roots, so we can eliminate choice D off the bat.

To evaluate the rest of the choices, graph the equation on the built-in calculator: the number of x-intercepts of a parabola is the number of distinct real roots of the function. For this function, there are two x-intercepts, so there must be 2 distinct real roots. That eliminates choices A and B, meaning the answer must be C.

Alternatively, we can solve this problem algebraically. The given equation, $y = 2x^2 - 3x - 7$, is written in standard $ax^2 + bx + c$ form, where $a = 2$, $b = -3$, and $c = -7$. The number of distinct real roots will be determined by the discriminant:

$$\text{discriminant} = b^2 - 4ac$$
$$\text{discriminant} = (-3)^2 - 4(2)(-7)$$
$$= 9 + 56$$
$$= 65$$

Because this value is greater than zero, the equation must have two distinct real roots.

4) B
For any quadratic function that is written in the form $f(x) = a(x - h)^2 + k$, the vertex is (h, k) and the axis of symmetry is the vertical line $x = h$. Thus, the axis of symmetry for the parabola given by $f(x) = (x - 1)^2 + 3$ is the vertical line $x = 1$.

If you like, you can confirm this using the built-in calculator. Graph the original function, and then graph each of the answer choices one at a time. Choice B is the vertical line that splits the parabola perfectly in half.

5) C
You don't need any specialized quadratics knowledge for this one. Use your understanding of basic function transformations: to move a graph 4 units down, we have to subtract 4 outside the parentheses. So:
$$f(x) = (x - 3)^2 + 1$$
$$g(x) = (x - 3)^2 + 1 - 4$$
$$g(x) = (x - 3)^2 - 3$$

6) C
Because we know the vertex of this parabola is at $(3, 4)$, we know that the height of the triangle is 4. We also know that, because parabolas are symmetrical, the base is $2(3) = 6$. So we use the formula for the area of a triangle:
$$\text{Area} = \frac{1}{2} \times \text{base} \times \text{height}$$
$$\text{Area} = \frac{1}{2}(6)(4)$$
$$\text{Area} = 12$$

Quadratic Functions: Practice Set 2 (p. 322)
1) -4
If $x = 4$ is a root of the equation, then $(4, 0)$ is an x-intercept of the graph. Plug in those values for x and y in the equation:
$$y = x^2 - 3x + k$$
$$0 = (4)^2 - 3(4) + k$$
$$0 = 16 - 12 + k$$
$$0 = 4 + k$$
$$-4 = k$$

2) 8
Since line l is parallel to the x-axis, we know that $c = 8$. We could use this information to find the values of a and b by plugging this information into the equation (that is, $8 = \frac{1}{2}x^2$), but we actually don't need those values! Because the graph is symmetrical about the y-axis, we know that a and b must be opposites: that is, $-a = b$. Therefore, $a + b + c$ is equal to $a + (-a) + c$, which is equal to c. The answer is 8.

3) B
Multiply the two terms together and set the product equal to -16.
$$(2n + 3)(2n - 5) = -16$$
Now FOIL and combine like terms, setting everything equal to zero to get the equation into standard form.
$$4n^2 - 4n - 15 = -16$$
$$4n^2 - 4n + 1 = 0$$
Since the question is only asking "how many distinct values of n" there are, we do not need to find the actual solutions. We just need to know how many there are. So, find the discriminant, $b^2 - 4ac$:
$$(-4)^2 - 4(4)(1)$$
That simplifies to $16 - 16 = 0$. Since the discriminant is equal to zero, there is only one distinct real solution.

Alternatively, graph $y = 4x^2 - 4x + 1$ using the built-in calculator. The graph has exactly one x-intercept, so there is one distinct real solution.

4) 1
We're looking for the intersection of two functions, so we need to set them equal to each other:
$$x^2 + 3 = mx + 3$$
We have two unknowns in this equation, but we have one other piece of information: the functions intersect at $(1, a)$. At the point of intersection, then, $x = 1$:
$$1^2 + 3 = m(1) + 3$$
$$4 = m + 3$$
$$1 = m$$

5) C
The value of c in the equation is the y-intercept of the graph, so the y-intercept must be positive. Eliminate choices A and D. To choose between B and C, consider the vertex of the parabola. The x-intercept of the vertex must be located at $x = -b/(2a)$. Given that a and b are both positive, this value must be negative. Therefore, the x-coordinate of the vertex must be negative: we can eliminate choice B. Choice C is the answer.

6) A
One option would be to simply graph all four answer choices and pick the one that looks symmetrical. You can skip that step if you're familiar with the basic shapes of the x^2 and x^3 functions as well as the effects of basic function transformations. The x^3 function will never be

Answer Explanations

symmetrical across the y-axis, so choices C and D are out. The basic x^2 function is symmetrical across the y-axis, but it won't be if we move it 2 units to the left (choice B). However, the x^2 function remains symmetrical across the y-axis if we simply move it up one unit, so choice A is the right answer.

7) B
The graph of $y = 1$ is a horizontal line, and the graph of $y = ax^2 + b$ is a parabola: specifically, it is a parabola that has been moved up b units but not moved left or right at all. The value of a determines whether the parabola opens up or down, and the value of b gives the y-coordinate of the vertex. For there to be exactly two solutions to this system of equations, the vertex of the parabola must be below $y = 1$ if it opens up, or above $y = 1$ if it opens down. Therefore, B is the correct answer: $a = -2$ means the parabola opens downwards, and $b = 4$ means the vertex is above 1.

Alternatively, one could graph all four answers. In the correct one, the line and the parabola will intersect exactly twice.

8) 12
First, draw the square:

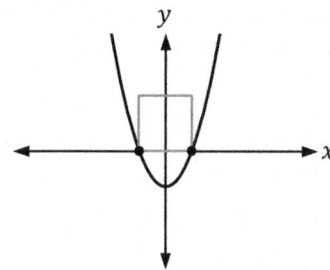

The length of one side of the square is equal to the distance between the x-intercepts of the graph. So what are the x-intercepts?

$$0 = x^2 - 3$$
$$3 = x^2$$
$$x = \sqrt{3} \text{ or } x = -\sqrt{3}$$

The distance from the negative x-intercept to the origin is $\sqrt{3}$, and the distance from the origin to the positive x-intercept is also $\sqrt{3}$. Therefore, the side length of the square is $\sqrt{3} + \sqrt{3} = 2\sqrt{3}$. The area of the square is $\left(2\sqrt{3}\right)^2 = 2^2 * 3 = 12$.

9) D
For any quadratic, the sum of the solutions is equal to $-b/a$. So, here:

$$\text{sum} = \frac{-(-5)}{1} = 5$$

Alternatively, you can solve the equation algebraically and add the solutions.

$$x^2 - 5x - 24 = 0$$
$$(x - 8)(x + 3) = 0$$
$$x = 8 \text{ or } x = -3$$
$$\text{sum} = 8 + (-3) = 5$$

10) B
The graph passes through the point $(0, -1)$, which is all we need. Plug those values into the equation:
$$-1 = 4(0) - (0)^2 - k$$
$$-1 = -k$$
$$k = 1$$

11) B
The equation is given in *standard form*, $y = ax^2 + bx + c$. We need to rewrite the equation to put into *vertex form*, $y = a(x - h)^2 + k$, where (h, k) are the coordinates of the parabola's vertex. The value of a is the same in both forms, so here, $a = 1$. Reading from the graph, the vertex is $(2, -9)$. So for this parabola, the equation in vertex form is $y = (x - 2)^2 - 9$.

If you picked choice C for this question, you did not read the entire problem! While choice C is equivalent to the original equation, it is not the specific equivalent form we were asked for. In fact, three of the four answer choices here are equivalent to the original equation: A, B, and C could all be simplified to $y = x^2 - 4x - 5$. But only choice B uses the coordinates of the vertex as constants in the equation, so only B can be the correct answer.

POLYNOMIAL, EXPONENTIAL, RADICAL, AND RATIONAL FUNCTIONS (p. 324)
Polynomial, Exponential, Radical, and Rational Functions: Try It

1) $(-1, 0), (2, 0),$ **and** $(3, 0)$
The x-intercepts of a graph are the points where the y-coordinate is zero. In function notation, $f(x)$ indicates the y value. So, plug zero in for $f(x)$.

$$f(x) = -(x + 1)(x - 2)(x - 3)$$
$$0 = -(x + 1)(x - 2)(x - 3)$$

Divide both sides by -1:

$$0 = (x + 1)(x - 2)(x - 3)$$

Set each factor equal to zero:

$$x + 1 = 0 \text{ or } x - 2 = 0 \text{ or } x - 3 = 0$$
$$x = -1 \text{ or } x = 2 \text{ or } x = 3$$

Alternatively, just graph the function in the built-in calculator and click on each point where the graph intersects the x-axis.

2) $(-1, 0), (2, 0),$ **and** $(3, 0)$
As in #1 above, we plug zero in for $f(x)$.

$$g(x) = -(x+1)(x-2)^2(x-3)$$
$$0 = -(x+1)(x-2)^2(x-3)$$

Divide both sides by -1:
$$0 = (x+1)(x-2)^2(x-3)$$

Set each factor equal to zero:
$$x+1 = 0 \text{ or } (x-2)^2 = 0 \text{ or } x-3 = 0$$

Solve the middle factor by taking the square root of both sides.

$$x+1 = 0 \text{ or } x-2 = 0 \text{ or } x-3 = 0$$
$$x = -1 \text{ or } x = 2 \text{ or } x = 3$$

Alternatively, just graph the function in the built-in calculator and click on each point where the graph intersects the x-axis.

3) **In the graph of $f(x)$, the curve crosses the x-axis at all three x-intercepts. In the graph of $g(x)$, the curve crosses the x-axis at $x = -1$ and $x = 3$ but only touches the x-axis (without crossing it) at $x = 2$.**

The graph of a polynomial function will cross the x-axis at all zeros that result from a factor with an odd-numbered exponent. Here, the exponents on all but one of the factors have no exponent written, which means their exponent is 1. That's an odd number, so the curve will cross the x-axis at each of those points.

The exception is the $(x-2)^2$ in the $g(x)$ function. This factor has an even-numbered exponent, so the curve will just touch the x-axis, without crossing it, at that point.

4) **$(0, 12)$**

The y-intercepts of a graph are the points where the x-coordinate is zero. So, plug 0 in for x.

$$g(x) = -(x+1)(x-2)^2(x-3)$$
$$g(0) = -(0+1)(0-2)^2(0-3)$$
$$= -(1)(-2)^2(-3)$$
$$= -(1)(4)(-3)$$
$$= 12$$

Alternatively, just graph the function in the built-in calculator and click on the point where the graph intersects the y-axis.

5) **The account was opened with an initial investment of $2000.**

Rewrite the equation in the form
$$A = P(1 + r)^t$$
where A is the final amount, P is the initial amount, r is the rate of change, and t is time.

$$f(x) = 2000(1.04)^x$$
$$A = 2000(1 + 0.04)^t$$

Now it's easier to see that the initial amount was $2000, while the rate of change was 4%.

6) **$2530.64**

Plug in 6 for x.
$$f(x) = 2000(1.04)^x$$
$$f(6) = 2000(1.04)^6$$

You can type that expression directly into the calculator to get the answer. Otherwise, take care to follow PEMDAS: we have to apply the exponent *before* we do any multiplying.

$$f(6) = 2000(1.2653)$$
$$= 2530.638$$

Rounded to the nearest cent, that's $2530.64.

7) **growth; rate = 50%**

The number in the parentheses is greater than 1, so this is exponential growth. The amount by which it differs from 1 is $1.5 - 1 = 0.5$, so the rate of change is $100(0.5) = 50\%$.

8) **neither**

The number in the parentheses is less than zero, so this is neither exponential growth nor exponential decay.

9) **decay; rate = 40%**

The number in the parentheses is between zero and 1, so this is exponential decay. The amount by which it differs from 1 is $1 - 0.6 = 0.4$, so the rate of change is $100(0.4) = 40\%$.

10) $f(x) = 1000(1.005)^{12x}$

Start by writing out the compound interest formula:
$$A = P\left(1 + \frac{r}{n}\right)^{nt}$$

The initial investment is $1000, so $P = 1000$. The annual interest rate is 6%, so $r = 0.06$. The interest is compounded monthly (12 times per year), so $n = 12$. Therefore:

$$A = 1000\left(1 + \frac{0.06}{12}\right)^{12(t)}$$
$$A = 1000(1 + 0.005)^{12t}$$
$$A = 1000(1.005)^{12t}$$

Now rewrite that in function notation:
$$f(x) = 1000(1.005)^{12x}$$

11) **$1093.93**

Remember, x represents the amount of time in <u>years</u>. So first, convert 18 months to years: since there are 12 months in 1 year, 18 months is equivalent to 1.5 years. Therefore, plug in 1.5 for x:

$$f(1.5) = 1000(1.005)^{12(1.5)}$$

Answer Explanations

Type that expression into the built-in calculator:

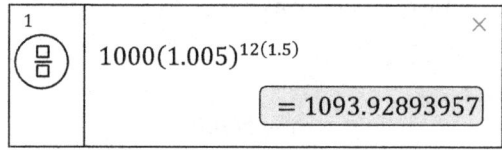

Rounded to the nearest cent, that's $1093.93.

12) $x \geq -4/3$
Take the part of the function that's under the square root and set it greater than or equal to zero.
$$3x + 4 \geq 0$$
$$3x \geq -4$$
$$x \geq -4/3$$

13) $(0, 3)$
Find $f(0)$ by plugging in 0 for x in the equation:
$$f(x) = 5 - \sqrt{3x + 4}$$
$$f(0) = 5 - \sqrt{3(0) + 4}$$
$$= 5 - \sqrt{0 + 4}$$
$$= 5 - \sqrt{4}$$
$$= 5 - 2$$
$$= 3$$

14) $x \neq -4/3$
Take the bottom of the fraction and set it unequal to zero.
$$3x + 4 \neq 0$$
$$3x \neq -4$$
$$x \neq -4/3$$

Note that this is <u>not</u> the same as the domain of $f(x)$. The domain of $g(x)$ includes all numbers that are less than $-4/3$ and all numbers that are greater than $-4/3$, but not $-4/3$ itself. The domain of $f(x)$ *does* include $-4/3$ itself, as well as all numbers greater than $-4/3$; it does *not* include the numbers that are less than $-4/3$.

15) $(-2, 0)$
$$g(x) = \frac{x + 2}{3x + 4}$$
$$0 = \frac{x + 2}{3x + 4}$$
$$(3x + 4) * (0) = \left(\frac{x + 2}{3x + 4}\right) * (3x + 4)$$
$$0 = x + 2$$
$$-2 = x$$

Polynomial, Exponential, Radical, and Rational Functions: Practice Set 1 (p. 334)
1) C
According to the table, when $a = 0$, the value of $p(a)$ is 14.7. Plug zero into the answer choices and you can quickly eliminate choices A and B. Now repeat the process with $a = 1$. Only choice C comes out to 12.8, so it must be the right answer.

Alternatively, we can use the built-in calculator to solve this problem. For each answer choice, type in the equation and then click the ✱ symbol above the equation-entering area. Click on the image that looks like a table, and the calculator will automatically generate a table of points. The choice that matches the values in the table we were given is the right answer.

2) D
In this ugly-looking polynomial, the 1.9 is simply the y-intercept. After all, if we plug in $t = 0$, all the other terms disappear. So that's our interpretation: when the value of t is zero, the value of $h(t)$ is 1.9. But 1.9 what? The problem told us that $h(t)$ "represents the plane's altitude, in kilometers above sea level," while t is just the time since takeoff, in minutes. Therefore, when zero minutes have passed (at takeoff), the plane's altitude was 1.9 kilometers above sea level. This lets us conclude that the plane took off at that altitude, and our answer is D.

3) 1.2
We can model this growth with an exponential function of the form $y = a(b)^x$. The starting value, a, is 1000. The constant b is equal to 1 plus the rate of change; the rate of change here is 20%, so the value of b is $1 + 0.2 = 1.2$. That gives us the equation $y = 1000(1.2)^x$. If that's equivalent to $p(t) = 1000r^t$, then the value of r in the latter equation must be 1.2.

4) B
In this equation, x represents the number of years that have passed since the census, which took place in 2000. In 2014, fourteen years have passed, so $x = 14$. All we have to do is plug in 14 for x.
$$y = 1.26(1.07)^{14} = 324.895$$
The y value represents the population in thousands, so a y value of 324.895 translates to a population of 324,895 people. The closest answer choice to that value is B.

5) C
Subtract straight down:
$$\begin{aligned} f(x) &= 2x^3 - 5x^2 + 8x - 1 \\ g(x) &= -x^3 + 2x^2 - x + 3 \\ &= 2x^3 + x^3 - 7x^2 + 8x + x - 4 \\ &= 3x^3 - 7x^2 + 9x - 4 \end{aligned}$$

6) D
One option is to graph the equation in the built-in calculator and look at the y-intercept.

Alternatively, we can solve algebraically. The y-intercept occurs at the point where $x = 0$, so write out the equation and plug in zero for x:

$$f(0) = 3.2(0.5)^0 + 1$$

Now be sure to carefully follow PEMDAS. We have to apply the exponent before we do any multiplication, so the next step is to calculate $(0.5)^0$. Any value raised to the zero power is 1, so that gives us this:

$$f(0) = 3.2(1) + 1$$
$$= 3.2 + 1$$
$$= 4.2$$

7) A
In any exponential equation of form $A = P(1 + r)^t$, the P represents the starting value. In this context, that means it's the value of $T(x)$, the number of toys sold, when x, the number of years since 2015, is zero. Therefore, the best interpretation of the 1200 is that it's the number of toys sold in 2015.

8) D
One way to solve is to graph both equations in the built-in calculator. The points where the graphs intersect are the answers.

Alternatively, we can back-solve by plugging the values from the roman numerals into the equation one at a time. Here's $x = 0$:

$$\sqrt{0 + 30} \stackrel{?}{=} \frac{0}{2} - 9$$
$$\sqrt{30} \neq -9$$

That doesn't work, so statement I is false. Eliminate choices A and B. Now try $x = 6$:

$$\sqrt{6 + 30} \stackrel{?}{=} \frac{6}{2} - 9$$
$$\sqrt{36} \stackrel{?}{=} 3 - 9$$
$$6 \neq -6$$

That doesn't work either, so statement II is false. Eliminate choice C, and choice D must be the answer.

If you'd like to solve the problem algebraically (not recommended), start by setting the original equations equal to each other:

$$\sqrt{x + 30} = \frac{x}{2} - 9$$

Now carefully square both sides:

$$\left(\sqrt{x + 30}\right)^2 = \left(\frac{x}{2} - 9\right)^2$$
$$x + 30 = \left(\frac{x}{2} - 9\right)\left(\frac{x}{2} - 9\right)$$
$$x + 30 = \frac{x^2}{4} - 9x + 81$$
$$0 = \frac{x^2}{4} - 10x + 51$$

Get rid of the fraction by multiplying both sides by 4:

$$0 = x^2 - 40x + 204$$

Now factor:

$$0 = (x - 6)(x - 34)$$
$$x = 6 \text{ or } x = 34$$

But do we really have two solutions? As we saw in the back-solving explanation above, $x = 6$ doesn't work: it's an extraneous solution. Now try $x = 34$:

$$\sqrt{34 + 30} \stackrel{?}{=} \frac{34}{2} - 9$$
$$\sqrt{64} \stackrel{?}{=} 17 - 9$$
$$8 = 8$$

That one works, so $x = 34$ is the one and only solution.

9) C
A rational function is undefined when the denominator is equal to zero. So, set the denominator of this function equal to zero and see what happens:

$$(x - 3)(x - 1) = 0$$
$$x = 3 \text{ or } x = 1$$

This tells us that the function is undefined at two values of x: when $x = 3$ and when $x = 1$. The fact that we can cancel out an $(x - 3)$ from the top and bottom of the fraction does not change this answer! That just alters what will happen to the graph at those points. The fact that $(x - 1)$ doesn't cancel out means we'll have a vertical asymptote at $x = 1$; since $(x - 3)$ does cancel out, we'll have a hole at $x = 3$ instead of an asymptote. But either way, the function is undefined at both values.

Alternatively, we can solve this problem using the built-in calculator. Type in the original equation, and then click on the ⚙ icon above the equation-entering area. This will bring up several options. Click on the one that looks like a table, and the calculator will automatically create a table of points for you:

1	$f(x) = \dfrac{(x+1)(x-3)}{(x-3)(x-1)}$	✕
2		✕

x	$f(x)$
-2	0.3333333
-1	0
0	-1
1	undefined
2	3

- 539 -

Answer Explanations

We can already see that $-2, -1, 0$, and 2 are included in the domain of this function, because when x equals any of those values, there is a corresponding value of $f(x)$. We can also see that 1 is <u>not</u> included in the domain, because when $x = 1$, $f(x)$ is undefined.

From this, we know statement I is false and statement II is true, so the answer must be C.

10) C
When an exponential equation takes the form $A = P(1 + r)^t$, the P represents the starting value, the r represents the rate expressed as a decimal, the t represents time, and the A represents the final value. In this problem, the starting value is $24,000, so that's P. The invesment <u>decreases</u> in value by 11% each year, so r must be negative: specifically, $r = -0.11$. So:

$$A = P(1 + r)^t$$
$$A = 24,000(1 - 0.11)^t$$
$$A = 24,000(0.89)^t$$

11) C
One option is to graph the equation in the built-in calculator. The points where the graph intersects the x-axis are the x-intercepts.

Alternatively, we can solve this algebraically. The x-intercepts occur at the points where $y = 0$. In function notation, $f(x)$ is just another way of expressing y. So, plug in zero for $f(x)$ in the equation:

$$0 = -2(x - 3)(2x - 3)(3x + 5)$$

To simplify, divide both sides by -2.

$$0 = (x - 3)(2x - 3)(3x + 5)$$

The equation is already factored for us, so now we just have to set each factor equal to zero and solve.

$$x - 3 = 0 \text{ or } 2x - 3 = 0 \text{ or } 3x + 5 = 0$$
$$x = 3 \quad \text{or} \quad 2x = 3 \quad \text{or} \quad 3x = -5$$
$$x = 3 \text{ or } x = 3/2 \text{ or } x = -5/3$$

There are three x-intercepts, but only one is included in the answer choices: $x = 3/2$. The answer is C.

Polynomial, Exponential, Radical, and Rational Functions: Practice Set 2 (p. 336)
1) C
According to the problem, interest is compounded n "times per year." If Kathy has noticed that her interest is now compounding every 2 months (6 times per year) instead of quarterly (4 times per year), n is what is changing.

2) D
The best way to solve this is to try and sketch the functions described in a way that does not touch all four quadrants.

Choice A: A linear function with a non-zero slope is simply a line that's not horizontal. Here's the graph of $y = x + 2$, which touches exactly three quadrants:

Choice B: An exponential function with a non-zero y-intercept can touch two or three quadrants, but not four.

Choice C: A polynomial with four real zeros *can* touch all four quadrants, but it does not *have* to. Here's one way to draw it so that it touches only three:

Choice D: No matter how you draw it, a quadratic function with both positive and negative roots will always touch all four quadrants. The answer must be D.

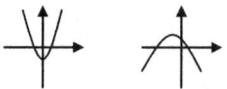

3) 624
The big rule of functions is that whatever's in the parentheses gets plugged in for x. We've been told that $g(k) = 50$. That gives us a k in the parentheses, so we plug k in for x.

$$g(x) = 2\sqrt{x + 1}$$
$$g(k) = 2\sqrt{k + 1}$$

We know that $g(k) = 50$, so:

$$50 = 2\sqrt{k + 1}$$

To solve, first divide both sides by 2.

$$25 = \sqrt{k + 1}$$

Don't move too fast here! To get rid of that square root, we have to <u>square</u> both sides. (If you got 4 for your answer, you square rooted here instead.)

$$25^2 = \left(\sqrt{k + 1}\right)^2$$
$$625 = k + 1$$
$$624 = k$$

Alternatively, you can solve this problem using the built-in calculator. Type in both of the given equations, then zoom out until you can see the point where the two graphs intersect. Click on that point and the calculator will automatically display the coordinates: $(624, 50)$. Thus, when $x = 624$, the corresponding value of $g(x)$ is

50. In other words, $g(624) = 50$. We know from the problem that $g(k) = 50$, so 624 must be the value of k.

4) A

Because this problem involves an annual rate that is compounded quarterly, we need the more complicated version of the compound interest formula:

$$A = P\left(1 + \frac{r}{n}\right)^{nt}$$

Let's adjust the variables to match this problem. Here, x represents time, so we'll use that instead of t. And $f(x)$ is the value of the endowment after x years, so we'll swap the A for $f(x)$. We also know that interest is compounded quarterly, so n (the number of compounding intervals per year) must be 4.

$$f(x) = P\left(1 + \frac{r}{4}\right)^{4x}$$

Compare that to the equation we've been given:

$$f(x) = 3256(1.02)^{4x}$$

We can now match up the contents of the parentheses in these two equations:

$$1 + \frac{r}{4} = 1.02$$
$$\frac{r}{4} = 0.02$$
$$r = 0.08$$

The rate of increase is 0.08, which is equivalent to 8%.

5) 17

Try not to get overwhelmed by all the abstraction in this problem. We have the equation for the function:

$$h(x) = a\sqrt{x - 1} + b$$

We also have some point values. For example, we know that when $x = 1, h(x) = 2$. Plug that information into the equation:

$$2 = a\sqrt{1 - 1} + b$$
$$2 = a\sqrt{0} + b$$
$$2 = a(0) + b$$
$$2 = b$$

That gives us the value of b. We can now rewrite the equation like this:

$$h(x) = a\sqrt{x - 1} + 2$$

Now, plug in the second point we were given: when $x = 5, h(x) = 10$.

$$10 = a\sqrt{5 - 1} + 2$$
$$10 = a\sqrt{4} + 2$$
$$10 = 2a + 2$$
$$8 = 2a$$
$$4 = a$$

Great, another constant solved. Now our equation looks like this:

$$h(x) = 4\sqrt{x - 1} + 2$$

Finally, let's turn to the third point we were given: when $x = k, h(x) = 18$.

$$18 = 4\sqrt{k - 1} + 2$$

Subtract 2:

$$16 = 4\sqrt{k - 1}$$

Divide by 4:

$$4 = \sqrt{k - 1}$$

Square both sides:

$$4^2 = \left(\sqrt{k - 1}\right)^2$$
$$16 = k - 1$$
$$17 = k$$

6) C

Since $g(x) = f(x - 1)$, we'll find the equation for $g(x)$ by plugging in $(x - 1)$ for x in the original $f(x)$ equation.

$$f(x) = 80(10)^x$$
$$g(x) = 80(10)^{(x - 1)}$$

Use the exponent rules to simplify.

$$g(x) = 80(10)^x(10)^{-1}$$
$$g(x) = 80(10)^x \left(\frac{1}{10}\right)$$
$$g(x) = \frac{80(10)^x}{10}$$
$$g(x) = 8(10)^x$$

Alternatively, we can solve this problem by plugging in numbers. Start the same way, by plugging in $(x - 1)$ for x in the original $f(x)$ equation to get this:

$$g(x) = 80(10)^{(x - 1)}$$

Now, make up a value for x. Let's say we decided to use $x = 2$. In that case, the value of $g(x)$ is

$$g(2) = 80(10)^{(2 - 1)}$$
$$= 80(10)^1$$
$$= 800$$

Next, plug $x = 2$ into each of the answer choices. The one that comes out to 800 is our answer.

A) $7(10)^2 = 7(100) = 700$
B) $8(9)^2 = 8(81) = 648$
C) $8(10)^2 = 8(100) = 800$
D) $80(1/10)^2 = 80(1/100) = 0.8$

Only choice C matches the 800 we were looking for, so the answer is C.

Answer Explanations

7) −2

First, subtract the given functions and combine like terms.

$$\begin{array}{r} f(x) = px^3 - 3x^2 + 2x + 5 \\ - \quad g(x) = 3x^3 + 5x^2 - qx + 2 \\ \hline = px^3 - 3x^3 - 8x^2 + 2x + qx + 3 \end{array}$$

To make the next step easier, try rewriting this so that the polynomial has exactly one x^3 term, exactly one x^2 term, and so on. Like this:

$$= (p - 3)x^3 - 8x^2 + (2 + q)x + 3$$

We've been told that this outcome is equal to the expression $-x^3 - 8x^2 + 6x + 3$. Match up the coefficients of like terms. For example, $(p - 3)x^3$ must be the same thing as $-x^3$. Therefore, $p - 3$ must equal -1:

$$p - 3 = -1$$
$$p = 2$$

Similarly, $(2 + q)x$ must be the same thing as $6x$, so $2 + q$ must equal 6:

$$2 + q = 6$$
$$q = 4$$

Therefore, the value of $p - q$ is $2 - 4 = -2$.

8) A

This problem tests your understanding of the concept of half-life. Let's examine one choice at a time, plugging in numbers where necessary.

Start with choice A. Let's say the initial amount of substance is 8 g. After one half-life, we know 1/2 of the substance will remain, so 4 g.

After two half-lives, half of that 4 g will have decayed, leaving 2 g. After three half-lives, half of that 2 g will have decayed, leaving 1 g. At this point, exactly 1 g remains of our original 8 g: in other words, 1/8 remains. A is correct.

Now try choice B, starting with an original amount of 8 g again. That means at time $t = 0$, the amount remaining is 8 g. At time $t = 1$, the amount remaining is 4 g. At time $t = 2$, the amount remaining is 2 g. But 2 g is 25% of 8 g, not 50%. Choice B is incorrect.

For choice C, check the definitions in the problem again. A is the amount remaining after some number of half-lives, while A_0 is the initial amount. In our example, $A_0 = 8$. But as we just saw, at time $t = 1$, the amount remaining is 4. So at time $t = 1$, $A = 4$ and $A_0 = 8$. Since $4 < 8$, choice C is incorrect.

Choice D is tricky. Read carefully! It's true that as the value of t increases, the *amount of remaining substance* decreases exponentially. But that's A, not A_0. Recall that A_0 was defined simply as the initial amount of the substance. That never changes, no matter what happens to t. In our examples above, while A changed, the value of A_0 was always 8. Since A_0 does not decrease, choice D is incorrect.

9) D

Try sketching this to see what's possible.

Choice A:

Choice B:

Choice C:

As we can see, depending on how the line and the exponential curve are oriented, it's possible for the graphs to intersect twice, once, or not at all. However, there's no way we can draw this such that the graphs will intersect more than twice, so D is the right answer.

10) C

Choice A is possible: a 3rd degree polynomial can have two x-intercepts if it crosses the x-axis at one of those points and just touches the x-axis (without crossing) at the other. This just means that in the equation, one of the factors will have an even-numbered exponent. For example, graph this equation on the built-in calculator:

$$y = -0.2(x - 2)^2(x - 5).$$

Choice B is possible. We are told that the x-intercepts *include* 2 and 5, but a 3rd degree polynomial can have up to 3 intercepts. Try graphing this equation:

$$y = 0.08(x - 2)(x - 5)(x + 5)$$

Choice D is possible. We know that the function must decrease at the least over the interval $0 < x < 2$, but we know nothing at all about the interval $-\infty < x < 0$. And in fact, we've already seen an example in which the graph was increasing over that interval! Take another look at the graph we created for choice B.

Only choice C remains. So why does this have to be false? Well, we know that 2 is an x-intercept of the function, which means that $(x - 2)$ is a factor. And by definition, when something is a factor, the remainder you get when you divide by that something is zero. So when $f(x)$ is divided by $(x - 2)$, the remainder must be zero, not 5. C must be false, which makes it the right answer.

11) D

First, find the equation for $h(x)$:

$$f(x) = 4\sqrt{x}, \quad g(x) = \frac{x + 2}{x - 9}$$

$$h(x) = g(f(x))$$

$$h(x) = \frac{4\sqrt{x} + 2}{4\sqrt{x} - 9}$$

There are two limitations on the domain of this function. First, we can only take the square root of nonnegative numbers, so $x \geq 0$. Second, we can't divide by zero, so set the denominator of the $h(x)$ fraction unequal to zero:

$$4\sqrt{x} - 9 \neq 0$$
$$4\sqrt{x} \neq 9$$
$$\sqrt{x} \neq \frac{9}{4}$$
$$(\sqrt{x})^2 \neq \left(\frac{9}{4}\right)^2$$
$$x \neq \frac{81}{16}$$

12) B
Plug in numbers. All we know about a, b, and c is that they are positive, so any positive number will work. Then graph the answer choices in the built-in calculator to see which one looks most like the graph.

Alternatively, start by considering the graph of $y = a^x$. If a is positive, the graph will take this general shape:

The graph in the figure has been shifted down, so the right answer choice has to subtract something outside the parentheses. Eliminate choices A and C. Also, the graph in the figure has been shifted to the left, so the right answer choice has to *add* something *inside* the parentheses. That leaves choice B as the only possible answer.

DATA INTERPRETATION (p. 339)
Data Interpretation: Try It
1) 1/18
There are 5 blue marbles owned by Cleo. The question is asking us this: those 5 marbles represent what fraction of *all* the marbles shown in the table? The "whole" for this problem is the overall total number of marbles, which is 90. The "part" is the number of marbles owned by Cleo, which is 5. So the answer is 5/90, which simplifies to 1/18.

2) 5/18
The "part" for this problem is still the 5 marbles owned by Cleo. But this time, the question is different. Now, we want to know this: the 5 marbles owned by Cleo represent what fraction of all the *blue marbles* shown in the table? Look at the "Blue" column: the total for that column is 18. Thus, the "whole" for this problem is the 18 blue marbles shown in the table, and the "part" is the 5 blue marbles owned by Cleo. The answer is 5/18.

3) 23 students
Add up the frequencies. The heights of the bars show us how many students received each score: there were 3 students who received the first score, then 5 who received the second score, and so on. The total number of students is $3 + 5 + 6 + 6 + 3 = 23$.

4) 19 feet
Read carefully and check the axes. We want the shark with the greatest jaw width, which is the measurement on the y-axis. So, which point has the greatest y-coordinate? It'll be the highest point on the graph:

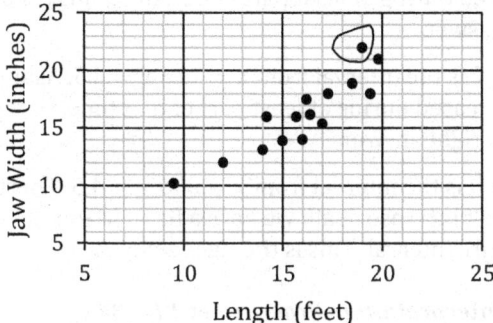

That's the point (19, 22). Checking the axes again, this point represents a shark with a length of 19 feet and a jaw width of 22 inches. The question asked for the length of this shark, so 19 feet is our answer.

5) 15 inches
This time, the question is asking about the predicted values, not the actual recorded values. So we can ignore the points on the scatterplot altogether: all we care about is the line. We want to know about the shark whose length is 15 feet, which is the measurement on the x-axis. So this quiestion is really asking us this: what's the y-coordinate for the point on the line where $x = 15$?

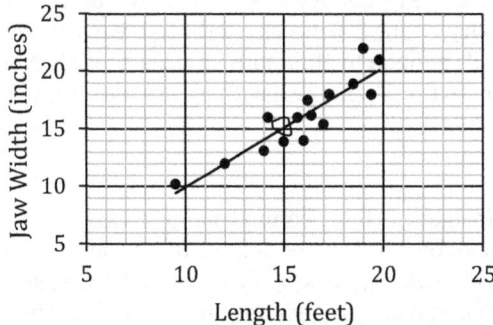

The line passes through the point (15, 15). This tells us that the line of best fit predicts that a shark whose length is 15 feet will have a jaw width of 15 inches, so 15 inches is our answer.

6) D
Check the choices one at a time. Since the x-axis represents the number of hours past 12 pm, the period

Answer Explanations

from 12 pm to 1:30 pm will be represented as the interval from $x = 0$ to $x = 1.5$. In that part of the graph, we have a line with a steady positive slope, which indicates that distance (the y-value) is steadily increasing over time. That means Ron is driving, so choice A is out.

Now we have a little more clarity on what we're looking for: during Ron's break, he shouldn't be driving, so the distance traveled should not change. Therefore, we're looking for a place on the graph where y doesn't change at all: that is, we'll see a flat horizontal line.

Choice B is the interval from $x = 1$ to $x = 2.5$. Since y has increased during at least part of that time, this is not the right answer.

Choice C is the interval from $x = 2$ to $x = 3.5$. Again, y has increased during at least part of that time, so this is not the right answer.

Choice D is the interval from $x = 3$ to $x = 4.5$. This time, y doesn't increase at all: we have a flat horizontal line for the entire interval. This is the right answer.

Data Interpretation: Practice Set 1 (p. 347)
1) 39.10
Break it down one package at a time. A package that weighs 0.5 pounds falls in the 0-1 lb range covered by the top row of the table: the fee is $12.50. A package that weighs 4.5 pounds falls in the 4.01-5 lb range covered by the last row of the table: the fee is $14.10. Since Sheldon ships two of the lighter packages and one of the heavier ones, his total fee is 2($12.50) + 1($14.10) = $39.10.

2) D
Each answer choice gives us a frequency table in which the left column contains the actual values, while the right column contains the corresponding frequency. For example, the first row of choice A says that for the number 2, the frequency is 4. In other words, this tells us that we have four 2's. But check the list: we have three 2's. That's enough to eliminate choices A and B. Now move on to the 3's. In the list, there are four 3's, so choice D must be right.

3) B
To begin, ignore all the context and just look at the graph. The line of best fit is a line sloping downwards, meaning as the value of x increases, the value of y decreases. Nothing is remaining constant, so we can eliminate choice C. And choices A and D are actually saying the same thing as each other: both are saying that x and y increase or decrease <u>together</u>. That relationship would be represented by a line that was sloping upwards, not downwards, so we can eliminate choices A and D. The only possible answer is B.

4) B
A dot plot is a way to visually present information about frequencies: the values are found along the x-axis, and the number of dots for a particular value tells you its frequency. For example, the dot plot for Data Set *A* has two dots for the 1, three dots for the 2, and so on; this tells us that Data Set *A* contains two 1's, three 2's, and so forth.

Let's evaluate the choices. The least value in data set *A* is 1, and the least value in data set *B* is 2. Since 1 is less than 2, we can eliminate choice A.

The greatest value in data set *A* is 5, and the greatest value in data set *B* is 6. Since 5 is less than 6, choice B is correct.

As for choices C and D, simply count the number of dots in each set to find the number of values in that set. In this case, the data sets show 12 dots each, so they both represent the same number of values.

5) B
This is a "part over whole" question, so the important thing is to be clear on exactly what is the "part" and exactly what is the "whole"—it won't necessarily be the overall total of the data. In this problem, we're asked for a fraction *of all the cups of tea sold*. So the bottom of the fraction is the total number of cups of tea sold: 109. The top of the fraction is the cups of tea sold that were size medium: that's 42. So 42/109 is the answer.

6) C
Don't be overwhelmed by all the data shown, most of which is irrelevant. Focus on the value in the question. How many new all-electric vehicles were sold in 2019? That's the dark bar for that year: about 220. Now move to the next part of the question: that 220 is supposed to be "approximately twice" something. So what number is approximately half of 220? That's easy: 110.

We're ready for the final part of the question, which is talking about plug-in hybrid cars. So the right answer should be the year in which the plug-in hybrid cars was about 110. The plug-in hybrids are represented by the gray bars. The year for which the gray bar is closest to 110 is 2018, so the answer is C.

7) 4
This question asks about the nine dates on which the crude oil price was within a specific range of values. That's a question about actual recorded values, so it's about the points on the scatterplot. Crude oil price is on the x-axis here, so find nine points where the x-values are between $75 and $100:

Problem Solving and Data Analysis

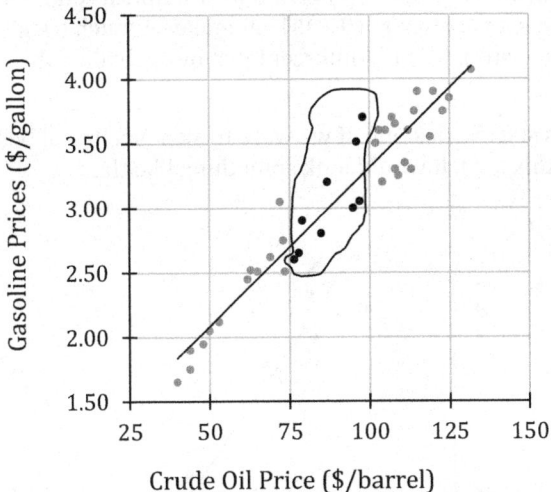

The *y*-axis of this graph represents gasoline price. So if a point is above the line, then the *actual* gasoline price is greater than the *predicted* gasoline price for that date. That's true for four of these points:

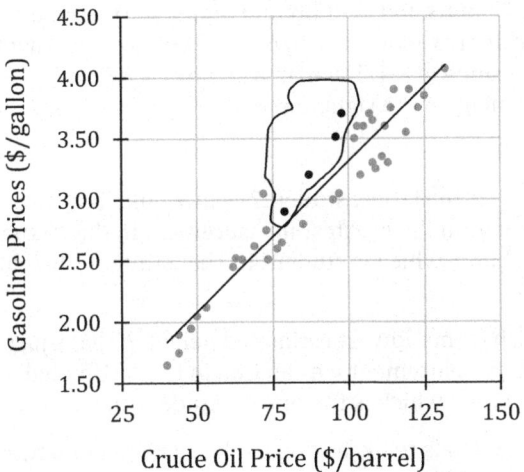

So the answer is 4.

Data Interpretation: Practice Set 2 (p. 349)
1) C
It's all the extraneous information that makes this problem more difficult than it would be otherwise. Ignore all the attractions on which Lupe took zero rides and add up the others. We need one ride on the Parachuter, two rides on the roller coasters, and two rides on the go-karts:

$$1(\$25) + 2(\$8) + 2(\$8) = \$57$$

That's what she actually spent. If she had bought the Fun Pass, she would have needed to pay $43.95; but she also would have needed to pay for the Parachuter, which isn't included in the Fun Pass price.

$$\$43.95 + \$25 = \$68.95$$

With the Fun Pass, then, she would have ended up paying $68.95 − $57.00 = $11.95 more than she actually did.

2) A
A line with a great average rate of change will look steep, while a line with a low average rate of change will look shallow. Even when the graph is not a line, the same general principle applies. From 1993 to 1996, the price hardly changed at all: it shows an increase of less than 50 cents. Compare that with the increases for all the other choices:

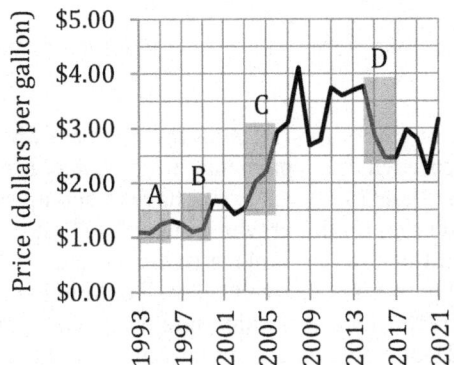

The answer is A.

3) D
This curve shows the minimum wage increasing over time. So if the trend continues, then the wage in 2010 would have to be greater than it was in 2000. That's enough to eliminate choices A and B.

To choose between choices C and D, consider the kind of increase we're seeing. This looks more like an exponential curve than a linear increase: the rate of increase is itself increasing.

Choice C gives us an increase, but a smaller increase than we saw from 1990 to 2000. That would flatten the curve, like this:

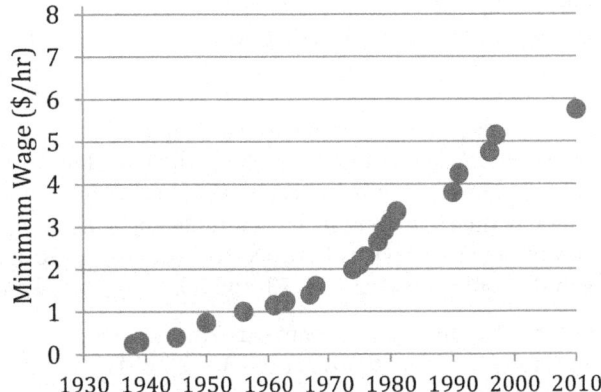

By contrast, choice D gives a bigger increase than we saw from 1990 to 2000, which is the most consistent with how this curve is working so far:

Answer Explanations

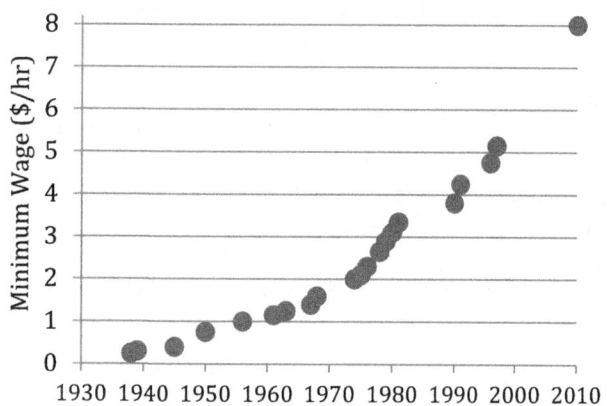

4) D
Each bar on this graph indicates the number of players whose score fell into a particular range. There is no bar for "fewer than 25 points," so we have to add up several bars to get that total. But which ones? The first two bars represent the number of players who earned 0-10 points or 11-20 points, respectively, so we'll definitely include those. The third bar is trickier: it tells us that 9 players earned 21-30 points each. But how many of those were under 25? We don't know—all we can do is establish a range of possibilities. If all 9 of these players earned 21 points, then we'd want to count them all. In that case, our answer would be the sums of the first three bars:

$$4 + 5 + 9 = 18$$

But if all 9 players in that middle bar earned 30 points, then we wouldn't want to count any of them. In that case, our answer would be just the sum of the first two bars:

$$4 + 5 = 9$$

It's also possible that only *some* of the 9 players in that middle bar scored under 25 points, while some didn't. In that case, our answer would be less than the 18 that we calculated first, but greater than the 9 that we calculated second. So, we've established a maximum and a minimum: the answer must be between 9 and 18, inclusive. The only answer in that range is D.

5) C
Read the stem and leaf plot one row at a time, constructing the list of data by applying the tens digit supplied by the left column to each of the ones digits supplied by the right column. For example, the ages represented in the top row here are 26, 26, and 27; the ages in the bottom row are 72, 73, and 73.

Therefore, the oldest participant was 73, and the youngest was 26. The difference is $73 - 26 = 47$.

6) A
This problem involves several classic SAT "gotcha" tricks for a scatterplot. First, the equations in the choices are written in a weird order, with the y-intercept first (instead of in regular $y = mx + b$ form). And second, the graph does not start at $(0, 0)$! That makes it much trickier for us to estimate the y-intercept just by eyeballing the graph.

So let's start with slope. If we were to sketch a line of best fit for this data, it would look something like this:

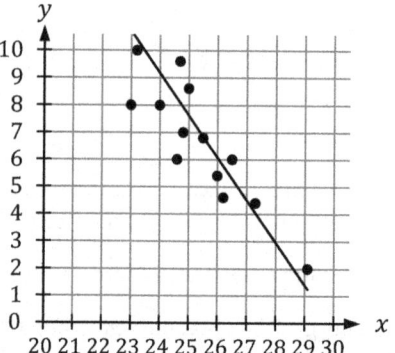

The line points downward, so it's a negative slope. Eliminate choices B and D. More specifically, the line goes up about 10 units and over about 6 units, so the slope should be approximately $-10/6 = -1.667$, which is a lot closer to a slope of -1.5 than to a slope of -3. That's enough to make A the right answer.

7) 9
First, which is the tallest student? That would have to be the student with the greatest measurement in the "actual height" column, which is student E. That student's height is 6 ft, 1 in.

Next, which is the "lowest estimated height"? That's just the lowest measurement we can find in the "estimated height" column, which is the one for student D: 5 ft, 4 in.

So this question is really asking us this: a height of 6 ft, 1 in is how much greater than a height of 5 ft, 4 in?

We'll need to subtract them to find out. But to make this simpler, convert both heights to inches first. 6 feet is $6(12) = 72$ inches, so the height of "6 ft, 1 in" is 73 inches.

5 feet is $5(12) = 60$ inches, so the height of "5 ft, 4 in" is 64 inches.

Now subtract: $73 - 64 = 9$ inches.

RATIOS, PROPORTIONS, AND UNIT CONVERSIONS (p. 351)
Ratios, Proportions, and Unit Conversions: Try It
1) $45.60

$$\frac{15}{28.50} = \frac{24}{x}$$

$$15x = 24(28.50)$$

Problem Solving and Data Analysis

$$x = \frac{24(28.50)}{15} = 45.60$$

2) 10.5 inches

$$\frac{4}{6} = \frac{7}{h}$$
$$4h = 7(6)$$
$$h = \frac{7(6)}{4} = 10.5$$

3) $287.28

$$\frac{3 \text{ tins}}{\Box} \times \frac{2 \text{ oz.}}{1 \text{ tin}} \times \frac{28 \text{ g}}{1 \text{ oz.}} \times \frac{\$1.71}{1 \text{ g}} = 3(2)(28)(\$1.71)$$
$$= \$287.28$$

4) 16:15

$$\frac{x}{y} = \frac{3}{4} \text{ and } \frac{x}{z} = \frac{4}{5}$$

We need a value for x that works in both fractions. The easiest value to use would be a multiple of both 3 and 4: $x = 12$.

$$\frac{x}{y} = \frac{3}{4} = \frac{12}{16}$$
$$\frac{x}{z} = \frac{4}{5} = \frac{12}{15}$$

If $x = 15$, then $y = 16$ and $z = 15$. The ratio of y to z is 16 to 15.

Ratios, Proportions, and Unit Conversions: Practice Set 1 (p. 357)

1) D
If 15 of the 32 emails were spam, we can conclude that $32 - 15 = 17$ were *not* spam. Therefore, the ratio of non-spam emails to spam emails is 17:15.

2) 18

$$\frac{\text{cookies}}{\text{brownies}} = \frac{3}{4}$$
$$\frac{c}{24} = \frac{3}{4}$$
$$c = \frac{3}{4}(24)$$
$$c = 18$$

3) 280

$$\frac{0.28 \text{ kg}}{\Box} \times \frac{1000 \text{ g}}{1 \text{ kg}} = 0.28(1000) \text{ g}$$
$$= 280 \text{ g}$$

4) C
Convert the mixed fraction 2½ to the decimal 2.5 to make this easier to set up.

$$\frac{x}{6} = \frac{50}{2.5}$$
$$x = \frac{50}{2.5}(6)$$
$$x = 120$$

5) D
We don't know the actual lengths of these line segments, but we do know the relationship of the lengths. So, plug in numbers, and make it simple by plugging in the exact numbers from the ratio. We'll say $\overline{FG}$ has a length of 2, and $\overline{GH}$ has a length of 5.

F • —2— • G —————5————— • H

In that case, the length of $\overline{FH}$ is $2 + 5 = 7$. So the ratio of the length of $\overline{GH}$ to the length of $\overline{FH}$ is 5 to 7.

6) C
Remember, a ratio is just a fraction. Calculate the value of each answer choice by dividing the "Yes" responses by the "No" responses for that county.

A) 25/92 = 0.27
B) 78/61 = 1.28
C) 45/18 = 2.5
D) 51/24 = 2.125

Choice C is the biggest, so it's the right answer.

7) A
Plug in numbers. If there are 100 books at the bookstore, then $0.30(100) = 30$ of them are on sale. Thus, the ratio of books on sale to total books is $30/100 = 3/10$.

8) D

$$\frac{180 \text{ mi}}{\Box} \times \frac{1 \text{ hr}}{45 \text{ mi}} \times \frac{60 \text{ min}}{1 \text{ hr}} = \frac{180(60)}{45} \text{ min}$$
$$= 240 \text{ min}$$

9) B
Of the 540 students in the dining hall, 36 requested a vegetarian meal, meaning that $540 - 36 = 504$ students did not. If the study group is a representative sample, then approximately the same fraction of the whole should be non-vegetarian meal requesters. Therefore:

$$\frac{x}{15} = \frac{504}{540}$$
$$x = \frac{504}{540}(15)$$
$$x = 14$$

10) 9
The friends share the sub in the ratio 1:2:3. This means that for every 6 inches of sub, 1 inch will go to the first friend, 2 inches will go to the second friend, and 3 inches

Answer Explanations

will go to the third friend (for a total of $1 + 2 + 3 = 6$ inches). Thus, out of every 6 inches of sub, the friend with the largest share will get 3 inches: in other words, the ratio of the third friend's portion to the whole is 3 to 6. So:

$$\frac{x}{18} = \frac{3}{6}$$

$$x = \frac{3}{6}(18)$$

$$x = 9$$

11) 6

First, write out the ratios:

$$\frac{a}{t} = \frac{2}{5}$$

$$\frac{t}{m} = \frac{5}{8}$$

The tulips are what the two equations have in common, and they're already the same number in both! If there are 5 tulips, then there are 2 azaleas and 8 marigolds. Thus, the ratio of azaleas to marigolds is 2 to 8. Therefore:

$$\frac{a}{24} = \frac{2}{8}$$

$$a = \frac{2}{8}(24)$$

$$a = 6$$

12) B

Plug in numbers. Let's say Cirrus Tech has 60 employees. Then $(3/5)(60) = 36$ employees are part-time, and $(3/4)(36) = 27$ of the part-time employees work fewer than twenty hours per week. In that case, the fraction who work fewer than twenty hours per week would be $27/60 = 9/20$.

13) C

When the SAT uses underlining or italics to emphasize something in the problem, they are actually trying to help you: they're drawing your attention to the fact that something has changed. Here, the issue is that the units are different in one part of the problem than they were in the other. The length of the rectangle is 3 feet, but the ratio we know uses the length of the rectangle in <u>inches</u>. So, convert the length first:

$$\text{length} = 3 \text{ feet} = 3(12) = 36 \text{ inches}$$

Now we can apply the given ratio.

$$\frac{\text{length in inches}}{\text{width in feet}} = \frac{18}{1}$$

$$\frac{36}{w} = \frac{18}{1}$$

$$36 = 18w$$

$$w = \frac{36}{18} = 2$$

Ratios, Proportions, and Unit Conversions: Practice Set 2 (p. 359)

1) 0.6 or 6/10 (or equivalent fraction)

$$\frac{x}{6} = \frac{y}{10}$$

$$10x = 6y$$

$$x = \frac{6y}{10}$$

Multiply both sides by $1/y$:

$$\frac{x}{y} = \frac{6}{10}$$

The answer is 6/10, which can be simplified to 3/5 (but doesn't have to be). The decimal 0.6 would also be accepted as correct.

Alternatively, you can solve this problem by plugging in a value for one of the variables. Let's say $y = 5$:

$$\frac{x}{6} = \frac{5}{10}$$

$$x = \frac{5}{10}(6)$$

$$x = 3$$

So if $y = 5$, then $x = 3$. Therefore, the value of x/y is 3/5, which is 0.6.

2) B

With this ratio, the smallest number of marbles we could have is eight: after all, 1 red marble plus 3 green marbles plus 4 blue marbles = 8 total marbles. The next smallest total would be 16, which we'd get by doubling all those values. This tells you that the only possible totals for this problem would be multiples of 8. The only multiple of 8 in the answer choices is 24, so B must be our answer.

3) D

This problem is trying to trip you up by giving you more information than you actually need. Did you spot what was irrelevant? It was the milk. All we need to know is the ratio of hot chocolate mix to number of people, which is 14 to 6:

$$\frac{x}{21} = \frac{14}{6}$$

$$x = \frac{14}{6}(21) = 49$$

4) C

Plug in values, starting with the variable that the two equations have in common: y. Let's say $y = 6$:

- 548 -

TM and © 2023 PrepMatters, Inc. All rights reserved.

$$2x = 3(6)$$
$$x = 18/2 = 9$$
$$2(6) = 3z$$
$$z = 12/3 = 4$$

So if $y = 6$, then $x = 9$ and $z = 4$. The ratio of x to z is 9 to 4.

5) D

$$\frac{343 \text{ m}}{1 \text{ sec}} \times \frac{0.001 \text{ km}}{1 \text{ m}} \times \frac{0.62 \text{ mi}}{1 \text{ km}} \times \frac{60 \text{ sec}}{1 \text{ min}} \times \frac{60 \text{ min}}{1 \text{ hr}}$$

$$= \frac{343(0.001)(0.62)(60)(60) \text{ mi}}{1 \text{ hr}}$$

$$= \frac{765.576 \text{ mi}}{1 \text{ hr}}$$

6) 1000

The ratio of the largest share to the total is

$$\frac{6}{4+5+6} = \frac{6}{15}$$

How much does the partner with the largest share make?

$$\frac{6}{15} = \frac{x}{7500}$$

$$x = \frac{6}{15}(7500) = 3000 \text{ dollars}$$

The ratio of the *smallest* share to the total is

$$\frac{4}{4+5+6} = \frac{4}{15}$$

So the partner with the smallest share makes $\frac{4}{15}(7500) = 2000$ dollars. The difference is

$3000 - 2000 = 1000$ dollars.

7) B

Plug in values.

Old:
$$\text{sugar} = 5 \text{ cups}$$
$$\text{flour} = 2 \text{ cups}$$

New:
$$\text{sugar} = 5 - 0.3(5) = 3.5 \text{ cups}$$
$$\text{flour} = 2 + 0.25(2) = 2.5 \text{ cups}$$
$$\text{ratio} = \frac{3.5}{2.5} = \frac{7}{5}$$

8) 18.5 or 37/2

The original solution has 1.5 cups of salt and 5 cups of water, for a total of 6.5 cups of solution. The fraction of the original solution that is water is 5/6.5. If we add x cups of water, the amount of water in the solution becomes $5 + x$, and the total amount of solution becomes $6.5 + x$. We need the fraction that is water to be 94%, which is 94/100. So:

$$\frac{5+x}{6.5+x} = \frac{94}{100}$$

$$100(5+x) = 94(6.5+x)$$
$$500 + 100x = 611 + 94x$$
$$500 + 6x = 611$$
$$6x = 111$$
$$x = 18.5$$

9) D

The ratio of savings to spendings is 4 to 1. But that means that the ratio of savings to *total* is 4 to 5.

$$\frac{x}{60{,}000} = \frac{4}{5}$$

$$x = \frac{4}{5}(60{,}000)$$

$$x = 48{,}000$$

Alternatively, you could back-solve this problem. Start with choice B. If he saves $24,000 and he saves 4 times as much as he spends, then he spends $24,000/4 = $6000. But $24,000 + $6,000 = $30,000. We need the total to be $48,000, so this is not enough. Eliminate choice B and choice A (which is even smaller) and try another choice. The only one that works is D.

10) B

$$\frac{11{,}186 \text{ m}}{1 \text{ sec}} \times \frac{1 \text{ km}}{1000 \text{ m}} \times \frac{1 \text{ mi}}{1.609 \text{ km}} \times \frac{60 \text{ sec}}{1 \text{ min}} \times \frac{60 \text{ min}}{1 \text{ hr}}$$

$$= \frac{11{,}186(60)(60) \text{ mi}}{1000(1.609) \text{ hr}}$$

$$= \frac{25{,}027.72 \text{ mi}}{1 \text{ hr}}$$

11) C

Draw the rectangle. We don't know the length and width, but we know their ratio is 3:5. So, label the dimensions $3x$ and $5x$.

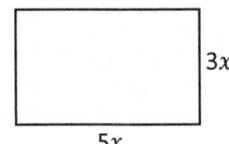

The area is 135:

$$(3x)(5x) = 135$$
$$15x^2 = 135$$
$$x^2 = 9$$
$$x = 3$$

From here, we can get the actual dimensions:

$$\text{length} = 3x = 3(3) = 9$$
$$\text{width} = 5x = 5(3) = 15$$

Therefore, the perimeter is

Answer Explanations

$$p = 2(9) + 2(15) = 48$$

12) A
Plug in numbers, starting with the non-fiction books since that's what the two given relationships have in common. Let's say there are 5 non-fiction books. There are 3 times as many fiction as non-fiction, so that gives us 15 fiction books. And if 1/5 of the 5 non-fiction books are biographies, then there is 1 biography. The ratio of fiction books to biographies is therefore 15 to 1.

13) D
There are 4916 visitors in the specified age group, out of 16,403 total visitors. That ratio of part to whole should also apply to the pie chart, where the "part" is the degree measure for the corresponding sector, and the "whole" is the full 360° of the circle.

$$\frac{x}{360} = \frac{4916}{16,403}$$
$$x = \frac{4916}{16,403}(360°)$$
$$x = 107.9°$$

PERCENTAGES (p. 361)
Percentages: Try It
1) 9
$$x = 0.18(50)$$
$$x = 9$$

To solve this problem using the built-in calculator, type in 18%, and the calculator will automatically supply the word "of." Then type in the 50.

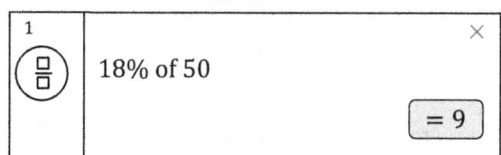

2) 12.5%
$$10 = (x/100)(80)$$
$$10 = 0.8x$$
$$x = 10/0.8 = 12.5$$

3) 75
$$30 = 0.40(x)$$
$$x = 30/0.40 = 75$$

4) 60
$$50 + 0.20(50) = x$$
$$50 + 10 = x$$
$$60 = x$$

5) 40
$$x - 0.15(x) = 34$$
$$1x - 0.15x = 34$$

$$0.85x = 34$$
$$x = 34/0.85 = 40$$

6) 12.5%
$$800 + (x/100)(800) = 900$$
$$8x = 100$$
$$x = 100/8 = 12.5$$

Percentages: Practice Set 1 (p. 365)
1) 4.5
Translate word-for-word: use x for the "what," followed by an equals sign for the "is," followed by $30/100 = 0.3$ for the "30%," followed by multiplication for the "of," followed by 15.

$$x = 0.3(15)$$
$$x = 4.5$$

To solve this problem using the built-in calculator, type in 30%, and the calculator will automatically supply the word "of." Then type in the 15.

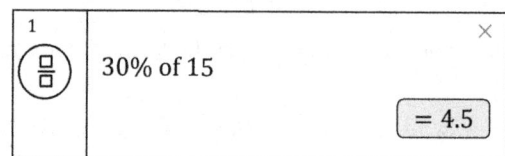

2) A
Translate word-for-word: use x for the "what," followed by an equals sign for the "is," followed by $0.4/100 = 0.004$ for the "0.4%," followed by multiplication for the "of," followed by 800.

$$x = 0.004(800)$$
$$x = 3.2$$

Be sure to translate carefully! If you got answer B, you found 4% of 800, not 0.4%.

To solve this problem using the built-in calculator, type in 0.4%, and the calculator will automatically supply the word "of." Then type in the 800.

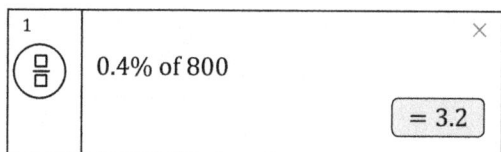

3) C
Translate word-for-word: use 15 for the "fifteen," followed by an equals sign for the "is," followed by $x/100$ for the "what percent," followed by multiplication for the "of," followed by 20.

$$15 = (x/100)(20)$$
$$15 = 0.2x$$
$$x = 15/0.2 = 75$$

Alternatively, you could back-solve this problem using the built-in calculator. For example, here's choice B:

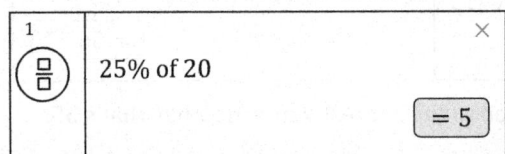

That's too small: we need it to equal 15. So, eliminate choice B as well as choice A (which is even smaller) and try choice C.

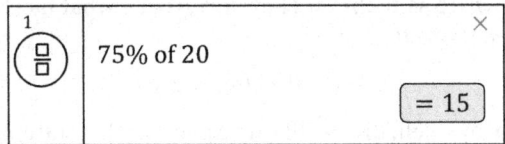

4) 60
Translate word-for-word: use $40/100 = 0.4$ for the "forty percent," followed by multiplication for the "of," followed by an x for the "what number," followed by an equals sign for the "is," followed by 24.

$$0.4x = 24$$
$$x = 24/0.4 = 60$$

5) A
Translate word-for-word: use $150/100 = 1.5$ for the "150%," followed by multiplication for the "of," followed by x, followed by an equals sign for the "is," followed by 24.

$$1.5x = 24$$
$$x = 24/1.5 = 16$$

Alternatively, you could back-solve this problem using the built-in calculator. For example, here's choice B:

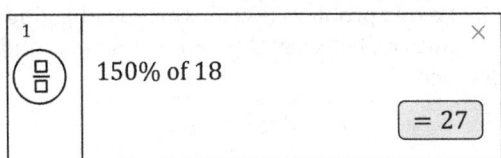

That's too big: we need it to equal 24. So, we can eliminate choice B as well as choices C and D (which are even bigger). The answer must be A.

6) B
Use the Original & Final formula:

$$\text{Original} \pm \text{Percent}(\text{Original}) = \text{Final}$$

Remember, the "original" is the value after the word "than."

$$40 + 0.3(40) = x$$
$$40 + 12 = x$$
$$52 = x$$

7) C
Use the Original & Final formula:

$$\text{Original} \pm \text{Percent}(\text{Original}) = \text{Final}$$
$$60 - 0.44(60) = x$$
$$60 - 26.4 = x$$
$$33.6 = x$$

8) C
Translate word-for-word: use 36 for the "$36.00," followed by an equals sign for the "is," followed by $120/100 = 1.2$ for the "120%," followed by multiplication for the "of," followed by x for the "what price."

$$36 = 1.2x$$
$$x = 36/1.2 = 30$$

9) A
Use the Original & Final formula:

$$\text{Original} \pm \text{Percent}(\text{Original}) = \text{Final}$$
$$20 - \frac{x}{100}(20) = 15$$
$$20 - 0.2x = 15$$
$$-0.2x = -5$$
$$x = -5/-0.2 = 25$$

10) C
Use the Original & Final formula:

$$\text{Original} \pm \text{Percent}(\text{Original}) = \text{Final}$$
$$15 + \frac{x}{100}(15) = 20$$
$$15 + 0.15x = 20$$
$$0.15x = 5$$
$$x = 5/0.15 = 33.\overline{33}$$

11) B
Use the Original & Final formula:

$$\text{Original} \pm \text{Percent}(\text{Original}) = \text{Final}$$

In this problem, $36 is the price after the discount, so it's the final. Use x for our unknown value, the original.

$$x - 0.25(x) = 36$$
$$1x - 0.25x = 36$$
$$0.75x = 36$$
$$x = 36/0.75 = 48$$

Alternatively, you can back-solve this problem. Start with choice B: if $48 is the price before the discount, then the price after the discount would be $48 - 0.25(48) = 36$ dollars. That's what we wanted it to be, so B is the right answer.

12) B
Use the Original & Final formula:

$$\text{Original} \pm \text{Percent}(\text{Original}) = \text{Final}$$

Answer Explanations

Remember, the Original is the value after the word "than." In this problem, 14 is the other number, the final. Use x for the original.

$$x - 0.3(x) = 14$$
$$1x - 0.3x = 14$$
$$0.7x = 14$$
$$x = 14/0.7 = 20$$

Alternatively, you can back-solve this problem. Start with choice B: 30% less than 20 is $20 - 0.3(20) = 14$. That's what we wanted it to be, so B is the right answer.

13) D

Translate the first half of the problem word-for-word: use $70/100 = 0.7$ for the "70%," followed by multiplication for the "of," followed by x, followed by an equals sign for the "is," followed by 42.

$$0.7x = 42$$
$$x = 42/0.7 = 60$$

Now that we know that $x = 60$, the second half of the problem is really just asking us this: "What is 30% of 60?" Translate that word-for-word, using a new variable for the unknown since x already represents something else. So, let's use y for the "what," followed by an equals sign for the

"is," followed by $30/100 = 0.3$ for the "30%," followed by multiplication for the "of," followed by 60.

$$y = 0.3(60)$$
$$y = 18$$

14) 80

Percent is part over whole. Here, the "part" is the number of problems answered correctly, which is $60 - 12 = 48$. The "whole" is the 60 problems. So:

$$\frac{48}{60} = \frac{p}{100}$$

$$4800 = 60p$$

$$p = 4800/60 = 80$$

Note: because of the way the question was set up, the correct answer is **80**, <u>not</u> 0.80. After all, the student didn't answer 0.8% of the problems correctly.

15) B

This is a good problem for back-solving using the built-in calculator. Here's choice C:

That rounds to 56, so this is too big. Eliminate choice C and choice D (which is even bigger). Let's try choice B:

Rounded to the nearest whole number, that's 55.

Alternatively, we could solve this with algebra by using an inequality. If we want the result to round to 55, then it must be greater than or equal to 54.5, and it must be less than 55.5. And the result is defined as 25% of x, which we can write as $0.25(x)$. Therefore, that's what has to be between those two values:

$$54.5 \leq 0.25(x) < 55.5$$

To get x by itself, divide all three parts of this statement by 0.25.

$$\frac{54.5}{0.25} \leq \frac{0.25(x)}{0.25} < \frac{55.5}{0.25}$$

$$218 \leq x < 222$$

Therefore, x must be greater than or equal to 218, and it must be less than 222. The only answer choice that satisfies both those conditions is B.

16) B

Percent is part over whole. The "whole" here is all the responses recorded for the first two questions, which is $160 + 160 = 320$. The "part" is the answers for the first two questions that were C. That's $125 + 9 = 134$. So:

$$x = 134/320 = 0.41875$$

That translates to 41.875%, which is closest to choice B.

17) B

We can make this problem less abstract by plugging in our own numbers. Let's say the radius is 3. Now find the circumference:

$$C = 2\pi(3) = 6\pi$$

The question is this: the radius is what percent of the circumference? Now that we have values for the radius and the circumference, we can translate word-for-word. Use 3 for "the radius," followed by an equals sign for the "is," followed by $x/100$ for the "what percent," followed by multiplication for the "of," followed by 6π for "the circumference."

$$3 = (x/100)(6\pi)$$
$$300 = x(6\pi)$$
$$x = 300/(6\pi)$$
$$x \approx 15.91549$$

That's closest to 15.9%, so the answer is B.

Alternatively, we can solve this problem algebraically without plugging in numbers. Here's that word-for-word translation again:

$$r = (x/100)(2\pi r)$$
$$100r = x(2\pi r)$$
$$x = \frac{100r}{2\pi r}$$

At this point, the r's cancel out, leaving us with $x = 100/(2\pi) \approx 15.91549$.

18) C
This is a good back-solving problem. Start with choice B. What is 20% more than 120?

$$120 + 0.20(120) = 144$$

Not quite enough. Eliminate choice B as well as choice A (which is even smaller). Let's try choice C. What is 20% more than 125?

$$125 + 0.20(125) = 150$$

Exactly what we needed, so C is the answer.

Alternatively, we solve this problem algebraically using the Original & Final formula. Just remember that the "original" is always the value after the word "than." The problem told us that Leslie currently has 20% more books than she had last week, meaning that last week's amount (our unknown value) is the Original here. So:

$$x + 0.20(x) = 150$$
$$1x + 0.2x = 150$$
$$1.2x = 150$$
$$x = 150/1.2 = 125$$

If you got choice B, you accidentally used the 150 books as the "original" instead of the final. The problem is, this question wasn't asking, "What number is 20% less than 150?" Instead, it was asking, "150 is 20% more than what number?" These two questions are not the same thing! They don't come out the same because what we're taking a percentage of is different.

Percentages: Practice Set 2 (p. 367)
1) 24
Take this multi-step problem one piece at a time. First, how many of Mike's red shirts are striped?

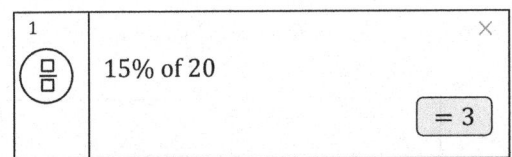

Next, how many of his black shirts are striped?

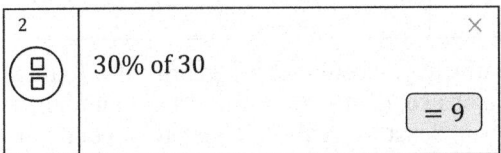

Altogether, then, Mike has $3 + 9 = 12$ striped shirts. And he has $20 + 30 = 50$ shirts total. Percent is part over whole, so divide 12 by 50:

$$\frac{12}{50} = 0.24 = 24\%$$

The question said that $p\%$ of Mike's shirts are striped. We now know that 24% of Mike's shirts are striped, so $p = 24$.

2) A
Again, taking this one piece at a time is the key. First, focus on Daniel's hourly wage. He earns $3 an hour, so how much does he earn in 6 hours?

$$\text{hourly wages} = \$3(6) = \$18$$

If he's earned a total of $45, that means he must have earned $45 - \$18 = \$27$ in tips. That $27 must equal 15% of the value of all the food he sold. So if he sold $x worth of food, we can say this:

$$27 = 0.15(x)$$
$$x = 27/0.15 = 180$$

3) B
The selling price, $102.87, was 35% greater than the wholesale price. Use the Original & Final formula, where the Original (always the value after the word "than") is the wholesale price:

$$x + 0.35(x) = 102.87$$
$$1x + 0.35x = 102.87$$
$$1.35x = 102.87$$
$$x = 102.87/1.35 = 76.2$$

Therefore, the wholesale price was $76.20.

Alternatively, you could back-solve this problem. Start with choice B. What amount is 35% greater than $76.20?

$$76.20 + 0.35(76.20) = 102.87$$

$102.87 is exactly what we needed, so B must be the right answer.

4) 153.6
This one is all about carefully translating word-for-word. Use x for the "what," followed by an equals sign for the "is," followed by $0.06/100 = 0.0006$ for the "0.06%," followed by multiplication for the "of," followed by 4/5, followed by multiplication for the "of," followed by $3.2 \times 10^5 = 320{,}000$.

$$x = 0.0006\left(\frac{4}{5}\right)(320{,}000)$$
$$x = 153.6$$

Remember, percent always means divide by 100! If your answer was 15360, you accidentally used 0.06 (which is 6%) instead of 0.0006 (which is 0.06%).

Answer Explanations

5) C

Let's say Ezekiel received $$x$ for his birthday and that he handed $$y$ to the cashier. The amount he handed to the cashier was 60% of what he received for his birthday, so:

$$y = 0.60x$$

We also know that the amount he received in change, $1.80, was 6% of the amount he handed to the cashier. So:

$$1.80 = 0.06y$$

Plug the first equation into the second one:

$$1.80 = 0.06(0.60x)$$
$$1.8 = 0.036x$$
$$x = 1.8/0.036 = 50$$

Alternatively, you can back-solve this problem. Start with choice B. If Ezekiel received $40 for his birthday, then the amount he handed to the cashier was $0.6(\$40) = \$24$. The change he received should be 6% of that amount, but $0.06(\$24) = \$1.44$, not $1.80, so this isn't enough. Eliminate choice B and choice A (which is even smaller) and try choice C. If he received $50 for his birthday, then the amount he handed to the cashier would be $0.6(\$50) = \$30$, and 6% of $30 is $0.06(\$30) = \$1.80$. Choice C is the right answer.

6) C

Start with choice B: if the original price was $238, then the discounted price was $\$238 - 0.4(\$238) = \$142.80$, and the price after the sales tax was applied was $\$142.80 + 0.05(\$142.80) = \$149.94$. This is less than the $176.40 we're looking for, so choice B is too small. Choice A, which is even smaller, is out as well.

Now move on to choice C. If the original price was $280, then the discounted price was $\$280 - 0.4(\$280) = \$168$, and the price after the sales tax was applied was $\$168 + 0.05(\$168) = \$176.40$. Choice C is the right answer.

To solve this algebraically, let's say x is the original price. Use the Original & Final formula to write out the discounted price:

$$\text{discounted price} = x - 0.4x$$
$$\text{discounted price} = 0.6x$$

Now we need to find 5% more than $0.6x$. So, use the Original & Final formula again, this time with $0.6x$ as the Original:

$$\text{post-tax price} = 0.6x + 0.05(0.6x)$$
$$\text{post-tax price} = 0.63x$$

Therefore:

$$176.40 = 0.63x$$
$$x = 176.40/0.63 = 280$$

7) C

Take this one step at a time. On Monday, the store received b bushels. The amount they sold on Monday was 20% of that value, so $0.2b$. Once they sold those, the number of bushels remaining was $b - 0.2b = 0.8b$. On Tuesday, they sold 20% of those remaining bushels, which would be $0.2(0.8b)$. That's choice C.

Alternatively, we could plug in our own numbers. Let's say the store originally received a delivery of 100 bushels of apples. Write that down somewhere:

$$b = 100$$

If the store sold 20% of those 100 bushels on Monday, then they sold 20 bushels on Monday. At that point, they have $100 - 20 = 80$ bushels remaining. Then they sold 20% of those 80 bushels on Tuesday: that's $0.2(80) = 16$ bushels. So, if $b = 100$, then our final answer should equal 16. Now try the answers. Choice A comes out to $0.2(100) = 20$ bushels: not a match. Choice B is $0.2(0.2(100)) = 4$ bushels: not a match. Choice C is $0.2(0.8(100)) = 16$ bushels. That works! Just to make sure, try choice D: that's $100 - 0.2(100) = 80$ bushels, which is not a match. Choice C is the right answer.

MEAN, MEDIAN, AND MODE (p. 368)
Mean, Median, and Mode: Try It

1) 83

To solve this problem in the built-in calculator, use the command `mean()`.

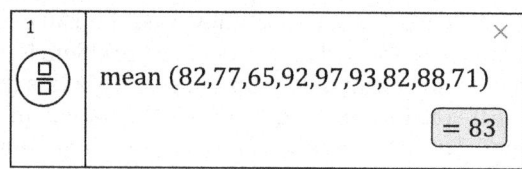

Alternatively, you could solve algebraically. The average of a set of numbers is the sum of the numbers divided by the number of numbers in the set. We have nine numbers in this set: 82, 77, 65, 92, 97, 93, 82, 88, and 71. The sum of these numbers is 747. We then divide this sum, 747, by the number of terms, 9, to get $747/9 = 83$.

2) 82

To solve this problem in the built-in calculator, use the command `median()`.

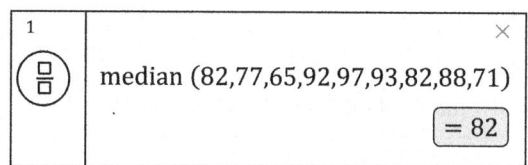

Alternatively, you could solve algebraically. To find the median of a set of numbers, first list the numbers in order from least to greatest. If we have an odd number of terms, the median is the term in the middle; if we have an even number of terms, the median is the average of the two middle terms. When we reorder the given numbers, we get 65, 71, 77, 82, 82, 88, 92, 93, and 97. Since we have nine terms (an odd number), the median is the term in the middle:

$$65, 71, 77, 82, 82, 88, 92, 93, 97$$

The median is 82.

3) 82
The mode is the most frequently appearing term in a set of data. In the given set, the number 82 appears twice; all the other numbers only appear once. Therefore, the mode of the set is 82.

4) 32
The range of a set of data is the result we get when we subtract the smallest term from the largest term. In our set, the smallest term is 65 and the largest term is 97. Therefore, the range is $97 - 65 = 32$.

5) $38,500
Start with the formula:

$$\text{mean} = \frac{\text{sum}}{\#}$$

The first sentence of the problem tells us that for the last ten weddings, the average was $25,000. So, we know the mean (25000) and the number of things (10). Plug those into the equation:

$$25,000 = \frac{\text{sum}}{10}$$
$$\text{sum} = 25,000(10)$$
$$\text{sum} = 250,000$$

So the sum of the first ten weddings' budgets was $250,000. Now move to the second sentence of the problem, which gives us a new mean (23,500) and a new # of things (9). Set up the equation again with our new information:

$$23,500 = \frac{\text{sum}}{9}$$
$$\text{sum} = 23,500(9)$$
$$\text{sum} = 211,500$$

This tells us that the sum of these 9 weddings' budgets was $211,500. Since we already know that the sum of all 10 weddings' budgets was $250,000, we can find the budget for the excluded wedding by subtracting:

$$250,000 - 211,500 = 38,500$$

The budget for the excluded wedding was $38,500.

6) 2.12
Start by writing out the equation for mean:

$$\text{mean} = \frac{\text{sum}}{\#}$$

For this problem, that means we need to find the sum of all the TVs owned by these families, and then divide that by the number of families. Let's deal with the sum first. Use the table to multiply each number of TVs by its frequency; then add up the results.

$$0(5) + 1(11) + 2(15) + 3(12) + 4(6) + 5(1)$$
$$= 0 + 11 + 30 + 36 + 24 + 5$$
$$= 106$$

So the sum of all the TVs represented in the table is 106. Next, we need to know how many families there are. Look above the table, and you'll find the problem already told us: there are fifty families. But if you didn't notice that, we can also calculate it from the table by adding up the frequencies:

$$5 + 11 + 15 + 12 + 6 + 1 = 50$$

Now we know that the sum of all the TVs is 106, and the total number of families is 50. The average number of TVs per family, therefore, is $106/50 = 2.12$.

7) 2
There are 50 families, so the median is the average of the 25th term and the 26th term. Check the frequencies in the table. The first row contains 5 terms, so we haven't gotten to the 25th term yet. The first and second rows combined contain $5 + 11 = 16$ terms: still not enough. But if we add in the third row, we get $5 + 11 + 15 = 31$ terms. That means both the 25th and the 26th term must be in that third row: that is, they're both 2's. Therefore, the median of the set is 2.

8) Set E
The mean of set E is $(2 + 9 + 10)/3 = 7$, while the mean of set F is $(10 + 11 + 12)/3 = 11$. Notice set F is quite closely grouped around its mean: none of its terms is more than 1 away from its mean. That's not the case with set E. In fact, all the terms in set E are 2 or more away from its mean. Therefore, set E has the greater standard deviation.

Mean, Median, and Mode: Practice Set 1 (p. 374)
1) B
To solve this problem in the built-in calculator, use the command `mean()`.

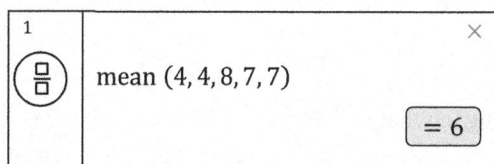

If you'd prefer to solve algebraically, start by writing out the equation for mean:

$$\text{mean} = \frac{\text{sum}}{\#}$$

Now plug in what we know:

Answer Explanations

$$\text{mean} = \frac{4+4+8+7+7}{5} = 6$$

2) A

To solve this problem in the built-in calculator, use the commands `mean()` and `median()`.

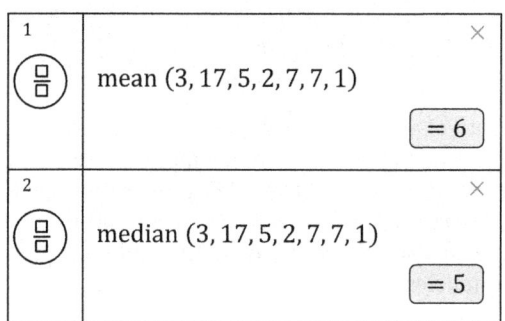

The positive difference is $6 - 5 = 1$.

If you'd prefer to solve algebraically, first re-write the list so that it's in order from least to greatest:

$$1, 2, 3, 5, 7, 7, 17$$

There are 7 numbers on the list. So to find the mean, add up the numbers and divide by 7.

$$\text{mean} = \frac{\text{sum}}{\#}$$

$$\text{mean} = \frac{1+2+3+5+7+7+17}{5}$$

$$\text{mean} = 42/7 = 6$$

Because our list has an odd number of terms, the median will be the single number in the middle. Cross out the numbers from both ends of the list until one value remains.

$$\cancel{1}, \cancel{2}, \cancel{3}, 5, \cancel{7}, \cancel{7}, \cancel{17}$$

The median is 5.

The problem asked for the positive difference between the mean (6) and the median (5). So, subtract those values:

$$6 - 5 = 1$$

3) 460

Start by writing out the equation for mean:

$$\text{mean} = \frac{\text{sum}}{\#}$$

Now plug in what we know:

$$92 = \frac{\text{sum}}{5}$$

$$92(5) = \text{sum}$$

$$460 = \text{sum}$$

4) B

Start by writing out the equation for mean:

$$\text{mean} = \frac{\text{sum}}{\#}$$

Now plug in what we know from the first sentence of the problem:

$$8.6 = \frac{\text{sum}}{10}$$

$$8.6(10) = \text{sum}$$

$$86 = \text{sum}$$

This tells us that the sum of the ten infants' ages is 86 months. Now, set up the equation again for the information in the second sentence:

$$9 = \frac{\text{sum}}{9}$$

$$9(9) = \text{sum}$$

$$81 = \text{sum}$$

This tells us that after infant A is removed, the sum of the remaining 9 infants' ages is 81 months. Therefore, to find infant A's age, we just subtract:

$$86 - 81 = 5$$

5) 16.75

Start by writing out the equation for mean:

$$\text{mean} = \frac{\text{sum}}{\#}$$

For this problem, that means we need to find the sum of all ages on the men's team, and then divide that by the number of people on the team. Let's deal with the sum first. Use the table to multiply each age by its frequency; then add up the results.

$$\text{sum} = 15(4) + 16(4) + 17(10) + 18(6)$$
$$\text{sum} = 60 + 64 + 170 + 108 = 402$$

So the sum of the ages of all the swimmers on the men's team is 402. Next, we need to know how many swimmers there are on the men's team. We can calculate that from the table by adding up the frequencies:

$$4 + 4 + 10 + 6 = 24$$

Now we know that the sum of the ages of all the swimmers on the men's team is 402, and the total number of swimmers is 24. The average age of the swimmers on the team is therefore $402/24 = 16.75$.

6) C

First, re-write the list in order from least to greatest:

$$6, 7, 8, 8, 9, 10, 11$$

Now write out the list as it would appear if we replaced the 10 and 11 with 9 and 9:

$$6, 7, 8, 8, 9, 9, 9$$

The question is this: out of mean, median, mode, and range, what has increased? Well, the sum of the list has decreased, which means the mean must have also decreased. Eliminate choice A.

As for the median, it hasn't changed at all! It was 8 in the first list and it's 8 in this one. Eliminate choice B.

The range of the original list was $11 - 6 = 5$, while the range of the new list is $9 - 6 = 3$. The range has decreased, so we can eliminate choice D.

That leaves choice C. In the original list, the mode was 8, because it was the only value that appeared more than once. But in the new list, 9 repeats more than once as well; in fact, there are more 9's than 8's. Therefore, the mode has increased from 8 to 9. Choice C is the answer.

7) B
Start by writing out the equation for mean:
$$\text{mean} = \frac{\text{sum}}{\#}$$
Now plug in what we know.
$$12 = \frac{(x + x + 1 + 2x - 5)}{3}$$
Let's solve for x. Start by multiplying both sides by 3:
$$12(3) = x + x + 1 + 2x - 5$$
Now combine like terms.
$$36 = 4x - 4$$
Add 4 to both sides:
$$40 = 4x$$
And finally, divide by 4:
$$10 = x$$
But be careful: 10 is not the answer! It's just the value of x. Now that we know that $x = 10$, we can rewrite our list of numbers:
$$x = 10$$
$$x + 1 = 11$$
$$2x - 5 = 15$$
So the list of numbers is 10, 11, 15. The median, or middle number, is 11.

Mean, Median, and Mode: Practice Set 2 (p. 375)
1) D
Let's say Ben is b years old. If Roger is three years younger than Ben, his age is $b - 3$. Howard, the eldest sibling, is 15.

The range of the ages is 5. Therefore, the greatest age (which is Howard's age, 15) minus the least age (which is Roger's age, $b - 3$) must be 5:
$$15 - (b - 3) = 5$$

$$15 - b + 3 = 5$$
$$18 - b = 5$$
$$-b = -13$$
$$b = 13$$

2) 5
Start by writing out the equation for mean:
$$\text{mean} = \frac{\text{sum}}{\#}$$
Now plug in what we know from the "if" clause:
$$0.6 = \frac{\text{sum}}{10}$$
$$0.6(10) = \text{sum}$$
$$6 = \text{sum}$$
So Maya scored a total of 6 goals in the first ten games. Now set up the equation again for the rest of the information in the problem:
$$1 = \frac{\text{sum}}{11}$$
$$1(11) = \text{sum}$$
$$11 = \text{sum}$$
This tells us that in order to achieve the average of 1 goal per game, Maya must score a total of 11 goals this season. She has only scored 6 goals so far, so the number of goals she would need to score in her final game is $11 - 6 = 5$.

3) B
The median, a, is the middle number of miles walked. Based on the table, there were ten 1-mile distances, thirteen 2-mile distances, and so on. Since there are 100 athletes, the median distance will be between the 50th athlete's distance and the 51st athlete's distance. Now, start adding the number of athletes in each row. The first three rows represent $10 + 13 + 18 = 41$ athletes: we haven't reached the 50th athlete yet. But if we add on the fourth row, we get to $41 + 35 = 71$ athletes. This tells us that both the 50th athlete and the 51st athlete are represented in that fourth row, meaning they each walked a distance of 4 miles. Thus, the median, a, is 4.

The mode is the most frequent number of miles walked. Looking at the chart, we can see that the single distance walked by the largest number of athletes (35) was 4 miles. The mode, b, is 4.

Thus, $a - b$ equals $4 - 4 = 0$.

4) B
This question asks for the average of x and y, which we could represent algebraically as $(x + y)/2$.

One way to handle this problem is to solve it algebraically.
$$2z = 2x + 2y - 6$$

Answer Explanations

Add 6 to both sides:
$$2z + 6 = 2x + 2y$$
Divide both sides by 2:
$$z + 3 = x + y$$
This tells us that the sum of x and y is equal to $z + 3$. Since the *average* of x and y would just be the sum divided by 2, we can conclude that the average of x and y is $(z + 3)/2$.

Alternatively, we can solve this by plugging in numbers for x and y. For example, if $x = 6$ and $y = 10$, then the equation becomes this:
$$2z = 2(6) + 2(10) - 6$$
$$2z = 12 + 20 - 6$$
$$2z = 26$$
$$z = 13$$
Now, check what the question was asking. What is the average of x and y? With our numbers, the answer is $(6 + 10)/2 = 8$. So, test $z = 3$ in each answer choice until we get 8 as an answer. The only one that works is B.

5) C
This question checks our knowledge of terms: median is the middle number when the set is lined up least to greatest; mode is the most frequent occurrence in the number set; range is the lowest value subtracted from the highest value; standard deviation is how varied the set is from the mean. Let's check the choices one at a time.

A) Set A's range (which is $9 - 2 = 7$) is less than set B's (which is $300 - 2 = 298$), so choice A is false.
B) Set A has no modes, since no number appears more than once in the set. Choice B is false.
C) The median of set A is 5, and the median of set B is 10. Since 5 is 1/2 of 10, choice C is true.
D) You can use the stddev() command to find the standard deviations using the built-in calculator, or you can just approximate. The mean of set A is about 5, and the terms are fairly closely grouped around that number: no value is more than 4 away from the mean. In set B, the mean is about 65, and *all* of the terms are more than 4 away from that! Therefore, the standard deviation of set B is larger than the standard deviation of set A, meaning choice D is false.

Only choice C is true.

6) B
The key here is to carefully follow the instructions. We're not just supposed to calculate the mean of the list of numbers we've been given; we have to delete two numbers from the list and then calculate the mean of the remaining numbers. So first, put the 7 scores in order from least to greatest:

$$15.73, 15.82, 15.99, 16.21, 18.14, 19.34, 19.40$$

Next, cross out the highest and lowest scores on the list. That leaves us with these:

$$15.82, 15.99, 16.21, 18.14, 19.34$$

Felicia's score is the mean of these 5 scores:
$$(15.82 + 15.99 + 16.21 + 18.14 + 19.34)/5$$
$$= 85.5/5$$
$$= 17.1$$

7) 88
Start by writing out the equation for mean:
$$\text{mean} = \frac{\text{sum}}{\#}$$
Now plug in the information for the 1st period class:
$$84 = \frac{\text{sum}}{21}$$
$$84(21) = \text{sum}$$
$$1764 = \text{sum}$$
Now set up the equation again for the rest of the 2nd period class:
$$91 = \frac{\text{sum}}{28}$$
$$91(28) = \text{sum}$$
$$2548 = \text{sum}$$
To find the average of both classes combined, we need to add up all the scores from both classes and divide that result by the total number of students.
$$\text{mean} = \frac{1764 + 2548}{21 + 28}$$
$$\text{mean} = \frac{4312}{49}$$
$$\text{mean} = 88$$

8) C
Start by writing out the equation for mean:
$$\text{mean} = \frac{\text{sum}}{\#}$$
This time, let's start with the last piece of information we've been given: the average of an unknown number of integers is 54. If x is the number of those integers, that gives us this:
$$54 = \frac{\text{sum}}{x}$$
$$54x = \text{sum}$$

So if there are x unknown integers, then the sum of the unknown integers is $54x$. But we also have three known integers: 12, 108, and 36. The sum of *all* the integers on the list is therefore $12 + 108 + 36 + 54x$. We also know that the average of all the integers on the list is 53. And if there are x unknown integers and 3 known integers, then the total number of integers on the list is $x + 3$. Now we can set up the equation again:

$$53 = \frac{12 + 108 + 36 + 54x}{x + 3}$$

To simplify, multiply both sides by $(x + 3)$:

$$53(x + 3) = 12 + 108 + 36 + 54x$$
$$53x + 159 = 156 + 54x$$
$$53x + 3 = 54x$$
$$3 = x$$

But wait! 3 isn't our final answer (which is good, because it's also not one of the answer choices). Remember, x represents the number of unknown integers on the list. The question was asking for the total number of integers. So we add our 3 unknown integers to our 3 known integers for a total of 6 integers on the list.

Alternatively, you can solve this problem by back-solving. Start with choice B. If there are 5 integers on the list, and 3 of them are 12, 108, and 36, then there are exactly two unknown integers. Call them x and y. Now we can do this:

$$53 = \frac{12 + 108 + 36 + x + y}{5}$$
$$53(5) = 156 + x + y$$
$$265 = 156 + x + y$$
$$109 = x + y$$

But if the sum of our two unknown integers is 109, then their average would have to be $109/2 = 54.5$. According to the problem, the actual average of the unknown integers is 54, so this doesn't work. Eliminate choice B.

Now try choice C. If there are 6 integers on the list, then we have three unknowns: let's call them x, y, and z.

$$53 = \frac{12 + 108 + 36 + x + y + z}{6}$$
$$53(6) = 156 + x + y + z$$
$$318 = 156 + x + y + z$$
$$162 = x + y + z$$

If the sum of three unknown integers is 162, then their average is $162/3 = 54$, exactly what we needed. Choice C is the right answer.

9) C
Standard deviation is a measure of how far the terms of the set are, on average, from the mean of the set. Choice C is quite tightly grouped around its mean, which is 7: none of the terms in the set are more than 2 away from that mean. By contrast, choice A is spread slightly wider from its mean, which is 6: some of the terms are as much as 4 away from that mean. Choices B and D are spread even wider from their means, so choices A, B, and D all have larger standard deviations than C's.

Alternatively, we can solve this problem using the built-in calculator. Use the command stddev() to directly calculate the standard deviation of each list.

$$\text{stddev}(2, 4, 6, 8, 10) = 3.16227766017$$

$$\text{stddev}(4, 4, 50, 90, 90) = 43.0209251411$$

$$\text{stddev}(5, 6, 7, 8, 9) = 1.58113883008$$

$$\text{stddev}(10, 20, 30, 40, 100) = 35.3553390593$$

Choice C is the smallest.

10) A
Try plugging in numbers. We know the average of a, b, and c is 12, so let's make it simple: set them all equal to 12.

$$\text{Old: } a = 12, b = 12, c = 12$$

Now, apply the changes in the problem: increase a by 1, decrease b by 4, and keep c the same. That gives us this:

$$\text{New: } a = 13, b = 8, c = 12$$

Now take the average:

$$\frac{(13 + 8 + 12)}{3} = 11$$

If you prefer the more abstract approach, we can do the same thing with algebra.

$$12 = \frac{a + b + c}{3}$$
$$a + b + c = 12(3) = 36$$

$$\text{New sum} = a + 1 + b - 4 + c$$
$$= a + b + c - 3$$

We already know that $a + b + c = 36$. So the new sum is $36 - 3 = 33$. Therefore, the new average is $33/3 = 11$.

Answer Explanations

11) 4

We're looking for the average of x, y, and z:

$$\text{mean} = \frac{x + y + z}{3}$$

We already know that $z = 6$, so we can rewrite that this way:

$$\text{mean} = \frac{x + y + 6}{3}$$

We also know that $x + y = z$. Since $z = 6$, that means that $x + y = 6$. Plug that in as well:

$$\text{mean} = \frac{(x + y) + 6}{3}$$

$$\text{mean} = \frac{(6) + 6}{3}$$

$$\text{mean} = 12/3 = 4$$

Alternatively, we can plug in numbers. Since $x + y = 6$, we could say that $x = 4$ and $y = 2$ (for example). In that case, average of x, y, and z is just the average of 4, 2, and 6:

$$\text{mean} = \frac{4 + 2 + 6}{3}$$

$$\text{mean} = 12/3 = 4$$

12) A

First, write out algebraic statements for each of the given relationships.

Peng has 5 more than Ali:

$$p = a + 5$$

Raj has twice as many as Peng:

$$r = 2p$$

Kaimana has 16 fewer than triple the number that Raj has:

$$k = 3r - 16$$

The problem tells us that Kaimana has 26 marbles. So, plug 26 in for k in the last equation:

$$26 = 3r - 16$$
$$42 = 3r$$
$$14 = r$$

Now plug in 14 for r in the second equation:

$$14 = 2p$$
$$7 = p$$

And now plug in 7 for p in the first equation:

$$7 = a + 5$$
$$2 = a$$

At this point, we know how many marbles each person has, so all we have to do is calculate the average of 2, 7, 14, and 26:

$$\text{mean} = \frac{2 + 7 + 14 + 26}{4}$$

$$\text{mean} = 49/4 = 12.25$$

13) A

Mean, median, and mode are all "measures of central tendency": they're different ways of estimating the central point of a set of data. Whether we add 2 to each term or multiply each term by 2, we're changing where the center of the data is. As a result, either action would cause the mean, median, and mode to all increase. Eliminate choices C and D.

By contrast, range and standard deviation are both "measures of dispersion": they're different ways of measuring how varied the set is. So what happens to those measures if you multiply by 2? Well, let's say we had a simple set like {1, 2, 3}. If we multiply all the terms by 2, the new set is {2, 4, 6}. The range has changed, and so has the standard deviation: in the original set, no term was more than 1 away from the mean, while in the new set, some terms are as much as 2 away from the mean. This is a different set from the one described in the problem, but it certainly casts doubt on choice B.

Now consider what happens if we *add* 2 to each term. Our {1, 2, 3} set would become {3, 5, 7}. The range is exactly the same as it was. And notice that although each term has increased by 2, the *mean* has increased by 2 as well, meaning the average distance from the mean has not changed. That's going to work the same way no matter how many terms the set has, so the right answer is A.

PROBABILITY (p. 377)
Probability: Try It
1) 12/52 or 0.231

Probability is part over whole: in this case, the 12 face cards over the 52 playing cards in the deck. Therefore, the answer is $12/52 = 0.231$.

2) 2/52 or 0.038

For this problem, the "whole" is still the 52 playing cards in the deck, as it was in the last problem. But the "part" is now the number of sevens in the deck that are not black. As the Note clarifies, there are 4 sevens in the deck: two black and two red. The number of sevens in the deck that are not black, then, is 2. Therefore, the answer is $2/52 = 0.038$.

3) 986/5403 or 0.182

This problem is about *a student* chosen at random, so the "whole" is the overall total number of students: 5403.

The "part" is the off-campus undergraduate students: 986. Therefore, the answer is 986/5403 = 0.182.

4) 986/4548 or 0.217
This time, we're told that *an undergraduate student* is chosen at random. The "whole" we need is therefore the total number of undergraduate students: that's 4548. The "part" is still the off-campus undergraduate students, so 986. But because of the different whole, the probability is different: for this one, it's 986/4548 = 0.217.

5) 9/100 or 0.09
To calculate the probability that the first marble is green, we divide the number of green marbles (that's the "part") by the total number of marbles, giving us 3/10. Since he returns that marble to the bag, when he draws the second marble, the bag still contains 3 green marbles and 10 total marbles, so the probability for the second marble is also 3/10. To find the probability that both events occur, multiply:

$$\frac{3}{10} * \frac{3}{10} = \frac{9}{100} = 0.09$$

6) 6/90 or $0.0\overline{66}$
The probability that the first marble is green is still 3/10, just as it was in #5 above. But consider what happens when he goes to draw the second marble. At this point, there are only 9 marbles left in the bag, and only 2 of them are green. Therefore, the probability that the second marble is green is 2/9. Now we multiply:

$$\frac{3}{10} * \frac{2}{9} = \frac{6}{90} = 0.0\overline{66}$$

Probability: Practice Set 1 (p. 382)
1) D
Probability is part over whole. In this case, the "part" is the number of NON-language teachers. Add up the teachers of other subjects: 6 math teachers + 5 history teachers + 4 science teachers = 15. The "whole" is the total number of teachers: that's 3 + 2 + 6 + 5 + 4 = 20. Therefore, the probability is 15/20 = 0.75.

2) A
Probability is part over whole. In this case, the "part" is the number of tote bags (x), while the "whole" is the total number of items (x tote bags + 12 t-shirts = $x + 12$ items). Therefore, the probability is $\frac{x}{x+12}$.

3) 30
Probability is part over whole. In this case, the "part" is the number of purple lollipops, while the "whole" is the total number of lollipops. If there are 18 yellow lollipops, 22 red lollipops, and p purple lollipops, the total number of lollipops is $18 + 22 + p$. Therefore:

$$\frac{p}{18 + 22 + p} = \frac{3}{7}$$

Now cross-multiply to solve.

$$7p = 3(18 + 22 + p)$$
$$7p = 3(40 + p)$$
$$7p = 120 + 3p$$
$$4p = 120$$
$$p = 30$$

4) D
First, find the number of juniors.

$$\frac{j}{720} = \frac{5}{16}$$
$$j = \frac{5}{16}(720) = 225$$

The total number of juniors and seniors is 720, so if there are 225 juniors, then there are 720 − 225 = 495 seniors.

5) A
Since there are six sides on a die, the probability of rolling a six on any one roll is exactly 1/6. But this is an "and" problem: we want the probability that Liam rolls a six the first time AND the second time. So, multiply the probability of the first event (rolling a six the first time) by the probability of the second event (rolling a six the second time).

$$\frac{1}{6} * \frac{1}{6} = \frac{1}{36}$$

6) C
Probability is part over whole. The mouse will be chosen at random from those that solved the puzzle in 3 to 5 minutes, so the "whole" for this problem is the 14 + 11 = 25 mice that solved it in that time frame. Now, out of those 25 mice, how many are in Group B? That's the "part": 11. The answer is 11/25 = 0.44.

Probability: Practice Set 2 (p. 383)
1) A
This is an "and" probability problem, so multiply: we need the probability of the first event (rolling a 2) times the probability of the second event (rolling a 3) times the probability of the third event (rolling a 4). Since the die has six different sides, the probability of any one result in a single roll is 1/6. Therefore, the probability is

$$\frac{1}{6} * \frac{1}{6} * \frac{1}{6}$$

2) C
Probability is part over whole. In this case, the "part" is the number of participants who are 16 or 17. Anyone who is either 16 or 17 should be included, so we just have to add the number of sixteen-year-olds and the number of seventeen-year-olds to get the top of the fraction. The heights of the bars tell us that there are 17

Answer Explanations

sixteen-year-olds and 15-year-olds, so the "part" for our fraction is 17 + 15. The "whole" is the 50 participants in the program, so (17 + 15)/50 is the answer.

3) B
This is not an "and" problem or an "or" problem, but rather something much simpler. The probability of something happening and the probability of it *not* happening will always add up to 1. So if the probability that event X will occur twice is 0.84, the probability that that does *not* happen is 1 − 0.84 = 0.16.

4) 1/4 or 0.25
Let's say the four lunch periods are labeled periods A, B, C, and D. Emma has an equal chance of being assigned to any one of them, so let's say she's assigned to period A. What's the probability that Zoe is there too? Well, there are four lunch periods, and Zoe has an equal chance of being assigned to any one of them, so the probability that she's in A specifically is 1/4.

That's it! The answer is 1/4.

If you're objecting that we don't actually know that Emma ends up in period A, of course you're right. But since she has an equal chance of landing in any of the periods, it works out the same way.

Technically, the probability that Emma is in period A *and* Zoe is in period A would be (1/4)(1/4) = 1/16. Similarly, the probability that Emma is in period B *and* Zoe is in period B would also be (1/4)(1/4) = 1/16. It's the same for all four periods. So the probability that they're both in A *or* they're both in B *or* they're both in C *or* they're both in D is

$$\frac{1}{16} + \frac{1}{16} + \frac{1}{16} + \frac{1}{16} = \frac{4}{16} = \frac{1}{4}$$

5) D
This is an "or" problem, so let's solve it by focusing on the opposite outcome first. What's the probability that Mr. Vega does NOT hit a red light on at least one day? We could reword that question like this: what's the probability that Mr. Vega hits a green light every day? That's just an "and" problem:

$$0.5 * 0.5 * 0.5 * 0.5 * 0.5 = 0.03125$$

The probability that he hits a green light every day is 3.125%. Therefore, the probability that he hits a red light at least once is 100% − 3.125% = 96.875%, which is closest to choice D.

STATISTICS (p. 384)
Statistics: Try It
1) No
The sample isn't random because the method may oversample some groups, such as those with internet access and those with interest in the city website.

2) Yes
As long as every worker has an employee ID number and the numbers are randomly assigned, this method produces a random sample.

3) No
Those who volunteer to participate are likely to have greater-than-average interest in the team.

4) C
The only population we can draw a conclusion about is the one from which we have a representative sample: the physics majors.

Statistics: Practice Set 1 (p. 388)
1) B
Since the problem told us we have a random sample, we can solve this with a simple proportion.

$$\frac{116}{200} = \frac{x}{35,700}$$

$$x = \frac{116}{200}(35,700) = 20,706$$

2) C
In choice A, the sample consists only of the extremes. People with GPAs in the middle are underrepresented.

In choice B, the sample consists only of English majors. We wanted a random sample of all the students in the university, not just the ones majoring in English.

Choice C is a random sample, assuming all students have ID numbers and that the ID numbers are randomly assigned.

Choice D is particularly problematic because of what the researcher is trying to evaluate. This sample consists only of the students who are already using the writing sample, which may oversample people who are satisfied with it.

3) B
Because the sample is random, we can use it to make reliable predictions about the larger population from which the sample is drawn. That eliminates choice A.

But what precisely is the larger population from which it is drawn? Look at the wording of how the sample was described: we have a random sample *of employees at a shoe department in a Virginia department store*. Choice B describes that population exactly. C and D go too far.

4) C
Because the sample is random, we can use it to make reliable predictions about the larger population from which the sample is drawn. The 3% margin of error gives us the level of precision for those predictions. Specifically, since 19% of the respondents were born outside the

state, the most likely percentage of residents who were born outside of state is between 19% − 3% = 16% and 19% + 3% = 22%. Thus, it is unlikely for the actual percentage to be either under 16% or over 22%. That's choice C.

Choice A applies these percentages to the wrong thing. The 16% and 22% are not measures of certainty about the overall accuracy; they are the outer bounds of the most likely range for the percentage of residents who were born out of state.

Choice B is too strongly worded. While it is *unlikely* that more than 22% of California residents were born out of state, we can't say that it's impossible.

Choice D applies the result too broadly. Our sample is drawn only from California residents, so we can only make reliable predictions about California residents. We have no basis to make predictions about any other populations, such as Americans in general.

5) D
Choice A is using information about one group (pedestrians on the campus at an elite university) to draw a conclusion about a different group (people in general). This isn't supported. For one thing, this method is likely to have oversampled people who were students at the elite university, and those students may have above-average levels of confidence in their mathematics abilities.

But choice B doesn't work either! The flaws in the study methodology don't prove that the *opposite* conclusion is true. We just don't have the grounds to make a conclusion either way.

Choice C is half right, half wrong. Yes, the survey design was inappropriate, but the sample size was not the issue; the real problem was that this sample is not necessarily representative of the larger population that the statistician wanted to study ("the general public"). All a small sample size does is increase the margin of error, meaning we'll have a less precise conclusion. But an unrepresentative sample means we really can't draw any conclusion at all.

Choice D is the winner for several reasons. It's nice and weak (the results *may* not be reliable), which is easier to support. And it focuses on the right issue: the sample was biased (meaning not truly random).

Statistics: Practice Set 2 (p. 389)
1) D
This problem is a lot like a Reading question, where we have to be very careful not to go too far. Choices A and B are both claiming we've proved causation (this supplement causes acne to decrease), which we haven't: all we know for sure is correlation (people who took the pill were more likely to experience a decrease in their acne).

Choice C is making a prediction, which is also unsupported. For one thing, this is ignoring margin of error. And more importantly, this is using the percentages wrong: we know that a decrease happened in 60% *more* of the supplement participants than in the sugar pill participants, not that 60% *of the participants who used the supplement* showed a decrease. It's possible, for example, that 100 of the sugar pill participants saw a decrease, and 160 of the Supplement X participants saw a decrease. In that case, the percentage of Supplement X participants who saw a decrease would have been 160/600 = 26.67%, not 60%.

Choice D is the choice with the weakest language and is thus the easiest to support. This is the most reliable conclusion of the four.

2) D
Because the sample is random, we can use it to make reliable predictions about the larger population from which the sample is drawn. Specifically, since the mean selling price of the sample was $12.20, the mean selling price for the action figures in the store is most likely some value in between $12.20 − $1.16 = $11.04 and $12.20 + $1.16 = $13.36.

Choice A is wrong because we have no way to conclude a minimum or maximum selling price for the toys in the sample. It's possible, for example, that the sample consisted of 25 toys that were each $5 less than the mean and 25 toys that were each $5 more than the mean. In that case, *none* of the toys in the sample would fall within choice A's range!

Choice B is wrong for the same reason as choice A. We can make conclusions about the mean selling price of the action figures at the store, but we don't know what their individual selling prices might be.

Choice C actually doesn't go quite far enough! It's not true that any value in this range is a plausible mean for the *sample*. We actually know the mean of the sample: it's $12.20.

Choice D is the one that uses margin of error correctly. It's drawing a conclusion about mean, not actual selling price, and it's appropriately using the margin of error to limit the precision of the conclusion we can draw about the mean of the larger population (the action figures at the store).

3) C
Because the sample is random, we can use it to make reliable predictions about the larger population from which the sample is drawn. But be careful: the 65% applied only to the 50 soccer players in the sample, not necessarily to the overall sample of varsity athletes.

Answer Explanations

Choice A draws a conclusion about the wrong group. Choice D is just all kinds of wrong: it draws a conclusion about the wrong group ("students" instead of varsity soccer players), it uses language that's too strong, and it actually goes the wrong way! We know at least that 65% of the 50 soccer players in the sample get *at least* 8 hours, so unless every single one in that group gets *exactly* 8 hours, this choice is wrong.

Choice B is a bit more subtle but it takes an additional step by introducing a new term: "sleep-deprived." Nothing in the problem gave us the grounds to make a conclusion using this term. For all we know, varsity soccer players require 9 hours of sleep each night. In that case, it's possible that 100% of the team is sleep-deprived!

Choice C is the one that gets it right. The 50 soccer players were a subset of a random sample of varsity athletes, so they must be varsity soccer players. And the word "most" is vague enough to cover the margin of error: this isn't claiming that exactly 65% of varsity soccer players get this much sleep, but rather that something more than 50% do.

4) A

Because the sample is random, we can use it to make reliable predictions about the larger population from which the sample is drawn. Specifically, since the survey results are from a random sample of dog owners, we can conclude that approximately 84% (plus or minus the margin of error) of dog owners take their dog to the vet once a year.

Statement I is wrong because it ignores the margin of error. We can't say that *exactly* 84% of dog owners do this. Eliminate choices C and D.

Statement II is wrong for the same reason. The margin of error means we can't say for sure that exactly 84% of another randomly chosen sample of the same group would come out the same way. Now we can eliminate choice B, meaning choice A must be the answer.

But just for the record, Statement III is wrong too. This one actually has even less support than the other two statements, because we know nothing at all about cat owners; the sample was drawn from dog owners, so that's the only population we can make any kind of conclusion about.

AREA AND VOLUME (p. 390)
Area and Volume: Try It
1) 81π

$$A = \pi r^2$$
$$A = \pi(9)^2$$
$$A = 81\pi \text{ square meters}$$

2) 26

Start by writing out the formula for area of a rectangle.

$$A = lw$$
$$36 = l(4)$$
$$9 = l$$

So this is a rectangle with a width of 4 and a length of 9. That means it has two 4-inch sides and two 9-inch sides. Its perimeter is the sum of those four sides:

$$p = 4 + 4 + 9 + 9$$
$$p = 26$$

3) 100

A square has four equal sides, so its perimeter can be written this way:

$$p = s + s + s + s$$
$$p = 4s$$

In this square, the perimeter is 40:

$$40 = 4s$$
$$10 = s$$

A square is a rectangle: just one where all four sides have the same length. So we can find the area of a square using the formula for area of a rectangle.

$$A = lw$$
$$A = (10)(10)$$
$$A = 100$$

4) 128

Problems about how many smaller shapes can fit into or be cut out of a larger shape are about all how much space the shapes take up. For two-dimensional shapes, then, this problem is about area: we have to divide the area of the larger shape by the area of the smaller shape. We already know that each of the squares has area 25. What about the rectangle?

$$A = lw$$
$$A = 10(320)$$
$$A = 3200$$

Now divide:

$$3200/25 = 128$$

5) 36

We've split this figure into a 10×3 rectangle and a 5×5 rectangle. Well, that's helpful—a 5×5 rectangle is a square. We can already fill in the rest of its side lengths.

Geometry and Trigonometry

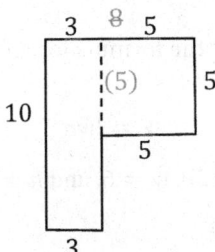

There's only one missing side length now: the vertical line on the bottom right. But that line segment plus the dashed line segment must be the same length as the vertical side of length 10 on the left. We know the dashed line segment has a length of 5, so the remaining side must have a length of $10 - 5 = 5$.

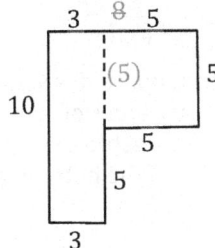

To find the perimeter, add up all those outer side lengths. (Don't count the dashed line we drew in; that's not part of the perimeter.) Starting from the top left and going around clockwise, that gives us this:

$$p = 3 + 5 + 5 + 5 + 5 + 3 + 10$$
$$p = 36$$

6) 90π

$$V = \pi r^2 h$$
$$V = \pi(3)^2(10)$$
$$V = \pi(9)(10)$$
$$V = 90\pi$$

7) 600
The formula for volume of a cube is the same as the formula for volume of a rectangular prism, except that the length, width, and height are all the same. So instead of writing the formula as $V = lwh$, we can write it as $V = s * s * s$ (where s represents the side length), or $V = s^3$.

$$V = s^3$$
$$1000 = s^3$$
$$10 = s$$

There are six faces to a cube: the top, bottom, front, back, left side, and right side. Each one has an area of s^2. So:

$$SA = 6s^2$$
$$SA = 6(10)^2$$
$$SA = 600$$

8) 4

$$V = \frac{1}{3}\pi r^2 h$$
$$32\pi = \frac{1}{3}\pi r^2(6)$$

Divide both sides by π:

$$32 = \frac{1}{3}r^2(6)$$
$$32 = 2r^2$$
$$16 = r^2$$
$$4 = r$$

9) 30
This problem is a lot like #4 from p. 395. We still need to take the amount of space taken up by the larger shape and divide it by the amount of space taken up by the smaller shape. Now, however, because we're in three dimensions, we're going to use volume to measure how much space each shape takes up. So first, find the volume of the rectangular prism:

$$V = lwh$$
$$V = (6)(4)(10)$$
$$V = 240$$

Now, we need the volume of the cube. Just as a square is a rectangle in which all the sides are the same length, a cube is a rectangular prism in which all the edges are the same length. So, we can find the volume of a cube using the formula for volume of a rectangular prism.

$$V = lwh$$
$$V = (2)(2)(2)$$
$$V = 8$$

Now divide:

$$240/8 = 30$$

Area and Volume: Practice Set 1 (p. 398)
1) C
Start by writing out the formula for area of a rectangle:

$$A = lw$$

In this problem, $A = 1$. The dimensions are x and 0.75, so one of those is the length and the other is the width (it doesn't matter which is which). Now plug those values into the equation you wrote out:

$$1 = 0.75(x)$$

To isolate x, divide both sides by 0.75.

$$1/0.75 = x$$
$$4/3 = x$$

2) A
Start by writing out the formula for area of a rectangle:

Answer Explanations

$$A = lw$$

In this problem, $A = 12$ and $l = 8$. Plug those values in:

$$12 = 8w$$

Now divide both sides by 8:

$$12/8 = w$$
$$1.5 = w$$

3) 11.25

To find the area of the shaded region, subtract the area of the smaller square from the area of the larger square.

$$\text{Area of larger square} = 4.5^2 = 20.25$$
$$\text{Area of smaller square} = 3^2 = 9$$
$$20.25 - 9 = 11.25$$

4) B

To find the area of a shape that we don't have a formula for, look to draw lines on the shape to split it up into easier shapes:

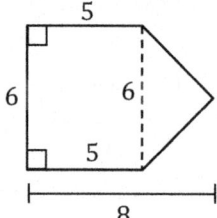

Now we have a rectangle and a triangle. Find the area of the rectangle first.

$$A = lw$$
$$A = 6(5) = 30$$

Now the triangle. The base is 6. As for the height, the horizontal length of the full pentagon was 8, and the rectangle used up 5 of that. The remaining horizontal distance must be $8 - 5 = 3$.

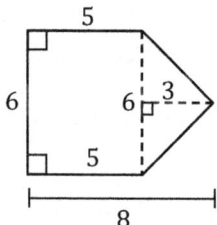

Now find the area of the triangle:

$$A = \frac{1}{2}bh$$
$$A = \frac{1}{2}(6)(3) = 9$$

To find the area of the pentagon, simply add the areas of the two shapes we divided it into (the rectangle and the triangle).

$$30 + 9 = 39$$

5) B

Start by writing out the formula for volume of a rectangular prism:

$$V = lwh$$

In this prism, $V = 120$, $w = 6$, and $h = \sqrt{50}$.

Plug those values in:

$$120 = l(6)(\sqrt{50})$$

Divide both sides by 6:

$$20 = l\sqrt{50}$$

Divide both sides by $\sqrt{50}$:

$$\frac{20}{\sqrt{50}} = l$$

Use the calculator to compare this value, which comes out to about 2.83, to the values of each of the answer choices. Or, you can use algebra to simplify the fraction. First multiply the top and the bottom of the fraction by $\sqrt{50}$:

$$l = \frac{20 * \sqrt{50}}{\sqrt{50} * \sqrt{50}}$$

$$l = \frac{20\sqrt{50}}{50}$$

We can simplify $\sqrt{50}$ as $\sqrt{25} * \sqrt{2} = 5\sqrt{2}$.

$$l = \frac{20(5)\sqrt{2}}{50}$$

$$l = \frac{100\sqrt{2}}{50}$$

$$l = 2\sqrt{2}$$

6) D

To find the perimeter, we have to fill in all the missing side lengths.

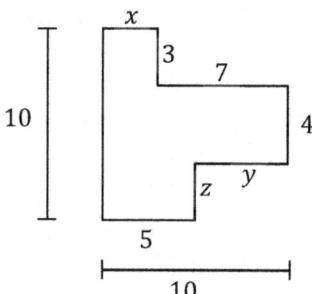

The horizontal length of this whole figure is 10. Look at the two "tops" of this figure: the x and the 7 must add up to 10.

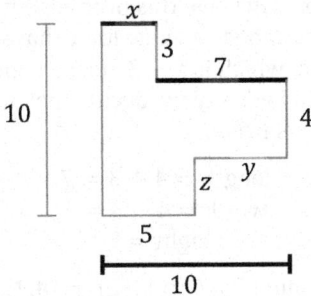

Therefore, x must equal 3.

Now look at the "bottoms" of the figure: the 5 and the y must also add up to 10.

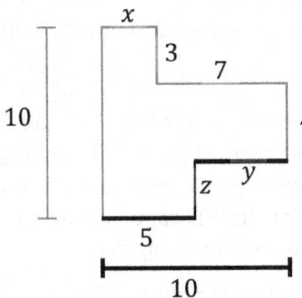

Therefore, y must equal 5.

Now consider vertical distances. The height of the whole figure is 10. Therefore, the three vertical pieces on the right side (3, 4, and z) must add up to 10.

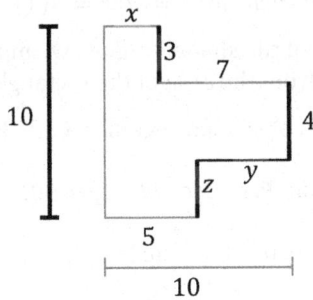

So:
$$3 + 4 + z = 10$$
$$7 + z = 10$$
$$z = 3$$

Now that we have all the side lengths, we just have to add them all up. Starting on the top left and going in clockwise order, that gives us this:
$$p = 3 + 3 + 7 + 4 + 5 + 3 + 5 + 10$$
$$p = 40$$

A shortcut on this problem is to realize that it doesn't actually matter what the values of x, y, and z are. After all, we already know what the top, right, bottom, and left sides of this figure must add up to, which is really all we need:

$$\begin{array}{cccc} \text{top} & \text{right} & \text{bottom} & \text{left} \\ p = (x + 7) + (3 + 4 + z) + (y + 5) + (10) \\ p = 10 + 10 + 10 + 10 \\ p = 40 \end{array}$$

7) D
Write out the formula for circumference of a circle:
$$C = 2\pi r$$

Plug in what we know:
$$16\pi = 2\pi r$$
Divide by π: $\quad 16 = 2r$
Divide by 2: $\quad 8 = r$

So the radius is 8. The problem asked for the area of the circle, so next, write out that formula:
$$A = \pi r^2$$

And plug in $r = 8$:
$$A = \pi(8)^2$$
$$A = 64\pi$$

8) 320
To calculate the number of tiles we'll need, we have to divide the area of the wall by the area of each tile. Make sure you're using the same unit for both. In this problem, the dimensions of the mosaic are given in feet, but the dimensions of the tiles are given in inches.

Let's start by converting everything to inches. If the length of the mosaic is 20 feet, then its length in inches is $20(12) = 240$ inches. Similarly, if the height of the mosaic is 4 feet, then its height in inches is $4(12) = 48$ inches. Now calculate the area:

$$\text{Area of mosaic} = (240)(48) = 11520 \text{ in}^2$$

The tiles are each 6 inches by 6 inches:

$$\text{Area of tile} = (6)(6) = 36 \text{ in}^2$$

Therefore, we need $11520/36 = 320$ tiles.

Note: be sure to do these unit conversions on the original linear dimensions (feet and inches) rather than finding the areas first and then trying to convert square feet to square inches. Remember, just because there are 12 inches in 1 foot, that doesn't mean there are 12 square inches in 1 square foot. It's a different unit, so a different conversion rate applies.

9) C
Write out the formula supplied by the problem:
$$S = 2\pi r^2 h + 2\pi r h$$

In this cylinder, $r = 4$ and $h = 6$. Plug those values in:
$$S = 2\pi(4)^2(6) + 2\pi(4)(6)$$
$$S = 2\pi(16)(6) + 2\pi(4)(6)$$

- 567 -

Answer Explanations

$$S = 192\pi + 48\pi$$
$$S = 240\pi$$

10) B
Redraw the figure, including a line to indicate the radius of the circle.

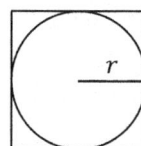

In this figure, the diameter of the circle is equal to the side length of the square. Since the diameter is equal to twice the radius, we can do this:

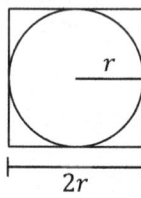

The perimeter of a square is the sum of the four sides. In this case, each side length is $2r$.

$$p = 2r + 2r + 2r + 2r$$

Now plug in the known perimeter, which is 24.

$$24 = 2r + 2r + 2r + 2r$$

Combine like terms:

$$24 = 8r$$

Divide both sides by 8:

$$3 = r$$

So the radius is 3. The problem asked for the area of the circle, so next, write out that formula:

$$A = \pi r^2$$

And plug in $r = 3$:

$$A = \pi(3)^2$$
$$A = 9\pi$$

11) D
Start by writing out the formula for volume of a rectangular prism:

$$V = lwh$$

In this prism, $l = (x + 3)$, $w = (x - 3)$, and $h = 2$. Plug all that information in:

$$V = (x + 3)(x - 3)(2)$$
$$V = 2(x + 3)(x - 3)$$

Now FOIL:

$$V = 2(x^2 - 9)$$
$$V = 2x^2 - 18$$

Alternatively, you can solve this problem by plugging in your own values. Choose a value for x that's bigger than 3 so that the width, which is $x - 3$, doesn't end up a negative number. Let's say we decide that $x = 4$. That means that for this prism:

$$\text{length} = 4 + 3 = 7$$
$$\text{width} = 4 - 3 = 1$$
$$\text{height} = 2$$

For our prism, volume $= (7)(1)(2) = 14$. Now check the answer choices. Since $x = 4$, choice A comes out to $2(4) - 6 = 2$. We didn't get 14, so this is not a match. Choice B comes out to $2(4) + 2 = 10$: also not a match. choice C is $2(4)^2 = 2(16) = 32$: no match. But choice D is $2(4)^2 - 18 = 2(16) - 18 = 32 - 18 = 14$. That matches the 14 we were looking for, so D must be the answer.

12) C
This problem is similar to #3 from this set: to find the area of the shaded region, we'll find the area of the larger shape and then subtract the area of the smaller (unshaded) regions. In this case, the larger shape is a rectangle with width 2 and length 6.

$$\text{Area of rectangle} = (2)(6) = 12$$

The height of each of the unshaded circles is the same as the width of the rectangle, which is 2. Therefore, the diameter of each circle is 2, which means the radius of each circle is 1.

$$\text{Area of each circle} = \pi r^2 = \pi(1)^2 = \pi$$

To find the area of the shaded region, we must subtract 3 of those circles from the area of the rectangle:

$$\text{Area of shaded region} = 12 - 3\pi$$

Area and Volume: Practice Set 2 (p. 400)
1) D
Redraw the figure, marking the length of each radius as r.

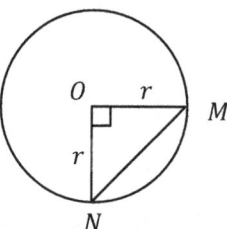

Now write out the formula for area of a triangle:

$$A = \frac{1}{2}bh$$

In this case, the area is 6, and both the base and the height have length r. Plug in that information:

$$6 = \frac{1}{2}(r)(r)$$
$$6 = \frac{1}{2}r^2$$

$$12 = r^2$$
$$\sqrt{12} = r$$

The problem asked for the area of the circle, so next, write out that formula:
$$A = \pi r^2$$

And plug in $r = \sqrt{12}$:
$$A = \pi\left(\sqrt{12}\right)^2$$
$$A = 12\pi$$

2) 8

Problems about how many of something fit into something else are about how much space the shapes take up. This means the relevant property is *area* if we're in two dimensions (as in #8 from practice set 1), or *volume* if we're in three dimensions (as we are here). We'll need to find the volume of the big cube, find the volume of the small cubes, and then divide.

All the problem is telling us is the surface area of each, not the volume. Well, surface area is just the sum of the areas of all the faces, and each face on a cube is a square. The area of a square is equal to the side length squared (s^2), and a cube has six faces: top, bottom, left, right, front, and back. Therefore, the total surface area of a cube is 6 times s^2.
$$SA = 6s^2$$

The formula for volume of a cube is the same as the formula for volume of a rectangular solid, except that length, width, and height are all the same, so they can each be represented by s:
$$V = s * s * s = s^3$$

Now let's apply those formulas.

Small cube:
$$SA = 6s^2$$
$$96 = 6s^2$$
$$16 = s^2$$
$$4 = s$$
$$V = s^3 = 4^3 = 64$$

Large cube:
$$SA = 6s^2$$
$$384 = 6s^2$$
$$64 = s^2$$
$$8 = s$$
$$V = s^3 = 8^3 = 512$$

Finally, to find the number of cubes of volume 64 that we can cut from a cube of volume 512, divide:
$$512/64 = 8$$

3) B

The perimeter of the square is 24. Perimeter is just the sum of the side lengths, and in a square, each side length is the same:

$$p = s + s + s + s$$
$$24 = 4s$$
$$6 = s$$

Therefore, the side length of the square is 6. The radius of each of these arcs is half the side length of the square, so $r = 3$. Each of these 4 arcs is 1/4 of a full circle with radius 3. So to find the area of the shaded region, we just have to subtract the area of 1 full circle with radius 3 from the area of the square.

$$\text{Area of square} = 6^2 = 36$$
$$\text{Area of circle} = \pi(3)^2 = 9\pi$$
$$\text{Area of shaded region} = 36 - 9\pi$$

4) B

The problem tells us that $\overline{AD}$ and $\overline{EF}$ are both *congruent*, meaning they have the same length, and *collinear*, meaning they lie on the same line. Let's say they each have length x.

The area of triangle CEF is equal to ½ times the base (which is x) times the height. But what's the height? We'd have to draw it in:

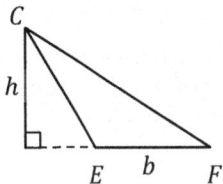

But wait, we already know that height! That's just another side of square $ABCD$, so its length is x. Therefore:

$$\text{Area of triangle } = \frac{1}{2}(b)(h)$$
$$\text{Area of triangle } CEF = \frac{1}{2}(x)(x)$$
$$\text{Area of triangle } CEF = \frac{1}{2}x^2$$

We already know that the area of the square is 10. Since x is the side length of square, that means $x^2 = 10$. Plug that information right in to the equation above:

$$\text{Area of triangle } CEF = \frac{1}{2}(10)$$
$$\text{Area of triangle } CEF = 5$$

5) 40

Let's start by drawing the blue rectangle.

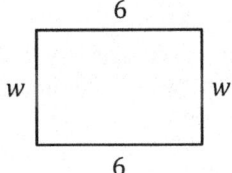

Answer Explanations

We can calculate the width of the blue rectangle using the given perimeter.

$$20 = 6 + 6 + w + w$$
$$20 = 12 + 2w$$
$$8 = 2w$$
$$4 = w$$

The width of the green rectangle is twice that width, so it's 8. The length of the green rectangle is equal to the side length of the yellow square. Since the area of the yellow square is 25, we can do this:

$$25 = s * s$$
$$25 = s^2$$
$$5 = s$$

Therefore, the green rectangle has a length of 5 and a width of 8. Its area is $A = 5 * 8 = 40$.

6) C

Start by calculating the area of the square.

$$A = s * s$$
$$A = 3 * 3$$
$$A = 9$$

So the square and the circle each have an area of 9. The circle has a diameter of d, so its radius is $d/2$. Now use the formula for area of a circle:

$$A = \pi r^2$$
$$9 = \pi \left(\frac{d}{2}\right)^2$$

Divide by π:

$$\frac{9}{\pi} = \left(\frac{d}{2}\right)^2$$

Take the square root of both sides:

$$\sqrt{\frac{9}{\pi}} = \sqrt{\left(\frac{d}{2}\right)^2}$$

$$\frac{3}{\sqrt{\pi}} = \frac{d}{2}$$

Multiply both sides by 2:

$$\frac{6}{\sqrt{\pi}} = d$$

Use your calculator to find the value of $6/\sqrt{\pi}$. The result comes out to approximately 3.385, which is closest to answer choice C.

7) A

The width of the outer rectangle is x. That includes a 1-inch border on both the left and the right, so the width of the inner rectangle is $x - 2$.

The height of the outer rectangle is $x + 2$. That includes a 1-inch border on both the top and the bottom, so the height of the inner rectangle is $(x + 2) - 2 = x$.

The area of the inner rectangle is its width, $x - 2$, multiplied by its height, x. That's choice A.

8) 12

Draw the rectangle as described:

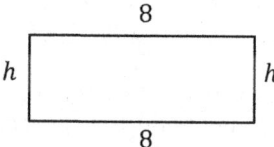

Now use the given perimeter to find the rectangle's height:

$$8 + 8 + h + h = 22$$
$$16 + 2h = 22$$
$$2h = 6$$
$$h = 3$$

Now fill in the height in your rectangle, and then draw a diagonal:

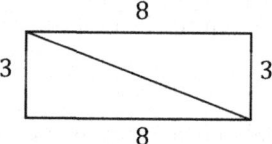

The diagonal divides the rectangle into two right triangles, each with height 3 and base 8. Use the formula for area of a triangle:

$$A = \frac{1}{2}bh$$
$$A = \frac{1}{2}(8)(3)$$
$$A = 12$$

9) A

Re-draw the figure, filling in the known side lengths.

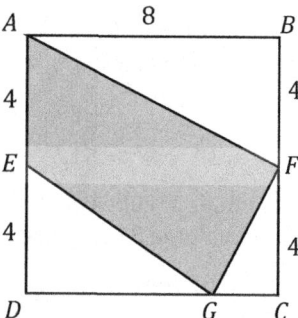

The shaded region is a shape we don't have a formula for, so look for a way to cut it up into easier shapes. Here, the simplest solution is to draw a line straight across the middle, from E to F. Because that line is parallel to the top and bottom of the square, we already know its length: 8.

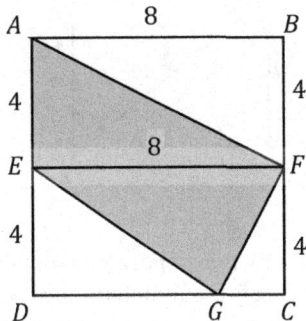

The top half of the shaded region is a right triangle with base 8 and height 4, so its area is $(1/2)(8)(4) = 16$. What about the bottom half of the shaded region? It's a triangle too, and if we use $\overline{EF}$ as the base, then its base is 8. Now draw in its height:

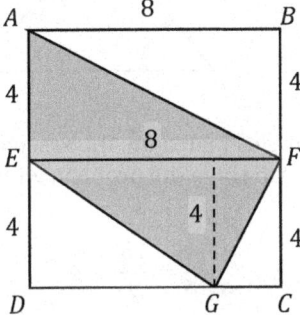

That height is parallel to $\overline{ED}$, so its height is 4! So the area of the bottom triangle is also $(1/2)(8)(4) = 16$.

Putting those components together, the total area of the shaded region must be $16 + 16 = 32$. The total area of the square is $8*8 = 64$. So the ratio of the shaded area to the total area is 32/64, which is equivalent to 1/2.

10) B
To calculate how many of a smaller shape will fit into a larger shape, divide the amount of space taken up by the larger shape by the amount of space taken up by the smaller shape. The shapes in this problem are three-dimensional, so we use volume to measure how much space is taken up. First calculate the volume of the small boxes:

$$V = lwh$$
$$V = (2)(3)(4)$$
$$V = 24$$

Each small box has a volume of 24 cubic inches, so 100 small boxes have a total volume of $100(24) = 2400$ cubic inches. Since we want the small boxes to fit into the larger box perfectly with no space left over, the volume of the larger box must also be 2400 cubic inches. Now test the choices.

A) $V = (20)(30)(40) = 24,000$
B) $V = (10)(12)(20) = 2400$
C) $V = (10)(15)(24) = 3600$
D) $V = (8)(27)(64) = 13,824$

Only choice B matches the 2400 cubic inches we need, so B must be the answer.

11) C
The area of square B is x, so B's side length is $\sqrt{x}$. The side length of square A is 3 inches less than twice the side length of square B. So:

$$\text{side length of square A} = 2\sqrt{x} - 3$$
$$\text{Area of square A} = (2\sqrt{x} - 3)^2$$
$$= (2\sqrt{x} - 3)(2\sqrt{x} - 3)$$
$$= 4x - 6\sqrt{x} - 6\sqrt{x} + 9$$
$$= 4x - 12\sqrt{x} + 9$$

ANGLES, LINES, AND TRIANGLES (p. 402)
Angles, Lines, and Triangles: Try It
1) ∠RQB, ∠SRD, and ∠CRQ
∠AQP and ∠RQB are opposite angles, so they must be congruent. ∠AQP and ∠CRQ are corresponding angles, so they must be congruent. Finally, ∠CRQ and ∠SRD are opposite angles, so they must be congruent as well.

2) 36°
∠AQR and ∠CRS are corresponding angles, so the measure of ∠CRS must be 144°. Redraw the figure and fill that in. Next, note that ∠CRS is adjacent to ∠SRD. Therefore, since the measure of ∠CRS is 144°, the measure of ∠SRD must be $180 - 144 = 36°$.

3) 720°
The sum of the interior angles of an n-sided polygon is given by the formula below:

$$\text{sum of angles} = 180(n - 2)$$

A hexagon has 6 sides, so plug in 6 for n:

$$\text{sum of angles} = 180(6 - 2)$$
$$= 180(4)$$
$$= 720$$

4) 120°
First find the sum of the interior angles as shown in #1 above. In a "regular" hexagon, all six angles have the same measure. So if each angle measures $x°$, we can say this:

$$x + x + x + x + x + x = 720$$
$$6x = 720$$
$$x = 720/6$$
$$x = 120$$

Answer Explanations

5) 16 or 17
Because this is an isosceles triangle, we know that two sides will have the same length. However, we don't know *which* two. If the sides are 5, 5, and 6, then the perimeter would be $5 + 5 + 6 = 16$. If the sides are 6, 6, and 5, then the perimeter is $6 + 6 + 5 = 17$.

6) B only
The lengths of the remaining sides must be greater than zero, so choice A is impossible. But they also must be less than 10: after all, the hypotenuse of a right triangle is across from the largest angle in the triangle, so it must be the largest side. Therefore, the perimeter must be less than 30, which eliminates choices C and D. Only choice B is possible.

7) A
If all we know about a pair of triangles is that they have the same *angle measurements* as each other, then all we can say for sure is that the triangles are similar; they may or may not be congruent.

However, in this problem, we've been told that the two triangles have the same *side lengths* as each other. Triangles with matching side lengths also have matching angles, so this is enough to establish that the triangles are congruent.

8) ∠DCE
Opposite angles are congruent.

9) ∠CDE
To make it easier to see the relationships, extend the parallel lines as well as transversal $\overline{AD}$. Do you see a corresponding angle to ∠BAC? Mark that and the angle opposite it, ∠CDE, as congruent to ∠BAC.

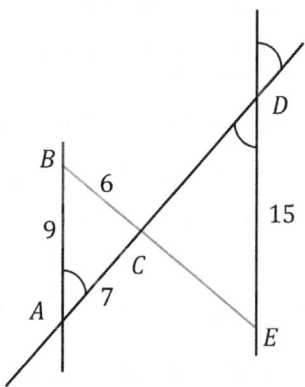

10) ∠CED
Now that we've matched up two of the three angles in these triangles, the third angle must match as well.

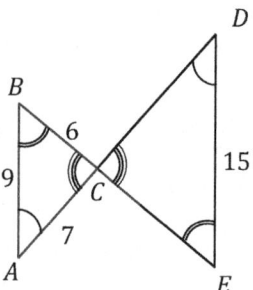

11) 10
Re-draw the figure as two separate triangles oriented the same way, being careful to match up the corresponding angles. This means we have to swing them around in opposite directions: think of swinging point A down to the right, and swinging point E down to the left.

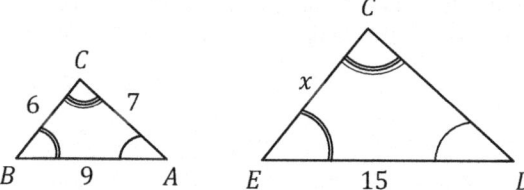

Because all the angles match up, this is a pair of similar triangles. So, we can solve the problem with a proportion:

$$\frac{x}{6} = \frac{15}{9}$$

$$x = (15/9)(6)$$

$$x = 10$$

Angles, Lines, and Triangles: Practice Set 1 (p. 412)
1) 22.5
The perimeter of a triangle is the sum of the lengths of its sides. In an equilateral triangle, all three sides have the same length. Since we know that one side length of the smaller triangle is 3, we can conclude that its other side lengths are also 3. Thus, its perimeter is $3 + 3 + 3 = 9$.

Similarly, we know that one side length of the larger triangle is 4.5, so its other side lengths must also be 4.5. The perimeter of the larger triangle is $4.5 + 4.5 + 4.5 = 13.5$.

So, the perimeter of the entire logo is $9 + 13.5 = 22.5$.

2) C
Re-draw the diagram, filling in what you know.

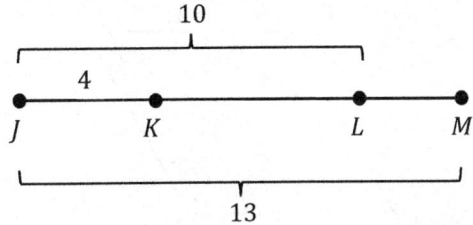

Now let's see what else has to be true. If the distance from point J to point L is 10, and $\overline{JK}$ covers 4 of that, then the distance from point K to point L must be $10 - 4 = 6$.

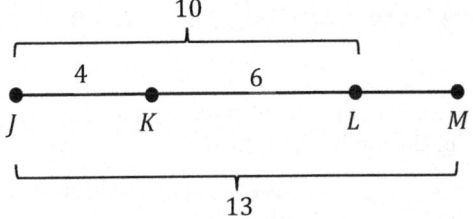

Similarly, if the distance from point J to point M is 13, and $\overline{JL}$ covers 10 of that, then the distance from point L to point M must be $13 - 10 = 3$.

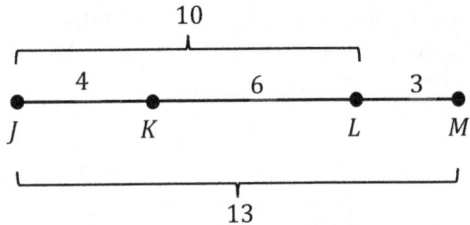

Therefore, the distance from point K to point M is $6 + 3 = 9$.

3) C
The given angle, ∠CRX, is adjacent to ∠CRQ. Therefore, they must add up to 180°. Since the measure of ∠CRX is 42°, the measure of ∠CRQ must be $180° - 42° = 138°$.

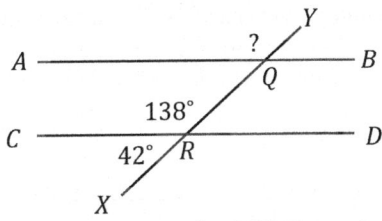

We need the measure of ∠AQY. From the figure, we can see that ∠AQY and ∠CRQ are corresponding angles: that is, they are in the same position as each other relative to the intersecting line $\overline{XY}$. Corresponding angles are congruent to each other, so if the measure of ∠CRQ is 138°, then the measure of ∠AQY must also be 138°.

4) D
Not sure how to start? A good way to get moving is to focus on filling in what you *do* know, even if you're not sure yet how it's going to get you to the answer. In this case, we have two of the angles in a triangle, so we can certainly calculate the remaining angle. After all, the angles of any triangle must add up to 180 degrees:

$$36 + 72 + x = 180$$
$$108 + x = 180$$
$$x = 72$$

So the measure of angle P must be 72°. Well, wait—so is the measure of angle Q! That means we have an isosceles triangle. And in an isosceles triangle, the two sides that are across from the matching angles must be the same length. So since angle Q is across from a side of length 8.1, the same must be true of angle P: the length of $\overline{MQ}$ is 8.1.

Alternatively, you can use an approximating & measuring strategy to solve this problem. Take a look at the figure. $\overline{MQ}$ is clearly longer than $\overline{PQ}$, so we can eliminate choice A. And triangle MPQ sure looks like an isosceles triangle, so it's reasonable to assume that the length of $\overline{MQ}$ is approximately the same as the length of $\overline{MP}$. That makes choice D the best guess, and as we saw above, it's the right answer.

5) C
In this figure, ∠PRS is adjacent to ∠PRQ, so they must add up to 180°. Therefore, the measure of ∠PRQ is $180° - 153° = 27°$.

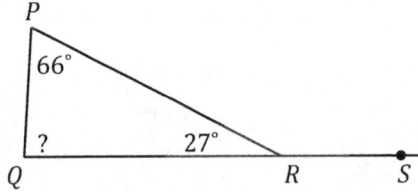

The three angles in a triangle must always add up to 180°, so if the measure of ∠PQR is $x°$, we can say this:

$$66 + 27 + x = 180$$
$$93 + x = 180$$
$$x = 87$$

You could also use an approximating & measuring strategy here. Hold the corner of your scratch paper up to the angle in the figure: the angle appears to be a little less than 90°. That makes choice C the best guess.

6) 140
The sum of the interior angles of an n-sided polygon is given by $180(n - 2)$. Therefore, the sum of the interior angles of a 9-sided polygon is $180(9 - 2) = 180(7) = 1260°$. In a "reglar" polygon, all angles are congruent, so the measure of any one angle in this nonagon would be $1260/9 = 140°$.

7) A
Re-draw the figure and think about what you can fill in already. If two sides of a triangle have the same lengths, then the angles across from those two sides must be

Answer Explanations

congruent. In triangle XYZ, we have two sides of length 3, one of which is across from a 60° angle. Therefore, the angle across from the other 3 must also be 60°.

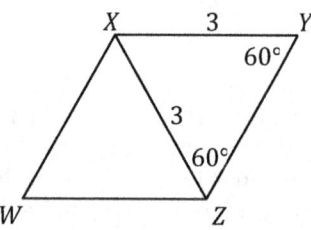

The three angles in triangle XYZ must add up to 180°. If two of them are 60° and 60°, the remaining one must be $180° - 120° = 60°$.

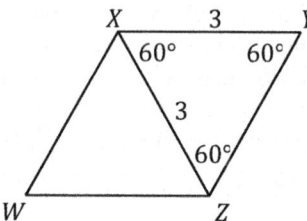

All three angles in triangle XYZ are the same, which means all three sides must be the same. Fill in a 3 for side $\overline{YZ}$.

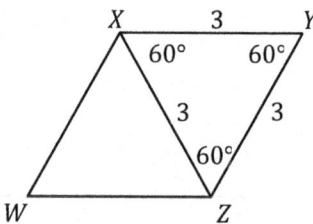

$WXYZ$ is a parallelogram, so $\overline{WZ}$ must be parallel to $\overline{XY}$. Thus, ∠WZX must match ∠ZXY, and ∠WXZ must match ∠XZY. Fill in 60° for both.

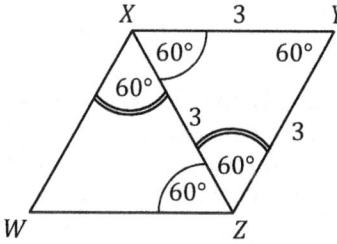

And now that triangle WXZ has two 60° angles, we can conclude that the remaining angle is also 60°. This means triangle WXZ is also an equilateral triangle with sides of length 3:

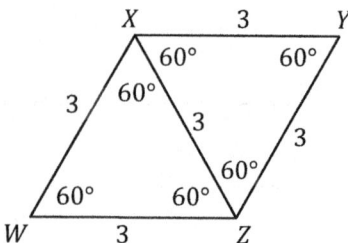

Now that we have all the side lengths, we can calculate the perimeter of parallelogram $WXYZ$. Ignoring the diagonal $\overline{XZ}$ (which is not a part of the perimeter), the sum of the four side lengths is $3 + 3 + 3 + 3 = 12$.

8) 45

The eight congruent central angles must add up to the full 360° of the circle. Therefore:

$$x + x + x + x + x + x + x + x = 360$$
$$8x = 360$$
$$x = 360/8$$
$$x = 45$$

9) C

Re-draw the figure, extending the lines of the parallelogram to make it easier to see the relationships created by the parallel lines.

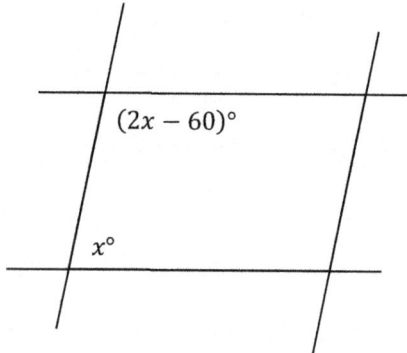

With the lines extended, it's easier to see that the angle right above the $(2x - 60)°$ angle corresponds to the angle marked $x°$. Go ahead and fill in $x°$ for that top angle.

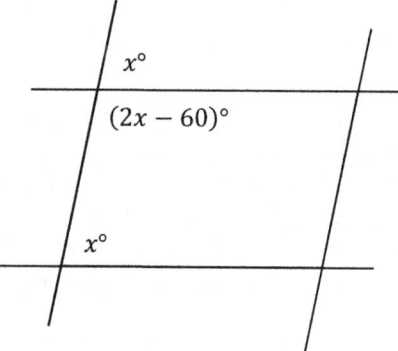

That top $x°$ angle is adjacent to the $(2x - 60)°$ angle, so they must add up to 180°.

$$x + 2x - 60 = 180$$
$$3x - 60 = 180$$

$$3x = 240$$
$$x = 80$$

Alternatively, you can use an approximating & measuring strategy to solve this problem. The angle marked as $x°$ is clearly not a right angle, so choice D is out. But it looks pretty close to 90°, so choice is the best guess.

10) D
Draw these out as two separate triangles to make it easier to see the relationships.

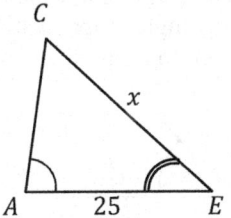 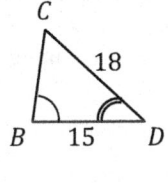

Because $\overline{BD}$ is parallel to $\overline{AE}$, the base angles of triangle CAE correspond with the base angles of triangle CBD. And both triangles contain angle C, so all three angles correspond. Therefore, these are similar triangles.

To find the length of $\overline{CE}$, then, we can use a proportion:

$$\frac{x}{25} = \frac{18}{15}$$

$$x = (18/15)(25) = 30$$

Alternatively, you can use an approximating & measuring strategy to solve this problem. $\overline{CE}$ appears to be the longest side of this triangle, so its length must be greater than 25. That lets us eliminate choices A and B. What about C? Well, if the length of $\overline{CE}$ was 27, then the length of $\overline{DE}$ would be 27 − 18 = 9, meaning $\overline{DE}$ would be half the length of $\overline{CD}$. That doesn't seem right: $\overline{CD}$ looks longer than that. That's reason enough to choose D as the best answer.

11) D
This problem tests your knowledge of some common geometry symbols. "$\overline{AC} \cong \overline{AD}$" means those two sides are congruent (they have the same length). "$\overline{AC} \perp \overline{AD}$" means the two sides are perpendicular (they intersect at a 90° angle). "$\overline{BE}$ bisects $\overline{AD}$" means that the length of $\overline{AD}$ is cut in half at point E: in other words, the length of $\overline{AE}$ is equal to the length of $\overline{ED}$. Finally, "$\overline{BE} \parallel \overline{CD}$" means that those two lengths are parallel to each other.

From all this, we can conclude that triangle ACD is an isosceles triangle (since $\overline{AC}$ and $\overline{AD}$ have the same length) and that angle A measures 90°. The remaining two angles in the big triangle must match each other and add up to 90°, so they are each 45°.

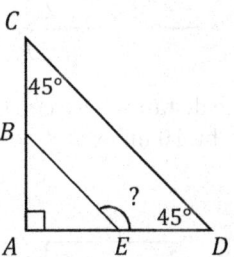

Because of the parallel lines, if the measure of ∠CDE is 45°, then so is the measure of ∠BEA:

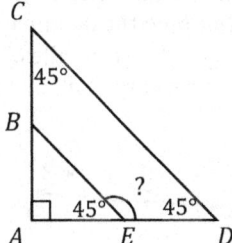

Since ∠AEB and ∠BED are adjacent, they must add up to 180°. Therefore, the measure of ∠BED is 180° − 45° = 135°.

Alternatively, you can use a measuring & approximating strategy to solve this problem. Everything on the SAT is drawn to scale unless the problem tells you otherwise, so start by simply looking at the angle in question. It's certainly more than 90°, so we can already cross out choices A and B. Choice C would be only slightly more than 90°, while choice D is significantly greater. This looks like a pretty big angle, so D seems the most likely candidate. And as it turns out, D was the right answer.

12) D
First, draw the points and line as described. Since point B bisects $\overline{AC}$, indicate on your drawing that the length of $\overline{AB}$ is equal to the length of $\overline{BC}$. Similarly, since C bisects $\overline{BD}$, the length of $\overline{BC}$ should equal the length of $\overline{CD}$.

```
    x    x    x
  •----•----•----•
  A    B    C    D
```

We're told that the length of $\overline{BC}$ is 4. Based on our figure, we now know that the lengths of $\overline{AC}$ and $\overline{CD}$ are 4 as well. Add that information to your sketch.

```
    4    4    4
  •----•----•----•
  A    B    C    D
```

The length of $\overline{AD}$ is 4 + 4 + 4 = 12.

Angles, Lines, and Triangles: Practice Set 2 (p. 414)
1) A
A figure is a good way to start this problem, but what should it look like? Here's one way the towns could be arranged.

Answer Explanations

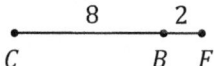

If that's the case, the distance between Cedarhurst and Farmingdale would be 10 miles. But here's another option.

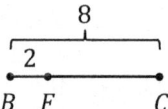

Bellmore is still 8 miles from Cedarhurst and 2 miles from Farmingdale, but now the distance from between Cedarhurst and Farmingdale is 6 miles. Eliminate choice B. And what if the 3 towns aren't all on the same straight line?

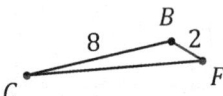

Because of the "third side of the triangle" rule, the distance between C and F in this scenario could be any number that's greater than 6 but less than 10. That eliminates choices C and D, leaving A as the only possible answer.

2) 30
The extra transversal in this picture is making the problem seem harder than it is. Try re-drawing the figure without the line that splits up the $x°$ angle and the 100° angle.

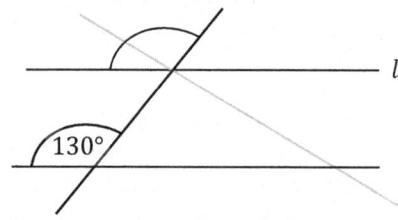

Now the relationship is clearer. Because of the parallel lines, the big angle we just created corresponds to the 130° angle. Therefore, $x + 100$ must equal 130, so $x = 30$.

3) D
Redraw the figure, extending the parallel lines and $\overline{AB}$ so you can better see the angle relationships.

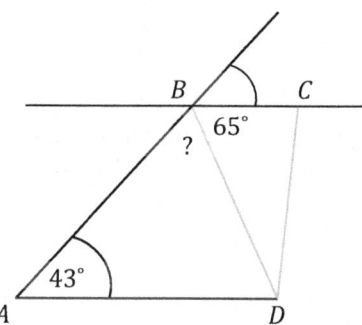

Angle BAD and the top marked angle are corresponding angles, so the measure of that top angle must be 43°. And now we have three angles adjacent to each other on the same line:

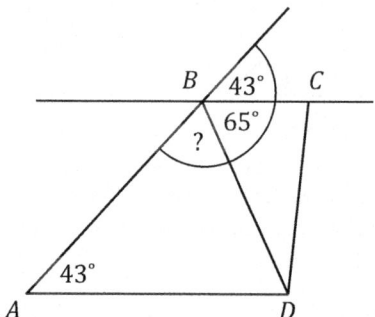

These three angles must add up to 180°. Therefore, the measure of angle ABD is $180 - (43 + 65) = 72°$.

4) 72
The sum of the interior angles in a pentagon is equal to $180(5 - 2) = 540°$. Since this is a regular pentagon, each angle has the same degree measure: specifically, each of the five angles must measure $540/5 = 108°$. In the figure, $\angle DEF$ is adjacent to one of the interior angles of the pentagon, so they must add up to 180°. Therefore, the measure of $\angle DEF$ is $180 - 108 = 72°$.

5) A
Redraw the figure, extending parallel lines $\overline{MS}$ and $\overline{NR}$ as well as transversal $\overline{SP}$ so you can better see the angle relationships.

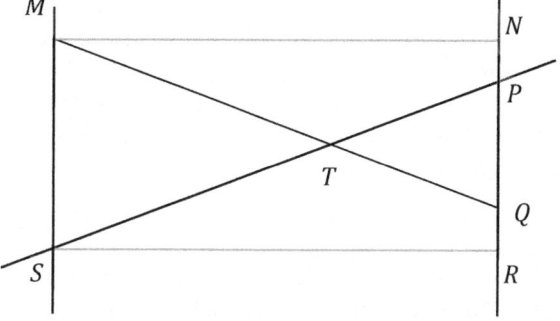

This makes it easier to see that angles MST and TPQ are alternate interior angles, so they must be congruent. Go ahead and indicate on your figure that vertical angles *MTS* and *QTP* match each other as well.

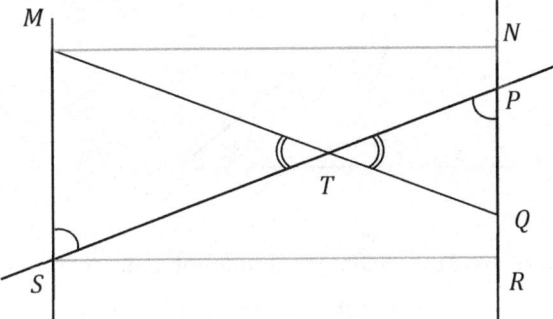

At this point, we've filled in two pairs of corresponding angles in triangles *MTS* and *QTP*. Thus, the remaining pair of angles must also correspond.

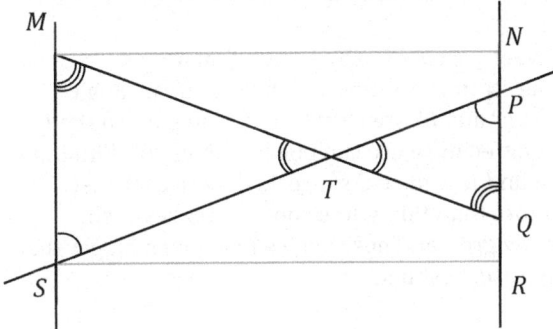

Fill in the side length information from the problem:

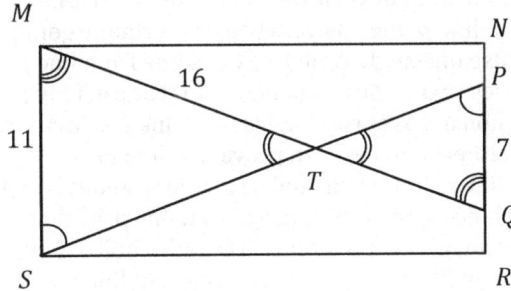

In order to see which sides match up with which, redraw the triangles so that they're oriented the same way as each other. To do this, draw triangle *MTS* first, keeping its orientation the same as it was, and carrying over everything we know about it. Then draw another triangle next to it, oriented the same way, and copy over the angle markings.

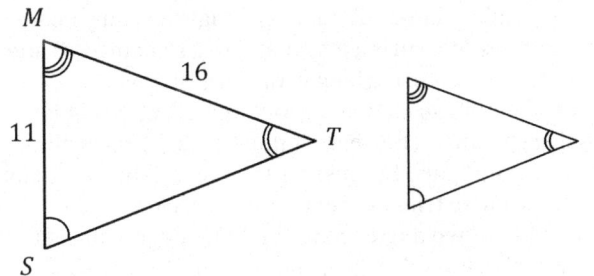

Next, label the vertices on the smaller triangle one at a time by matching up the angle markings to the larger figure we drew before. The angle with 3 curves was angle *Q*; the angle with 2 curves was *T*; the angle with one curve was *P*. Fill in that information, along with the one known side length.

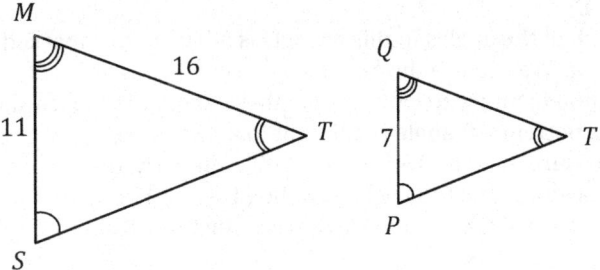

Now, the relationship between these side lengths is clearer. The 11 in the larger triangle corresponds with the 7 in the smaller triangle, and the 16 in the larger triangle corresponds with side $\overline{QT}$ in the smaller triangle. So, if $\overline{QT}$ has length x:

$$\frac{11}{7} = \frac{16}{x}$$

Now cross-multiply to solve.

$$11x = 16(7)$$
$$x = \frac{16(7)}{11} = \frac{112}{11}$$

6) B
Yes, this problem is trying to trick you. In similar triangles, the *side lengths* are proportional, not the angles. The corresponding angles of similar triangles are congruent, so if the smallest angle in triangle *DEF* measures 24°, then the smallest angle in triangle *ABC* measures 24° as well.

7) 85
Because the bases are parallel, the lower left angle in the big triangle (which measures $(4a - 10)°$) must be congruent to the lower left angle in the top triangle (which measures $(a + 50)°$).

$$a + 50 = 4a - 10$$
$$-3a = -60$$
$$a = 20$$

The figure also shows a pair of supplementary angles: the angle marked $(a + 50)°$ is adjacent to the angle marked $(3b - 85)°$. Therefore, those two angles must add up to 180°.

$$(a + 50) + (3b - 85) = 180$$

Moreover, we already figured out that $a = 20$, so we can go ahead and plug that in:

$$(20 + 50) + (3b - 85) = 180$$
$$70 + 3b - 85 = 180$$

Answer Explanations

$$3b - 15 = 180$$
$$3b = 195$$
$$b = 65$$

Since $a = 20$ and $b = 65$, the value of $a + b$ is $20 + 65 = 85$.

8) D
Each of the angles in this triangle is adjacent to a marked angle. We can use the fact that adjacent angles are supplementary to label each of these angles. For example, the bottom left angle is adjacent to a 73° angle, so its measure must be $180 - 73 = 107°$. Similarly, the measure of the top angle must be $(180 - a)°$, and the measure of the bottom right angle must be $(180 - b)°$.

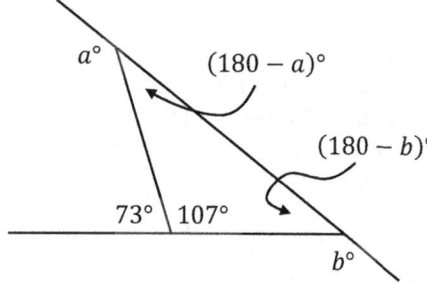

Since these are three angles in a triangle, their sum must be 180°.

$$(180 - a) + (180 - b) + 107 = 180$$
$$180 + 180 + 107 - a - b = 180$$
$$467 - a - b = 180$$
$$-a - b = -287$$
$$a + b = 287$$

We don't have enough information to figure out the values of a or b, but don't let that bother you—that's not what we were asked! All we need is the *average* of a and b. And how do you find the average of two numbers? You add them up and divide that sum by 2. We already know that the sum of a and b is 287. Therefore, the average of a and b must be $287/2 = 143.5$.

Alternatively, you could solve this problem by plugging in your own numbers. Let's start from the top again. We'd still start by calculating that the bottom left angle measures $180 - 73 = 107°$. Now, plug in a value for the top angle in the triangle. Let's say we use 20°. In that case, the degree measure of the angle on the bottom right must be $180 - 20 - 107 = 53°$.

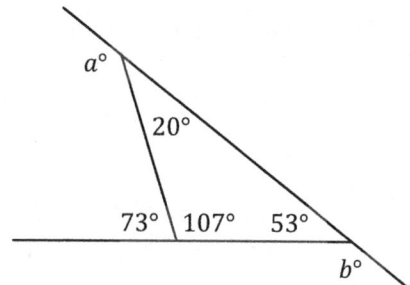

From there, we can calculate the values of a and b:

$$a = 180 - 20 = 160$$
$$b = 180 - 53 = 127$$

Now calculate the average of a and b:

$$\frac{160 + 127}{2} = 143.5$$

Alternatively, we could use an approximating & measuring strategy to solve this problem. The angles marked as $a°$ and $b°$ are clearly obtuse angles, so their average degree measure can't be less than 90°. Eliminate choices A and B. Choice C suggests they're each just slightly more than 90°, while choice D makes them significantly greater. These angles look much bigger than 90°, so D is the best bet.

9) C
This is a tricky problem, so work slowly and use process of elimination. First of all, if we want to prove that line l is parallel to line p, the answer choice is certainly going to have to use one angle from line l and one from line p. Choice A uses two angles from line p, so that can't help. But wait: choice B uses two angles from line l, so that can't help either! Choice B can prove that line m is parallel to line n, but it can't tell us anything about line p. Similarly, choice D uses two angles from line p, so that can't tell us anything about line l. The only choice that uses one angle from each of the two relevant lines is choice C, so that must be the right answer.

10) A
Use the two given angles to calculate the measure of the third angle.

$$180 - (42 + 48) = 90$$

The third angle must measure 90°, which means this must be a right triangle. An acute triangle has only acute angles (angles measuring less than 90°), so choices B and C are out. In an obtuse triangle, the largest angle is greater than 90°, so choice D is out as well. Choice A is the only remaining choice, so it must be right regardless of the "scalene" part. But just for the record, that's true as well. In a scalene triangle, no two sides are the same length, and no two angles have the same degree measure. The angles here are 42°, 48°, and 90°, so they're all different. The triangle is scalene.

11) D
This problem requires a little creative visualization. Go one choice at a time, using the test given in the problem: if the line segment in the answer choice either intersects with $\overline{AB}$ or lies in the same plane, it can't be right.

Choice A is out because $\overline{AH}$ intersects with $\overline{AB}$ at vertex A.

Choice B is out because $\overline{AB}$ and $\overline{GM}$ lie in the same plane (the "back" face of the prism).

Choice C is harder, but it's out for the same reason as choice B: $\overline{AB}$ and $\overline{FE}$ lie in the same plane. This time, the plane they share is not one of the faces of the prism, but we could slice through the prism with a new plane that contains both those lines, creating a single quadrilateral in which $\overline{AB}$ is parallel to $\overline{FE}$. That's enough to eliminate C.

Choice D is the odd one out. There's no way in which this $\overline{ME}$ is parallel to $\overline{AB}$, and there's no plane we could draw that would capture them both. But they'll also never intersect each other—if we extended both line segments to infinity, $\overline{ME}$ would run back into the distance and forwards towards us, while $\overline{AB}$ would soar above it stretching infinitely from left to right. They'd never come into contact. Choice D must be the answer.

RIGHT TRIANGLES AND TRIGONOMETRY (p. 416)
Right Triangles and Trigonometry: Try It
1) 4
Use the Pythagorean theorem to find the missing side length:
$$a^2 + b^2 = c^2$$
$$4^2 + x^2 = \left(\sqrt{20}\right)^2$$
$$16 + x^2 = 20$$
$$x^2 = 4$$
$$x = \pm 2$$

It makes no sense for the height to be a negative value, so $x = 2$. Therefore, this is a right triangle with a base of 4 and a height of 2. Now we can use the formula for area of a triangle:
$$A = \frac{1}{2}bh$$
$$A = \frac{1}{2}(4)(2)$$
$$A = 4$$

2) B
Use the Pythagorean theorem:
$$a^2 + b^2 = c^2$$
Fill in k and n for the legs:

$$k^2 + n^2 = c^2$$
Now take the square root of both sides:
$$\sqrt{k^2 + n^2} = c$$

3) 18
In an isosceles right triangle (a 45-45-90 triangle), the pattern of side lengths is $x, x,$ and $x\sqrt{2}$. We have the hypotenuse, which is the $x\sqrt{2}$ part of that pattern. So:
$$x\sqrt{2} = 6\sqrt{2}$$
Divide both sides by $\sqrt{2}$:
$$x = 6$$
So this is a right triangle with a base of 6 and a height of 6. Now use the formula for area of a triangle:
$$A = \frac{1}{2}bh$$
$$A = \frac{1}{2}(6)(6) = 18$$

4) $2\sqrt{3}$
Re-draw the figure and fill in the angles. All angles in an equilateral triangle are 60°. The height is perpendicular to the base, so that's a 90° angle. And the height splits the top angle in half, so those are two 30° angles.

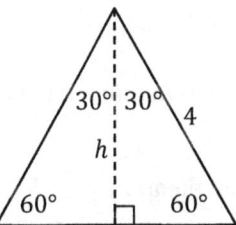

Therefore, drawing a height in an equilateral triangle splits it into two 30-60-90 triangles. Focus on the one on the right. The hypotenuse of this triangle is 4, so that's $2x$.
$$2x = 4$$
$$x = 2$$
The height is the side across from the 60° angle, so that's $x\sqrt{3}$. Since $x = 2$, the height must be $2\sqrt{3}$.

5) $\dfrac{5}{\sqrt{74}}$ or 0.581
Use CAH from SOH-CAH-TOA: cosine equals adjacent over hypotenuse. For this angle, the adjacent leg is 5. But what's the hypotenuse? We'll have to use the Pythagorean theorem to figure it out.
$$a^2 + b^2 = c^2$$
$$5^2 + 7^2 = c^2$$
$$25 + 49 = c^2$$
$$74 = c^2$$
$$\sqrt{74} = c$$

Answer Explanations

$$\cos a = \frac{\text{adjacent}}{\text{hypotenuse}} = \frac{5}{\sqrt{74}}$$

6) 20
First, write out the TOA part of SOH-CAH-TOA: tangent equals opposite over hypotenuse. For this triangle:

$$\tan k = \frac{x}{16}$$

From the problem, we also know this:

$$\tan k = \frac{5}{4}$$

So, set those equal to each other:

$$\frac{x}{16} = \frac{5}{4}$$
$$x = \frac{5}{4}(16)$$
$$x = 20$$

7) 450°

$$\frac{5\pi}{2} \text{radians} \times \frac{180°}{\pi \text{ radians}}$$
$$= \frac{5\pi(180)°}{2\pi}$$
$$= 450°$$

Right Triangles and Trigonometry: Practice Set 1 (p. 422)
1) D
Use the Pythagorean theorem: $a^2 + b^2 = c^2$.

$$5^2 + 8^2 = c^2$$
$$25 + 64 = c^2$$
$$89 = c^2$$
$$\sqrt{89} = c$$

2) B
First, re-draw the figure. Draw in new lines for $\overline{EA}$ and $\overline{AF}$; fill in their lengths and the length of $\overline{AB}$. Since $\overline{EF}$ is tangent to the circle, it must intersect at a right angle, so mark angle B as 90°.

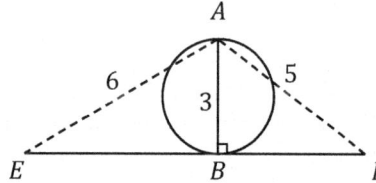

We can find the lengths of $\overline{EB}$ and $\overline{BF}$ using the Pythagorean theorem: $a^2 + b^2 = c^2$.

For $\overline{EB}$:

$$x^2 + 3^2 = 6^2$$
$$x^2 + 9 = 36$$

$$x^2 = 27$$
$$x = \sqrt{27} = \sqrt{9} * \sqrt{3}$$
$$x = 3\sqrt{3}$$

For $\overline{BF}$:

$$3^2 + y^2 = 5^2$$
$$9 + y^2 = 25$$
$$y^2 = 16$$
$$y = 4$$

The length of $\overline{EF}$ is equal to the sum of those two lengths, so the answer is $4 + 3\sqrt{3}$.

3) 25/4 or 6.25
Re-draw the figure. Note that the symbols in the problem give us several pieces of important information. First, "$\overline{AB} \perp \overline{BC}$" means those two sides are perpendicular, so we can mark angle B as 90°. Second, $\overline{AB} \cong \overline{BC}$ means those sides are congruent, meaning they have the same length: indicate that with hash marks. And if two sides in a triangle are congruent, then the angles across from them must be congruent, so this is a 45-45-90 triangle.

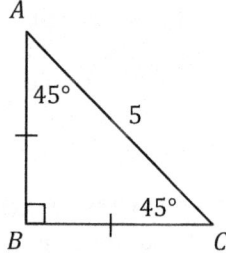

Therefore, we can use the special triangle proportions to find the lengths of the legs:

$$5 = x\sqrt{2}$$
$$\frac{5}{\sqrt{2}} = x$$

Don't bother simplifying that fraction, because our next step may take care of that for us. Check the reference section for the formula for area of a triangle:

$$A = \frac{1}{2}bh$$
$$A = \frac{1}{2}\left(\frac{5}{\sqrt{2}}\right)\left(\frac{5}{\sqrt{2}}\right)$$
$$A = \frac{1 * 5 * 5}{2 * \sqrt{2} * \sqrt{2}}$$
$$A = \frac{25}{4}$$

4) B
Since $BCDE$ is a square, $\overline{CD}$, the diameter of the circle, must be equal in length to $\overline{BE}$, the height of the triangle. Triangle AEB is a right triangle, so we can find the length of $\overline{BE}$ using the Pythagorean theorem.

Geometry and Trigonometry

$$a^2 + b^2 = c^2$$
$$3^2 + x^2 = 5^2$$
$$9 + x^2 = 25$$
$$x^2 = 16$$
$$x = 4$$

(As a time saver, you can skip using the Pythagorean theorem if you spot that this triangle is a 3-4-5 triangle, one of the Pythagorean triples.)

If the diameter of the circle is 4, then the radius is 2. Now, use the formula for circumference of a circle, as given in the reference section:

$$C = 2\pi r$$
$$C = 2\pi(2)$$
$$C = 4\pi$$

5) 60/65 (or any equivalent fraction, such as 12/13) or 0.923

Use SOH-CAH-TOA:

$$\cos = \frac{\text{adjacent}}{\text{hypotenuse}}$$

$$\cos x = \frac{60}{65}$$

6) C

Use the special right triangle proportions for a 45-45-90 triangle:

$$x = 3$$
$$x\sqrt{2} = 3\sqrt{2}$$

Therefore, the sides of this triangle are 3, 3, and $3\sqrt{2}$. To find the perimeter, add those values:

$$p = 3 + 3 + 3\sqrt{2}$$
$$p = 6 + 3\sqrt{2}$$

7) C

First, draw the figure. The angle between the wall and the level ground must be 90°. We were given another angle, 60°. Since the angles in a triangle must add up to 180°, the remaining angle must be 30°.

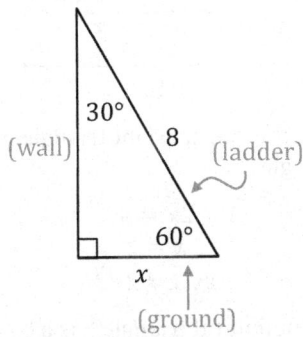

Now we can use the special right triangle proportions for a 30-60-90 triangle.

$$2x = 8$$

$$x = 4$$

Alternatively, you could use SOH-CAH-TOA to solve this:

$$\cos 60 = \frac{x}{8}$$
$$8(\cos 60) = x$$
$$8\left(\frac{1}{2}\right) = x$$
$$4 = x$$

8) D

Use SOH-CAH-TOA. For this angle, the correct values for sine and cosine would be:

$$\sin \theta = \frac{x}{7}$$

$$\cos \theta = \frac{y}{7}$$

Only choice D gets that right.

9) C

In any right triangle, the largest angle is the 90° angle. Since $180° = \pi$ radians, a measurement of 90° must equal $\pi/2$ radians.

10) C

The angles in a triangle must add up to 180°. Since we know two of the angles are 30° and 90°, the remaining angle must be 60°. We can use the special right triangle proportions for a 30-60-90 triangle to find the lengths of the legs.

$$2x = 16$$
$$x = 8 = BC$$
$$x\sqrt{3} = 8\sqrt{3} = AC$$

Check the reference section to find the formula for area of a triangle:

$$A = \frac{1}{2}bh$$
$$A = \frac{1}{2}(8)(8\sqrt{3})$$
$$A = 32\sqrt{3}$$

11) C

Use the Pythagorean theorem: $a^2 + b^2 = c^2$.

$$5^2 + b^2 = 14^2$$
$$25 + b^2 = 196$$
$$b^2 = 171$$
$$b = \sqrt{171}$$

12) 3/5 or 0.6

The paths traveled by the two ants form a right triangle, with the path taken by ant A forming the legs of the triangle, and the path taken by ant B forming the hypotenuse.

Answer Explanations

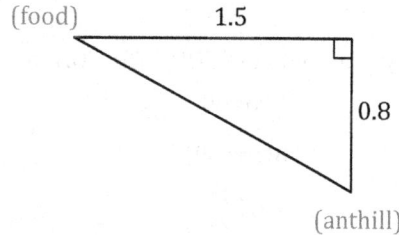

We can find the length of the path traveled by B using the Pythagorean theorem.

$$a^2 + b^2 = c^2$$
$$0.8^2 + 1.5^2 = c^2$$
$$0.64 + 2.25 = c^2$$
$$2.89 = c^2$$
$$1.7 = c$$

So ant B traveled 1.7 meters. Ant A traveled a total of 0.8 + 1.5 = 2.3 meters. So ant A traveled 2.3 − 1.7 = 0.6 meters further than ant B did.

Right Triangles and Trigonometry: Practice Set 2 (p. 424)
1) D
Use SOH-CAH-TOA. Since this problem involves the side *opposite* the 48° angle as well as the *hypotenuse*, use the SOH portion:

$$\sin = \frac{\text{opposite}}{\text{hypotenuse}}$$

First write out that relationship for the 48° angle, filling in everything we know:

$$\sin 48 = \frac{x}{8}$$

Now multiply both sides by 8 to isolate x.

$$8 \sin 48 = x$$

2) B
We can split this quadrilateral into two different right triangles.

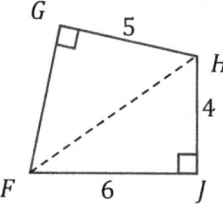

Area of $\triangle FHJ$:

$$A = \frac{1}{2}(6)(4)$$
$$A = 12$$

$\triangle FGH$ is a little trickier, since we only know one leg. But we can figure out the other sides by first using the Pythagorean theorem on $\triangle FHJ$, which shares a hypotenuse with $\triangle FGH$:

$$6^2 + 4^2 = c^2$$
$$36 + 16 = c^2$$
$$52 = c^2$$
$$c = \sqrt{52}$$

Now use the Pythagorean theorem again, this time on $\triangle FGH$:

$$a^2 + 5^2 = \left(\sqrt{52}\right)^2$$
$$a^2 + 25 = 52$$
$$a^2 = 27$$
$$a = \sqrt{27}$$

So we can now calculate the area of $\triangle FGH$:

$$A = \frac{1}{2}(5)\left(\sqrt{27}\right) = 2.5\sqrt{27}$$

Therefore, the area of $\triangle FHJ = 12 + 2.5\sqrt{27}$, which comes out to about 25.

3) B
The perimeter of a triangle is simply the sum of the three sides. In this case, all three sides are the same length:

$$s + s + s = 12$$
$$3s = 12$$
$$s = 4$$

Now we know the base of the triangle is 4. But in order to calculate the area, we need to know the height as well. Draw an equilateral triangle with a base of 4 and drop a height straight down the middle. Since the angles were originally each 60°, this splits the top angle into two 30° angles. Therefore, we now have two 30-60-90 triangles:

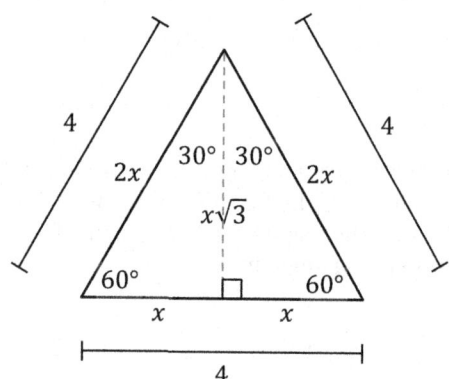

Now we can use the special right triangle proportions for a 30-60-90 triangle.

$$2x = 4$$
$$x = 2$$
$$x\sqrt{3} = 2\sqrt{3}$$

Therefore, the equilateral triangle has a base of 4 and a height of $2\sqrt{3}$:

Geometry and Trigonometry

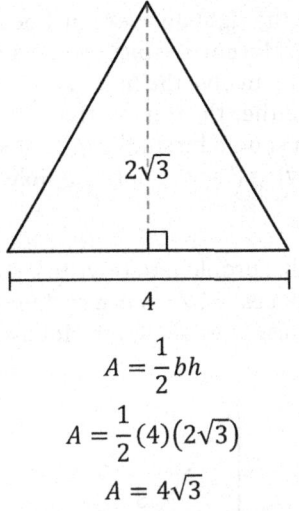

$$A = \frac{1}{2}bh$$
$$A = \frac{1}{2}(4)(2\sqrt{3})$$
$$A = 4\sqrt{3}$$

By the way, there is also a shortcut available here. The area of an equilateral triangle with side length s is always equal to $\frac{s^2\sqrt{3}}{4}$. So, in this case:

$$A = \frac{4^2\sqrt{3}}{4} = \frac{16\sqrt{3}}{4} = 4\sqrt{3}$$

4) B
The smallest side is always opposite the smallest angle, and the hypotenuse is opposite the largest angle. Therefore, this is our triangle:

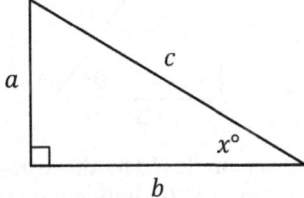

Now use SOH-CAH-TOA:

$$\tan x = \frac{\text{opposite}}{\text{adjacent}}$$
$$\tan x = \frac{a}{b}$$

5) 3/5 or 0.6
First, re-draw the figure, filling in all the side length information.

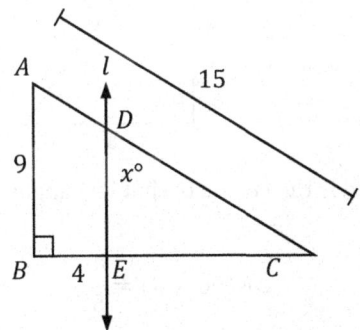

Because line l is parallel to $\overline{AB}$, the measure of $\angle BAD$ must match the measure of $\angle EDC$, and the measure of $\angle ABE$ must match the measure of $\angle DEC$.

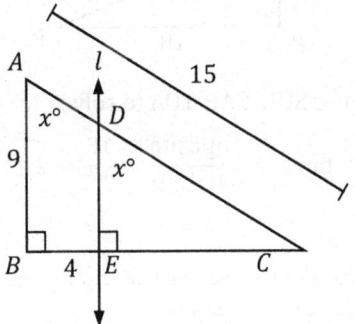

This means $\triangle ABC$ and $\triangle DEC$ are similar triangles. Redraw them as separate triangles to see the relationship:

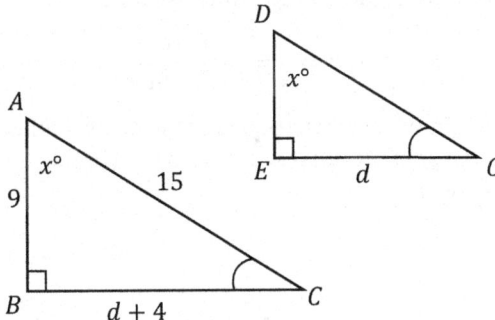

At this point, we could use the Pythagorean theorem and a couple of proportions to fill in more side lengths, but we don't need to bother. To find $\cos x$, just apply SOH-CAH-TOA to the larger triangle.

$$\cos x = \frac{9}{15} = \frac{3}{5}$$

6) B
As you already know, if a, b, and c are the sides of a right triangle with hypotenuse c, then $a^2 + b^2 = c^2$. What you may not realize is that the theorem works both ways. That is, if $a^2 + b^2 = c^2$, then a, b, and c are the sides of a right triangle with hypotenuse c.

If PQR is a right triangle, the hypotenuse would have to be 19.5, since that's the longest side. So, let's check:

$$a^2 + b^2 = c^2$$
$$7.5^2 + 18^2 = 19.5^2$$
$$380.25 = 380.25$$

It works! Therefore, PQR is a right triangle. Go ahead and sketch it, taking care to make $\overline{QR}$ the hypotenuse:

Answer Explanations

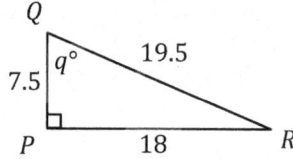

Now we can use SOH-CAH-TOA to solve.

$$\tan q = \frac{\text{opposite}}{\text{adjacent}} = \frac{18}{7.5} = 2.4$$

7) B
Convert the radian measure to degrees to make this problem easier to understand.

$$0 < P < \pi/2$$
$$0 < P < 90°$$

This tells us that angle P is an acute angle, meaning we can fit it into a right triangle. Now use SOH-CAH-TOA:

$$\cos P = \frac{r}{q} = \frac{\text{adjacent}}{\text{hypotenuse}}$$

Draw a right triangle where one of the acute angles is labeled P. Label the adjacent leg r, and label the hypotenuse q.

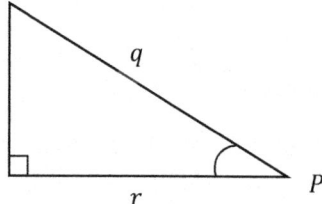

To find the remaining side, use the Pythagorean theorem:

$$x^2 + r^2 = q^2$$
$$x^2 = q^2 - r^2$$
$$x = \sqrt{q^2 - r^2}$$

Add that side length to your figure:

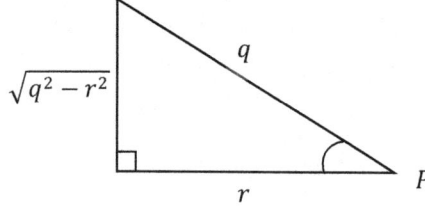

Now use SOH-CAH-TOA to find the tangent of angle P.

$$\tan P = \frac{\text{opposite}}{\text{adjacent}}$$
$$\tan P = \frac{\sqrt{q^2 - r^2}}{r}$$

Alternatively, you could deduce that answer B must be correct by the process of elimination. Once we know that r is the adjacent leg, we can conclude that the denominator of the right answer must be r, eliminating choices C and D. Moreover, since the TOA part of SOH-CAH-TOA doesn't involve the hypotenuse, we can also conclude that neither the top nor the bottom of the right answer fraction should be simply q. That's enough to eliminate A, leaving B as the only possible answer.

8) 4/5 or 0.8
It's helpful for this problem to rewrite 0.6 as a fraction: 6/10, which reduces to 3/5. Since cosine is adjacent/hypotenuse, we can now sketch the following right triangle:

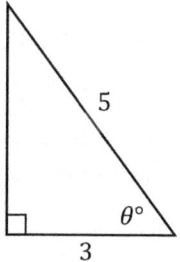

This is a 3-4-5 triangle, one of the Pythagorean triples, so the remaining side must be 4.

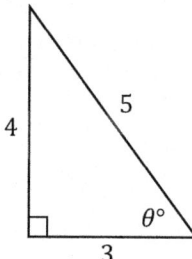

Now, what about the angles? The three angles in a triangle must add up to 180°, which means that in this triangle, the sum of 90°, θ, and the remaining angle (let's call it x) must be 180:

$$90 + \theta + x = 180$$
$$\theta + x = 90$$
$$x = 90 - \theta$$

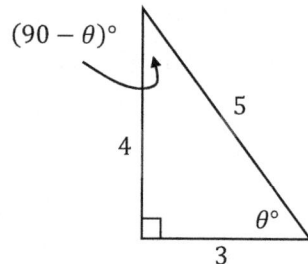

So all we need is the cosine of that last angle. Use SOH-CAH-TOA:

$$\cos(90 - \theta) = \frac{4}{5}$$

Alternatively, you could use the $\cos^{-1}$ function on your calculator to determine θ directly:

$$\cos\theta = 0.6$$
$$\theta = \cos^{-1}(0.6)$$
$$\theta = 53.1301$$
$$90 - 53.1301 = 36.8699$$
$$\cos 36.8699 = 0.8$$

But if you take this approach, be careful to make sure your calculator is giving an answer in degrees and not radians!

9) C

The volume of a triangular prism is equal to the area of the triangular base times the height of the prism. Since we know the base is an isosceles right triangle, we can determine the lengths of the legs by using the special right triangle proportions for a 45-45-90 triangle:

$$x\sqrt{2} = 6\sqrt{2}$$
$$x = 6$$

Each leg of the triangle has a length of 6. Now we can calculate the area of the triangle:

$$A = \frac{1}{2}(6)(6)$$
$$A = 18$$

We already know that the volume of the prism is 108. Now plug that information and the area of the base into the formula for volume of a prism:

$$V = (\text{area of base})(\text{height of prism})$$
$$108 = (18)h$$
$$h = \frac{108}{18} = 6$$

10) C

If you are familiar with the unit circle or the ASTC acronym, this question can be answered quickly by recognizing that cosine is negative in the 2nd and 3rd quadrants: that is, from $\pi/2$ to $3\pi/2$. Therefore, C must be the answer.

Alternatively, you could use the $\cos^{-1}$ function on your calculator to determine x directly:

$$\cos x = -0.707$$
$$x = \cos^{-1}(-0.707)$$
$$x \approx 2.356$$

The value 2.356 is between $\pi/2$ (which equals about 1.5708) and $3\pi/2$ (which equals about 4.7124). But if you take this approach, be careful to make sure your calculator is giving an answer in radians and not degrees!

11) B

Use SOH-CAH-TOA:

$$\sin\theta = \frac{\text{opposite}}{\text{hypotenuse}}$$
$$\sin\theta = \frac{x}{7}$$

We also know that $\sin\theta = 0.45$. Therefore:

$$0.45 = \frac{x}{7}$$
$$7(0.45) = x$$
$$3.15 = x$$

12) D

This is a SOH-CAH-TOA problem. From the point of view of the 70° angle, the problem involves the *opposite* leg and the *hypotenuse*, so we should use sine:

$$\sin 70 = \frac{x}{10}$$
$$10 \sin 70 = x$$

Unfortunately, 10 sin 70 is not one of our answer choices! But, because the angles of a triangle have to add up to 180°, we know that the measure of the other acute angle here must be 20°. From the point of view of that 20° angle, the problem involves the *adjacent* leg and the *hypotenuse*, so we should use cosine:

$$\cos 20 = \frac{x}{10}$$
$$10 \cos 20 = x$$

CIRCLES (p. 426)
Circles: Try It
1) 2π

Write out the formula for arc length:

$$\text{Arc length} = \frac{\text{central angle}}{360}(2\pi r)$$

Now plug in what we know:

$$\text{Arc length} = \frac{40}{360}(2\pi(9))$$
$$\text{Arc length} = \frac{1}{9}(18\pi)$$
$$\text{Arc length} = 2\pi$$

2) 20

Write out the formula for sector area:

$$\text{Sector area} = \frac{\text{central angle}}{360}(\pi r^2)$$

Now plug in what we know:

$$8\pi = \frac{d}{360}\left(\pi(12^2)\right)$$
$$8\pi = \frac{d}{360}(144\pi)$$

Answer Explanations

Multiply both sides by 360:
$$2880\pi = d(144\pi)$$

Divide by 144π:
$$20 = d$$

3) B
There are 360° in a circle, so the degree measure of a semicircle is $360/2 = 180°$. Arc QR is intercepted by inscribed angle P, so the measure of angle P must be $180/2 = 90°$. Therefore, triangle PQR is a right triangle.

4) $(-1, 0)$
The equation $(x-h)^2 + (y-k)^2 = r^2$ gives a circle centered at (h, k) and with a radius of length r. To better match that form, we could rewrite the equation we've been given in this problem like this:
$$\left(x-(-1)\right)^2 + (y-0)^2 = 2^2$$
Now it's easier to see that $h = -1$ and $k = 0$. Therefore, the center is located at $(-1, 0)$.

Alternatively, you could solve this problem using the built-in calculator. Type in the equation:

$(x+1)^2 + y^2 = 4$

The calculator will graph the circle, highlighting helpful (x, y) points. We can see that the points $(-3, 0)$ and $(1, 0)$ are directly across the circle from each other, so the center must be the point immediately between them: $(-1, 0)$.

5) $(x+9)^2 + (y-5)^2 = 16$
Start by writing out the form of the circle equation:
$$(x-h)^2 + (y-k)^2 = r^2$$
Now plug in the given information:
$$\left(x-(-9)\right)^2 + \left(y-(5)\right)^2 = 4^2$$
And simplify:
$$(x+9)^2 + (y-5)^2 = 16$$

6) 6
First, write out the equation:
$$(x-3)^2 + (y-1)^2 = 25$$
We know the graph of this equation passes through the point $(k, -3)$. So, plug in k for the x value in the equation and -3 for the y.
$$(k-3)^2 + (-3-1)^2 = 25$$
$$(k-3)^2 + (-4)^2 = 25$$
$$(k-3)^2 + 16 = 25$$
$$(k-3)^2 = 9$$
$$\sqrt{(k-3)^2} = \pm\sqrt{9}$$
$$k - 3 = 3 \text{ or } k - 3 = -3$$
$$k = 6 \text{ or } k = 0$$

This tells us that the circle passes through two different points that have a y-coordinate of -3: $(6, -3)$ and $(0, -3)$. However, we were told that k is a *positive* constant, so its value cannot be zero. Therefore, the value of k must be 6.

7) $(-2, 5)$
Type the equation into the built-in calculator.

$x^2 + 4x + y^2 - 10y = 2$

The calculator will graph the circle, highlighting helpful (x, y) points. We can see that the points $(-2, -0.568)$ and $(-2, 10.568)$ are directly across the circle from each other, so the center must be the point immediately between them. The x-coordinate must be -2, and the center must be the average of the two known y-coordinates:
$$\frac{-0.568 + 10.568}{2} = \frac{10}{2} = 5$$
So the center is located at $(-2, 5)$.

Alternatively, we can "complete the square" to solve the problem algebraically.
$$x^2 + 4x + y^2 - 10y = 2$$
The terms are already grouped correctly. For the x quadratic, $(b/2)^2 = (4/2)^2 = 2^2 = 4$.

For the y's, $(b/2)^2 = (-10/2)^2 = (-5)^2 = 25$.

Therefore:
$$x^2 + 4x + \mathbf{4} + y^2 - 10y + \mathbf{25} = 2 + \mathbf{4} + \mathbf{25}$$
$$(x+2)^2 + (y-5)^2 = 31$$
This is a circle centered at $(-2, 5)$ with a radius of $\sqrt{31}$.

Circles: Practice Set 1 (p. 431)
1) B
The equation $(x-h)^2 + (y-k)^2 = r^2$ gives a circle centered at (h, k) and with a radius of length r. Notice the minuses in the parentheses. The equation we've been given in this problem is
$$(x+3)^2 + (y-1)^2 = 16$$
To match the form above, we could rewrite the given equation like this:
$$\left(x-(-3)\right)^2 + (y-1)^2 = 4^2$$

Now it matches: $h = -3$ and $k = 1$. Therefore, the center is located at $(-3, 1)$.

Alternatively, you could solve this problem using the built-in calculator. Type in the equation:

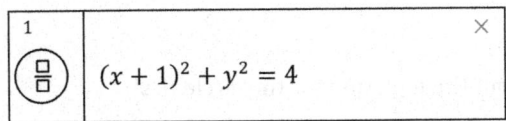

The calculator will graph the circle, highlighting helpful (x, y) points. We can see that the points $(-3, 5)$ and $(-3, -3)$ are directly across the circle from each other, so the center must be the point immediately between them: $(-3, 1)$.

2) D
Use the formula for area of a circle:
$$A = \pi r^2$$
$$49\pi = \pi r^2$$

Divide both sides by π:
$$49 = r^2$$

Take the square root of both sides:
$$7 = r$$

The radius of this circle is 7, so the diameter is $2(7) = 14$. The diameter is always the longest chord that can be drawn in a circle. Since this chord is not a diameter, it must be less than 14. No line segment can have a length that's less than or equal to zero, so the length of this chord must be between 0 and 14. That's choice D.

3) B
The easiest way to handle this problem is to graph each of the given equations in the built-in calculator. Just be sure to copy over the equations carefully! There is no exponent on the x in choice D.

Alternatively, you can solve this problem using your knowledge of the forms of various types of equations. In choice A, there is no way to manipulate the equation so that it would end up matching the form of a circle equation, which has no coefficients on either the x expression or the y expression. This is in fact the equation of an ellipse, which is an elongated circular shape that has horizontal and vertical radii of different lengths.

Choice C has a minus between the x term and the y term instead of a plus. This is the equation of a hyperbola, which is a pair of parabolas stretching away from each other.

Choice D has no squared x term. This is the equation of a horizontal parabola.

Only choice B fits the circle form: this is a circle centered at $(1, 0)$ with a radius of 1.

4) 5
Start by writing out the form of the circle equation:
$$(x - h)^2 + (y - k)^2 = r^2$$

Now plug in the given center:
$$(x - 6)^2 + (y + 4)^2 = r^2$$

The graph passes through the point $(9, 0)$, which means those values of x and y must satisfy this equation. So, plug in 9 for x and 0 for y:
$$(9 - 6)^2 + (0 + 4)^2 = r^2$$

Now simplify and solve for r.
$$(3)^2 + (4)^2 = r^2$$
$$9 + 16 = r^2$$
$$25 = r^2$$
$$5 = r$$

5) B
Write out the formula for arc length:
$$\text{Arc length} = \frac{\text{central angle}}{360}(2\pi r)$$

Now plug in what we know:
$$\text{Arc length} = \frac{90}{360}(2\pi(18))$$
$$\text{Arc length} = \frac{1}{4}(36\pi)$$
$$\text{Arc length} = 9\pi$$

6) B
The easiest way to handle this problem is to graph each of the given equations in the built-in calculator. Choice B is the circle that matches the given requirements.

Alternatively, you can use your knowledge of the basic form of the circle equation to solve this. The equation $(x - h)^2 + (y - k)^2 = r^2$ gives a circle centered at (h, k) and with a radius of length r. This circle is centered at $(2, 5)$, so $h = 2$ and $k = 5$. The radius is 9, so $r = 9$.

Therefore:
$$(x - 2)^2 + (y - 5)^2 = 9^2$$
$$(x - 2)^2 + (y - 5)^2 = 81$$

7) C
Start by writing out the formula for area of a circle.
$$A = \pi r^2$$

Now plug in what we know:
$$81\pi = \pi r^2$$
$$81 = r^2$$

Answer Explanations

$$9 = r$$

Now use the formula for arc length.

$$\text{Arc length} = \frac{\text{central angle}}{360}(2\pi r)$$

$$\text{Arc length} = \frac{80}{360}(2\pi(9))$$

$$\text{Arc length} = \frac{80(18\pi)}{360}$$

$$\text{Arc length} = \frac{1440\pi}{360}$$

$$\text{Arc length} = 4\pi$$

8) B

The equation $(x - h)^2 + (y - k)^2 = r^2$ gives a circle centered at (h, k) and with a radius of length r. The equation we've been given in this problem is

$$x^2 + (y + 9)^2 = 100$$

To match the form above, we could rewrite the given equation like this:

$$(x - 0)^2 + \left(y - (-9)\right)^2 = 10^2$$

Now it's easier to see that $h = 0$, and $k = -9$, and $r = 10$. We want the circumference of the circle, so all we need from that is the radius:

$$C = 2\pi r$$
$$C = 2\pi(10)$$
$$C = 20\pi$$

Circles: Practice Set 2 (p. 432)
1) B

Write out the equation for the circle first:

$$(x - h)^2 + (y - k)^2 = r^2$$
$$(x - 2)^2 + (y - 4)^2 = 16$$

Next, type that equation into the built-in calculator. On the next line, type in the equation $y = 8$. Click on the point of intersection on the graph and the calculator will automatically display the coordinates: $(2, 8)$.

Alternatively, once you have the equation for the circle, you can solve the problem algebraically. The circle will intersect with the line $y = 8$ at a point that has a y-coordinate of 8. So:

$$(x - 2)^2 + (8 - 4)^2 = 16$$
$$(x - 2)^2 + (4)^2 = 16$$
$$(x - 2)^2 + 16 = 16$$
$$(x - 2)^2 = 0$$

Now take the square root of both sides:

$$x - 2 = 0$$
$$x = 2$$

2) 72

If the shaded region is 20% of the area of the circle, then the degree measure of the central angle is 20% of the full 360° of the circle. Therefore, the measure of the angle is $0.2(360) = 72°$.

3) D

Write out the equation for the circle first:

$$(x - h)^2 + (y - k)^2 = r^2$$
$$(x - 3)^2 + y^2 = 25$$

Next, type that equation into the built-in calculator. Click on each of the points where the graph intersects the x-axis, and the calculator will automatically display the coordinates: $(-2, 0)$ and $(8, 0)$. Only the latter point is included in the answer choices, so the answer is D.

Alternatively, once you have the equation for the circle, you can solve the problem algebraically. After all, an x-intercept is just a point on the graph with a y-coordinate of zero. So, plug in $y = 0$:

$$(x - 3)^2 + 0^2 = 25$$
$$(x - 3)^2 = 25$$
$$\sqrt{(x - 3)^2} = \pm\sqrt{25}$$
$$x - 3 = 5 \text{ or } x - 3 = -5$$
$$x = 8 \text{ or } x = -2$$

The circle has two x-intercepts: one at $(8, 0)$ and the other at $(-2, 0)$. Only one of them is in the answer choices: choice D.

4) C

Type the equation into the built-in calculator.

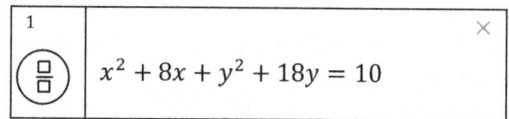

The calculator will graph the circle, highlighting helpful (x, y) points. We can see that the points $(-4, 1.344)$ and $(-4, -19.344)$ are directly across the circle from each other, so the center must be the point immediately between them. The x-coordinate must be -4, and the center must be the average of the two known y-coordinates:

$$\frac{1.344 + (-19.344)}{2} = \frac{-18}{2} = -9$$

So the center is located at $(-4, -9)$.

Alternatively, we can "complete the square" to solve the problem algebraically.

$$x^2 + 8x + y^2 + 18y = 10$$
$$x^2 + 8x + \mathbf{4^2} + y^2 + 18y + \mathbf{9^2} = 10 + \mathbf{4^2} + \mathbf{9^2}$$
$$(x + 4)^2 + (y + 9)^2 = 10 + 16 + 81$$
$$(x + 4)^2 + (y + 9)^2 = 107$$

This is a circle centered at $(-4, -9)$ with a radius of $\sqrt{107}$.

5) D

All radii in a circle have the same length, so we can set these two radii equal to each other:

$$2x - 3 = x + 1$$
$$2x = x + 4$$
$$x = 4$$

But be careful not to move too fast! This tells that the value of x is 4, not that the *radius* is 4. To get the radius, we have to plug 4 back into either $2x - 3$ or $x + 1$:

$$\text{radius} = 4 + 1 = 5$$

Therefore, the area is $\pi(5)^2 = 25\pi$.

6) B

Redraw the figure, and draw in three diameters of the circle: $\overline{VY}, \overline{WZ},$ and $\overline{UX}$. Notice that these diameters intersect at the center of the circle, splitting the central 360° into six congruent 60° angles.

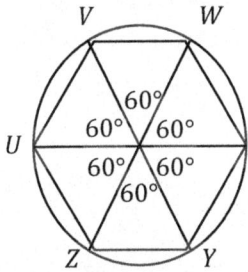

The central angle that intercepts arc XYZ consists of two of these 60° angles, so it measures 120°.

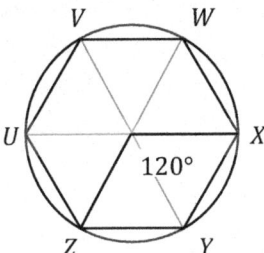

Therefore, what this question is really asking for is the length of a 120° arc of a circle with radius 9.

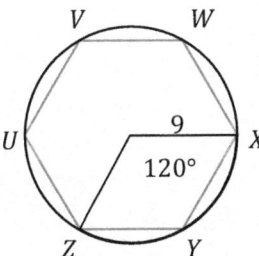

Now use the formula for arc length.

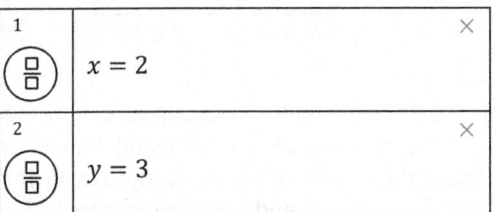

$$\text{Arc length} = \frac{\text{central angle}}{360}(2\pi r)$$

$$\text{Arc length} = \frac{120}{360}(2\pi(9))$$

$$\text{Arc length} = 6\pi$$

7) A

Type the equations for both of the tangent lines into the built-in calculator:

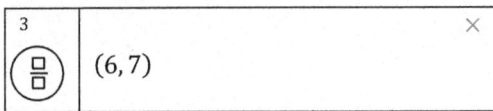

Now, keeping those equations where they are, test one choice at a time by typing in the point into the next line in the calculator. For example, here's choice A:

Now, count the gridlines on the graph. This point is exactly 4 units away from both lines. Therefore, A must be the answer.

Alternatively, we can solve this by sketching it. First, sketch an xy-plane. Draw in the vertical line $x = 2$ and the horizontal line $y = 3$.

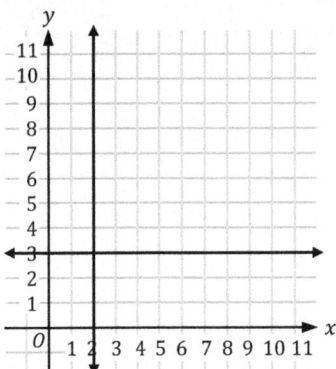

Now, where can we place a circle so that it's tangent to both lines? Theoretically, there are four possible positions: the circle might touch the lines on its top and left side, or on its top and right, or on its bottom and left, or on its bottom and right. But with a radius of 4, all but one of those positions would give us a circle that would cross over into one of the other quadrants. There's only one position in which we have enough room for the entire circle to remain within Quadrant I:

Answer Explanations

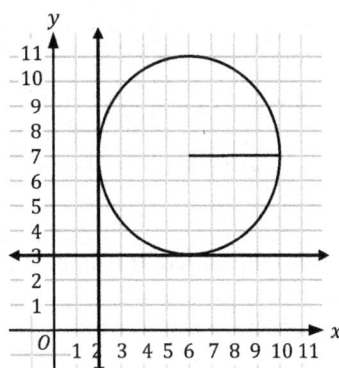

The circle must be positioned so that its center is 4 units to the right of the vertical line $x = 2$ and 4 units above the horizontal line $y = 3$. Therefore, the x-coordinate of the center is $2 + 4 = 6$, and the y-coordinate is $3 + 4 = 7$.

Made in the USA
Columbia, SC
17 June 2025